"THERE IS STRENGTH IN THE VISION OF A SISTERHOOD THAT HAS ROOTS IN THE PAST AND EXTENDS INTO THE FUTURE."

—Alice S. Rossi

Beginning with a letter from Abigail Adams dated 1771, Dr. Rossi has assembled a comprehensive anthology of major feminist writings from the late eighteenth century to the mid-twentieth. In these pages we meet religious women as well as atheists; conservative moralists as well as radicals; women in deep rebellion from their families and society as well as women in comfortable, happy circumstances. There are calls not only for political rights, but also for economic, sexual, educational and reproductive liberation. The variety of lives and circumstances and styles of feminist effort is striking. Dr. Rossi's careful choice of material and her extended introductory essays for each writer bring this rich heritage vividly to life.

ALICE S. ROSSI

is a noted sociologist and feminist who has been in the forefront of the current women's movement in America. She is professor of sociology and chairperson of the Department of Sociology and Anthropology at Goucher College. She is the author of one of the famous early essays of the women's movement, "Equality between the Sexes: An Immodest Proposal," and her edited works include **Essays on Sex Equality** by John Stuart Mill and Harriet Taylor Mill (1970), and **Academic Women on the Move** (1973).

THE FEMINIST PAPERS

From Adams to de Beauvoir

Edited and with Introductory
Essays by Alice S. Rossi

THE FEMINIST PAPERS
A Bantam Book

PRINTING HISTORY
Columbia University Press edition published October 1973
Bantam edition published January 1974
2nd printing

Contents

v

List of Figures

Preface: Feminist Lives And Works

This book has been in the making for not quite two years. When the publisher approached me about editing the "essential works of feminism" in October 1970, my first response was the claim that it would be more appropriate to seek a historian rather than a sociologist as editor. The magnitude of the task—to select and abridge the critical documents in feminist history over the past two centuries—seemed overwhelming. On the other hand, there were few intellectual tasks that had given me as much pleasure as the research and writing for an introduction to John Stuart Mill's *The Subjection of Women* (Rossi 1970). The enlarged scope suggested for this book held the promise of more of the same intellectual pleasure of discovery and analysis. Then, too, perhaps it was precisely because I was *not* trained as a historian that I had the audacity to undertake the project.

Most anthologies have a format of an interpretive introductory essay followed by a series of abridged documents, with at most a brief headnote for each entry, and a concluding bibliography. In preparation for writing such headnotes, I began to read memoirs and biographies of the feminists whose work I had abridged. In the course of this reading the plan for the book changed. My sociologist's and feminist's imagination was fully engaged by the attempt to trace out the connections among the ideas expressed in a published work, the personal life behind an essay or book, and the larger time and place in history in which both the life and the work were anchored. The idea grew to precede each abridged selection with an essay that would serve one or more of several ends, depending on the nature of the selection. In some cases the mode was a chronology of the personal life, placing the work in the context of that life and selecting a few issues for special exploration that seemed to speak in a lively way to our contemporary situation. In other cases it seemed more appropriate to write a sociographic rather than a biographic analysis. Here the focus was not the life of one person, but of two or more: sisters, in the case of Sarah and Angelina

Grimké; friends, in the case of Susan Anthony and Elizabeth Stanton; a whole sibling set, in the case of the Blackwells.

It was not certain that this attempt to integrate the personal lives with the published essays and books would have as much appeal to others as it clearly did to me. To test this question, I conducted an experiment in undergraduate seminars during the spring of 1971 and again in 1972. The first seminar was on the sociology of the family, and its object was to explore the family backgrounds of a number of women prominent in the nineteenth century, applying what was known from sociology and psychology about family structure and personality formation to see if these findings provided clues to the subsequent achievement of the individual women we studied. Both the students and I found this venture fascinating, and seminar discussions which tried to compare the individual cases suggested a number of additional themes to be explored with yet another sample of lives. By the spring of 1972 the work on the book was further advanced, and a different experiment was undertaken in a seminar on women's movements. For two of the early nineteenth-century feminists, the seminar members read their work first and then learned about the lives of the authors. For the next two feminists we reversed the order, and I described the personal lives before the students read the published work. The seminar members unanimously concluded that both their interest and comprehension were increased when they knew something of the personal lives before grappling with the published work.

The third test was a harsher one. Since I was neither a historian nor a biographer, I submitted samples of the essays to several friends experienced in biographic analysis. Here, too, their reaction confirmed my hope that a sociologist could indeed illuminate new aspects of familiar fields of historical inquiry. This was particularly the case when the focus was closest to the sociological tradition—in studies of such social relationships as marriage, sisterhood, parenthood, or friendship—or on a larger scale, in a search for the social structural roots of the woman's-rights movement in the decade before 1848. My colleagues also concurred with my experience that contemporary readers find the early feminist works far more interesting if they are first acquainted with the lives of the authors.

The search for selections and the writing of the essays for

this volume was a source of great personal and intellectual gratification. For one thing, it represented a return to an old love for history, but of a very different quality from previous excursions into the past. Except for the work on John Stuart Mill and his relationship to Harriet Taylor, I had never studied history with a focus on women; the more I read, therefore, the greater was my sense that there was a whole host of like-minded women who had preceded my generation in American history. I had never before experienced so keenly a sense of continuity with previous generations. The closest analogy was my mother's visit shortly after the birth of my first daughter, when there was a tangible awareness in the house of three generations of females whose lives were closely connected and which would span more than a century. I did not then appreciate what a "woman's culture" meant, and hence I could not understand then, as I do now, why my mother said it meant something more special to her for me to have a daughter than it had when my son was born the year before. As an activist and a feminist scholar, I have felt the wish for continuity, but until this project, it had been only a continuity from the present through my daughters and women students to some hoped-for future when our contemporary visions might be realized. Now I have acquired a long line of feminists in the past. There is strength in the vision of a sisterhood that has roots in the past and extends into the future. I hope this volume enables its readers to share in that vision.

The second ingredient of the intellectual pleasure was the release from the confines of my own particular training as a sociologist. Sex and age are such fundamental human attributes that they are central to almost any field of human inquiry, from physiology through sociology to art and literature. The training we have received in higher education these past forty years has been so excessively specialized that a scholar is poorly prepared to undertake any synthesis of problems involving the variables of age or sex; instead she is often paralyzed in trying to deal properly with a major variable that cuts across the artificial boundaries separating the disciplines. The emergence of departments of human development released much intellectual energy for addressing problems involving aging and human maturation. It is the hope of many feminist scholars that the emergence of women's-studies courses and research programs may do the same for problems involving sex roles. Having had the good fortune to count historians and literary scholars among my friends, my own professional work as a research sociologist was compensated for by contact with their lively interests. But in the work for this volume I had a first experience of moving naturally across whole bodies of materials and engaging in a dialogue that drew ideas from history, psychology, sociology, and literature. It was like a whole women's-studies program inside my head —a program in which I was both student and teacher, bringing to bear countless questions from one discipline after another on the lives of the many women of the past whom I studied. Precious summer nights of the most gratifying intellectual experience I have ever known have gone into the making of this book.

One decision concerning the content of the volume was clear from the start. If a feminist in the past considered her ideas in need of two or more hundred pages to develop, it would not do at all to try to compress those ideas into a few abridged pages. I have found for myself, and my students concur, that such shallow treatment has the effect of blurring all distinctions among the early writers. Any abridgment is a violation of an author's intent, no matter how judicious an editor tries to be. But at least there should be enough of Mary Wollstonecraft or Margaret Fuller or Sarah Grimké for the reader in the 1970s to gain a sense of how these women thought, what arguments they brought to bear on their analysis, and so on. The selections, therefore, would have to be extensive enough to give each author a fair hearing. Accordingly, however, either the book would have to move into several volumes, which it could not do, or very careful screening would have to be applied to the final selections.

A second critical issue was the framework within which the selection would be made. My first surprise was to realize that after more than a month of reading nineteenth-century feminists, I had not found a single one who used the word "feminism" or "feminist." I had been misled by O'Neill's claim that "feminism is an older term and was always used to describe the woman's rights movement as such" (O'Neill 1969:x). In point of fact, the term "feminism" was rarely used in the mid-nineteenth century and referred simply to the "qualities of females." It was not until the 1890s that a concept of feminism emerged; it meant, as we mean it today, the "opinions and principles of the advocates of the extended recognition of the achievements and claims of women," to use the somewhat awkward language of the unabridged Oxford dictionary. As near as we know, the term "feminism" was first used in print in a book review in the April 27, 1895, issue of a British journal, *The Athenaeum*. The review dealt with a novel by Miss Sidgwick, a popular writer of the day. *The Grasshoppers* tells the story of three "delicately nurtured women" who are plunged into an "abyss of poverty, privation and dependence." One of the central characters was a young woman:

> whose intellectual evolution and . . . coquettings with the doctrines of "feminism" are traced with real humour, while the poignancy of her subsequent troubles is enhanced by the fact that . . . she, alone . . . has in her the capacity of fighting her way back to independence. [Anonymous 1895].

There were assorted usages of the terms "feminism," "feministic," "feminist," and even "femininism" in European periodicals during 1895. By the turn of the century—but not until then—feminism and feminist no longer required quotation marks in the public press.

Until very recently it has been traditional to consider feminist history the equivalent of the story of the American woman's rights or suffrage movement, with perhaps a bit of attention to the more militant Pankhurst movement in England or the Woman's Party led by Alice Paul in the United States. This view seemed totally inadequate to me as a sociologist and a contemporary feminist. The emancipation or liberation of women involves more than political participation and the change of any number of laws. Liberation is equally important in areas other than politics; economic, reproductive, educational, household, sexual, and cultural emancipation are also relevant. A feminist history must include Emma Goldman as well as Elizabeth Stanton, Margaret Sanger as well as Susan Anthony, Virginia Woolf as well as Lucretia Mott—despite the fact that anarchism clearly had priority over feminism to Emma Goldman, as temperance had priority to Frances Willard and literature to Virginia Woolf. This implied that the framework of the selections would have to include not just writers and activists for whom woman's liberation was a central passion, but also those who were

equally if not more concerned with issues other than the
rights of their own sex.

These considerations suggested two criteria by which to
judge candidates for inclusion. For one, the book would not
be confined to the movement for political rights for women
but would include feminist efforts to secure economic, sexual,
educational, and reproductive liberation as well. Secondly,
room would have to be made for those whose contribution
was made by activity, rather than including only those with
skillful pens, who left books and essays for us to examine. In
this book, then, an "essential work" could be a published
book or a life or outstanding participation in some pioneering
action dedicated to expanding the life options of women.

There was, of course, a primary list of "musts" from the
very beginning of the project. A volume of "essential works"
had to include selections from Mary Wollstonecraft, Margaret
Fuller, Sarah Grimké, Elizabeth Cady Stanton, John Stuart
Mill, Charlotte Gilmán, Virginia Woolf, and Simone de
Beauvoir. By the first criterion, which broadened the spheres
of concern from politics to education, sex, maternity and the
economy, this basic list was quickly supplemented by Friedrich Engels, Harriet Martineau, Elizabeth Blackwell, Emma
Goldman, and Jane Addams. The second criterion, which
urged inclusion of activist as well as writing feminists,
brought in Frances Wright, Lucy Stone, Lucretia Mott, Susan
Anthony, and Margaret Sanger. Along the way I encountered
figures unknown to me whose work and whose lives were of
sufficient interest to merit inclusion; Judith Murray, August
Bebel, Antoinette Brown, and Suzanne LaFollette joined the
list in this way.

The lives of the feminists represented in this book span
the years from 1744 to 1972, from the birth of Abigail Adams
to the three women still alive and well in 1972—Suzanne La-
Follette, Margaret Mead, and Simone de Beauvoir. Figure 1
may help readers to link individuals to this larger historical
canvas.

There were many other feminists one would have liked
to include, but to do so would have detracted from the balance sought in the design of the book. It is with great regret
that I have had to omit entries for Florence Kelley, Emmeline
Pankhurst, Olive Schreiner, Isadora Duncan, Margaret Dreier
Robins, Mother Jones, Alice Paul, Elise Clews Parsons, Carrie
Chapman Catt, and many, many more. In some cases there

Name	Life line
Abigail Adams	1744 → 6 16 26 36 46 56 66 → 1818
Judith Murray	1751 → 9 19 29 39 49 59 69 → 1820
Mary Wollstonecraft	1759 → 1 11 21 31 → 1797
Frances Wright	1795 → 5 17 25 35 45 55 → 1852
Lucretia Mott	1793 → 7 17 27 37 47 57 67 77 87 → 1880
Harriet Martineau	1802 → 8 18 28 38 48 58 68 → 1876
Margaret Fuller	1810 → 10 20 30 40 → 1850
John Stuart Mill	1806 → 4 14 24 34 44 54 64 → 1873
Sarah Grimké	1792 → 8 18 28 38 48 58 68 78 → 1873
Angelina Grimké	1805 → 5 15 25 35 45 55 65 75 → 1876
Elizabeth Blackwell	1821 → 9 19 29 39 49 59 69 79 89 → 1910
Antoinette Brown	1825 → 5 15 25 35 45 55 65 75 85 95 → 1921
Lucy Stone	1818 → 2 12 22 32 42 52 62 72 → 1893
Susan Anthony	1820 → 10 20 30 40 50 60 70 80 → 1906
Elizabeth Stanton	1815 → 5 15 25 35 45 55 65 75 85 → 1902
Friedrich Engels	1820 → 10 20 30 40 50 60 70 → 1895
August Bebel	1840 → 10 20 30 40 50 60 70 → 1913
Alice Blackwell	1857 → 3 13 23 33 43 53 63 73 83 93 → 1950
Emma Goldman	1869 → 1 11 21 31 41 51 61 71 → 1940
Jane Addams	1860 → 10 20 30 40 50 60 70 → 1935
Charlotte Gilman	1860 → 10 20 30 40 50 60 70 → 1935
Margaret Sanger	1883 → 7 17 27 37 47 57 67 77 → 1960
Suzanne LaFollette	1893 → 7 17 27 37 47 57 67 77
Virginia Woolf	1882 → 8 18 28 38 48 58 → 1941
Margaret Mead	1901 → 9 19 29 39 49 59 69
Simone de Beauvoir	1908 → 2 12 22 32 42 52 62

FIGURE 1: Life Lines of Major Writers and Activists Covered in this Volume

were no good or easily available written works or accounts of their activity. In other cases, they duplicated too closely a kind of work already better represented by someone else.

It is also with some regret that I have omitted the contemporary period. The most recent selection is from Simone de Beauvoir's *The Second Sex*, which in my view stands as the end of an older feminism, during a transitional period that is described in the introduction to Part 4. But we are probably too close to the contemporary scene to judge what will merit inclusion in a collection of "essential works of feminism," and in the interim a great many books and journals are now easily available in bookstores and libraries.

It is hoped that the selections, together with the interpretive essays that accompany them, will communicate the diversity that has existed under the feminist banner in the past. The feminist movement has included deeply religious women as well as atheists; conservative moralists as well as radical reformers and revolutionaries; women in deep rebellion from their families and the larger society as well as women in comfortable happy circumstances, who chipped away gently at some social expectation of appropriate behavior for women. As Margaret Fuller pointed out more than a hundred years ago, some pioneers in the cause of women are passionate rebels who serve as harbingers of future change, while others are leaders of reform who must be "severe lawgivers to themselves" if they are to seek change in the legal and social structure of their society.

Pioneers in any movement for social change will include persons with disturbed family histories and sometimes unusual personality tendencies, for the wellsprings of societal change tend to be fed, not by conformists, but by individuals who are alienated from the world around them. That is as true of men pioneers as of women pioneers, though there has been an unfortunate tendency to view such men as deeply *creative* and the women as deeply *neurotic*. It serves no purpose to sketch our feminist predecessors in rosy colors or to write filiopietistic biographies suggesting a Great Woman theory of feminist history. Such a hypothesis will serve us no better than the Great Man theory of history has done. No interpretation we place on a life or a social movement can detract from the past achievement, sometimes made at great personal cost. If we hope to see increasing numbers of lives touched by feminist ideas, we need to see our predecessors sharply as the women they actually were, with all their weak-nesses as well as their strengths. There is charisma enough in their lives and writings to pass along to another generation. If those records and the lives behind them are also to stimu-late a new generation to "go and do likewise," then they must be portrayed in terms that facilitate identification with them. Since none of us is flawless, it is comforting to sense human weaknesses as well as strengths in those we admire.

Acknowledgments

There are a number of people and facilities whose assist-ance contributed to the making of this book. I have relied almost exclusively on the library resources of Baltimore, Maryland for the numerous books and journals necessary to the project. When I first began this work, I doubted that this source would be adequate, but I had underestimated the con-tributions of past generations of Baltimorians. The Enoch Pratt Library is one of the finest public libraries in the coun-try, and its staff gave enthusiastic help to me and my princi-pal student assistant, Sally Zulver, in tracking down numerous materials, particularly from the early nineteenth century. Secondly, my own institution, Goucher College, is a women's college, and the library holdings give silent testimony to that fact. The Goucher library is rich in all the mainstream suf-frage-movement materials from the Civil War period to the early 1920s. Then there is a sad falling off, and only a rare holding from the radical and reformist tradition of feminism. The period from 1940 to 1969 projects a silent message by the sheer absence of literature on women: the college did not consider the sex of its student body relevant to a liberal edu-cation. It was a good feeling, however, to establish connections with my predecessors on the faculty from an earlier period. I do not know if they dealt very much with women's rights in their courses, but they filled the shelves of the library with feminist books, in which students could find some analysis of their own history as women. The Johns Hopkins University library was of very little use on the subject of women, re-flecting the male bias of that worthy institution of higher education, though its general history holdings were of enor-mous help in preparation for the writing of the introductory essay to Part 2, on the social roots of the women's-rights movement in the nineteenth century. Neither time nor funds permitted the use of special collections, unless they held a particular manuscript it seemed important to examine. Thus the Schlesinger Library was used to secure a copy of an unpublished biography of Antoinette Brown, and the Library of Congress for a famous pamphlet on family limitation by Margaret Sanger.

Goucher College was a most congenial context in which to conduct the research underlying this book. As a small college with easy access to colleagues in fields other than one's own, it was a great help to pop across a hall or climb one flight of stairs to seek an answer to a question of a history or literature colleague. I am in particular debt to Rhoda M. Dorsey, academic dean and herself an American historian, and to the Committee on Publication and Research, which awarded me the Mary Wilhelmine Williams Fellowship that permitted me to pay my dedicated assistant, Sally Zulver, during the summer of 1971.

Special thanks to the students who experimented with me in the two seminars described above. Their papers and discussions contributed in numerous ways to the progress of the book. These included, in the seminar on the sociology of the family: Lucy Amerman, Barbara Antonazzi, Nancy Brandt, Sharon Freiberg, Angela Gilbert, Amy Hurwitz, Gayle Johnson, Ellen Lipton, Sherry Nelson, Anne Ostroff, Robin Schoen, Marilyn Schwartz, Joan Urken, and Sally Zulver. More recently, in the seminar on women's movements, the collaborating students were: Joan Barth, Phyllis Braudy, Laura Cram, Katherine Edmunds, Deborah Goldberg, Caryl Goodman, Heidi Hanson, Donna Leach, Sydney Roby, Marsha Sterns, and Barbara Zetlin.

I am deeply indebted to my friend, former colleague at Goucher College and sister-feminist, Florence Howe. Her own standards of excellence in biographic and feminist analysis have been an important source of encouragement to an essentially loner-type scholar like myself. At several critical junctures in the course of my work she gave freely of her emotional support and intellectual encouragement. Her knowledge of and commitment to the growing field of women's studies has been an important prod to the sense of urgency that helped keep me at my typewriter when other commitments tempted me away.

I would also like to express my gratitude to Toni Burbank, whose editorial support contributed yet another source of pleasure to the work, and to Ruth Hein, whose superb pen caught errors, suggested important additions, and smoothed many sentences.

Finally, I have the rare good fortune to have a very tender comrade in my husband, Peter, and three warmly supportive children, Peter, Kris, and Nina. They have seen little but the back of my head bent over a book or a typewriter for the past two summers. Behind my own head and ten fingers were four other heads and forty fingers that washed, cleaned, sewed, picked up, Xeroxed endless pages, and listened with interest as I shared with them the lives and ideas of past feminists and my attempts to find meaning and connections among them. "The book," as it was known on the domestic turf, has been in many ways a family enterprise.

Jemand and Julius gave a friendly and furry presence to many a night of work that ended at dawn.

ALICE S. ROSSI

Baltimore, Maryland

For my mother and daughters

PART 1

Reason Shall Set Us Free:
Feminism and the
Enlightenment Perspective

PART TWO

Reason Shall Set Us Free:
Feminism and the
Enlightenment Perspective

Introduction: Analysis versus Action

The eight selections included in this first section span the hundred-year period from 1770 to 1870 and range from the young Abigail Adams' letter to her husband, "Remember the Ladies," to John Stuart Mill's *The Subjection of Women*. The authors include some of the earliest women radical thinkers in English and American history (Wollstonecraft, Wright, and Martineau); one of the few male intellectual and political figures of the nineteenth century to espouse the cause of women's rights (Mill); a previously little-known eighteenth-century American woman who wrote on sex equality (Murray); and a woman who deserves to be known as the first sociologist, though the field was not labeled "sociology" for twenty years after she defined and illustrated the scientific analysis of society (Martineau).

Despite their diversity of style and values, the authors of these first eight selections share several characteristics. Most of all, they were heirs to the happy Enlightenment conviction that reason would lead the way to a progressively better social order, free of the superstitions that had in the past bogged down mankind. Throughout their writings there is an expectation that "free enquiry" is the simple path to truth which, once arrived at, must absolutely persuade and easily translate into social reality. Their enthusiastic, if naive, belief in education as the cure-all for human ignorance and corruption flowed directly from their confidence in the human cognitive faculty. While their language was often passionate and expressive, underneath it there was a rationalist philosophy and a shared set of libertarian ideals. These writers believed deeply that reason, if properly cultivated through education, could set men and women free. What "reasonable" person, they seemed to ask, could fail to be convinced by their analysis of the position of women, and once convinced, what "reasonable" man could fail to encourage women to cultivate a wider range of options and skills?

Prominent in the thought of many early English feminists was an ongoing concern for the implications of the French and American revolutions. Like many Englishmen of their day, they tried to find the means to achieve many of the revolutionary goals without the revolutionary bloodshed. The feminist ideas of Wollstonecraft, Wright, Martineau, and Fuller have a flavor one associates with the earlier revolutionary ferment, transmuted into an earnest hope that rational persuasion may substitute for overt conflict. Viewing male power as analogous to political tyranny, they directed their appeal concerning women to the democratic political beat in English political thought of their day. This theme appears later in the century among socialists in England and the United States, but its strongly feminist form reemerges only with the renascence of feminism in the 1960s. It was rarely visible among the American nineteenth-century feminists, whose moral perspective focused on the analogy between women's oppression and that of the slave rather than that of the worker.

The flexing of rationalist muscles often led to extreme ideological positions. Some became so convinced that the villain of the past was the church, which they viewed as steeped in superstition and irrationality, and its closely allied institution, the state, that a "reasonable" route to freedom required the disestablishment of both institutions. Those who took this direction from their rationalist starting point tended to polarize into two different intellectual and political camps. At one extreme was the *philosophic anarchist*, exemplified by William Godwin, husband of Mary Wollstonecraft. The anarchist was critical of all human institutions and dedicated to the belief that once people were liberated from false gods and repressive training, they could live in a golden state of freedom and happiness. In this view, the "law" was a major impediment to freedom and must be discarded. From here it was an easy step for Godwin to denounce marriage, the state, and the church. In a similar vein, though not quite so extreme as Godwin, Wollstonecraft attempted to do for woman what Rousseau tried to do for the natural man and Paine for the rights of man. A combination of eighteenth-century rationalism and nineteenth-century Victorian sexual repression may have constituted the twin foundations for the naive confidence expressed by these early writers in the potential for smoothly implementing social change following their rational analyses. In 1973 our intellectual perspective is far more complex, formed as it has been by the all too frequent exposure during this century to the continuing power of myth and aggression in human affairs and to the emotional intensity with which men and women resist fundamental change in their intimate relations with each other.

A second extreme manifestation of Enlightenment thinking was the belief that a perfect society could be rationally ordered by the rationalists themselves. This was the route of the *social planner,* well illustrated by those who became committed to cooperative-community models, such as Robert Owen early in the nineteenth century and Marxist-Leninists later on. The planners were committed to a manipulation of the environment so that the crippling effects of the present bad environment on human character would be remedied. More pragmatic than the anarchists, they were convinced that an intermediary stage, consisting of a generation or two of specially trained people, would be necessary before individuals and society were ready for natural association (Brinton 1959:300–302). Fanny Wright was clearly attracted to this side of the Enlightenment impulse in her plans for the experimental community, Nashoba, and the activities sponsored by her Hall of Science in New York. Martineau and Mill, by contrast, put much greater emphasis on the power of thought and education to do the job of releasing men and women from the confines of the past. Their environmentalism left little room in the theories of Mill and Martineau for either psychological or physiological assumptions concerning sex differences.

The early libertarian feminist thinkers tended to be located in similar social positions. They were members of the more forward-looking intellectual circles of their society. As publicists, critics, novelists, political economists, they literally lived by their pens, marginal to the centers of economic and social power of their day. They were cosmopolitan members of an urban intelligentsia.

Such early feminists as Wright, Fuller, Mill, and Martineau began their commitment to feminism, as to many other causes of their day, first as theorists and writers. In the case of some, ideas and published works led to involvement in political activity. Though the balance between their analysis and action was heavily tipped toward analysis, several of these early feminist writers also participated in efforts at social and political change. Wright tried to implement her proposed solutions to the problem of slavery through the

establishment of Nashoba. Mill took the route from political
writing to political action as an elected member of the House
of Commons and sponsor of the first bill to enfranchise English women. Fuller moved from journalistic writing in New
York to personal participation in political rebellion in Italy.

In Part 2 we shall see that the balance between analysis
and action was quite different for most of the pioneers who
founded the woman's-rights movement in the mid-nineteenth
century. They were activists to a far greater extent than they
were analysts. While a general feminist orientation was their
starting point, it was quickly transformed into active political
organization. Throughout the lives of such women as Anthony, Mott, Stanton, and Stone the accent was far more on
action and organization than it was on any confidence in the
power of the written word alone. The discussion of the social
origins of the woman's-rights movement which introduces
Part 2 shows that the impulse of these early American feminists was rooted in the revivalist dedication to benevolent
reform of society. They were conservative and moralistic,
exerting organized political pressure for legal reform. Their
symbols were petitions, marches, and conventions. By contrast, the Enlightenment feminists represented in this first
section were libertarian and rationalist, concentrating their
efforts on the power of the written word. Essays, reviews, and
books were their symbols and tools.

"Remember the Ladies":
Abigail Adams vs. John Adams

Abigail Adams' famous "Remember the Ladies" letter to her husband has been referred to in numerous histories of women's rights in America. In this letter she half-jestingly suggests that if the lawmakers of the Second Continental Congress do not direct attention to the "Ladies," they are "determined to foment a Rebellion." Rebellion was of course much on the minds of both John and Abigail Adams in the spring of 1776. Abigail's letter was written shortly after the English occupation of Boston had been lifted, and she also queries her husband about the military and political situation in Virginia.

It seems highly appropriate to begin this collection with this lively exchange between Abigail and John Adams. Abridgments of three additional letters from the Adams correspondence have also been included, to supplement the passages from the three key ones in the husband-wife exchange of views on women's political rights.

The first selection, written in 1771, is from a letter written to a friend of the family, Isaac Smith, while he was on a trip to England. It supplies some personal background for Abigail Adams' plea to her husband five years later, for here she describes her own desire to have been what her sex prevents her from being: as she put it, "a rover." She specifically requests Smith to find out more about Catherine Macaulay, the English woman historian who enjoyed a spectacular popularity in England during the 1770s and 1780s. Catherine Macaulay will appear again in the discussion of Mary Wollstonecraft, who was much influenced by Macaulay's *Letters on Education.*

The second of the supplementary letters is to Abigail Adams' friend Mercy Otis Warren, who later followed the model of Catherine Macaulay by writing a three-volume work on the American Revolution. In writing to Warren, Abigail Adams lets off some steam over her husband's mocking response to her plea for "the Ladies." She claims that she will write him that she had been testing the disinterestedness of his virtue and "when weigh'd in the balance have found it wanting." She does indeed respond to John Adams, but not at all along the lines she outlined to her friend. From her original prediction of rebellion she has moved to a passive assertion of women's "sway"; thus an early skirmish over women's rights to representation ends on this tame note.

Finally, John Adams' letter to James Sullivan is of special interest because of the very different tone it takes in responding to Sullivan's questions about the qualification of voters. In writing to Sullivan, Adams develops his reason for holding to a property qualification—that men without property are typically directed by some man of property "who has attached their minds to his interest." Since few women could hold property in those days, women would be excluded from the franchise on property grounds. Adams, however, did not see fit to expand this point in responding to his wife—that is, that women would vote in accord with those men who have attached women's minds to their interest, presumably their husbands and fathers. He gives no logical argument of any kind in responding to Abigail Adams.

There is an interesting omission in the categories of persons John Adams sees rebelling during this period of the 1770s: to children, college students, apprentices, Indians, Negroes, he links women as the rebellious upstarts of the day. He does not mention mature men who did not own property. A century later, when the fourteenth and fifteenth amendments were passed, Abigail Adams' female descendants were most vigorous in their response to the idea that women were linked with the "lunatic, ignorant and criminal" classes, in being excluded from the new definition of citizens qualified to vote.

Abigail Adams to Isaac Smith Jr.

Braintree April the 20 1771

Dear Sir

I write you, not from the Noisy Buisy Town, but from my humble Cottage in Braintree, where I arrived last Saturday and here again am to take up my abode.

"Where Contemplation p[l]umes her rufled Wings
And the free Soul look's down to pitty Kings."

Suffer me to snatch you a few moments from all the Hurry and tumult of London and in immagination place you by me that I may ask you ten thousand Questions, and bear with me Sir, tis the only recompence you can make for the loss of your Company.

From my Infancy I have always felt a great inclination to visit the Mother Country as tis call'd and had nature formed me of the other Sex, I should certainly have been a rover. And altho this desire has greatly diminished owing partly I believe to maturer years, but more to the unnatural treatment which this our poor America has received from her, I yet retain a curiosity to know what ever is valuable in her. I thank you Sir for the particular account you have already favour'd me with, but you always took pleasure in being communicatively good.

Women you know Sir are considered as Domestick Beings, and altho they inherit an Eaquel Share of curiosity with the other Sex, yet but few are hardy eno' to venture abroad, and explore the amaizing variety of distant Lands. The Natural tenderness and Delicacy of our Constitutions, added to the many Dangers we are subject too from your Sex, renders it almost imposible for a Single Lady to travel without injury to her character. And those who have a protecter in an Husband, have generally speaking obstacles sufficent to prevent their Roving, and instead of visiting other Countries; are

First five letters from L. H. Butterfield, ed., *The Adams Papers*, Series II, *Adams Family Correspondence*. Cambridge, Mass., Harvard University Press, 1963. Pp. 76–402. Final letter from Charles Francis Adams, ed., *The Works of John Adams: With Life of the Author*. Boston, Little, Brown, 1854. Vol. IX, pp. 375–378.

obliged to content themselves with seeing but a very small part of their own. To your Sex we are most of us indebted for all the knowledg we acquire of Distant lands. As to a Knowledg of Humane Nature, I believe it may as easily be obtained in this Country, as in England, France or Spain. Education alone I conceive Constitutes the difference in Manners. Tis natural I believe that every person to have a partiality for their own Country. Dont you think this little Spot of ours better calculated for happiness than any other you have yet seen or read of. Would you exchange it for England, France, Spain or Ittally? Are not the people here more upon an Eaquality in point of knowledg and of circumstances—there being none so immensly rich as to Lord it over us, neither any so abjectly poor as to suffer for the necessaries of life provided they will use the means. . . .

. . . I have a great desire to be made acquainted with Mrs. Maccaulays own history. One of my own Sex so eminent in a tract so uncommon naturally raises my curiosity and all I could ever learn relative to her, is this that she is a widdow Lady and Sister to Mr. Sawbridge. I have a curiosity to know her Education, and what first prompted her to engage in a Study never before Exhibited to the publick by one of her own Sex and Country, tho now to the honour of both so admirably performed by her. As you are now upon the Spot, and have been entroduced to her acquaintance, you will I hope be able to satisfie me with some account, in doing which you will confer an oblagation upon your assured Friend,

Abigail Adams.

Abigail Adams to John Adams

Braintree March 31 1776

—I long to hear that you have declared an independancy —and by the way in the new Code of Laws which I suppose it will be necessary for you to make I desire you would Remember the Ladies, and be more generous and favourable to them than your ancestors. Do not put such unlimited power into the hands of the Husbands. Remember all Men would be tyrants if they could. If perticuliar care and attention is not paid to the Laidies we are determined to foment a

Rebelion, and will not hold ourselves bound by any Laws in which we have no voice, or Representation.

That your Sex are Naturally Tyrannical is a Truth so thoroughly established as to admit of no dispute, but such of you as wish to be happy willingly give up the harsh title of Master for the more tender and endearing one of Friend. Why then, not put it out of the power of the vicious and the Lawless to use us with cruelty and indignity with impunity. Men of Sense in all Ages abhor those customs which treat us only as the vassals of your Sex. Regard us then as Beings placed by providence under your protection and in immitation of the Supreem Being make use of that power only for our happiness.

John Adams to Abigail Adams

Ap. 14. 1776

As to Declarations of Independency, be patient. Read our Privateering Laws, and our Commercial Laws. What signifies a Word.

As to your extraordinary Code of Laws, I cannot but laugh. We have been told that our Struggle has loosened the bands of Government every where. That Children and Apprentices were disobedient—that schools and Colledges were grown turbulent—that Indians slighted their Guardians and Negroes grew insolent to their Masters. But your Letter was the first Intimation that another Tribe more numerous and powerfull than all the rest were grown discontented.—This is rather too coarse a Compliment but you are so saucy, I wont blot it out.

Depend upon it, We know better than to repeal our Masculine systems. Altho they are in full Force, you know they are little more than Theory. We dare not exert our Power in its full Latitude. We are obliged to go fair, and softly, and in Practice you know We are the subjects. We have only the Name of Masters, and rather than give up this, which would compleatly subject Us to the Despotism of the Peticoat, I hope General Washington, and all our brave Heroes would fight. I am sure every good Politician would plot, as long as he would against Despotism, Empire, Monarchy, Aristocracy, Oligarchy, or Ochlocracy.

Abigail Adams to Mercy Otis Warren

Braintree April 27 1776

He is very sausy to me in return for a List of Female Grievances which I transmitted to him. I think I will get you to join me in a petition to Congress. I thought it was very probable our wise Statesmen would erect a New Government and form a new code of Laws. I ventured to speak a word in behalf of our Sex, who are rather hardly dealt with by the Laws of England which gives such unlimitted power to the Husband to use his wife Ill.

I requested that our Legislators would consider our case and as all Men of Delicacy and Sentiment are averse to Ex-cercising the power they possess, yet as there is a natural propensity in Humane Nature to domination, I thought the most generous plan was to put it out of the power of the Arbitrary and tyranick to injure us with impunity by Estab-lishing some Laws in our favour upon just and Liberal prin-cipals.

I believe I even threatned fomenting a Rebellion in case we were not considerd, and assured him we would not hold ourselves bound by any Laws in which we had neither a voice, nor representation.

In return he tells me he cannot but Laugh at My Ex-trodonary Code of Laws. That he had heard their Struggle had loosned the bands of Government, that children and ap-prentices were dissabedient, that Schools and Colledges were grown turbulant, that Indians slighted their Guardians, and Negroes grew insolent to their Masters. But my Letter was the first intimation that another Tribe more numerous and powerfull than all the rest were grown discontented. This is rather too coarse a complement, he adds, but that I am so sausy he wont blot it out.

So I have help'd the Sex abundantly, but I will tell him I have only been making trial of the Disintresstedness of his Virtue, and when weigh'd in the balance have found it wanting.

It would be bad policy to grant us greater power say they since under all the disadvantages we Labour we have the assendancy over their Hearts.

And charm by accepting, by submitting sway.

Abigail Adams to John Adams

B[raintre]e May 7 1776

I can not say that I think you very generous to the Ladies, for whilst you are proclaiming peace and good will to Men, Emancipating all Nations, you insist upon retaining an absolute power over Wives. But you must remember that Arbitrary power is like most other things which are very hard, very liable to be broken—and notwithstanding all your wise Laws and Maxims we have it in our power not only to free ourselves but to subdue our Masters, and without voilence throw both your natural and legal authority at our feet—

"Charm by accepting, by submitting sway
Yet have our Humour most when we obey."

John Adams to James Sullivan

Philadelphia, 26 May, 1776

It is certain, in theory, that the only moral foundation of government is, the consent of the people. But to what an extent shall we carry this principle? Shall we say that every individual of the community, old and young, male and female, as well as rich and poor, must consent, expressly, to every act of legislation? No, you will say, this is impossible. How, then, does the right arise in the majority to govern the minority, against their will? Whence arises the right of the men to govern the women, without their consent? Whence the right of the old to bind the young, without theirs?

But let us first suppose that the whole community, of every age, rank, sex, and condition, has a right to vote. This community is assembled. A motion is made, and carried by a majority of one voice. The minority will not agree to this. Whence arises the right of the majority to govern, and the obligation of the minority to obey?

From necessity, you will say, because there can be no other rule.

But why exclude women?

You will say, because their delicacy renders them unfit for practice and experience in the great businesses of life, and the hardy enterprises of war, as well as the arduous cares of state. Besides, their attention is so much engaged with the necessary nurture of their children, that nature has made them fittest for domestic cares. And children have not judgment or will of their own. True. But will not these reasons apply to others? Is it not equally true, that men in general, in every society, who are wholly destitute of property, are also too little acquainted with public affairs to form a right judgment, and too dependent upon other men to have a will of their own? If this is a fact, if you give to every man who has no property, a vote, will you not make a fine encouraging provision for corruption, by your fundamental law? Such is the frailty of the human heart, that very few men who have no property, have any judgment of their own. They talk and vote as they are directed by some man of property, who has attached their minds to his interest.

Upon my word, Sir, I have long thought an army a piece of clock-work, and to be governed only by principles and maxims, as fixed as any in mechanics; and, by all that I have read in the history of mankind, and in authors who have speculated upon society and government, I am much inclined to think a government must manage a society in the same manner; and that this is machinery too. . . .

Your idea that those laws which affect the lives and personal liberty of all, or which inflict corporal punishment, affect those who are not qualified to vote, as well as those who are, is just. But so they do women, as well as men; children, as well as adults. What reason should there be for excluding a man of twenty years eleven months and twenty-seven days old, from a vote, when you admit one who is twenty-one? The reason is, you must fix upon some period in life, when the understanding and will of men in general, is fit to be trusted by the public. Will not the same reason justify the state in fixing upon some certain quantity of property, as a qualification?

The same reasoning which will induce you to admit all men who have no property, to vote, with those who have, for those laws which affect the person, will prove that you ought to admit women and children; for, generally speaking, women and children have as good judgments, and as independent minds, as those men who are wholly destitute of property; these last being to all intents and purposes as much dependent upon others, who will please to feed, clothe, and employ them, as women are upon their husbands, or children on their parents. . . .

Depend upon it, Sir, it is dangerous to open so fruitful a source of controversy and altercation as would be opened by attempting to alter the qualifications of voters; there will be no end of it. New claims will arise; women will demand a vote; lads from twelve to twenty-one will think their rights not enough attended to; and every man who has not a farthing, will demand an equal voice with any other, in all acts of state. It tends to confound and destroy all distinctions, and prostrate all ranks to one common level.

Away From Puddings and Garments:
Judith Sargent Murray (1751–1820)

Judith Sargent was born in Gloucester, Massachusetts, in 1751, the daughter of a prosperous merchant and sea captain. As often happened in these early years, the fact that she had a brother was crucial for her own early educational preparation, for during the years her brother studied at home in preparation for entry to Harvard College, she was permitted to study by his side and share the training he received. The Sargent family held liberal views in both religious and political matters. Judith's father strongly supported the Revolutionary forces in the colonies and later sat as a delegate to the Massachusetts convention which ratified the Constitution in 1788. The family's religious views were deeply affected by the preaching of Reverend John Murray, who converted the family to the Universalist creed.

Judith Sargent married John Stevens in 1769, when she was eighteen years old. After his death and several years of verse and prose writing, she married John Murray, the same preacher who had earlier converted her family. The first publication from her pen was a volume of verse in 1784, four years before her marriage to Murray. The next decade represents a very productive period in her writing career: she wrote for the *Universalist Quarterly*, numerous essays for the *Massachusetts Magazine*, and two plays, *Virtue Triumphant* and *The Traveller Returned*. She is the first native-born woman dramatist in America to have had her plays professionally performed.

Murray's essay "On the Equality of the Sexes" was first published in the *Massachusetts Magazine* in 1790; there is some evidence, however, that a first draft considerably predates publication. In a footnote to the 1790 version, Murray comments that "if it hath been anticipated, the testimony of many respectable persons, who saw it in manuscript as early as the year 1779, can obviate the imputation of plagiarism." One surmises that essays on women's education, which began to appear in English and American journals in the late 1780s, made her anxious to publish her own essay on sex equality but that she feared that her ideas might be seen as borrowed from other contemporary writers.

Judith Murray returned to the topic of the education of women in later writings for the *Massachusetts Magazine*, in a section entitled "The Gleaner," which she wrote over a considerable period of time. These essays, which appeared in a separate, third volume of her collected writings in 1798, cover a wide range of topics treated in a variety of ways: in the guise of letters to which she responds in print—anticipating the question-and-answer columns that were later to take hold in American newspapers and magazines; fictional stories in which she develops her ideas on the proper education of a woman in the medium of a central female character; essays on such topics as philanthropy, household economy, and hospitality. At the end of the "Gleaner" essays she explained that she used the pseudonym "Constantia" to assure that her writing would be viewed as independently as possible, unaffected by the fact of her marriage to John Murray.

The addendum to Murray's 1790 essay is of special interest. She admits that she has not adhered closely to Scripture in developing her main argument in the essay; but knowing that many people do build their case against equality of women on the Bible, she attempts a rebuttal to a strict scriptural interpretation of the Fall. No doubt with tongue in cheek, Murray taunts men with the idea that Adam was not motivated by any high pure motive, as was Eve, but by attachment to a woman. "Strong-minded" women of the nineteenth century later embellished and varied this reinterpretation of Scripture in their efforts to meet the opposition of the clergy to any change in the status of women. A hundred years later Elizabeth Cady Stanton tried her hand at a "Woman's Bible," much to the embarrassment and dismay of her conservative suffragist friends. Close to two hundred years later feminists in the 1960s again returned to theology and the structure of the church in an analysis and denunciation of the demeaning and distorted treatment women had received from both Catholic and Protestant churchmen (Daly 1968, Callahan 1965, Lauer 1963).

Murray's essay stands as the earliest example of this argument that I have found in my search of the American feminist literature. This is its first republication since its 1790 appearance.

---

৯ On the Equality of the Sexes ৯

Is it upon mature consideration we adopt the idea, that nature is thus partial in her distributions? Is it indeed a fact, that she hath yielded to one half of the human species so unquestionable a mental superiority? I know that to both sexes elevated understandings, and the reverse, are common. But, suffer me to ask, in what the minds of females are so notoriously deficient, or unequal. May not the intellectual powers be ranged under their four heads—imagination, reason, memory and judgement. The province of imagination has long since been surrendered up to us, and we have been crowned undoubted sovereigns of the regions of fancy. Invention is perhaps the most arduous effort of the mind; this branch of imagination hath been particularly ceded to us, and we have been time out of mind invested with that creative faculty. Observe the variety of fashions (here I bar the contemptuous smile) which distinguish and adorn the female world; how continually are they changing, insomuch that they almost render the whole man's assertion problematical, and we are ready to say, *there is something new under the sun.* Now, what a playfulness, what an exuberance of fancy, what strength of inventive imagination, doth this continual variation discover? Again, it hath been observed, that if the turpitude of the conduct of our sex, hath been ever so enormous, so extremely ready are we that the very first thought presents us with an apology so plausible, as to produce our actions even in an amiable light. Another instance of our creative powers, is our talent for slander; how ingenious are we at inventive scandal? what a formidable story can we in a moment fabricate merely from the force of a prolifick imagi-

---

From Judith Sargent Murray, "On the Equality of the Sexes," *The Massachusetts Magazine*, March 1790, pp. 132–135, and April 1790, pp. 223–226.

nation? how many reputations, in the fertile brain of a female, have been utterly despoiled? how industrious are we at improving a hint? suspicion how easily do we convert into conviction, and conviction, embellished by the power of eloquence, stalks abroad to the surprise and confusion of unsuspecting innocence. Perhaps it will be asked if I furnish these facts as instances of excellency in our sex. Certainly not; but as proofs of a creative faculty, of a lively imagination. Assuredly great activity of mind is thereby discovered, and was this activity properly directed, what beneficial effects would follow. Is the needle and kitchen sufficient to employ the operations of a soul thus organized? I should conceive not. Nay, it is a truth that those very departments leave the intelligent principle vacant, and at liberty for speculation. Are we deficient in reason? We can only reason from what we know, and if opportunity of acquiring knowledge hath been denied us, the inferiority of our sex cannot fairly be deduced from thence. Memory, I believe, will be allowed us in common, since every one's experience must testify, that a loquacious old woman is as frequently met with, as a communicative old man; their subjects are alike drawn from the fund of other times, and the transactions of their youth, or of maturer life, entertain, or perhaps fatigue you, in the evening of their lives. "But our judgment is not so strong— we do not distinguish so well." Yet it may be questioned, from what doth this superiority, in thus discriminating faculty of the soul, proceed. May we not trace its source in the difference of education, and continued advantages? Will it be said that the judgment of a male of two years old, is more sage than that of a female's of the same age? I believe the reverse is generally observed to be true. But from that period what partiality! how is the one exalted and the other depressed, by the contrary modes of education which are adopted! the one is taught to aspire, and the other is early confined and limited. As their years increase, the sister must be wholly domesticated, while the brother is led by the hand through all the flowery paths of science. Grant that their minds are by nature equal, yet who shall wonder at the *apparent* superiority, if indeed custom becomes *second nature;* nay if it taketh place of nature, and that it doth the experience of each day will evince. At length arrived at womanhood, the uncultivated fair one feels a void, which the employments allotted her are by no means capable of filling. What can she do? to books, she may not apply; or if she doth, *to those only of the novel kind*, lest she merit the appellation of a *learned lady*; and what ideas have been affixed to this term, the observation of many can testify. Fashion, scandal and sometimes what is still more reprehensible, are then called in to her relief; and who can say to what lengths the liberties she takes may proceed. Meantime she herself is most unhappy; she feels the want of a cultivated mind. Is she single, she in vain seeks to fill up time from sexual employments or amusements. Is she united to a person whose soul nature made equal to her own, education hath set him so far above her, that in those entertainments which are productive of such rational felicity, she is not qualified to accompany him. She experiences a mortifying consciousness of inferiority, which embitters every enjoyment. Doth the person to whom her adverse fate hath consigned her, possess a mind incapable of improvement, she is equally wretched, in being so closely connected with an individual whom she cannot but despise. Now, was she permitted the same instructors as her brother, (with an eye however to their particular departments) for the employment of a rational mind an ample field would be opened. In astronomy she might catch a glimpse of the immensity of the Deity, and thence she would form amazing conceptions of the august and supreme Intelligence. In geography she would admire Jehova in the midst of his benevolence; thus adapting this globe to the various wants and amusements of its inhabitants. In natural philosophy she would adore the infinite majesty of heaven, clothed in condescension; and as she traversed the reptile world, she would hail the goodness of a creating God. A mind, thus filled, would have little room for the trifles with which our sex are, with too much justice, accused of amusing themselves, and they would thus be rendered fit companions for those, who should one day wear them as their crown. Fashions, in their variety, would then give place to conjectures, which might perhaps conduce to the improvement of the literary world; and there would be no leisure for slander or detraction. Reputation would not then be blasted, but serious speculations would occupy the lively imaginations of the sex. Unnecessary visits would be precluded, and that custom would only be indulged by way of relaxation, or to answer the demands of consanguinity and friendship. Females would become discreet, their judgments would be invigorated, and their partners for life being circumspectly chosen, an unhappy Hymen would then be as rare, as is now the reverse.

Will it be urged that those acquirements would supersede our domestick duties, I answer that every requisite in female economy is easily attained; and, with truth I can add, that when once attained, they require no further *mental attention*. Nay, while we are pursuing the needle, or the superintendency of the family, I repeat, that our minds are at full liberty for reflection; that imagination may exert itself in full vigor; and that if a just foundation early laid, our ideas will then be worthy of rational beings. If we were industrious we might easily find time to arrange them upon paper, or should avocations press too hard for such an indulgence, the hours allotted for conversation would at least become more refined and rational. Should it still be vociferated, "Your domestick employments are sufficient"—I would calmly ask, is it reasonable, that a candidate for immortality, for the joys of heaven, an intelligent being, who is to spend an eternity in contemplating the works of Deity, should at present be so degraded, as to be allowed no other ideas, than those which are suggested by the mechanism of a pudding, or the sewing of the seams of a garment? Pity that all such censurers of female improvement do not go one step further, and deny their future existence; to be consistent they surely ought.

Yes, ye lordly, ye haughty sex, our souls are by nature *equal* to yours; the same breath of God animates, enlivens, and invigorates us; and that we are not fallen lower than yourselves, let those witness who have greatly towered above the various discouragements by which they have been so heavily oppressed; and though I am unacquainted with the list of celebrated characters on either side, yet from the observations I have made in the contracted circle in which I have moved, I dare confidently believe, that from the commencement of time to the present day, there hath been as many females, as males, who, by the *mere force of natural powers*, have merited the crown of applause; who *thus unassisted*, have seized the wreath of fame. I know there are who assert, that as the animal powers of the one sex are superiour, of course their mental faculties also must be stronger; thus attributing strength of mind to the transient organization of this earth born tenement. But if this reasoning is just, man must be content to yield the palm to many of the brute creation, since by not a few of his brethren of the field, he is far surpassed

in bodily strength. Moreover, was this argument admitted, it
would prove too much, for occular demonstration evinceth,
that there are many robust masculine ladies, and effeminate
gentlemen. Yet I fancy that Mr. Pope, though clogged with an
enervated body, and distinguished by a diminutive stature,
could nevertheless lay claim to greatness of soul; and perhaps
there are many other instances which might be adduced to
combat so unphilosophical an opinion. Do we not often see,
that when the clay built tabernacle is well nigh dissolved,
when it is just ready to mingle with the parent soil, the immortal inhabitant aspires to, and even attaineth heights the
most sublime, and which were before wholly unexplored. Besides, were we to grant that animal strength proved anything, taking into consideration the accustomed impartiality
of nature, we should be induced to imagine, that she had
invested the female mind with superiour strength as an equivalent for the bodily powers of man. But waving this however
palpable advantage, for *equality* only, we wish to contend.

CONSTANTIA

· · ·

By way of supplement to the forgoing pages, I subjoin the
following extract from a letter wrote to a friend in the
December of 1780.

AND now assist me, O thou genius of my sex, while I
undertake the arduous task of endeavouring to combat that
vulgar, that almost universal errour, which hath, it seems
enlisted even Mr. P—— under its banners. The superiority of
your sex hath, I grant, been time out of mind esteemed a
truth incontrovertible; in consequence of which persuasion,
every plan of education hath been calculated to establish this
favourite tenet. Not long since, weak and presuming as I was,
I amused myself with selecting some arguments from nature,
reason and experience, against this so generally received idea.
I confess that to sacred testimonies I had not recourse. I held
them to be merely metaphorical, and thus regarding them, I
could not persuade myself that there was any propriety in
bringing them to decide in this *very important debate*. However, as you, sir, confine yourself entirely to the sacred ora-
cles, I mean to bend the whole of my artillery against those

supposed proofs, which you have from thence provided, and from which you have formed an intrenchment *apparently* so invulnerable. And first, to begin with our great progenitors; but here, suffer me to promise, that it is for mental strength I mean to contend, for with respect to animal powers, I yield them undisputed to that sex, which enjoys them in common with the lion, the tyger, and many other beasts of prey; therefore your observations respecting *the rib, under the arm, at a distance from the head, &c.&c.* in no sort militate against my view. Well, but the woman was first in the transgression. Strange how blind *self love* renders you men; were you not wholly absorbed in a partial admiration of your own abilities, you would long since have acknowledged the force of what I am now going to urge. It is true some ignoramuses have, absurdly enough informed us, that the beauteous fair of paradise, was seduced from her obedience, by a malignant demon, *in the guise of a baleful serpent;* but we, who are better informed, know that the fallen spirit presented himself to her view, *a shining angel still;* for thus, saith the criticks in the Hebrew tongue, ought the word to be rendered. Let us examine her motive—Hark! the seraph declares that she shall attain a perfection of knowledge; for is there aught which is not comprehended under one or other of the terms *good* and *evil.* It doth not appear that she was governed by any one sensual appetite; but merely by a desire of adorning her mind; a laudable ambition fired her soul, and a thirst for knowledge impelled the predilection so fatal in its consequences. Adam could not plead the same deception; assuredly he was not deceived; nor ought we to admire his superiour strength, or wonder at his sagacity, when we so often confess that example is much more influential than precept. His gentle partner stood before him, a melancholy instance of the direful effects of disobedience; he saw her not possessed of that wisdom which she had fondly hoped to obtain, but he beheld the once blooming female, disrobed of that innocence, which had heretofore rendered her so lovely. To him then deception became impossible, as he had proof positive of the fallacy of the argument, which the deceiver had suggested. What then could be his inducement to burst the barriers, and to fly directly in the face of that command, which *immediately* from the mouth of Deity *he* had received, since, I say, he could not plead the fascinating stimulus, the accumulation of knowledge, as indisputable conviction was so visibly portrayed before him.

What mighty cause impelled him to sacrifice myriads of beings
yet unborn, and by one impious act, which *he saw* would be
productive of such fatal effect, entail undistinguished ruin
upon a race of beings, which he was yet to produce. Blush, ye
vaunters of fortitude; ye boasters of resolution; ye haughty
lords of the creation; blush when ye remember, that he was
influenced by no other motive than a bare pusillanimous attachment to a woman! by sentiments so exquisitely soft, that
all his sons have, from that period, when they have designed
to degrade them, described as highly feminine. Thus it should
see, that all the arts of the grand deceiver (since means adequate to the purpose are, I conceive, invariably pursued)
were requisite to mislead our general mother, while the father
of mankind forfeited his own, and relinquished the happiness
of posterity, merely in compliance with the blandishments of
a female.

Champion of Womankind:
Mary Wollstonecraft (1759–1797)

Mary Wollstonecraft was born in London in 1759, the second child and first daughter of Edward John and Elizabeth Dixon Wollstonecraft. Shortly before her birth her father had inherited a sizable amount of money from his family. He had aspirations to become a gentleman farmer with this financial cushion, but he proved unsuited to the work required for an independent farmer to succeed in those years of the Enclosure Acts. Children were born in rapid succession, and the family moved from farm to farm as the father sought some magical site where he could wrest a financial return from the earth and halt the depletion of his inheritance. As family responsibilities grew and the family finances worsened, he inflicted his fury and despair on his wife, and she in turn responded with growing impatience and excessive demands for obedience from her oldest daughter, Mary.

The family situation never improved, and Mary grew into an unhappy, introspective youngster, hungry for affection and guidance, but rarely experiencing any to meet her needs. The frequent moves themselves prevented the cultivation of any lasting friendships outside the family. As she neared her teens, Mary found that she could best confront the difficult family scenes by reacting to her father with independence and contempt and to her mother with as much avoidance as possible. She roamed the wild country of Wales or the English towns they lived near, absorbing the physical and social variety of the English scene. While living at Hoxton, she befriended one elderly reverend and his wife, who shared their books and welcomed Mary to their home. There she perhaps had her first taste of an affectionate relationship between husband and wife and of a peaceful domestic setting. Mrs. Clare was in turn responsible for introducing Mary to a young girl, Fanny Blood, who became a close friend and mentor to the younger Mary. Fanny was accomplished in the arts, well read, and domestically competent in her own family, which was headed by a father as impecunious as Mary's. Fanny was

skillful at sewing and drawing, from which she earned enough
to sustain the household and feed her younger siblings. The
two girls corresponded, and soon Mary set herself to improving her writing and extending her reading under Fanny's
instruction.

In 1778, over her parents' objection, Mary struck out on
her own in a search for both independence and income. The
choice was a narrow one for a girl of nineteen: not yet competent to teach, she could therefore only serve as a companion
to an elderly widow. In Mary's case this was a Mrs. Dawson,
who lived in Bath, England's most fashionable watering place.
While the town itself provided Mary with exposure to yet
another dimension of English life, the wealthy pleasure-
seeking aristocracy and a retinue of fortune seekers, her position in the Dawson household was a difficult one—above the
servants yet not acceptable as a peer in the widow's own
social circle. Wollstonecraft's letters during this year show
two characteristics: a growing despondency and a strain to
acquire some polish and style in her writing. When her mother
became fatally ill, she left the Dawson household and took on
her mother's care until her death.

With a father who had given up all hope of doing anything
but exist very meagerly on his shrinking financial reserves,
Mary, like so many women whose lives we shall examine in
this collection, was the member of the family to assume responsibility. For all the claims of strident egocentricism that
greeted her in later years, any review of the responsibilities
she willingly assumed during these early years makes it
apparent that in fact she had a generous and willing heart.
Being of service to others may be psychologically congenial to
those who have been deprived of affection and trust in their
early life, since indebtedness of others is a consequence of
such service; but it is hardly the only possible outcome of an
emotionally impoverished childhood. There was strength and
a capacity to manage difficulties in the commitments Mary
Wollstonecraft accepted with such good grace. After her
mother's death she worked for a year as a governess in Ireland
and then established what became a moderately successful
day and boarding school, with her friend Fanny and two sisters serving as her teaching associates. The money she earned
from this venture, beyond supporting the four women, was
also freely given to help Fanny's parents and Mary's father
and younger brother. Her loyalty to her sister Eliza and to her

dearest friend Fanny is shown not merely in the teaching collaboration and financial help, but also in far more taxing efforts on their behalf. It was Mary who flew to her sister's home after the birth of a first child, when from all accounts the sister seems to have undergone a severe postpartum depression. Mary nursed her sister, became convinced that the trouble was rooted in marital unhappiness, and effected an adventurous "rescue mission" by secreting her sister away, while fearing the wrath of both the law and her brother-in-law. When Fanny later married and moved to Lisbon, it was again Mary Wollstonecraft who undertook the long trip to be with her ill friend at her confinement, and took care of Fanny and the child until they both died shortly after the birth.

For many women in the nineteenth century it was a financial prod that started them on the path to a writing career. Wollstonecraft's first published work was a collection of essays entitled *Thoughts on the Education of Daughters*, which she wrote in 1786 in order to meet the rent that was coming due on the building she used for her school. Even this was not enough, however, and she decided to risk all for a chance at a very different and new life by moving to London in 1787. The years from 1787 to 1790 were lean but fruitful; she learned German and Italian, thus acquiring the skills to work as a translator and reviewer for the *Analytical Review*, a journal put out by her first bookseller, Joseph Johnson. In her first year in London she also wrote a novel—*Mary*, a thinly disguised autobiography—and planned a collection of stories for children, *Original Stories*.

Though Wollstonecraft was clearly productive in her writings during these first two years in London, she continued to show dramatic swings in general mood and confidence, from overly dramaticizing her importance—as when she wrote to a sister, "You know I am not born to tread in the beaten track —the peculiar bent of my nature pushes me on"—to plunging into a mood of considerable depression, during which she felt a loss of control over her emotions. A recent biographer quotes a revealing letter she wrote to Johnson in 1788 that shows considerable insight into herself in this period:

I am a strange compound of weakness and resolution! . . . There is certainly a great defect in my mind—my wayward heart creates its own misery.—Why I am made thus I cannot tell; and, till I can form some idea of the whole

of my existence, I must be content to weep and dance like
a child—long for a toy, and be tired of it as soon as I get
it. [Wardle 1951:97]

This vacillation continued to characterize Wollstonecraft over
the next decade, for she remained to the end of her brief life
a mercurial creature shifting rapidly between emotional ups
and downs. She learned through her increasingly skilled pen,
to direct and channel the strong and passionate moods she
experienced, while enough of the passion showed through to
penetrate the reasoning surface of her readers' minds and stir
responses intense enough to almost match her own.

It was predictable that Wollstonecraft would be stirred by
the storming of the Bastille in France in July 1789. The high
hopes that this was the first act of a revolution that would
take Europe a step further toward the emancipation of man
were quickly adopted by Wollstonecraft. Abstract discussions
about the rights of man had had little appeal to her in the
preceding year. Now that they were combined with reason in
action across the channel, she was a ready convert to the new
political beliefs. As Wardle suggests in the biography, she was

> attracted to democratic principles not by her intelligence
> alone but by her sympathies; she subscribed to the rights
> of man not because they were reasonable but because they
> were humane. [Wardle 1951:120]

The direct stimulus for the pamphlet that earned her
instant public attention, was the publication of Edmund
Burke's *Reflections on the Revolution in France*. Wollstonecraft's response, *A Vindication of the Rights of Man, in a
Letter to the Right Honourable Edmund Burke*, was not a
reasoned analysis of Burke's denunciation of the plans for the
new French government but a scathing rejection of his seeming acceptance of social injustice and support for the spirit of
religion and the spirit of chivalry on which, he believed,
European civilization had long been founded. Here she found
her voice and her forte: her pamphlet, though weakly organized and discursive, is powerful in its appeal to political and
human sentiments. All the leading journals took immediate
note of the Wollstonecraft response and she was swept to
center stage in the political debates of the day.

This was precisely the boost she needed to support her self-
confidence and launch her into the writing of the book that

was to make her well known in feminist history—*A Vindication of the Rights of Woman*. Like its predecessor, *A Vindication* was written in response to a pamphlet by someone else, Talleyrand in this case. Talleyrand's book, a *Report on Public Instruction*, laid out his proposals for national education under the new French constitution. Central to Wollstonecraft's response was Talleyrand's proposal that French girls be educated with their brothers in public schools only to the age of eight, and that, thereafter, they were to remain at home, where their interests and activities would normally center for the rest of their lives. Wollstonecraft dedicated her own book to Talleyrand, urging him in a preface to revise his educational plan and not bar women from their democratic rights.

Wollstonecraft was well prepared to respond quickly to Talleyrand's views. Little noted at the time was a fourteen-page review Wollstonecraft had published in the November 1790 issue of the *Analytical Review*, of Catherine Macaulay's *Letters on Education*. Wollstonecraft quoted extensively from the book, defended it point for point, and paid high tribute to Catherine Macaulay's talents, "so unusual in a woman." More importantly, in her own book she expanded on much the same points Macaulay had developed a few years earlier: both texts denied any fundamental difference in character between the sexes and argued strongly that there should be identical education for both boys and girls; both books took the view that the weakness of contemporary women was attributable to their faulty education and social position and urged that special emphasis be given to physical education; both authors believed that a strong healthy body was a necessary basis for the strains of motherhood as well as other less conventional undertakings by women. So, too, both women argued for the "rights" of women and believed that women would gladly sacrifice special privilege in exchange for those rights.

It is an interesting question why Macaulay's essay was neglected while Wollstonecraft's caused a great stir. This is all the more puzzling when it is realized that Catherine Macaulay had already enjoyed popularity as a historian before her tract on education was published in the late 1780s. The eight volumes of her *History of England*, published between 1763 and 1783, were acclaimed in both England and France. An early enthusiast of "liberty," Macaulay and her book were warmly greeted in Paris, translated into French, and reputed

to be the inspiration for Madame Roland, who wanted to do a
similar history of France, to be "la Macaulay de son pays."
This is the same Macaulay about whom Abigail Adams had
asked in 1771.

A critical reason for the public neglect is a familiar one.
Throughout the nineteenth century the publishing world and
the reading public were keenly attuned to conventional morality. Any hint of gossip quickly circulated in the London world
of these years, perhaps very much as it does today in Washington or New York. Unlike the situation in our period, however, the written work of those whose personal morality was
in question became the object of a powerful sanction exercised
by public opinion—neglect. In Macaulay's case, an important
event intervened between the publication of the early volumes
of her *History*, which established her reputation as a woman
scholar, and the publication of her *Letters on Education*: her
second marriage in 1778. Her unforgiveable "sin" in the eyes
of her contemporaries was to marry "beneath her." The
daughter of a London banking family on her mother's side,
Macaulay had in 1760 married a Brownlee Street physician
fifteen years her senior. When he died six years later, she
threw herself into a combination of a very gay life, with a
house in Bath and trips to Paris, and very productive years of
work on the second through the fifth volumes of her *History*.
During this period she was the subject of sculpture and paintings, and odes were written in her honor by some of her
admirers. But in 1778, at the age of forty-seven, she married
William Graham, aged twenty-one. This in itself was clearly
a violation of accepted behavior: to marry a man fifteen years
her senior was "proper," but to become the wife of one
twenty-six years her junior was extremely "improper." Furthermore, Graham was the brother of a quack doctor and was
himself a "surgeon's mate." There was a stormy response in
the social world that had previously admired her. Lost to view,
but of interest to those of us concerned with the kinds of
marriages contracted by the early feminists, was the fact that
the marriage lasted until her death thirteen years later. During
these years she finished the remaining three volumes of her
History of England (Stephen and Lee, 1922:407–409).

It seems likely that Wollstonecraft knew something of
Macaulay's history, and it may be that she quoted so extensively from the book in her review to give the idea and the
fact of the authorship wider circulation than other discus-

sions would do. Thus, in her own Vindication, Wollstonecraft may have been unconsciously attempting to compensate for the neglect Macaulay's work and person had
received by her own excessive praise of Macaulay as a
"woman of the greatest abilities, undoubtedly, that this country has ever produced." Unfortunately when Wollstonecraft's
own turn came to be the recipient of public ridicule and scorn,
there was no one but her husband, William Godwin, to defend her, with the result that her work and her life were lost
to view for many decades.

Wollstonecraft's book, like her preceding one, burns with
indignation. Given to exaggeration as it was, by taking exceptional abuses as though they typified the experiences of all
women, it had rhetorical power and persuasiveness, and for
its time it was a remarkably fearless book to write and publish. Like her contemporaries and immediate descendants in
political thinking on social problems, she felt both cause and
solution to lie in education: ignorance, poverty, prejudice,
and sin arise in the absence of knowledge and will be solved
by the spread of education. In this view there are no innate
racial, sexual, or social class differences among men and
women; all differences are rooted in the social environment
and can be eradicated by changes in that environment. Workers would learn their "true" class interest and fight for equality under a communist or socialist banner. Women would
learn (or could be taught) their true interest, the root of their
subjection, and similarly fight for a true equality of the sexes.
Wollstonecraft was as much a daughter of the Enlightenment
as were Fuller or Stanton later in the nineteenth century, or
Millett and women advocates of "consciousness-raising" in
our own day.

Though addressed to Talleyrand, a good deal of Wollstonecraft's comments were devoted to Rousseau in the course
of her Vindication of the Rights of Woman. Both her reason
and her sentiment were strongly on the side of a naturalistic
approach to child rearing. She urged not only that there be
more similarity in the rearing of boys and girls, but also that
such rearing be of a simple and natural variety. Her own
strong defense of nursing, simple clothing, physical exercise,
and a healthy approach to human sexuality was foreshadowed
in the Original Stories which she published in 1788 and
would probably have been even more apparent in the book
on child rearing that she planned to coauthor with a physician

had she lived to write it. What she objected to in Rousseau, as in Talleyrand, was not the content of their views of education, but the confinement of educational reform to boys and the exclusion of concern for girls. Wollstonecraft seems to have been strongly attracted to Rousseau's image of man as an element in nature, which she then blended with her political rejection of aristocracy and her strong endorsement of human rights and the equality of the sexes.

For a woman to write with the bite, the frankness, and the conviction of Wollstonecraft made for a predictable English response. Horace Walpole described her as a "hyena in petticoats" and classed her with Tom Paine (hardly destined to displease Wollstonecraft, since Paine was a hero of hers) as one of the "philosophizing serpents we have in our bosom." (Wardle 1951:159) In a tradition familiar to women in the 1970s, one response was the "put-down"; for Wollstonecraft it took the form of satires in which her arguments were applied to children and to animals. In her own circle of liberal thinkers, however, the book received a kindlier reception, and she herself was hailed as the champion of womankind. By 1792 she was established in a pleasant house, had a growing circle of admirers, and seemed assured of a future career as an author of note.

But she was also, by that date, a woman of thirty-three. Her success was a feather in her cap, but there was no gratification for the passionate private woman behind the accomplished writer. There may well be a connection between the relaxation of intellectual effort she could now afford, following her two successes, and the emotional storms she experienced over the remaining five years of her life. There are early hints of the severe strain she felt in keeping a rational, controlling hand over her tendency to depression and melancholy. The reality of her earlier circumstances tipped the emotional balance toward depression. When the economic pressure and intellectual effort were somewhat relaxed, her circumstances may have tipped the emotional balance toward infatuation and passionate enthusiasm.

In 1792 she had a foolish infatuation with a white-haired, temperamental artist, Henry Fuseli, which she presented as a platonic enthusiasm for the man; the episode peaked when Wollstonecraft sought permission of the Fuselis to live with them—a request Mrs. Fuseli turned down in no uncertain terms. Shortly thereafter Wollstonecraft left for France to write a brief history of the French Revolution. Paris was then a stormy center from which she wrote observant on-the-scene reports of political events as the moderate Girondins began to lose control to the Montagnards. From her window she watched the king brought through the streets under heavy guard, riding in a hackney coach on his way to his death. She was temporarily safe, since she was known as a liberal thinker and supporter of the Revolution, but she faced serious problems as her stay extended beyond her plans, prices rose, and political tension increased the danger to an unaccompanied English woman on the Paris streets.

This was the setting in which she met Gilbert Imlay, a tall, awkward young American. From an initial dislike her feelings changed until she found herself in a passionate affair. What seems to have been a passing matter for Imlay was quite otherwise for Wollstonecraft. She became pregnant, gave birth in Havre in 1794 to a daughter she named Fanny, after her early close friend, and pursued Imlay for months in a vain hope of establishing their relationship on firmer grounds. Less than two years after her flaming vindication of women's rights, she wrote to Imlay:

> Cherish me with that dignified tenderness, which I have only found in you; and your own dear girl will try to keep under a quickness of feeling, that has sometimes given you pain. [Wardle 1951:191]

Painful months of protest, hopes raised and then dashed, and an attempt at suicide by drowning intervene before she accepted the fact that the relationship had ended as far as Imlay was concerned. In fact, he was already established with her successor in a London apartment.

With rare insight Wollstonecraft once wrote to Imlay that "on examining my heart, I find that it is so constituted, I cannot live without some particular affection—I am afraid not without a passion" (Wardle 1951:258). One suspects that this observation holds not only for affairs of the heart but also for those of the intellect. There clearly seems to have been a similar profile to her most intimate relations in life and to her ideological and intellectual involvements. There is no gradual build-up of either argument or feeling. Ideas, like people, are the objects of spontaneous enthusiasms in the life of Mary Wollstonecraft: the rights of man, the rights of women, the French revolutionary cause were ideas she spontaneously and enthusiastically accepted with much the same immediacy as persons, whether Fanny Blood, the Clares, Tom Paine, or Gilbert Imlay and William Godwin.

Yet there remains a haunting suspicion that, had fate been kinder, Wollstonecraft's relationship with Godwin might have been spared the sharp disenchantment and abrupt termination that marked her earlier love relations. Knowledge of the tragic end—her death ten days following the birth of their daughter Mary—makes it a sad experience to read the notes exchanged between Godwin and Wollstonecraft over the short year or so of their relationship in 1796–1797. Godwin, the first philosophical anarchist in English history, offered a far better intellectual match than Mary's previous relations. There was much to constitute a base of shared values between them and much in personal style and thought process to add the spice of difference. Wollstonecraft did not live to describe the stimulation she experienced in their intellectual exchanges, but Godwin did, in the *Memoirs of Mary Wollstonecraft*, which he wrote within six months after her death:

> I have been stimulated, as long as I can remember, by an ambition for intellectual distinction; but . . . I have been discouraged . . . by finding that I did not possess, in the degree of some other men, an intuitive perception of intellectual beauty. I have perhaps a strong and lively sense of the pleasures of the imagination; but I have seldom been right in assigning to them their proportionate value. . . . What I wanted in this respect, Mary possessed, in a degree superior to any other person I ever knew. . . . In a robust and unwavering judgment of this sort, there is a kind of witchcraft; when it decides justly, it produces a responsive vibration in every ingenuous mind. In this sense, my oscillation and scepticism were fixed by her boldness. . . . This light was lent to me for a very short period, and is now extinguished for ever!
> [Godwin 1930:124–126]

Of the quality of their personal relationship, there is much better evidence, partially as a result of their style of residence. At no point, either before or after marriage, did they share the same household completely, for Godwin maintained a separate apartment "about twenty doors from our house" where he spent the greater part of his day and sometimes evenings.

This was a consciously adopted pattern, which Godwin explained in the *Memoirs*:

> we were both of us of opinion, that it was possible for two persons to be too uniformly in each other's society. . . . We spent the latter half of each day in one another's society, yet we were in no danger of satiety. We seemed to combine, in a considerable degree, the novelty and lively sensation of a visit, with the more delicious and heartfelt pleasures of domestic life. [Godwin 1930:109–110]

This arrangement may not seem odd in the 1970s, used as we are to the separation of the home from the workplace even for intellectual pursuits, but it was unusual in the late eighteenth century. Godwin had expressed himself along very radical lines before he fell in love with Mary Wollstonecraft, opposing marriage and many other institutional patterns; he was the butt of no little humor from his contemporaries when it became known that he and Wollstonecraft married in the spring of 1797. The decision to marry took place after it was clear that Mary was pregnant. Referring to the earlier stage of their love affair, Godwin expressed their views:

> We did not marry. It is difficult to recommend any thing to indiscriminate adoption, contrary to the established rules and prejudices of mankind; but certainly nothing can be so ridiculous upon the face of it, or so contrary to the genuine march of sentiment, as to require the overflowing of the soul to wait upon a ceremony, and that at which, wherever delicacy and imagination exist, is of all things most sacredly private, to blow a trumpet before it, and to record the moment when it has arrived at its climax. [Godwin 1930:101]

Because of their separate dwellings (and the absence of a telephone!), a constant stream of notes went back and forth between the two apartments during their year together. There were even three brief notes sent by Mary on the day of her confinement, keeping Godwin informed of the progress of her labor. As a result, one can sense the gradual development of the relationship over these brief months, and a deepening and ever more tender concern for each other. In November 1796, before Mary suspected her pregnancy, she sent the following brief note one morning:

If the felicity of last night has had the same effect on your health as on my countenance, you have no cause to lament your failure of resolution: for I have seldom seen so much live fire running about my features as this morning when recollections—very dear, called forth the blush of pleasure, as I adjusted my hair. [Wardle 1966:46–47]

A month later she wrote:

Was not yesterday a very pleasant evening? There was a tenderness in your manner, as you seemed to be opening your heart, to a new born affection, that rendered you very dear to me. There are other pleasures in the world, you perceive, besides those know[n] to your philosophy. [Wardle 1966:57]

Two of her notes during this latter part of December hint at her suspicion of a pregnancy: "As to other perhaps—they must rest in the womb of time"; and three days later: "of myself I am still at a loss what to say". (Wardle 1966:57).

A more domestic note and the sharing of a growing tenderness toward their unborn child (referred to in the letters as "Master William") are reflected in the letters following their marriage in late March 1797. While Godwin was traveling with his friend Montagu, Wollstonecraft wrote him:

I was not quite well the day after you left me; but it is past and I am well and tranquill, excepting the disturbance produced by Master William's joy, who took it into his head to frisk a little at being informed of your remembrance. I begin to love this little creature, and to anticipate his birth as a fresh twist to a knot, which I do not wish to untie. Men are spoilt by frankness, I believe, yet I must tell you that I love you better than I supposed I did, when I promised to love you for ever—and I will add . . . that on the whole I may be termed happy. You are a tender, affectionate creature; and I feel it thrilling through my frame giving and promising pleasure. [Wardle 1966:82]

In the *Memoirs* Godwin refers to this period and what it meant to both of them:

She was a worshipper of domestic life. She loved to observe the growth of affection between me and her daughter, then three years of age, as well as my anxiety respect-

ing the child not yet born. Pregnancy itself, unequal as
the decree of nature seems to be in this respect, is the
source of a thousand endearments. No one knew better
than Mary how to extract sentiments of exquisite delight,
from trifles, which a suspicious and formal wisdom would
scarcely deign to remark. [Godwin 1930:108–109]

Both the solicitous tone of the letters they exchanged and
the tender, delicate quality of Godwin's *Memoirs* were clearly
not appealing to the early-nineteenth-century readers of the
Memoirs. Instead, the public reacted to the book as crowning
proof of Godwin's "moral turpitude." This extreme response
was not confined to that long-past era, however; one of the
most outrageous assessments of Wollstonecraft was written
in 1947. Conventional morality may have prevented any
human understanding or warm response to the Godwin-Woll-
stonecraft relationship in the late 1790s, but the counterpart
in our own century has often been a narrow psychoanalytic
framework of personality interpretation. Across 150 years
and a more fancied than factually based account of her life,
Lundberg and Farnham "analyzed" Wollstonecraft in the following terms:

Mary Wollstonecraft hated men. She had every personal
reason possible known to psychiatry for hating them. Hers
was hatred of creatures she greatly admired and feared,
creatures that seemed to her capable of doing everything
while women to her seemed capable of doing nothing
whatever, in their own nature being pitifully weak in
comparison with the strong lordly male. . . . Mary Wollstonecraft's life reads like a psychiatric case history. So,
for that matter, do the lives of many later feminists. . . .
[She] was afflicted with a severe case of penis-envy. . . .
that she was an extreme neurotic of a compulsive type
there can be no doubt. Out of her illness arose the ideology of feminism, which was to express the feelings of so
many women in years to come. [Lundberg and Farnham
1947:145, 149, 150, 159]

It is perhaps the fate of pioneers to press hard on the
cake of custom and to suffer attacks on their ideas and their
personal lives from the established powers in the mainstream
of their society. What tools are used in these attacks will vary
by time and culture: ridicule, social exclusion, damnation,

accusation of penis envy, imprisonment, have all been used against those fearless enough to move outside the confines of thought and action approved by their society. Significant social change does not take place overnight, but through a long series of pressures against the normative boundaries of society. Women and men in the 1970s who enjoy a wider range of sexual and social options are indebted for their greater latitude and freedom to such pioneers as Wollstonecraft and Godwin.

After Wollstonecraft's death Godwin gave up his separate dwelling and took residence in Mary's apartment, the better to supervise the household and the care of the two little daughters, Fanny and Mary. He felt completely incapable of filling this role adequately and was long tormented by his loss of his wife. For a while a friend of his sister directed the household, while he threw himself into the writing of the *Memoirs*, tried to compile a *Posthumous Works*, and wrote a novel, *St. Leon*, whose heroine was thought to be an idealized version of Mary. A great change can be noted in this work, compared to the exclusive focus on rationality of his earlier work. In the Preface Godwin admitted that his views had changed since the publication of his *Political Justice*:

> I apprehend domestic and private affections inseparable from the nature of man, and from what may be styled the culture of the heart, and am fully persuaded that they are not incompatible with a profound and active sense of justice in the mind of him that cherishes them. [Wardle 1951:323]

Wollstonecraft's biographer notes that this change had the effect of loosening Godwin's commitment to a rational system of philosophy; that from 1797 on he was to retract, but rarely to reconstruct, his theories. As Wardle put it, "though he was a better man for having been Mary's husband, he was a worse philosopher" (Wardle 1951:323).

Though a modern reader finds an enchanting quality to Godwin's *Memoirs* of his wife Mary, his contemporaries thought otherwise. They seized upon his revelations of her relation to Imlay and denounced her as immoral—a "philosophical wanton" as the *European Magazine* put it. In the index to another magazine the phrase "See Mary Wollstonecraft" was inserted as an entry under the heading "Prostitution" (Wardle 1951:318).

This sad aftermath to the life of a charming and courageous feminist was echoed in the lives of her husband and her
two daughters. Godwin eventually married again—a widow
with two children of her own. The household was then a
strange assortment of children: Fanny, Mary, Charles, and
Claire, and eventually a fifth child, William. In 1812, when
Mary was fifteen, Percy Bysshe Shelley learned that Godwin
was still alive and the young poet, who admired Godwin as
well as Wollstonecraft, came with his wife to visit Godwin.
Over the next two years, these visits recurred, and Shelley
persuaded the young Mary to run off with him to Paris. They
moved about, hounded by debt and infamy, and eventually
returned to England. They were married in 1816, shortly after
the death by drowning of Shelley's first wife. It is with no
little irony that one notes that after the death of Percy
Shelley, Mary Wollstonecraft Godwin Shelley devoted the
larger part of her life not to a vindication of the rights of
women, but to a strenuous effort to make herself, Shelley,
and her parents "respectable" enough to not disgrace the
title and fortune her son inherited.

Mary Wollstonecraft's first daughter, Fanny, had an even
sadder fate. A melancholic child according to the descriptions
of those who knew her after her mother's death, she grew up
into a quiet and introspective young woman. While still in
her late teens, she left home, ostensibly to visit her aunts in
Dublin, but in fact she traveled to Bristol where she committed suicide. She left a note that found its way to Godwin
and Shelley in which she wrote: "Perhaps to hear of my
death will give you pain, but you will soon have the blessing
of forgetting that such a creature ever existed" (Wardle
1951:335).

The furor created by Godwin's publication of the *Memoirs* no doubt contributed to the neglect of *A Vindication of
the Rights of Woman* in the early decades of the nineteenth
century. The book underwent four editions between 1833 and
1856, then none until 1890. The few feminists of the mid-
century who knew of Wollstonecraft's work—such as Harriet
Martineau, Emma Willard, and Margaret Fuller—were uniform in their disapproval. Martineau commented that she did
not regard Mary Wollstonecraft as "a safe example, nor as a
successful champion of Woman and her Rights" (Chapman
1877, I:303). Consistent with her rejection of conventional
social codes, Fanny Wright differed from this general denunci-

ation of Wollstonecraft, for she wrote to Mary Shelley in 1827 to enlist her interest in Nashoba, commenting that she was prompted by her respect for William Godwin and Mary Wollstonecraft (Wardle 1951:340). By 1889, when Susan Anthony and Elizabeth Cady Stanton published the first three volumes of the *History of Woman Suffrage*, Mary Wollstonecraft's name stood first in the list of earlier feminists to whom the suffrage history was dedicated.

ᨒ A Vindication of the Rights of Woman ᨒ

Introduction to the First Edition.

I have turned over various books written on the subject of education, and patiently observed the conduct of parents and the management of schools; but what has been the result? —a profound conviction that the neglected education of my fellow-creatures is the grand source of the misery I deplore; and that women, in particular, are rendered weak and wretched by a variety of concurring causes, originating from one hasty conclusion. The conduct and manners of women, in fact, evidently prove that their minds are not in a healthy state; for, like the flowers which are planted in too rich a soil, strength and usefulness are sacrificed to beauty; and the flaunting leaves, after having pleased a fastidious eye, fade, disregarded on the stalk, long before the season when they ought to have arrived at maturity. One cause of this barren blooming I attribute to a false system of education, gathered from the books written on this subject by men who, considering females rather as women than human creatures, have been more anxious to make them alluring mistresses than affectionate wives and rational mothers; and the understanding of the sex has been so bubbled by this specious homage, that the civilized women of the present century, with a few exceptions, are only anxious to inspire love, when they

---

From Mary Wollstonecraft, *A Vindication of the Rights of Woman*. New York, W. W. Norton, 1967.

ought to cherish a nobler ambition, and by their abilities and virtues exact respect.

In a treatise, therefore, on female rights and manners, the works which have been particularly written for their improvement must not be overlooked; especially when it is asserted, in direct terms, that the minds of women are enfeebled by false refinement; that the books of instruction, written by men of genius, have had the same tendency as more frivolous productions; and that, in the true style of Mahometanism, they are treated as a kind of subordinate beings, and not as a part of the human species, when improveable reason is allowed to be the dignified distinction which raises men above the brute creation, and puts a natural sceptre in a feeble hand.

Yet, because I am a woman, I would not lead my readers to suppose that I mean violently to agitate the contested question respecting the quality or inferiority of the sex; but as the subject lies in my way, and I cannot pass it over without subjecting the main tendency of my reasoning to misconstruction, I shall stop a moment to deliver, in a few words, my opinion. In the government of the physical world it is observable that the female in point of strength is, in general, inferior to the male. This is the law of nature; and it does not appear to be suspended or abrogated in favour of woman. A degree of physical superiority cannot, therefore, be denied—and it is a noble prerogative! But not content with this natural pre-eminence, men endeavour to sink us still lower, merely to render us alluring objects for a moment; and women, intoxicated by the adoration which men, under the influence of their senses, pay them, do not seek to obtain a durable interest in their hearts, or to become the friends of the fellow creatures who find amusement in their society.

I am aware of an obvious inference:—from every quarter have I heard exclamations against masculine women; but where are they to be found? If by this appellation men mean to inveigh against their ardour in hunting, shooting, and gaming, I shall most cordially join in the cry; but if it be against the imitation of manly virtues, or, more properly speaking, the attainment of those talents and virtues, the exercise of which ennobles the human character, and which raise females in the scale of animal being, when they are comprehensively termed mankind;—all those who view them with a philosophic eye must, I should think, wish with me, that they may every day grow more and more masculine. . . .

I wish also to steer clear of an error which many respectable writers have fallen into; for the instruction which has
hitherto been addressed to women, has rather been applicable
to *ladies,* if the little indirect advice, that is scattered through
Sandford and Merton, be excepted; but addressing my sex in
a firmer tone, I pay particular attention to those in the middle
class, because they appear to be in the most natural state. Perhaps the seeds of false-refinement, immorality, and vanity,
have ever been shed by the great. Weak, artificial beings,
raised above the common wants and affections of their race,
in a premature unnatural manner, undermine the very foundation of virtue, and spread corruption through the whole mass
of society! As a class of mankind they have the strongest
claim to pity; the education of the rich tends to render them
vain and helpless, and the unfolding mind is not strengthened
by the practice of those duties which dignify the human character. They only live to amuse themselves, and by the same
law which in nature invariably produces certain effects, they
soon only afford barren amusement. . . .

My own sex, I hope, will excuse me, if I treat them like
rational creatures, instead of flattering their *fascinating*
graces, and viewing them as if they were in a state of perpetual childhood, unable to stand alone. I earnestly wish to
point out in what true dignity and human happiness consists
—I wish to persuade women to endeavour to acquire strength,
both of mind and body, and to convince them that the soft
phrases, susceptibility of heart, delicacy of sentiment, and
refinement of taste, are almost synonymous with epithets of
weakness, and that those beings who are only the objects of
pity and that kind of love, which has been termed its sister,
will soon become objects of contempt.

Dismissing, then, those pretty feminine phrases, which the
men condescendingly use to soften our slavish dependence,
and despising that weak elegancy of mind, exquisite sensibility, and sweet docility of manners, supposed to be the sexual
characteristics of the weaker vessel, I wish to shew that elegance is inferior to virtue, that the first object of laudable ambition is to obtain a character as a human being, regardless
of the distinction of sex; and that secondary views should be
brought to this simple touchstone. . . .

The education of women has, of late, been more attended
to than formerly; yet they are still reckoned a frivolous sex,

and ridiculed or pitied by the writers who endeavour by satire or instruction to improve them. It is acknowledged that they spend many of the first years of their lives in acquiring a smattering of accomplishments; meanwhile strength of body and mind are sacrificed to libertine notions of beauty, to the desire of establishing themselves,—the only way women can rise in the world,—by marriage. And this desire making mere animals of them, when they marry they act as such children may be expected to act:—they dress; they paint, and nick-name God's creatures. Surely these weak beings are only fit for a seraglio!—Can they be expected to govern a family with judgment, or take care of the poor babes whom they bring into the world?

If then it can be fairly deduced from the present conduct of the sex, from the prevalent fondness for pleasure which takes place of ambition and those nobler passions that open and enlarge the soul; that the instruction which women have hitherto received has only tended, with the constitution of civil society, to render them insignificant objects of desire— mere propagators of fools!—if it can be proved that in aiming to accomplish them, without cultivating their understandings, they are taken out of their sphere of duties, and made ridiculous and useless when the short-lived bloom of beauty is over, I presume that *rational* men will excuse me for endeavouring to persuade them to become more masculine and respectable.

Indeed the word masculine is only a bugbear: there is little reason to fear that women will acquire too much courage or fortitude; for their apparent inferiority with respect to bodily strength, must render them, in some degree, dependent on men in the various relations of life; but why should it be increased by prejudices that give a sex to virtue, and confound simple truths with sensual reveries?

Women are, in fact, so much degraded by mistaken notions of female excellence, that I do not mean to add a paradox when I assert, that this artificial weakness produces a propensity to tyrannize, and gives birth to cunning, the natural opponent of strength, which leads them to play off those contemptible infantine airs that undermine esteem even whilst they excite desire. Let men become more chaste and modest, and if women do not grow wiser in the same ratio, it will be clear that they have weaker understandings. It seems scarcely necessary to say, that I now speak of the sex in general. Many individuals have more sense than their male relatives; and, as nothing preponderates where there is a constant struggle for an equilibrium, without it has naturally more gravity, some women govern their husbands without degrading themselves, because intellect will always govern.

The Prevailing Opinion of a Sexual Character Discussed.

To account for, and excuse the tyranny of man, many ingenious arguments have been brought forward to prove, that the two sexes, in the acquirement of virtue, ought to aim at attaining a very different character; or, to speak explicitly, women are not allowed to have sufficient strength of mind to acquire what really deserves the name of virtue. Yet it should seem, allowing them to have souls, that there is but one way appointed by Providence to lead *mankind* to either virtue or happiness.

If then women are not a swarm of ephemeron triflers, why should they be kept in ignorance under the specious name of innocence? Men complain, and with reason, of the follies and caprices of our sex, when they do not keenly satirize our headstrong passions and grovelling vices. Behold, I should answer, the natural effect of ignorance! The mind will ever be unstable that has only prejudices to rest on, and the current will run with destructive fury when there are no barriers to break its force. Women are told from their infancy, and taught by the example of their mothers, that a little knowledge of human weakness, justly termed cunning, softness of temper, *outward* obedience, and a scrupulous attention to a puerile kind of propriety, will obtain for them the protection of man; and should they be beautiful, everything else is needless, for, at least, twenty years of their lives. . . .

Children, I grant, should be innocent; but when the epithet is applied to men, or women, it is but a civil term for weakness. For if it be allowed that women were destined by Providence to acquire human virtues, and by the exercise of their understandings, that stability of character which is the firmest ground to rest our future hopes upon, they must be permitted to turn to the fountain of light, and not forced to shape their course by the twinkling of a mere satellite. . . .

In treating, therefore, of the manners of women, let us, disregarding sensual arguments, trace what we should endeavour to make them in order to co-operate, if the expression be not too bold, with the supreme Being.

By individual education, I mean, for the sense of the word is not precisely defined, such an attention to a child as will slowly sharpen the senses, form the temper, regulate the passions as they begin to ferment, and set the understanding to work before the body arrives at maturity; so that the man may only have to proceed, not to begin, the important task of learning to think and reason.

To prevent any misconstruction, I must add, that I do not believe that a private education can work the wonders which some sanguine writers have attributed to it. Men and women must be educated, in a great degree, by the opinions and manners of the society they live in. In every age there has been a stream of popular opinion that has carried all before it, and given a family character, as it were, to the century. It may then fairly be inferred, that, till society be differently constituted, much cannot be expected from education. It is, however, sufficient for my present purpose to assert, that, whatever effect circumstances have on the abilities, every being may become virtuous by the exercise of its own reason; for if but one being was created with vicious inclinations, that is positively bad, what can save us from atheism? or if we worship a God, is not that God a devil?

Consequently, the most perfect education, in my opinion, is such an exercise of the understanding as is best calculated to strengthen the body and form the heart. Or, in other words, to enable the individual to attain such habits of virtue as will render it independent. In fact, it is a farce to call any being virtuous whose virtues do not result from the exercise of its own reason. This was Rousseau's opinion respecting men: I extend it to women, and confidently assert that they have been drawn out of their sphere by false refinement, and not by an endeavour to acquire masculine qualities. Still the regal homage which they receive is so intoxicating, that till the manners of the times are changed, and formed on more reasonable principles, it may be impossible to convince them that the illegitimate power, which they obtain, by degrading themselves, is a curse, and that they must return to nature and equality, if they wish to secure the placid satisfaction that unsophisticated affections impart. But for this epoch we must wait—wait, perhaps, till kings and nobles, enlightened by reason, and, preferring the real dignity of man to childish state, throw off their gaudy hereditary trappings: and if then women do not resign the arbitrary power of beauty—they will prove that they have *less* mind than man. . . .

Though, to reason on Rousseau's ground, if man did attain a degree of perfection of mind when his body arrived at maturity, it might be proper, in order to make a man and his wife *one*, that she should rely entirely on his understanding; and the graceful ivy, clasping the oak that supported it, would form a whole in which strength and beauty would be equally conspicuous. But, alas! husbands, as well as their helpmates, are often only overgrown children; nay, thanks to early debauchery, scarcely men in their outward form—and if the blind lead the blind, one need not come from heaven to tell us the consequence.

Many are the causes that, in the present corrupt state of society, contribute to enslave women by cramping their understandings and sharpening their senses. One, perhaps, that silently does more mischief than all the rest, is their disregard of order.

To do everything in an orderly manner, is a most important precept, which women, who, generally speaking, receive only a disorderly kind of education, seldom attend to with that degree of exactness that men, who from their infancy are broken into method, observe. This negligent kind of guess-work, for what other epithet can be used to point out the random exertions of a sort of instinctive common sense, never brought to the test of reason? prevents their generalizing matters of fact—so they do to-day, what they did yesterday, merely because they did it yesterday.

This contempt of the understanding in early life has more baneful consequences than is commonly supposed; for the little knowledge which women of strong minds attain, is, from various circumstances, of a more desultory kind than the knowledge of men, and it is acquired more by sheer observations on real life, than from comparing what has been individually observed with the results of experience generalized by speculation. Led by their dependent situation and domestic employments more into society, what they learn is rather by snatches; and as learning is with them, in general, only a secondary thing, they do not pursue any one branch with that persevering ardour necessary to give vigour to the faculties, and clearness to the judgment. In the present state of society, a little learning is required to support the character of a gentleman; and boys are obliged to submit to a few years of discipline. But in the education of women, the cultivation of the understanding is always subordinate to the acquirement of some corporeal accomplishment; even while enervated by confinement and false notions of modesty, the body is prevented from attaining that grace and beauty which relaxed half-formed limbs never exhibit. Besides, in youth their faculties are not brought forward by emulation; and having no serious scientific study, if they have natural sagacity it is turned too soon on life and manners. They dwell on effects, and modifications, without tracing them back to causes; and complicated rules to adjust behaviour are a weak substitute for simple principles.

As a proof that education gives this appearance of weakness to females, we may instance the example of military men, who are, like them, sent into the world before their minds have been stored with knowledge or fortified by principles. The consequences are similar; soldiers acquire a little superficial knowledge, snatched from the muddy current of conversation, and, from continually mixing with society, they gain, what is termed a knowledge of the world; and this acquaintance with manners and customs has frequently been confounded with a knowledge of the human heart. But can the crude fruit of casual observation, never brought to the test of judgment, formed by comparing speculation and experience, deserve such a distinction? Soldiers, as well as women, practice the minor virtues with punctilious politeness. Where is then the sexual difference, when the education has been the same? All the difference that I can discern, arises from the superior advantage of liberty, which enables the former to see more of life. . . .

Standing armies can never consist of resolute robust men; they may be well disciplined machines, but they will seldom contain men under the influence of strong passions, or with very vigorous faculties. And as for any depth of understanding, I will venture to affirm, that it is as rarely to be found in the army as amongst women; and the cause, I maintain, is the same. It may be further observed, that officers are also particularly attentive to their persons, fond of dancing, crowded rooms, adventures, and ridicule. Like the *fair* sex, the business of their lives is gallantry. They were taught to please, and they only live to please. Yet they do not lose their rank in the distinction of sexes, for they are still reckoned superior to women, though in what their superiority consists, beyond what I have just mentioned, it is difficult to discover.

The great misfortune is this, that they both acquire manners before morals, and a knowledge of life before they have, from reflection, any acquaintance with the grand ideal outline of human nature. The consequence is natural; satisfied with common nature, they become a prey to prejudices, and taking all their opinions on credit, they blindly submit to authority. So that, if they have any sense, it is a kind of instinctive glance, that catches proportions, and decides with respect to manners; but fails when arguments are to be pursued below the surface, or opinions analyzed.

May not the same remark be applied to women? Nay, the argument may be carried still further, for they are both thrown out of a useful station by the unnatural distinctions established in civilized life. Riches and hereditary honours have made cyphers of women to give consequence to the numerical figure; and idleness has produced a mixture of gallantry and despotism into society, which leads the very men who are the slaves of their mistresses to tyrannize over their sisters, wives, and daughters. This is only keeping them in rank and file, it is true. Strengthen the female mind by enlarging it, and there will be an end to blind obedience; but, as blind obedience is ever sought for by power, tyrants and sensualists are in the right when they endeavour to keep women in the dark, because the former only want slaves, and the latter a plaything. The sensualist, indeed, has been the most dangerous of tyrants, and women have been duped by their lovers as princes by their ministers, whilst dreaming that they reigned over them. . . .

Women are, therefore, to be considered either as moral beings, or so weak that they must be entirely subjected to the superior faculties of men.

Let us examine this question. Rousseau declares that a woman should never, for a moment, feel herself independent, that she should be governed by fear to exercise her *natural* cunning, and made a coquettish slave in order to render her a more alluring object of desire, a *sweeter* companion to man, whenever he chooses to relax himself. He carries the arguments, which he pretends to draw from the indications of nature, still further, and insinuates that truth and fortitude, the corner stones of all human virtue, should be cultivated with certain restrictions, because, with respect to the female character, obedience is the grand lesson which ought to be impressed with unrelenting rigour.

What nonsense! when will a great man arise with sufficient strength of mind to puff away the fumes which pride and sensuality have thus spread over the subject! If women are by nature inferior to men, their virtues must be the same in quality, if not in degree, or virtue is a relative idea; consequently, their conduct should be founded on the same principles, and have the same aim.

Connected with man as daughters, wives, and mothers, their moral character may be estimated by their manner of fulfilling those simple duties; but the end, the grand end of their exertions should be to unfold their own faculties and acquire the dignity of conscious virtue. They may try to render their road pleasant; but ought never to forget, in common with man, that life yields not the felicity which can satisfy an immortal soul. I do not mean to insinuate that either sex should be so lost in abstract reflections or distant views, as to forget the affections and duties that lie before them, and are, in truth, the means appointed to produce the fruit of life; on the contrary, I would warmly recommend them, even while I assert, that they afford most satisfaction when they are considered in their true, sober light. . . .

To speak disrespectfully of love is, I know, high treason against sentiment and fine feelings; but I wish to speak the simple language of truth, and rather to address the head than the heart. To endeavour to reason love out of the world, would be to out Quixote Cervantes, and equally offend against common sense; but an endeavour to restrain this tumultuous passion, and to prove that it should not be allowed to dethrone superior powers, or to usurp the sceptre which the understanding should ever coolly wield, appears less wild.

Youth is the season for love in both sexes; but in those days of thoughtless enjoyment provision should be made for the more important years of life, when reflection takes place of sensation. But Rousseau, and most of the male writers who have followed his steps, have warmly inculcated that the whole tendency of female education ought to be directed to one point:—to render them pleasing.

Let me reason with the supporters of this opinion who have any knowledge of human nature, do they imagine that marriage can eradicate the habitude of life? The woman who has only been taught to please will soon find that her charms

are oblique sunbeams, and that they cannot have much effect
on her husband's heart when they are seen every day, when
the summer is passed and gone. Will she then have sufficient
native energy to look into herself for comfort, and cultivate
her dormant faculties? or, is it not more rational to expect
that she will try to please other men; and, in the emotions
raised by the expectation of new conquests, endeavour to
forget the mortification her love or pride has received? When
the husband ceases to be a lover—and the time will inevitably
come, her desire of pleasing will then grow languid, or become a spring of bitterness; and love, perhaps, the most
evanescent of all passions, gives place to jealousy or vanity.

I now speak of women who are restrained by principle or
prejudice; such women, though they would shrink from an
intrigue with real abhorrence, yet, nevertheless, wish to be
convinced by the homage of gallantry that they are cruelly
neglected by their husbands; or, days and weeks are spent in
dreaming of the happiness enjoyed by congenial souls till
their health is undermined and their spirits broken by discontent. How then can the great art of pleasing be such a necessary study? it is only useful to a mistress; the chaste wife, and
serious mother, should only consider her power to please as
the polish of her virtues, and the affection of her husband as
one of the comforts that render her task less difficult and her
life happier. But, whether she be loved or neglected, her first
wish should be to make herself respectable, and not to rely
for all her happiness on a being subject to like infirmities with
herself. . . .

Women ought to endeavour to purify their heart; but can
they do so when their uncultivated understandings make
them entirely dependent on their senses for employment and
amusement, when no noble pursuit sets them above the little
vanities of the day, or enables them to curb the wild emotions
that agitate a reed over which every passing breeze has
power? To gain the affections of a virtuous man, is affectation necessary? Nature has given woman a weaker frame than
man; but, to ensure her husband's affections, must a wife,
who by the exercise of her mind and body whilst she was discharging the duties of a daughter, wife, and mother, has allowed her constitution to retain its natural strength, and her
nerves a healthy tone, is she, I say, to condescend to use art
and feign a sickly delicacy in order to secure her husband's
affection? Weakness may excite tenderness, and gratify the

arrogant pride of man; but the lordly caresses of a protector will not gratify a noble mind that pants for, and deserves to be respected. Fondness is a poor substitute for friendship!

In a seraglio, I grant, that all these arts are necessary; the epicure must have his palate tickled, or he will sink into apathy; but have women so little ambition as to be satisfied with such a condition? Can they supinely dream life away in the lap of pleasure, or the languor of weariness, rather than assert their claim to pursue reasonable pleasures and render themselves conspicuous by practising the virtues which dignify mankind? Surely she has not an immortal soul who can loiter life away merely employed to adorn her person, that she may amuse the languid hours, and soften the cares of a fellow-creature who is willing to be enlivened by her smiles and tricks, when the serious business of life is over.

Besides, the woman who strengthens her body and exercises her mind will, by managing her family and practising various virtues, become the friend, and not the humble dependent of her husband; and if she, by possessing such substantial qualities, merit his regard, she will not find it necessary to conceal her affection, nor to pretend to an unnatural coldness of constitution to excite her husband's passions. In fact, if we revert to history, we shall find that the women who have distinguished themselves have neither been the most beautiful nor the most gentle of their sex.

• • •

Gentleness of manners, forbearance and long-suffering are such amiable God-like qualities, that in sublime poetic strains the Deity has been invested with them; and, perhaps, no representation of his goodness so strongly fastens on the human affections as those that represent him abundant in mercy and willing to pardon. Gentleness, considered in this point of view, bears on its front all the characteristics of grandeur, combined with the winning graces of condescension; but what a different aspect it assumes when it is the submissive demeanour of dependence, the support of weakness that loves, because it wants protection; and is forbearing, because it must silently endure injuries; smiling under the lash at which it dare not snarl. Abject as this picture appears, it is the portrait of an accomplished woman, according to the received opinion of female excellence, separated by specious reasoners from human excellence. Or, they kindly restore the rib, and make one moral being of a man and woman; not forgetting to give her all the "submissive charms."

How women are to exist in that state where there is to be neither marrying or giving in marriage, we are not told. For though moralists have agreed that the tenor of life seems to prove that *man* is prepared by various circumstances for a future state, they constantly concur in advising *woman* only to provide for the present. Gentleness, docility, and a spaniel-like affection are, on this ground, consistently recommended as the cardinal virtues of the sex; and, disregarding the arbitrary economy of nature, one writer has declared that it is masculine for a woman to be melancholy. She was created to be the toy of man, his rattle, and it must jingle in his ears whenever, dismissing reason, he chooses to be amused.

To recommend gentleness, indeed, on a broad basis is strictly philosophical. A frail being should labour to be gentle. But when forbearance confounds right and wrong, it ceases to be a virtue; and, however convenient it may be found in a companion—that companion will ever be considered as an inferior, and only inspire a vapid tenderness, which easily degenerates into contempt. Still, if advice could really make a being gentle, whose natural disposition admitted not of such a fine polish, something towards the advancement of order would be attained; but if, as might quickly be demonstrated, only affectation be produced by this indiscriminate counsel, which throws a stumbling-block in the way of gradual improvement, and true melioration of temper, the sex is not much benefited by sacrificing solid virtues to the attainment of superficial graces, though for a few years they may procure the individuals regal sway. . . .

But to view the subject in another point of view. Do passive indolent women make the best wives? Confining our discussion to the present moment of existence, let us see how such weak creatures perform their part? Do the women who, by the attainment of a few superficial accomplishments, have strengthened the prevailing prejudice, merely contribute to the happiness of their husbands? Do they display their charms merely to amuse them? And have women, who have early imbibed notions of passive obedience, sufficient character to manage a family or educate children? So far from it, that, after surveying the history of woman, I cannot help, agreeing with the severest satirist, considering the sex as the weakest as well as the most oppressed half of the species. What does history disclose but marks of inferiority, and how few women have emancipated themselves from the galling yoke of sovereign man?—So few, that the exceptions remind me of an ingenious conjecture respecting Newton: that he was probably a being of superior order, accidentally caged in a human body. Following the same train of thinking, I have been led to imagine that the few extraordinary women who have rushed in eccentrical directions out of the orbit prescribed to their sex, were *male* spirits, confined by mistake in female frames. But if it be not philosophical to think of sex when the soul is mentioned, the inferiority must depend on the organs; or the heavenly fire, which is to ferment the clay, is not given in equal portions.

But avoiding, as I have hitherto done, any direct comparison of the two sexes collectively, or frankly acknowledging the inferiority of woman, according to the present appearance of things, I shall only insist that men have increased that inferiority till women are almost sunk below the standard of rational creatures. Let their faculties have room to unfold, and their virtues to gain strength, and then determine where the whole sex must stand in the intellectual scale. Yet let it be remembered, that for a small number of distinguished women I do not ask a place.

· · ·

I love man as my fellow; but his sceptre, real, or usurped, extends not to me, unless the reason of an individual demands my homage; and even then the submission is to reason, and not to man. In fact, the conduct of an accountable being must be regulated by the operations of its own reason; or on what foundation rests the throne of God?

It appears to me necessary to dwell on these obvious truths, because females have been insulated, as it were; and, while they have been stripped of the virtues that should clothe humanity, they have been decked with artificial graces that enable them to exercise a short-lived tyranny. Love, in their bosoms, taking place of every nobler passion, their sole ambition is to be fair, to raise emotion instead of inspiring respect; and this ignoble desire, like the servility in absolute monarchies, destroys all strength of character. Liberty is the mother of virtue, and if women be, by their very constitution, slaves, and not allowed to breathe the sharp invigorating air of freedom, they must ever languish like exotics, and be reckoned beautiful flaws in nature.

. . .

. . . [B]odily strength seems to give man a natural superiority over woman; and this is the only solid basis on which the superiority of the sex can be built. But I still insist, that not only the virtue, but the *knowledge* of the two sexes should be the same in nature, if not in degree, and that women, considered not only as moral, but rational creatures, ought to endeavour to acquire human virtues (or perfections) by the *same* means as men, instead of being educated like a fanciful kind of *half* being—one of Rousseau's wild chimeras.

But, if strength of body be, with some show of reason, the boast of men, why are women so infatuated as to be proud of a defect? Rousseau has furnished them with a plausible excuse, which could only have occurred to a man, whose imagination had been allowed to run wild, and refine on the impressions made by exquisite senses;—that they might, forsooth, have a pretext for yielding to a natural appetite without violating a romantic species of modesty, which gratifies the pride and libertinism of man.

Women, deluded by these sentiments, sometimes boast of their weakness, cunningly obtaining power by playing on the *weakness* of men; and they may well glory in their illicit sway, for, like Turkish bashaws, they have more real power than their masters: but virtue is sacrificed to temporary gratifications, and the respectability of life to the triumph of an hour.

Women, as well as despots, have now, perhaps, more power than they would have if the world, divided and subdivided into kingdoms and families, were governed by laws deduced from the exercise of reason; but in obtaining it, to carry on the comparison, their character is degraded, and licentiousness spread through the whole aggregate of society. The many become pedestal to the few. I, therefore, will venture to assert, that till women are more rationally educated, the progress of human virtue and improvement in knowledge must receive continual checks. And if it be granted that woman was not created merely to gratify the appetite of man, or to be the upper servant, who provides his meals and takes care of his linen, it must follow, that the first care of those mothers or fathers, who really attend to the education of females, should be, if not to strengthen the body, at least, not to destroy the constitution by mistaken notions of beauty and female excellence; nor should girls ever be allowed to imbibe the pernicious notion that a defect can, by any chemical process of reasoning, become an excellence. In this respect, I am happy to find, that the author of one of the most instructive books, that our country has produced for children, coincides with me in opinion; I shall quote his pertinent remarks to give the force of his respectable authority to reason.

But should it be proved that woman is naturally weaker than man, whence does it follow that it is natural for her to labour to become still weaker than nature intended her to be? Arguments of this cast are an insult to common sense, and savour of passion. The *divine right* of husbands, like the divine right of kings, may, it is to be hoped, in this enlightened age, be contested without danger, and, though conviction may not silence many boisterous disputants, yet, when any prevailing prejudice is attacked, the wife will consider, and leave the narrow-minded to rail with thoughtless vehemence at innovation.

The mother, who wishes to give true dignity of character to her daughter, must, regardless of the sneers of ignorance, proceed on a plan diametrically opposite to that which Rousseau has recommended with all the deluding charms of eloquence and philosophical sophistry: for his eloquence renders absurdities plausible, and his dogmatic conclusions puzzle, without convincing, those who have not ability to refute them.

Throughout the whole animal kingdom every young creature requires almost continual exercise, and the infancy of children, conformable to this intimation, should be passed in harmless gambols, that exercise the feet and hands, without requiring very minute direction from the head, or the constant attention of a nurse. In fact, the care necessary for self-preservation is the first natural exercise of the understanding, as little inventions to amuse the present moment unfold the imagination. But these wise designs of nature are counteracted by mistaken fondness or blind zeal. The child is not left a moment to its own direction, particularly a girl, and thus rendered dependent—dependence is called natural.

To preserve personal beauty, woman's glory! the limbs and faculties are cramped with worse than Chinese bands, and the sedentary life which they are condemned to live, whilst boys frolic in the open air, weakens the muscles and relaxes the nerves. As for Rousseau's remarks, which have since been echoed by several writers, that they have naturally, that is from their birth, independent of education, a fondness for dolls, dressing, and talking—they are so puerile as not to merit a serious refutation. That a girl, condemned to sit for hours together listening to the idle chat of weak nurses, or to attend to her mother's toilet, will endeavour to join the conversation, is, indeed, very natural; and that she will imitate her mother or aunts, and amuse herself by adorning her lifeless doll, as they do in dressing her, poor innocent babe! is undoubtedly a most natural consequence. For men of the greatest abilities have seldom had sufficient strength to rise above the surrounding atmosphere; and, if the page of genius have always been blurred by the prejudices of the age, some allowance should be made for a sex, who, like kings, always see things through a false medium.

Pursuing these reflections, the fondness for dress, conspicuous in women, may be easily accounted for, without supposing it the result of a desire to please the sex on which they are dependent. The absurdity, in short, of supposing that a girl is naturally a coquette, and that a desire connected with the impulse of nature to propagate the species, should appear even before an improper education has, by heating the imagination, called it forth prematurely, is so unphilosophical, that such a sagacious observer as Rousseau would not have adopted it, if he had not been accustomed to make reason give way to his desire of singularity, and truth to a favourite paradox. . . .

I have, probably, had an opportunity of observing more girls in their infancy than J. J. Rousseau—I can recollect my own feelings, and I have looked steadily around me; yet, so far from coinciding with him in opinion respecting the first dawn of the female character, I will venture to affirm, that a girl, whose spirits have not been damped by inactivity, or innocence tainted by false shame, will always be a romp, and the doll will never excite attention unless confinement allows her no alternative. Girls and boys, in short, would play harmlessly together, if the distinction of sex was not inculcated long before nature makes any difference. I will go further, and affirm, as an indisputable fact, that most of the women, in the circle of my observation, who have acted like rational creatures, or shown any vigour of intellect, have accidentally been allowed to run wild—as some of the elegant formers of the fair sex would insinuate.

The baneful consequences which flow from inattention to health during infancy, and youth, extend further than is supposed—dependence of body naturally produces dependence of mind; and how can she be a good wife or mother, the greater part of whose time is employed to guard against or endure sickness? Nor can it be expected that a woman will resolutely endeavour to strengthen her constitution and abstain from enervating indulgences, if artificial notions of beauty, and false descriptions of sensibility, have been early entangled with her motives of action. Most men are sometimes obliged to bear with bodily inconveniences, and to endure, occasionally, the inclemency of the elements; but genteel women are, literally speaking, slaves to their bodies, and glory in their subjection.

I once knew a weak woman of fashion, who was more than commonly proud of her delicacy and sensibility. She thought a distinguishing taste and puny appetite the height of all human perfection, and acted accordingly. I have seen this weak sophisticated being neglect all the duties of life, yet recline with self-complacency on a sofa, and boast of her want of appetite as a proof of delicacy that extended to, or, perhaps, arose from, her exquisite sensibility: for it is difficult to render intelligible such ridiculous jargon.—Yet, at the moment, I have seen her insult a worthy old gentlewoman, whom unexpected misfortunes had made dependent on her ostentatious bounty, and who, in better days, had claims on her gratitude. Is it possible that a human creature could have become such a weak and depraved being, if, like the Sybarites, dissolved in luxury, everything like virtue had not been worn away, or never impressed by precept, a poor substitute, it is true, for cultivation of mind, though it serves as a fence against vice? . . .

Women are everywhere in this deplorable state; for, in order to preserve their innocence, as ignorance is courteously termed, truth is hidden from them, and they are made to assume an artificial character before their faculties have acquired any strength. Taught from their infancy that beauty is woman's sceptre, the mind shapes itself to the body, and, roaming round its gilt cage, only seeks to adore its prison. Men have various employments and pursuits which engage their attention, and give a character to the opening mind; but women, confined to one, and having their thoughts constantly directed to the most insignificant part of themselves, seldom extend their views beyond the triumph of the hour. But were their understanding once emancipated from the slavery to which the pride and sensuality of man and their short-sighted desire, like that of dominion in tyrants, of present sway, has subjected them, we should probably read of their weaknesses with surprise. . . .

Let not men then in the pride of power, use the same arguments that tyrannic kings and venal ministers have used, and fallaciously assert that woman ought to be subjected because she has always been so. But, when man, governed by reasonable laws, enjoys his natural freedom, let him despise woman, if she do not share it with him; and, till that glorious period arrives, in descanting on the folly of the sex, let him not overlook his own.

Women, it is true, obtaining power by unjust means, by practising or fostering vice, evidently lose the rank which reason would assign them, and they become either abject slaves or capricious tyrants. They lose all simplicity, all dignity of mind, in acquiring power, and act as men are observed to act when they have been exalted by the same means.

It is time to effect a revolution in female manners—time to restore to them their lost dignity—and make them, as a part of the human species, labour by reforming themselves to reform the world. It is time to separate unchangeable morals from local manners. If men be demi-gods—why let us serve them! And if the dignity of the female soul be as disputable as that of animals—if their reason does not afford sufficient light to direct their conduct whilst unerring instinct is denied—they are surely of all creatures the most miserable! and, bent beneath the iron hand of destiny, must submit to be a *fair defect* in creation. But to justify the ways of Providence respecting them, by pointing out some irrefragable reason for thus making such a large portion of mankind accountable and not accountable, would puzzle the subtilest casuist. . . .

. . . It were to be wished that women would cherish an affection for their husbands, founded on the same principle that devotion ought to rest upon. No other firm base is there under heaven—for let them beware of the fallacious light of sentiment; too often used as a softer phrase for sensuality. It follows then, I think, that from their infancy women should either be shut up like eastern princes, or educated in such a manner as to be able to think and act for themselves.

Why do men halt between two opinions, and expect impossibilities? Why do they expect virtue from a slave, from a being whom the constitution of civil society has rendered weak, if not vicious?

Still I know that it will require a considerable length of time to eradicate the firmly rooted prejudices which sensualists have planted; it will also require some time to convince women that they act contrary to their real interest on an enlarged scale, when they cherish or affect weakness under the name of delicacy, and to convince the world that the poisoned source of female vices and follies, if it be necessary, in compliance with custom, to use synonymous terms in a lax sense, has been the sensual homage paid to beauty:—to beauty of features; for it has been shrewdly observed by a German writer, that a pretty woman, as an object of desire, is generally allowed to be so by men of all descriptions; whilst a fine woman, who inspires more sublime emotions by displaying intellectual beauty, may be overlooked or observed with indifference by those men who find their happiness in the gratification of their appetites. I foresee an obvious retort—whilst man remains such an imperfect being as he appears hitherto to have been, he will, more or less, be the slave of his appetites; and those women obtaining most power who gratify a predominant one, the sex is degraded by a physical, if not by a moral necessity.

This objection has, I grant, some force; but while such a sublime precept exists, as, "Be pure as your heavenly Father is pure;" it would seem that the virtues of man are not limited by the Being who alone could limit them; and that he may press forward without considering whether he steps out of his sphere by indulging such a noble ambition. To the wild billows it has been said, "Thus far shalt thou go, and no further; and here shall thy proud waves be stayed." Vainly then do they beat and foam, restrained by the power that confines the struggling planets in their orbits, matter yields to the great governing Spirit. But an immortal soul, not restrained by mechanical laws and struggling to free itself from the shackles of matter, contributes to, instead of disturbing, the order of creation, when, co-operating with the Father of spirits, it tries to govern itself by the invariable rule that, in a degree, before which our imagination faints, regulates the universe.

Besides, if women be educated for dependence; that is, to act according to the will of another fallible being, and submit, right or wrong, to power, where are we to stop? Are they to be considered as vicegerents allowed to reign over a small domain, and answerable for their conduct to a higher tribunal, liable to error?

It will not be difficult to prove that such delegates will act like men subjected by fear, and make their children and servants endure their tyrannical oppression. As they submit without reason, they will, having no fixed rules to square their conduct by, be kind, or cruel, just as the whim of the moment directs; and we ought not to wonder if sometimes, galled by their heavy yoke, they take a malignant pleasure in resting it on weaker shoulders.

But, supposing a woman, trained up to obedience, be married to a sensible man, who directs her judgment without making her feel the servility of her subjection, to act with as much propriety by this reflected light as can be expected when reason is taken at second hand, yet she cannot ensure the life of her protector; he may die and leave her with a large family.

A double duty devolves on her: to educate them in the character of both father and mother; to form their principles and secure their property. But alas! she has never thought, much less acted for herself. She has only learned to please men, to depend gracefully on them; yet, encumbered with children, how is she to obtain another protector—a husband to supply the place of reason? A rational man, for we are not treading on romantic ground, though he may think her a pleasing docile creature, will not choose to marry a *family* for love, when the world contains many more pretty creatures. What is then to become of her? She either falls an easy prey to some mean fortune-hunter, who defrauds her children of their paternal inheritance, and renders her miserable; or becomes the victim of discontent and blind indulgence. Unable to educate her sons, or impress them with respect; for it is not a play on words to assert, that people are never respected, though filling an important station, who are not respectable; she pines under the anguish of unavailing impotent regret. The serpent's tooth enters into her very soul, and the vices of licentious youth bring her with sorrow, if not with poverty also, to the grave.

This is not an overcharged picture; on the contrary, it is a very possible case, and something similar must have fallen under every attentive eye.

I have, however, taken it for granted, that she was well-disposed, though experience shows, that the blind may as easily be led into a ditch as along the beaten road. But supposing, no very improbable conjecture, that a being only taught to please must still find her happiness in pleasing;—what an example of folly, not to say vice, will she be to her innocent daughters! The mother will be lost in the coquette, and, instead of making friends of her daughters, view them with eyes askance, for they are rivals—rivals more cruel than any other, because they invite a comparison, and drive her from the throne of beauty, who has never thought of a seat on the bench of reason.

It does not require a lively pencil, or the discriminating outline of a caricature, to sketch the domestic miseries and petty vices which such a mistress of a family diffuses. Still she only acts as a woman ought to act, brought up according to Rousseau's system. She can never be reproached for being masculine, or turning out of her sphere; nay, she may observe another of his grand rules, and, cautiously preserving her reputation free from spot, be reckoned a good kind of woman. Yet in what respect can she be termed good? She abstains, it is true, without any great struggle, from committing gross crimes; but how does she fulfil her duties? Duties!—in truth she has enough to think of to adorn her body and nurse a weak constitution.

With respect to religion, she never presumed to judge for herself; but conformed, as a dependent creature should, to the ceremonies of the church which she was brought up in, piously believing that wiser heads than her own have settled that business:—and not to doubt is her point of perfection. She therefore pays her tithe of mint and cummin—and thanks her God that she is not as other women are. These are the blessed effects of a good education! These the virtues of man's help-mate!

I must relieve myself by drawing a different picture.

Let fancy now present a woman with a tolerable understanding, for I do not wish to leave the line of mediocrity,

whose constitution, strengthened by exercise, has allowed her
body to acquire its full vigour; her mind, at the same time,
gradually expanding itself to comprehend the moral duties of
life, and in what human virtue and dignity consist.

Formed thus by the discharge of the relative duties of her
station, she marries from affection, without losing sight of
prudence, and looking beyond matrimonial felicity, she secures her husband's respect before it is necessary to exert
mean arts to please him and feed a dying flame, which nature
doomed to expire when the object became familiar, when
friendship and forbearance take place of a more ardent affection. This is the natural death of love, and domestic peace is
not destroyed by struggles to prevent its extinction. I also
suppose the husband to be virtuous; or she is still more in
want of independent principles.

Fate, however, breaks this tie. She is left a widow, perhaps, without a sufficient provision; but she is not desolate!
The pang of nature is felt; but after time has softened sorrow
into melancholy resignation, her heart turns to her children
with redoubled fondness, and anxious to provide for them,
affection gives a sacred heroic cast to her maternal duties. She
thinks that not only the eye sees her virtuous efforts from
whom all her comfort now must flow, and whose approbation
is life; but her imagination, a little abstracted and exalted by
grief, dwells on the fond hope that the eyes which her trembling hand closed, may still see how she subdues every wayward passion to fulfil the double duty of being the father as
well as the mother of her children. Raised to heroism by misfortunes, she represses the first faint dawning of a natural
inclination, before it ripens into love, and in the bloom of
life forgets her sex—forgets the pleasure of an awakening
passion, which might again have been inspired and returned.
She no longer thinks of pleasing, and conscious dignity prevents her from priding herself on account of the praise which
her conduct demands. Her children have her love, and her
brightest hopes are beyond the grave, where her imagination
often strays.

I think I see her surrounded by her children, reaping the
reward of her care. The intelligent eye meets hers, whilst
health and innocence smile on their chubby cheeks, and as
they grow up the cares of life are lessened by their grateful
attention. She lives to see the virtues which she endeavoured

to plant on principles, fixed into habits, to see her children attain a strength of character sufficient to enable them to endure adversity without forgetting their mother's example.

The task of life thus fulfilled, she calmly waits for the sleep of death, and rising from the grave, may say—Behold, thou gavest me a talent—and here are five talents.

I wish to sum up what I have said in a few words, for I here throw down my gauntlet, and deny the existence of sexual virtues, not excepting modesty. For man and woman, truth, if I understand the meaning of the word, must be the same; yet to the fanciful female character, so prettily drawn by poets and novelists, demanding the sacrifice of truth and sincerity, virtue becomes a relative idea, having no other foundation than utility, and of that utility men pretend arbitrarily to judge, shaping it to their own convenience.

Women, I allow, may have different duties to fulfil; but they are *human* duties, and the principles that should regulate the discharge of them, I sturdily maintain, must be the same.

To become respectable, the exercise of their understanding is necessary, there is no other foundation for independence of character; I mean explicitly to say that they must only bow to the authority of reason, instead of being the *modest* slaves of opinion.

In the superior ranks of life how seldom do we meet with a man of superior abilities, or even common acquirements? The reason appears to me clear, the state they are born in was an unnatural one. The human character has ever been formed by the employments the individual, or class, pursues; and if the faculties are not sharpened by necessity, they must remain obtuse. The argument may fairly be extended to women; for, seldom occupied by serious business, the pursuit of pleasure gives that insignificancy to their character which renders the society of the *great* so insipid. The same want of firmness, produced by a similar cause, forces them both to fly from themselves to noisy pleasures, and artificial passions, till vanity takes place of every social affection, and the characteristics of humanity can scarcely be discerned. Such are the blessings of civil governments, as they are at present organized, that wealth and female softness equally tend to debase mankind, and are produced by the same cause; but allowing women to be rational creatures, they should be

incited to acquire virtues which they may call their own, for
how can a rational being be ennobled by anything that is not
obtained by its *own* exertions?

Of the Pernicious Effects Which Arise From the Unnatural Distinctions Established in Society.

From the respect paid to property flow, as from a poisoned
fountain, most of the evils and vices which render this world
such a dreary scene to the contemplative mind. . . .

One class presses on another; for all are aiming to procure respect on account of their property: and property, once
gained, will procure the respect due only to talents and virtue.
Men neglect the duties incumbent on man, yet are treated like
demi-gods; religion is also separated from morality by a ceremonial veil, yet men wonder that the world is almost, literally speaking, a den of sharpers or oppressors. . . .

It is vain to expect virtue from women till they are in
some degree independent of men; nay, it is vain to expect that
strength of natural affection which would make them good
wives and mothers. Whilst they are absolutely dependent on
their husbands they will be cunning, mean, and selfish, and
the men who can be gratified by the fawning fondness of
spaniel-like affection have not much delicacy, for love is not
to be bought, in any sense of the words; its silken wings are
instantly shrivelled up when anything beside a return in kind
is sought. Yet whilst wealth enervates men, and women live,
as it were, by their personal charms, how can we expect them
to discharge those ennobling duties which equally require
exertion and self-denial? Hereditary property sophisticates the
mind, and the unfortunate victims to it, if I may so express
myself, swathed from their birth, seldom exert the locomotive
faculty of body or mind; and, thus viewing everything
through one medium, and that a false one, they are unable to
discern in what true merit and happiness consist. False, indeed, must be the light when the drapery of situation hides
the man, and makes him stalk in masquerade, dragging from
one scene of dissipation to another the nerveless limbs that
hang with stupid listlessness, and rolling round the vacant eye
which plainly tells us that there is no mind at home.

I mean, therefore, to infer that the society is not properly
organized which does not compel men and women to discharge

their respective duties, by making it the only way to acquire that countenance from their fellow-creatures which every human being wishes some way to attain. The respect, consequently, which is paid to wealth and mere personal charms, is a true north-east blast that blights the tender blossoms of affection and virtue. Nature has wisely attached affections to duties to sweeten toil, and to give that vigour to the exertions of reason which only the heart can give. But the affection which is put on merely because it is the appropriated insignia of a certain character, when its duties are not fulfilled, is one of the empty compliments which vice and folly are obliged to pay to virtue and the real nature of things.

To illustrate my opinion, I need only observe that when a woman is admired for her beauty, and suffers herself to be so far intoxicated by the admiration she receives as to neglect to discharge the indispensable duty of a mother, she sins against herself by neglecting to cultivate an affection that would equally tend to make her useful and happy. True happiness, I mean all the contentment and virtuous satisfaction that can be snatched in this imperfect state, must arise from well regulated affections; and an affection includes a duty. Men are not aware of the misery they cause and the vicious weakness they cherish by only inciting women to render themselves pleasing; they do not consider that they thus make natural and artificial duties clash by sacrificing the comfort and respectability of a woman's life to voluptuous notions of beauty when in nature they all harmonize.

Cold would be the heart of a husband, were he not rendered unnatural by early debauchery, who did not feel more delight at seeing his child suckled by its mother, than the most artful wanton tricks could ever raise; yet this natural way of cementing the matrimonial tie and twisting esteem with fonder recollections, wealth leads women to spurn. To preserve their beauty and wear the flowery crown of the day, which gives them a kind of right to reign for a short time over the sex, they neglect to stamp impressions on their husbands' hearts that would be remembered with more tenderness when the snow on the head began to chill the bosom than even their virgin charms. The maternal solicitude of a reasonable affectionate woman is very interesting, and the chastened dignity with which a mother returns the caresses that she and her child receive from a father who has been fulfilling the serious duties of his station, is not only a respectable but a beautiful sight. So singular indeed are my feelings, and I have endeavoured not to catch factitious ones, that after having been fatigued with the sight of insipid grandeur and the slavish ceremonies that with cumbrous pomp supplied the place of domestic affections, I have turned to some other scene to relieve my eye by resting it on the refreshing green everywhere scattered by nature. I have then viewed with pleasure a woman nursing her children, and discharging the duties of her station with, perhaps, merely a servant maid to take off her hands the servile part of the household business. I have seen her prepare herself and children, with only the luxury of cleanliness, to receive her husband, who returning weary home in the evening found smiling babes and a clean hearth. My heart has loitered in the midst of the group, and has even throbbed with sympathetic emotion, when the scraping of the well known foot has raised a pleasing tumult.

* * *

The preposterous distinctions of rank, which render civilization a curse by dividing the world between voluptuous tyrants and cunning envious dependents, corrupt, almost equally, every class of people, because respectability is not attached to the discharge of the relative duties of life, but to the station, and when the duties are not fulfilled the affections cannot gain sufficient strength to fortify the virtue of which they are the natural reward. Still there are some loopholes out of which a man may creep, and dare to think and act for himself; but for a woman it is a herculean task, because she has difficulties peculiar to her sex to overcome which require almost superhuman powers.

A truly benevolent legislator always endeavours to make it the interest of each individual to be virtuous; and thus private virtue becoming the cement of public happiness, an orderly whole is consolidated by the tendency of all the parts towards a common centre. But, the private or public virtue of woman is very problematical; for Rousseau, and a numerous list of male writers, insist that she should all her life be subjected to a severe restraint, that of propriety. Why subject her to propriety—blind propriety, if she be capable of acting from a nobler spring, if she be an heir of immortality? Is sugar always to be produced by vital blood? Is one half of the human species, like the poor African slaves, to be subject to prejudices that brutalize them, when principles would be a

surer guard, only to sweeten the cup of man? Is not this indirectly to deny woman reason? for a gift is a mockery, if it
be unfit for use.

Women are, in common with men, rendered weak and
luxurious by the relaxing pleasures which wealth procures;
but added to this they are made slaves to their persons, and
must render them alluring that man may lend them his reason
to guide their tottering steps aright. Or should they be ambitious, they must govern their tyrants by sinister tricks, for
without rights there cannot be any incumbent duties. The laws
respecting woman, which I mean to discuss in a future part,
make an absurd unit of a man and his wife; and then, by the
easy transition of only considering him as responsible, she is
reduced to a mere cypher.

The being who discharges the duties of its station is independent; and, speaking of women at large, their first duty is
to themselves as rational creatures, and the next in point of
importance, as citizens, is that which includes so many, of a
mother. The rank in life which dispenses with their fulfilling
this duty necessarily degrades them by making them mere
dolls. Or, should they turn to something more important than
merely fitting drapery upon a smooth block, their minds are
only occupied by some soft platonic attachment; or, the actual
management of an intrigue may keep their thoughts in motion; for when they neglect domestic duties, they have it not
in their own power to take the field and march and counter-
march like soldiers, or wrangle in the senate to keep their
faculties from rusting. . . .

But, to render her really virtuous and useful, she must not,
if she discharge her civil duties, want, individually, the protection of civil laws; she must not be dependent on her husband's bounty for her subsistence during his life or support
after his death—for how can a being be generous who has
nothing of its own? or virtuous, who is not free? The wife, in
the present state of things, who is faithful to her husband,
and neither suckles nor educates her children, scarcely deserves the name of a wife, and has no right to that of a
citizen. But take away natural rights, and duties become null.

Women then must be considered as only the wanton solace
of men when they become so weak in mind and body that
they cannot exert themselves, unless to pursue some frothy
pleasure or to invent some frivolous fashion. What can be a
more melancholy sight to a thinking mind than to look into

the numerous carriages that drive helter-skelter about this metropolis in a morning full of pale-faced creatures who are flying from themselves. I have often wished, with Dr. Johnson, to place some of them in a little shop with half a dozen children looking up to their languid countenances for support. I am much mistaken if some latent vigour would not soon give health and spirit to their eyes, and some lines drawn by the exercise of reason on the blank cheeks, which before were only undulated by dimples, might restore lost dignity to the character, or rather enable it to attain the true dignity of its nature. Virtue is not to be acquired even by speculation, much less by the negative supineness that wealth naturally generates.

Besides, when poverty is more disgraceful than even vice, is not morality cut to the quick? Still to avoid misconstruction, though I consider that women in the common walks of life are called to fulfil the duties of wives and mothers, by religion and reason, I cannot help lamenting that women of a superior cast have not a road open by which they can pursue more extensive plans of usefulness and independence. I may excite laughter by dropping a hint which I mean to pursue some future time, for I really think that women ought to have representatives, instead of being arbitrarily governed without having any direct share allowed them in the deliberations of government.

But, as the whole system of representation is now in this country only a convenient handle for despotism, they need not complain, for they are as well represented as a numerous class of hard-working mechanics, who pay for the support of royalty when they can scarcely stop their children's mouths with bread. How are they represented whose very sweat supports the splendid stud of an heir apparent, or varnishes the chariot of some female favourite who looks down on shame? Taxes on the very necessaries of life enable an endless tribe of idle princes and princesses to pass with stupid pomp before a gaping crowd, who almost worship the very parade which costs them so dear. This is mere gothic grandeur, something like the barbarous useless parade of having sentinels on horseback at Whitehall, which I could never view without a mixture of contempt and indignation. . . .

But what have women to do in society? I may be asked, but to loiter with easy grace; surely you would not condemn them all to suckle fools and chronicle small beer! No. Women might certainly study the art of healing, and be physicians as well as nurses. And midwifery, decency seems to allot to them, though I am afraid the word midwife in our dictionaries will soon give place to *accoucheur*, and one proof of the former delicacy of the sex be effaced from the language.

They might also study politics, and settle their benevolence on the broadest basis; for the reading of history will scarcely be more useful than the perusal of romances, if read as mere biography; if the character of the times, the political improvements, arts, &c., be not observed. In short, if it be not considered as the history of man; and not of particular men, who filled a niche in the temple of fame, and dropped into the black rolling stream of time, that silently sweeps all before it, into the shapeless void called—eternity. For shape, can it be called, "that shape hath none"?

Business of various kinds they might likewise pursue, if they were educated in a more orderly manner, which might save many from common and legal prostitution. Women would not then marry for a support, as men accept of places under government, and neglect the implied duties; nor would an attempt to earn their own subsistence—a most laudable one!—sink them almost to the level of those poor abandoned creatures who live by prostitution. For are not milliners and mantua-makers reckoned the next class? The few employments open to women, so far from being liberal, are menial; and when a superior education enables them to take charge of the education of children as governesses, they are not treated like the tutors of sons, though even clerical tutors are not always treated in a manner calculated to render them respectable in the eyes of their pupils, to say nothing of the private comfort of the individual. But as women educated like gentlewomen are never designed for the humiliating situation which necessity sometimes forces them to fill, these situations are considered in the light of a degradation; and they know little of the human heart, who need to be told that nothing so painfully sharpens sensibility as such a fall in life.

Some of these women might be restrained from marrying by a proper spirit or delicacy, and others may not have had it in their power to escape in this pitiful way from servitude; is not that government then very defective, and very unmindful of the happiness of one half of its members, that does not provide for honest, independent women, by encouraging them to fill respectable stations? But in order to render their private

virtue a public benefit, they must have a civil existence in the
state, married or single; else we shall continually see some
worthy woman, whose sensibility has been rendered painfully
acute by undeserved contempt, droop like "the lily broken
down by a plow-share."

It is a melancholy truth—yet such is the blessed effect of
civilization!—the most respectable women are the most oppressed; and, unless they have understandings far superior to
the common run of understandings, taking in both sexes, they
must, from being treated like contemptible beings, become
contemptible. How many women thus waste life away the
prey of discontent, who might have practised as physicians,
regulated a farm, managed a shop, and stood erect, supported
by their own industry, instead of hanging their heads sur-
charged with the dew of sensibility, that consumes the beauty
to which it at first gave lustre; nay, I doubt whether pity and
love are so near akin as poets feign, for I have seldom seen
much comparison excited by the helplessness of females,
unless they were fair; then, perhaps, pity was the soft handmaid of love, or the harbinger of lust. . . .

Proud of their weakness, however, they must always be
protected, guarded from care, and all the rough toils that
dignify the mind. If this be the fiat of fate, if they will make
themselves insignificant and contemptible, sweetly to waste
"life away," let them not expect to be valued when their
beauty fades, for it is the fate of the fairest flowers to be admired and pulled to pieces by the careless hand that plucked
them. In how many ways do I wish, from the purest benevolence, to impress this truth on my sex; yet I fear that they
will not listen to a truth that dear-bought experience has
brought home to many an agitated bosom, nor willingly
resign the privileges of rank and sex for the privileges of
humanity, to which those have no claim who do not discharge
its duties.

Those writers are particularly useful, in my opinion, who
make man feel for man, independent of the station he fills,
or the drapery of factitious sentiments. I then would fain
convince reasonable men of the importance of some of my
remarks; and prevail on them to weigh dispassionately the
whole tenor of my observations. I appeal to their understandings; and, as a fellow-creature, claim, in the name of my sex,
some interest in their hearts. I entreat them to assist to emancipate their companion, to make her a *help meet* for them!

Would men but generously snap our chains, and be content with rational fellowship instead of slavish obedience, they would find us more observant daughters, more affectionate sisters, more faithful wives, more reasonable mothers—in a word, better citizens. We should then love them with true affection, because we should learn to respect ourselves; and the peace of mind of a worthy man would not be interrupted by the idle vanity of his wife, nor the babes sent to nestle in a strange bosom, having never found a home in their mother's.

Parental Affection.

Parental affection is, perhaps, the blindest modification of perverse self-love. . . . Parents often love their children in the most brutal manner, and sacrifice every relative duty to promote their advancement in the world.—To promote, such is the perversity of unprincipled prejudices, the future welfare of the very beings whose present existence they embitter by the most despotic stretch of power. Power, in fact, is ever true to its vital principle, for in every shape it would reign without control or inquiry. Its throne is built across a dark abyss, which no eye must dare to explore, less the baseless fabric should totter under investigation. Obedience, unconditional obedience, is the catch-word of tyrants of every description, and to render "assurance doubly sure," one kind of despotism supports another. Tyrants would have cause to tremble if reason were to become the rule of duty in any of the relations of life, for the light might spread till perfect day appeared. And when it did appear, how would men smile at the sight of the bugbears at which they started during the night of ignorance, or the twilight of timid inquiry.

Parental affection, indeed, in many minds, is but a pretext to tyrannize where it can be done with impunity, for only good and wise men are content with the respect that will bear discussion. Convinced that they have a right to what they insist on, they do not fear reason, or dread the sifting of subjects that recur to natural justice: because they firmly believe that the more enlightened the human mind becomes the deeper root will just and simple principles take. . . .

Woman, however, a slave in every situation to prejudice, seldom exerts enlightened maternal affection; for she either neglects her children, or spoils them by improper indulgence. Besides, the affection of some women for their children is, as I have before termed it, frequently very brutish: for it eradicates every spark of humanity. Justice, truth, everything is sacrificed by these Rebekahs, and for the sake of their *own* children they violate the most sacred duties, forgetting the common relationship that binds the whole family on earth together. Yet, reason seems to say, that they who suffer one duty, or affection, to swallow up the rest, have not sufficient heart or mind to fulfil that one conscientiously. It then loses the venerable aspect of a duty, and assumes the fantastic form of a whim.

As the care of children in their infancy is one of the grand duties annexed to the female character by nature, this duty would afford many forcible arguments for strengthening the female understanding, if it were properly considered.

The formation of the mind must be begun very early, and the temper, in particular, requires the most judicious attention—an attention which women cannot pay who only love their children because they are their children, and seek no further for the foundation of their duty, than in the feelings of the moment. It is this want of reason in their affections which makes women so often run into extremes, and either be the most fond or most careless and unnatural mothers.

To be a good mother—a woman must have sense, and that independence of mind which few women possess who are taught to depend entirely on their husbands. Meek wives are, in general, foolish mothers; wanting their children to love them best, and take their part, in secret, against the father, who is held up as a scarecrow. When chastisement is necessary, though they have offended the mother, the father must inflict the punishment; he must be the judge in all disputes: but I shall more fully discuss this subject when I treat of private education; I now only mean to insist, that unless the understanding of woman be enlarged, and her character rendered more firm, by being allowed to govern her own conduct, she will never have sufficient sense or command of temper to manage her children properly. Her parental affection, indeed, scarcely deserves the name, when it does not lead her to suckle her children, because the discharge of this duty is equally calculated to inspire maternal and filial affection: and it is the indispensable duty of men and women to fulfil the duties which give birth to affections that are the surest preservatives against vice. Natural affection, as it is termed, I believe to be a very faint tie; affections must grow out of the habitual exercise of a mutual sympathy: and what sympathy does a mother exercise who sends her babe to a nurse, and only takes it from a nurse to send it to a school?

In the exercise of their maternal feelings providence has furnished women with a natural substitute for love, when the lover becomes only a friend, and mutual confidence takes place of overstrained admiration—a child then gently twists the relaxing cord, and a mutual care produces a new mutual sympathy. But a child, though a pledge of affection, will not enliven it, if both father and mother be content to transfer the charge to hirelings; for they who do their duty by proxy should not murmur if they miss the reward of duty—parental affection produces filial duty.

On National Education.

The good effects resulting from attention to private education will ever be very confined, and the parent who really puts his own hand to the plough will always, in some degree, be disappointed, till education becomes a grand national concern. A man cannot retire into a desert with his child, and if he did he could not bring himself back to childhood, and become the proper friend and playfellow of an infant or youth. And when children are confined to the society of men and women, they very soon acquire that kind of premature manhood which stops the growth of every vigorous power of mind or body. In order to open their faculties they should be excited to think for themselves; and this can only be done by mixing a number of children together, and making them jointly pursue the same objects.

A child very soon contracts a benumbing indolence of mind, which he has seldom sufficient vigour afterwards to shake off, when he only asks a question instead of seeking for information, and then relies implicitly on the answer he receives. With his equals in age this could never be the case, and the subjects of inquiry, though they might be influenced, would not be entirely under the direction of men, who frequently damp, if not destroy, abilities, by bringing them for-

ward too hastily: and too hastily they will infallibly be
brought forward, if the child be confined to the society of a
man, however sagacious that man may be.

Besides, in youth the seeds of every affection should be
sown, and the respectful regard which is felt for a parent, is
very different from the social affections which are to constitute the happiness of life as it advances. Of these equality is
the basis, and an intercourse of sentiments unclogged by that
observant seriousness which prevents disputation, though it
may not enforce submission. Let a child have ever such an
affection for his parent, he will always languish to play and
prattle with children; and the very respect he feels—for filial
esteem always has a dash of fear mixed with it—will, if it do
not teach him cunning, at least prevent him from pouring out
the little secrets which first open the heart to friendship and
confidence, gradually leading to more expansive benevolence.
Added to this, he will never acquire that frank ingenuousness
of behaviour which young people can only attain by being
frequently in society where they dare to speak what they
think; neither afraid of being reproved for their presumption,
nor laughed at for their folly.

Forcibly impressed by the reflections which the sight of
schools, as they are at present conducted, naturally suggested,
I have formerly delivered my opinion rather warmly in favour
of a private education; but further experience has led me to
view the subject in a different light. I still, however, think
schools, as they are now regulated, the hot-beds of vice and
folly, and the knowledge of human nature supposed to be
attained there, merely cunning selfishness. . . .

The only way to avoid two extremes equally injurious to
morality, would be to contrive some way of combining a
public and private education. Thus to make men citizens two
natural steps might be taken, which seem directly to lead to
the desired point; for the domestic affections, that first open
the heart to the various modifications of humanity, would be
cultivated, whilst the children were nevertheless allowed to
spend a great part of their time, on terms of equality, with
other children.

I still recollect, with pleasure, the country day school;
where a boy trudged in the morning, wet or dry, carrying his
books, and his dinner, if it were at a considerable distance; a
servant did not then lead master by the hand, for, when he
had once put on coat and breeches, he was allowed to shift

for himself, and return alone in the evening to recount the feats of the day close at the parental knee. His father's house was his home, and was ever after fondly remembered; nay, I appeal to many superior men, who were educated in this manner, whether the recollection of some shady lane where they conned their lesson, or of some stile, where they sat making a kite, or mending a bat, has not endeared their country to them?

But, what boy ever recollected with pleasure the years he spent in close confinement at an academy near London? unless, indeed, he should, by chance, remember the poor scarecrow of an usher, whom he tormented; or the tart-man, from whom he caught a cake, to devour it with a cattish appetite of selfishness. At boarding-schools of every description, the relaxation of the junior boys is mischief; and of the senior, vice. Besides, in great schools, what can be more prejudicial to the moral character than the system of tyranny and abject slavery which is established amongst the boys, to say nothing of the slavery to forms, which makes religion worse than a farce? . . .

. . .

In order then to inspire a love of home and domestic pleasures, children ought to be educated at home, for riotous holidays only make them fond of home for their own sakes. Yet, the vacations, which do not foster domestic affections, continually disturb the course of study, and render any plan of improvement abortive which includes temperance; still, were they abolished, children would be entirely separated from their parents, and I question whether they would become better citizens by sacrificing the preparatory affections, by destroying the force of relationships that render the marriage state as necessary as respectable. But, if a private education produce self-importance, or insulate a man in his family, the evil is only shifted, not remedied.

This train of reasoning brings me back to a subject on which I mean to dwell, the necessity of establishing proper day schools.

But these should be national establishments, for whilst schoolmasters are dependent on the caprice of parents, little exertion can be expected from them, more than is necessary to please ignorant people. Indeed, the necessity of a master's giving the parents some sample of the boy's abilities, which during the vacation is shown to every visitor, is productive of more mischief than would at first be supposed. For it is seldom done entirely, to speak with moderation, by the child itself; thus the master countenances falsehood, or winds the poor machine up to some extraordinary exertion, that injures the wheels, and stops the progress of gradual improvement. The memory is loaded with unintelligible words, to make a show of, without the understanding's acquiring any distinct ideas: but only that education deserves emphatically to be termed cultivation of mind which teaches young people how to begin to think. The imagination should not be allowed to debauch the understanding before it gained strength, or vanity will become the forerunner of vice: for every way of exhibiting the acquirements of a child is injurious to its moral character. . . .

. . . The pure animal spirits, which make both mind and body shoot out, and unfold the tender blossoms of hope, are turned sour, and vented in vain wishes or pert repinings, that contract the faculties and spoil the temper; else they mount to the brain, and sharpening the understanding before it gains proportionable strength, produce that pitiful cunning which disgracefully characterizes the female mind—and I fear will ever characterize it whilst women remain the slaves of power!

The little respect paid to chastity in the male world is, I am persuaded, the grand source of many of the physical and moral evils that torment mankind, as well as of the vices and follies that degrade and destroy women; yet at school, boys infallibly lose that decent bashfulness which might have ripened into modesty at home. . . .

I have already animadverted on the bad habits which females acquire when they are shut up together; and I think that the observation may fairly be extended to the other sex, till the natural inference is drawn which I have had in view throughout—that to improve both sexes they ought, not only in private families, but in public schools, to be educated together. If marriage be the cement of society, mankind should all be educated after the same model, or the intercourse of the sexes will never deserve the name of fellowship, nor will women ever fulfil the peculiar duties of their sex, till they become enlightened citizens, till they become free by being enabled to earn their own subsistence, independent of men; in the same manner, I mean, to prevent misconstruction, as one man is independent of another. Nay, marriage will never be held sacred till women, by being brought up with men, are prepared to be their companions rather than their mistresses; for the mean doublings of cunning will ever render them contemptible, whilst oppression renders them timid. . . .

Were boys and girls permitted to pursue the same studies together, those graceful decencies might early be inculcated which produce modesty without those sexual distinctions that taint the mind. Lessons of politeness, and that formulary of decorum which treads on the heels of falsehood, would be rendered useless by habitual propriety of behaviour. Not, indeed, put on for visitors like the courtly robe of politeness, but the sober effect of cleanliness of mind. Would not this simple elegance of sincerity be a chaste homage paid to domestic affections, far surpassing the meretricious compliments that shine with false lustre in the heartless intercourse of fashionable life? But, till more understanding preponderates in society, there will ever be a want of heart and taste, and the harlot's *rouge* will supply the place of that celestial suffusion which only virtuous affections can give to the face. Gallantry, and what is called love, may subsist without simplicity of character; but the main pillars of friendship are respect and confidence—esteem is never founded on it cannot tell what! . . .

True taste is ever the work of the understanding employed in observing natural effects; and till women have more understanding, it is vain to expect them to possess domestic taste. Their lively senses will ever be at work to harden their hearts, and the emotions struck out of them will continue to be vivid and transitory, unless a proper education store their mind with knowledge.

It is the want of domestic taste, and not the acquirement of knowledge, that takes women out of their families, and tears the smiling babe from the breast that ought to afford it nourishment. Women have been allowed to remain in ignorance, and slavish dependence, many, very many years, and still we hear of nothing but their fondness of pleasure and sway, their preference of rakes and soldiers, their childish attachment to toys, and the vanity that makes them value accomplishments more than virtues. . . .

Let an enlightened nation then try what effect reason would have to bring them back to nature, and their duty; and allowing them to share the advantages of education and government with man, see whether they will become better as they grow wiser and become free. They cannot be injured by the experiment; for it is not in the power of man to render them more insignificant than they are at present.

To render this practicable, day schools, for particular ages, should be established by government, in which boys and girls might be educated together. The school for the younger children, from five to nine years of age, ought to be absolutely free and open to all classes. A sufficient number of masters should also be chosen by a select committee, in each parish, to whom any complaint of negligence, &c., might be made, if signed by six of the children's parents. . . .

. . . [T]o prevent any of the distinctions of vanity, they should be dressed alike, and all obliged to submit to the same discipline, or leave the school. The school-room ought to be surrounded by a large piece of ground, in which the children might be usefully exercised, for at this age they should not be confined to any sedentary employment for more than an hour at a time. But these relaxations might all be rendered a part of elementary education, for many things improve and amuse the senses, when introduced as a kind of show, to the principles of which, dryly laid down, children would turn a deaf ear. For instance, botany, mechanics, and astronomy. Reading, writing, arithmetic, natural history, and some simple experiments in natural philosophy, might fill up the day; but these pursuits should never encroach on gymnastic plays in the open air. The elements of religion, history, the history of man, and politics, might also be taught by conversations, in the socratic form.

After the age of nine, girls and boys, intended for domestic employments, or mechanical trades, ought to be removed to other schools, and receive instruction in some measure appropriated to the destination of each individual, the two sexes being still together in the morning; but in the afternoon the girls should attend a school where plain-work, mantua-making, millinery, &c., would be their employment.

The young people of superior abilities, or fortune, might now be taught, in another school, the dead and living languages, the elements of science, and continue the study of history and politics, on a more extensive scale, which would not exclude polite literature.

Girls and boys still together? I hear some readers ask: yes. And I should not fear any other consequence than that some early attachment might take place; which, whilst it had the best affect on the moral character of the young people, might not perfectly agree with the views of the parents, for it will be a long time, I fear, before the world will be so far enlightened that parents, only anxious to render their children virtuous, shall allow them to choose companions for life themselves. . . .

In this plan of education the constitution of boys would not be ruined by the early debaucheries which now make men so selfish, or girls rendered weak and vain by indolence and frivolous pursuits. But, I presuppose that such a degree of equality should be established between the sexes as would shut out gallantry and coquetry, yet allow friendship and love to temper the heart for the discharge of higher duties.

These would be schools of morality—and the happiness of man, allowed to flow from the pure springs of duty and affection, what advances might not the human mind make? Society can only be happy and free in proportion as it is virtuous; but the present distinctions, established in society, corrode all private and blast all public virtue.

I have already inveighed against the custom of confining girls to their needle, and shutting them out from all political and civil employments; for by thus narrowing their minds they are rendered unfit to fulfil the peculiar duties which nature has assigned them.

Only employed about the little incidents of the day, they necessarily grow up cunning. My very soul has often sickened at observing the sly tricks practised by women to gain some foolish thing on which their silly hearts were set. Not allowed to dispose of money, or call anything their own, they learn to turn the market penny; or, should a husband offend, by staying from home, or give rise to some emotions of jealousy—a new gown, or any pretty bawble, smooths Juno's angry brow.

But these *littlenesses* would not degrade their character, if women were led to respect themselves, if political and moral subjects were opened to them; and I will venture to affirm that this is the only way to make them properly attentive to their domestic duties. An active mind embraces the whole circle of its duties, and finds time enough for all. It is not, I assert, a bold attempt to emulate masculine virtues; it is not the enchantment of literary pursuits, or the steady investigation of scientific subjects, that leads women astray from duty. No, it is indolence and vanity—the love of pleasure and the love of sway, that will reign paramount in an empty mind.

I say empty emphatically, because the education which women now receive scarcely deserves the name. For the little knowledge that they are led to acquire, during the important years of youth, is merely relative to accomplishments; and accomplishments without a bottom, for unless the understanding be cultivated, superficial and monotonous is every grace. Like the charms of a made up face, they only strike the senses in a crowd; but at home, wanting mind, they want variety. The consequence is obvious; in gay scenes of dissipation we meet the artificial mind and face, for those who fly from solitude dread, next to solitude, the domestic circle; not having it in their power to amuse or interest, they feel their own insignificance, or find nothing to amuse or interest themselves.

Besides, what can be more indelicate than a girl's *coming out* in the fashionable world? Which, in other words, is to bring to market a marriageable miss, whose person is taken from one public place to another, richly caparisoned. Yet, mixing in the giddy circle under restraint, these butterflies long to flutter at large, for the first affection of their souls is their own persons, to which their attention has been called with the most sedulous care whilst they were preparing for the period that decides their fate for life. Instead of pursuing this idle routine, sighing for tasteless show and heartless state, with what dignity would the youths of both sexes form attachments in the schools that I have cursorily pointed out; in which, as life advanced, dancing, music, and drawing might be admitted as relaxations, for at these schools young people of fortune ought to remain, more or less, till they were of age. Those who were designed for particular professions might attend, three or four mornings in the week, the schools appropriated for their immediate instruction. . . .

I know that libertines will also exclaim, that woman would be unsexed by acquiring strength of body and mind, and that beauty, soft bewitching beauty! would no longer adorn the daughters of men. I am of a very different opinion, for I think that, on the contrary, we should then see dignified beauty, and true grace; to produce which, many powerful physical and moral causes would concur. Not relaxed beauty, it is true, or the graces of helplessness; but such as appears to make us respect the human body as a majestic pile fit to receive a noble inhabitant, in the relics of antiquity. . . .

My observations on national education are obviously hints; but I principally wish to enforce the necessity of educating the sexes together to perfect both, and of making children sleep at home that they may learn to love home; yet to make private support, instead of smothering, public affections, they should be sent to school to mix with a number of equals, for only by the jostlings of equality can we form a just opinion of ourselves.

To render mankind more virtuous, and happier of course, both sexes must act from the same principle; but how can that be expected when only one is allowed to see the reasonableness of it? To render also the social compact truly equitable, and in order to spread those enlightening principles which alone can meliorate the fate of man, women must be allowed to found their virtue on knowledge, which is scarcely possible unless they be educated by the same pursuits as men. For they are made so inferior by ignorance and low desires, as not to deserve to be ranked with them; or, by the serpentine wrigglings of cunning they mount the tree of knowledge, and only acquire sufficient to lead men astray.

It is plain from the history of all nations, that women cannot be confined to merely domestic pursuits, for they will not fulfil family duties, unless their minds take a wider range, and whilst they are kept in ignorance they become in the same proportion the slaves of pleasure as they are the slaves of man. Nor can they be shut out of great enterprises, though the narrowness of their minds often make them mar, what they are unable to comprehend.

The libertinism, and even the virtues of superior men, will always give women, of some description, great power over them; and these weak women, under the influence of childish passions and selfish vanity, will throw a false light over the objects which the very men view with their eyes, who ought to enlighten their judgment. Men of fancy, and those sanguine characters who mostly hold the helm of human affairs, in general, relax in the society of women; and surely I need not cite to the most superficial reader of history the numerous examples of vice and oppression which the private intrigues of female favourites have produced; not to dwell on the mischief that naturally arises from the blundering interposition of well-meaning folly. . . . The power which vile and foolish women have had over wise men, who possessed sensibility, is notorious; I shall only mention one instance.

Who ever drew a more exalted female character than Rousseau? though in the lump he constantly endeavoured to

degrade the sex. And why was he thus anxious? Truly to
justify to himself the affection which weakness and virtue
had made him cherish for that fool Theresa. He could not
raise her to the common level of her sex; and therefore he
laboured to bring woman down to hers. He found her a
convenient humble companion, and pride made him determine to find some superior virtues in the being whom he
chose to live with; but did not her conduct during his life,
and after his death, clearly show how grossly he was mistaken who called her a celestial innocent. Nay, in the bitterness of his heart he himself laments, that when his bodily
infirmities made him no longer treat her like a woman, she
ceased to have an affection for him. And it was very natural
that she should, for having so few sentiments in common,
when the sexual tie was broken, what was to hold her? To
hold her affection whose sensibility was confined to one sex,
nay, to one man, it requires sense to turn sensibility into the
broad channel of humanity; many women have not mind
enough to have an affection for a woman, or a friendship for
a man. But the sexual weakness that makes woman depend
upon a man for subsistence, produces a kind of cattish affection which leads a wife to purr about her husband as she
would about any man who fed and caressed her.

Men are, however, often gratified by this kind of fondness,
which is confined in a beastly manner to themselves; but
should they ever become more virtuous, they will wish to
converse at their fireside with a friend, after they cease to
play with a mistress.

Besides, understanding is necessary to give variety and
interest to sensual enjoyments, for low, indeed, in the intellectual scale is the mind that can continue to love when
neither virtue nor sense give a human appearance to an
animal appetite. But sense will always preponderate; and if
women be not, in general, brought more on a level with men,
some superior women, like the Greek courtezans, will assemble the men of abilities around them, and draw from their
families many citizens who would have stayed at home had
their wives had more sense, or the graces which result from
the exercise of understanding and fancy, the legitimate parents of taste. A woman of talents, if she be not absolutely
ugly, will always obtain great power, raised by the weakness
of her sex; and in proportion as men acquire virtue and delicacy, by the exertion of reason, they will look for both in

women, but they can only acquire them in the same way that men do.

In France or Italy, have the women confined themselves to domestic life? though they have not hitherto had a political existence, yet, have they not illicitly had great sway? corrupting themselves and the men with whose passions they played. In short, in whatever light I view the subject, reason and experience convince me that the only method of leading women to fulfil their peculiar duties, is to free them from all restraint by allowing them to participate in the inherent rights of mankind. . . .

I speak of the improvement and emancipation of the whole sex, for I know that the behaviour of a few women, who, by accident, or following a strong bent of nature, have acquired a portion of knowledge superior to that of the rest of their sex, has often been overbearing; but there have been instances of women who, attaining knowledge, have not discarded modesty, nor have they always pedantically appeared to despise the ignorance which they laboured to disperse in their own minds. The exclamations then which any advice respecting female learning commonly produces, especially from pretty women, often arise from envy. When they chance to see that even the lustre of their eyes and the flippant sportiveness of refined coquetry will not always secure them attention, during a whole evening, should a woman of a more cultivated understanding endeavour to give a rational turn to the conversation, the common source of consolation is, that such women seldom get husbands. What arts have I not seen silly women use to interrupt by *flirtation*—a very significant word to describe such a manœuvre—a rational conversation which made the men forget that they were pretty women.

But, allowing what is very natural to man, that the possession of rare abilities is really calculated to excite overweening pride, disgusting in both men and women—in what a state of inferiority must the female faculties have rusted when such a small portion of knowledge as those women attained, who have sneeringly been termed learned women, could be singular?—Sufficiently so to puff up the possessor, and excite envy in her contemporaries, and some of the other sex. Nay, has not a little rationality exposed many women to the severest censure? I advert to well known facts, for I have frequently heard women ridiculed, and every little weakness exposed, only because they adopted the advice of some medi-

cal men, and deviated from the beaten track in their mode of
treating their infants. I have actually heard this barbarous
aversion to innovation carried still further, and a sensible
woman stigmatized as an unnatural mother, who has thus
been wisely solicitous to preserve the health of her children,
when in the midst of her care she has lost one by some of the
casualties of infancy, which no prudence can ward off. Her
acquaintance has observed, that this was the consequence of
new-fangled notions—the new-fangled notions of ease and
cleanliness. And those who pretending to experience, though
they have long adhered to prejudices that have, according to
the opinions of the most sagacious physicians, thinned the
human race, almost rejoiced at the disaster that gave a kind
of sanction to prescription.

Indeed, if it were only on this account, the national education of women is of the utmost consequence, for what a
number of human sacrifices are made to that moloch prejudice! And in how many ways are children destroyed by the
lasciviousness of man? The want of natural affection in many
women, who are drawn from their duty by the admiration of
men, and the ignorance of others, render the infancy of man
a much more perilous state than that of brutes; yet men are
unwilling to place women in situations proper to enable them
to acquire sufficient understanding to know how even to nurse
their babes.

So forcibly does this truth strike me, that I would rest
the whole tendency of my reasoning upon it, for whatever
tends to incapacitate the maternal character, takes woman
out of her sphere. . . .

In public schools women, to guard against the errors of
ignorance, should be taught the elements of anatomy and
medicine, not only to enable them to take proper care of
their own health, but to make them rational nurses of their
infants, parents, and husbands; for the bills of mortality are
swelled by the blunders of self-willed old women, who give
nostrums of their own without knowing anything of the
human frame. It is likewise proper only in a domestic view,
to make women acquainted with the anatomy of the mind, by
allowing the sexes to associate together in every pursuit; and
by leading them to observe the progress of the human understanding in the improvement of the sciences and arts; never
forgetting the science of morality, or the study of the political
history of mankind. . . .

. . . The conclusion which I wish to draw is obvious; make women rational creatures, and free citizens, and they will quickly become good wives and mothers; that is—if men do not neglect the duties of husbands and fathers.

Discussing the advantages which a public and private education combined, as I have sketched, might rationally be expected to produce, I have dwelt most on such as are particularly relative to the female world, because I think the female world oppressed; yet the gangrene, which the vices engendered by oppression have produced, is not confined to the morbid part, but pervades society at large: so that when I wish to see my sex become more like moral agents, my heart bounds with the anticipation of the general diffusion of that sublime contentment which only morality can diffuse.

Woman of Action:
Frances Wright (1795–1852)

Strange is the course I run, and far the goal.
I sweep th'arena and no eye beholds,
Yet soon with daring hand and fearless soul
I seize the crown that Fame there distant holds. . . .

Start—but 'tis truth. There is a soul on earth,
Twin-born, the same, the counterpart of thine;
As strange, as proud, as lonely from its birth—
With powers as vast. Harold, that soul is mine!
[Perkins and Wolfson 1939:25]

Frances Wright wrote these lines in 1818, when she was
twenty-three years old. Part of a poem she dedicated to
Byron's *Childe Harold*, they capture several key characteristics of Fanny Wright herself: pride, loneliness, ambition,
and utter confidence that fame would be hers in the future.
Shortly after the lines were written, Frances and her sister
Camilla sailed for America on their first visit. Three years
later she wrote *Views of Society and Manners in America*,
which started her on the road to the fame she yearned for.

Along that road Frances Wright attempted many things:
as an intimate friend of General Lafayette, she served as a
courier for him in England to exiled Carbonari, members of a
secret revolutionary society in opposition to the Bourbons in
France. As an idealist who believed in translating her ideas
into action, she founded an experimental commune in Tennessee—Nashoba, dedicated to the goal of gradual emancipation by helping slaves to buy their freedom through their
own surplus labor. A charismatic public speaker and reformer, she spoke and published innumerable lectures urging
a national system of education, and she was instrumental in
the transition of a workingman's movement into a political
party. As an activist in New York, she bought and maintained
a Hall of Science—a center for community groups, a school
for special courses for workers, and a dispensary for free
physical examinations and health care. All these activities

took place before 1835. Wright's concern for women was only part of her larger concern for education as a necessary base for a fully democratic society. She argued eloquently for more schooling and less churchgoing for American women, thereby earning an intense opposition from all sectors of the American clergy. Though Scotch by birth, she was American by style and scene of action. In both word and deed she is perhaps the first woman radical leader in the long struggle for women's rights in American history.

Frances Wright was the second of three children born to James and Camilla Campbell Wright in Dundee, Scotland. Her father's family were tradesmen in linen for several generations, while her mother's family, the Campbells, had long been of a higher, landowning class in Scotland. The parents had a very happy but brief life together, for the young wife died in her fifth year of marriage and her husband two months later. The Wright children—Richard, Fanny, and Camilla—were left without parents while all were under five. Richard was settled with a maternal great-aunt while Fanny and Camilla became the legal wards of their mother's sister, Frances Campbell.

Fanny's parents seem to have been somewhat rebellious against their own rather staid middle-class families. Her father was much taken with Tom Paine's *Rights of Man* and had contributed funds toward a cheap edition of Paine's work for distribution among the poor. In her Aunt Frances' aristocratic home Fanny had an upbringing very different from the one she would have had in her father's home, for her aunt adhered to a strict and rigid training in the values of her social class. There is little evidence that this upbringing had any deep impact on Fanny's social ideas, for she seems to have been rebellious and critical of her environment from her earliest years. As a young adolescent she came upon a history of the American Revolution, written in Italian, which fired her deepest enthusiasm and began a long search in the libraries available to her for evidence that America was a real country and not a fantasy of the Italian author. In her Scots-English upper-class world, America might as well have been nonexistent, for it was hardly ever discussed. Though she rebelled against her environment on social and political grounds, there is reason to believe that Fanny Wright soaked up some aspects of it despite herself: the confidence and assurance that always marked her presence and her belief that she could easily be the peer of anyone in the world, coupled with her need and her ability to procure the services of others to handle the minutiae of daily life, are characteristics of her future self that may well have been acquired in her early years in an aristocratic household. Self-confidence is harder to come by when adult status must be earned completely on one's own.

There is no evidence of the exact source of difficulty which led to a break between Fanny and her Aunt Frances, but it was serious enough to cause the two sisters to leave the aunt's household abruptly and to spend the next few years, until they came of age, with Professor James Milne, their father's maternal uncle and a professor of moral philosophy at Glasgow College. Here Fanny was exposed to the free-thinking rationalist philosophy of her great-uncle and his colleagues, undoubtedly laying the broad foundation for the views she developed subsequently in America. Here, too, she had the free run of the college library, where she soaked up everything she could find about her greatest enthusiasm, America.

It was also during her late teens in Professor Milne's home that Fanny Wright did her first writing. Smitten with Epicurean philosophy, she wrote a tract modeled on the style of Plato's Dialogues, *A Few Days in Athens*, which appeared in print in several editions. Her second venture was stimulated by seeing the actor John Kemble perform one of his finest roles, Coriolanus. Her enthusiasm spilled over into a feverish several days' effort, during which she wrote a three-act play in Shakespearean blank verse entitled *Altorf*. What is particularly characteristic of Fanny Wright was her immediate decision, once the play was written, to get John Kemble himself to read it, and failing that, to get a copy of her play to Kemble's theater manager in London. She was crushed when the play was returned, apparently unread. What is significant is her confident assumption that this first play from her pen was worthy of the attention of the great actor and his manager. Such confidence she later showed in her contacts with Lafayette, the aging Jefferson, and other prominent Americans.

Perhaps the most significant personal event during these few years in Glasgow was the development of a deep friendship with Mrs. Craig Millar. Millar and his wife had spent two years in political exile in Philadelphia and New York during the last years of Washington's administration. Fanny's link with Mrs. Millar was crucial on two counts. One was the personal attachment she formed with the older woman, who seemed to satisfy Fanny's unmet need for a loving mother, but in a relationship free of the authority of a mother, which might well have been a barrier to intimacy for the rebellious young Fanny. Second was the fact that Mrs. Millar had spent two years in America, which made her a sympathetic source of detailed information about the United States and of personal references to people she had known in Philadelphia and New York.

Shortly after the sisters reached their majority, Fanny decided on a trip to the United States. With letters of introduction to several important families in New York, she and Camilla set sail in 1818. Not long after their arrival, Fanny was busy seeking a way to have *Altorf* produced on a New York stage. As an unknown, young, and female playwright, she had no chance to achieve this on her own, but through the intermediary of a young Irishman, she managed to get the play produced.

Mrs. Millar had cautioned Fanny to change a number of scenes, on the ground that they would offend people by their frank depiction of passion, to say nothing of political ideas. Fanny Wright did not pay very close attention to such sage advice, for when her play was performed in Philadelphia, she was openly listed as its author. For the rest of her stay, she and her sister traveled in New York State and Pennsylvania, gathering impressions she turned to good account in the book she published upon her return to England in 1820.

This book, *Views of Society and Manners in America*, was her passport out of obscurity to some considerable public attention. Sharply critical of England, and extremely enthusiastic about most aspects of America, the book was loved by radical Whigs and denounced by extreme Tories; had wide sales in both countries; was translated into several languages; and brought to Fanny the attention she so desired and the friends who were to shape the next phases in her adventurous life. A selection from this volume will give the reader a direct sampling of the young Fanny's observations.

Among the letters of praise she received from readers, two were perhaps of most significance to her: one from Jeremy Bentham, who wrote inviting her to his home, the Hermitage, if she should come to London. This, of course,

she did as soon as possible, and Bentham's opinion of Fanny
was recorded in a letter she kept to the end of her life: "the
strongest sweetest mind that ever [was] cased in a human
body." The second letter was from General Lafayette, then
sixty-seven years old, living at his country estate of La
Grange, the beloved center of an intense and complex net of
relatives. He was at the same time a constant source of irritation to his kin because of his devotion to the ideals of the
revolution in the very postrevolutionary world of 1821.
Nothing could have pleased and flattered the young Fanny
more than a letter of praise for her book from this famous
devotee of the young America.

Fanny was soon on her way to France and in due time
met the revolutionary hero. What drew them together was
ostensibly their mutual love for America; what held them
together is more difficult to say. La Grange became a home
away from home for Fanny during her stays in France. Complete with moated walls and five-pointed round towers, in
one of which the General had his private quarters, the ancient house was the setting for a growing intimacy between
Fanny and the elderly Lafayette. The complex friendship was
clearly modeled on a tender and intellectually stimulating
father-daughter relationship, yet there were at least under-
tones, perhaps unclear to the two partners, that suggest
something more than paternal and filial tenderness. On the
other hand, Lafayette was Fanny's confidante when her own
heart was stirred by a first lover, with no suggestion of
jealousy or conflict at the disclosure of this venture. While at
La Grange, the two spent hours alone together in his study,
where the General hung a portrait of Fanny he had ordered
painted; directly underneath the study, Fanny had her own
room whenever she stayed at La Grange.

The years 1821–1823 found Fanny traveling back and
forth between England and France, sometimes as a courier
for Lafayette in his efforts to help exiled Frenchmen in England, at other times to handle manuscript processing in
connection with her own publications. In 1823 Lafayette received an invitation from President Monroe to visit the
United States, and this precipitated a hostile disagreement
between the Lafayette family and Fanny. She favored the
trip and wished to accompany him. The family, aware that
she was young enough to be his daughter but old enough to
be his wife, felt that the whole relationship was unsuitable

to such a public display as a trip to the United States. After long and heated debate, including the rejection of Fanny's proposal that Lafayette legally adopt her, it was finally decided that they would go at about the same time but that Fanny and Camilla would be traveling on a different boat.

Lafayette's tour of America was that of a beloved hero returned to the scene of battle and victory; he was feted all up and down the east coast, took numerous trips inland, with bands and dinners everywhere he stopped. Throughout the trip he met wherever possible for some quiet times with Fanny and Camilla, if they were not invited to official occasions in his honor. One of the highlights of the trip was a two-week visit with Jefferson at Monticello. The invitation for the two young women was arranged by Lafayette, who informed Jefferson that "you and I are the two persons in the world whose esteem she values most" (Perkins and Wolfson 1939:115).

Some time before this visit to Monticello Fanny had her first direct confrontation with the worst of American slavery. While in a Virginian seaport she saw a vessel overloaded with slaves born in Virginia, chained two by two, sailing for the Savannah slave markets. She was soon convinced that slavery was a cancer in the America she loved and that it needed removal. Jefferson himself was on the board of an early national group working toward the colonization of the slave population of the United States. She discussed the issue with him at Monticello and seemed to agree with his view that to give liberty to a slave before he understood its nature would be to withhold the "protection of a master without securing the guardianship of the law." While in Washington, Robert Owen gave a series of lectures on cooperatives, and it was not long before Fanny put his ideas together with her concern for the gradual emancipation of the slaves. Her argument (and later her plan for Nashoba) was based on the idea that the slave's surplus labor could be applied toward gradual repayment of his original purchase price plus the cost of colonization in some country outside the United States; a plan for education went along with the rural labor, so that the ex-slave would be prepared to survive economically once free.

Next Fanny plowed through all the southern statutes in Washington libraries to discover any legal impediments to her plans. By early 1825 Lafayette started a tour of the southern states which was to culminate in a large celebration in his honor in New Orleans. Fanny and her sister took off separately in a move through the western territories, stopping at the new communities of Economy and New Harmony in Ohio, before going down the Mississippi by steamboat to join Lafayette in New Orleans. Along the way Fanny drafted her plan, at first proposing that Congress set aside certain portions of the public lands in the southern states as experimental farms where Blacks could work and receive specialized schooling. Never one to leave an idea untested, she sent copies of her plan everywhere and had Lafayette send a copy to Jefferson himself. Jefferson showed considerable adroitness in his diplomatic response:

> At the age of 82 with one foot in the grave and the other lifted to follow it, I do not permit myself to take part in any new enterprise, not even in the great one which is the subject of your letter, and which has been through life one of my greatest anxieties. . . . I leave its accomplishment as the work of another generation. . . . You are young, dear Madame, and have powers of mind which may do much in exciting others in this arduous task. [Perkins and Wolfson 1939:141]

Fanny was clearly not satisfied to merely motivate others to work toward her goal. Lafayette set sail for France, but Fanny and Camilla stayed behind to find land, purchase slaves, and get the first experiment under way. Nashoba, the resulting community, lasted from October 1825 to 1829, when it ceased as a going concern. Here Fanny and her sister were joined by a director—Richardson—and George Flower, a man who had caught Fanny's enthusiasm at one of the Ohio cooperative communities, with Flower's wife and three children, and eight slaves purchased in Nashville; the group set to the backbreaking job of land clearing and planting in 1826.

Never one to remain for long in any one place, Fanny herself did not stay to supervise this early stage of community building. Since she was a publicist and reformer at this period, the pitiful little effort at Nashoba was widely known from her writings and was thought to be far more successful than it actually was. Readers took the plan for the reality. Nor was Fanny prepared for the contrast in public reaction to her ideas on religion and marriage in the highly moral atmosphere of America, compared to the sophisticated thinking of her associates in Paris. In Paris the more advanced of the French Carbonari had adopted the socialistic theories of Saint-Simon and had implemented them in a community they founded near Paris. They held views on sex relations even more advanced than those Fanny endorsed in 1827. But to argue as she did for the gradual blending of the white man and the black "till their children became one in blood, in hue," was hardly accepted in Ohio and Tennessee with the equanimity it encountered among her radical friends in Paris. In 1828 Wright published her views on marriage in the *Memphis Advocate*, stating in part:

> The marriage law existing without the pale of the institution [Nashoba] is of no force within that pale. No woman can forfeit her individual rights or independent existence, and no man assert over her any rights or power whatsoever beyond what he may exercise over her free and voluntary affection.

In full consistency, Fanny also stressed the fact that women could not expect special privileges:

> Nor on the other hand, may any woman assert claims to the society or peculiar protection of any individual of the other sex, beyond what mutual inclination dictates and sanctions; while to every individual member of either sex, is secured the protection and friendly aid of all. [Perkins and Wolfson 1939:193]

Predictably, most Americans pounced upon these ideas as evidence that the experiment was not the worthy goal Wright professed it to be; it was instead nothing but a "free love colony." Wright had taken a step beyond the "respectable" world whose opinion she really wished to affect and in whose eyes she wished to establish her reputation.

As if racial miscegenation and equality in man-woman relations were not "offensive" enough, Wright took one further position in describing the educational philosophy of Nashoba that was surely calculated to trigger the most heated response of middle-class Americans in 1828. In an era when religious revivals were sweeping the country, she wrote that religion occupied no place in the Nashoba community. In as good an example of applied Benthamism as one could find, she argued that her philosophy centered on human happiness: whatever tended to promote that happiness was virtuous, whatever hindered it was sinful; children would receive no religious training but would be left to develop freely, examining all opinions and values openly, free to accept or reject as reason and sentiment would dictate.

With some justice, substantiated only later by historians, Wright put her finger on one of the motivations underlying clerical sponsorship of these revivals of the late 1820s: that the eastern churches, disturbed by the waning of religious adherence in the western territories, found it possible in light of this threat to join hands with denominations with which they had previously vigorously quarreled and to establish such nationwide associations as the American Tract Society and the American Bible Society. Behind the religious revivals, Wright argued, was the clergy's attempt to excite popular interest in individual salvation. Cincinnati was a center for such religious heat in 1828, and it was to Cincinnati that Fanny herself went to wage yet another battle; this time she was the defender of reason against the religious fervor of the times. Her language suggests the intensity with which she waged her opposition:

> The victims of this odious experiment on human credulity and nervous weakness were invariably women. Helpless age was made a public spectacle, youth driven to raving insanity, mothers and daughters carried lifeless from the presence of the ghostly expounders of damnation, all ranks shared the contagion, while the despair of Calvin's hell itself seemed to have fallen upon every heart and discord to have taken possession of every mansion. [Perkins and Wolfson 1939:211]

Arriving in July 1828, Fanny Wright took Cincinnati by storm; she gave three Sunday lectures in the courthouse and another in August in the town theater, setting out her argument in a brilliant style that can hardly be captured by the mere reading of her words. A good part of her impact stemmed from her style of delivery and her physical presence. We are indebted to Frances Trollope for an account of Fanny at this time. Mrs. Trollope had every reason to write a scathing denunciation of Fanny, for it was under her charismatic spell that Mrs. Trollope had traveled to America to explore the possibility of her son Henry's settling at Nashoba. After the long trip, Mrs. Trollope found a pitiful rude settlement in malaria-infested lowlands, with unfinished buildings and little by way of food provisions. She also experienced the social shock of finding Fanny's sister pregnant and ill and the settlement director, Richardson, married to one of the black women. Mrs. Trollope left as soon as possible and found her way to Cincinnati. Yet she had the fairness to report the impact Fanny Wright had on her audiences. In her famous book, *Domestic Manners of the Americans*, she observed that Fanny had "the power of commanding attention and enchanting the ear of any audience before whom it was her pleasure to appear." Of Fanny herself she wrote with a discerning feminine eye to detail:

> All my expectations fell far short of the splendor, the brilliance, the overwhelming eloquence of this extraordinary orator. . . . It is impossible to imagine anything more striking than her appearance. Her tall and majestic figure, the deep and almost solemn expression of her eyes, the simple contour of her finely formed head, unadorned excepting by its own natural ringlets. Her garment of plain white muslin which hung about her in folds that recalled the drapery of a Grecian statue, all contributed to produce an effect unlike anything I had ever seen before, or ever expect to see again. [Trollope 1832:97, 99–100]

Wright gave these same lectures—in defense of reason, in support of widespread education, and in accusations of wickedness on the part of a scheming American clergy—in a series all the way from Cincinnati eastward to Philadelphia, Baltimore, and New York. She was roundly denounced by religious conservatives as the "Priestess of Beelzebub," but she went on to New York and published these lectures as a *Course of Popular Lectures*, one of which is included in this collection.

Turning from the campaigns against slavery and against religious revivals, Fanny now concentrated on the poverty and ignorance of the urban American scene. She was appalled by the changes that had taken place in the American city since her earlier visit in the years 1818–1820: filth, poverty, ignorance were everywhere; and she threw herself into a campaign to eradicate such evils. Settling temporarily in New York, she edited the *Free Enquirer*, succeeded in secretly buying an old Methodist church that was up for sale, and converted it into her Hall of Science. Here she set up the offices for the *Free Enquirer*, organized trustees charged with

arranging lecturers on scientific and moral subjects, organized
a day-school and a Sunday school, and established a dispensary with an attending physician. In her public lectures,
aimed at the urban working class, she analyzed the "existing
evils" of American society and proposed her own remedies
for them. The first American workingmen's party was formed
in this period; it called for a ten-hour workday and public
education for all children. Fanny Wright was active in the
party, particularly on educational matters. She proposed a
state system of education, at the heart of which was a "State
Guardianship" plan for boarding schools for children from
two to twelve years of age, which she defended as the only
plan which could rear a generation "fit to carry on in the
true spirit of the American republic."

In 1830 Wright found time to fulfill her obligations to
the slaves she had bought for Nashoba. Despite the hazards,
she traveled to New Orleans, met the slaves who came down
from Nashoba, and traveled with them to Haiti, where she
had worked out arrangements for their settlement with the
government. Her companion on this trip was Phiquepal
D'Arusmont, a Frenchman who had traveled to America to
develop his own innovative educational plan which would
combine study with actual work and the learning of trades.
Fanny Wright had had previous contact with D'Arusmont
through the publication of the *New Harmony Gazette* and
the *Free Enquirer*, which he and his students printed.

Fanny's other, more personal concern from Nashoba days
was her sister Camilla. Fanny's biographers are sensitive to
the price Camilla paid for her devotion to Fanny and her
ideals. From early childhood Camilla was a loyal follower of
her bold and fearless sister, following her wherever Fanny's
ideas took her, and undoubtedly performing the services
Fanny always needed from others: to handle the daily chores
of life—the thousand details of cooking, cleaning, copying
manuscripts, keeping records, packing, and shipping—as the
two traveled through America in the 1820s. It would be fair
to say that Camilla fulfilled the duties usually associated
with the wife role. Clearly she was the passive follower in
the relationship between the sisters. By 1829 Camilla, ill
from repeated malarial fever contracted in the mosquito-in-
fested lowlands of the Mississippi valley in Tennessee, came
east with her child to live at Fanny's home in New York.
But her child died, and ill and despairing, Camilla returned to

England and an early death in 1831 at the age of thirty. Upon Fanny's return from Haiti she found herself in the middle of a political battle within the Workingman's Party. It centered in part on her State Guardianship plan, which was endorsed by one faction of the party but hotly opposed by a larger faction, which rejected the idea of separating a young child from its family at the tender age Fanny recommended. Another brave bold experiment began to fall apart, and Fanny Wright returned to Europe with her grieving sister.

Her life during her remaining years was a blend of personal conflict and tragedy on the one hand and feeble attempts to recapture at least a small sector of public opinion to her ideas on the other.

In the personal realm, she was deeply grieved by her sister's death and turned to D'Arusmont in Paris for comfort and support. Their relationship had become personal during their isolated stay in Haiti, and now in Paris in 1831 they lived together, making no attempt to legalize the relationship until Fanny became pregnant. The first child died; a second, Frances Sylva, was born in 1832.

Over the next decade or more the D'Arusmont family was frequently separated as they traveled, individually or in pairs rather than as a threesome, to England or America. Most often it was the father who remained with the daughter while Fanny traveled to earn money by lecturing and supervising her publications. The correspondence of these years suggests that D'Arusmont gradually took over all the significant responsibility for the rearing of his daughter and the care of their home. His letters are full of warmth and of pride in his ability to handle the household without a "femme de menage." By 1835 Fanny was back in America, settling in Philadelphia for 1836–1837; there she started a new paper, *Manual of American Principles*, financed, edited, and largely written by herself.

It is in Philadelphia that she must have met Lucretia Mott, the only American woman she knew and liked who was later to become active in the American woman's suffrage movement. Like radical women much later in American history, Fanny Wright had little sympathy for the middle-class woman's movement that grew up in America. Her concern was with education, general reform, and most particularly, improvement of the lot of the working class. Long before the 1848 uprisings and before the emergence of the first national

Workingman's Party in the United States, she predicted to
Lafayette that the future would center on class war as the
working classes of the world began to reason and to join
hands across the nations in a common cause against their
oppressors.

Financial pressure had been the prod for much of Wright's
traveling and writing in the late 1830s and early 1840s.
Ironically, in light of her political beliefs, these financial problems were solved in 1844 by the news that, as the last surviving Wright, she had fallen heir to the Wright holdings in
Scotland. Over the next few years she was back in Scotland
and France, settling the legal aspects of her inheritance, shocking her husband by placing her Dundee holdings in a trust
that excluded him from any share in its management or power
to dispose of it should he survive her. This move triggered
D'Arusmont's attempt to make American law work in his
favor by securing all Fanny's properties in his name in 1847.
As a wife Fanny could not bring suit against her husband;
so she obtained a divorce and then succeeded in regaining
control of her property through legal action against D'Arusmont in 1850.

There was much bitterness within the family over these
legal quarrels and some justice and considerable psychological astuteness in D'Arusmont's argument with his wife. In
an illuminating letter to her he observed:

> Your life was essentially an external life. You loved virtue
> deeply, but you loved also, and perhaps even more,
> grandeur and glory; and in your estimation, unknown, I
> am sure, to your innermost soul, your husband and child
> ranked only as mere appendages to your personal exist-
> ence. You could not even conceive their individuality, as
> distinct from your own; you imagined you possessed
> . . . the right of stopping their personal development
> and forcing them to live your life without examining
> whether that existence coincided with their wishes or
> their ideal. [Perkins and Wolfson 1939:378–379]

If one changed the sexes in the profile D'Arusmont sketched
in this passage, one would have a portrait perfectly consistent with approved social behavior.

A last personal detail softens the image of these passages.
In 1852 Wright fell on the ice in her Cincinnati front yard
and broke her hip. Removed to a friend's house, she lingered

for ten agonizing months with her leg in traction. On the day she died, she made her will, leaving everything she possessed to her only daughter, Frances Sylva D'Arusmont.

Any final assessment of Fanny Wright's place in history, however, must be centered on her unique public contributions rather than on her personal life. Impulsive, flamboyant, and ambitious Fanny Wright clearly was; but she was also an enormously charismatic woman of intelligence and boundless energy, dedicated to the translation of her ideas into political and social action. In the programs she instituted in her New York Hall of Science, we can see the forerunners of the community action programs, job training, free public education, and neighborhood medical centers which became familiar on the American scene many decades after her death. Twenty years before women were socially accepted as public speakers, Fanny Wright drew large and responsive audiences that included men as well as women, the poor as well as the rich. Though her State Guardianship plan for the education of young children was far more radical than her contemporaries in the workingman's movement could accept, thousands of workers responded to her general call for a free public school system. The workingman's movement of the 1820s, in fact, evolved into a political party which was often referred to as the Fanny Wright Party. No other woman in the nineteenth century had the distinction of having a political party and numerous political societies named after her.

Two decades before the sermons and public lectures of northern abolitionists, Fanny Wright saw slavery not as a sin but as a social cancer that would corrupt the young democratic nation. Though she lacked persistence to match her enthusiasms, the key idea of her Nashoba experiment—that emancipation of the slaves without training in economic skills or provision of land would work a dreadful hardship on the black men and women of America—is an insight that only a few abolitionists shared. It is difficult to imagine Fanny Wright turning away from the economic and political misery of southern blacks as most abolitionists did in the post-Civil War period. She had respect for the personhood of blacks as she had for working-class men and women that was seldom found among the clergymen, intellectuals, or politicians of her day and perhaps, one is tempted to say, of our day as well.

⊱ Education ⊰

New York, March 1820.

My Dear Friend,

The education of youth, which may be said to form the basis of American government, is in every state of the Union made a national concern. Upon this subject, therefore, the observations that apply to one may be considered as, more or less, applying to all. The portion of this widespread community that paid the earliest and most anxious attention to the instruction of its citizens was New England. This probably originated in the greater democracy of her colonial institutions. Liberty and knowledge ever go hand in hand.

If the national policy of some of the New England states has been occasionally censurable, the internal arrangement of all amply redeems her character. There is not a more truly virtuous community in the world than that found in the democracies of the East. The beauty of their villages, the neatness and cleanliness of their houses, the simplicity of their manners, the sincerity of their religion, despoiled in a great measure of its former Calvinistic austerity, their domestic habits, pure morals, and well-administered laws must command the admiration and respect of every stranger. I was forcibly struck in Connecticut with the appearance of the children, neatly dressed, with their satchels on their arms and their faces blooming with health and cheerfulness, dropping their courtesy to the passenger as they trooped to school. The obeisance thus made is not rendered to station but to age. Like the young Spartans, the youth are taught to salute respectfully their superiors in years, and the artlessness and modesty with which the intelligent young creatures reply to the stranger's queries might give pleasure to Lycurgus himself.

The state of Connecticut has appropriated a fund of a million and a half of dollars to the support of public schools. In Vermont, a certain portion of land has been laid off in

From Frances Wright, *Views of Society and Manners in America—in a Series of Letters From That Country To A Friend in England, During the Years 1818, 1819, 1820*. London, 1821. Letter XXIII (pp. 215–222).

every township, whose proceeds are devoted to the same purpose. In the other states, every township taxes itself to such amount as is necessary to defray the expense of schools, which teach reading, writing, and arithmetic to the whole population. In larger towns these schools teach geography and the rudiments of Latin. These establishments, supported at the common expense, are open to the whole youth, male and female, of the country. Other seminaries of a higher order are also maintained in the more populous districts, half the expense being discharged by appropriated funds and the remainder by a small charge laid on the scholar. The instruction here given fits the youth for the state colleges, of which there is one or more in every state. The university of Cambridge, in Massachusetts, is the oldest and, I believe, the most distinguished establishment of the kind existing in the Union.

Perhaps the number of colleges founded in this widespread family of republics may not, in general, be favourable to the growth of distinguished universities. It best answers, however, the object intended, which is not to raise a few very learned citizens but a well-informed and liberal-minded community.

It is unnecessary that I should enter into a particular detail of the internal regulations of all the different states relative to the national instruction. The child of every citizen, male or female, white or black, is entitled by right to a plain education, and funds sufficient to defray the expense of his instruction are raised either from public lands appropriated to the purpose, or by taxes sometimes imposed by the legislature and sometimes by the different townships. . . .

If we must seek the explanation of national manners in national institutions and early education, all the characteristics of the American admit of an easy explanation. The foreigner is at first surprised to find in the ordinary citizen that intelligence and those sentiments which he had been accustomed to seek in the writings of philosophers and the conversation of the most enlightened. The better half of our education in the Old World consists of unlearning: we have to unlearn when we come from the nursery, to unlearn again when we come from the school, and often to continue unlearning through life, and to quit the scene at last without having rid ourselves of half the false notions which had been implanted in our young minds. All this trouble is saved here.

The impressions received in childhood are few and simple, as are all the elements of just knowledge. Whatever ideas may be acquired are learned from the page of truth and embrace principles often unknown to the most finished scholar of Europe. Nor is the *manner* in which education is here conducted without its influence in forming the character. I feel disposed at least to ascribe to it that mild friendliness of demeanor which distinguishes the American. It is violence that begets violence, and gentleness, gentleness. I have frequently heard it stated by West Indians that a slave invariably makes the hardest slave driver. In English schools it is well known that the worst-used *fag* becomes, in his turn, the most cruel tyrant, and in a British ship of war it will often be found that the merciless disciplinarian has learned his harshness in the school of suffering. The American, in his infancy, manhood, or age, never feels the hand of oppression. Violence is positively forbidden in the schools, in the prisons, on shipboard, in the army; everywhere, in short, where authority is exercised, it must be exercised without appeal to the argument of a blow. . . .

In the education of women, New England seems hitherto to have been peculiarly liberal. The ladies of the eastern states are frequently possessed of the most solid acquirements, the modern and even the dead languages, and a wide scope of reading; the consequence is that their manners have the character of being more composed than those of my gay young friends in this quarter. I have already stated, in one of my earlier letters, that the public attention is now everywhere turned to the improvement of female education. In some states, colleges for girls are established under the eye of the legislature. . . .

In other countries it may seem of little consequence to inculcate upon the female mind "the principles of government, and the obligations of patriotism," but it was wisely foreseen by that venerable apostle of liberty that in a country where a mother is charged with the formation of an infant mind that is to be called in future to judge of the laws and support the liberties of a republic, the mother herself should well understand those laws and estimate those liberties. Personal accomplishments and the more ornamental branches of knowledge should certainly in America be made subordinate to solid information. This is perfectly the case with respect to the men; as yet the women have been educated too much after the European manner. French, Italian, dancing, drawing engage the hours of the one sex (and this but too commonly in a lax and careless way), while the more appropriate studies of the other are philosophy, history, political economy, and the exact sciences. It follows, consequently, that after the spirits of youth have somewhat subsided, the two sexes have less in common in their pursuits and turn of thinking than is desirable. A woman of a powerful intellect will of course seize upon the new topics presented to her by the conversation of her husband. The less vigorous or the more thoughtless mind is not easily brought to forego trifling pursuits for those which occupy the stronger reason of its companion.

I must remark that in no particular is the liberal philosophy of the Americans more honorably evinced than in the place which is awarded to women. The prejudices still to be found in Europe, though now indeed somewhat antiquated, which would confine the female library to romances, poetry, and belles-lettres, and female conversation to the last new publication, new bonnet, and *pas seul*, are entirely unknown here. The women are assuming their place as thinking beings, not in despite of the men, but chiefly in consequence of their enlarged views and exertions as fathers and legislators.

I may seem to be swerving a little from my subject, but as I have adverted to the place accorded to women in one particular, I may as well now reply to your question regarding their general condition. It strikes me that it would be impossible for women to stand in higher estimation than they do here. The deference that is paid to them at all times and in all places has often occasioned me as much surprise as pleasure.

In domestic life there is a tenderness on the part of the husband to his weaker helpmate, and this in all situations of life that I believe in no country is surpassed and in few equalled. No *cavaliere servente* of a lady of fashion, no sighing lover, who has just penned a sonnet to his "mistress's eyebrow," ever rendered more delicate attentions to the idol of his fancy than I have seen rendered by an American farmer or mechanic, not to say gentleman, to the companion of his life. The wife and daughters of the labouring citizen are always found neatly dressed and occupied at home in household concerns; no field labour is ever imposed upon a woman, and I believe that it would outrage the feelings of an

American, whatever be his station, should he see her engaged in any toil seemingly unsuited to her strength. In travelling, I have myself often met with a refinement of civility from men, whose exterior promised only the roughness of the mechanic or working farmer, that I should only have looked for from the polished gentleman.

Perhaps the condition of women affords, in all countries, the best criterion by which to judge of the character of men. Where we find the weaker sex burdened with hard labour, we may ascribe to the stronger something of the savage, and where we see the former deprived of free agency, we shall find in the latter much of the sensualist. I know not a circumstance which more clearly marks in England the retrograde movement of the national morals than the shackles now forged for the rising generation of women. Perhaps these are as yet more exclusively laid upon what are termed the highest class, but I apprehend that thousands of our countrywomen in the middle ranks, whose mothers, or certainly whose grandmothers, could ride unattended from the Land's End to the border and walk abroad alone or with an unmarried friend of the other sex armed with all the unsuspecting virtue of Eve before her fall—I apprehend that the children and grandchildren of these matrons are now condemned to walk in leading strings from the cradle to the altar, if not to the grave, taught to see in the other sex a race of seducers rather than protectors and of masters rather than companions. Alas for the morals of a country when female dignity is confounded with helplessness and the guardianship of a woman's virtue transferred from herself to others! If any should doubt the effect produced by the infringement of female liberty upon the female mind, let them consider the dress of the present generation of English women. This will sufficiently settle the question without a reference to the pages of the daily journals. Of the two extremes it is better to see a woman, as in Scotland, bent over the glebe, mingling the sweat of her brow with that of her churlish husband or more churlish son, than to see her gradually sinking into the childish dependence of a Spanish *donna*.

The liberty here enjoyed by the young women often occasions some surprise to foreigners, who, contrasting it with the constraint imposed on the female youth of Paris or London, are at a loss to reconcile the freedom of the national manners with the purity of the national morals; but confidence and innocence are twin sisters, and should the American women ever resign the guardianship of their own virtue, the lawyers of these democracies will probably find as good occupation in prosecuting suits for divorce as those of any of the monarchies of Europe.*

I often lament that in the rearing of women so little attention should be commonly paid to the exercise of the bodily organs; to invigorate the body is to invigorate the mind, and Heaven knows that the weaker sex have much cause to be rendered strong in both. In the happiest country their condition is sufficiently hard. Have they talents? It is difficult to turn them to account. Ambition? The road to honorable distinction is shut against them. A vigorous intellect? It is broken down by sufferings, bodily and mental. The lords of creation receive innumerable, incalculable advantages from the hand of nature, and it must be admitted that they everywhere take sufficient care to foster the advantages with which they are endowed. There is something so flattering to human vanity in the consciousness of superiority that it is little surprising if men husband with jealousy that which nature has enabled them to usurp over the daughters of Eve. Love of power more frequently originates in vanity than pride (two qualities, by the way, which are often confounded) and is, consequently, yet more peculiarly the sin of little than of great minds. Now an overwhelming proportion of human minds appertain to the former class and must be content to soothe their self-love by considering the weakness of others rather than their own strength. You will say this is severe; is it not true? In what consists the greatness of a despot? In

---

* The law of divorce is one so little referred to in America that it never occurred to me to hear or enquire how it stood. In the state of Rhode Island, however, there is a very singular regulation. As it was explained to me: if a married couple shall give in to the civil magistrate a mutual declaration that they are desirous of separating from (as the French would express it) *incompatibilité*, and shall then live entirely apart, but within the precincts of the state, for two full years, conducting themselves with propriety during that period, they may obtain, upon application, a disannulment of the marriage contract. I was surprised to hear that few had ever sought *the benefit of the act*, and that of those who had applied for it, some had broken the exacted stipulations before the expiration of the two years. Might it not tend to cement rather than weaken the marriage tie throughout the world if every country had a Rhode Island?

his own intrinsic merits? No, in the degradation of the multitude who surround him. What feeds the vanity of a patrician? The consciousness of any virtue that he inherits with his blood? The list of his senseless progenitors would probably soon cease to command his respect if it did not enable him to command that of his fellow creatures. "But what," I hear you ask, "has this to do with the condition of women? Do you mean to compare men collectively to the despot and the patrician?" Why not? The vanity of the despot and the patrician is fed by the folly of their fellow men, and so is that of their sex collectively soothed by the dependence of women: it pleases them better to find in their companion a fragile vine, clinging to their firm trunk for support, than a vigorous tree with whose branches they may mingle theirs. I believe they sometimes repent of their choice when the vine has weighed the oak to the ground. It is difficult, in walking through the world, not to laugh at the consequences which, sooner or later, overtake men's follies, but when these are visited upon women I feel more disposed to sigh. Born to endure the worst afflictions of fortune, they are enervated in soul and body lest the storm should not visit them sufficiently rudely. Instead of essaying to counteract the unequal law of nature, it seems the object of man to visit it upon his weaker helpmate more harshly. It is well, however, that his folly recoils upon his own head, and that the fate of the sexes is so entwined that the dignity of the one must rise or fall with that of the other.

In America much certainly is done to ameliorate the condition of women, and as their education shall become, more and more, the concern of the state, their character may aspire in each succeeding generation to a higher standard. The republic, I am persuaded, will be amply repaid for any trouble or expense that may be thus bestowed. In her struggles for liberty much of her virtue emanated from the wives and daughters of her senators and soldiers, and to preserve to her sons the energy of freemen and patriots she must strengthen that energy in her daughters.*

To invigorate the character, however, it is not sufficient to cultivate the mind. The body also must be trained to whole-

* In the Revolutionary War the enthusiasm of the women is acknowledged to have greatly assisted that of the men. In all successful struggles for liberty I believe the same co-operation of the sexes will be found to have existed.

some exercise, and the nerves braced to bear those extremes of climate which here threaten to enervate the more weakly frame. It is the union of bodily and mental vigor in the male population of America which imparts to it that peculiar energy of character which in its first infancy drew forth so splendid a panegyric from the British orator: "What in the world is equal to it?" exclaimed Mr. Burke. "Whilst we follow them (the colonists) among the tumbling mountains of ice, and behold them penetrating into the deepest frozen recesses of Hudson's Bay and Davis' Straits, whilst we are looking for them beneath the Arctic Circle, we hear that they have pierced into the opposite region of polar cold, that they are at the antipodes, and engaged under the frozen serpent of the South. Falkland Island, which seemed too remote and romantic an object for the grasp of national ambition, is but a stage and resting place in the progress of their victorious industry; nor is the equinoctial heat more discouraging to them than the accumulated winter of both the poles. We know that while some of them draw the line and strike the harpoon on the coast of Africa, others run the longitude, and pursue their gigantic game along the coast of Brazil. No sea but what is vexed by their fisheries; no climate that is not witness to their toils." *

Now, though it is by no means requisite that the American women should emulate the men in the pursuit of the whale, the felling of the forest, or the shooting of wild turkeys, they might, with advantage, be taught in early youth to excel in the race, to hit a mark, to swim, and in short to use every exercise which could impart vigor to their frames and independence to their minds. But I have dwelt enough upon this subject, and you will, perhaps, apprehend that I am about to subjoin a Utopian plan of national education: no, I leave this to the republic herself, and, wishing all success to her endeavours, I bid you farewell.

---

* [Edmund Burke], "Speech on Conciliation with America" [March 22, 1775].

⤷ Of Free Enquiry ⤶

There is a common error that I feel myself called upon
to notice; nor know I the country in which it is more prevalent than in this. Whatever indifference may generally prevail
among men, still there are many eager for the acquisition of
knowledge; willing to enquire, and anxious to base their
opinions upon correct principles. In the curiosity which motives their exertions, however, the vital principle is but too
often wanting. They come selfishly, and not generously, to
the tree of knowledge. They eat, but care not to impart of
the fruit to others. Nay, there are who, having leaped the
briar fence of prejudice themselves, will heap new thorns in
the way of those who would venture the same. . . .

But will this imputation startle my hearers? Will they
say, America is the home of liberty, and Americans brethren
in equality. Is it so? and may we not ask here, as elsewhere,
how many are there, not anxious to monopolize, but to
universalize knowledge? how many, that consider their own
improvement in relation always with that of their fellow
beings, and who feel the imparting of truth to be not a work
of supererogation, but a duty; the withholding it, not a
venial omission, but a treachery to the race. Which of us
have not seen fathers of families pursuing investigations
themselves, which they hide from their sons, and, more especially, from their wives and daughters? As if truth could
be of less importance to the young than to the old; or as if
the sex which in all ages has ruled the destinies of the world,
could be less worth enlightening than that which only follows
its lead!

The observation I have hazarded may require some explanation. Those who arrogate power usually think themselves superior *de facto* and *de jure*. Yet justly might it be
made a question whether those who ostensibly govern are
not always unconsciously led. Should we examine closely into
the state of things, we might find that, in all countries, the
governed decide the destinies of the governors, more than
the governors those of the governed; even as the labouring

From Frances Wright, *Course of Popular Lectures*. New York,
Free Enquirer, 1829. Lecture II (pp. 41–62).

classes influence more directly the fortunes of a nation than does the civil officer, the aspiring statesman, the rich capitalist, or the speculative philosopher.

However novel it may appear, I shall venture the assertion, that, until women assume the place in society which good sense and good feeling alike assign to them, human improvement must advance but feebly. It is in vain that we would circumscribe the power of one half of our race, and that half by far the most important and influential. If they exert it not for good, they will for evil; if they advance not knowledge, they will perpetuate ignorance. Let women stand where they may in the scale of improvement, their position decides that of the race. Are they cultivated?—so is society polished and enlightened. Are they ignorant?—so is it gross and insipid. Are they wise?—so is the human condition prosperous. Are they foolish?—so is it unstable and unpromising. Are they free?—so is the human character elevated. Are they enslaved?—so is the whole race degraded. . . .

. . . It is my object to show, that, before we can engage successfully in the work of enquiry, we must engage in a body; we must engage collectively; as human beings desirous of attaining the highest excellence of which our nature is capable; as children of one family, anxious to discover the true and the useful for the common advantage of all. It is my farther object to show that no co-operation in this matter can be effective which does not embrace the two sexes on a footing of equality; and, again, that no co-operation in this matter can be effective, which does not embrace human beings on a footing of equality. Is this a republic—a country whose affairs are governed by the public voice—while the public mind is unequally enlightened? Is this a republic, where the interests of the many keep in check those of the few—while the few hold possession of the courts of knowledge, and the many stand as suitors at the door? Is this a republic, where the rights of all are equally respected, the interests of all equally secured, the ambitions of all equally regulated, the services of all equally rendered? Is this such a republic—while we see endowed colleges for the rich, and barely *common schools* for the poor; while but one drop of colored blood shall stamp a fellow creature for a slave, or, at the least, degrade him below sympathy; and while one half of the whole population is left in civil bondage, and, as it were, sentenced to mental imbecility?

Let us pause to enquire if this be consistent with the being of a republic. Without knowledge, could your fathers have conquered liberty? and without knowledge, can you retain it? Equality! where is it, if not in education? Equal rights! they cannot exist without equality of instruction. "All men are born free and equal!" they are indeed so *born*, but do they so *live*? Are they educated as equals? and, if not, can they *be* equal? and, if not equal, can they be free? Do not the rich command instruction? and they who have instruction, must they not possess the power? and when they have the power, will they not exert it in their own favor? I will ask more; I will ask, *do* they not exert it in their own favor? I will ask if two professions do not now rule the land and its inhabitants? I will ask, whether your legislatures are not governed by lawyers and your households by priests? And I will farther ask, whether the deficient instruction of the mass of your population does not give to lawyers their political ascendancy; and whether the ignorance of women be not the cause that your domestic hearths are invaded by priests? . . .

. . . Your political institutions have taken equality for their basis; your declaration of rights, upon which your institutions rest, sets forth this principle as vital and inviolate. Equality is the soul of liberty; there is, in fact, no liberty without it—none that cannot be overthrown by the violence of ignorant anarchy, or sapped by the subtilty of professional craft. That this is the case your reasons will admit; that this is the case your feelings *do* admit—even those which are the least amiable and the least praiseworthy. The jealousy betrayed by the uncultivated against those of more polished address and manners, has its source in the beneficial principle to which we advert, however, (in this, as in many other cases,) misconceived and perverted. Cultivation of mind will ever lighten the countenance and polish the exterior. This external superiority, which is but a faint emanation of the superiority within, vulgar eyes can see and ignorant jealousy will resent. This, in a republic, leads to brutality; and, in aristocracies, where this jealously is restrained by fear, to servility. Here it will lead the wagoner to dispute the road with a carriage; and, in Europe, will make the foot passenger doff his hat to the lordly equipage which spatters him with mud, while there he mutters curses only in his heart. The unreasoning observer will refer the conduct of the first to the *republican institutions*—the reflecting observer, to the *anti-republican education*. The instruction befitting free men is that which gives the sun of knowledge to shine on all; and which at once secures the liberties of each individual, and disposes each individual to make a proper use of them.

Equality, then, we have shown to have its seat in the mind. A proper cultivation of the faculties would ensure a sufficiency of that equality for all the ends of republican government, and for all the modes of social enjoyment. The diversity in the natural powers of different minds, as decided by physical organization, would be then only a source of interest and agreeable variety. All would be capable of appreciating the peculiar powers of each; and each would perceive that his interests, well understood, were in unison with the interests of all. Let us now examine whether liberty, properly interpreted, does not involve, among your unalienable rights as citizens and human beings, the right of equal means of instruction.

Have ye given a pledge, sealed with the blood of your fathers, for the equal rights of all human kind sheltered within your confines? What means the pledge? or what understand ye by human rights? But understand them as ye will, define them as ye will, how are men to be secured in *any* rights without instruction? how to be secured in the *equal exercise* of those rights without *equality of instruction*? By instruction understand me to mean, knowledge—*just knowledge*; not talent, not genius, not inventive mental powers. These will vary in every human being; but knowledge is the same for every mind, and every mind may and *ought to be* trained to receive it. If, then, ye have pledged, at each anniversary of your political independence, your lives, properties, and honor, to the securing your common liberties, ye have pledged your lives, properties, and honor, to the securing of *your common instruction*. Or will you secure the end without securing the means? ye shall do it, when ye reap the harvest without planting the seed. . . .

All men are born free and equal! That is: *our moral feelings acknowledge it to be just and proper, that we respect those liberties in others, which we lay claim to for ourselves; and that we permit the free agency of every individual, to any extent which violates not the free agency of his fellow creatures.*

There is but one honest limit to the rights of a sentient being; it is where they touch the rights of another sentient being. Do we exert our own liberties without injury to others —we exert them justly; do we exert them at the expense of others—unjustly. And, in thus doing, we step from the sure platform of liberty upon the uncertain threshold of tyranny. Small is the step; to the unreflecting so imperceptibly small, that they take it every hour of their lives as thoughtlessly as they do it unfeelingly. . . .

Who among us but has had occasion to remark the ill-judged, however well intentioned government of children by their teachers; and, yet more especially, by their parents? In what does this mismanagement originate? In a misconception of the relative position of the parent or guardian, and of the child; in a departure, by the parent, from the principle of liberty, in his assumption of rights destructive of those of the child; in his exercise of authority, as by right divine, over the judgment, actions, and person of the child; in his forgetfulness of the character of the child, as a human being, born "free and equal" among his compeers; that is, having equal claims to the exercise and development of all his senses, faculties, and powers, with those who brought him into existence, and with all sentient beings who tread the earth. Were a child thus viewed by his parent, we should not see him, by turns, made a plaything and a slave; we should not see him commanded to believe, but encouraged to reason; we should not see him trembling under the rod, nor shrinking from a frown, but reading the wishes of others in the eye, gathering knowledge wherever he threw his glance, rejoicing in the present hour, and treasuring up sources of enjoyment for future years. We should not then see the youth launching into life without compass or quadrant. We should not see him doubting at each emergency how to act, shifting his course with the shifting wind, and, at last, making shipwreck of mind and body on the sunken rocks of hazard and dishonest speculation, nor on the foul quicksands of debasing licentiousness.

What, then, has the parent to do, if he would conscientiously discharge that most sacred of all duties, that weightiest of all responsibilities, which ever did or ever will devolve on a human being? What is he to do, who, having brought a creature into existence, endowed with varied faculties, with tender susceptibilities, capable of untold wretchedness or equally of unconceived enjoyment; what is he to do, that he may secure the happiness of that creature, and make the life he has given blessing and blessed, instead of cursing and cursed? What is he to do?—he is to encourage in his child a spirit of enquiry, and equally to encourage it in himself. He is never to advance an opinion without showing the facts upon which it is grounded; he is never to assert a fact, without proving it to be a fact. He is not to teach a code of morals, any more than a creed of doctrines; but he is to direct his young charge to observe the consequences of actions on himself and on others; and to judge of the propriety of those actions by their ascertained consequences. He is not to command his feelings any more than his opinions or his actions; but he is to assist him in the analysis of his feelings, in the examination of their nature, their tendencies, their effects. Let him do this, and have no anxiety for the result. In the free exercise of his senses, in the fair development of his faculties, in a course of simple and unrestrained enquiry, he will discover truth, for he will ascertain facts; he will seize upon virtue, for he will have distinguished beneficial from injurious actions; he will cultivate kind, generous, just, and honourable feelings, for he will have proved them to contribute to his own happiness and to shed happiness around him.

Who, then, shall say, enquiry is good for him and not good for his children? Who shall cast error from himself, and allow it to be grafted on the minds he has called into being? Who shall break the chains of his own ignorance, and fix them, through his descendants, on his race? But, there are some who, as parents, make one step in duty, and halt at the second. We see men who will aid the instruction of their sons, and condemn only their daughters to ignorance. "Our sons," they say, "will have to exercise political rights, may aspire to public offices, may fill some learned profession, may struggle for wealth and acquire it. It is well that we give them a helping hand; that we assist them to such knowledge as is going, and make them as sharp witted as their neighbors. But for our daughters," they say—if indeed respecting them they say any thing—"for our daughters, little trouble or expense is necessary. They can never *be any thing*; in fact, they *are nothing*. We had best give them up to their mothers, who may take them to Sunday's preaching; and, with the aid of a little music, a little dancing, and a few fine gowns, fit them out for the market of marriage."

Am I severe? It is not my intention. I know that I am honest, and I fear that I am correct. Should I offend, however I may regret, I shall not repent it; satisfied to incur displeasure, so that I render service.

But to such parents I would observe, that with regard to

their sons, as to their daughters, they are about equally mistaken. If it be their duty, as we have seen, to respect in their children the same natural liberties which they cherish for themselves—if it be their duty to aid as guides, not to dictate as teachers—to lend assistance to the reason, not to command its prostration,—then have they nothing to do with the blanks or the prizes in store for them, in the wheel of worldly fortune. Let possibilities be what they may in favor of their sons, they have no calculations to make on them. It is not for them to ordain their sons magistrates nor statesmen; nor yet even lawyers, physicians, or merchants. They have only to improve the one character which they receive at the birth. They have only to consider them as *human beings,* and to ensure them the fair and thorough developement of all the faculties, physical, mental, and moral, which distinguish their nature. In like manner, as respects their daughters, they have nothing to do with the injustice of laws, nor the absurdities of society. Their duty is plain, evident, decided. In a daughter they have in charge a human being; in a son, the same. Let them train up these *human beings,* under the expanded wings of liberty. Let them seek *for* them and *with* them just knowledge; encouraging, from the cradle upwards, that useful curiosity which will lead them unbidden in the paths of free enquiry; and place them, safe and superior to the storms of life, in the security of well regulated, self-possessed minds, well grounded, well reasoned, conscientious opinions, and self-approved, consistent practice.

I have as yet, in this important matter, addressed myself only to the reason and moral feelings of my audience; I could speak also to their interests. Easy were it to show, that in proportion as your children are enlightened, will they prove blessings to society and ornaments to their race. But if this be true of all, it is more especially true of the now more neglected half of the species. Were it only in our power to enlighten part of the rising generation, and should the interests of the whole decide our choice of the portion, it were the females, and not the males, we should select.

When, now a twelvemonth since, the friends of liberty and science pointed out to me, in London, the walls of their rising university, I observed, with a smile, that they were beginning at the wrong end: "Raise such an edifice for your young women, and ye have enlightened the nation." It has already been observed, that women, wherever placed, however high or low in the scale of cultivation, hold the destinies of humankind. Men will ever rise or fall to the level of the other sex; and from some causes in their conformation, we find them, however armed with power or enlightened with knowledge, still held in leading strings even by the least cultivated female. Surely, then, if they knew their interests, they would desire the improvement of those who, if they do not advantage, will injure them; who, if they elevate not their minds and meliorate not their hearts, will debase the one and harden the other; and who, if they endear not existence, most assuredly will dash it with poison. How many, how omnipotent are the interests which engage men to break the mental chains of women! How many, how dear are the interests which engage them to exalt rather than lower their condition, to multiply their solid acquirements, to respect their liberties, to make them their equals, to wish them even their superiors! Let them enquire into these things. Let them examine the relation in which the two sexes stand, and ever must stand, to each other. Let them perceive, that, mutually dependent, they must ever be giving and receiving, or they must be losing;—receiving or losing in knowledge, in virtue, in enjoyment. Let them perceive how immense the loss, or how immense the gain. Let them not imagine that they know aught of the delights which intercourse with the other sex can give, until they have felt the sympathy of mind with mind, and heart with heart; until they bring into that intercourse every affection, every talent, every confidence, every refinement, every respect. Until power is annihilated on one side, fear and obedience on the other, and both restored to their birthright—equality. Let none think that affection can reign without it; or friendship, or esteem. Jealousies, envyings, suspicions, reserves, deceptions—these are the fruits of inequality. Go, then! and remove the evil first from the minds of women, then from their condition, and then from your laws. Think it no longer indifferent whether the mothers of the rising generation are wise or foolish. . . .

There is a vulgar persuasion, that the ignorance of women, by favoring their subordination, ensures their utility. 'Tis the same argument employed by the ruling few against the subject many in aristocracies; by the rich against the poor in democracies; by the learned professions against the people in all countries. And let us observe, that if good in one case, it should be good in all; and that, unless you are prepared to admit that you are yourselves less industrious in proportion to your intelligence, you must abandon the position with respect to others. But, in fact, who is it among men that best struggle with difficulties?—the strong minded or the weak? Who meet with serenity adverse fortune?—the wise or the foolish? Who accommodate themselves to irremediable circumstances? or, when remediable, who control and mould them at will?—the intelligent or the ignorant? Let your answer in your own case, be your answer in that of women. . . .

. . . Let us understand what knowledge is. Let us clearly perceive that accurate knowledge regards all equally; that truth, or fact, is the same thing for all human-kind; that there are not truths for the rich and truths for the poor, truths for men and truths for women; there are simply *truths*, that is, *facts*, which all who open their eyes and their ears and their understandings can perceive. There is no mystery in these facts. There is no witchcraft in knowledge. Science is not a trick; not a puzzle. The philosopher is not a conjuror. The observer of nature who envelopes his discoveries in mystery, either knows less than he pretends, or feels interested in *withholding* his knowledge. The teacher whose lessons are difficult of comprehension, is either clumsy or he is dishonest.

We observed . . . that it was the evident interest of our appointed teachers to disguise the truth. We discovered this to be a matter of necessity, arising out of their dependence upon the public favor. We may observe yet another cause, now operating far and wide—universally, omnipotently—a cause pervading the whole mass of society, and springing out of the existing motive principle of human action—competition. Let us examine, and we shall discover it to be the object of each individual to obscure the first elements of the knowledge he professes—be that knowledge mechanical and operative, or intellectual and passive. It is thus that we see the simple manufacture of a pair of shoes magnified into an art, demanding a seven years apprenticeship, when all its intricacies might be mastered in as many months. It is thus that cutting out a coat after just proportions is made to involve more science, and to demand more study, than the anatomy of the body it is to cover. And it is thus, in like manner, that all the branches of knowledge, involved in what is called scholastic learning, are wrapped in the fogs of pompous pedantry; and that every truth, instead of being presented in naked innocence, is obscured under a weight of elaborate words, and lost and buried in a medley of irrelevant ideas, useless amplifications, and erroneous arguments. Would we unravel this confusion—would we distinguish the true from the false, the real from the unreal, the useful from the useless —would we break our mental leading strings—would we know the uses of all our faculties—would we be virtuous, happy, and intelligent beings—would we be useful in our generation—would we possess our own minds in peace, be secure in our opinions, be just in our feelings, be consistent in our practice—would we command the respect of others, and—far better—would we secure our own—let us enquire.

Let us enquire! What mighty consequences, are involved in these little words! Whither have they not led? To what are they not yet destined to lead? Before them thrones have given way. Hierarchies have fallen, dungeons have disclosed their secrets. Iron bars, and iron laws, and more iron prejudices, have given way; the prison house of the mind hath burst its fetters; science disclosed her treasures; truth her moral beauties; and civil liberty, sheathing her conquering sword, hath prepared her to sit down in peace at the feet of knowledge. . . .

Did the knowledge of each individual embrace all the discoveries made by science, all the truths extracted by philosophy from the combined experience of ages, still would enquiry be in its infancy, improvement in its dawn. Perfection for man is in no time, in no place. The law of his being, like that of the earth he inhabits, is *to move always, to stop never*. From the earliest annals of tradition, his movement has been in advance. The tide of his progress hath had ebbs and flows, but hath left a thousand marks by which to note its silent but tremendous influx. . . .

If this be so—and who that looks abroad shall gainsay the assertion?—if this be so—and who that looks to your jails, to your penitentiaries, to your houses of refuge, to your hospitals, to your asylums, to your hovels of wretchedness, to your haunts of intemperance, to your victims lost in vice and hardened in profligacy, to childhood without protection, to youth without guidance, to the widow without sustenance, to the female destitute and female outcast, sentenced to shame and sold to degradation—who that looks to these shall say, that enquiry hath not a world to explore, and improvement yet a world to reform!

The First Woman Sociologist:
Harriet Martineau (1802–1876)

Harriet Martineau was one of many foreign visitors who came to the United States during the first decades of the nineteenth century, eager to explore the new democracy at first hand. But of the dozens of European accounts of travels in America, Martineau's *Society in America* and de Tocqueville's *Democracy in America* are probably the most outstanding. After 140 years these two volumes remain primary sources for students of early American society. Neither volume attempted to explain American society in terms of its historical development, as scholars examined French or English society at that time. There is no parade of great men and their deeds in the pages of Martineau or de Tocqueville. Rather, both authors described and tried to explain the points of difference and similarity between the young American nation and their own, more caste-ridden European countries. This comparative focus gives Martineau's analysis a tone that is familiar to social scientists of today, for her mode of analysis is very close to what is now known as the comparative analysis of social structure.

The institutional framework is apparent in the very chapter headings of Martineau's book: the apparatus of government, agriculture, economy, parties, marriage, children, religion. For each of these topics her emphasis is on tracing the way in which the basic moral values of the young nation determined its institutional structure. Because the focus was not simply on political history, there are rich observations of Americans and their families in the 1830s, which permit the reader today to observe through Martineau's eyes and values the lives led by women and men in their family roles and in the private social world of their communities.

Harriet Martineau was a young woman of thirty-two when she set sail from England in 1834 for her two-year visit to the United States. Her reputation as a writer on the liberal left of her day preceded her to America, for she had already published a number of essays and books that had

had lively sales on both sides of the Atlantic. She traveled through the South, up and down the east coast, and into the expanding territories to the west in Ohio and Michigan. A typical description of her reception, in her own words, was of her stay in Stockbridge with Mrs. Sedgwick, an American writer whom Martineau admired:

I was "Layfayetted," as they say, to great advantage. All business was suspended, and almost the whole population was busy in giving me pleasure and information. I never before was the cause of such a jubilee. [Chapman 1877, I:245]

This universal welcome and admiration did not hold, however, for the last part of her stay in the United States. She caused a minor upheaval by publicly endorsing Garrison and the courageous abolitionists of this early period. Reaction to her endorsement of abolition was so intense, with talk of a public lynching should she set foot again in slave territory, that her plans for travel into the western territories during the last three months of her American trip were altered to a more northerly route. Twenty years later Martineau described the anxiety of this trip in vivid terms:

The woods of Michigan were very beautiful; but danger was about us there, as everywhere during those three months of travel. It was out of such glades as those of Michigan that mobs had elsewhere issued to stop the coach, and demand the victim, and inflict the punishment earned by compassion for the negro, and assertion of true republican liberty. I believe there was scarcely a morning during those three months when it was not my first thought on waking whether I should be alive at night. [Chapman 1877, I:369]

Even before the word "sociology" had been coined by Auguste Comte to describe the study of society, Martineau was "preaching sociology without the name" (Webb 1960: 308). She paved the way for the emerging field by the care with which she handled her observations of social behavior and the terms in which she analyzed them. What makes her work even more outstanding is the self-consciousness with which she advocated the view that the study of societies constitutes a separate scientific discipline. Less well known either to the general reading public or to historians of sociology itself is the volume she published in 1838, *How to Observe Manners and Morals*. This slim volume, which Lipset (1962:7) characterizes as the "first book on the methodology of social research," was drafted aboard ship during her voyage to America. It is easy to assume from a reading of this manuscript that the methodology she prescribed was Martineau's own preparation for field observation in America and, by extension, that she planned in advance to write a book on America. In her autobiography, however, she explicitly denies such intentions.

Before her departure she turned down several publishers' offers for a book on her American experiences. In the autobiography she claimed:

> I am sure that no traveler seeing things through author spectacles can see them as they are; and it was not till I looked over my journal on my return that I decided to write "Society in America." (I never can bear to think of the title. My own title was "Theory and Practice of Society in America," but the publishers would not sanction it.)[Chapman 1877, I:330]

Inveterate writer that she was, her months of travel and conversation in America included the keeping of a voluminous journal, in which she meticulously recorded the names of all the people she met and the occasions on which she met them and added pages of observation and commentary. Her traveling companion, Louisa Jeffrey, assisted her in this enterprise, checking the accuracy and detail in a way that must have been particularly important for someone handicapped by partial deafness, as Martineau was.

What background produced this remarkable Victorian radical woman? Accounts of her formative years do little to suggest the tenacity with which she later pursued her writing career, producing some fifty volumes and countless essays and reviews in the course of her long but ailing life. The sixth of eight children of Thomas Martineau and his wife Elizabeth, she was a delicate child suffering from weak digestion and a high-strung nervous system. In the account of her childhood and early adulthood her mother emerges as the more dominant partner in the parents' marriage and in the lives of the children. Harriet's father was a Norwich manufacturer with sporadic financial success, who stood in the shadow of his brother, an eminent surgeon of that period.

Harriet was frequently sent to the country in the hope of improving her health but was apparently not spared any of the rigorous domestic apprenticeship or intellectual studies despite her continuing poor health. From the record, the young Harriet received a remarkably intensive education, even for the liberal Unitarian circles to which her family belonged.

In later years Harriet cited her younger brother James as the one person in her life for whom she had a very intense and special affection—though she met all her filial obligations as long as her mother lived. The intensity that marked the relationship with James is clear in her autobiography:

All who have ever known me are aware that the strongest passion I have ever entertained was in regard to my youngest brother, who has certainly filled the largest space in the life of my affections of any person whatever. . . . [But] in the history of human affections . . . the least satisfactory is the fraternal. Brothers are to sisters what sisters can never be to brothers as objects of engrossing and devoted affection. [Chapman 1877, I: 76–77]

Harriet Martineau never married, though when she was in her mid-twenties she was briefly engaged to a young man who died within the year. In looking back over her life as an unmarried woman, she showed no regrets on this score. The tone with which she described that life is in marked contrast to the depth of feeling she hints at when speaking of her brother. She summed up her marital status in these words:

I am in truth very thankful for not having married at all. I have never since been tempted nor have suffered any thing at all in relation to that matter which is held to be all-important to woman,—love and marriage. . . . The veneration in which I hold domestic life has always shown me that that life was not for those whose self respect had been early broken down, or had never grown. . . . My strong will, combined with anxiety of conscience, makes me fit only to live alone; and my taste and liking are for living alone. The older I have grown, the more serious and irremediable have seemed to me the evils and disadvantages of married life as it exists among us at this time. [Chapman 1877, I:100, 101]

Beneath the somewhat stilted Victorian prose is a shrewd self-awareness that her particular personal history had cheated her of those qualities necessary for the formation of intimate and trusting relations in marriage and maternity without loss of self. Martineau was in no sense, however, an embittered woman in her later years. She retained a youthful and zestful delight in children that was apparent in her earlier response to American children. She stands as one of the few European visitors to America who was not "turned off" by American children for their independence and (from the English perspective) impudence and boldness. Like Fanny Wright, she sensed very properly that to produce an independent, adventurous, and aspiring adult required a childhood rooted in trust and love and a varied experience with independence and assertion of self.

A good illustration of Martineau's ability to project into the lives of others, and to appreciate the transformation that love can make in a life, can be found in her assessment of Margaret Fuller. The two women met during Martineau's stay in Boston, at a point when the younger Margaret was lost in the heady idealist world of the Transcendentalists. Martineau reports that in correspondence, in conversation, and in later public criticism of *Society in America*, Fuller took strong exception to Martineau's involvement with the antislavery cause as a "low and disagreeable one, which should be left to unrefined persons to manage, while others were occupied with higher things" (Chapman 1877, I:381). In the years after her return to England, Martineau watched the intellectual and personal development of the younger woman as Fuller published or loomed in correspondence that flowed across the ocean. Once she finally broke away from America to fulfill her dream of visiting Europe, Fuller visited Harriet Martineau. Martineau revealed her sense of the kind of woman Margaret Fuller might have been had her early adulthood been spent away from Boston:

> She was not content with pursuing, and inducing others to pursue, a metaphysical idealism destructive of all genuine feeling and sound activity; she mocked at objects and efforts of a higher order than her own, and despised those who, like myself, could not adopt her scale of valuation. All this might have been spared, a world of mis-

chief saved, and a world of good effected, if she had found her heart a dozen years sooner, and in America instead of Italy. It is the most grievous loss I have almost ever known in private history—the deferring of Margaret Fuller's married life so long. . . . I regard her American life as a reflexion , . . of the prevalent social spirit of her time and place; and the Italian life as the true revelation of the tender and high-souled woman, who had till then been as curiously concealed from herself as from others. [Chapman 1877, I:382–383]

Martineau was one of the few people in the 1850s to sympathize with the vast change that took place in Fuller's thinking once she breathed the political and personal air of Europe, which was freer than any she had ever known in America.

At one point in her observations of American women Martineau notes that "the prosperity of America is a circumstance unfavourable to its women. It will be long before they are put to the proof as to what they are capable of thinking and doing." She contrasts this circumstance with the reality confronting Englishwomen, thousands of whom were sorely tested by economic adversity and its effect upon their families' income following the crash of 1825. Martineau herself must be counted among such Englishwomen, for it was the collapse of her father's business in 1825 that triggered her efforts to establish herself as a writer, and it was continued economic need that kept her pen at work each day from early morning to midafternoon for years on end. In the course of that long writing career she touched on political and literary issues of her day; was the first to translate and abridge Comte's *Positive Philosophy*; penned numerous pamphlets on political economy in an effort to reach a wide audience of English workers; wrote several stories for children and a volume on "household education" that urged a more rational form of child care; and proposed the publication of a 200-volume library of good cheap books for the working classes, of which 140 were actually published. She was an ardent defender of women's rights throughout her life, though her plan to found a journal dedicated to the cause of women did not succeed. Long before Marx and Engels were to depict women as household slaves oppressed by the bourgeois patriarchal family system analogous to the oppression of the proletariat by the ruling class, Martineau wrote of the analogy between the position of women in England and America and that of the American slave. She showed a careful eye for the impact of marriage on American women, noting the contrast between their healthy vigor before marriage and their rapid aging and the shallowness of their lives thereafter. She showed a sociological sensitivity to the consequences of the universal social pressure in America on women toward marriage and motherhood, commenting drily that "where all women have only one serious object, many of them will be unfit for the object." She was astonished by the pervasive influence of religion on American women, though she drops the acid comment that

> their charity is overflowing, if it were but more enlightened; and it may be supposed that they could not exist without religion. It appears to superabound; but it is not usually of a healthy character.

Martineau made countless friends and had innumerable admirers during her American tour, only to lose many of them, and to confirm the views of those who denounced her support of abolitionism during her visit, when her book on America was published. Her hopes for the new nation remained high, but she feared that the cancer of slavery might yet rip the society apart or so corrupt it that it would be deflected from fulfilling its own professed destiny as the land of the free. She put a sensitive finger on the same character tendencies in the American that de Tocqueville in her own era and Riesman more than a century later pointed out, chief among them the overwhelming concern of Americans for the opinions of others. She interpreted this "other-directedness" as the reflection of an open society, where social status must be achieved. English men and women, by contrast, in a society where social position was more apt to be ascribed at birth, could indulge in greater eccentricity and individuality.

Crusty, garrulous, a prodigious writer, a forerunner of the discipline of sociology not yet born, Harriet Martineau stands as an early ardent defender of women's rights, the first woman sociologist, and a sympathetic observer of the social condition of women in a society that proclaimed freedom and justice for all but did not grant it to more than half its population.

⨳ Society in America ⨳

Woman

If a test of civilisation be sought, none can be so sure as the condition of that half of society over which the other half has power,—from the exercise of the right of the strongest. Tried by this test, the American civilisation appears to be of a lower order than might have been expected from some other symptoms of its social state. The Americans have, in the treatment of women, fallen below, not only their own democratic principles, but the practice of some parts of the Old World.

The unconsciousness of both parties as to the injuries suffered by women at the hands of those who hold the power is a sufficient proof of the low degree of civilisation in this important particular at which they rest. While woman's intellect is confined, her morals crushed, her health ruined, her weaknesses encouraged, and her strength punished, she is told that her lot is cast in the paradise of women: and there is no country in the world where there is so much boasting of the "chivalrous" treatment she enjoys. That is to say,—she has the best place in stage-coaches: when there are not chairs enough for everybody, the gentlemen stand: she hears oratorical flourishes on public occasions about wives and home, and apostrophes to women: her husband's hair stands on end at the idea of her working, and he toils to indulge her with money: she has liberty to get her brain turned by religious excitements, that her attention may be diverted from morals, politics, and philosophy; and, especially, her morals are guarded by the strictest observance of propriety in her presence. In short, indulgence is given her as a substitute for justice. Her case differs from that of the slave, as to the principle, just so far as this; that the indulgence is large and universal, instead of petty and capricious. In both cases, justice is denied on no better plea than the right of the strongest. In both cases, the acquiescence of the many, and the burning discon-

From Harriet Martineau, *Society in America*. London, Saunders & Otley, 1837. Vol. III, pp. 105–151.

tent of the few, of the oppressed testify, the one to the actual
degradation of the class, and the other to its fitness for the
enjoyment of human rights. . . .

The intellect of woman is confined by an unjustifiable
restriction of both methods of education,—by express teaching, and by the discipline of circumstance. The former, though
prior in the chronology of each individual, is a direct consequence of the latter, as regards the whole of the sex. As
women have none of the objects in life for which an enlarged
education is considered requisite, the education is not given.
Female education in America is much what it is in England.
There is a profession of some things being taught which are
supposed necessary because everybody learns them. They
serve to fill up time, to occupy attention harmlessly, to improve conversation, and to make women something like companions to their husbands, and able to teach their children
somewhat. But what is given is, for the most part, passively
received; and what is obtained is, chiefly, by means of the
memory. There is rarely or never a careful ordering of influences for the promotion of clear intellectual activity. Such
activity, when it exceeds that which is necessary to make the
work of the teacher easy, is feared and repressed. This is natural enough, as long as women are excluded from the objects
for which men are trained. While there are natural rights
which women may not use, just claims which are not to be
listened to, large objects which may not be approached, even
in imagination, intellectual activity is dangerous: or, as the
phrase is, unfit. Accordingly, marriage is the only object left
open to woman. Philosophy she may pursue only fancifully,
and under pain of ridicule: science only as a pastime, and
under a similar penalty. Art is declared to be left open: but
the necessary learning, and, yet more, the indispensable experience of reality, are denied to her. Literature is also said
to be permitted: but under what penalties and restrictions? . . .

. . . Nothing is thus left for women but marriage.—Yes;
Religion, is the reply.—Religion is a temper, not a pursuit.
It is the moral atmosphere in which human beings are to
live and move. Men do not live to breathe: they breathe to
live. A German lady of extraordinary powers and endowments, remarked to me with amazement on all the knowledge
of the American women being based on theology. She observed that in her own country theology had its turn with

other sciences as a pursuit: but nowhere, but with the American women, had she known it make the foundation of all other knowledge. Even while thus complaining, this lady stated the case too favourably. American women have not the requisites for the study of theology. The difference between theology and religion, the science and the temper, is yet scarcely known among them. It is religion which they pursue as an occupation; and hence its small results upon the conduct, as well as upon the intellect. We are driven back upon marriage as the only appointed object in life: and upon the conviction that the sum and substance of female education in America, as in England, is training women to consider marriage as the sole object in life, and to pretend that they do not think so.

The morals of women are crushed. If there be any human power and business and privilege which is absolutely universal, it is the discovery and adoption of the principle and laws of duty. As every individual, whether man or woman, has a reason and a conscience, this is a work which each is thereby authorised to do for him or herself. But it is not only virtually prohibited to beings who, like the American women, have scarcely any objects in life proposed to them; but the whole apparatus of opinion is brought to bear offensively upon individuals among women who exercise freedom of mind in deciding upon what duty is, and the methods by which it is to be pursued. There is nothing extraordinary to the disinterested observer in women being so grieved at the case of slaves,—slave wives and mothers, as well as spirit-broken men,—as to wish to do what they could for their relief: there is nothing but what is natural in their being ashamed of the cowardice of such white slaves of the north as are deterred by intimidation from using their rights of speech and of the press, in behalf of the suffering race, and in their resolving not to do likewise: there is nothing but what is justifiable in their using their moral freedom, each for herself, in neglect of the threats of punishment: yet there were no bounds to the efforts made to crush the actions of women who thus used their human powers in the abolition question, and the convictions of those who looked on, and who might possibly be warmed into free action by the beauty of what they saw. It will be remembered that they were women who asserted the right of meeting and of discussion, on the day when Garrison was mobbed in Boston. Bills were

posted about the city on this occasion, denouncing these
women as casting off the refinement and delicacy of their
sex: the newspapers, which laud the exertions of ladies in all
other charities for the prosecution of which they are wont to
meet and speak, teemed with the most disgusting reproaches
and insinuations: and the pamphlets which related to the
question all presumed to censure the act of duty which the
women had performed in deciding upon their duty for themselves.—One lady, of high talents and character, whose books
were very popular before she did a deed greater than that of
writing any book, in acting upon an unusual conviction of
duty, and becoming an abolitionist, has been almost excom-
municated since. A family of ladies, whose talents and con-
scientiousness had placed them high in the estimation of
society as teachers, have lost all their pupils since they declared their anti-slavery opinions. The reproach in all the
many similar cases that I know is, not that the ladies hold
anti-slavery opinions, but that they act upon them. The incessant outcry about the retiring modesty of the sex proves
the opinion of the censors to be, that fidelity to conscience is
inconsistent with retiring modesty. If it be so, let the modesty
succumb. It can be only a false modesty which can be thus
endangered. No doubt, there were people in Rome who were
scandalised at the unseemly boldness of christian women
who stood in the amphitheatre to be torn in pieces for their
religion. No doubt there were many gentlemen in the British
army who thought it unsuitable to the retiring delicacy of
the sex that the wives and daughters of the revolutionary
heroes should be revolutionary heroines. But the event has a
marvellous efficacy in modifying the ultimate sentence. The
bold christian women, the brave American wives and daughters of half a century ago are honoured, while the intrepid
moralists of the present day, worthy of their grandmothers,
are made the confessors and martyrs of their age.

· · ·

How fearfully the morals of woman are crushed, appears
from the prevalent persuasion that there are virtues which
are peculiarly masculine, and others which are peculiarly
feminine. It is amazing that a society which makes a most
emphatic profession of its Christianity, should almost universally entertain such a fallacy: and not see that, in the
case they suppose, instead of the character of Christ being

the meeting point of all virtues, there would have been a separate gospel for women, and a second company of agents for its diffusion. It is not only that masculine and feminine employments are supposed to be properly different. No one in the world, I believe, questions this. But it is actually supposed that what are called the hardy virtues are more appropriate to men, and the gentler to women. . . .

. . . [T]he consequences are what might be looked for. Men are ungentle, tyrannical. They abuse the right of the strongest, however they may veil the abuse with indulgence. They want the magnanimity to discern woman's human rights; and they crush her morals rather than allow them. Women are, as might be anticipated, weak, ignorant and subservient, in as far as they exchange self-reliance for reliance on anything out of themselves. Those who will not submit to such a suspension of their moral functions, (for the work of self-perfection remains to be done, sooner or later,) have to suffer for their allegiance to duty. They have all the need of bravery that the few heroic men who assert the highest rights of women have of gentleness, to guard them from the encroachment to which power, custom, and education, incessantly conduce.

Such brave women and such just men there are in the United States, scattered among the multitude, whose false apprehension of rights leads to an enormous failure of duties. There are enough of such to commend the true understanding and practice to the simplest minds and most faithful hearts of the community, under whose testimony the right principle will spread and flourish. If it were not for the external prosperity of the country, the injured half of its society would probably obtain justice sooner than in any country of Europe. But the prosperity of America is a circumstance unfavourable to its women. It will be long before they are put to the proof as to what they are capable of thinking and doing: a proof to which hundreds, perhaps thousands of Englishwomen have been put by adversity, and the result of which is a remarkable improvement in their social condition, even within the space of ten years. Persecution for opinion, punishment for all manifestations of intellectual and moral strength, are still as common as women who have opinions and who manifest strength: but some things are easy, and many are possible of achievement, to women of ordinary powers, which it would have required genius to accomplish but a few years ago.

Marriage.

If there is any country on earth where the course of true love may be expected to run smooth, it is America. It is a country where all can marry early, where there need be no anxiety about a worldly provision, and where the troubles arising from conventional considerations of rank and connexion ought to be entirely absent. It is difficult for a stranger to imagine beforehand why all should not love and marry naturally and freely, to the prevention of vice out of the marriage state, and of the common causes of unhappiness within it. The anticipations of the stranger are not, however, fulfilled: and they never can be while the one sex overbears the other. Marriage is in America more nearly universal, more safe, more tranquil, more fortunate than in England: but it is still subject to the troubles which arise from the inequality of the parties in mind and in occupation. It is more nearly universal, from the entire prosperity of the country: it is safer, from the greater freedom of divorce, and consequent discouragement of swindling, and other vicious marriages: it is more tranquil and fortunate from the marriage vows being made absolutely reciprocal; from the arrangements about property being generally far more favorable to the wife than in England; and from her not being made, as in England, to all intents and purposes the property of her husband. The outward requisites to happiness are nearly complete, and the institution is purified from the grossest of the scandals which degrade it in the Old World: but it is still the imperfect institution which it must remain while women continue to be ill-educated, passive, and subservient: or well-educated, vigorous, and free only upon sufferance.

The institution presents a different aspect in the various parts of the country. I have spoken of the early marriages of silly children in the south and west, where, owing to the disproportion of numbers, every woman is married before she well knows how serious a matter human life is. She has an advantage which very few women elsewhere are allowed: she has her own property to manage. It would be a rare sight elsewhere to see a woman of twenty-one in her second widowhood, managing her own farm or plantation; and managing it well, because it had been in her own hands during her marriage. In Louisiana, and also in Missouri, (and probably in other States,) a woman not only has half her husband's property by right at his death, but may always be considered as possessed of half his gains during his life; having at all times power to bequeath that amount. The husband interferes much less with his wife's property in the south, even through her voluntary relinquishment of it, than is at all usual where the cases of women having property during their marriage are rare. In the southern newspapers, advertisements may at any time be seen, running thus:— "Mrs. A, wife of Mr. A, will dispose of &c. &c." When Madame Lalaurie was mobbed in New Orleans, no one meddled with her husband or his possessions; as he was no more responsible for her management of her human property than anybody else. On the whole, the practice seems to be that the weakest and most ignorant women give up their property to their husbands; the husbands of such women being precisely the men most disposed to accept it: and that the strongest-minded and most conscientious women keep their property, and use their rights; the husbands of such women being precisely those who would refuse to deprive their wives of their social duties and privileges. . . .

I have mentioned that divorce is more easily obtained in the United States than in England. In no country, I believe, are the marriage laws so iniquitous as in England, and the conjugal relation, in consequence, so impaired. Whatever may be thought of the principles which are to enter into laws of divorce, whether it be held that pleas for divorce should be one, (as narrow interpreters of the New Testament would have it;) or two, (as the law of England has it;) or several, (as the Continental and United States' laws in many instances allow,) nobody, I believe, defends the arrangement by which, in England, divorce is obtainable only by the very rich. The barbarism of granting that as a privilege to the extremely wealthy, to which money bears no relation whatever, and in which all married persons whatever have an equal interest, needs no exposure beyond the mere statement of the fact. It will be seen at a glance how such an arrangement tends to vitiate marriage: how it offers impunity to adventurers, and encouragement to every kind of mercenary marriages: how absolute is its oppression of the injured party: and how, by vitiating marriage, it originates and aggravates licentiousness to an incalculable extent. To England alone belongs the disgrace of such a method of legislation. . . .

Of the American States, I believe New York approaches

nearest to England in its laws of divorce. It is less rigid, in as far as that more is comprehended under the term "cruelty." The husband is supposed to be liable to cruelty from the wife, as well as the wife from the husband. There is no practical distinction made between rich and poor by the process being rendered expensive: and the cause is more easily resumable after a reconciliation of the parties. In Massachusetts, the term "cruelty" is made so comprehensive, and the mode of sustaining the plea is so considerately devised, that divorces are obtainable with peculiar ease. The natural consequence follows: such a thing is never heard of. A long-established and very eminent lawyer of Boston told me that he had known of only one in all his experience. Thus it is wherever the law is relaxed, and, *cæteris paribus,* in proportion to its relaxation: for the obvious reason, that the protection offered by law to the injured party causes marriages to be entered into with fewer risks, and the conjugal relation carried on with more equality. Retribution is known to impend over violations of conjugal duty. When I was in North Carolina, the wife of a gamester there obtained a divorce without the slightest difficulty. When she had brought evidence of the danger to herself and her children,—danger pecuniary and moral,—from her husband's gambling habits, the bill passed both Houses without a dissenting voice.

It is clear that the sole business which legislation has with marriage is with the arrangement of property; to guard the reciprocal rights of the children of the marriage and the community. There is no further pretence for the interference of the law, in any way. An advance towards the recognition of the true principle of legislative interference in marriage has been made in England, in the new law in which the agreement of marriage is made a civil contract, leaving the religious obligation to the conscience and taste of the parties. It will be probably next perceived that if the civil obligation is fulfilled, if the children of the marriage are legally and satisfactorily provided for by the parties, without the assistance of the legislature, the legislature has, in principle, nothing more to do with the matter. . . .

It is assumed in America, particularly in New England, that the morals of society there are peculiarly pure. I am grieved to doubt the fact: but I do doubt it. Nothing like a comparison between one country and another in different circumstances can be instituted: nor would any one desire to enter upon such a comparison. The bottomless vice, the all-pervading corruption of European society cannot, by possibility, be yet paralleled in America: but neither is it true that any outward prosperity, any arrangement of circumstances, can keep a society pure while there is corruption in its social methods, and among its principles of individual action. Even in America, where every young man may, if he chooses, marry at twenty-one, and appropriate all the best comforts of domestic life,—even here there is vice. Men do not choose to marry early, because they have learned to think other things of more importance than the best comforts of domestic life. A gentleman of Massachusetts, who knows life and the value of most things in it, spoke to me with deep concern of the alteration in manners which is going on: of the increase of bachelors, and of mercenary marriages; and of the fearful consequences. It is too soon for America to be following the old world in its ways. In the old world, the necessity of thinking of a maintenance before thinking of a wife has led to requiring a certain style of living before taking a wife; and then, alas! to taking a wife for the sake of securing a certain style of living. That this species of corruption is already spreading in the new world is beyond a doubt;—in the cities, where the people who live for wealth and for opinion congregate.

I was struck with the great number of New England women whom I saw married to men old enough to be their fathers. One instance which perplexed me exceedingly, on my entrance into the country, was explained very little to my satisfaction. The girl had been engaged to a young man whom she was attached to: her mother broke off the engagement, and married her to a rich old man. This story was a real shock to me; so persuaded had I been that in America, at least, one might escape from the disgusting spectacle of mercenary marriages. But I saw only too many instances afterwards. The practice was ascribed to the often-mentioned fact of the young men migrating westwards in large numbers, leaving those who should be their wives to marry widowers of double their age. The Auld Robin Gray story is a frequently enacted tragedy here, and one of the worst symptoms that struck me was, that there was usually a demand upon my sympathy in such cases. I have no sympathy for those who, under any pressure of circumstances, sacrifice their heart's-love for legal prostitution, and no environment of beauty or sentiment can deprive the fact of its coarseness: and least of all could I sympathise with women who set the example of marrying for an establishment in a new country, where, if anywhere, the conjugal relation should be found in its purity.

The unavoidable consequence of such a mode of marrying is, that the sanctity of marriage is impaired, and that vice succeeds. Any one must see at a glance that if men and women marry those whom they do not love, they must love those whom they do not marry. There are sad tales in country villages, here and there, which attest to this; and yet more in towns, in a rank of society where such things are seldom or never heard of in England. I rather think that married life is immeasurably purer in America than in England: but that there is not otherwise much superiority to boast of. I can only say, that I unavoidably knew of more cases of lapse in highly respectable families in one State than ever came to my knowledge at home; and that they were got over with a disgrace far more temporary and superficial than they could have been visited with in England. I am aware that in Europe the victims are chosen, with deliberate selfishness, from classes which cannot make known their perils and their injuries; while in America, happily, no such class exists. I am aware that this destroys all possibility of a comparison: but the fact remains, that the morals of American society are less pure than they assume to be. If the common boast be meant to apply to the rural population, at least let it not be made, either in pious gratitude, or patriotic conceit, by the aristocratic city classes, who, by introducing the practice of mercenary marriages, have rendered themselves responsible for whatever dreadful consequences may ensue.

The ultimate and very strong impression on the mind of a stranger, pondering the morals of society in America, is that human nature is much the same everywhere, whatever may be its environment of riches or poverty; and that it is justice to the human nature, and not improvement in fortunes, which must be looked to as the promise of a better time. Laws and customs may be creative of vice; and should be therefore perpetually under process of observation and correction: but laws and customs cannot be creative of virtue: they may encourage and help to preserve it; but they cannot originate it.

Occupation.

The greater number of American women have home and its affairs, wherewith to occupy themselves. Wifely and motherly occupation may be called the sole business of woman there. If she has not that, she has nothing. The only alternative, as I have said, is making an occupation of either religion or dissipation; neither of which is fit to be so used: the one being a state of mind; the other altogether a negation when not taken in alternation with business.

It must happen that where all women have only one serious object, many of them will be unfit for that object. In the United States, as elsewhere, there are women no more fit to be wives and mothers than to be statesmen and generals; no more fit for any responsibility whatever, than for the maximum of responsibility. There is no need to describe such: they may be seen everywhere. I allude to them only for the purpose of mentioning that many of this class shirk some of their labours and cares, by taking refuge in boarding-houses. It is a circumstance very unfavourable to the character of some American women, that boarding-house life has been rendered compulsory by the scarcity of labour,—the difficulty of obtaining domestic service. The more I saw of boarding-house life, the worse I thought of it; though I saw none but the best. Indeed, the degrees of merit in such establishments weigh little in the consideration of the evil of their existence at all. In the best it is something to be secure of respectable company, of a good table, a well-mannered and courteous hostess, and comfort in the private apartments: but the mischiefs of the system throw all these objects into the background.

To begin with young children. There can be no sufficient command of proper food for them; nor any security that they will eat it naturally at the table where fifty persons may be sitting, a dozen obsequious blacks waiting, and an array of tempting dishes within sight. The child is in imminent danger of being too shy and frightened to eat at all, or of becoming greedy to eat too much. Next, it is melancholy to see girls of twelve years old either slinking down beside their parents, and blushing painfully as often as any one of fifty strangers looks towards them; or boldly staring at all that is going on, and serving themselves, like little women of the world. After tea, it is a common practice to hand the young ladies to the piano, to play and sing to a party, composed chiefly of gentlemen, and brought together on no principle of selection except mere respectability. Next comes the mischief to the young married ladies, the most numerous class of women found in boarding-houses. The uncertainty about domestic service is so great, and the economy of boarding-house life so tempting to people who have not provided themselves with house and furniture, that it is not to be wondered at that many young married people use the accommodation provided. But no sensible husband, who could beforehand become acquainted with the liabilities incurred, would willingly expose his domestic peace to the fearful risk. I saw enough when I saw the elegantly dressed ladies repair to the windows of the common drawing-room, on their husbands' departure to the counting-house, after breakfast. There the ladies sit for hours, doing nothing but gossiping with one another, with any gentlemen of the house who may happen to have no business, and with visitors. It is true that the sober-minded among the ladies can and do withdraw to their own apartments for the morning: but they complain that they cannot settle to regular employments as they could in a house of their own. Either they are not going to stay long; or they have not room for their books, or they are broken in upon by their acquaintances in the house. The common testimony is, that little can be done in boarding-houses: and if the more sober-minded find it so, the fate of the thoughtless, who have no real business to do, may be easily anticipated. They find a dear friend or two among the boarders, to whom they confide their husbands' secrets. A woman who would do this once would do it twice, or as often as she changes her boarding-house, and finds a new dear friend in each. I have been assured that there is no end to the difficulties in which gentlemen have been involved, both as to their commercial and domestic affairs, by the indiscretion of their thoughtless young wives, amidst the idleness and levities of boarding-house life. . . .

The study of the economy of domestic service was a continual amusement to me. What I saw would fill a volume. Many families are, and have for years been, as well off for domestics as any family in England; and I must say that among the loudest complainers there were many who, from fault of either judgment or temper, deserved whatever difficulty they met with. This is remarkably the case with English ladies settled in America. They carry with them habits of command, and expectations of obedience; and when these are found utterly to fail, they grow afraid of their servants. Even when they have learned the theory that domestic service is a matter of contract, an exchange of service for recompense, the authority of the employer extending no further than to require the performance of the service promised,— when the ladies have learned to assent in words to this, they are still apt to be annoyed at things which in no way concern them. If one domestic chooses to wait at table with no cap over her scanty chevelure, and in spectacles,—if another goes to church on Sunday morning, dressed exactly like her mistress, the lady is in no way answerable for the bad taste of her domestics. But English residents often cannot learn to acquiesce in these things; nor in the servants doing their work in their own way; nor in their dividing their time as they please between their mistress's work and their own. The consequence is, that they soon find it impossible to get American help at all, and they are consigned to the tender mercies of the low Irish; and every one knows what kind of servants they commonly are. Some few of them are the best domestics in America: those who know how to value a respectable home, a steady sufficient income, the honour of being trusted, and the security of valuable friends for life: but too many of them are unsettled, reckless, slovenly; some dishonest, and some intemperate. . . .

Many ladies, in the country especially, take little girls to train; having them bound to a certain term of service. In such a case, the girl is taken at about eleven years old, and bound to remain till she is eighteen. Her mistress engages to clothe her; to give her Sunday-schooling, and a certain amount of weekday schooling in the year; and to present her at the end of the term (except in case of bad behaviour) with fifty dollars, or a cow, or some equivalent. Under a good mistress, this is an excellent bargain for the girl; but mistresses complain that as soon as the girls become really serviceable, by the time they are fourteen or fifteen, they begin to grow restless, having usually abundance of kind friends to tell them what good wages they might get if they were free.

In several abodes in which I resided for a longer or shorter time, the routine of the house was as easy and agreeable as any Englishman's; elsewhere, the accounts of domestic difficulties were both edifying and amusing. At first, I heard but

little of such things; there being a prevalent idea in America
that English ladies concern themselves very little about household affairs. This injurious misapprehension the ladies of
England owe, with many others, to the fashionable novels
which deluge the country from New York to beyond the
Mississippi. Though the Americans repeat and believe that
these books are false pictures of manners, they cannot be
wholly upon their guard against impressions derived from
them. Too many of them involuntarily image to themselves
the ladies of England as like the duchesses and countesses of
those low books: and can scarcely believe that the wives of
merchants, manufacturers, and shopkeepers, and of the
greater number of professional men, buy their own provision,
keep household accounts, look to the making and mending,
the baking, making of preserves, &c., and sometimes cook,
with their own hands, any dish of which their husbands may
be fond. When it was found, from my revelations, that English and American ladies have, after all, much the same sort
of things to do, the real state of household economy was laid
open to me.

All American ladies should know how to clear-starch and
iron: how to keep plate and glass: how to cook dainties: and,
if they understand the making of bread and soup likewise, so
much the better. The gentlemen usually charge themselves
with the business of marketing; which is very fair. A lady,
highly accomplished and very literary, told me that she had
lately been left entirely without help, in a country village
where there was little hope of being speedily able to procure
any. She and her daughter made the bread, for six weeks,
and entirely kept the house, which might vie with any nobleman's for true luxury; perfect sufficiency and neatness. She
mentioned one good result from the necessity: that she
should never again put up with bad bread. She could now
testify that bread might always be good, notwithstanding
changes of weather, and all the excuses commonly given. I
heard an anecdote from this lady which struck me. She was
in the habit of employing, when she wanted extra help, a
poor woman of colour, to do kitchen-work. The domestics
had always appeared on perfectly good terms with this
woman till, one day, when there was to be an evening party,
the upper domestic declined waiting on the company; giving
as a reason that she was offended at being required to sit
down to table with the coloured woman. Her mistress gently

rebuked her pride, saying "If you are above waiting on my
company, my family are not. You will see my daughter carry
the tea-tray, and my niece the cake." The girl repented, and
besought to be allowed to wait; but her assistance was declined; at which she cried heartily. The next day, she was
very humble, and her mistress reasoned with her, quite successfully. The lady made one concession in silence. She had
the coloured woman come after dinner, instead of before.

. . .

. . . For my own part, I had rather suffer any inconvenience from having to work occasionally in chambers and
kitchen, and from having little hospitable designs frustrated,
than witness the subservience in which the menial class is
held in Europe. In England, servants have been so long accustomed to this subservience; it is so completely the established custom for the mistress to regulate their manners,
their clothes, their intercourse with their friends, and many
other things which they ought to manage for themselves,
that it has become difficult to treat them any better. Mistresses who abstain from such regulation find that they are
spoiling their servants; and heads of families who would
make friends of their domestics find them little fitted to reciprocate the duty. In America it is otherwise: and may it
ever be so! All but those who care for their selfish gratification more than for the welfare of those about them will be
glad to have intelligent and disinterested friends in the domestics whom they may be able to attach, though there may
be difficulty at first in retaining them; and some eccentricities
of manner and dress may remain to be borne with. . . .

As for the occupations with which American ladies fill up
their leisure; what has been already said will show that there
is no great weight or diversity of occupation. Many are
largely engaged in charities, doing good or harm according to
the enlightenment of mind which is carried to the work. In
New England, a vast deal of time is spent in attending preach-
ings, and other religious meetings: and in paying visits, for
religious purposes, to the poor and sorrowful. The same results follow from this practice that may be witnessed wherever
it is much pursued. In as far as sympathy is kept up, and
acquaintanceship between different classes in society is occasioned, the practice is good. In as far as it unsettles the
minds of the visitors, encourages a false craving for religious

excitement, tempts to spiritual interference on the one hand, and cant on the other, and humours or oppresses those who need such offices least, while it alienates those who want them most, the practice is bad. I am disposed to think that much good is done, and much harm: and that, whenever women have a greater charge of indispensable business on their hands, so as to do good and reciprocate religious sympathy by laying hold of opportunities, instead of by making occupation, more than the present good will be done, without any of the harm.

All American ladies are more or less literary: and some are so to excellent purpose: to the saving of their minds from vacuity. Readers are plentiful: thinkers are rare. Minds are of a very passive character: and it follows that languages are much cultivated. If ever a woman was pointed out to me as distinguished for information, I might be sure beforehand that she was a linguist. I met with a great number of ladies who read Latin; some Greek; some Hebrew; some German. With the exception of the last, the learning did not seem to be of much use to them, except as a harmless exercise. I met with more intellectual activity, more general power, among many ladies who gave little time to books, than among those who are distinguished as being literary. I did not meet with a good artist among all the ladies in the States. I never had the pleasure of seeing a good drawing, except in one instance; or, except in two, of hearing good music. The entire failure of all attempts to draw is still a mystery to me. The attempts are incessant; but the results are below criticism. Natural philosophy is not pursued to any extent by women. There is some pretension to mental and moral philosophy; but the less that is said on that head the better.

This is a sad account of things. It may tempt some to ask "what then are the American women?" They are better educated by Providence than by men. The lot of humanity is theirs: they have labour, probation, joy, and sorrow. They are good wives; and, under the teaching of nature, good mothers. They have, within the range of their activity, good sense, good temper, and good manners. Their beauty is very remarkable; and, I think, their wit no less. Their charity is overflowing, if it were but more enlightened: and it may be supposed that they could not exist without religion. It appears to superabound; but it is not usually of a healthy character. It may seem harsh to say this: but is it not the fact that religion emanates from the nature, from the moral state of the individual? Is it not therefore true that unless the nature be completely exercised, the moral state harmonised, the religion cannot be healthy?

One consequence, mournful and injurious, of the "chivalrous" taste and temper of a country with regard to its women is that it is difficult, where it is not impossible, for women to earn their bread. Where it is a boast that women do not labour, the encouragement and rewards of labour are not provided. It is so in America. In some parts, there are now so many women dependent on their own exertions for a maintenance, that the evil will give way before the force of circumstances. In the meantime, the lot of poor women is sad. Before the opening of the factories, there were but three resources; teaching, needle-work, and keeping boarding-houses or hotels. Now, there are the mills; and women are employed in printing-offices; as compositors, as well as folders and stitchers.

I dare not trust myself to do more than touch on this topic. There would be little use in dwelling upon it; for the mischief lies in the system by which women are depressed, so as to have the greater number of objects of pursuit placed beyond their reach, more than in any minor arrangements which might be rectified by an exposure of particular evils. I would only ask of philanthropists of all countries to inquire of physicians what is the state of health of sempstresses; and to judge thence whether it is not inconsistent with common humanity that women should depend for bread upon such employment. Let them inquire what is the recompense of this kind of labour, and then wonder if they can that the pleasures of the licentious are chiefly supplied from that class. Let them reverence the strength of such as keep their virtue, when the toil which they know is slowly and surely destroying them will barely afford them bread, while the wages of sin are luxury and idleness. During the present interval between the feudal age and the coming time, when life and its occupations will be freely thrown open to women as to men, the condition of the female working classes is such that if its sufferings were but made known, emotions of horror and shame would tremble through the whole of society.

For women who shrink from the lot of the needle-woman, —almost equally dreadful, from the fashionable milliner down to the humble stocking-darner,—for those who shrink through pride, or fear of sickness, poverty, or temptation, there is little resource but pretension to teach. What office is there which involves more responsibility, which requires more qualifications, and which ought, therefore, to be more honourable, than that of teaching? What work is there for which a decided bent, not to say a genius, is more requisite? Yet are governesses furnished, in America as elsewhere, from among those who teach because they want bread; and who certainly would not teach for any other reason. Teaching and training children is, to a few, a very few, a delightful employment, notwithstanding all its toils and cares. Except to these few it is irksome; and, when accompanied with poverty and mortification, intolerable. Let philanthropists inquire into the proportion of governesses among the inmates of lunatic asylums. The answer to this question will be found to involve a world of rebuke and instruction. What can be the condition of the sex when such an occupation is overcrowded with candidates, qualified and unqualified? What is to be hoped from the generation of children confided to the cares of a class, conscientious perhaps beyond most, but reluctant, harassed, and depressed?

The most accomplished governesses in the United States may obtain 600 dollars a-year in the families of southern planters; provided they will promise to teach everything. In the north they are paid less; and in neither case, is there a possibility of making provision for sickness and old age. Ladies who fully deserve the confidence of society may realise an independence in a few years by school-keeping in the north: but, on the whole, the scanty reward of female labour in America remains the reproach to the country which its philanthropists have for some years proclaimed it to be. I hope they will persevere in their proclamation, though special methods of charity will not avail to cure the evil. It lies deep; it lies in the subordination of the sex: and upon this the exposures and remonstrances of philanthropists may ultimately succeed in fixing the attention of society; particularly of women. The progression or emancipation of any class usually, if not always, takes place through the efforts of individuals of that class: and so it must be here. All women should inform themselves of the condition of their sex, and of their own position. It must necessarily follow that the noblest of them will, sooner or later, put forth a moral power which shall prostrate cant, and burst asunder the bonds, (silken to some, but cold iron to others,) of feudal prejudices and usages. In the meantime, is it to be understood that the principles of the Declaration of Independence bear no relation to half of the human race? If so, what is the ground of the limitation? If not so, how is the restricted and dependent state of women to be reconciled with the proclamation that "all are endowed by their Creator with certain inalienable rights; that among these are life, liberty, and the pursuit of happiness?"

The Making of a Cosmopolitan Humanist:
Margaret Fuller (1810–1850)

Edgar Allan Poe said of Margaret Fuller's *Woman in the Nineteenth Century* that it was "a book which few women in the country could have written, and no woman in the country would have published, with the exception of Miss Fuller." Poe's intriguing observation stimulates a reader to learn more not only about Margaret Fuller's ideas, as expressed in this book, but also about Margaret Fuller as a person. It is far easier to describe her ideas than to fathom the many-sided person that unfolded over the short forty years of her life. A contemporary said of her that "Margaret had so many selves that you can peel her like an onion" (Wade 1940:xv).

Familiarity with her life, correspondence, and writings gives a few clues to why her contemporaries found her so complex a personality: she never seemed to settle down to the steady state of a "finished" adult woman. I believe Fuller underwent more change in intellectual and political development, to say nothing of her personal development, in the short fifteen years between her twenty-fifth and her fortieth birthdays than she had undergone during the first twenty-five years of childhood through early adulthood. To know her in 1840 would be to know a quite different woman than the Fuller of 1846 and the still different woman of 1849. Those who knew her when she was closely associated with the Boston Transcendentalist circle between 1840 and 1844 knew one kind of woman: highly intellectual, closely attuned to the rarified atmosphere of the stimulating, flowering world of Emerson, Hawthorne, Channing, Ripley, and their friends. To meet her or to reestablish contact with her in 1846 was to encounter a rather different woman: a practicing New York journalist working as a critic for Horace Greeley's *Tribune*, alert and informed about a wide spectrum of American life. Yet a third woman would emerge if the years of the encounter were 1847 to 1850. By that time Fuller had become more cosmopolitan as a result of her travels in England,

France, and Italy; greatly politicized, befriending the Italian patriot Mazzini in London and later in Italy during the 1848 uprising; serving as a hospital director during the siege of Rome. Those who knew her in her Boston days and who themselves remained in that Transcendentalist cocoon could scarcely be expected to recognize the cosmopolitan humanist of 1848, when Fuller was not only deeply involved in the political crisis in Italy, but also pregnant and in love with a young Italian rebel from an aristocratic but impoverished family, Angelo Ossoli. By 1850 she was living and writing from the center of a turbulent political and personal whirlpool, with a deep attraction to the people and culture of Italy similar to the hold Italy had over Elizabeth Browning during these same years, though Fuller was an active participant while Browning was a passive invalid observer of the Italian scene.

What experiences went into the molding of this complex and fascinating woman? Are there clues in her early life of the adult woman she was to become? Can we sense any connection between her personal biography and the ideas that startled her contemporaries when her first essay on women appeared in 1843?

Margaret Fuller, the first daughter of Timothy and Margaret Fuller, was born in Cambridgeport, Massachusetts, in 1810. Her father was a graduate of Harvard College, class of 1801, an idealistic republican whose political career took him to Congress as a representative from Massachusetts in 1817 and to the House of Representatives in Massachusetts, where he served as Speaker of the House, in 1825. Ten years older than his wife when he married at the age of thirty-one, he has been described as a stern patriarch who completely dominated his wife and household. He is said to have paid lip service to a belief in the equality of the sexes, but if so, this belief was not apparent in his relations to his wife, whom he clearly did not treat as though she were a partner with rights equal to his own. By contrast, he poured much of his hope and his own abilities into the training he gave his daughter Margaret. No detail of her life as a child was left unsupervised by her stern father, from her dress to her social behavior to her arduous studies. Fuller's memoirs of early childhood note a long series of nightmares stimulated by her reading in the Latin classics. A repetitive dream, apparently triggered by vivid passages from Virgil, was of trampling horses, trees dripping with blood, and herself drowning in pools of blood. Treating her not as a child but a living mind, Timothy Fuller paid little attention to the girl's physical fragility or her own inner drive for excellence that manifested itself at a very early age, and clearly no attention to the effects of her isolation from other girls her own age. Years later, in editing her collected papers, her brother Arthur was moved to write a long footnote on his father's treatment of Margaret in which he tried to soften the image of his father given in the autobiographic sketch by his sister:

> It is doubtless true, also, that he did not perfectly comprehend the rare mind of his daughter, or see for some years that she required no stimulating to intellectual effort as do most children, but rather the reverse. But how many fathers are there who would have understood at once such a child as Margaret Fuller was, or would have done even as wisely as he? . . . She needed, doubtless, to be *urged* into the usual sports of children, and the company of those of her own age. She needed to be kept from books for a period. . . . This simply was not done, but the error arose from no lack of tenderness or consideration, . . . but from the simple fact that the laws of physiology as connected with those of mind were not understood then as now. . . . Our father was indeed exact and strict with himself and others; but none has ever been more devoted to his children than he or more painstaking with their education, nor more fondly loved them. [Fuller 1855: 353–354]

After a breakdown of Margaret's health, her father decided that her studious regimen and isolation from girls her own age might have been responsible, and he sent her to a school at Groton, forty miles from Cambridge. Her incredible knowledge and lack of social skills made her an easy prey to ridicule and rejection at the school, and Margaret returned to her home a year later. Now fourteen, her journal shows, she quickly returned to the same demanding schedule she had followed earlier. To read her account of her daily routine is to be reminded of a close parallel in another family, across the sea, in which the father supervised every detail of a child's education—that of John Stuart Mill. Here is one entry from Fuller's journal for these mid-adolescent years:

I rise a little before five, walk an hour, and then practice on the piano until seven, when we breakfast. Next I read French . . . til eight, then two or three lectures in Brown's Philosophy. About half-past nine I go to Mr. Perkins' school and study Greek until twelve, when, the school being dismissed, I recite, go home, and practice again until dinner, at two. Sometimes, if the conversation is very agreeable, I lounge for half an hour over the dessert, though rarely so lavish of time. Then, when I can, I read two hours in Italian, but I am often interrupted. At six I walk or take a drive. Before going to bed I play or sing for half an hour or so, to make all sleepy, and about eleven, retire to write a while in my journal, exercises on what I have read, or a series of characteristics which I am filling up according to advice. Thus, you see, I am learning Greek, and making acquaintance with metaphysics, and French and Italian literature. [Wade 1940: 13–14]

With such an exposure to both classical and modern languages, philosophy, and literature, it comes as no surprise when Fuller notes in one letter of this period that she wishes to model herself after the "brilliant Madame de Stael."

The Fuller family lived in Cambridge from 1824 to 1833, spanning the critical years in Margaret's life, from the age of fourteen to twenty-three. In Cambridge she knew many members of the Harvard and Divinity School classes of the late 1820s; she befriended, among others, William Channing and James Freeman Clarke. Her father's political persuasions did not fare very well during the early 1830s, since he was a supporter and advocate of John Quincy Adams while Andrew Jackson had swept western ideas and patronage into the eastern hub of politics. By 1833 the family withdrew to a quiet and less expensive life on a farm at Groton. Margaret Fuller's duties then included teaching the four younger children and writing, the latter resulting in her first published articles in 1834. Her father died suddenly from cholera in 1835, leaving the family in far from comfortable financial circumstances. The wife he had dominated had little ability to hold things together, and the burden of responsibility for the support of the family fell upon Margaret Fuller, where it remained for many years. She met this challenge by teaching, first at a progressive school in Boston headed by Bronson Alcott and later in Providence, Rhode Island. In 1839 she moved back to the Boston area, where she took boarding students, published a translation from the German of Eckermann's *Conversations with Goethe*, and reestablished social connections with the intellectual elite she had known earlier in the decade. As early as 1830, when she was only twenty, she had participated in discussion group gatherings in Cambridge that included Emerson, Ripley, George Putnam, Frederick Henry Hedge—the circle that came to be known as the Transcendental Club. Fuller was not the only woman in this circle, for it included Elizabeth Peabody and Sarah Ripley as well. This was perhaps the first time in America that women were admitted on a plane of intellectual equality with men.

When Fuller returned to Boston after a number of years' teaching young girls, her interests had coalesced on the problem of how to compensate for the narrow education women in the Boston area had received. Her first attempt to share her own unusual education with other women was to establish a lecture series, which she called "Conversations," open by subscription to women and structured around a series of prearranged topics for discussion, led by Fuller. Her pedagogic intent behind these Conversations is clear from her remarks at the opening of the first series in 1839:

> Women are now taught at school all that men are. They run over superficially even *more* studies, without being really taught anything. But with this difference: men are called on from a very early period to reproduce all that they learn. Their college exercises, their political duties, their professional studies, the first actions of life in any direction, call on them to put to use what they have learned. But women learn without any atttempt to reproduce. Their only reproduction is for purposes of display. It is to supply this defect that these conversations have been planned. [Wade 1940:74]

These were not typical adult-education lectures, however. Priced at twenty dollars for a series of ten Conversations, compared to the two dollars charged for a comparable Lyceum Lecture series, they attracted women from all the prominent Boston social and intellectual families: names such as Emerson, Peabody, Parker, Quincy, Lowell, Channing, Shaw, and

Whiting figured among them. Fuller provided an important circle of Boston women with skill in public speaking, in defending their viewpoints, in marshalling evidence. Fuller's efforts helped pave the way for what has been called the "feminine fifties"—the decade of the 1850s, when New England women became prominent in letters, abolition, and women's rights causes.

As a further source of income, Fuller assumed the editorship of *The Dial*, a Transcendental literary quarterly; she edited the journal from its establishment in 1840 until 1842. It was in this same publication that her first major essay on women appeared in the July 1843 issue. Under the awkward title "The Great Lawsuit. Man versus Men. Woman versus Women" Fuller's essay was widely read and strongly reacted to in both America and England. She later revised and expanded the essay into the book *Woman in the Nineteenth Century*, which she published two years later.

A trip to the western states with James and Sarah Clarke in 1844 provided the basis for yet another book, *Summer on the Lakes*, and a further shift in Fuller's perspective on life and society. Her travels in the West made her somewhat skeptical of the Boston and Concord scale of values; she was attracted to the openness of the western society, though distressed by the "comfortless and laborious indoor life" women led there. Despite this latter pessimistic note, Fuller was drawn to the quality of the West, a land "still nearer the acorn" than her native New England. The book sold well, attracted the attention of Horace Greeley, himself an ardent devotee of the West, and led to an invitation from him to join his *Tribune* staff as a literary critic and to take up residence in his own suburban home on the East River.

Fuller's two published books and her work as a literary critic opened doors to the intellectual circles of New York. Much to Mary Greeley's delight, Fuller also served as a social prize for numerous Greeley afternoon teas and a smaller-scale series of Conversations. This added activity was not always without displeasure to Horace Greeley, who felt Fuller was neglecting her journalistic duties and queening it a bit too much in his own home. He was quick to find a verbal knife with which to prick her social bubble on such occasions: taking a phrase from Fuller's book on women in which she argued that women could enter just about any occupation at all, Greeley would tease her by crying out,

"Let them be sea captains if they will" whenever Fuller waited for him to open a door for her (Wade 1940:142).

The New York experience, like the western trip, was a good corrective to the mystical and idealistic talk of the Transcendentalist world of Boston. Fuller learned to write simply and well, to move in wider social circles, to become involved in political issues in a way she had rarely done in Boston. Some of her best essays were written during these few years as a *Tribune* critic. A collection of her critical essays, including reviews of the new romantic poets (Barrett, Browning, Shelley, Tennyson, Longfellow, Lowell, Hawthorne, and so on), appeared in 1846 as *Papers on Literature and Art*.

There is an astringent, striking quality to many of the essays Fuller wrote during the 1844–1846 period in New York. She placed a subtle and perceptive finger on the pulse of her society and reported in a lovely clear language what she observed. While the New England literati still faced a long weaning process from English and Continental thought and standards of taste, Fuller reviewed several books written for and by relatively uneducated rural Americans and commented that in them one could find "the very life; the most vulgar prose, and the most exquisite poetry" (Fuller 1855: 272). She suggested that such books, though still "rude charcoal sketches," exhibited the beginnings of an American literature, though still "gold-fishes amid the moss in the still waters" (Fuller 1855:274). In a brief article on travel books she observed that the best of them were written by women and suggested that one of the pleasures in reading a travel book by a woman is that "you can see their minds grow by what they feed on, when they travel" (Fuller 1855:286). In an incisive set of comments on children's books she noted that too many of them are monotonously "tender," with too much attention to "moral influence," and urged that "a larger proportion of the facts of natural or human history" be allowed to speak for themselves (Fuller 1855:313).

Of considerable sociological interest are articles she wrote on the Irish character, domestic servants, and the employer-employee relationship. Reader response to the first essay on the Irish was so great that she wrote a second. Concerning the Irish, she commented: "by their ready service to do all the hard work, they make it easier for the rest of the population to grow effeminate, and help the country to grow too fast" (Fuller 1855:322). This remark is followed by further comments showing her quick grasp of the power of society to mold character. She wrote:

> They [the Irish] are looked upon with contempt for their want of aptitude in learning new things; their ready and ingenious lying; their eye-service. These are the faults of an oppressed race, which must require the aid of better circumstances through two or three generations to eradicate. . . . Will you not believe it, merely because that bog-bred youth you placed in the mud-hole tells you lies, and drinks to cheer himself in those endless diggings? [Fuller 1855:323]

It seems clear from these *Tribune* articles that exposure to the reality of the social circumstances in which the poor and the immigrant were living in American cities in the 1840s was paving the way for the radical sympathies that blossomed once Fuller reached Europe. Her desire for such a trip had been frustrated by her father in earlier years; now her dream was realized in 1846, when she sailed for England with her friends Marcus and Rebecca Spring. Her reputation had preceded her, and she spent a stimulating year befriending Carlyle and Mazzini in London and meeting George Sand and the Polish poet Adam Mickiewicz in Paris, before she reached the country she was to love best of all, Italy.

The political events and experiences of Fuller's stay in Italy are of less concern to our purposes than her more private affairs, for it is here that she met Angelo Ossoli, with whom she had a love affair that resulted in a pregnancy and a secret marriage to protect Ossoli's papal connections and family relations. To understand this relationship in Fuller's life, we must return to her early adult years. Despite the stern and one-sided nature of her early training, centering as it did on arduous study, there is ample evidence that Fuller, like most young women, had heterosexual encounters that stirred her romantically. She had an early adolescent crush on her Harvard tutor, Henry Hedge, and later fell in love with her cousin George Davis. At twenty she was worried that she was no longer young, for her friends had all married and Davis had proved fickle. At twenty-five she had a brief infatuation with Samuel Ward. By 1840, when she was thirty, her memoirs record a good deal of inner turmoil concerning her future. Like many other intellectual women of her day (or ours), Fuller yearned for love but resisted the narrowness of its fulfillment. Soon she wrote, "womanhood is at present too closely bounded to give me scope." It is at this period that she plunged into what seems like a decision on the side of art and writing: running the Conversations, editing *The Dial*, writing her essays on women. While on Greeley's staff, she had a brief romance with James Rathan, a German Jew, complete with secret meetings and passionate exchanges of love letters, but this too ended when Rathan left for Europe and gave no response to her letters.

Fuller's biographer, Mason Wade, has suggested that there was a strain of homosexuality in Fuller's personality, which he bases on the quality of her feelings toward her own sex. He suggests that her "masculinized personality" led to an attraction to women who had the beauty and feminine charm she lacked, while they were drawn to her intelligence and firmer will power. By way of evidence, he quotes Fuller's comments on love between adults of the same sex:

> It is so true that a woman may be in love with a woman, and a man with a man. It is pleasant to be sure of it, because it is undoubtedly the same love that we shall feel when we are angels, when we ascend to the only fit place for the Mignons, where *sie fragen nicht nach Mann und Weib*. It is regulated by the same laws as that of love between persons of different sexes, only it is purely intellectual and spiritual, unprofaned by any mixture of lower instincts, undisturbed by any need of consulting temporal interests; its law is the desire of the spirit to realize a whole, which makes it seek in another being that which it finds not in itself. [Wade 1940:90–91]

Homosexuality has such complex semantic and psychoanalytic associations that the use of the word stops the pursuit of an idea rather than opening a deeper channel of understanding. If one entertains the possibility that all human beings, men and women, have a deep desire to do and achieve in the world and an equally strong desire to relate intimately and meaningfully with others, then each member of any man-woman pair can satisfy the other partner in one or both dimensions, but if only one dimension is fulfilled, the individual will seek fulfillment in the other dimension outside the relationship. For men in Fuller's time, as in our own, intimacy could be partially fulfilled in marriage and family

relations and the needs for achievement could be met in the
outside world of work and male associates and friends. Because religious and cultural restrictions against a free and
open sexuality no doubt placed serious limitations on the
physical fulfillment of intimacy needs, relations to children
on the one hand and religious excitation in prayer and revivals on the other hand were important sources of emotional
gratification in the lives of nineteenth-century women and
men. But for such women as Margaret Fuller there was little
likelihood of establishing a relationship with a man of the
time and the same social world in which there was scope for a
meshing without conflict in either the achievement or intimacy areas of life. Where was the man in New England
who could take pride and pleasure in a life with an ambitious,
intellectually brilliant woman unless he was absolutely confident that he was her superior? And in the absence of such a
relationship, where would one expect a Margaret Fuller to
turn for emotional gratification if not to members of her
own sex? With warmth and tenderness denied her in heterosexual relationships, she could only turn to women or live a
deprived emotional life.

It is revealing in this connection to note Fuller's comments on George Sand after she met her in Paris. She wrote
in her journal that Sand

> might have loved one man permanently if she could have
> found one contemporary . . . who could interest and
> command her throughout her range; but there was hardly
> any possibility of that, for such a person. Thus she has
> naturally changed the objects of her affections several
> times. [Wade 1940:197]

This meeting took place in Paris in 1847. Four years earlier,
in writing the essay on women for *The Dial*, Fuller showed
the same awareness of the restraints of a given time and
place upon the development of individual women. She pointed
out that it is the *lives* of such women as Mary Wollstonecraft
and George Sand, even more than their *writings*, that give
proof of the need for some new interpretation of woman's
rights and options, and argued that such women "rich in
genius . . . ought not to find themselves by birth in a place
so narrow, that in breaking bonds they become outlaws."
Were the world less confining in the expectations held for
women, Fuller argues, "they would not run their heads so

wildly against its laws." Only four years after Fuller wrote those words, she herself joined Wollstonecraft, Sand, and Wright in running her own head against the laws of her time and place, as Charlotte Gilman, Margaret Sanger, Florence Kelley, and Bernadette Devlin, among others, have done in the decades since Fuller's death. It is nothing short of astonishing that biographers of the very women who argued so persuasively about the restrictions of conventional definitions of appropriate roles for women seem unable to break through their own cultural blinders to sense that these same pioneer women were highly likely to give testimony in their own lives to the changes required in the social codes.

One pertinent example of needed change in social codes concerning sex roles is the relative balance of intellectual ability, accomplishment, or social status of a husband and wife. Our social code has long favored an edge in status, intelligence, accomplishment, and age on the part of the husband. Though the intensity with which this code is held has lessened in recent years, most contemporary young people, even in the 1970s, feel conflicted about any excess of intelligence, earning power, or accomplishment on the part of the wife. Numerous men find it perfectly natural to make a sharp differentiation between the creature comfort and sexual gratification possible in a widely disparate marital relationship, while they fulfill their intellectual needs in relations with male peers. Why, then, is it so difficult to imagine that the same complementarity might be found in marriages contracted by ambitious, intellectual women? It is only by following the thought of the pioneer women such as Fuller in her formal essay and on into her life that we can see the possibility that in her relationship with Ossoli she found a sufficiently gratifying pattern of a new sort. The Fuller-Ossoli relationship is an exact replica of the typical marriage of her day, except that it is the woman rather than the man who would have to gratify intellectual needs outside the marriage.

Social codes apart, one could even argue that the stress of daily life at home and work can be more easily sustained when one marriage partner, whether husband or the wife, is deeply committed to intellectual pursuits than when both partners are so committed. Liberated young women in the 1970s have not begun to break this cultural molding of heterosexual expectations. The most ambitious of such women seek and are now granted admission to such prestigious institutions as Yale, Princeton, and Harvard, where the probabilities are strong that the men they meet will be as ambitious for autonomy and accomplishment as themselves. A really radical break from the confinement of sex roles might lie in women's search for mates from very different social and intellectual circles, men who are not vain, self-centered, and ambitious but tenderly devoted to home and children and the living of life. The sexual game until the 1970s has left women of all social classes competing for high-status men. One can well imagine the shock to status sensibilities of high-status men if they had to compete with men of lower classes for the women of their own class. How much better, from a masculine perspective, to believe that intelligent women will remain single because they are neurotically disturbed!

Several entries in Fuller's journal, written in February 1850, suggest that she had the capacity to think and to act along such unconventional lines. These entries were written just a few months before she embarked on her fateful trip back to America with her husband and son. She was perfectly aware of the respects in which her husband would not "fit" either the society or the expectations of a proper husband for her that were held in her Boston and New York world:

> I have said as little as possible about Ossoli and our relation, wishing my old friends to form their own impression naturally, when they see us together. I have faith that all who ever knew me will feel that I have become somewhat milder, kinder, and more worthy to serve all who need, for my new relations. I have expected that those who have cared for me chiefly for my activity of intellect, would not care for him; but that those in whom the moral nature predominates would gradually learn to love and admire him, and see what a treasure his affection must be to me. But even that would be only gradually; for it is by acts, not by words, that one so simple, true, delicate and retiring, can be known. . . . His enthusiasm is quiet. . . . He is very unlike most Italians, but very unlike most Americans, too. I do not expect all who cared for me to care for him, nor is it of importance to him that they should. He is wholly without vanity. [Fuller 1855:381–382]

In a letter to her brother she is thinking ahead to the problem of where in America they should settle. She wrote:

> Climate is one thing I must think of. The change from the Roman winter to that of New England might be very trying for Ossoli. In New York he would see Italians often, hear his native tongue, and feel less exiled. If we had our affairs in New York and lived in the neighboring country, we could find places as quiet as C——, more beautiful, and from which access to a city would be as easy by means of steam. [Fuller 1855:379]

There is a gentle solicitude and tenderness in these fragments concerning Ossoli that reveal new qualities in Fuller and suggest chains of thought she never lived to develop. She is now a rebel from the Yankee intellectual elite, just as Ossoli is a rebel from the aristocratic class of Italy. For Margaret Fuller, her man was Italian; for Frances Wright, French; for Florence Kelley, Polish; for Kate Millett, Japanese. A society, or a stratum within a society, which places rigid restrictions on the definitions of "proper" heterosexual liaisons may require of its innovators that they seek outside the confines of their culture and stratum.

Scholars all too often move in a world as restricted as that in which their subjects lived or from which they escaped. Bearing in mind the gentle quality Margaret Fuller projected about her relationship with Ossoli, note the tone and phrasing one American scholar applied to this same relationship: "Margaret Fuller moved in 1846 to Italy, where she fell in love with Angelo Ossoli, titled, handsome, penniless, dissipated, and younger than Margaret by ten years. A son was born to the couple on September 5, 1848, and a year later came the announcement that they were married, with the date unspecified" (Riegel 1963:102).

Margaret Fuller was a woman who never stopped growing and changing; she seemed, in this last year of her life, to be bringing the suppressed and unfulfilled sides of herself into balance with her drive for accomplishment and recognition. This is nowhere more apparent than in the letters describing her son, Nino. In 1849 she wrote to friends:

> I thank you warmly for your sympathy about my little boy. What he is to me even you can hardly dream; you that have three, in whom the natural thirst of the heart

was earlier satisfied, can scarcely know what my one ewe lamb is to me. [Fuller 1855:376–377]

A few weeks later she commented:

What a difference it makes to come home to a child! . . . How it fills up all the gaps of life just in the way that is most consoling, most refreshing. Formerly I used to feel sad at that hour . . . and I felt so lonely! Now I never feel lonely. . . . Seeing how full he is of life, how much he can afford to throw away, I feel the inexhaustibleness of nature, and console myself for my own incapacities. [Fuller 1855:380–381]

Both Fuller and her husband dreaded the trip to America in the spring of 1850. Ossoli had been warned in his youth by a fortune-teller to beware of the sea. Margaret Fuller did not seem able to assuage his fears, since she shared them on other grounds herself, perhaps because so many unresolved problems of finances and social acceptance lay ahead for her and her family. In one of her last letters she wrote that her only consolation was that, in case of mishap, "I shall perish with my husband and my child" (Wade 1940:265). Their ship crashed against rocks within sight of Fire Island, off the shore of Long Island, during a storm. People on shore refused to send out a boat in the rough sea, and Margaret refused to leave the boat separately from her husband or child. All three were drowned on July 19, 1850. The same scholar quoted earlier erroneously claims that this trip was taken only by Margaret and her son; this is one of the endless number of errors of fact and absence of empathy that characterize his portrait of American feminists (Riegel 1963:102).

It is precisely because one senses so much change in Margaret Fuller during these crowded last ten years of her life that one feels keenly the loss occasioned by her premature death. Her first essay on women was written before her trip to the American West; before she had honed her writing skill as a critic; before her sympathies had been deepened by contact with the urban American scene; before her political development in Europe; and before her experience of love and maternity. When she finished the revision of what became *Woman in the Nineteenth Century*, she wrote her friend William Channing of her delight in the final stages of the writing, when it seemed to "spin out beneath my hand," and she felt a delightful glow,

> as if I had put a good deal of my true life in it, as if, suppose I went away now, the measure of my foot print would be left on the earth. [Wade 1941:567]

Her wish in 1844 had been that publication be limited to one edition, so that she could "make it constantly better while I live."

Had she lived; had she been able to deflect the scorn of her straight-laced contemporaries where her marriage was concerned; had she been able to weave together all the new elements of her experiences in the late 1840s and apply her matured perspective to the problems of women—then we in the 1970s might be even more indebted to Margaret Fuller than we are. The seeds of her potential are in the pages she left behind. To catch an anticipatory sense of how her life and thought flowed together and evolved in the years after she left Boston, listen to the woman in Boston, in 1843:

> Ye cannot believe it, men; but the only reason why women ever assume what is more appropriate to you, is because you prevent them from finding out what is fit for themselves. Were they free, were they wise fully to develop the strength and beauty of woman, they would never wish to be men.

The Great Lawsuit. Man versus Men. Woman versus Women.

. . . [N]ot a few believe, and men themselves have expressed the opinion, that the time is come when Euridice is to call for an Orpheus, rather than Orpheus for Euridice; that the idea of man, however imperfectly brought out, has been far more so than that of woman, and that an improvement in

---

From Margaret Fuller, "The Great Lawsuit. Man versus Men. Woman versus Women," *The Dial*, Vol. IV, No. 1 (July 1843), pp. 1–47.

the daughters will best aid the reformation of the sons of this age.

It is worthy of remark, that, as the principle of liberty is better understood and more nobly interpreted, a broader protest is made in behalf of woman. As men become aware that all men have not had their fair chance, they are inclined to say that no women have had a fair chance. The French revolution, that strangely disguised angel, bore witness in favor of woman, but interpreted her claims no less ignorantly than those of man. Its idea of happiness did not rise beyond outward enjoyment, unobstructed by the tyranny of others. The title it gave was Citoyen, Citoyenne, and it is not unimportant to woman that even this species of equality was awarded her. Before, she could be condemned to perish on the scaffold for treason, but not as a citizen, but a subject. The right, with which this title then invested a human being, was that of bloodshed and license. The Goddess of Liberty was impure. Yet truth was prophesied in the ravings of that hideous fever induced by long ignorance and abuse. Europe is conning a valued lesson from the blood stained page. The same tendencies, farther unfolded, will bear good fruit in this country.

Yet, in this country, as by the Jews, when Moses was leading them to the promised land, everything has been done that inherited depravity could, to hinder the promise of heaven from its fulfilment. The cross, here as elsewhere, has been planted only to be blasphemed by cruelty and fraud. The name of the Prince of Peace has been profaned by all kinds of injustice towards the Gentile whom he said he came to save. But I need not speak of what has been done towards the red man, the black man. These deeds are the scoff of the world; and they have been accompanied by such pious words, that the gentlest would not dare to intercede with, "Father forgive them, for they know not what they do.". . .

Though the national independence be blurred by the servility of individuals; though freedom and equality have been proclaimed only to leave room for a monstrous display of slave dealing, and slave keeping; though the free American so often feels himself free, like the Roman, only to pamper his appetites and his indolence through the misery of his fellow beings, still it is not in vain, that the verbal statement has been made, "All men are born free and equal." There it stands, a golden certainty, wherewith to encourage the good, to shame the bad. The new world may be called clearly to perceive that it incurs the utmost penalty, if it reject the sorrowful brother. And if men are deaf, the angels hear. But men cannot be deaf. It is inevitable that an external freedom, such as has been achieved for the nation, should be so also for every member of it. That, which has once been clearly conceived in the intelligence, must be acted out. . . .

Of all its banners, none has been more steadily upheld, and under none has more valor and willingness for real sacrifices been shown, than that of the champions of the enslaved African. And this band it is, which, partly in consequence of a natural following out of principles, partly because many women have been prominent in that cause, makes, just now, the warmest appeal in behalf of woman.

Though there has been a growing liberality on this point, yet society at large is not so prepared for the demands of this party, but that they are, and will be for some time, coldly regarded as the Jacobins of their day.

"Is it not enough," cries the sorrowful trader, "that you have done all you could to break up the national Union, and thus destroy the prosperity of our country, but now you must be trying to break up family union, to take my wife away from the cradle, and the kitchen hearth, to vote at polls, and preach from a pulpit? Of course, if she does such things, she cannot attend to those of her own sphere. She is happy enough as she is. She has more leisure than I have, every means of improvement, every indulgence."

"Have you asked her whether she was satisfied with these indulgences?"

"No, but I know she is. She is too amiable to wish what would make me unhappy, and too judicious to wish to step beyond the sphere of her sex. I will never consent to have our peace disturbed by any such discussions."

" 'Consent'—you? it is not consent from you that is in question, it is assent from your wife."

"Am not I the head of my house?"

"You are not the head of your wife. God has given her a mind of her own."

"I am the head and she the heart."

"God grant you play true to one another then. If the head represses no natural pulse of the heart, there can be no question as to your giving your consent. Both will be of one accord, and there needs but to present any question to get a full and true answer. There is no need of precaution, of indulgence, or consent. But our doubt is whether the heart consents with the head, or only acquiesces in its decree; and it is to ascertain the truth on this point, that we propose some liberating measures."

Thus vaguely are these questions proposed and discussed at present. But their being proposed at all implies much thought, and suggests more. Many women are considering within themselves what they need that they have not, and what they can have, if they find they need it. Many men are considering whether women are capable of being and having more than they are and have, and whether, if they are, it will be best to consent to improvement in their condition.

The numerous party, whose opinions are already labelled and adjusted too much to their mind to admit of any new light, strive, by lectures on some model-woman of bridal-like beauty and gentleness, by writing or lending little treatises, to mark out with due precision the limits of woman's sphere, and woman's mission, and to prevent other than the rightful shepherd from climbing the wall, or the flock from using any chance gap to run astray.

Without enrolling ourselves at once on either side, let us look upon the subject from that point of view which to-day offers. No better, it is to be feared, than a high house-top. A high hill-top, or at least a cathedral spire, would be desirable.

It is not surprising that it should be the Anti-Slavery party that pleads for woman, when we consider merely that she does not hold property on equal terms with men; so that, if a husband dies without a will, the wife, instead of stepping at once into his place as head of the family, inherits only a part of his fortune, as if she were a child, or ward only, not an equal partner.

We will not speak of the innumerable instances, in which profligate or idle men live upon the earnings of industrious wives; or if the wives leave them and take with them the children, to perform the double duty of mother and father, follow from place to place, and threaten to rob them of the children, if deprived of the rights of a husband, as they call them, planting themselves in their poor lodgings, frightening them into paying tribute by taking from them the children, running into debt at the expense of these otherwise so overtasked helots. Though such instances abound, the public opinion of his own sex is against the man, and when cases of extreme tyranny are made known, there is private action in

the wife's favor. But if woman be, indeed, the weaker party,
she ought to have legal protection, which would make such
oppression impossible.

And knowing that there exists, in the world of men, a
tone of feeling towards women as towards slaves, such as is
expressed in the common phrase, "Tell that to women and
children;" that the infinite soul can only work through them
in already ascertained limits; that the prerogative of reason,
man's highest portion, is allotted to them in a much lower
degree; that it is better for them to be engaged in active labor,
which is to be furnished and directed by those better able to
think, &c. &c.; we need not go further, for who can review
the experience of last week, without recalling words which
imply, whether in jest or earnest, these views, and views like
these? Knowing this, can we wonder that many reformers
think that measures are not likely to be taken in behalf of
women, unless their wishes could be publicly represented by
women?

That can never be necessary, cry the other side. All men
are privately influenced by women; each has his wife, sister,
or female friends, and is too much biassed by these relations
to fail of representing their interests. And if this is not
enough, let them propose and enforce their wishes with the
pen. The beauty of home would be destroyed, the delicacy of
the sex be violated, the dignity of halls of legislation destroyed, by an attempt to introduce them there. Such duties
are inconsistent with those of a mother; and then we have
ludicrous pictures of ladies in hysterics at the polls, and senate chambers filled with cradles.

But if, in reply, we admit as truth that woman seems destined by nature rather to the inner circle, we must add that
the arrangements of civilized life have not been as yet such
as to secure it to her. Her circle, if the duller, is not the
quieter. If kept from excitement, she is not from drudgery.
Not only the Indian carries the burdens of the camp, but the
favorites of Louis the Fourteenth accompany him in his
journeys, and the washerwoman stands at her tub and carries
home her work at all seasons, and in all states of health.

As to the use of the pen, there was quite as much opposition to woman's possessing herself of that help to free-agency
as there is now to her seizing on the rostrum or the desk; and
she is likely to draw, from a permission to plead her cause

that way, opposite inferences to what might be wished by those who now grant it.

As to the possibility of her filling, with grace and dignity, any such position, we should think those who had seen the great actresses, and heard the Quaker preachers of modern times, would not doubt, that woman can express publicly the fulness of thought and emotion, without losing any of the peculiar beauty of her sex.

As to her home, she is not likely to leave it more than she now does for balls, theatres, meetings for promoting missions, revival meetings, and others to which she flies, in hope of an animation for her existence, commensurate with what she sees enjoyed by men. Governors of Ladies' Fairs are no less engrossed by such a charge, than the Governor of the State by his; presidents of Washingtonian societies, no less away from home than presidents of conventions. If men look straitly to it, they will find that, unless their own lives are domestic, those of the women will not be. The female Greek, of our day, is as much in the street as the male, to cry, What news? We doubt not it was the same in Athens of old. The women, shut out from the market-place, made up for it at the religious festivals. For human beings are not so constituted, that they can live without expansion; and if they do not get it one way, must another, or perish.

And, as to men's representing women fairly, at present, while we hear from men who owe to their wives not only all that is comfortable and graceful, but all that is wise in the arrangement of their lives, the frequent remark, "You cannot reason with a woman," when from those of delicacy, nobleness, and poetic culture, the contemptuous phrase, "Women and children," and that in no light sally of the hour, but in works intended to give a permanent statement of the best experiences, when not one man in the million, shall I say, no, not in the hundred million, can rise above the view that woman was made *for man*, when such traits as these are daily forced upon the attention, can we feel that man will always do justice to the interests of woman? Can we think that he takes a sufficiently discerning and religious view of her office and destiny, ever to do her justice, except when prompted by sentiment; accidentally or transiently, that is, for his sentiment will vary according to the relations in which he is placed. The lover, the poet, the artist, are likely to view her nobly. The father and the philosopher have some chance of liberality; the man of the world, the legislator for expediency, none.

Under these circumstances, without attaching importance in themselves to the changes demanded by the champions of woman, we hail them as signs of the times. We would have every arbitrary barrier thrown down. We would have every path laid open to woman as freely as to man. Were this done, and a slight temporary fermentation allowed to subside, we believe that the Divine would ascend into nature to a height unknown in the history of past ages, and nature, thus instructed, would regulate the spheres not only so as to avoid collision, but to bring forth ravishing harmony.

Yes then, and only then, will human beings be ripe for this, when inward and outward freedom for woman, as much as for man, shall be acknowledged as a right, not yielded as a concession. As the friend of the negro assumes that one man cannot, by right, hold another in bondage, so should the friend of woman assume that man cannot, by right, lay even well-meant restrictions on woman. If the negro be a soul, if the woman be a soul, apparelled in flesh, to one master only are they accountable. There is but one law for all souls, and, if there is to be an interpreter of it, he comes not as man, or son of man, but as Son of God.

Were thought and feeling once so far elevated that man should esteem himself the brother and friend, but nowise the lord and tutor of woman, were he really bound with her in equal worship, arrangements as to function and employment would be of no consequence. What woman needs is not as a woman to act or rule, but as a nature to grow, as an intellect to discern, as a soul to live freely, and unimpeded to unfold such powers as were given her when we left our common home. If fewer talents were given her, yet, if allowed the free and full employment of these, so that she may render back to the giver his own with usury, she will not complain, nay, I dare to say she will bless and rejoice in her earthly birthplace, her earthly lot.

Let us consider what obstructions impede this good era, and what signs give reason to hope that it draws near.

I was talking on this subject with Miranda, a woman, who, if any in the world, might speak without heat or bitterness of the position of her sex. Her father was a man who cherished no sentimental reverence for woman, but a firm belief in the equality of the sexes. She was his eldest child, and came to him at an age when he needed a companion. From the time she could speak and go alone, he addressed her not as a plaything, but as a living mind. Among the few verses he ever wrote were a copy addressed to this child, when the first locks were cut from her head, and the reverence expressed on this occasion for that cherished head he never belied. It was to him the temple of immortal intellect. He respected his child, however, too much to be an indulgent parent. He called on her for clear judgment, for courage, for honor and fidelity, in short for such virtues as he knew. In so far as he possessed the keys to the wonders of this universe, he allowed free use of them to her, and by the incentive of a high expectation he forbade, as far as possible, that she should let the privilege lie idle.

Thus this child was early led to feel herself a child of the spirit. She took her place easily, not only in the world of organized being, but in the world of mind. A dignified sense of self-dependence was given as all her portion, and she found it a sure anchor. Herself securely anchored, her relations with others were established with equal security. She was fortunate, in a total absence of those charms which might have drawn to her bewildering flatteries, and of a strong electric nature, which repelled those who did not belong to her, and attracted those who did. With men and women her relations were noble; affectionate without passion, intellectual without coldness. The world was free to her, and she lived freely in it. Outward adversity came, and inward conflict, but that faith and self-respect had early been awakened, which must always lead at last to an outward serenity, and an inward peace.

Of Miranda I had always thought as an example, that the restraints upon the sex were insuperable only to those who think them so, or who noisily strive to break them. She had taken a course of her own, and no man stood in her way. Many of her acts had been unusual, but excited no uproar. Few helped, but none checked her; and the many men, who knew her mind and her life, showed to her confidence as to a brother, gentleness as to a sister. And not only refined, but very coarse men approved one in whom they saw resolution and clearness of design. Her mind was often the leading one, always effective.

When I talked with her upon these matters, and had said

very much what I have written, she smilingly replied, And yet we must admit that I have been fortunate, and this should not be. My good father's early trust gave the first bias, and the rest followed of course. It is true that I have had less outward aid, in after years, than most women, but that is of little consequence. Religion was early awakened in my soul, a sense that what the soul is capable to ask it must attain, and that, though I might be aided by others, I must depend on myself as the only constant friend. This self-dependence, which was honored in me, is deprecated as a fault in most women. They are taught to learn their rule from without, not to unfold it from within.

This is the fault of man, who is still vain, and wishes to be more important to woman than by right he should be.

Men have not shown this disposition towards you, I said.

No, because the position I early was enabled to take, was one of self-reliance. And were all women as sure of their wants as I was, the result would be the same. The difficulty is to get them to the point where they shall naturally develop self-respect, the question how it is to be done.

Once I thought that men would help on this state of things more than I do now. I saw so many of them wretched in the connections they had formed in weakness and vanity. They seemed so glad to esteem women whenever they could!

But early I perceived that men never, in any extreme of despair, wished to be women. Where they admired any woman they were inclined to speak of her as above her sex. Silently I observed this, and feared it argued a rooted skepticism, which for ages had been fastening on the heart, and which only an age of miracles could eradicate.

Ever I have been treated with great sincerity; and I look upon it as a most signal instance of this, that an intimate friend of the other sex said in a fervent moment, that I deserved in some star to be a man. Another used as highest praise, in speaking of a character in literature, the words "a manly woman."

It is well known that of every strong woman they say she has a masculine mind.

This by no means argues a willing want of generosity towards woman. Man is as generous towards her, as he knows how to be.

Wherever she has herself arisen in national or private history, and nobly shone forth in any ideal of excellence, men have received her, not only willingly, but with triumph. Their encomiums indeed are always in some sense mortifying, they show too much surprise.

In every-day life the feelings of the many are stained with vanity. Each wishes to be lord in a little world, to be superior at least over one; and he does not feel strong enough to retain a life-long ascendant over a strong nature. Only a Brutus would rejoice in a Portia. . . .

But not only is man vain and fond of power, but the same want of development, which thus affects him morally in the intellect, prevents his discerning the destiny of woman. The boy wants no woman, but only a girl to play ball with him, and mark his pocket handkerchief. . . .

The sexes should not only correspond to and appreciate one another, but prophesy to one another. In individual instances this happens. Two persons love in one another the future good which they aid one another to unfold. This is very imperfectly done as yet in the general life. Man has gone but little way, now he is waiting to see whether woman can keep step with him, but instead of calling out like a good brother; You can do it if you only think so, or impersonally; Any one can do what he tries to do, he often discourages with school-boy brag; Girls cant do that, girls cant play ball. But let any one defy their taunts, break through, and be brave and secure, they rend the air with shouts.

No! man is not willingly ungenerous. He wants faith and love, because he is not yet himself an elevated being. He cries with sneering skepticism; Give us a sign. But if the sign appears, his eyes glisten, and he offers not merely approval, but homage.

The severe nation which taught that the happiness of the race was forfeited through the fault of a woman, and showed its thought of what sort of regard man owed her, by making him accuse her on the first question to his God, who gave her to the patriarch as a handmaid, and, by the Mosaical law, bound her to allegiance like a serf, even they greeted, with solemn rapture, all great and holy women as heroines, prophetesses, nay judges in Israel; and, if they made Eve listen to the serpent, gave Mary to the Holy Spirit. In other nations it has been the same down to our day. To the woman, who could conquer, a triumph was awarded. And not only those whose strength was recommended to the heart by association with goodness and beauty, but those who were bad, if they were steadfast and strong, had their claims allowed. In any age a Semiramis, an Elizabeth of England, a Catharine of Russia makes her place good, whether in a large or small circle.

How has a little wit, a little genius, always been celebrated in a woman! What an intellectual triumph was that of the lonely Aspasia, and how heartily acknowledged! She, indeed, met a Pericles. But what annalist, the rudest of men, the most plebeian of husbands, will spare from his page one of the few anecdotes of Roman women?—Sappho, Eloisa! The names are of thread-bare celebrity. The man habitually most narrow towards women will be flushed, as by the worst assault on Christianity, if you say it has made no improvement in her condition. Indeed, those most opposed to new acts in her favor are jealous of the reputation of those which have been done.

We will not speak of the enthusiasm excited by actresses, improvistatrici, female singers, for here mingles the charm of beauty and grace, but female authors, even learned women, if not insufferably ugly and slovenly, from the Italian professor's daughter, who taught behind the curtain, down to Mrs. Carter and Madame Dacier, are sure of an admiring audience, if they can once get a platform on which to stand.

But how to get this platform, or how to make it of reasonably easy access is the difficulty. Plants of great vigor will almost always struggle into blossom, despite impediments. But there should be encouragement, and a free, genial atmosphere for those of more timid sort, fair play for each in its own kind. Some are like the little, delicate flowers, which love to hide in the dripping mosses by the sides of mountain torrents, or in the shade of tall trees. But others require an open field, a rich and loosened soil, or they never show their proper hues.

It may be said man does not have his fair play either; his energies are repressed and distorted by the interposition of artificial obstacles. Aye, but he himself has put them there; they have grown out of his own imperfections. If there is a misfortune in woman's lot, it is in obstacles being interposed by men, which do *not* mark her state, and if they express her past ignorance, do not her present needs. As every man is of woman born, she has slow but sure means of redress, yet the sooner a general justness of thought makes smooth the path, the better.

. . . .

It is not the transient breath of poetic incense, that women want; each can receive that from a lover. It is not life-long sway; it needs but to become a coquette, a shrew, or a good cook, to be sure of that. It is not money, nor notoriety, nor the badges of authority, that men has appropriated to themselves. If demands made in their behalf lay stress on any of these particulars, those who make them have not searched deeply into the need. It is for that which at once includes all these and precludes them; which would not be forbidden power, lest there be temptation to steal and misuse it; which would not have the mind perverted by flattery from a worthiness of esteem. It is for that which is the birthright of every being capable to receive it,—the freedom, the religious, the intelligent freedom of the universe, to use its means, to learn its secret as far as nature has enabled them, with God alone for their guide and their judge.

Ye cannot believe it, men; but the only reason why women ever assume what is more appropriate to you, is because you prevent them from finding out what is fit for themselves. Were they free, were they wise fully to develop the strength and beauty of woman, they would never wish to be men, or manlike. The well-instructed moon flies not from her orbit to seize on the glories of her partner. No; for she knows that one law rules, one heaven contains, one universe replies to them alike. It is with women as with the slave.

"Vor dem Sklaven, wenn er die Kette bricht,
Vor dem freien Menschen erzittert nicht."

Tremble not before the free man, but before the slave who has chains to break.

In slavery, acknowledged slavery, women are on a par with men. Each is a work-tool, an article of property,—no more! In perfect freedom, such as is painted in Olympus, in Swedenborg's angelic state, in the heaven where there is no marrying nor giving in marriage, each is a purified intelligence, an enfranchised soul,—no less! . . . .

That an era approaches which shall approximate nearer to such a temper than any has yet done, there are many tokens, indeed so many that only a few of the most prominent can here be enumerated.

The reigns of Elizabeth of England and Isabella of Castile foreboded this era. They expressed the beginning of the new state, while they forwarded its progress. These were strong characters, and in harmony with the wants of their time. One showed that this strength did not unfit a woman for the duties of a wife and mother; the other, that it could enable her to live and die alone. Elizabeth is certainly no pleasing example. In rising above the weakness, she did not lay aside the weaknesses ascribed to her sex; but her strength must be respected now, as it was in her own time.

We may accept it as an omen for ourselves, that it was Isabella who furnished Columbus with the means of coming hither. This land must pay back its debt to woman, without whose aid it would not have been brought into alliance with the civilized world.

• • •

. . . [C]ivilized Europe is still in a transition state about marriage, not only in practice, but in thought. A great majority of societies and individuals are still doubtful whether earthly marriage is to be a union of souls, or merely a contract of convenience and utility. Were woman established in the rights of an immortal being, this could not be. She would not in some countries be given away by her father, with scarcely more respect for her own feelings than is shown by the Indian chief, who sells his daughter for a horse, and beats her if she runs away from her new home. Nor, in societies where her choice is left free, would she be perverted, by the current of opinion that seizes her, into the belief that she must marry, if it be only to find a protector, and a home of her own.

Neither would man, if he thought that the connection was of permanent importance, enter upon it so lightly. He would not deem it a trifle, that he was to enter into the closest relations with another soul, which, if not eternal in themselves, must eternally affect his growth.

Neither, did he believe woman capable of friendship, would he, by rash haste, lose the chance of finding a friend in the person who might, probably, live half a century by his side. Did love to his mind partake of infinity, he would not miss his chance of its revelations, that he might the sooner rest from his weariness by a bright fireside, and have a sweet and graceful attendant, "devoted to him alone." Were he a step higher, he would not carelessly enter into a relation, where he might not be able to do the duty of a friend, as well as a protector from external ill, to the other party, and have a being in his power pining for sympathy, intelligence, and aid, that he could not give.

Where the thought of equality has become pervasive, it shows itself in four kinds.

The household partnership. In our country the woman looks for a "smart but kind" husband, the man for a "capable, sweet-tempered" wife.

The man furnishes the house, the woman regulates it. Their relation is one of mutual esteem, mutual dependence. Their talk is of business, their affection shows itself by practical kindness. They know that life goes more smoothly and cheerfully to each for the other's aid; they are grateful and content. The wife praises her husband as a "good provider," the husband in return compliments her as a "capital housekeeper." This relation is good as far as it goes.

Next comes a closer tie which takes the two forms, either of intellectual companionship, or mutual idolatry. The last, we suppose, is to no one a pleasing subject of contemplation. The parties weaken and narrow one another; they lock the gate against all the glories of the universe that they may live in a cell together. To themselves they seem the only wise, to all others steeped in infatuation, the gods smile as they look forward to the crisis of cure, to men the woman seems an unlovely syren, to women the man an effeminate boy.

The other form, of intellectual companionship, has become more and more frequent. Men engaged in public life, literary men, and artists have found in their wives companions and confidants in thought no less than in feeling. And, as in the course of things the intellectual development of woman has spread wider and risen higher, they have, not unfrequently, shared the same employment. As in the case of Roland and his wife, who were friends in the household and the nation's councils, read together, regulated home affairs, or prepared public documents together indifferently.

It is very pleasant, in letters begun by Roland and finished by his wife, to see the harmony of mind and the difference of nature, one thought, but various ways of treating it.

This is one of the best instances of a marriage of friendship. It was only friendship, whose basis was esteem; probably neither party knew love, except by name.

Roland was a good man, worthy to esteem and be esteemed, his wife as deserving of admiration as able to do

without it. Madame Roland is the fairest specimen we have
yet of her class, as clear to discern her aim, as valiant to pursue it, as Spenser's Britomart, austerity set apart from all that
did not belong to her, whether as woman or as mind. She is
an antetype of a class to which the coming time will afford a
field, the Spartan matron, brought by the culture of a book-
furnishing age to intellectual consciousness and expansion.

Self-sufficing strength and clear-sightedness were in her
combined with a power of deep and calm affection. The page
of her life is one of unsullied dignity.

Her appeal to posterity is one against the injustice of
those who committed such crimes in the name of liberty. She
makes it in behalf of herself and her husband. I would put
beside it on the shelf a little volume, containing a similar
appeal from the verdict of contemporaries to that of mankind,
that of Godwin in behalf of his wife, the celebrated, the by
most men detested Mary Wollstonecraft. In his view it was an
appeal from the injustice of those who did such wrong in the
name of virtue.

Were this little book interesting for no other cause, it
would be so for the generous affection evinced under the
peculiar circumstances. This man had courage to love and
honor this woman in the face of the world's verdict, and of
all that was repulsive in her own past history. He believed he
saw of what soul she was, and that the thoughts she had
struggled to act out were noble. He loved her and he defended her for the meaning and tendency of her inner life. It
was a good fact.

Mary Wollstonecraft, like Madame Dudevant (commonly
known as George Sand) in our day, was a woman whose existence better proved the need of some new interpretation of
woman's rights, than anything she wrote. Such women as
these, rich in genius, of most tender sympathies, and capable
of high virtue and a chastened harmony, ought not to find
themselves by birth in a place so narrow, that in breaking
bonds they become outlaws. Were there as much room in the
world for such, as in Spenser's poem for Britomart, they
would not run their heads so wildly against its laws. They
find their way at last to purer air, but the world will not
take off the brand it has set upon them. The champion of the
rights of woman found in Godwin one who plead her own
cause like a brother. George Sand smokes, wears male attire,
wishes to be addressed as Mon frère; perhaps, if she found

those who were as brothers indeed, she would not care whether she were brother or sister. . . .

Women like Sand will speak now, and cannot be silenced; their characters and their eloquence alike foretell an era when such as they shall easier learn to lead true lives. But though such forebode, not such shall be the parents of it. Those who would reform the world must show that they do not speak in the heat of wild impulse; their lives must be unstained by passionate error; they must be severe lawgivers to themselves. As to their transgressions and opinions, it may be observed, that the resolve of Eloisa to be only the mistress of Abelard, was that of one who saw the contract of marriage a seal of degradation. Wherever abuses of this sort are seen, the timid will suffer, the bold protest. But society is in the right to out-law them till she has revised her law, and she must be taught to do so, by one who speaks with authority, not in anger and haste. . . .

We might mention instances, nearer home, of mind-partners in work and in life, sharing together, on equal terms, public and private interests, and which have not on any side that aspect of offence which characterizes the attitude of the last named; persons who steer straight onward, and in our freer life have not been obliged to run their heads against any wall. But the principles which guide them might, under petri-fied or oppressive institutions, have made them warlike, paradoxical, or, in some sense, Pariahs. The phenomenon is different, the law the same, in all these cases. Men and women have been obliged to build their house from the very foundation. If they found stone ready in the quarry, they took it peaceably, otherwise they alarmed the country by pull-ing down old towers to get materials.

These are all instances of marriage as intellectual com-panionship. The parties meet mind to mind, and a mutual trust is excited which can buckler them against a million. They work together for a common purpose, and, in all these instances, with the same implement, the pen. . . .

. . . [W]e do not mean to imply that community of em-ployment is an essential to union of this sort, more than to the union of friendship. Harmony exists in difference no less than in likeness, if only the same key-note govern both parts. Woman the poem, man the poet; woman the heart, man the head; such divisions are only important when they are never to be transcended. If nature is never bound down, nor the voice of inspiration stifled, that is enough. We are pleased that women should write and speak, if they feel the need of it, from having something to tell; but silence for a hundred years would be as well, if that silence be from divine command, and not from man's tradition. . . .

I have not spoken of the higher grade of marriage union, the religious, which may be expressed as pilgrimage towards a common shrine. This includes the others; home sympathies, and household wisdom, for these pilgrims must know how to assist one another to carry their burdens along the dusty way; intellectual communion, for how sad it would be on such a journey to have a companion to whom you could not communicate thoughts and aspirations, as they sprang to life, who would have no feeling for the more and more glorious prospects that open as we advance, who would never see the flowers that may be gathered by the most industrious traveller. It must include all these. . . .

Another sign of the time is furnished by the triumphs of female authorship. These have been great and constantly increasing. They have taken possession of so many provinces for which men had pronounced them unfit, that though these still declare there are some inaccessible to them, it is difficult to say just *where* they must stop.

The shining names of famous women have cast light upon the path of the sex, and many obstructions have been removed. When a Montague could learn better than her brother, and use her lore to such purpose afterwards as an observer, it seemed amiss to hinder women from preparing themselves to see, or from seeing all they could when prepared. Since Somerville has achieved so much, will any young girl be prevented from attaining a knowledge of the physical sciences, if she wishes it? De Staël's name was not so clear of offence; she could not forget the woman in the thought; while she was instructing you as a mind, she wished to be admired as a woman; sentimental tears often dimmed the eagle glance. Her intellect, too, with all its splendor, trained in a drawing room, fed on flattery, was tainted and flawed; yet its beams make the obscurest school house in New England warmer and lighter to the little rugged girls, who are gathered together on its wooden bench. They may never through life hear her name, but she is not the less their benefactress.

This influence has been such that the aim certainly is, how, in arranging school instruction for girls, to give them as fair a field as boys. These arrangements are made as yet with little judgment or intelligence, just as the tutors of Jane Grey, and the other famous women of her time, taught them Latin and Greek, because they knew nothing else themselves, so now the improvement in the education of girls is made by giving them gentlemen as teachers, who only teach what has been taught themselves at college, while methods and topics need revision for those new cases, which could better be made by those who had experienced the same wants. Women are often at the head of these institutions, but they have as yet seldom been thinking women, capable to organize a new whole for the wants of the time, and choose persons to officiate in the departments. And when some portion of education is got of a good sort from the school, the tone of society, the much larger proportion received from the world, contradicts its purport. Yet books have not been furnished, and a little elementary instruction been given in vain. Women are better aware how large and rich the universe is, not so easily blinded by the narrowness and partial views of a home circle.

Whether much or little has or will be done, whether women will add to the talent of narration, the power of systematizing, whether they will carve marble as well as draw, is not important. But that it should be acknowledged that they have intellect which needs developing, that they should not be considered complete, if beings of affection and habit alone, is important.

Yet even this acknowledgment, rather obtained by woman than proffered by man, has been sullied by the usual selfishness. So much is said of women being better educated that they may be better companions and mothers *of men!* They should be fit for such companionship, and we have mentioned with satisfaction instances where it has been established. Earth knows no fairer, holier relation than that of a mother. But a being of infinite scope must not be treated with an exclusive view to any one relation. Give the soul free course, let the organization be freely developed, and the being will be fit for any and every relation to which it may be called. The intellect, no more than the sense of hearing, is to be cultivated, that she may be a more valuable companion to man, but because the Power who gave a power by its mere existence signifies that it must be brought out towards perfection.

In this regard, of self-dependence and a greater simplicity and fulness of being, we must hail as a preliminary the increase of the class contemptuously designated as old maids.

We cannot wonder at the aversion with which old bachelors and old maids have been regarded. Marriage is the natural means of forming a sphere, of taking root on the earth: it requires more strength to do this without such an opening, very many have failed of this, and their imperfections have been in every one's way. They have been more partial, more harsh, more officious and impertinent than others. Those, who have a complete experience of the human instincts, have a distrust as to whether they can be thoroughly human and humane, such as is hinted at in the saying, "Old maids' and bachelors' children are well cared for," which derides at once their ignorance and their presumption.

Yet the business of society has become so complex, that it could now scarcely be carried on without the presence of these despised auxiliaries, and detachments from the army of aunts and uncles are wanted to stop gaps in every hedge. They rove about, mental and moral Ishmaelites, pitching their tents amid the fixed and ornamented habitations of men.

They thus gain a wider, if not so deep, experience. They are not so intimate with others, but thrown more upon themselves, and if they do not there find peace and incessant life, there is none to flatter them that they are not very poor and very mean. . . .

Saints and geniuses have often chosen a lonely position, in the faith that, if undisturbed by the pressure of near ties they could give themselves up to the inspiring spirit, it would enable them to understand and reproduce life better than actual experience could.

How many old maids take this high stand, we cannot say; it is an unhappy fact that too many of those who come before the eye are gossips rather, and not always good-natured gossips. But, if these abuse, and none make the best of their vocation, yet, it has not failed to produce some good fruit. It has been seen by others, if not by themselves, that beings likely to be left alone need to be fortified and furnished within themselves, and education and thought have tended more and more to regard beings as related to absolute Being, as well as to other men. It has been seen that as the loss of no bond ought to destroy a human being, so ought the missing of none to hinder him from growing. And thus a circumstance of the time has helped to put woman on the true platform. Perhaps the next generation will look deeper into this matter, and find that contempt is put on old maids, or old women at all, merely because they do not use the elixir which will keep the soul always young. No one thinks of Michael Angelo's Persican Sibyl, or St. Theresa, or Tasso's Leonora, or the Greek Electra as an old maid, though all had reached the period in life's course appointed to take that degree.

Even among the North American Indians, a race of men as completely engaged in mere instinctive life as almost any in the world, and where each chief, keeping many wives as useful servants, of course looks with no kind eye on celibacy in woman, it was excused in the following instance mentioned by Mrs. Jameson. A woman dreamt in youth that she was betrothed to the sun. She built her a wigwam apart, filled it with emblems of her alliance and means of an independent life. There she passed her days, sustained by her own exertions, and true to her supposed engagement.

In any tribe, we believe, a woman, who lived as if she was betrothed to the sun, would be tolerated, and the rays which made her youth blossom sweetly would crown her with a halo in age. . . .

. . . The world at large is readier to let woman learn and manifest the capacities of her nature than it ever was before, and here is a less encumbered field, and freer air than anywhere else. And it ought to be so; we ought to pay for Isabella's jewels.

The names of nations are feminine. Religion, Virtue, and Victory are feminine. To those who have a superstition as to outward signs, it is not without significance that the name of the Queen of our mother-land should at this crisis be Victoria. Victoria the First. Perhaps to us it may be given to disclose the era there outwardly presaged.

Women here are much better situated than men. Good books are allowed with more time to read them. They are not so early forced into the bustle of life, nor so weighed down by demands for outward success. The perpetual changes, incident to our society, make the blood circulate freely through the body politic, and, if not favorable at present to the grace and bloom of life, they are so to activity, resource, and would be to reflection but for a low materialist tendency, from which the women are generally exempt.

They have time to think, and no traditions chain them,

and few conventionalities compared with what must be met in other nations. There is no reason why the fact of a constant revelation should be hid from them, and when the mind once is awakened by that, it will not be restrained by the past, but fly to seek the seeds of a heavenly future.

Their employments are more favorable to the inward life than those of the men.

Woman is not addressed religiously here, more than elsewhere. She is told to be worthy to be the mother of a Washington, or the companion of some good man. But in many, many instances, she has already learnt that all bribes have the same flaw; that truth and good are to be sought for themselves alone. And already an ideal sweetness floats over many forms, shines in many eyes.

Already deep questions are put by young girls on the great theme, What shall I do to inherit eternal life?

Men are very courteous to them. They praise them often, check them seldom. There is some chivalry in the feeling towards "the ladies," which gives them the best seats in the stage-coach, frequent admission not only to lectures of all sorts, but to courts of justice, halls of legislature, reform conventions. The newspaper editor "would be better pleased that the Lady's Book were filled up exclusively by ladies. It would then, indeed, be a true gem, worthy to be presented by young men to the mistresses of their affections." Can gallantry go farther?

In this country is venerated, wherever seen, the character which Goethe spoke of as an Ideal. "The excellent woman is she, who, if the husband dies, can be a father to the children." And this, if rightly read, tells a great deal.

Women who speak in public, if they have a moral power, such as has been felt from Angelina Grimke and Abby Kelly, that is, if they speak for conscience' sake, to serve a cause which they hold sacred, invariably subdue the prejudices of their hearers, and excite an interest proportionate to the aversion with which it had been the purpose to regard them.

· · ·

For woman, if by a sympathy as to outward condition, she is led to aid the enfranchisement of the slave, must no less so, by inward tendency, to favor measures which promise to bring the world more thoroughly and deeply into harmony with her nature. When the lamb takes place of the lion as the emblem of nations, both women and men will be as children of one spirit, perpetual learners of the word and doers thereof, not hearers only.

A writer in a late number of the New York Pathfinder, in two articles headed "Femality," has uttered a still more pregnant word than any we have named. He views woman truly from the soul, and not from society, and the depth and leading of his thoughts is proportionately remarkable. He views the feminine nature as a harmonizer of the vehement elements, and this has often been hinted elsewhere; but what he expresses most forcibly is the lyrical, the inspiring and inspired apprehensiveness of her being. . . .

There are two aspects of woman's nature, expressed by the ancients as Muse and Minerva. It is the former to which the writer in the Pathfinder looks. It is the latter which Wordsworth has in mind, when he says,

"With a placid brow,
Which woman ne'er should forfeit, keep thy vow."

The especial genius of woman I believe to be electrical in movement, intuitive in function, spiritual in tendency. She is great not so easily in classification, or re-creation, as in an instinctive seizure of causes, and a simple breathing out of what she receives that has the singleness of life, rather than the selecting or energizing of art.

More native to her is it to be the living model of the artist, than to set apart from herself any one form in objective reality; more native to inspire and receive the poem than to create it. In so far as soul is in her completely developed, all soul is the same; but as far as it is modified in her as woman, it flows, it breathes, it sings, rather than deposits soil, or finishes work, and that which is especially feminine flushes in blossom the face of earth, and pervades like air and water all this seeming solid globe, daily renewing and purifying its life. Such may be the especially feminine element, spoken of as Femality. But it is no more the order of nature that it should be incarnated pure in any form, than that the masculine energy should exist unmingled with it in any form.

Male and female represent the two sides of the great radical dualism. But, in fact, they are perpetually passing into one another. Fluid hardens to solid, solid rushes to fluid. There is no wholly masculine man, no purely feminine woman.

History jeers at the attempts of physiologists to bind great original laws by the forms which flow from them. They make a rule; they say from observation, what can and cannot be. In vain! Nature provides exceptions to every rule. She sends women to battle, and sets Hercules spinning; she enables women to bear immense burdens, cold, and frost; she enables the man, who feels maternal love, to nourish his infant like a mother. Of late she plays still gayer pranks. Not only she deprives organizations, but organs, of a necessary end. She enables people to read with the top of the head, and see with the pit of the stomach. Presently she will make a female Newton, and a male Syren.

Man partakes of the feminine in the Apollo, woman of the masculine as Minerva.

Let us be wise and not impede the soul. Let her work as she will. Let us have one creative energy, one incessant revelation. Let it take what form it will, and let us not bind it by the past to man or woman, black or white. Jove sprang from Rhea, Pallas from Jove. So let it be.

If it has been the tendency of the past remarks to call woman rather to the Minerva side,—if I, unlike the more generous writer, have spoken from society no less than the soul,—let it be pardoned. It is love that has caused this, love for many incarcerated souls, that might be freed could the idea of religious self-dependence be established in them, could the weakening habit of dependence on others be broken up.

Every relation, every gradation of nature, is incalculably precious, but only to the soul which is poised upon itself, and to whom no loss, no change, can bring dull discord, for it is in harmony with the central soul.

If any individual live too much in relations, so that he becomes a stranger to the resources of his own nature, he falls after a while into a distraction, or imbecility, from which he can only be cured by a time of isolation, which gives the renovating fountains time to rise up. With a society it is the same. Many minds, deprived of the traditionary or instinctive means of passing a cheerful existence, must find help in self-impulse or perish. It is therefore that while any elevation, in the view of union, is to be hailed with joy, we shall not decline celibacy as the great fact of the time. It is one from which no vow, no arrangement, can at present save a thinking mind. For now the rowers are pausing on their oars, they wait a change before they can pull together. All tends to illustrate the thought of a wise contemporary. Union is only possible to those who are units. To be fit for relations in time, souls, whether of man or woman, must be able to do without them in the spirit.

It is therefore that I would have woman lay aside all thought, such as she habitually cherishes, of being taught and led by men. I would have her, like the Indian girl, dedicate herself to the Sun, the Sun of Truth, and go no where if his beams did not make clear the path. I would have her free from compromise, from complaisance, from helplessness, because I would have her good enough and strong enough to love one and all beings, from the fulness, not the poverty of being.

Men, as at present instructed, will not help this work, because they also are under the slavery of habit. I have seen with delight their poetic impulses. A sister is the fairest ideal, and how nobly Wordsworth, and even Byron, have written of a sister.

There is no sweeter sight than to see a father with his little daughter. Very vulgar men become refined to the eye when leading a little girl by the hand. At that moment the right relation between the sexes seem established, and you feel as if the man would aid in the noblest purpose, if you ask him in behalf of his little daughter. Once two fine figures stood before me, thus. The father of very intellectual aspect, his falcon eye softened by affection as he looked down on his fair child, she the image of himself, only more graceful and brilliant in expression. I was reminded of Southey's Kehama, when lo, the dream was rudely broken. They were talking of education, and he said,

"I shall not have Maria brought too forward. If she knows too much, she will never find a husband; superior women hardly ever can."

"Surely," said his wife, with a blush, "you wish Maria to be as good and wise as she can, whether it will help her to marriage or not."

"No," he persisted, "I want her to have a sphere and a home, and some one to protect her when I am gone."

It was a trifling incident, but made a deep impression. I felt that the holiest relations fail to instruct the unprepared and perverted mind. If this man, indeed, would have looked

at it on the other side, he was the last that would have been
willing to have been taken himself for the home and protection he could give. . . .

But men do *not* look at both sides, and women must
leave off asking them and being influenced by them, but
retire within themselves, and explore the groundwork of being
till they find their peculiar secret. Then when they come
forth again, renovated and baptized, they will know how to
turn all dross to gold, and will be rich and free though they
live in a hut, tranquil, if in a crowd. Then their sweet singing
shall not be from passionate impulse, but the lyrical overflow
of a divine rapture, and a new music shall be elucidated from
this many-chorded world.

Grant her then for a while the armor and the javelin. Let
her put from her the press of other minds and meditate in
virgin loneliness. The same idea shall reappear in due time
as Muse, or Ceres, the all-kindly, patient Earth-Spirit. . . .

A profound thinker has said "no married woman can
represent the female world, for she belongs to her husband.
The idea of woman must be represented by a virgin."

But that is the very fault of marriage, and of the present
relation between the sexes, that the woman does belong to
the man, instead of forming a whole with him. Were it otherwise there would be no such limitation to the thought.

Woman, self-centred, would never be absorbed by any
relation; it would be only an experience to her as to man.
It is a vulgar error that love, *a* love to woman is her whole
existence; she also is born for Truth and Love in their universal energy. Would she but assume her inheritance, Mary
would not be the only Virgin Mother. . . .

And will not she soon appear? The woman who shall
vindicate their birthright for all women; who shall teach them
what to claim, and how to use what they obtain? Shall not
her name be for her era Victoria, for her country and her
life Virginia? Yet predictions are rash; she herself must teach
us to give her the fitting name.

Prestige From the Other Sex:
John Stuart Mill (1806–1873)

John Stuart Mill's *The Subjection of Women* has been a major classic of feminist writing for a century. Its publication in England in 1869 was followed by an American edition in a matter of months, and it was quickly adopted by the leaders of the suffrage movement as a definitive analysis of the position of women in society. In the ensuing decades of the nineteenth century, American suffragists sold copies of the book at suffrage conventions and made ceremonial references to it in their speeches. At the age of seventy-nine, Sarah Grimké personally canvassed from house to house in her New England town to sell a hundred copies of the book.

The publication of the essay was propitious for the American woman's rights movement, since it appeared during the difficult post-Civil War period, when some of the staunchest early male supporters of woman's rights in the United States—such men as Horace Greeley and Frederick Douglass—withdrew their political support to argue that the vote must first be secured for the Negro. John Stuart Mill's stature as an eminent Englishman, renowned for his liberal stands on numerous issues, and his intellectual accomplishments over a forty-year period of prolific publication were an essential boost to the American suffrage movement in these postwar years. It takes nothing from the intrinsic contribution of Mill's analysis to point out that *The Subjection of Women* lent the American suffrage cause the concrete prestige it needed precisely because it was written by an eminent *man*. As late as 1911 a republication carried an introduction by Carrie Chapman Catt, who hailed the new edition as a "happy incident" that would prove of "untold value to the movement."

Mill was sixty-three when *The Subjection of Women* was published in 1869, and it is doubtful that he would ever have written the essay if it were not for the role that Harriet Taylor had played in his personal and intellectual life. Though Mill did the actual writing in 1861—three years after his wife's death—it should properly be viewed as a joint endeavor. The ideas formulated in the essay were discussed innumerable times during the twenty-odd years of intimacy and intellectual collaboration between the two. Mill himself explained that before he became an intimate friend of Harriet's his views on the position of women had consisted of nothing but an abstract principle: he saw no more reason for women than for men to be held in legal subjection to others. He explained Harriet's contribution as a wide range of perceptions of the vast practical bearings of women's disabilities:

> But for her rare knowledge of human nature and comprehension of moral and social influences, I should have had a very insufficient perception of the mode in which the consequences of the inferior position of women intertwine themselves with all the evils of existing society and with all the difficulties of human improvement. [Coss 1924:170]

In what follows I shall give a brief account of the personal and political background to Mill's essay on women, with a special focus on the contribution of Harriet Taylor Mill and the controversy surrounding their intellectual collaboration (see Rossi 1970 for a more extended treatment).

John Stuart Mill was a precocious child who received a remarkable education under his father's tutelage. His father James Mill, together with his intellectual mentor Jeremy Bentham, set out a course of study that would produce a "worthy successor" to carry on their work in Utilitarian economics and politics. This study regimen began with Greek at the age of three, Latin in his eighth year, supplemented with mathematics, philosophy, and the experimental sciences as he approached his teens. By his fourteenth year, Mill had completed a course of education that would normally stretch into young adulthood.

It is scarcely surprising, in light of the rigorous long days of study Mill was subjected to as a child, that neither his emotional self nor his social skills were given much chance for cultivation. In addition to his own demanding study, he was gradually charged with the responsibility of tutoring his numerous younger siblings. In later years he described himself at eighteen as a "dry, hard logical machine." It was to the emotional impoverishment of his early life that Mill attributed his aloof reserve, a quality he frequently referred to as an impediment to intimate relations with others.

The formal phase of Mill's unconventional education ended in 1820, when he went abroad for a year of study in France. There he lived with Jeremy Bentham's brother, Sir Samuel Bentham, and concentrated his studies on the sciences, French, and music. On his return, he began his lifelong association with the East India Company, starting as a clerk directly under his father in 1822 and retiring from the company in 1858 as chief of the office of the examiner of India correspondence. Almost simultaneously with the beginning of his employment, John Mill and a group of young radicals formed the Utilitarian Society. James Mill was the intellectual and political mentor to this talented circle of politically ambitious young men, bent upon modeling themselves after the French *philosophes* of the eighteenth century.

Beneath the surface of Mill's busy life during the 1820's, however, a storm was brewing: Mill was attempting to define his own identity and to differentiate it from that of his father. This involved a severe mental depression in 1826 and a subsequent transformation of his intellectual and personal orientation. He began to depart from the "pure" world of rationalism at the heart of his father's ideas on education and politics, turning with a new responsiveness to the work of Coleridge, Carlyle, the French Saint Simonians, Comte, and Macaulay.

Historical evidence is vague about the exact circumstances which first brought John Mill and Harriet Taylor together. Mill's new-found responsiveness to poetry and literature and his long-standing interest in radical politics were clearly in the background of the encounter. The connecting link is thought to have been William J. Fox, Unitarian minister of the South Place Chapel, whose parish included Harriet and her husband John. Tradition has it that Mill and Harriet Taylor met at a dinner party at William Fox's home in the summer or fall of 1830. Harriet Martineau was a member of the party, and it was she who was fond of telling and embroidering upon the occasion of John and Harriet's first meeting. From an examination of personal correspondence, one scholar of John Mill and Harriet Taylor suggests that their relationship was already intimate by the summer of 1831, a year or so later (Hayek 1951:36–37). At the time of their meeting, Harriet was twenty-three, already married for more than four years, and the mother of two sons. Her last child, Helen, was born the following year, in July 1831.

Concern for the status of women and the relations between

the sexes was no new idea in the social circle of the Unitarian Radicals in the early 1830s. Mary Wollstonecraft had herself been a Unitarian intellectual, and down through the years of the Unitarian journal, the *Monthly Repository*, there are numerous articles both friendly to and persistent in their demands for the education of women. Harriet Martineau had written one such article, "On Female Education," in 1823, in which she argued that women must be educated to be "companions to men, instead of playthings or servants." The Utilitarian *Westminster Review* had similarly been a champion for the cause of women almost from the first issue. This background makes somewhat curious Mill's later explicit denial that his views on the relations between the sexes had been adopted or learnt from Harriet. It would be more accurate to say that ideas on sex equality were not unique to either John Mill or Harriet Taylor. They had both absorbed much of the thinking on this issue from the two main social circles within which they moved, the Philosophic Radicals and the Unitarian Radicals.

The year 1833 was critical in the relationship between John Mill and Harriet Taylor. For Harriet the dilemma centered on whether and how a pattern could be established that would permit her to continue her close contact with John Mill yet fulfill her obligations to her husband. For Mill the dilemma was more complex, for he was continuing to explore the new intellectual world opened to him following his earlier mental crisis as well as trying to cope with his new personal relationship with Harriet. The Taylors agreed to a trial separation for approximately six months, apparently with the hope on her husband's part that Harriet would decide to cut her tie to John Mill and return fully to him as his wife. Mill joined Harriet in Paris in the fall of 1833 for several weeks. The result of the separation was that Harriet did not renounce the liberty of seeing John Mill, and her husband agreed to such an arrangement in exchange for retaining the external formality of residing as his wife in his household. From 1834 until their marriage in 1851 (two years after the death of her husband), John Mill and Harriet Taylor continued this pattern, seeing each other for dinner at Harriet's home when John Taylor was absent, and spending frequent weekends at summer places along the English coast, as Harriet moved restlessly about from place to place with her daughter Helen. Mill continued to live at home with his mother, working at

India House, tutoring his younger siblings, and writing widely on numerous political topics of the day.

Controversy has raged for more than a century over Harriet Taylor's personality and intellectual capability, as it has over the nature of her relationship to Mill and her contribution to his published writings. Mill himself was lavish in his praise of her as a woman and as an intellectual, comparing her with prominent intellectual and artistic figures in English history. The praise was so lavish as to tax the credibility of many of Mill's contemporaries. Alexander Bain, Mill's friend and first biographer, wrote to Mill's stepdaughter:

> I venture to express the opinion that no such combination has ever been realized in the history of the human race. [Stillinger 1961:23]

William Fox, the Mills' mutual friend, was one contemporary who was warm in his feeling toward Harriet and high in his assessment of her ability, moral commitment, and devotion to Mill. A more recent scholar, Francis Mineka, shares the sympathetic view of Harriet's influence:

> However over colored by emotion his estimate of her powers may have been, there can be no doubt that she was the saving grace of his inner life. Without her, John Mill might well have been a different person, but one can doubt that he would have been as fine, as understanding or as great a man. [Mineka 1944:274–275]

Positive assessments of Harriet Taylor such as this have been few, and they are far outweighed by harshly negative judgments. Harold Laski thought Mill was "literally the only person who was in the least impressed by her" (Stillinger 1961:24–25). Keith Rinehart has portrayed Mill as a submissive man whose autobiography shows a movement from the "aegis of one demi-god, his father, to another, his wife" (Rinehart 1953:265–273). Stillinger suggests that Mill "enjoyed her more as a correspondent than as a companion" (Stillinger 1961:27). Max Lerner took a curious attitude toward the relationship between the two, suggesting that Mill himself was a proper Victorian in his attitudes toward sex and that Harriet Taylor was probably a frigid woman as a matter of principle rather than of neurosis (Lerner 1961:xiv), though one may wonder what the difference is between a "proper Victorian attitude" and "principled frigidity."

One must be cautious in assessing the views held of Harriet by either her male contemporaries or the scholars who read the scattered fragments of evidence from those contemporaries. Assertive women were undoubtedly an even greater irritation to Victorian men than they are to men today. In a man single-mindedness of purpose has always been considered admirable; in a woman, whether in Victorian England or contemporary America, it has usually been thought a sign of selfishness, a distasteful departure from conventional ideals of femininity. Harriet Taylor was no shrinking violet, no soft and compliant woman. She had, after all, lived against the grain of Victorian London in an unconventional liaison with John Mill for twenty years before their marriage. Under his tutelage she had a most unusual opportunity to grow intellectually, and we may assume that over the years of their collaboration Harriet's self-confidence also grew as she tested her mettle against the strength of Mill's intellect and fund of knowledge. That a woman was the collaborator of so logical and intellectual a thinker as Mill, much less that she influenced the development of his thought, has clearly been disquieting to male expectations concerning women's intellect.

There is another, more sociological, approach to interpreting the contradictory assessments of Harriet Taylor. If one links the assessment to the social circle to which the writer, friend, or scholar belonged or was intellectually and politically attuned, one begins to see the influence of social structure upon attitude and belief. The negative assessments of Harriet turn out to be held mainly by members of the Philosophic Radicals or scholars interested in that circle, whereas the positive assessments are held by those associated with the Unitarian Radicals. Significant differences existed between these two circles in theory, politics, and morality. The Philosophic Radicals represented a pole of moral righteousness, theoretical commitment to Utilitarianism, and political concern for parliamentary reform. The Unitarian Radicals, by contrast, were individually more unconventional, more artistic, and passionately committed to a wide range of political and social reforms in the area of domestic affairs and the institution of the family. This was the social set with which Harriet Taylor was personally affiliated. Mill's association with the Unitarian Radicals was seen by his political associates as a threat to his allegiance to the Utilitarian cause, and Harriet was the symbol of that association. At the time, the Philosophic Radicals knew nothing of the intellectual distance Mill had traveled from Utilitarian theory, quite on his own, following his mental crisis in 1826. They may well have attributed the subsequent changes in Mill's thinking to the influence of Harriet and her social circle rather than to the intellectual ferment within Mill himself. By contrast, Harriet's friends among the Unitarian Radicals were warm in their support of the view that she contributed significantly to Mill's work.

The division in assessments of Harriet among her contemporaries is echoed in similar divisions among later scholars who have studied the individuals and political movements of these years in England. Thus Friedrich Hayek, himself opposed to socialism (the "road to serfdom"), conceded considerable influence to Harriet, since he could then interpret Mill's socialist phase as a temporary aberration due to Harriet's influence over him (Hayek 1951:266). In contrast, Harold Laski, a socialist, did not wish to view Mill's socialist thinking as a product of a woman's influence and hence followed the earlier trend toward a negative view of Harriet and of her contribution to Mill's thinking (Lerner 1961:6). One senses in Mill scholars an unwitting desire to reject Harriet Taylor as capable of contributing significantly to the vigor of Mill's social and political analysis—except when that analysis included some tinge of sentiment or political thought the scholar disapproved of, in which case the disliked element was seen as Harriet's influence.

Mill himself referred to many of his publications from 1840 on as "joint productions" of Harriet and himself. That he expressly exempted his *System of Logic* from Harriet's collaboration makes this claim more believable. It is the *Principles of Political Economy* which Mill cited as their first joint effort, pointing out that what was abstract and purely scientific was generally his, while the more human elements and lively practical illustrations were from her. He acknowledged that his first draft of the book had no chapter on the future condition of the working class, and that the one which was finally included was "wholly an exposition of her thoughts, often in words taken from her own lips" (Coss 1924:174). *On Liberty* Mill claimed was even more fully a joint effort:

[It was] more directly and literally our joint production than anything else which bears my name, for there was not a sentence of it that was not several times gone through by us together, turned over in many ways, and carefully weeded of any faults, either in thought or expression, that we detected in it. [Coss 1924:176]

It remains a puzzle why, if her contribution was so great, everything appeared under Mill's name alone. Social expediency probably ruled out such joint authorship during the long years of their unconventional relationship, and by the time they married, they may have felt that his "established" name would draw larger readership and sales than her lesser-known name. There is some evidence that Harriet was not completely satisfied with such a state of affairs. When it came time to publish the *Principles of Political Economy*, Mill wrote a footnote comment that "her dislike of publicity alone" prevented the insertion of dedications in all but the gift copies of the first edition. In actual fact, Harriet had approached her husband, John Taylor, about such a dedication, indicating pleasure at the prospect, and suggesting precedents for it in other recently published work. Taylor, however, was profoundly opposed to the idea on the ground that under their circumstances it showed a want of "taste and tact." One can imagine Harriet chafing at the social conventions that required her to remain unknown and unacknowledged by the reading public.

Harriet Taylor and John Mill had known each other for twenty-one years when they were finally married in the London Register's Office in April 1851. There is no better example of their commitment to the proper relations between the sexes than the remarkable statement Mill wrote two months before his marriage. There is no record of what Mill did with this statement, nor of any discussion between them prior to his drafting the document, but it is so fine an example of principles put to practice that it is worth inclusion here. The necessity for drafting a personal declaration in the form of an individuated marriage "pledge" applies to our own time as it did in 1851, for legal and ecclesiastical strictures continue to be alien to the spirit in which many men and women committed to sex equality wish to join their lives:

Being about, if I am so happy as to obtain her consent, to enter into the marriage relation with the only woman I have ever known, with whom I would have entered into

that state; and the whole character of the marriage relation as constituted by law being such as both she and I
entirely and conscientiously disapprove, for this among
other reasons, that it confers upon one of the parties to
the contract, legal power and control over the person,
property, and freedom of action of the other party, independent of her own wishes and will; I, having no means
of legally divesting myself of these odious powers (as I
most assuredly would do if an engagement to that effect
could be made legally binding on me), feel it my duty to
put on record a formal protest against the existing law of
marriage, in so far as conferring such powers; and a
solemn promise never in any case or under any circumstances to use them. And in the event of marriage between Mrs. Taylor and me I declare it to be my will and
intention, and the condition of the engagement between
us, that she retains in all respects whatever the same
absolute freedom of action and freedom of disposal of herself and of all that does or may at any time belong to her,
as if no such marriage had taken place; and I absolutely
disclaim and repudiate all pretension to have acquired any
rights whatever by virtue of such marriage.

6 March 1851   J. S. Mill

[Elliot 1910, Vol. 1:58]

The Mills had had twenty-one years before their marriage
in which to establish the style of their relationship. It was an
intellectual and sentimental communion through discussion
and written correspondence. From their own views of the
place of physical sex in individual lives and the larger society,
there is no reason to assume that sheer physical togetherness
was as necessary to their relationship as it would be to us in
our day. The Mills espoused very advanced and radical ideas
about the status of women, marriage and divorce laws, the
right of women to education and the franchise, and the injustice of denying basic human rights to the female half of
humanity; but in the area of human sexuality they were very
much the products of their Victorian era.

A good example of Mill's advanced thought is his awareness of the connection between the status of women and the
problem of population growth. In the chapter he attributed
to Harriet on the future condition of the working classes in
his *Political Economy*, Mill observed:

The ideas and institutions by which the accident of sex is made the groundwork of an inequality of legal rights, and a forced dissimilarity of social functions, must ere long be recognized as the greatest hindrance to moral, social and even intellectual improvement. On the present occasion I shall only indicate, among the probable consequences of the industrial and social independence of women, a great diminution of the evil of over population. It is by devoting one half of the human species to that exclusive function, by making it fill the entire life of one sex and interweave itself with almost all the objects of the other, that the "animal" instinct in question is nursed into the disproportionate preponderance which it has hitherto exercised in human life. [Robson 1965, Vol. 3:765–766]

When in 1848 an American reviewer of the *Political Economy* objected to Mill's ideas on population growth, Mill responded in biting fashion, linking the objections to the reviewer's nationality:

On the population question, my difference with the reviewer is fundamental, and in the incidental reference which he makes to my assertion of equality of political rights and of social position in behalf of women, the tone assumed by him is really below contempt. But I fear that a country where institutions profess to be founded on equality, and which yet maintains the slavery of black men and of all women will be one of the last to relinquish that other servitude. [Mineka 1963, Vol. 13:741]

John Mill retired from the East India Company in the autumn of 1858, and the Mills left England with a plan to spend the winter in France and the spring in Italy. They never reached their first destination, for a cold that Harriet had caught developed into severe lung congestion, and she died in Avignon on November 3. Mill's own words are the best description of the aftermath of her death:

Since then I have sought for such alleviation as my state admitted of, by the mode of life which most enables me to feel her still near me. I bought a cottage as close as possible to the place where she is buried, and there her daughter (my fellow-sufferer and now my chief comfort) and I, live constantly during a great portion of the year. My objects in life are solely those which were hers; my pursuits and occupations those in which she shared, or sympathized, and which are indissolubly associated with her. [Coss 1924:170]

In his autobiography, Mill explained that he turned to the drafting of *The Subjection of Women* in 1860 upon his stepdaughter's suggestion that there might be a "written exposition of my opinions on that great question, as full and conclusive as I could make it." He finished this first draft in 1861 but did not revise it until he retired from the House of Commons in 1868. In describing how he drew upon his wife's ideas in writing the essay, he explained:

As ultimately published it was enriched with some important ideas of my daughter's, and passages of her writing. But in what was of my own composition, all that is most striking and profound belongs to my wife; coming from the fund of thought which had been made common to us both, by our innumerable conversations and discussions on a topic which filled so large a place in our minds. [Coss 1924:186]

An important idea in Mill's view of the equality of the sexes is tapped in this passage: the "fund of thought made common" to Harriet and himself. Mill shied away from any direct personal account of his marital relationship, but the reader feels he was speaking from a personal basis when he described a marriage between equals toward the end of the *Subjection* essay. Although he first rejected the desirability of giving such a description (on the ground that those who can conceive such a marriage need no description, and to those who cannot conceive such a marriage, it would appear but the dream of an enthusiast), he proceeded to describe just such a relationship—a marriage between

two persons of cultivated faculties, identical in opinions and purposes, between whom there exists that best of equality, similarity of powers and capacities with reciprocal superiority in them so that each can enjoy the luxury of looking up to the other, and can have alternately the pleasure of leading and of being led in the path of development. . . . This and this only is the ideal of marriage; . . . all opinions, customs and institutions which favor any other notion of it . . . are relics of primitive barbarism.

The idea of complementary skills and knowledge, such that each spouse can be both leader and follower, teacher and student, on a firm base of shared values and goals, reads like a description of the Mills' own marriage. Yet Mill had a poor view of the capacity of men in his time to live out a marriage on a basis of equality. In fact he argued that the reason barriers are maintained against the liberation of women from their caste status is that "the generality of the male sex cannot yet tolerate the idea of living with an equal." John Stuart Mill clearly could and did.

There are several reasons why *The Subjection of Women* continues to be a powerfully effective essay, which people in the 1970s can find as stimulating as those who read it for the first time in the 1870s. It is grounded in basic libertarian values that ring as true today as then—"we have had the morality of submission and the morality of chivalry and generosity: the time is ripe for the morality of justice." To the generations of the twentieth century who have seen tyranny and the suppression of human liberty in all forms of government—Fascist, Communist, and democratic—John Stuart Mill's invocation of the rights of men and women to liberty and justice have a strong, continuing appeal. And to the women of the twentieth century, who have seen very little difference in the actual condition, if not the formal rights, of women under any existing form of government, *The Subjection of Women* continues to serve as a resounding affirmation of their human right to full equality and a sophisticated analysis of the obstacles that bar their way to it.

A second basic reason for the continuing relevance of Mill's essay on women is that it is not burdened with the dead weight of any of the social and psychological theories that have emerged during the hundred years separating us from the Mills: no Darwinism to encourage an unthinking expectation of unilinear progress of mankind through "natural selection" or "selective breeding"; no Freudian theory to belittle women's sexuality and encourage their acceptance as the "second sex"; no functional anthropology or sociology to justify a conservative acceptance of the status quo; no Marxist theory to encourage a narrow concentration on economic variables. What the Mills had as their guide is what we have only begun to recapture in our counterpart efforts to expand the horizons of men and women to fuller realization of their human potential: a blend of compassion and logic and a commitment to the view that liberty cannot exist in the absence of the power to use it.

Although Mill's essay was published as late as 1869, and although it was much praised by the English and American woman's-rights movements over the following half-century, its argument and style identify it as properly classified with the other entries in this section on the Enlightenment perspective. Mill himself stands as a significant figure in the history of ideas, straddling the eighteenth and nineteenth centuries and anticipating the twentieth, yet his underlying intellectual mode is an Enlightenment rationalism committed to the power of reason—a belief that education could cure all human ignorance, that rational argument could unsettle the most deeply entrenched human belief. His stance throughout the essay poses an implicit question: what "reasonable" man or woman could fail to abandon a narrow view of woman's potential, who could resist encouraging women to cultivate a wider sphere of options and skills, once they finished reading his logical analysis of the position of women?

Mill was, of course, a more complex political being than this portrait of his attitude suggests. He clearly appreciated political "timing" for ideas, and in fact left out of his essay any discussion of such topics as divorce and child custody on precisely the ground that the times were not "ripe" for public acceptance of liberal ideas for reform of English law in these matters. He did believe the time had come for woman suffrage, and he had in fact submitted the first bill on the enfranchisement of women to the House of Commons just a few years before his book on women appeared. But we are here dealing with the kind of argument he offered in the written essay rather than the full range of the man as political activist as well as writer. As such, the essay belongs in spirit and style to the earlier period of feminist writing.

One suspects that even in the last half of the nineteenth century the book had greater appeal for the older founders of the woman's-rights movement in the United States than for the younger feminists and reformers. Their biographies attest to the impact of the book on such women as Elizabeth Cady Stanton, Sarah Grimké, and Lucretia Mott, the hardy pioneers

who had twenty to forty years of women's-rights activity
behind them when Mill's essay appeared. Those women seeking a widening of liberal democratic rights for women, so
that they might share in the privileges and responsibilities of
full citizenship, could feel that the essay lent a glow of prestige from the other sex to their cause. For the younger women
activists by the turn of the century, who were stimulated by
the more radical and socialist thought of their day, Mill was
far less of an intellectual mentor or political hero. From the
perspective of 1972 *The Subjection of Women* stands as a
landmark in the history of liberal feminism.

☙ The Subjection of Women ❧

1

The object of this Essay is to explain as clearly as I am
able, the grounds of an opinion which I have held from the
very earliest period when I had formed any opinions at all
on social or political matters, and which, instead of being
weakened or modified, has been constantly growing stronger
by the progress of reflection and the experience of life: That
the principle which regulates the existing social relations
between the two sexes—the legal subordination of one sex
to the other—is wrong in itself, and now one of the chief
hindrances to human improvement; and that it ought to be
replaced by a principle of perfect equality, admitting no
power or privilege on the one side, nor disability on the
other.

• • •

The generality of a practice is in some cases a strong presumption that it is, or at all events once was, conducive to
laudable ends. This is the case, when the practice was first
adopted, or afterwards kept up, as a means to such ends, and
was grounded on experience of the mode in which they could

From John Stuart Mill, *The Subjection of Women*, in Alice S.
Rossi, ed., *Essays on Sex Equality*. Chicago, University of Chicago
Press, 1970. Pp. 125–242.

be most effectually attained. If the authority of men over women, when first established, had been the result of a conscientious comparison between different modes of constituting the government of society; if, after trying various other modes of social organization—the government of women over men, equality between the two, and such mixed and divided modes of government as might be invented—it had been decided, on the testimony of experience, that the mode in which women are wholly under the rule of men, having no share at all in public concerns, and each in private being under the legal obligation of obedience to the man with whom she has associated her destiny, was the arrangement most conducive to the happiness and well being of both; its general adoption might then be fairly thought to be some evidence that, at the time when it was adopted, it was the best: though even then the considerations which recommended it may, like so many other primeval social facts of the greatest importance, have subsequently, in the course of ages, ceased to exist. But the state of the case is in every respect the reverse of this. In the first place, the opinion in favour of the present system, which entirely subordinates the weaker sex to the stronger, rests upon theory only; for there never has been trial made of any other: so that experience, in the sense in which it is vulgarly opposed to theory, cannot be pretended to have pronounced any verdict. And in the second place, the adoption of this system of inequality never was the result of deliberation, or forethought, or any social ideas, or any notion whatever of what conduced to the benefit of humanity or the good order of society. It arose simply from the fact that from the very earliest twilight of human society, every woman (owing to the value attached to her by men, combined with her inferiority in muscular strength) was found in a state of bondage to some man. Laws and systems of polity always begin by recognising the relations they find already existing between individuals. They convert what was a mere physical fact into a legal right, give it the sanction of society, and principally aim at the substitution of public and organized means of asserting and protecting these rights, instead of the irregular and lawless conflict of physical strength. . . .

. . . We now live—that is to say, one or two of the most advanced nations of the world now live—in a state in which the law of the strongest seems to be entirely abandoned as the regulating principle of the world's affairs: nobody professes it, and, as regards most of the relations between human beings, nobody is permitted to practise it. When any one succeeds in doing so, it is under cover of some pretext which gives him the semblance of having some general social interest on his side. This being the ostensible state of things, people flatter themselves that the rule of mere force is ended; that the law of the strongest cannot be the reason of existence of anything which has remained in full operation down to the present time. However any of our present institutions may have begun, it can only, they think, have been preserved to this period of advanced civilization by a well-grounded feeling of its adaptation to human nature, and conduciveness to the general good. They do not understand the great vitality and durability of institutions which place right on the side of might; how intensely they are clung to; how the good as well as the bad propensities and sentiments of those who have power in their hands, become identified with retaining it; how slowly these bad institutions give way, one at a time, the weakest first, beginning with those which are least interwoven with the daily habits of life; and how very rarely those who have obtained legal power because they first had physical, have ever lost their hold of it until the physical power had passed over to the other side. Such shifting of the physical force not having taken place in the case of women; this fact, combined with all the peculiar and characteristic features of the particular case, made it certain from the first that this branch of the system of right founded on might, though softened in its most atrocious features at an earlier period than several of the others, would be the very last to disappear. It was inevitable that this one case of a social relation grounded on force, would survive through generations of institutions grounded on equal justice, an almost solitary exception to the general character of their laws and customs; but which, so long as it does not proclaim its own origin, and as discussion has not brought out its true character, is not felt to jar with modern civilization, any more than domestic slavery among the Greeks jarred with their notion of themselves as a free people.

. . .

. . . Whatever gratification of pride there is in the possession of power, and whatever personal interest in its exercise, is in this case not confined to a limited class, but common to the whole male sex. Instead of being, to most of its supporters, a thing desirable chiefly in the abstract, or, like the political ends usually contended for by factions, of little private importance to any but the leaders; it comes home to the person and hearth of every male head of a family, and of every one who looks forward to being so. The clodhopper exercises, or is to exercise, his share of the power equally with the highest nobleman. And the case is that in which the desire of power is the strongest: for every one who desires power, desires it most over those who are nearest to him, with whom his life is passed, with whom he has most concerns in common, and in whom any independence of his authority is oftenest likely to interfere with his individual preferences. If, in the other cases specified, power manifestly grounded only on force, and having so much less to support them, are so slowly and with so much difficulty got rid of, much more must it be so with this, even if it rests on no better foundation than those. We must consider, too, that the possessors of the power have facilities in this case, greater than in any other, to prevent any uprising against it. Every one of the subjects lives under the very eye, and almost, it may be said, in the hands, of one of the masters—in closer intimacy with him than with any of her fellow-subjects; with no means of combining against him, no power of even locally overmastering him, and, on the other hand, with the strongest motives for seeking his favour and avoiding to give him offence. In struggles for political emancipation, everybody knows how often its champions are bought off by bribes, or daunted by terrors. In the case of women, each individual of the subject-class is in a chronic state of bribery and intimidation combined. In setting up the standard of resistance, a large number of the leaders, and still more of the followers, must make an almost complete sacrifice of the pleasures or the alleviations of their own individual lot. If ever any system of privilege and enforced subjection had its yoke tightly riveted on the necks of those who are kept down by it, this has. . . .

Some will object, that a comparison cannot fairly be made between the government of the male sex and the forms of unjust power which I have adduced in illustration of it, since these are arbitrary, and the effect of mere usurpation, while it on the contrary is natural. But was there ever any domination which did not appear natural to those who possessed it? There was a time when the division of mankind into two classes, a small one of masters and a numerous one of slaves, appeared, even to the most cultivated minds, to be a natural, and the only natural, condition of the human race. . . .

. . . Again, the theorists of absolute monarchy have always affirmed it to be the only natural form of government; issuing from the patriarchal, which was the primitive and spontaneous form of society, framed on the model of the paternal, which is anterior to society itself, and, as they contend, the most natural authority of all. . . .

. . . So true is it that unnatural generally means only uncustomary, and that everything which is usual appears natural. The subjection of women to men being a universal custom, any departure from it quite naturally appears unnatural. But how entirely, even in this case, the feeling is dependent on custom, appears by ample experience. Nothing so much astonishes the people of distant parts of the world, when they first learn anything about England, as to be told that it is under a queen: the thing seems to them so unnatural as to be almost incredible. To Englishmen this does not seem in the least degree unnatural, because they are used to it; but they do feel it unnatural that women should be soldiers or members of parliament. In the feudal ages, on the contrary, war and politics were not thought unnatural to women, because not unusual; it seemed natural that women of the privileged classes should be of manly character, inferior in nothing but bodily strength to their husbands and fathers. . . .

But, it will be said, the rule of men over women differs from all these others in not being a rule of force: it is accepted voluntarily; women make no complaint, and are consenting parties to it. In the first place, a great number of women do not accept it. Ever since there have been women able to make their sentiments known by their writings (the only mode of publicity which society permits to them), an increasing number of them have recorded protests against their present social condition: and recently many thousands of them, headed by the most eminent women known to the public, have petitioned Parliament for their admission to the Parliamentary Suffrage. The claim of women to be educated as solidly, and in the same branches of knowledge, as men, is urged with growing intensity, and with a great prospect of success; while the demand for their admission into professions and occupations hitherto closed against them, becomes every year more urgent. Though there are not in this country, as there are in the United States, periodical Conventions and an organized party to agitate for the Rights of Women, there is a numerous and active Society organized and managed by women, for the more limited object of obtaining the political franchise. Nor is it only in our own country and in America that women are beginning to protest, more or less collectively, against the disabilities under which they labour. France, and Italy, and Switzerland, and Russia now afford examples of the same thing. How many more women there are who silently cherish similar aspirations, no one can possibly know; but there are abundant tokens how many *would* cherish them, were they not so strenuously taught to repress them as contrary to the proprieties of their sex. It must be remembered, also, that no enslaved class ever asked for complete liberty at once. . . .

. . . It is a political law of nature that those who are under any power of ancient origin, never begin by complaining of the power itself, but only of its oppressive exercise. There is never any want of women who complain of ill usage by their husbands. There would be infinitely more, if complaint were not the greatest of all provocatives to a repetition and increase of the ill usage. It is this which frustrates all attempts to maintain the power but protect the woman against its abuses. In no other case (except that of a child) is the person who has been proved judicially to have suffered an injury, replaced under the physical power of the culprit who inflicted it. Accordingly wives, even in the most extreme and protracted cases of bodily ill usage, hardly ever dare avail themselves of the laws made for their protection: and if, in a moment of irrepressible indignation, or by the interference of neighbours, they are induced to do so, their whole effort afterwards is to disclose as little as they can, and to beg off their tyrant from his merited chastisement.

All causes, social and natural, combine to make it unlikely that women should be collectively rebellious to the power of men. They are so far in a position different from all other subject classes, that their masters require something more from them than actual service. Men do not want solely the obedience of women, they want their sentiments. All men, except the most brutish, desire to have, in the woman most nearly connected with them, not a forced slave but a willing

one, not a slave merely, but a favourite. They have therefore put everything in practice to enslave their minds. The
masters of all other slaves rely, for maintaining obedience, on
fear; either fear of themselves, or religious fears. The masters
of women wanted more than simple obedience, and they
turned the whole force of education to effect their purpose.
All women are brought up from the very earliest years in the
belief that their ideal of character is the very opposite to
that of men; not self-will, and government by self-control,
but submission, and yielding to the control of others. All the
moralities tell them that it is the duty of women, and all the
current sentimentalities that it is their nature, to live for
others; to make complete abnegation of themselves, and to
have no life but in their affections. And by their affections
are meant the only ones they are allowed to have—those to
the men with whom they are connected, or to the children
who constitute an additional and indefeasible tie between
them and a man. When we put together three things—first,
the natural attraction between opposite sexes; secondly, the
wife's entire dependence on the husband, every privilege or
pleasure she has being either his gift, or depending entirely
on his will; and lastly, that the principal object of human
pursuit, consideration, and all objects of social ambition, can
in general be sought or obtained by her only through him, it
would be a miracle if the object of being attractive to men had
not become the polar star of feminine education and formation of character. And, this great means of influence over the
minds of women having been acquired, an instinct of selfishness made men avail themselves of it to the utmost as a means
of holding women in subjection, by representing to them
meekness, submissiveness, and resignation of all individual
will into the hands of a man, as an essential part of sexual
attractiveness. Can it be doubted that any of the other yokes
which mankind have succeeded in breaking, would have
subsisted till now if the same means had existed, and had
been as sedulously used, to bow down their minds to it? . . .

The preceding considerations are amply sufficient to
show that custom, however universal it may be, affords, in
this case no presumption, and ought not to create any prejudice, in favour of the arrangements which place women in
social and political subjection to men. But I may go farther,
and maintain that the course of history, and the tendencies
of progressive human society, afford not only no presumption

in favour of this system of inequality of rights, but a strong one against it; and that, so far as the whole course of human improvement up to this time, the whole stream of modern tendencies, warrants any inference on the subject, it is, that this relic of the past is discordant with the future, and must necessarily disappear.

* * *

Neither does it avail anything to say that the *nature* of the two sexes adapts them to their present functions and position, and renders these appropriate to them. Standing on the ground of common sense and the constitution of the human mind, I deny that any one knows, or can know, the nature of the two sexes, as long as they have only been seen in their present relation to one another. If men had ever been found in society without women, or women without men, or if there had been a society of men and women in which the women were not under the control of the men, something might have been positively known about the mental and moral differences which may be inherent in the nature of each. What is now called the nature of women is an eminently artificial thing—the result of forced repression in some directions, unnatural stimulation in others. It may be asserted without scruple, that no other class of dependents have had their character so entirely distorted from its natural proportions by their relation with their masters; for, if conquered and slave races have been, in some respects, more forcibly repressed, whatever in them has not been crushed down by an iron heel has generally been let alone, and if left with any liberty of development, it has developed itself according to its own laws; but in the case of women, a hot-house and stove cultivation has always been carried on of some of the capabilities of their nature, for the benefit and pleasure of their masters. . . .

Even the preliminary knowledge, what the differences between the sexes now are, apart from all questions as to how they are made what they are, is still in the crudest and most incomplete state. Medical practitioners and physiologists have ascertained, to some extent, the differences in bodily constitution; and this is an important element to the psychologist: but hardly any medical practitioner is a psychologist. Respecting the mental characteristics of women; their observations are of no more worth than those of common men. It is a subject on which nothing final can be known, so long as those who alone can really know it, women themselves, have given but little testimony, and that little, mostly suborned. It is easy to know stupid women. Stupidity is much the same all the world over. A stupid person's notions and feelings may confidently be inferred from those which prevail in the circle by which the person is surrounded. Not so with those whose opinions and feelings are an emanation from their own nature and faculties. It is only a man here and there who has any tolerable knowledge of the character even of the women of his own family. I do not mean, of their capabilities; these nobody knows, not even themselves, because most of them have never been called out. I mean their actually existing thoughts and feelings. Many a man thinks he perfectly understands women, because he has had amatory relations with several, perhaps with many of them. If he is a good observer, and his experience extends to quality as well as quantity, he may have learnt something of one narrow department of their nature—an important department, no doubt. But of all the rest of it, few persons are generally more ignorant, because there are few from whom it is so carefully hidden. The most favourable case which a man can generally have for studying the character of a woman, is that of his own wife: for the opportunities are greater, and the cases of complete sympathy not so unspeakably rare. And in fact, this is the source from which any knowledge worth having on the subject has, I believe, generally come. But most men have not had the opportunity of studying in this way more than a single case: accordingly one can, to an almost laughable degree, infer what a man's wife is like, from his opinions about women in general. To make even this one case yield any result, the woman must be worth knowing, and the man not only a competent judge, but of a character so sympathetic in itself, and so well adapted to hers, that he can either read her mind by sympathetic intuition, or has nothing in himself which makes her shy of disclosing it. Hardly anything, I believe, can be more rare than this conjunction. It often happens that there is the most complete unity of feeling and community of interests as to all external things, yet the one has as little admission into the internal life of the other as if they were common acquaintance. Even with true affection, authority on the one side and subordination on the other prevent perfect confidence. Though nothing may be intentionally withheld, much is not shown. . . . When we further consider that to understand one woman is not necessarily to understand any other woman; that even if he could study many women of one rank, or of one country, he would not thereby understand women of other ranks or countries; and even if he did, they are still only the women of a single period of history; we may safely assert that the knowledge which men can acquire of women, even as they have been and are, without reference to what they might be, is wretchedly imperfect and superficial, and always will be so, until women themselves have told all that they have to tell. . . .

One thing we may be certain of—that what is contrary to women's nature to do, they never will be made to do by simply giving their nature free play. The anxiety of mankind to interfere in behalf of nature, for fear lest nature should not succeed in effecting its purpose, is an altogether unnecessary solicitude. What women by nature cannot do, it is quite superfluous to forbid them from doing. What they can do, but not so well as the men who are their competitors, competition suffices to exclude them from; since nobody asks for protective duties and bounties in favour of women; it is only asked that the present bounties and protective duties in favour of men should be recalled. If women have a greater natural inclination for some things than for others, there is no need of laws or social inculcation to make the majority of them do the former in preference to the latter. . . .

The general opinion of men is supposed to be, that the natural vocation of a woman is that of a wife and mother. I say, is supposed to be, because, judging from acts—from the whole of the present constitution of society—one might infer that their opinion was the direct contrary. They might be supposed to think that the alleged natural vocation of women was of all things the most repugnant to their nature; insomuch that if they are free to do anything else—if any other means of living, or occupation of their time and faculties, is open, which has any chance of appearing desirable to them—there will not be enough of them who will be willing to accept the condition said to be natural to them. If this is the real opinion of men in general, it would be well that it should be spoken out. I should like to hear somebody openly enunciating the doctrine (it is already implied in much that is written on the subject)—"It is necessary to society that women should marry and produce children. They will not do so unless they are compelled. Therefore it is necessary to compel them.". . .

. . . It is not a sign of one's thinking the boon one offers very attractive, when one allows only Hobson's choice, "that or none." And here, I believe, is the clue to the feelings of those men, who have a real antipathy to the equal freedom of women. I believe they are afraid, not lest women should be unwilling to marry, for I do not think that any one in reality has that apprehension; but lest they should insist that marriage should be on equal conditions; lest all women of spirit and capacity should prefer doing almost anything else, not in their own eyes degrading, rather than marry, when marrying is giving themselves a master, and a master too of all their earthly possessions. . . . But, in that case, all that has been done in the modern world to relax the chain on the minds of women, has been a mistake. They never should have been allowed to receive a literary education. Women who read, much more women who write, are, in the existing con-stitution of things, a contradiction and a disturbing element: and it was wrong to bring women up with any acquirements but those of an odalisque, or of a domestic servant.

2

It will be well to commence the detailed discussion of the subject by the particular branch of it to which the course of our observations has led us: the conditions which the laws of this and all other countries annex to the marriage contract. Marriage being the destination appointed by society for women, the prospect they are brought up to, and the object which it is intended should be sought by all of them, except those who are too little attractive to be chosen by any man as his companion; one might have supposed that everything would have been done to make this condition as eligible to them as possible, that they might have no cause to regret being denied the option of any other. Society, however, both in this, and, at first, in all other cases, has preferred to attain its object by foul rather than fair means: but this is the only case in which it has substantially persisted in them even to the present day . . .

. . . I am far from pretending that wives are in general no better treated than slaves; but no slave is a slave to the same lengths, and in so full a sense of the word, as a wife is. Hardly any slave, except one immediately attached to the master's person, is a slave at all hours and all minutes; in general he has, like a soldier, his fixed task, and when it is done, or when he is off duty, he disposes, within certain limits, of his own time, and has a family life into which the master rarely intrudes. "Uncle Tom" under his first master had his own life in his "cabin," almost as much as any man whose work takes him away from home, is able to have in his own family. But it cannot be so with the wife. Above all, a female slave has (in Christian countries) an admitted right, and is considered under a moral obligation, to refuse to her master the last familiarity. Not so the wife: however brutal a tyrant she may unfortunately be chained to—though she may know that he hates her, though it may be his daily pleasure to torture her, and though she may feel it impossible not to loathe him —he can claim from her and enforce the lowest degradation of a human being, that of being made the instrument of an animal function contrary to her inclinations. While she is held in this worst description of slavery as to her own person, what is her position in regard to the children in whom she and her master have a joint interest? They are by law *his* children. He alone has any legal rights over them. No one act can she do towards or in relation to them, except by delegation from him. Even after he is dead she is not their legal guardian, unless he by will has made her so. He could even send them away from her, and deprive her of the means of seeing or corresponding with them, until this power was in some degree restricted by Serjeant Talfourd's Act. This is her legal state. And from this state she has no means of withdrawing herself. If she leaves her husband, she can take nothing with her, neither her children nor anything which is rightfully her own. If he chooses, he can compel her to return, by law, or by physical force; or he may content himself with seizing for his own use anything which she may earn, or which may be given to her by her relations. It is only legal separation by a decree of a court of justice, which entitles her to live apart, without being forced back into the custody of an exasperated jailer—or which empowers her to apply any earnings to her own use, without fear that a man whom perhaps she has not seen for twenty years will pounce upon

her some day and carry all off. This legal separation, until
lately, the courts of justice would only give at an expense
which made it inaccessible to any one out of the higher ranks.
Even now it is only given in cases of desertion, or of the extreme of cruelty; and yet complaints are made every day that
it is granted too easily. Surely, if a woman is denied any lot in
life but that of being the personal body-servant of a despot,
and is dependent for everything upon the chance of finding
one who may be disposed to make a favourite of her instead
of merely a drudge, it is a very cruel aggravation of her fate
that she should be allowed to try this chance only once. The
natural sequel and corollary from this state of things would
be, that since her all in life depends upon obtaining a good
master, she should be allowed to change again and again
until she finds one. I am not saying that she ought to be
allowed this privilege. That is a totally different consideration. The question of divorce, in the sense involving liberty of
remarriage, is one into which it is foreign to my purpose to
enter. All I now say is, that to those to whom nothing but
servitude is allowed, the free choice of servitude is the only,
though a most insufficient, alleviation. Its refusal completes
the assimilation of the wife to the slave—and the slave under
not the mildest form of slavery: for in some slave codes the
slave could, under certain circumstances of ill usage, legally
compel the master to sell him. But no amount of ill usage,
without adultery superadded, will in England free a wife from
her tormentor.

I have no desire to exaggerate, nor does the case stand in
any need of exaggeration. I have described the wife's legal
position, not her actual treatment. The laws of most countries
are far worse than the people who execute them, and many
of them are only able to remain laws by being seldom or
never carried into effect. If married life were all that it might
be expected to be, looking to the laws alone, society would
be a hell upon earth. Happily there are both feelings and
interests which in many men exclude, and in most, greatly
temper, the impulses and propensities which lead to tyranny:
and of those feelings, the tie which connects a man with his
wife affords, in a normal state of things, incomparably the
strongest example. The only tie which at all approaches to it,
that between him and his children, tends, in all save exceptional cases, to strengthen, instead of conflicting with, the
first. Because this is true; because men in general do not

inflict, nor women suffer, all the misery which could be inflicted and suffered if the full power of tyranny with which the man is legally invested were acted on; the defenders of the existing form of the institution think that all its iniquity is justified, and that any complaint is merely quarrelling with the evil which is the price paid for every great good. But the mitigations in practice, which are compatible with maintaining in full legal force this or any other kind of tyranny, instead of being any apology for despotism, only serve to prove what power human nature possesses of reacting against the vilest institutions, and with what vitality the seeds of good as well as those of evil in human character diffuse and propagate themselves. Not a word can be said for despotism in the family which cannot be said for political despotism. . . .

Whether the institution to be defended is slavery, political absolution, or the absolutism of the head of a family, we are always expected to judge of it from its best instances; and we are presented with pictures of loving exercise of authority on one side, loving submission to it on the other—superior wisdom ordering all things for the greatest good of the dependents, and surrounded by their smiles and benedictions. All this would be very much to the purpose if any one pretended that there are no such things as good men. Who doubts that there may be great goodness, and great happiness, and great affection, under the absolute government of a good man? Meanwhile, laws and institutions require to be adapted, not to good men, but to bad. Marriage is not an institution designed for a select few. Men are not required, as a preliminary to the marriage ceremony, to prove by testimonials that they are fit to be trusted with the exercise of absolute power. The tie of affection and obligation to a wife and children is very strong with those whose general social feelings are strong, and with many who are little sensible to any other social ties; but there are all degrees of sensibility and insensibility to it, as there are all grades of goodness and wickedness in men, down to those whom no ties will bind, and on whom society has no action but through its *ultima ratio,* the penalties of the law. In every grade of this descending scale are men to whom are committed all the legal powers of a husband. The vilest malefactor has some wretched woman tied to him, against whom he can commit any atrocity except killing her, and, if tolerably cautious, can do that without much danger of the legal penalty. And how many thousands are there among the lowest classes in every country, who, without being in a legal sense malefactors in any other respect, because in every other quarter their aggressions meet with resistance, indulge the utmost habitual excesses of bodily violence towards the unhappy wife, who alone, at least of grown persons, can neither repel nor escape from their brutality; and towards whom the excess of dependence inspires their mean and savage natures, not with a generous forbearance, and a point of honour to behave well to one whose lot in life is trusted entirely to their kindness, but on the contrary with a notion that the law has delivered her to them as their thing, to be used at their pleasure, and that they are not expected to practise the consideration towards her which is required from them towards everybody else. . . .

. . .

What is it, then, which really tempers the corrupting effects of the power, and makes it compatible with such amount of good as we actually see? Mere feminine blandishments, though of great effect in individual instances, have very little effect in modifying the general tendencies of the situation; for their power only lasts while the woman is young and attractive, often only while her charm is new, and not dimmed by familiarity; and on many men they have not much influence at any time. The real mitigating causes are, the personal affection which is the growth of time, in so far as the man's nature is susceptible of it, and the woman's character sufficiently congenial with his to excite it; their common interests as regards the children, and their general community of interest as concerns third persons (to which however there are very great limitations); the real importance of the wife to his daily comforts and enjoyments, and the value he consequently attaches to her on his personal account, which, in a man capable of feeling for others, lays the foundation of caring for her on her own; and lastly, the influence naturally acquired over almost all human beings by those near to their persons (if not actually disagreeable to them): who, both by their direct entreaties, and by the insensible contagion of their feelings and dispositions, are often able, unless counteracted by some equally strong personal influence, to obtain a degree of command over the conduct of the superior, altogether excessive and unreasonable. Through these various means, the wife frequently exercises even too much power over the man; she is able to affect his conduct in things in which she may not be qualified to influence it for good—in which her influence may be not only unenlightened, but employed on the morally wrong side; and in which he would act better if left to his own prompting. But neither in the affairs of families nor in those of states is power a compensation for the loss of freedom. Her power often gives her what she has no right to, but does not enable her to assert her own rights. A Sultan's favourite slave has slaves under her, over whom she tyrannizes; but the desirable thing would be that she should neither have slaves nor be a slave. By entirely sinking her own existence in her husband; by having no will (or persuading him that she has no will) but his, in anything which regards their joint relation, and by making it the business of her life to work upon his sentiments, a wife may gratify herself by influencing, and very probably perverting, his conduct, in those of his external relations which she has never qualified herself to judge of, or in which she is herself wholly influenced by some personal or other partiality or prejudice. Accordingly, as things now are, those who act most kindly to their wives, are quite as often made worse, as better, by the wife's influence, in respect to all interests extending beyond the family. She is taught that she has no business with things out of that sphere; and accordingly she seldom has any honest and conscientious opinion on them; and therefore hardly ever meddles with them for any legitimate purpose, but generally for an interested one. She neither knows nor cares which is the right side in politics, but she knows what will bring in money or invitations, give her husband a title, her son a place, or her daughter a good marriage.

. . .

There are, no doubt, women, as there are men, whom equality of consideration will not satisfy; with whom there is no peace while any will or wish is regarded but their own. Such persons are a proper subject for the law of divorce. They are only fit to live alone, and no human beings ought to be compelled to associate their lives with them. But the legal subordination tends to make such characters among women more, rather than less, frequent. If the man exerts his whole power, the woman is of course crushed: but if she is treated with indulgence, and permitted to assume power, there is no

rule to set limits to her encroachments. The law, not deter-
mining her rights, but theoretically allowing her none at all,
practically declares that the measure of what she has a right
to, is what she can contrive to get.

The equality of married persons before the law, is not
only the sole mode in which that particular relation can be
made consistent with justice to both sides, and conducive to
the happiness of both, but it is the only means of rendering
the daily life of mankind, in any high sense, a school of moral
cultivation. Though the truth may not be felt or generally
acknowledged for generations to come, the only school of
genuine moral sentiment is society between equals. . . . We
have had the morality of submission, and the morality of
chivalry and generosity; the time is now come for the morality of justice. Whenever, in former ages, any approach has
been made to society in equality, Justice has asserted its
claims as the foundation of virtue. . . . The family, justly
constituted, would be the real school of the virtues of freedom. It is sure to be a sufficient one of everything else. It will
always be a school of obedience for the children, of command
for the parents. What is needed is, that it should be a school
of sympathy in equality, of living together in love, without
power on one side or obedience on the other. This it ought to
be between the parents. It would then be an exercise of those
virtues which each requires to fit them for all other association, and a model to the children of the feelings and conduct
which their temporary training by means of obedience is designed to render habitual, and therefore natural, to them. The
moral training of mankind will never be adapted to the conditions of the life for which all other human progress is a
preparation, until they practise in the family the same moral
rule which is adapted to the normal constitution of human
society. Any sentiment of freedom which can exist in a man
whose nearest and dearest intimacies are with those of whom
he is absolute master, is not the genuine or Christian love of
freedom, but, what the love of freedom generally was in the
ancients and in the middle ages—an intense feeling of the
dignity and importance of his own personality; making him
disdain a yoke for himself, of which he has no abhorrence
whatever in the abstract, but which he is abundantly ready to
impose on others for his own interest or glorification.

●   ●   ●

After what has been said respecting the obligation of obedience, it is almost superfluous to say anything concerning the more special point included in the general one—a woman's right to her own property; for I need not hope that this treatise can make any impression upon those who need anything to convince them that a woman's inheritance or gains ought to be as much her own after marriage as before. The rule is simple: whatever would be the husband's or wife's if they were not married, should be under their exclusive control during marriage; which need not interfere with the power to tie up property by settlement, in order to preserve it for children. Some people are sentimentally shocked at the idea of a separate interest in money matters, as inconsistent with the ideal fusion of two lives into one. For my own part, I am one of the strongest supporters of community of goods, when resulting from an entire unity of feeling in the owners, which makes all things common between them. But I have no relish for a community of goods resting on the doctrine, that what is mine is yours but what is yours is not mine; and I should prefer to decline entering into such a compact with any one, though I were myself the person to profit by it. . . .

. . . When the support of the family depends, not on property, but on earnings, the common arrangement, by which the man earns the income and the wife superintends the domestic expenditure, seems to me in general the most suitable division of labour between the two persons. If, in addition to the physical suffering of bearing children, and the whole responsibility of their care and education in early years, the wife undertakes the careful and economical application of the husband's earnings to the general comfort of the family; she takes not only her fair share, but usually the larger share, of the bodily and mental exertion required by their joint existence. If she undertakes any additional portion, it seldom relieves her from this, but only prevents her from performing it properly. The care which she is herself disabled from taking of the children and the household, nobody else takes; those of the children who do not die, grow up as they best can, and the management of the household is likely to be so bad, as even in point of economy to be a great drawback from the value of the wife's earnings. In an otherwise just state of things, it is not, therefore, I think, a desirable custom, that the wife should contribute by her labour to the income of the family. In an unjust state of things, her doing so may be useful to her, by making her of more value in the eyes of the man who is legally her master; but, on the other hand, it enables him still farther to abuse his power, by forcing her to work, and leaving the support of the family to her exertions, while he spends most of his time in drinking and idleness. The *power* of earning is essential to the dignity of a woman, if she has not independent property. But if marriage were an equal contract, not implying the obligation of obedience; if the connexion were no longer enforced to the oppression of those to whom it is purely a mischief, but a separation, on just terms (I do not now speak of a divorce), could be obtained by any woman who was morally entitled to it; and if she would then find all honourable employments as freely open to her as to men; it would not be necessary for her protection, that during marriage she should make this particular use of her faculties. Like a man when he chooses a profession, so, when a woman marries, it may in general be understood that she makes choice of the management of a household, and the bringing up of a family, as the first call upon her exertions, during as many years of her life as may be required for the purpose; and that she renounces, not all other objects and occupations, but all which are not consistent with the requirements of this. . . . But the utmost latitude ought to exist for the adaptation of general rules to individual suitabilities; and there ought to be nothing to prevent faculties exceptionally adapted to any other pursuit, from obeying their vocation notwithstanding marriage: due provision being made for supplying otherwise any falling-short which might become inevitable, in her full performance of the ordinary functions of mistress of a family. These things, if once opinion were rightly directed on the subject, might with perfect safety be left to be regulated by opinion, without any interference of law.

3

On the other point which is involved in the just equality of women, their admissibility to all the functions and occupations hitherto retained as the monopoly of the stronger sex, I should anticipate no difficulty in convincing any one who has gone with me on the subject of the equality of women in the family. I believe that their disabilities elsewhere are only clung to in order to maintain their subordination in domestic life; because the generality of the male sex cannot yet tolerate the idea of living with an equal. Were it not for that, I think that almost every one, in the existing state of opinion in politics and political economy, would admit the injustice of excluding half the human race from the greater number of lucrative occupations, and from almost all high social functions; ordaining from their birth either that they are not, and cannot by any possibility become, fit for employments which are legally open to the stupidest and basest of the other sex, or else that however fit they may be, those employments shall be interdicted to them, in order to be preserved for the exclusive benefit of males. In the last two centuries, when (which was seldom the case) any reason beyond the mere existence of the fact was thought to be required to justify the disabilities of women, people seldom assigned as a reason their inferior mental capacity; which, in times when there was a real trial of personal faculties (from which all women were not excluded) in the struggles of public life, no one really believed in. The reason given in those days was not women's unfitness, but the interest of society, by which was meant the interest of men: just as the *raison d'état*, meaning the convenience of the government, and the support of existing authority, was deemed a sufficient explanation and excuse for the most flagitious crimes. In the present day, power holds a smoother language, and whomsoever it oppresses, always pretends to do so for their own good: accordingly, when anything is forbidden to women, it is thought necessary to say, and desirable to believe, that they are incapable of doing it, and that they depart from their real path of success and happiness when they aspire to it. But to make this reason plausible (I do not say valid), those by whom it is urged must be prepared to carry it to a much greater length than any one ventures to do in the face of present experience. It is not sufficient to maintain that women on the average are less gifted than men on the average, with certain of the higher mental faculties, or that a smaller number of women than of men are fit for occupations and functions of the highest intellectual character. It is necessary to maintain that no women at all are fit for them, and that the most eminent women are inferior in mental faculties to the most mediocre of the men on whom those functions at present devolve. For if the performance of the function is decided either by competition, or by any mode of choice which secures regard to the public interest, there needs to be no apprehension that any important employments will fall into the hands of women inferior to average men, or to the average of their male competitors. The only result would be that there would be fewer women than men in such employments; a result certain to happen in any case, if only from the preference always likely to be felt by the majority of women for the one vocation in which there is nobody to compete with them. Now, the most determined depreciator of women will not venture to deny, that when we add the experience of recent times to that of ages past, women, and not a few merely, but many women, have proved themselves capable of everything, perhaps without a single exception, which is done by men, and of doing it successfully and creditably. The utmost that can be said is, that there are many things which none of them have succeeded in doing as well as they have been done by some men—many in which they have not reached the very highest rank. But there are extremely few, dependent only on mental faculties, in which they have not attained the rank next to the highest. Is not this enough, and much more than enough, to make it a tyranny to them, and a detriment to society, that they should not be allowed to compete with men for the exercise of these functions? Is it not a mere truism to say, that such functions are often filled by men far less fit for them than numbers of women, and who would be beaten by women in any fair field of competition? What difference does it make that there may be men somewhere, fully employed about other things, who may be still better qualified for the things in question than these women? Does not this take place in all competitions? Is there so great a superfluity of men fit for high duties, that society can afford to reject the service of any competent person? Are we so certain of always finding a man made to our hands for any duty or function of social importance which falls vacant, that we lose nothing by putting a ban upon one-half of mankind, and refusing beforehand to make their faculties available, however distinguished they may be? And even if we could do without them, would it be consistent with justice to refuse to them their fair share of honour and distinction, or to deny to them the equal moral right of all human beings to choose their occupation (short of injury to others) according to their own preferences, at their own risk?

Nor is the injustice confined to them: it is shared by those who are in a position to benefit by their services. To ordain that any kind of persons shall not be physicians, or shall not be advocates, or shall not be members of parliament, is to injure not them only, but all who employ physicians or advocates, or elect members of parliament, and who are deprived of the stimulating effect of greater competition on the exertions of the competitors, as well as restricted to a narrower range of individual choice.

It will perhaps be sufficient if I confine myself, in the details of my argument, to functions of a public nature: since, if I am successful as to those, it probably will be readily granted that women should be admissible to all other occupations to which it is at all material whether they are admitted or not. And here let me begin by marking out one function, broadly distinguished from all others, their right to which is entirely independent of any question which can be raised concerning their faculties. I mean the suffrage, both parliamentary and municipal. The right to share in the choice of those who are to exercise a public trust, is altogether a distinct thing from that of competing for the trust itself. If no one could vote for a member of parliament who was not fit to be a candidate, the government would be a narrow oligarchy indeed. To have a voice in choosing those by whom one is to be governed, is a means of self-protection due to every one, though he were to remain for ever excluded from the function of governing: and that women are considered fit to have such a choice, may be presumed from the fact, that the law already gives it to women in the most important of all cases to themselves: for the choice of the man who is to govern a woman to the end of life, is always supposed to be voluntarily made by herself. In the case of election to public trusts, it is the business of constitutional law to surround the right of suffrage with all needful securities and limitations; but whatever securities are sufficient in the case of the male sex, no others need be required in the case of women. Under whatever conditions, and within whatever limits, men are admitted to the suffrage, there is not a shadow of justification for not admitting women under the same. The majority of the women of any class are not likely to differ in political opinion from the majority of the men of the same class, unless the question be one in which the interests of women, as such, are in some way involved; and if they are so, women require

the suffrage, as their guarantee of just and equal consideration. This ought to be obvious even to those who coincide in
no other of the doctrines for which I contend. Even if every
woman were a wife, and if every wife ought to be a slave, all
the more would these slaves stand in need of legal protection:
and we know what legal protection the slaves have, where the
laws are made by their masters.

With regard to the fitness of women, not only to participate in elections, but themselves to hold offices or practise
professions involving important public responsibilities; I have
already observed that this consideration is not essential to the
practical question in dispute: since any woman, who succeeds
in an open profession, proves by that very fact that she is
qualified for it. And in the case of public offices, if the political
system of the country is such as to exclude unfit men, it will
equally exclude unfit women: while if it is not, there is no
additional evil in the fact that the unfit persons whom it
admits may be either women or men. As long therefore as it
is acknowledged that even a few women may be fit for these
duties, the laws which shut the door on those exceptions cannot be justified by any opinion which can be held respecting
the capacities of women in general. . . .

If anything conclusive could be inferred from experience,
without psychological analysis, it would be that the things
which women are not allowed to do are the very ones for
which they are peculiarly qualified; since their vocation for
government has made its way, and become conspicuous,
through the very few opportunities which have been given;
while in the lines of distinction which apparently were freely
open to them, they have by no means so eminently distinguished themselves. We know how small a number of reigning queens history presents, in comparison with that of kings.
Of this smaller number a far larger proportion have shown
talents for rule; though many of them have occupied the
throne in difficult periods. It is remarkable, too, that they
have, in a great number of instances, been distinguished by
merits the most opposite to the imaginary and conventional
character of women: they have been as much remarked for
the firmness and vigour of their rule, as for its intelligence.
When, to queens and empresses, we add regents, and viceroys
of provinces, the list of women who have been eminent rulers
of mankind swells to a great length. This fact is so undeniable, that some one, long ago, tried to retort the argument,

and turned the admitted truth into an additional insult, by saying that queens are better than kings, because under kings women govern, but under queens, men. . . .

Is it reasonable to think that those who are fit for the greater functions of politics, are incapable of qualifying themselves for the less? Is there any reason in the nature of things, that the wives and sisters of princes should, whenever called on, be found as competent as the princes themselves to *their* business, but that the wives and sisters of statesmen, and administrators, and directors of companies, and managers of public institutions, should be unable to do what is done by their brothers and husbands? The real reason is plain enough; it is that princesses, being more raised above the generality of men by their rank than placed below them by their sex, have never been taught that it was improper for them to concern themselves with politics; but have been allowed to feel the liberal interest natural to any cultivated human being, in the great transactions which took place around them, and in which they might be called on to take a part. The ladies of reigning families are the only women who are allowed the same range of interests and freedom of development as men; and it is precisely in their case that there is not found to be any inferiority. Exactly where and in proportion as women's capacities for government have been tried, in that proportion have they been found adequate.

This fact is in accordance with the best general conclusions which the world's imperfect experience seems as yet to suggest, concerning the peculiar tendencies and aptitudes characteristic of women, as women have hitherto been. I do not say, as they will continue to be; for . . . I consider it presumption in any one to pretend to decide what women are or are not, can or cannot be, by natural constitution. They have always hitherto been kept, as far as regards spontaneous development, in so unnatural a state, that their nature cannot but have been greatly distorted and disguised; and no one can safely pronounce that if women's nature were left to choose its direction as freely as men's, and if no artificial bent were attempted to be given to it except that required by the conditions of human society, and given to both sexes alike, there would be any material difference, or perhaps any difference at all, in the character and capacities which would unfold themselves. . . . Let us consider the special nature of the mental capacities most characteristic of a woman of talent. They are all of a kind which fits them for practice, and makes them tend towards it. What is meant by a woman's capacity of intuitive perception? It means, a rapid and correct insight into present fact. It has nothing to do with general principles. Nobody ever perceived a scientific law of nature by intuition, nor arrived at a general rule of duty or prudence by it. These are results of slow and careful collection and comparison of experience; and neither the men nor the women of intuition usually shine in this department, unless, indeed, the experience necessary is such as they can acquire by themselves. For what is called their intuitive sagacity makes them peculiarly apt in gathering such general truths as can be collected from their individual means of observation. When, consequently, they chance to be as well provided as men are with the results of other people's experience, by reading and education, . . . they are better furnished than men in general with the essential requisites of skilful and successful practice. Men who have been much taught, are apt to be deficient in the sense of present fact; they do not see, in the facts which they are called upon to deal with, what is really there, but what they have been taught to expect. This is seldom the case with women of any ability. Their capacity of "intuition" preserves them from it. With equality of experience and of general faculties, a woman usually sees much more than a man of what is immediately before her. Now this sensibility to the present, is the main quality on which the capacity for practice, as distinguished from theory, depends. To discover general principles, belongs to the speculative faculty: to discern and discriminate the particular cases in which they are and are not applicable, constitutes practical talent: and for this, women as they now are have a peculiar aptitude. I admit that there can be no good practice without principles, and that the predominant place which quickness of observation holds among a woman's faculties, makes her particularly apt to build over-hasty generalizations upon her own observation; though at the same time no less ready in rectifying those generalizations, as her observation takes a wider range. But the corrective to this defect, is access to the experience of the human race; general knowledge—exactly the thing which education can best supply. A woman's mistakes are specifically those of a clever self-educated man, who often sees what men trained in routine do not see, but falls into errors for want of knowing things which have long been known. Of course he has acquired much of the pre-existing knowledge, or he could not have got on at all; but what he knows of it he has picked up in fragments and at random, as women do.

But this gravitation of women's minds to the present, to the real, to actual fact, while in its exclusiveness it is a source of errors, is also a most useful counteractive of the contrary error. The principal and most characteristic aberration of speculative minds as such, consists precisely in the deficiency of this lively perception and ever-present sense of objective fact. For want of this, they often not only overlook the contradiction which outward facts oppose to their theories, but lose sight of the legitimate purpose of speculation altogether, and let their speculative faculties go astray into regions not peopled with real beings, animate or inanimate, even idealized, but with personified shadows created by the illusions of metaphysics or by the mere entanglement of words, and think these shadows the proper objects of the highest, the most transcendant, philosophy. . . . A woman seldom runs wild after an abstraction. The habitual direction of her mind to dealing with things as individuals rather than in groups, and (what is closely connected with it) her more lively interest in the present feelings of persons, which makes her consider first of all, in anything which claims to be applied to practice, in what manner persons will be affected by it—these two things make her extremely unlikely to put faith in any speculation which loses sight of individuals, and deals with things as if they existed for the benefit of some imaginary entity, some mere creation of the mind, not resolvable into the feelings of living beings. Women's thoughts are thus as useful in giving reality to those of thinking men, as men's thoughts in giving width and largeness to those of women. In depth, as distinguished from breadth, I greatly doubt if even now, women, compared with men, are at any disadvantage. . . .

. . . Let us now consider another of the admitted superiorities of clever women, greater quickness of apprehension. Is not this pre-eminently a quality which fits a person for practice? In action, everything continually depends upon deciding promptly. In speculation, nothing does. A mere thinker can wait, can take time to consider, can collect additional evidence; he is not obliged to complete his philosophy at once, lest the opportunity should go by. The power of drawing the best conclusion possible from insufficient data is not indeed useless in philosophy; the construction of a provisional hypothesis consistent with all known facts is often the needful basis for further inquiry. . . . He who has not his faculties under immediate command, in the contingencies of action, might as well not have them at all. He may be fit to criticize, but he is not fit to act. Now it is in this that women, and the men who are most like women, confessedly excel. The other sort of man, however pre-eminent may be his faculties, arrives slowly at complete command of them: rapidity of judgment and promptitude of judicious action, even in the things he knows best, are the gradual and late result of strenuous effort grown into habit.

It will be said, perhaps, that the greater nervous susceptibility of women is a disqualification for practice, in anything but domestic life, by rendering them mobile, changeable, too vehemently under the influence of the moment, incapable of dogged perseverance, unequal and uncertain in the power of using their faculties. I think that these phrases sum up the greater part of the objections commonly made to the fitness of women for the higher class of serious business. Much of all this is the mere overflow of nervous energy run to waste, and would cease when the energy was directed to a definite end. Much is also the result of conscious or unconscious cultivation; as we see by the almost total disappearance of "hysterics" and fainting fits, since they have gone out of fashion. Moreover, when people are brought up, like many women of the higher classes (though less so in our own country than in any other) a kind of hothouse plants, shielded from the wholesome vicissitudes of air and temperature, and untrained in any of the occupations and exercises which give stimulus and development to the circulatory and muscular system, while their nervous system, especially in its emotional department, is kept in unnaturally active play; it is no wonder if those of them who do not die of consumption, grow up with constitutions liable to derangement from slight causes, both internal and external, and without stamina to support any task, physical or mental, requiring continuity of effort. But women brought up to work for their livelihood show none of these morbid characteristics, unless indeed they are chained to an excess of sedentary work in confined and unhealthy rooms. Women who in their early years have shared in the healthful physical education and bodily freedom of their brothers, and who obtain a sufficiency of pure air and exercise in after-life, very rarely have any excessive susceptibility of nerves which can disqualify them for active pursuits. There is indeed a certain proportion of persons, in both sexes, in whom an unusual degree of nervous sensibility is constitutional, and of so marked a character as to be the feature of their organization which exercises the greatest influence over the whole character of the vital phenomena. . . . We will assume this as a fact: and let me then ask, are men of nervous temperament found to be unfit for the duties and pursuits usually followed by men? If not, why should women of the same temperament be unfit for them? The peculiarities of the temperament are, no doubt, within certain limits, an obstacle to success in some employments, though an aid to it in others. But when the occupation is suitable to the temperament, and sometimes even when it is unsuitable, the most brilliant examples of success are continually given by the men of high nervous sensibility. They are distinguished in their practical manifestations chiefly by this, that being susceptible of a higher degree of excitement than those of another physical constitution, their powers when excited differ more than in the case of other people, from those shown in their ordinary state: they are raised, as it were, above themselves, and do things with ease which they are wholly incapable of at other times. . . . It is the character of the nervous temperament to be capable of *sustained* excitement, holding out through long continued efforts. It is what is meant by *spirit*. It is what makes the high-bred racehorse run without slackening speed till he drops down dead. It is what has enabled so many delicate women to maintain the most sublime constancy not only at the stake, but through a long preliminary succession of mental and bodily tortures. It is evident that people of this temperament are particularly apt for what may be called the executive department of the leadership of mankind. They are the material of great orators, great preachers, impressive diffusers of moral influences. Their constitution might be deemed less favourable to the qualities required from a statesman in the cabinet, or from a judge. It would be so, if the consequence necessarily followed that because people are excitable they must always be in a state of excitement. But this is wholly a question of training. Strong feeling is the instrument and element of strong self-control: but it requires to be cultivated in that direction. . . .

Supposing it, however, to be true that women's minds are by nature more mobile than those of men, less capable of persisting long in the same continuous effort, more fitted for dividing their faculties among many things than for travelling in any one path to the highest point which can be reached by it: this may be true of women as they now are (though not without great and numerous exceptions), and may account for their having remained behind the highest order of men in precisely the things in which this absorption of the whole mind in one set of ideas and occupations may seem to be most requisite. Still, this difference is one which can only affect the kind of excellence, not the excellence itself, or its practical worth: and it remains to be shown whether this exclusive working of a part of the mind, this absorption of the whole thinking faculty in a single subject, and concentration of it on a single work, is the normal and healthful condition of the human faculties, even for speculative uses. I believe that what is gained in special development by this concentration, is lost in the capacity of the mind for the other purposes of life; and even in abstract thought, it is my decided opinion that the mind does more by frequently returning to a difficult problem, than by sticking to it without interruption. For the purposes, at all events, of practice, from its highest to its humblest departments, the capacity of passing promptly from one subject of consideration to another, without letting the active spring of the intellect run down between the two, is a power far more valuable; and this power women pre-eminently possess, by virtue of the very mobility of which they are accused. . . .

. . .

To so ridiculous an extent are the notions formed of the nature of women, mere empirical generalizations, framed, without philosophy or analysis, upon the first instances which present themselves, that the popular idea of it is different in different countries, according as the opinions and social circumstances of the country have given to the women living in it any specialty of development or non-development. An Oriental thinks that women are by nature peculiarly voluptuous; see the violent abuse of them on this ground in Hindoo writings. An Englishman usually thinks that they are by nature cold. The sayings about women's fickleness are mostly of French origin; from the famous distich of Francis the First, upward and downward. In England it is a common remark, how much more constant women are than men. Inconstancy has been longer reckoned discreditable to a woman, in England than in France; and Englishwomen are besides, in their inmost nature, much more subdued to opinion. It may be remarked by the way, that Englishmen are in peculiarly unfavourable circumstances for attempting to judge what is or is not natural, not merely to women, but to men, or to human beings altogether, at least if they have only English experience to go upon: because there is no place where human nature shows so little of its original lineaments. Both in a good and a bad sense, the English are farther from a state of nature than any other modern people. They are, more than any other people, a product of civilization and discipline. England is the country in which social discipline has most succeeded, not so much in conquering, as in suppressing, whatever is liable to conflict with it. The English, more than any other people, not only act but feel according to rule. In other countries, the taught opinion, or the requirement of society, may be the stronger power, but the promptings of the individual nature are always visible under it, and often resisting it: rule may be stronger than nature, but nature is still there. In England, rule has to a great degree substituted itself for nature. The greater part of life is carried on, not by following inclination under the control of rule, but by having no inclination but that of following a rule. . . .

I have said that it cannot now be known how much of the existing mental differences between men and women is natural, and how much artificial; whether there are any natural differences at all; or, supposing all artificial causes of difference to be withdrawn, what natural character would be revealed. I am not about to attempt what I have pronounced impossible: but doubt does not forbid conjecture, and where certainty is unattainable, there may yet be the means of arriving at some degree of probability. . . .

Let us take, then, the only marked case which observation affords, of apparent inferiority of women to men, if we except the merely physical one of bodily strength. No production in philosophy, science, or art, entitled to the first rank, has been the work of a woman. Is there any mode of accounting for this, without supposing that women are naturally incapable of producing them?

In the first place, we may fairly question whether experience has afforded sufficient grounds for an induction. It is scarcely three generations since women, saving very rare exceptions, have begun to try their capacity in philosophy, science, or art. It is only in the present generation that their attempts have been at all numerous; and they are even now extremely few, everywhere but in England and France. It is a relevant question, whether a mind possessing the requisites of first-rate eminence in speculation or creative art could have been expected, on the mere calculation of chances, to turn up during that lapse of time, among the women whose tastes and personal position admitted of their devoting themselves to these pursuits. In all things which there has yet been time for —in all but the very highest grades in the scale of excellence, especially in the department in which they have been longest engaged, literature (both prose and poetry)—women have done quite as much, have obtained fully as high prizes as many of them, as could be expected from the length of time and the number of competitors. . . .

If we consider the works of women in modern times, and contrast them with those of men, either in the literary or the artistic department, such inferiority as may be observed resolves itself essentially into one thing: but that is a most material one; deficiency of originality. . . . Thoughts original, in the sense of being unborrowed—of being derived from the thinker's own observations or intellectual processes— are abundant in the writings of women. But they have not yet produced any of those great and luminous new ideas which form an era in thought, nor those fundamentally new conceptions in art, which open a vista of possible effects not before thought of, and found a new school. Their compositions are mostly grounded on the existing fund of thought, and their creations do not deviate widely from existing types. This is the sort of inferiority which their works manifest: for in point of execution, in the detailed application of thought, and the perfection of style, there is no inferiority. Our best novelists in point of composition, and of the management of detail, have mostly been women; and there is not in all modern literature a more eloquent vehicle of thought than the style of Madame de Stael, nor, as a specimen of purely artistic excellence, anything superior to the prose of Madame Sand, whose style acts upon the nervous system like a symphony of Haydn or Mozart. High originality of conception is, as I have said, what is chiefly wanting. And now to examine if there is any manner in which this deficiency can be accounted for. . . .

It no doubt often happens that a person, who has not

widely and accurately studied the thoughts of others on a subject, has by natural sagacity a happy intuition, which he can suggest, but cannot prove, which yet when matured may be an important addition to knowledge: but even then, no justice can be done to it until some other person, who does possess the previous acquirements, takes it in hand, tests it, gives it a scientific or practical form, and fits it into its place among the existing truths of philosophy or science. Is it supposed that such felicitous thoughts do not occur to women? They occur by hundreds to every woman of intellect. But they are mostly lost, for want of a husband or friend who has the other knowledge which can enable him to estimate them properly and bring them before the world: and even when they are brought before it, they generally appear as his ideas, not their real author's. Who can tell how many of the most original thoughts put forth by male writers, belong to a woman by suggestion, to themselves only by verifying and working out? If I may judge by my own case, a very large proportion indeed.

If we turn from pure speculation to literature in the narrow sense of the term, and the fine arts, there is a very obvious reason why women's literature is, in its general conception and in its main features, an imitation of men's. Why is the Roman literature, as critics proclaim to satiety, not original, but an imitation of the Greek? Simply because the Greeks came first. If women lived in a different country from men, and had never read any of their writings, they would have had a literature of their own. As it is, they have not created one, because they found a highly advanced literature already created. If there had been no suspension of the knowledge of antiquity, or if the Renaissance had occurred before the Gothic cathedrals were built, they never would have been built. We see that, in France and Italy, imitation of the ancient literature stopped the original development even after it had commenced. All women who write are pupils of the great male writers. A painter's early pictures, even if he be a Raffaelle, are undistinguishable in style from those of his master. Even a Mozart does not display his powerful originality in his earliest pieces. What years are to a gifted individual, generations are to a mass. If women's literature is destined to have a different collective character from that of men, depending on any difference of natural tendencies, much longer time is necessary than has yet elapsed, before it can emancipate itself from the influence of accepted models, and guide itself by its own impulses. But if, as I believe, there will not prove to be any natural tendencies common to women, and distinguishing their genius from that of men, yet every individual writer among them has her individual tendencies, which at present are still subdued by the influence of precedent and example: and it will require generations more, before their individuality is sufficiently developed to make head against the influence. . . .

There are other reasons, besides those which we have now given, that help to explain why women remain behind men, even in the pursuits which are open to both. For one thing, very few women have time for them. This may seem a paradox; it is an undoubted social fact. The time and thoughts of every woman have to satisfy great previous demands on them for things practical. There is, first, the superintendence of the family and the domestic expenditure, which occupies at least one woman in every family, generally the one of mature years and acquired experience; unless the family is so rich as to admit of delegating that task to hired agency, and submitting to all the waste and malversation inseparable from that mode of conducting it. The superintendence of a household, even when not in other respects laborious, is extremely onerous to the thoughts; it requires incessant vigilance, an eye which no detail escapes, and presents questions for consideration and solution, foreseen and unforeseen, at every hour of the day, from which the person responsible for them can hardly ever shake herself free. If a woman is of a rank and circumstances which relieve her in a measure from these cares, she has still devolving on her the management for the whole family of its intercourse with others—of what is called society, and the less the call made on her by the former duty, the greater is always the development of the latter: the dinner parties, concerts, evening parties, morning visits, letter writing, and all that goes with them. . . .

There is another consideration to be added to all these. In the various arts and intellectual occupations, there is a degree of proficiency sufficient for living by it, and there is a higher degree on which depend the great productions which immortalize a name. To the attainment of the former, there are adequate motives in the case of all who follow the pursuit professionally: the other is hardly ever attained where there is not, or where there has not been at some period of life, an ardent desire of celebrity. Nothing less is commonly a sufficient stimulus to undergo the long and patient drudgery, which, in the case even of the greatest natural gifts, is absolutely required for great eminence in pursuits in which we already possess so many splendid memorials of the highest genius. Now, whether the cause be natural or artificial, women seldom have this eagerness for fame. Their ambition is generally confined within narrower bounds. The influence they seek is over those who immediately surround them. Their desire is to be liked, loved, or admired, by those whom they see with their eyes: and the proficiency in knowledge, arts, and accomplishments, which is sufficient for that, almost always contents them. This is a trait of character which cannot be left out of the account in judging of women as they are. I do not at all believe that it is inherent in women. It is only the natural result of their circumstances. The love of fame in men is encouraged by education and opinion: to "scorn delights and live laborious days" for its sake, is accounted the part of "noble minds," even if spoken of as their "last infirmity," and is stimulated by the access which fame gives to all objects of ambition, including even the favour of women; while to women themselves all these objects are closed, and the desire of fame itself considered daring and unfeminine. Besides, how could it be that a woman's interests should not be all concentrated upon the impressions made on those who come into her daily life, when society has ordained that all her duties should be to them, and has contrived that all her comforts should depend on them? The natural desire of consideration from our fellow creatures is as strong in a woman as in a man; but society has so ordered things that public consideration is, in all ordinary cases, only attainable by her through the consideration of her husband or of her male relations, while her private consideration is forfeited by making herself individually prominent, or appearing in any other character than that of an appendage to men. Whoever is in the least capable of estimating the influence on the mind of the entire domestic and social position and the whole habit of a life, must easily recognise in that influence a complete explanation of nearly all the apparent differences between women and men, including the whole of those which imply any inferiority.

4

There remains a question, not of less importance than those already discussed, and which will be asked the most importunately by those opponents whose conviction is somewhat shaken on the main point. What good are we to expect from the changes proposed in our customs and institutions? Would mankind be at all better off if women were free? If not, why disturb their minds, and attempt to make a social revolution in the name of an abstract right? . . .

. . . In regard . . . to the larger question, the removal of women's disabilities—their recognition as the equals of men in all that belongs to citizenship—the opening to them of all honourable employments, and of the training and education which qualifies for those employments—there are many persons for whom it is not enough that the inequality has no just or legitimate defence; they require to be told what express advantage would be obtained by abolishing it.

To which let me first answer, the advantage of having the most universal and pervading of all human relations regulated by justice instead of injustice. The vast amount of this gain to human nature, it is hardly possible, by any explanation or illustration, to place in a stronger light than it is placed by the bare statement, to any one who attaches a moral meaning to words. All the selfish propensities, the self-worship, the unjust self-preference, which exist among mankind, have their source and root in, and derive their principal nourishment from, the present constitution of the relation between men and women. Think what it is to a boy, to grow up to manhood in the belief that without any merit or any exertion of his own, though he may be the most frivolous and empty or the most ignorant and stolid of mankind, by the mere fact of being born a male he is by right the superior of all and every one of an entire half of the human race: including probably some whose real superiority to himself he has daily or hourly occasion to feel; but even if in his whole conduct he habitually follows a woman's guidance, still, if he is a fool, she thinks that of course she is not, and cannot be, equal in ability and judgment to himself; and if he is not a fool, he does worse— he sees that she is superior to him, and believes that, notwithstanding her superiority, he is entitled to command and she is bound to obey. What must be the effect on his character, of this lesson? And men of the cultivated classes are often not aware how deeply it sinks into the immense majority of male minds. For, among right-feeling and well-bred people, the inequality is kept as much as possible out of sight; above all, out of sight of the children. As much obedience is required from boys to their mother as to their father: they are not permitted to domineer over their sisters, nor are they accustomed to see these postponed to them, but the contrary; the compensations of the chivalrous feeling being made prominent, while the servitude which requires them is kept in the background. Well brought-up youths in the higher classes thus often escape the bad influences of the situation in their early years, and only experience them when, arrived at manhood, they fall under the dominion of facts as they really exist. Such people are little aware, when a boy is differently brought up, how early the notion of his inherent superiority to a girl arises in his mind; how it grows with his growth and strengthens with his strength; how it is inoculated by one schoolboy upon another; how early the youth thinks himself superior to his mother, owing her perhaps forbearance, but no real respect; and how sublime and sultan-like a sense of superiority he feels, above all, over the woman whom he honours by admitting her to a partnership of his life. Is it imagined that all this does not pervert the whole manner of existence of the man, both as an individual and as a social being? . . . [W]hen the feeling of being raised above the whole of the other sex is combined with personal authority over one individual among them; the situation, if a school of conscientious and affectionate forbearance to those whose strongest points of character are conscience and affection, is to men of another quality a regularly constituted Academy or Gymnasium for training them in arrogance and overbearingness; which vices, if curbed by the certainty of resistance in their intercourse with other men, their equals, break out towards all who are in a position to be obliged to tolerate them, and often revenge themselves upon the unfortunate wife for the involuntary restraint which they are obliged to submit to elsewhere. . . .

. . . If no authority, not in its nature temporary, were allowed to one human being over another, society would not be employed in building up propensities with one hand which it has to curb with the other. The child would really, for the first time in man's existence on earth, be trained in the way he should go, and when he was old there would be a chance that he would not depart from it. But so long as the right of the strong to power over the weak rules in the very heart of society, the attempt to make the equal right of the weak the principle of its outward actions will always be an uphill struggle; for the law of justice, which is also that of Christianity, will never get possession of men's inmost sentiments; they will be working against it, even when bending to it.

The second benefit to be expected from giving to women the free use of their faculties, by leaving them the free choice of their employments, and opening to them the same field of occupation and the same prizes and encouragements as to other human beings, would be that of doubling the mass of mental faculties available for the higher service of humanity. Where there is now one person qualified to benefit mankind and promote the general improvement, as a public teacher, or an administrator of some branch of public or social affairs, there would then be a chance of two. . . .

This great accession to the intellectual power of the species, and to the amount of intellect available for the good management of its affairs, would be obtained, partly, through the better and more complete intellectual education of women, which would then improve *pari passu* with that of men. Women in general would be brought up equally capable of understanding business, public affairs, and the higher matters of speculation, with men in the same class of society; and the select few of the one as well as of the other sex, who were qualified not only to comprehend what is done or thought by others, but to think or do something considerable themselves, would meet with the same facilities for improving and training their capacities in the one sex as in the other. In this way, the widening of the sphere of action for women would operate for good, by raising their education to the level of that of men, and making the one participate in all improvements made in the other. . . .

Besides the addition to the amount of individual talent available for the conduct of human affairs . . . the opinion of women would then possess a more beneficial, rather than a greater, influence upon the general mass of human belief and sentiment. I say a more beneficial, rather than a greater influence; for the influence of women over the general tone of opinion has always, or at least from the earliest known period, been very considerable. The influence of mothers on the early character of their sons, and the desire of young men to recommend themselves to young women, have in all recorded times been important agencies in the formation of character, and have determined some of the chief steps in the progress of civilization. . . . The other mode in which the effect of women's opinion has been conspicuous, is by giving a powerful stimulus to those qualities in men, which, not being themselves trained in, it was necessary for them that they should find in their protectors. Courage, and the military virtues generally, have at all times been greatly indebted to the desire which men felt of being admired by women: and the stimulus reaches far beyond this one class of eminent qualities, since, by a very natural effect of their position, the best passport to the admiration and favour of women has always been to be thought highly of by men. From the combination of the two kinds of moral influence thus exercised by women, arose the spirit of chivalry: the peculiarity of which is, to aim at combining the highest standard of the warlike qualities with the cultivation of a totally different class of virtues—those of gentleness, generosity, and self-abnegation, towards the nonmilitary and defenceless classes generally, and a special submission and worship directed towards women; who were distinguished from the other defenceless classes by the high rewards which they had it in their power voluntarily to bestow on those who endeavoured to earn their favour, instead of extorting their subjection. Though the practice of chivalry fell even more sadly short of its theoretic standard than practice generally falls below theory, it remains one of the most precious monuments of the moral history of our race; as a remarkable instance of a concerted and organized attempt by a most disorganized and distracted society, to raise up and carry into practice a moral ideal greatly in advance of its social condition and institutions; so much so as to have been completely frustrated in the main object, yet never entirely inefficacious, and which has left a most sensible, and for the most part a highly valuable impress on the ideas and feelings of all subsequent times.

. . .

It is often said that in the classes most exposed to temptation, a man's wife and children tend to keep him honest and respectable, both by the wife's direct influence, and by the concern he feels for their future welfare. This may be so, and no doubt often is so, with those who are more weak than wicked; and this beneficial influence would be preserved and strengthened under equal laws; it does not depend on the woman's servitude, but is, on the contrary, diminished by the disrespect which the inferior class of men always at heart feel towards those who are subject to their power. But when we ascend higher in the scale, we come among a totally different set of moving forces. The wife's influence tends, as far as it goes, to prevent the husband from falling below the common standard of approbation of the country. It tends quite as strongly to hinder him from rising above it. The wife is the auxiliary of the common public opinion. A man who is married to a woman his inferior in intelligence, finds her a perpetual dead weight, or, worse than a dead weight, a drag, upon every aspiration of his to be better than public opinion requires him to be. It is hardly possible for one who is in these bonds, to attain exalted virtue. If he differs in his opinion from the mass—if he sees truths which have not yet dawned upon them, or if, feeling in his heart truths which they nominally recognise, he would like to act up to those truths more conscientiously than the generality of mankind—to all such thoughts and desires, marriage is the heaviest of drawbacks, unless he be so fortunate as to have a wife as much above the common level as he himself is.

For, in the first place, there is always some sacrifice of personal interest required; either of social consequence, or of pecuniary means; perhaps the risk of even the means of subsistence. These sacrifices and risks he may be willing to encounter for himself; but he will pause before he imposes them on his family. And his family in this case means his wife and daughters; for he always hopes that his sons will feel as he feels himself, and that what he can do without, they will do without, willingly, in the same cause. But his daughters—their marriage may depend upon it: and his wife, who is unable to enter into or understand the objects for which these sacrifices are made—who, if she thought them worth any sacrifice, would think so on trust, and solely for his sake—who can participate in none of the enthusiasm or the self-approbation he himself may feel, while the things which he is disposed to sacrifice are all in all to her; will not the best and most unselfish man hesitate the longest before bringing on her this consequence? If it be not the comforts of life, but only social consideration, that is at stake, the burthen upon his conscience and feelings is still very severe.

Whoever has a wife and children has given hostages to Mrs. Grundy. . . . The almost invariable tendency of the wife to place her influence in the same scale with social consideration, is sometimes made a reproach to women, and represented as a peculiar trait of feebleness and childishness of character in them: surely with great injustice. Society makes the whole life of a woman, in the easy classes, a continued self-sacrifice; it exacts from her an unremitting restraint of the whole of her natural inclinations, and the sole return it makes to her for what often deserves the name of a martyrdom, is consideration. . . .

There is another very injurious aspect in which the effect, not of women's disabilities directly, but of the broad line of difference which those disabilities create between the education and character of a woman and that of a man, requires to be considered. Nothing can be more unfavourable to that union of thoughts and inclinations which is the ideal of married life. Intimate society between people radically dissimilar to one another, is an idle dream. Unlikeness may attract, but it is likeness which retains; and in proportion to the likeness is the suitability of the individuals to give each other a happy life. While women are so unlike men, it is not wonderful that selfish men should feel the need of arbitrary power in their own hands, to arrest *in limine* the life-long conflict of inclinations, by deciding every question on the side of their own preference. When people are extremely unlike, there can be no real identity of interest. . . . [T]hough it may stimulate the amatory propensities of men, it does not conduce to married happiness, to exaggerate by differences of education whatever may be the native differences of the sexes. If the married pair are well-bred and well-behaved people, they tolerate each other's tastes; but is mutual toleration what people look forward to, when they enter into marriage? These differences of inclination will naturally make their wishes different, if not restrained by affection or duty, as to almost all domestic questions which arise. What a difference there must be in the society which the two persons will wish to frequent, or be frequented by! Each will desire associates who share their own tastes: the persons agreeable to one, will be indifferent or positively disagreeable to the other; yet there can be none who are not common to both, for married people do not now live in different parts of the house and have totally different visiting lists, as in the reign of Louis XV. They cannot help

having different wishes as to the bringing up of the children:
each will wish to see reproduced in them their own tastes and
sentiments: and there is either a compromise, and only a half-
satisfaction to either, or the wife has to yield—often with
bitter suffering; and, with or without intention, her occult
influence continues to counterwork the husband's purposes.

It would of course be extreme folly to suppose that these
differences of feeling and inclination only exist because
women are brought up differently from men, and that there
would not be differences of taste under any imaginable circumstances. But there is nothing beyond the mark in saying
that the distinction in bringing-up immensely aggravates
those differences, and renders them wholly inevitable. While
women are brought up as they are, a man and a woman will
but rarely find in one another real agreement of tastes and
wishes as to daily life. . . . [W]hen each of two persons,
instead of being a nothing, is a something; when they are
attached to one another, and are not too much unlike to
begin with; the constant partaking in the same things, assisted by their sympathy, draws out the latent capacities of
each for being interested in the things which were at first
interesting only to the other; and works a gradual assimilation
of the tastes and characters to one another, partly by the
insensible modification of each, but more by a real enriching
of the two natures, each acquiring the tastes and capacities of
the other in addition to its own. This often happens between
two friends of the same sex, who are much associated in their
daily life: and it would be a common, if not the commonest,
case in marriage, did not the totally different bringing-up of
the two sexes make it next to an impossibility to form a really
well-assorted union. Were this remedied, whatever differences
there might still be in individual tastes, there would at least
be, as a general rule, complete unity and unanimity as to the
great objects of life. When the two persons both care for great
objects, and are a help and encouragement to each other in
whatever regards these, the minor matters on which their
tastes may differ are not all-important to them; and there is
a foundation for solid friendship, of an enduring character,
more likely than anything else to make it, through the whole
of life, a greater pleasure to each to give pleasure to the other,
than to receive it.

. . . The association of men with women in daily life is
much closer and more complete than it ever was before. Men's

life is more domestic. Formerly, their pleasures and chosen occupations were among men, and in men's company: their wives had but a fragment of their lives. At the present time, the progress of civilization, and the turn of opinion against the rough amusements and convivial excesses which formerly occupied most men in their hours of relaxation—together with (it must be said) the improved tone of modern feeling as to the reciprocity of duty which binds the husband towards the wife—have thrown the man very much more upon home and its inmates, for his personal and social pleasures: while the kind and degree of improvement which has been made in women's education, has made them in some degree capable of being his companions in ideas and mental tastes, while leaving them, in most cases, still hopelessly inferior to him. His desire of mental communion is thus in general satisfied by a communion from which he learns nothing. An unimproving and unstimulating companionship is substituted for (what he might otherwise have been obliged to seek) the society of his equals in powers and his fellows in the higher pursuits. We see, accordingly, that young men of the greatest promise generally cease to improve as soon as they marry, and, not improving, inevitably degenerate. If the wife does not push the husband forward, she always holds him back. He ceases to care for what she does not care for; he no longer desires, and ends by disliking and shunning, society congenial to his former aspirations, and which would now shame his falling-off from them; his higher faculties both of mind and heart cease to be called into activity. And this change coinciding with the new and selfish interests which are created by the family, after a few years he differs in no material respect from those who have never had wishes for anything but the common vanities and the common pecuniary objects.

What marriage may be in the case of two persons of cultivated faculties, identical in opinions and purposes, between whom there exists that best kind of equality, similarity of powers and capacities with reciprocal superiority in them—so that each can enjoy the luxury of looking up to the other, and can have alternately the pleasure of leading and of being led in the path of development—I will not attempt to describe. To those who can conceive it, there is no need; to those who cannot, it would appear the dream of an enthusiast. But I maintain, with the profoundest conviction, that this, and this only, is the ideal of marriage; and that all opinions, customs, and institutions which favour any other notion of it, or turn the conceptions and aspirations connected with it into any other direction, by whatever pretences they may be coloured, are relics of primitive barbarism. The moral regeneration of mankind will only really commence, when the most fundamental of the social relations is placed under the rule of equal justice, and when human beings learn to cultivate their strongest sympathy with an equal in rights and in cultivation.

Thus far, the benefits which it has appeared that the world would gain by ceasing to make sex a disqualification for privileges and a badge of subjection, are social rather than individual; consisting in an increase of the general fund of thinking and acting power, and an improvement in the general conditions of the association of men with women. But it would be a grievous understatement of the case to omit the most direct benefit of all, the unspeakable gain in private happiness to the liberated half of the species; the difference to them between a life of subjection to the will of others, and a life of rational freedom. After the primary necessities of food and raiment, freedom is the first and strongest want of human nature. . . .

. . .

When we consider the positive evil caused to the disqualified half of the human race by their disqualification—first in the loss of the most inspiriting and elevating kind of personal enjoyment, and next in the weariness, disappointment, and profound dissatisfaction with life, which are so often the substitute for it; one feels that among all the lessons which men require for carrying on the struggle against the inevitable imperfections of their lot on earth, there is no lesson which they more need, than not to add to the evils which nature inflicts, by their jealous and prejudiced restrictions on one another. Their vain fears only substitute other and worse evils for those which they are idly apprehensive of: while every restraint on the freedom of conduct of any of their human fellow creatures, (otherwise than by making them responsible for any evil actually caused by it), dries up *pro tanto* the principal fountain of human happiness, and leaves the species less rich, to an inappreciable degree, in all that makes life valuable to the individual human being.

PART 2

Pioneers on a Moral
Crusade: Feminism
and Status Politics

Introduction: Social Roots of the Woman's Movement in America

Seneca Falls, 1848

The first woman's-rights meeting in American history took place in a Methodist church in Seneca Falls, New York, on July 19 and 20, 1848. The women responsible for calling this historic meeting had met for a social occasion only six days earlier, in Waterloo, a few miles from Seneca Falls. There, in the home of Jane Hunt, they prepared their now famous Declaration of Sentiments and eleven resolutions covering their aims for presentation at the meeting. The ninth was the demand, revolutionary for its time: "Resolved, That it is the duty of the women of this country to secure to themselves the sacred right to the elective franchise" (Stanton and Blatch 1922:I, 146). The most controversial of the eleven resolutions in 1848, suffrage for women, was destined to become a central rallying point as the woman's-rights movement developed over the ensuing decades.

The two central figures in the Seneca Falls drama were Elizabeth Cady Stanton and Lucretia Mott. Legend has it that the seeds of the meeting were planted eight years earlier, in 1840, when these two women met for the first time in London. Lucretia and James Mott were delegates from an antislavery association to the World Anti-Slavery Society convention in London. Henry Stanton, also a delegate, brought his wife, Elizabeth, on the trip which doubled as their honeymoon. Lucretia was then a mature woman of forty-seven, mother of five children ranging in age from twelve to twenty-eight. She had many years of experience in several reform movements that had swept the country in the 1830s, and she was an active participant in antislavery agitation in Philadelphia. Elizabeth Stanton, by contrast, was a young bride of twenty-five, fresh from a rather sheltered life in a small town in New York State. The American women delegates were denied official seats at the London convention, over the vigorous objections of at least some of the American male delegates.

(Significantly, Henry Stanton was *not* among the prowomen delegates, though James Mott was.) This situation triggered much discussion of the sex issue as well as the slavery issue, and Elizabeth was swept into heady admiration for the older Lucretia, who held her own in argument, "skillfully parried all their attacks . . . turning the laugh on them, and then by her earnestness and dignity silencing their ridicule and jeers" (Hare 1937:192). Mott's biographer suggests that the young Elizabeth had never met a woman like Lucretia, who "dared to question the opinion of popes, kings, and parliamentarians with the same freedom she would have criticized an editorial in the London 'Times' " (Hare 1937:193). The two women spent many hours together in private conversation and are reported to have reached a decision during a walk through London that they would hold a woman's-rights convention on their return to America, since "the men to whom they had just listened had manifested their great need of some education on that question" (HWS:I, 61).

Yet a call for such a convention was not sounded for eight years. The Motts returned to Philadelphia and the Stantons to Johnstown, New York, where Henry undertook a legal apprenticeship with Elizabeth's father, Daniel Cady, a distinguished lawyer and judge in central New York. Even their shared commitment to the antislavery cause did not bring the two women in touch with each other, since they and their husbands belonged to two separate wings of the anti-slavery movement. Though there were more important reasons why a woman's-rights movement was not likely to develop in 1841, as compared to 1848, on the personal plane the immediate precipitant for the first convention was the occasion on which Lucretia and Elizabeth renewed their friendship in Waterloo. The Motts were in the area to combine a visit to Lucretia's sister, Martha Wright, in Auburn with attendance at a Society of Friends meeting in Waterloo. (Figure 2 shows that these little New York State villages were very close by, at the northern end of the Finger Lakes.) Elizabeth was invited to spend an afternoon at Jane Hunt's home to renew acquaintance with Lucretia.

The personal clue to what took place at that social gathering lies in events in Elizabeth's life during the preceding few years. Her first son was born in the spring of 1842, and that fall the young family settled in Boston, where Henry Stanton opened a law office. With financial help from Judge Cady, the

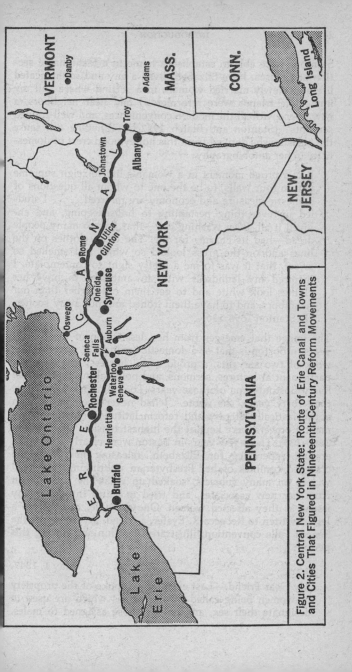

Figure 2. Central New York State: Route of Erie Canal and Towns and Cities That Figured in Nineteenth-Century Reform Movements

Stantons were able to establish a home in a fashionable section of Chelsea. Here Elizabeth lived a gay and sophisticated life as a newly married woman, in a setting where "all my immediate friends were reformers, I had near neighbors, a new house with all the modern conveniences, and well-trained servants" (Stanton and Blatch 1922:I, 142). One can sense the pleasure she derived from this honeymoon crest of domesticity in her autobiography:

> It is a proud moment in a woman's life to reign supreme within four walls, to be the one to whom all questions of domestic pleasure and economy are referred. . . . I studied up everything pertaining to housekeeping, and enjoyed it all. Even washing day—that day so many people dread—had its charms for me. The clean clothes on the lines and on the grass looked so white and smelled so sweet, that it was to me a pretty sight to contemplate. I inspired my laundress with an ambition to have her clothes look white and to get them out earlier than our neighbors, and to have them ironed and put away sooner. [E. Stanton 1898:136]

The image that emerges from her description of these early years in Boston is that of a domestic "manager" directing the work of two servants, a proud social hostess, and an eager participant at lectures, sermons, and political meetings in the lively Boston scene of those years. Looking back after more than forty years, she wrote, "I had never been in such an enthusiastically literary and reform latitude before, and my mental powers were kept at the highest tension" (E. Stanton 1898:133). Those few years in Boston were clearly a very liberating experience for Elizabeth, releasing her from the cramped confines of her Presbyterian upbringing. She read widely on many subjects, soaked up what she could learn from her new associates, and tried to think through many issues as they affected women. One example, taken from a letter written to Rebecca R. Eyster, a friend, a year before the Seneca Falls convention, illustrates her thinking during this period:

May 1, 1847.

My Dear Friend,—Last evening we spoke of the propriety of women being called by the names which are used to designate their sex, and not by those assigned to males.

You differed with me on the ground that custom had established the rule that a woman must take the whole of her husband's name, particularly when public mention is made of her. But you are mistaken about this. It is the custom now, since women have commenced forming themselves into independent societies, to use names of the feminine gender. . . . If you will glance through the public prints containing accounts of the formation of female societies, you will find no titles such as Miss and Mrs., and no Joseph, or Ichabod, but Elizabeth and Rebecca; . . . I have very serious objections, dear Rebecca, to being called Henry. There is a great deal in a name. It often signifies much, and may involve a great principle. Ask our colored brethren if there is nothing in a name. Why are the slaves nameless unless they take that of their master? Simply because they have no independent existence. . . . The custom of calling women Mrs. John This and Mrs. Tom That, and colored men Sambo and Zip Coon, is founded on the principle that white men are lords of all. I cannot acknowledge this principle as just; therefore, I cannot bear the name of another. [Stanton and Blatch 1922:II, 15–16]

With only a slight change in the language, one can still, today, read such arguments in correspondence between contemporary feminists.

Life changed dramatically for Elizabeth when the Stantons returned to New York State in 1846. Although they were again financially helped by Elizabeth's father, who gave them a house and a gift of money to renovate it, Elizabeth was no longer simply a domestic manager; she had become a hardworking homemaker with growing family responsibilities. In a tale of woe that may sound familiar to today's suburban housewives, she described her Seneca Falls life in 1847:

In Seneca Falls my life was comparatively solitary, and the change from Boston was somewhat depressing . . . our residence was on the outskirts of the town. . . . Mr. Stanton was frequently from home, I had poor servants, and an increasing number of children. To keep a house and grounds in good order, purchase every article for daily use, keep the wardrobes of half a dozen human beings in proper trim, take the children to dentists, shoemakers, and different schools, or find teachers at home, altogether made

> sufficient work to keep one brain busy, as well as all the
> hands I could impress into the service. Then, too, the nov-
> elty of housekeeping had passed away, and much that was
> once attractive in domestic life was now irksome. [Stanton
> and Blatch 1922:I, 142–143]

Generalizing from the experience of these years, she recalled
that she could finally understand not only the practical difficulties most women had to deal with in an isolated household, but also the "impossibility of woman's best development if in contact, the chief part of her life, with servants and
children" (Stanton 1898:147).

At the time the invitation arrived from Waterloo, in
July 1848, Elizabeth was in a mood of considerable discontent, with "a strong feeling that some active measures
should be taken to remedy the wrongs of society in general,
and of women in particular" (Stanton and Blatch 1922:I, 145).
She gave vent to her acute feelings of frustration and discontent during the visit with Lucretia Mott and her Quaker
friends. Since Lucretia was then fifty-five years old and her
youngest daughter already twenty, Elizabeth's complaints
concerning her isolated life as a mother of three active boys
under six would have to strike a chord in Lucretia's memory
rather than her current situation. Mott's biographer comments
that Lucretia was pleased to find Elizabeth "no longer an
unsophisticated bride with Calvinistic complexes, hoping
someone would tell her that girls had a right to go to college
or pursue careers" (Hare 1937:194). Elizabeth retained the
flashing wit Lucretia remembered, but it was now clothed
with personal maturity and a more informed intellect. In any
event, the striking blend of insightful reflection and indignation that shows through in Elizabeth's letter was probably
much in evidence in that Waterloo women's discussion. These
were women schooled in the art of "doing something" about
issues they could define as in need of "reform."

Enlightenment Versus Moral Crusader Feminists

It is what they decided to "do" that marks the special
quality of the American woman's-rights movement over the
course of the rest of the nineteenth century; this mark links it
to other social movements that had previously absorbed the

energies of the women in Waterloo. These were not Enlightenment feminists—familiar to the reader from Part 1—who
would proceed individually to write books and give lectures
on woman's rights, as Wollstonecraft, Fuller, and Martineau
had done in the earlier period. As Elizabeth Stanton put it, "I
could not see what to do or where to begin—my only
thought was a public meeting for protest and discussion"
(Stanton and Blatch 1922:I, 145). Well-worn grooves of political habit and experience were activated as the American
women took the step from personal discontent to organized
social action.

There are several interesting respects in which the Enlightenment feminists differ from the women I call the Moral
Crusader feminists, exemplified by Elizabeth Stanton and
Lucretia Mott. While there is an overall difference in generation, age is not the most significant contrast between the two
groups. The ages of individuals in the two groups in 1848
were as follows:

Enlightenment Feminists		Moral Crusader Feminists	
Frances Wright	53	Lucretia Mott	55
Margaret Fuller	38	Sarah Grimké	56
Harriet Martineau	46	Angelina Grimké	43
John Stuart Mill	42	Elizabeth Stanton	33
		Susan Anthony	28
		Lucy Stone	30
		Antoinette Brown	23

The Grimké sisters and Lucretia Mott shared many qualities
and experiences with the younger American women, such as
Stanton and Lucy Stone, yet they were, in fact, roughly the
same age in 1848 as such Enlightenment feminists as Martineau and Wright. Though born in South Carolina to a
slave-owning family, and though they wrote in the decade
preceding the Seneca Falls meeting, in both spirit and personal history the Grimké sisters had much more in common
with the younger Stanton-Stone group than with the Wright-
Fuller group of feminists. Indeed, in 1848 Margaret Fuller
was in Italy participating in the political uprising there—an
involvement it is difficult to imagine any of the American
Moral Crusader feminists sharing in spirit, much less in the
flesh.

What, then, differentiates the two sets of feminists? We have noted that the Enlightenment feminists were highly urban, sophisticated, solitary thinkers and writers. By contrast, the Moral Crusader feminists were almost all native-born, middle-class Americans from rural areas or small towns. They were decidedly not cosmopolitan, urban, worldly in their thinking or life styles. What motivated their efforts in behalf of women was less a radical impulse expressed through their pens than a moral impulse acted out in the political arena. In both social origins and the deepest premises of their thinking, most early native-born American feminists were profoundly conservative and moralistic. Fanny Wright, for example, was not only opposed to slavery and an ardent public lecturer defending emancipation, she was also an activist who tried to accomplish her ends through social experimentation at Nashoba. The American moral crusaders were just as ardently opposed to slavery, and some of them were active in the Underground Railroad assisting slaves to escape from their owners, but they were not involved in the actual work of integrating freed slaves into their own communities and their own social lives. Fanny Wright defended the rights of women and she herself secured a divorce, while Elizabeth Stanton, who sought reform in divorce laws, seems never to have considered separation or divorce as a solution to the unhappiness that clearly characterized her own marriage. Such women as Wollstonecraft, Wright, and Martineau had to make their own way in life to achieve economic security; when they wrote about the lack of opportunities for women to achieve economic security by their own labor, they knew personally what such restrictions were like. Elizabeth Stanton and Lucretia Mott shared their concern for the plight of working women, but they themselves were not "oppressed" in the ways they described in their speeches. They did not have to work to earn their own way of life, and they were little attracted to ideas that involved very basic changes in the economic or family system they viewed as oppressive to women. Wollstonecraft and Wright were extremely suspicious of religious institutions, quick to see scheming on the part of the clergy for their own personal and institutional advantage, and skeptical of any "truth" concerning man or woman in the Bible itself. Stanton, the Grimké sisters, Mott, and Anthony were critical of clerical interpretations of the Bible, and in varying degrees they favored the more liberal interpretations of theology in their day, but they fully accepted the view that great moral teachings were to be found in the Bible. Where Wright denounced the religious revivals as self-interested attempts by the clergy to fan a waning interest in religion, Mott, Stanton, Brown, and Anthony were themselves responsive to the message of these revivals, drawing from them their convictions about the need for the moral reform of society which they channeled into abolition and woman's-rights activity. Thus, the Enlightenment feminists showed an underlying perspective of skepticism toward social institutions, while the Crusader feminists showed piety and a moral passion for the reform of social institutions.

A second critical difference between the two groups is the contrast between solitary intellectual work and active participation in a social movement. The Enlightenment feminists were essentially "loners," while the Moral Crusader feminists were "joiners." The former reached out to the world through the instrument of their pens, while Elizabeth Stanton's impulse was to give a "call," hold meetings, draw up resolutions, form local societies to implement the resolutions, and organize the network of local societies into a national organization. As solitary and urbane intellectuals, the Enlightenment feminists developed their ideas on paper, for publication. As morally committed small-town women, the Moral Crusader feminists developed their ideas in social interaction and delivered them in Lyceum lectures, convention speeches, and legislative committee hearings.

What was crucial for the quality of the American woman's-rights movement was its roots in other, related social movements. Overlapping patterns of involvement for these early feminist leaders existed among four such movements: moral reform (by which they meant the closing down of brothels and the curbing of men's sexual appetites); temperance (which really meant, not moderation, but total abstinence); antislavery (which quickly moved from colonization of slaves outside the United States to gradual emancipation and then to total, immediate abolition); and woman's rights. Only in the last movement, which applied directly to the involved women, was there no progression over time from moderate to more radical solutions. To reform the world "out there"— men, slave owners, and drinkers—was one thing; to transform themselves, to alienate beyond tolerance the men and women in their personal lives—parents, spouses, neighbors—was quite another. That their contemporaries often denounced them as disturbing radicals should not mislead us to apply the same label to them.

It would, however, be an error to exaggerate these differences between the two groups of feminists, for they shared many traits as well. They were all libertarian, rational, and committed to an enlargement of the aspirations and the opportunities of women. They drew intellectual and political sustenance from the egalitarian ideals expressed in the American and French revolutions of the eighteenth century. Indeed, many of them, or their families before them, were left adrift in their society as a consequence of the translation of those very egalitarian ideas into the stuff of social and economic structure during the early part of the nineteenth century.

Colonial Versus Early-Nineteenth-Century America

It is this larger context of the social and economic transformation of American society during the early decades of the nineteenth century that we must briefly examine, for out of it grew all the social movements that absorbed the energies of the Moral Crusader feminists during the middle and last half of the nineteenth century.

In sketching these changes, it is convenient to compare the early nineteenth century with the colonial period. Colonial America consisted of a more stable and stratified society: families migrated to the colonies, purchased land, cultivated their crops, and if they were successful, passed enlarged properties on to their children. It was a society in which status was largely assigned at birth and in which the shortage of labor made meaningful the Puritan work ethic that all must contribute to the extent of their ability. Under such circumstances, women and children were not idle dependents but working contributors to all the efforts on farms and in trades that helped to sustain life. With a shortage of women, the pressures on them were great to marry or, if widowed, to remarry. But marriage meant to become a coworker beside a husband, if necessary learning new trade skills in butchering, silversmith work, printing, or upholstering—whatever special skills the husband's work required (Calhoun 1918; M.

Benson 1935). In addition, women had to have a wide range of skills to run their households, since the production of cloth and clothing, as of canning and preserving, was in their hands completely. Dexter (1931; 1950) has described the wide range of occupations at which women labored during the colonial period, using skills they learned in the same way men learned them—through apprenticeship training, usually within their own families.

Besides women's domestic competence, their fathers' status was valued when men sought wives in the colonial period. Since in a hierarchical society, organized on an ascriptive basis, women are chosen on the basis of the standing represented by their fathers, among the many unsettling effects of the revolution—and the spirit of egalitarianism it set loose in the society—was the far wider range of choice possible in mate selection. Once men had to achieve on their own, apart from inherited land and other wealth, the social standing of the families from which women were chosen as wives decreased in social significance. Urban occupational skills and wives were portable in a way that inherited land was not. As long as men took the lead in initiating courtship and marriage, men in the middle class of an urbanizing society had a wider pool of women to choose their wives from, while women in the middle class were in a competitive position for husbands with women from lower-status families.

While the colonial woman shared many of the same grounds for the cultivation of a sense of self-worth as a man, such as pride in family and the possession and exercise of productive work skills, the woman in the expanding era of Jacksonian democracy had a far less adequate basis for self-satisfaction than her brother had. From the perspective of a man, American society in 1820 was an open vista of opportunity: by dint of hard work he could hope to improve his position in society; if he did not succeed in one locality, he could move on to another, carrying his skills with him; with opportunity opening through education and the professionalization of many occupations such as medicine and law, his family could give him a head start on future success. These same changes had an opposite effect on women. With work separated from the household, with shops expanded into larger establishments, with cloth manufactured in factories, and with social status generally something to be "achieved," women were effectively cut off from participation in the significant work of their society. A woman's labor at home was less valued, and her husband was apt to invest large amounts of time and energy in economic efforts away from the household. As a result, the grounds for a woman's sense of self-worth narrowed during the decades when men's expanded.

As women's "real" contributions declined in worth, it seems that her qualities as a "woman" expanded, paving the way for the emergence of the cult of True Womanhood in the 1820–1860 period (Welter 1966). What mattered for a woman by the late 1820s were four qualities: piety, purity, submissiveness, and domesticity. The new prevalent values in the larger Jacksonian society—education, success at work, and political participation—were denied to women. As economic affluence increased with the growth of the new industrialism and expansion of trade, women's worth declined as producers and increased as consumers. While an unattached woman in colonial America was granted land or access to work to support herself, the Jacksonian woman was restricted. While schools were opening for young males, physicians and educators were arguing that the female brain and nervous system were insufficiently stable to sustain intellectual effort. Even an occupation as traditionally female as midwifery was being transformed into the field of obstetrics, controlled by male physicians. (The number of medical school graduates increased over fifty times from the turn of the century to the 1840s; by the 1850s physicians rather than midwives delivered most American babies [Rothstein 1972: 108–109].) While a colonial woman could take pride in her ability to manage a farm or run a business with her husband and to continue such management after his death, her Jacksonian descendant was far more restricted to domestic arts and skills (Rosenberg 1971; Lerner 1966).

But the cult of True Womanhood, focusing on submission and patience, was no preparation for women's real responsibilities within a family. Fragility and submission might suffice in courtship or in marital sex, but they did not prepare a woman for the physical and emotional stamina required by repeated pregnancies and the rearing of a large family of children. The conflict inherent in the lack of fit between the cultural ideal of True Womanhood and the social reality of homemaking and maternal roles has been thought by some historians to be at the root of the widespread rise of hysteria among women as the nineteenth century unfolded (Smith

1971; Rosenberg 1972). Rosenberg interprets this phenomenon as a withdrawal into the role of invalid, in which dependency and fragility are legitimate expectations consistent with
the cultural stereotype of a wife but which protected the
woman from the sexual demands of her husband and the
heavy physical and emotional demands of household and
child-care duties.

Thus the transformation of the egalitarian ethos from a
political ideal in the revolution into the fabric of society
meant an expansion of many opportunities for an increasing
number of men but a shrinking sphere of participation for
women in education, work, and political affairs. But as Rosenberg (1971:563) has pointed out, "Though many aspects of
Jacksonianism have been subjected to historical investigation,
the possibly stressful effects of such structural change upon
family and sex roles have not."

One important institutional sphere in which liberalized
ideas had a profound impact was that of religion. The Second
Great Awakening at the turn of the century (1795 to 1835)
can be viewed as a second wave that pushed American
Protestantism further away from the arid rationalism of the
English church toward the pietistic evangelicalism of a
uniquely American religion. It involved a reorientation of
social and religious belief, in which Jesus became a moral
teacher rather than the son of God, and the clergy became
revivalist soul winners rather than remote pastors. The gap
between parishioner and minister narrowed and the concept
of the proper duty of the religious person underwent change:
individual salvation was no longer the result of passive patience waiting for the spirit to descend, but of morally responsible contributions to the community through individual
efforts or concerted social action. The Jeffersonian and Jacksonian ideas of democracy swept through theology and church
organization and released a mighty surge of human effort
toward the benevolent reform of society and its members
(McLoughlin 1959).

It is relatively easy to see how men caught up in such an
evangelical spirit could express themselves through political
and economic efforts on their own and their communities'
behalf. But what would women do who were inspired by
such appeals to individual effort and benevolent reform in an
era when their opportunities for personal achievement had
narrowed? Many were clearly willing to follow the cultural

pressure to a narrower sphere of life, to follow the lead of
the women's magazines in the art of conspicuous consumption and the elaboration of the rituals surrounding social entertainment. Other middle-class women who caught the spirit
but not the ability to conform to the new cult of the lady
withdrew into depression, hysteria, or fainting fits. Where
social and religious codes did not proscribe women's participation, however, the rapidly proliferating societies which were
a major outcome of the Second Great Awakening (Ahlstrom
1972:403–414) gave scope for some women to pour their
energies into reform. Such agencies included missionary societies, publication and education societies, moral-reform movements, organizations dedicated to humanitarian interests,
antislavery societies, and eventually, woman's-rights organizations.

Nothing in this sketch of the changes between colonial
days and the early nineteenth century can be taken as well-established historical "fact." Too little of the history of
American women, or the impact of larger social historical
processes upon women, has been investigated as yet by
scholars. We can therefore speak only of "probable" impact
and "possible" interpretations in this larger backward look.
In turning to the more specific questions of the emergence of
movements for social reform during these early decades of
the nineteenth century, we are on somewhat firmer ground.
Several generations of American scholars have studied in
detail the religious revivals that swept the United States during these years and the temperance and abolition movements
that followed in their wake, although historians have not been
in agreement in the interpretations to be placed on the connections among these phenomena.

We shall attempt a selective review of the several social
movements which preceded the mid-century woman's-rights
movement, highlighting the ideas and experiences that
help to explain the emergence and the special characteristics
of the early woman's-rights movement in the United States.

Religious Revivalism in the 1820s

The Second Great Awakening had its beginning in boisterous camp meetings in Kentucky and Tennessee during the
period from 1795 to 1810. Theological reform, from 1810 to

1825, centered in the pruning of old beliefs by such men as
Lyman Beecher, Timothy Dwight, and Nathaniel Taylor, who
reinterpreted Calvinist dogma to fit the changed social and
intellectual climate of the early nineteenth century. Of major
importance to our theme is the locale of the third phase of
the Second Great Awakening in western and central New
York State (Barnes 1957). Within a brief few months the
revival spirit spread from Auburn, New York, in the west (at
the upper end of the eastern Finger Lakes) to Troy in the east
(just across the Hudson River from Albany). The man behind
this movement in New York State was Charles Grandison
Finney, a lawyer who had been converted just a few years
earlier. Finney's revivals firmly established evangelicalism.
Unlike the revivalism of the First Great Awakening, which
saw God as the center of the universe, Finney's revivalism
placed man at this center. McLoughlin (1959:12) characterizes
the contrast between eighteenth- and nineteenth-century
revivalism as one between spontaneous "praying down" in
the earlier period and carefully organized "working up" with
pragmatically contrived techniques which Finney consolidated into modern mass evangelism in the later period.

A good description of Finney's hold on an audience is
provided by Henry Stanton, who heard Finney preach in
1830 while he was working in Rochester and Finney served
as the minister of the Third Presbyterian Church. Stanton's
first impression of Finney, recalled with great vividness even
fifty years later, was as follows:

> A tall, grave looking man, dressed in an unclerical suit
> of gray, ascended the pulpit. Light hair covered his fore-
> head; his eyes were of a sparkling blue, and his pose and
> movement dignified. . . . The discourse was a chain of
> logic, brightened by felicity of illustration and enforced
> by urgent appeals from a voice of great compass and
> melody. . . . He illustrated his points frequently and
> happily by references to legal principles . . . not singu-
> lar, perhaps, for the speaker had been a lawyer before he
> became a clergyman. [H. B. Stanton 1887:40–41]

During the time Finney held the Rochester pulpit, he
preached three times on Sunday and three or four times during the week. The crowds he drew were not confined to the
usual middle-class members of the Presbyterian Church.
Members of Baptist and Methodist congregations came to

hear him and brought back his spirit of evangelism to their
own churches. Stanton (1887:41) suggests that Finney's first
effect was among the judges, lawyers, and physicians of the
community and worked its way down to the "bottom of
society." An account of Finney in action is again provided by
Stanton's memoirs:

> While depicting the glories or the terrors of the world to
> come he trod the pulpit like a giant. His action was dra-
> matic. . . . He gave his imagination full play. . . . As
> he would stand with his face towards the side gallery,
> and then involuntarily wheel around, the audience in that
> part of the house towards which he threw his arm would
> dodge as if he were hurling something at them. In describ-
> ing the sliding of a sinner to perdition, he would lift his
> long finger towards the ceiling and slowly bring it down
> till it pointed to the area in front of the pulpit, when half
> his hearers in the rear of the house would rise uncon-
> sciously to their feet to see him descend into the pit below.
> [H. B. Stanton 1887:41–42]

Finney argued against the view of original sin as a "constitutional depravity" and the idea of conversion as a miracle
to be patiently waited for. Instead he viewed conversion as
the result of the right use of mankind's natural powers and
believed that the new convert's faith should be tested through
good works in this life rather than expectations of his salvation in an after life. Barnes (1957:11) aptly summarizes
the significance of this shift in doctrine:

> This break with orthodoxy changed for Finney's converts
> the whole emphasis of religious experience. . . . Finney
> made salvation the beginning of religious experience in-
> stead of its end. The emotional impulse which Calvinism
> had concentrated upon a painful quest for a safe escape
> from life, Finney thus turned toward benevolent activity.
> . . . [This gospel] encourages mankind to work as well
> as to believe . . . and [thus] released a mighty impulse
> toward social reform.

It is significant that the "work" Finney called for was not the
work involved in earning a living but community "work" of
reform in morality and social values; this legitimized the involvement of middle-class women in volunteer reform work
in an era when paid employment was frowned upon for

them; it also provided the nouveau riche with visible good works to round out their new social positions and gave to middle-class farmers and professional men compensatory outlets for their sense of status deprivation.

An early hint of the connection between the Finney-inspired revival movement in the 1820s and 1830s and the later woman's-rights movement can be seen in the tactics of an early Finney convert, Theodore Weld. At the time Finney was "working" the Utica area, Weld was a student at nearby Hamilton College in Clinton. He was somewhat older than most of the students, having already traveled through the South as a temperance lecturer. Weld was also something of a student leader, and hence his initial opposition to Finney's new gospel made him an arch target in Finney's attempts to convert the students. The Finney magic eventually worked on Weld, who left college to become one of Finney's Holy Band of agents, roaming the valleys and towns of central New York State with the new gospel. One of the early towns he worked was Utica itself, and it was here that Weld continued Finney's simple but radical step of urging women to participate vocally at the revival meetings. He believed women should both pray and speak if they felt deeply enough and should not be prevented from such actions just because they were women. This move caused some discussion at first, but Weld argued that it was better to establish the practice before discussing the principle. As he put it,

> let intelligent women begin to pray and speak, and men begin to be converted to the true doctrine; and when they get familiar with it, they like it and lose all scruples. [Barnes 1957:13]

This pattern of women who prayed and spoke up in mixed meetings grew steadily and was soon a widespread practice in western and central New York revival meetings. Thus Congregational-Presbyterian women began to do in the late 1820s what only Quaker women had been able to do up to this juncture—to speak in public. Hence a decade before he met his future wife, Angelina Grimké, Weld made a contribution to the "softening-up" process that contributed to the subsequent emergence of women public speakers in central New York. Having dared to loosen their self-control in public, to express themselves freely "in promiscuous meetings," may have eased the way for other public participation by women in both the abolition and the woman's-rights movements to follow.

By 1826 the New England clergymen grew increasingly disturbed by these evangelical developments in New York State. Lyman Beecher, of the opinion that the devil was at work in New York, proposed a meeting between the eastern and western forces of the church. The following year Beecher traveled from Boston with a committee of his fellow clergymen and theologians to meet Finney and his western associates in New Lebanon, New York.

As was the style in such confrontations, a set of resolutions was presented for discussion and a vote. One of the first submitted by the Beecher forces read: "Resolved that in social meetings of men and women for religious worship, females are not to pray." The western Finney men defended the right of the "female brethren" to self-expression, and the resolution was defeated. Nor was ground for agreement found on any of the other resolutions. Toward the end, Beecher accused Finney of planning to descend on Connecticut and to "carry a streak of fire to Boston." But, he warned, if Finney were to attempt this, "I'll meet you at the State line, and call out all the artillery-men, and fight every inch of the way to Boston, and I'll fight you there" (see Barnes 1957:8–9).

Finney and his band did not heed Beecher's warnings. They carried their revivals to Pennsylvania and Connecticut and on to Boston itself. Beecher had to swallow his words under pressure from his congregation to invite Finney to the Hanover Church. From Boston, Finney returned to New York City and swept two wealthy philanthropists into the fold— Arthur and Lewis Tappan. In due time they contributed to the establishment of the Broadway Tabernacle, the largest house of worship in the country, built especially for Finney, as well as to the funding of the first antislavery societies. By the mid-1830s the revival movement had spread across the country, and the way was paved for putting content into the reformism implied by "expansive benevolence."

Evangelism and Antislavery

While these developments were taking place in America, the debate on slavery had reached a climax in England, culminating in the abolition of slavery by the English in the West Indies. A lively stream of letters was sent out by the British advocates of abolition to their denominational friends in America. The American newspapers, and especially religious weeklies and monthlies, adopted the theme, and soon the call was widespread: "let all who are opposed to the system . . . unite in associations for the abolition of slavery." Weld poured over the hundreds of antislavery pamphlets reaching America; he began his role as tactician and encyclopedist of the antislavery movement that was to extend through the petition campaign to Congress in the early 1840s. Weld was a man of great personal charm, with a powerful, spellbinding voice and enormous physical stamina. He was able to survive weeks of touring as a revivalist preacher, often involving five hours a night for a half-dozen or more consecutive evenings, despite heckling, the stoning of buildings, and physical abuse toward himself. His fame spread during the early 1830s as an evangelical revival speaker and later as an antislavery agent in the northern movement.

The young men who comprised the Finney Holy Band were deemed in need of further theological training, and Weld was sent out by the New York antislavery and benevolent societies to locate a site for a new theological seminary. The site eventually chosen was in Cincinnati, Ohio, and seventy-odd young men, most of them from central and western New York State, were soon enrolled at the Lane Theological Seminary there. Among them were Theodore Weld and Henry Stanton. By this point Lyman Beecher had been won over by the popularity and success of the revivals and accepted an invitation to be the seminary's first head.

When Beecher settled his family in Cincinnati, he did not realize he was headed for as intense a confrontation with Theodore Weld as he had experienced earlier with Charles Finney. Weld, implementing his new commitment to abolition, began a quiet campaign of converting those opposed to slavery and then enlarging this circle by turning the new converts into effective agents. By mid-winter of 1834 the students requested a debate on the slavery issue. This debate occupied some eighteen nights, during which the students discussed a series of questions beginning with "Ought the people of the slaveholding states to abolish slavery immediately?" Southern students contributed their personal observations, and northern students described atrocities to slaves they learned about from the British antislavery tracts. On the ninth evening of the debates a vote was taken, and the student body voted unanimously for "immediate abolition." The remaining nights followed the same pattern, centering on the question of whether Christians should support the goals of the colonization societies. Again this proposition was voted down, and the debates resulted in a united student body, totally committed to immediate abolition. Like some of their counterparts in recent times, the students did not let matters rest here but plunged into social action to "elevate the free blacks of Cincinnati." They equipped a reading room and library and established social clubs, temperance societies, an employment service, outdoor relief, and a "freedom bureau" to assist free blacks in purchasing the freedom of relatives still in bondage (Barnes 1957:64–69).

As if such actions were not incendiary enough in a town sitting on the river border of slave territory in 1834, the students also insisted that a proper Christian "should love the Negro as himself." It was not long before trouble began to brew in the town. There had been bloody riots in Cincinnati just a few years earlier as free black and fugitive slave populations began to increase. Lyman Beecher left the city for a trip east, optimistically hoping that there would be no trouble. But news of the Lane debates had spread through the national press, with the result that college students on many other campuses were debating the same issue, to the distress of their faculty and administrators. "Benevolence" was coming a bit too close to home for many of them. At an emergency conference Beecher agreed to a resolution drafted by the eastern college representatives that called for the suppression of all antislavery agitation. When the Lane officials implemented this resolution by abolishing the students' antislavery society and censoring their community activities for free Negroes, the students, almost to a man, resigned from the seminary. Many of them, along with some of their faculty, came together again later, as students and faculty of the newly founded Oberlin College. Charles Finney came west in 1835 to join this Oberlin faculty.

The year 1834 was also noteworthy as the year the first antislavery organization, the American Anti-Slavery Society, began its formal agitation. Henry Stanton, sent by the society to recruit seventy public speakers for the cause, enrolled many who had been classmates at the Lane Seminary. Weld and Finney trained them to their task as abolition agents before they entered the field. Weld gave them two weeks of training in abolition lore, complete with detailed tactics for coping with irate mobs of citizens. Revivalist preaching and "working-up" skills were now applied to the abolition campaign as they had been to soul winning earlier. The task of an agent, Weld told them, was to hold their ground in silence during the first flush of anger and attacks on their ideas or their persons from the citizens of a town. One agent described this stage of an agent's visit as a terribly "dispiriting experience," marked by "harsh words, stale eggs, and brick-bats and tar," and often by "indignities too gross to be printed" (Barnes 1957:77). Once the violence had been defused, the agents could get down to the job of persuasion on the issue of slavery and its abolition. These youthful agents were firm in the belief that they were doing their part "toward the moral conquest of the world."

The appeal they made was consistently evangelical. As Weld described his goal, he was after the "heart of the nation," not after converts who merely adopted "principles as dry theories" (Barnes 1957:79). Such an appeal precludes any endorsement of moderate "reforms" in the institution of slavery. As with adultery or prostitution, a bit of reform would not do. What is defined as a "sin" requires total denunciation. Once someone had been converted to this view, denouncing slavery as a sin could be a spiritually intoxicating experience in an all-white, nonslave-owning northern church or community. This is what Gusfield (1963) calls the early "benevolent" stage of a social movement. A later phase shifts attention from the sin to the sinner, appealing to the slave owner to give up the sin of slavery and the drinker his sinful visits to the grogshop. This was the basic appeal Angelina Grimké made a few years later in addressing the Christian women of the South.

Weld's procedures in trying to win a community or a church to his abolition views are interesting, for they reveal the model the Grimké sisters were taught to follow. Weld often began his campaign in a community with lectures on temperance, and only later, when his audience was won over by his personal magnetism and persuaded that he was a good and moral man, did he shift to his major goal—to win his listeners over to abolition. Stanton described the use of the same technique during his own agency:

> We resorted to odd expedients to get in Antislavery speeches. The temperance cause was popular. In 1835, in Rhode Island, I agreed to address an audience an hour and a half on temperance if they would then let me speak an hour and a half on slavery. On the next Sabbath the compact was faithfully fulfilled on both sides. [H. B. Stanton 1887:51]

(Fanny Wright had used the same technique in the 1820s, by beginning her lecture series on the topic of "free enquiry" and "education" and gradually moving to an attack on the churches in her final lecture. The same approach was used by the Grimké sisters in the late 1830s; a series of lectures on abolition shifted toward the end to focus on the topic of women and sex equality.) The form and spirit of these approaches were those of a protracted revival meeting. In towns with a particularly entrenched resistance to his message—and there were many of them—Weld spent as many as twenty consecutive evenings of two to five hours of preaching a night before achieving the conversion to abolition he sought.

In the wake of the conversions sparked by Weld and the "band of Seventy," as his group became known, local abolition societies were established, linked to national societies through subscription and delegate participation in annual conventions. From 1834 through the early 1840s these local societies played an important role in the petition campaigns to the national Congress waged by sympathizers with abolition year after year. The right of petition was one of the few political rights women had, and the petition campaigns of these years on the slavery question were important testing grounds on which northern women acquired political experience and skills. Weld had paved the way in Ohio and New York by his insistence that women participate at revival meetings. Now, with the need to enlist thousands of volunteers to circulate the petitions for submission to Congress, he organized the local abolition societies, encouraging women as often as men to undertake the actual door-to-door canvassing for signatures. Men had ceased to question women's right to speak in mixed assemblies in the revivalist counties. Now women began to gain practical political experience in nu-

merous towns across the country. Year after year these petitions were sent off to Washington, and women gained
familiarity with the residents of their communities, practiced
their verbal skills of persuasion, and learned about the political process.

This new political role for women was the cause of much
heated comment in Washington. Southern congressmen typically reacted with a sense of "outraged propriety." One
northern representative wrote that he was

> pained to see the names of so many American females to
> these petitions. It appeared . . . exceedingly indelicate
> that sensitive females of shrinking modesty should pre-
> sent their names here as petitioners. [Quoted in Barnes
> 1957:141]

Yet the women continued to form women's auxiliaries to
local abolition societies and corresponded with each other
about their work. By 1837 there was a national system of
female societies to support the petition campaigns. Critical to
this experience was the fact that in their cause women
brought to bear house-to-house agitation and hence face-to-
face influence in their own neighborhoods. They learned
names, details of families, and political views in their community. Among the women prominent in these campaigns
were Lucretia Mott and Lydia Maria Child, who organized
the women's efforts in Pennsylvania and Massachusetts;
Susan Anthony was an indefatigable volunteer in New York,
and Elizabeth Cady joined the effort in New York and, after
her marriage, in Boston. It was in the abolition movement of
the 1830s, therefore, that American women first showed
some corporate expression of their political will, and it was
from this movement that the woman's-rights leaders acquired the ideas about political organization which they
applied to their own cause in the late 1840s.

The petition campaign came to a halt in 1843, when the
issue of slavery gained a legitimate place in the debates in
Congress itself. Thereafter the focus of abolitionist activity
remained in the national Congress, reducing the need for the
vast network of local petition organizers. The end of the
petition campaigns may have produced a political vacuum in
the lives of many women, suddenly cut off from a sense of
contribution to the abolition cause and from participation in

the political process. To the more energetic leaders among the women organizers it may have been a bitter frustration to find that their voices no longer reached the hub of national politics in Washington—thus underlining the extremely limited basis for women in political participation. The crusading zeal stimulated by the religious revivals had been expressed in the abolition cause, and within a short time it flowed into the movement to expand woman's rights.

Still another source of disappointment in these early years of the 1840s was the defeat of Henry Clay in the election of 1844, as the Whigs and the Liberty Party lost out to the Democratic Party in New York State. Votes for the Liberty Party are of special interest, since abolition was its central issue. A decade earlier Weld had argued that abolition agents should stay away from the big cities and concentrate on the country and small towns; indeed, except for Utica, New York, no city in New York State gave the Liberty Party as much as 5 percent of its total vote, while within a radius of fifty miles of the town of Smithfield in central New York State, the Liberty Party won a majority of the votes cast in seventeen of the thirty-five small towns (Benson 1961:209–213). Smithfield gave 48 percent of its vote to the Liberty Party, the highest in the state. (Smithfield is interesting as the family seat of Gerrit Smith's father, whose family was closely tied by kinship and politics to Elizabeth Cady Stanton's family.) In 1887 Henry Stanton wrote: "for many years an influence on behalf of the slave radiated from the central counties of New York which was felt beyond the borders of the state" (H. B. Stanton 1887:65). Eighty years later Benson (1961) substantiated this observation by more sophisticated analyses of the 1844 vote pattern in the state.

The Whig and Liberty Party voters shared many moral and social values, some of which were derived from the earlier religious revivals of the 1820s and 1830s. Cross (1950: 201) characterized these beliefs as reflecting an "ultraist state of mind" which rose from an implicit reliance upon the direct "guidance of the Holy Ghost." Ultraists assumed that once they saw the "inner light," they had no choice but to reveal God's will to others and thus to bring about the ultimate perfection of mankind (Benson 1961:211).

Historians have varied in their interpretation of this missionary zeal to reform the world. Cross tends to the view that the ultraists dedicated to antislavery carried the "yankee holy enterprise of minding other people's business to its logical extreme." Benson suggests that lurking behind the religious zeal may be a substratum of "guilt and a hyperactive superego." The outpourings of the abolition movement and of the temperance movement certainly suggest the presence of a mighty intrusive conscience at work in their leaders. Not content with pronouncing the virtues of temperance, nor tolerant of the view that what is sin to some is pleasure and custom to others, temperance leaders waged a campaign to cleanse the land of the sin of drinking. Some of this same quality of moral righteousness flowed into the woman's-rights movement in the 1850s.

Socioeconomic Change and Benevolent Reform

More was involved than guilt and superego. Psychological manifestations are often responses to hard economic and social structural changes occurring in the society. The close connections in both ideas and personnel that existed between the evangelical movement and the abolition movement must be seen in the light of the economic and social causes for the spread of the revivals themselves which explain, for example, why they caught on so readily in central New York State in the mid-1820s.

Part of the reason may lie in the fact that this was a region of prosperous farms and comfortable small towns, very different from Boston to the east and the Kentucky and Tennessee frontier to the southwest. Boston was the seat of the sophisticated, educated Congregational clergy, the majority of whom resisted the revivalist spirit and its attack on religious determinism, only bowing to lay demand for revival preachers several years later. The southwest camp meetings were loud and boisterous affairs held outdoors; appropriate to the frontier circumstances of the territory, they hardly developed a style congenial to the more sophisticated easterners. Central New York State, by contrast, was at an intermediary stage compared to these two extremes: growing towns and cities contained newly successful merchants and manufacturers and a generation of young people restless for change but still sufficiently close to their religious heritage to avoid breaking away from the church altogether. Finney's message had its greatest appeal on such soil. Well-organized protracted meetings, which lasted for several days and nights, were possible in small towns as they were not in such large cities as Boston and New York; they therefore facilitated the contagious spread of individual and communal efforts at winning souls for Christ. The device of "anxious seats"—where individuals who felt on the verge of conversion could present themselves at the close of the sermon—was brought from the southwestern Baptist and Methodist revivals and was adaptable to the small town context.

A second reason for the responsiveness of central New York State to Finney's evangelical appeal is rooted in its economic development and the social consequences which followed. It was here, through the valley stretching from Buffalo in the west to Albany in the east, that the first major step in what was later called the Transportation Revolution took place: the construction of the Erie Canal, which provided a direct water route between the breadbasket midwestern plains and the Atlantic Ocean (Taylor 1951). The canal was officially opened to traffic in 1825, after many years of labor in the malarial lowland valley. Economic change in the state did not, however, have to wait for the official opening of the canal. Each new stage of the canal as it was completed made for enlarged markets for goods produced in the growing towns along the route. After serving merely as rural trade centers for an agricultural market, these towns could now reach New York City and other eastern seaports in one direction and the Great Lakes towns in the other. The towns throughout the valley became magnets for enterprising manufacturers, traders, and business speculators, and with them came a serious challenge to the system of social status and class that had long characterized the state's rural heartland. Landed property owners, wealthy farmers, preachers, physicians, and lawyers, who had been the backbone of the upper and middle classes of central New York State, were now being challenged by a new bourgeoisie—men with financial and manufacturing savvy who had a disturbing ability to strike it rich. As a group, the wealthy farmers and moderately comfortable professional men of these rural counties did not experience a decline in their own social position, but they did suffer a status deprivation and a challenge to their long-held values of piety and a Puritan work ethic.*

On the other hand, though the nouveaux riches might have income with which to live in a grander style than their more pious neighbors with well established positions through kinship or inherited wealth, they might yet feel insecure about their general social status. The old Puritan training they had received in their youth stood ready to make them feel guilty about their new wealth. McLoughlin points out that these newly rich families were simple sons and daughters of farmers who had emigrated westward from the poorer rural sections of New England at the turn of the century:

> the wealth and social position of this circle was so new that they almost felt guilty about it or fearful that it might suddenly be taken from them because they did not deserve it. By constantly assailing the sins of pride, social climbing, and the perils of laying up treasure on earth, Finney touched the nouveaux riches at their most tender point.
> [McLoughlin 1959:57]

Self-made men, as well as long-term settlers of means, had many reasons for being attracted to the new voice of the gospel that Finney spread through the canal valley.

---

* By social classes, sociologists mean variation in the degree of control over products and people. Income, occupation, education—singly or in combination—have been the chief indices sociologists have used to define social classes. By social status, sociologists have meant the distribution of prestige in a society—social-psychological variation in deference given to or received from others. While social class rests on economic factors of income and power, social status rests on less tangible cultural factors and life styles. A native-born Baptist textile worker may have been in the same social class as his Irish Catholic coworker, but there were many status differences between them in politics, family, religious values, and life style. In the long run sociologists expect a high correlation between social class and status, but in periods of very rapid social change there can be a short-run discrepancy between class and status which motivates people to behave in new and unexpected ways. Social scientists deal largely with the "long run," but people live their lives in the "short run," and their feelings, political actions, and receptivity to new ideas may be affected by the gap between their social class and the status they enjoy. Historical analysis of the kind we are attempting calls far more for a "short run" perspective on stratification.

Revivalism was not the only movement linked geographically to the path of the Erie Canal. Just south of the canal a cluster of small towns was the scene of abolition, temperance, and woman's-rights activities as well; they were Henrietta, Waterloo, Seneca Falls, Auburn, Syracuse, Oneida, Rome, Utica, Johnstown, Troy, Albany (see Figure 2). As manufacturing and commerce boomed in these towns, some portion of the middle-class, professional, farming, and small merchant families underwent a loss of relative social status, caught in the squeeze between the newly rich entrepreneurs and the increasing numbers of working-class laborers in the growing factory towns of the northeast. Such status loss can generate intense feelings of frustration and a receptivity to a shift in political or religious beliefs. Barnes' analysis (1957) of the Finney ideology suggests a congenial turning away from the emphasis on economic effort to a concentration on benevolent reform. The shift from visible community effort, linked not to an occupation but to volunteer participation in reform, may also have had a special attraction to married couples as a cohesive contribution to the marriage of the kind that work had provided in the colonial period. The history of abolition, moral reform, temperance, and woman's rights is striking in the frequency with which such married teams participated in the work of reform.

Cross (1950) analyzed New York counties in which antislavery sentiment was widespread and found that abolition agitation was strongest in those counties which had once been economically dominant but which by the 1830s had fallen behind their more advantageously situated neighbors; this finding is consistent with the view that the "once-hads" found reform a compensatory outlet through which an alternative form of status could be achieved.

The social backgrounds of Finney's band of evangelists have not been studied, but many of the same men were among the 100 prominent abolitionist leaders of the 1830s whom Donald (1956) has analyzed from this perspective. He found that they were mostly young—their median age in 1831, when Garrison's The Liberator was first published, was twenty-nine. They are described as "of Pilgrim descent," "of the best New England stock," and "descended from old and socially dominant Northeastern families." Their fathers were typically farmers, preachers, doctors, and teachers, with hardly any representation from manufacturing or banking interests.

Virtually all their parents were substantial members of their communities, with strong Federalist or Whig political sympathies. Congregational-Presbyterian and Quaker religious affiliations were most prominent among them. Only one was connected with the rising industrialism of the 1830s, and only thirteen were born in the principal cities of the United States at the turn of the nineteenth century (Donald 1956:19–36).

Henry Stanton is a good illustration of the profile Donald has drawn of the abolitionist. He was born in 1805 in a small town in Congregationalist-dominated Connecticut. His father was an enterprising farmer and merchant, with three stores under his charge and commercial interests in trade with the West Indies. Stanton described his father as a political leader of the "Jefferson" school. His grandfather had been an officer in the Revolutionary War and later a farmer and Congressman from Rhode Island. His mother also came from a long line of Puritan families; her father was both a farmer and a Rhode Island magistrate. Stanton's first job was as a clerk in the canal office in Rochester, which he took the year after the Erie Canal opened. Although his job exposed him to the new breed of manufacturing and commercial interests associated with canal traffic, socially he sought out people like his parents in background—wealthy landowners and lawyers active in state politics. Stanton was not attracted to a career in the burgeoning economy of central New York. He toyed with religion and law and was drawn to the rural elite and local politics. Along the way he was converted to the new school of Congregationalism by Finney, and soon afterward he became a student at the Lane Seminary in Ohio, where he was won to the abolition cause (H. B. Stanton 1887).

Stanton never achieved any significant degree of economic success, certainly none to compare with his wife's father, Judge Cady, or her wealthy relatives, such as Gerrit Smith, who was reputed to own some 800,000 acres of New York State land. Both Elizabeth and Henry Stanton threw their energies into temperance and abolition societies. They both illustrate very well Donald's point that social visibility in worthy moral causes could serve to compensate for the slip in relative economic status of a generation that could not match the economic success of their parents or the more enterprising peers of their own generation. They also fit Lipset's theory (1963) that a major force in political movements in American history has been the status anxiety experienced by groups of either "never-hads" or "once-hads." The Stantons, like many New England transcendentalists and New York abolitionists, temperance and woman's-rights leaders, were among the "once-hads."

In yet another study of the 1820–1840 period in New York State history, Benson (1961) argues that the transportation revolution had the effect of raising the level of aspirations of New York citizens to unprecedented heights and that those whose aspirations were frustrated became easy converts to Antimasonic sentiments. The Masonic orders included a wide range of middle-class men of upright character and long-term residence in their communities. During the period of rapid economic growth and upward social mobility, those native-born men who failed were particularly bitter, left behind in the economic struggle at lower-status levels, where they were joined by neighbors and fellow workers from among the new immigrants who filled the lower ranks of their communities in this period. Such unsuccessful men were ripe for attacks against any organization that seemed to dispense special privileges. Psychologically they could argue that "if it were not for the special privileges bestowed by X, I could be a wealthy man too." The chief argument in attacking the Masons was that the order "created odious aristocracies by its obligations to support the interests of its members in preference to others of equal qualifications" (Benson 1961:18). The Antimasonites described Masonry by the term "Monster Institution," the same term that a few years later was applied to slavery by the abolitionists. Like the abolitionists, the Antimasonites were sober citizens who valued piety, propriety, thrift, and steady habits, none of which had paid off for them personally.

The temperance movement can also be viewed in this interpretive framework, as in part a response to the sense of threat felt by the industrious Protestants in rural areas and small towns from the growing number of urbane, secular industrialists at the top of the status hierarchy and the increasing number of immigrants at the bottom. The native-born middle- and working-class devout Protestants fell back defensively upon their own values and waged an intense campaign to convert these new elements to moral and religious adherence to moderation or total abstinence. If they could not succeed in making teetotalers of everyone, they tried to at least acquire admirers of their own abstinence from among their neighbors (Gusfield 1963).

Discussions of status deprivation, like those concerning class stratification, typically imply a *male* perspective. Thus we have argued that men farmers, lawyers, and merchants in small-town Protestant America felt a loss of status and men in the nouveau-riche class an insecurity of status as social and economic processes changed the structure of social life around them. But such changes were bound to affect middle-class *women* as well; in fact, status deprivation may have had an even greater impact on them. Matters of ethics, life style, dress, religious affiliation and observance, housing, and domestic management would be of major importance to women; one can assume that, given their greater involvement in religious matters, women shared the value commitments to industriousness, steady habits, and moral uprightness. If men of rural and small-town Protestant America felt threatened by the new bourgeois elite and the growing numbers of immigrants, therefore, their wives and daughters may have felt status deprivation even more keenly. This differential impact on the sexes may have widened even further as the century wore on and educational opportunities and an extended franchise were available to men but not to women. Gainful employment drew increasing numbers of working-class women to factories and shops, while upper-class women and the women of the new bourgeoisie enjoyed more leisure, more domestic help, and greater opportunities for travel than the small-town, middle-class, old-style women could hope to experience. Their husbands' wounded vanity may have triggered an increase in male assertiveness in family roles as well. Under such circumstances, the ground seems ripe for women to seek outlets for their own frustrated status aspirations. A host of factors may have come together to shake the early-nineteenth-century woman out of her complacency and conformity; the narrowing of her social world, the depression of self-worth as products needed in the household were purchased rather than produced at home, the increased gap between men and women in educational opportunities, the cutting off of a sense of political participation through the petition campaigns to Congress, the vacuum created once the heady intoxication of evangelical revivals ended, and the strains of a birth rate pressing against the outer limits of potential female fertility—all may have combined to frustrate middle-class women who neither reaped the material and social benefits of the new bourgeois affluence nor shared in widening opportunities. If they were intelligent and aware, it is little wonder that increasing numbers of small-town middle-class women in the 1840s and 1850s felt that their world had become very narrow and restricted.

A further element in this picture is the increasingly negative view toward sexuality as the century progressed. Physicians warned against frequent sexual intercourse and the harmful consequences of masturbation. Early signs of repressive views toward human sexuality were already visible in the 1830s, in the formation of female moral reform societies, which urged the closing of houses of prostitution, the reform and education of prostitutes, and greater control by men over their sexual appetites. Women were urged to watch over the moral development of their young sons and to teach them strict self-control in sexual matters. A generation of such maternal teaching may have contributed to the increasingly negative view of sexuality by the 1850s; the burden of guilt drummed into them by mothers may have contributed to problems of sexual impotence for some sons. We read of hysteria among women in the nineteenth century, but that hysteria may have masked, not only sexual aversion and hostility to men, but also less overt problems of sexually inadequate husbands. There may even be a kernel of truth to the claim of some opponents of reform in the nineteenth century that male reformers were unmasculine—"man milliners," as Senator Ingalls of Kansas once called them, men "unable to beget or to bear; possessing neither fecundity nor virility" (Hofstadter 1954:177).

The temperance movement itself may have served the latent function of control over sexuality, for in the absence of effective contraceptives, such control can only be by social and psychological sanctions. In an era when male physicians argued that women's reproductive systems were so closely linked to their nervous systems that their intellect was "naturally unstable," women may have felt that only a thin veneer of moral training held in check men's inordinate sexual appetites. Alcohol was a threat to women, for it released men from the moral control they had learned from a diet of preaching and scolding from ministers and mothers alike.

Studies of the Women's Christian Temperance Union and its predecessors earlier in the century suggest that the movement leaders had as their target, not the upper class, but their own middle class and the working class. The flurry with Committees on Drawing Room Conversions, which tried to reach the upper class, had a very short-lived history (Gusfield 1963). Rosenberg (1972) suggests that the great concern with drinking shown by middle-class women reformers, as was the case with their earlier concern for sexual immorality, was probably rooted in general antimale sentiment and aversion to their own sexuality. Since the cult of womanhood gained strength during the nineteenth century, such reforms may also be indirect expressions by women of their long-standing but emerging resentment and fear concerning their numerous pregnancies and painful childbirths. It might also be noted that while mid-century woman's-rights reformers were later criticized by more radical feminists for being overly concerned with women of their own class, their efforts in both the moral reform and temperance movements were of specific benefit to working-class women who suffered even more from alcoholic husbands, frequent pregnancies, and disease than middle-class women did.

Thus we have seen overlap and continuity in the sequence of reform movements that emerged between the 1820s and the 1850s: from evangelical revivals to moral reform, abolition, temperance, and woman's rights. There was nevertheless a distinct contrast between the cause of women and all the other movements. Benevolent reform, applied to people "out there," was not threatening to the primary groups within which people lived: the slave owner was far away in the South, and heavy drinkers were more frequent among working-class and upper-class men than among men of the middle class. But when middle-class women demanded changes in the law to give them control over their own persons, their property, or their children, or to receive more and better education, or to participate in government through the franchise, the demands were not only closer to home—they were *in* the home. Men who would have to yield ground in complying with such change were men already suffering from a sense of status deprivation or insecurity on other grounds.

Clergymen, like fathers and husbands, were often intensely hostile to the new demands of women, for women were important to them as the mainstay of their congregations and the source of whatever deference a clergyman could enjoy in the community. Susan Anthony once remarked with bitterness that the "pin-cushion ministers" (i.e. clergymen whose education was financed by women's sewing societies) always turned out the "most narrow and bigoted in [their] teachings" (HWS:I, 539). Gratitude may be a thin mask hiding hostility in relationships in which men are dependent on the aid of women.

When the early woman's-rights leaders refused to accept the authority of the clergy as interpreters of the Bible and insisted on offering their own reinterpretation of the biblical conception of woman's role, as the Grimké sisters, Lucretia Mott and Elizabeth Stanton did, they were adding further insults to the already status-deprived Protestant clergy. While the women participated with their men in the abolition movement, their reform activities were a social and political reinforcement of family and church solidarity between the sexes. When the women brought their passion, intelligence, and resentment to bear upon their own cause, they threatened the shaky and status-deprived men in their families and churches. This is where the analogy so often drawn between slaves and women, or the position of contemporary blacks and women, breaks down. Little would change in the personal lives of northern abolitionist men if southern slaves were freed, but a great many changes would have to occur in the lives of such men if their women were freed.

Participation of Early Woman's-Rights Leaders in Reform Movements

The women who attended the first woman's-rights meetings in 1848, at Seneca Falls in July and at Rochester in August, were not novices to meetings of this kind. While the topic was a new one for many, most of those attracted to the cause of woman's rights had been active in other reform movements themselves, or they had grown up in families where such movements were discussed and often supported by their parents. Revival and temperance meetings in the 1820s and abolition societies in the 1830s paved the way for woman's-rights conventions in the 1840s and 1850s.

In this account of the interconnections among the reform movements, more mention was made of men who became involved in reform societies than of women. In turning to the mid-nineteenth-century feminist movement, it is of interest to examine the extent to which its early leaders were themselves involved in reform activity before their entry into the woman's movement in the 1850s. Figure 3 indicates the relationships among the seven women who were most important in the early stages of the woman's movement in the nineteenth century. Several aspects of the relationships among these women are portrayed in Figure 3, but attention is now directed merely to the reform movements each of them was involved in at some point during her life. The symbols shown above or below each of the boxes in Figure 3 indicate which of the five social movements each woman was associated with.

The oldest of the women, Lucretia Mott and Sarah Grimké, were involved in all five of the reform movements active between the 1820s and the 1860s. Lucretia Mott, who served as a delegate from a female antislavery society in Philadelphia to the London world convention in 1840, had already devoted several years to work as an abolitionist and had been a founder and first secretary of the Philadelphia Female Moral Reform Society in the mid-1830s. As a Quaker, she had not been swept into the earlier Finney evangelism but had taken the step of affiliating with his Quaker equivalent, Elias Hicks. Hicks had seceded from the more orthodox Quaker society in 1828 to rid theology of antiquated ideas and the Society of Friends of too rigid a structure of power over the lives of its members. Mott saw in Hicks a close approximation to the primitive Quakerism of George Fox and William Penn and was in agreement with Hicks' view that heaven and hell were "states of the soul" and the divinity of Jesus only the "indwelling of the eternal word within him" (Hare 1937). This openness to new ideas characterized Lucretia Mott throughout her life; even as a woman of eighty, in 1873, she attended a meeting of a Free Religious Association and was pleased to find that the association had endorsed her suggestion that its statement of purpose be changed from the scientific study of "theology" to the "scientific study of the religious element in man" (Hare 1937:288). Down through the years she remained a vigorous participant in moral reform, temperance, abolition, and woman's-rights agitation.

Figure 3.
Sociometry of Women's-Movement Leaders in the Nineteenth Century

	LUCRETIA MOTT	SARAH GRIMKÉ / ANGELINA GRIMKÉ	ELIZABETH CADY STANTON	SUSAN B. ANTHONY	ANTOINETTE BROWN	LUCY STONE
LUCRETIA MOTT(55) (James Mott) R T M A W 14*						
SARAH GRIMKE(56) ANGELINA GRIMKE(43) (Theodore Weld) R T M A W 14*						
ELIZABETH CADY STANTON(33) (Henry B. Stanton) T A W 18*						
SUSAN B. ANTHONY(28) T M A W 16*						
ANTOINETTE BROWN(23) (Samuel Blackwell) R T A W 20*						
LUCY STONE(30) (Henry Blackwell) T A W 10*						

Match name(s) at left with name(s) at top. Box where names cross gives Quality of Interpersonal Relationship.

Symbols for Social Movements

R Religious Revivalism
T Temperance
M Moral Reform
A Antislavery
W Woman's Rights

Quality of Interpersonal Relationship **

■	Very intimate	6
▦	Good friends	4
▨	Movement acquaintances	2
▤	Some strain and tension	0

( ) Age in 1848 at time of Seneca Falls Convention
* Cohesion Score Total for Five Relationships
** Cohesion Score Weight

Sarah Grimké and her sister Angelina shared the same profile of multiple participation in reform, though their level of leadership was not as consistently high as Lucretia Mott's. The most radical of the three women on the sex issue, Sarah Grimké contributed only sporadically as a writer and partici-pant after the 1850s.

Rosenberg's study of the New York Female Moral Reform Society showed very close ties between women on its execu-tive committee and the Finney wing of American Protestant-ism. Finney's wife was the Society's first president; its second head was the wife of one of Finney's closest supporters; financial support came from the Tappan brothers and clerical support from Finney disciples in New York. The society launched a weekly publication, the *Advocate of Moral Reform*, an extremely popular paper that gained some 20,000 sub-scribers within a few years of its founding in 1835 (Rosenberg 1971:570). Over the course of its first eight years the women gradually took over more and more of the jobs connected with publication. They hired a woman to travel through New England and New York State to organize auxiliaries, appointed two women as editors in 1836, replaced their male financial agent with a woman bookkeeper in 1841, and by 1843 were setting type and folding the journal themselves—all jobs which, they "proudly, indeed aggressively stressed, were ap-propriate tasks for women" (Rosenberg 1971:580). Rosenberg suggests that the legitimation of very conservative moral com-mitments enabled these women to engage in activities that were so daring for their day as the reform of prostitutes, the denunciation of men for sexual immorality, and the estab-lishment of pacesetting "firsts" for women in terms of oc-cupational tasks and community organization (Rosenberg 1971:567).

The younger women's leaders—Stanton, Anthony, Brown, and Stone—were only children during the ferment of the religious revivals in the 1820s and 1830s. It was their parents who were swept up in these exciting events. They had grown up near Henrietta to the west of the Finger Lakes in New York (Antoinette Brown); in Johnstown, New York, just northwest of Albany (Elizabeth Stanton); in western Massa-chusetts; or just east of Albany (Lucy Stone and Susan Anthony). Religious and moral reform were issues for their parents as young adults. As these four women entered adult-

hood, it was temperance and abolition that involved them,
woman's rights being added several years later.

A detailed analysis of the families in which these early
leaders grew up must await the statements that introduce
their writings and activity in the cause of women. Here it is
of interest only to highlight a few of the similarities and
contrasts among the four families. There is more continuity
of values between the parents and their daughters than one
might expect, perhaps because Elizabeth Stanton's life story
has been the most familiar to American readers. Elizabeth
has been portrayed as the "rebel" from her family, the
feminist who acquired a very early sense of the injustice
suffered by women. But Judge Cady was not at all like the
fathers of Susan Anthony or Antoinette Brown. Closer to the
cultural stereotype of the father, he was authoritative, firm,
more feared than loved by his children. Nettie Brown and
Susan Anthony were more fortunate, for their fathers in-
corporated the egalitarian ethos of their age into their expectations for their daughters. In fact, an interesting continuity
is found in the reform commitments of the parents, daughters,
and daughters' husbands for our small set of four woman's-
rights leaders. Using the movement symbols shown in Figure
3, this can be seen below:

	Elizabeth Stanton	Susan Anthony	Antoinette Brown	Lucy Stone
Parents	T	T–A–W	R–T–A–W	T–A
Self	T–A–W	M–T–A–W	R–T–A–W	T–A–W
Husband	T–A	not md	R–T–A–W	T–A–W

There was clearly a good base in a shared commitment to the
goals of the four social movements by both parents and
daughter in the cases of Susan Anthony and Antoinette
Brown. Elizabeth Stanton and Lucy Stone, on the other hand,
were the rebellious daughters of parents who did not approve
of wider spheres of education or political freedom for women.
Like her father, Elizabeth's husband did not share her commitment to woman's rights, while Antoinette Brown could
share with her husband Sam Blackwell and Lucy Stone with
her husband Henry Blackwell. As will be seen in the essay on
the Blackwell clan, it was Antoinette Brown who seemed to
have the most secure emotional roots from her early family
life, the happiest marriage, and the deepest sense of pleasure
and pride in her own sex.

Selections

Figure 3's tracing of the quality of social relationships that bound the early woman's-rights leaders together makes it quickly apparent that there are two relationships of an extremely close and intimate sort: the friendship between Elizabeth Stanton and Susan Anthony and that between Antoinette Brown and Lucy Stone. Antoinette Brown has not loomed as prominently in previous accounts of the nineteenth-century woman's movement as she does in this volume. Yet she emerged from my study as one of the movement's most interesting women, with a lively intelligence that she put to work in both her writings and her work in reform movements. She was among the first women to earn an Oberlin College degree and the first to be ordained a minister after completing theological studies at Oberlin. When she married into the Blackwell family, she added to her college friendship with Lucy Stone the further bond of marriage to the brother of Lucy's husband. Figure 3 also shows that such strain and tension as existed among these early leaders was between Lucy Stone and Stanton and Anthony. I believe Antoinette Brown, who had good relations with Stanton and Anthony and an intimate bond with Lucy, served an important role as mediating link among these early activists. Since Nettie and her husband Sam settled in New Jersey, she was also in relatively frequent contact with the Grimké sisters and had a long-standing admiration for and occasional contact with Lucretia Mott. As suggested by the total "cohesion score" of 20 (compared to 10 for the better-known Lucy Stone), Nettie Brown played an important role within this small circle of leaders.

Since the lives of these women are so closely tied to each other, an introduction to them and to their work is more properly approached with a sociographic than a biographic perspective. They were friends of long standing and co-workers in the complex history of the suffrage movement for several decades. Recognition of this fact is given by the four sets of selections in this section. Sarah and Angelina Grimké are introduced as a sister-sister pair, since their lives, writings, and political activity were so closely intertwined. The Blackwells are treated as a sibling set, since an analysis of this large group of nine brothers and sisters and the two famous sisters-in-law, Nettie Brown and Lucy Stone, can shed an interesting perspective on the life and work of the individuals.

Stanton and Anthony are handled as a friendship pair and
movement tactician team. Finally, since these women are
above all activists, the best introduction to their contributions
are the accounts they themselves have left of some of their
suffrage campaigns; the final selections are therefore abridged
accounts of some of the early campaigns, taken from the first
two volumes of the *History of Woman Suffrage*. These are
intended to permit the reader to participate vicariously in the
trials and tribulations and occasional successes of the many
women who devoted so many years to securing the vote for
American women.

It is with some regret that I have had to omit selections
on later stages of the suffrage movement. In part this omission
reflects the greater interest I have had in the pioneer women
of the first generation and in part results from the fact that
scholarly analyses of the last stages of the suffrage movement
are surprisingly slim. One largely untouched problem is the
impact of the Civil War upon the women who participated
in it. Scott (1970) has traced part of this story in her study
of Southern women, but much remains to be explored for the
generation of women who served in wartime nursing, government agencies and bureaus, and those who held their families,
homesteads, and community organizations together during
the years their men were away. Though kept out of decision-
making positions during their wartime service, they were
allowed to abandon some of the Victorian restrictions that
hampered them. One wants to know how the abrupt postwar
withdrawal from such unusual participation affected the perspectives such women subsequently brought to politics, work,
and the rearing of their children. Much historical work also
needs to be done before we can fully understand the social
and political influences that affected the course of the campaigns to secure the vote for women between 1880 and 1920.
Catt and Shuler (1926) have given one piece of this analysis
in their account of the role of the liquor interests in fighting
women's suffrage; Grimes (1967) has given us another in his
account of the anti-immigrant political pressures that helped
to gain the vote for women. But much more remains to be
done by the next generation of scholars.

In a curious way, Anthony and Stanton's massive work,
History of Woman Suffrage, may have had an unintended
result. Knowing only too well that women's achievements,
like women's history, rarely received attention from historians,

they were motivated in writing the *History* by a wish to assure a permanent record of the efforts of their movement. But the sheer existence of this record stands as a temptation to historians to focus on the suffrage movement as the sole story concerning American women in the latter half of the nineteenth and the first few decades of the twentieth century. The view that "feminism died" with the passage of the suffrage amendment is encouraged by the circumstance that so much of women's history has been the history of their attempt to secure the vote. It may be that we need more historical explorations of what was happening in the lives of American women apart from the struggle for the political right to vote in order to reach some final understanding of the suffrage movement itself.

From Abolition to Sex Equality:
Sarah Grimké (1792–1873) and
Angelina Grimké (1805–1879)

The Grimké sisters were born into an upper-class slave-owning family with deep roots in the colonial and state history of South Carolina. Their lives spanned over three-quarters of the nineteenth century, for Angelina lived to her seventy-fourth year and Sarah to her eighty-first. It is somewhat startling, in the light of this longevity, to realize that the activities and writings they became best-known for were all compressed into a brief three years of their lives, from 1835 to 1838. They were the only women in the band of seventy abolition agents trained by Theodore Weld for lecture tours under the sponsorship of the American Anti-Slavery Society in the late 1830s; Angelina Grimké was the first woman to address a state legislative committee in Massachusetts (1838) and the only Southern woman to make a public appeal to Southerners to abandon the institution of slavery (1836); and both sisters are among the earliest American writers on sex equality (1837). Angelina's marriage to Theodore Weld in 1838 symbolized the joining of the two reform movements of antislavery and woman's rights.

What sequence of experiences impelled these sisters to leave their home and state for the North, to change their religious affiliation, to join the abolition movement, to advocate sex equality? And why—since more than half a lifetime lay before Angelina after her marriage and since her sister Sarah never married—did the two sisters not continue in the forefront of the two movements to which they were so deeply committed? In pursuing the first question, we shall look into the family in which the Grimké sisters grew up. For the second question we must explore the impact of marriage, maternity, and finances on the lives of the sisters and of Theodore Weld.

Sarah was the older of the two sisters by twelve years. Born in Charleston in 1792, Sarah was the sixth child of John and Mary Grimké while Angelina was the fourteenth child. Sarah was an intensely serious, bright youngster, who admired her older brother Thomas enormously. She received a better-than-average education by studying his lessons along with her own. Her childhood had a surface veneer of busyness that goes with the social prominence and large size of her family, but beneath that surface Sarah seems to have been an introspective, lonely child. The importance Angelina was to have in her sister's life is apparent from her birth, for Sarah begged her parents for permission to be the infant's godmother. For the early years of Angelina's life, and to a certain extent thereafter, her sister Sarah stood as part sister, part mother to her. The frustration Sarah experienced from her father's refusal to permit her to learn Latin and later to study law was probably partially compensated for by the emotional gratification and admiration she derived from the special role she played in her younger sister's life.

Whatever resentment Sarah felt toward her father, she was intelligent enough to realize that the restrictions placed upon her were not peculiar to her father's views of appropriate education for a girl but were a reflection of wider social beliefs in the Charleston world around her. When her father was suffering from ill health, it was Sarah who accompanied him North for medical advice, and it was Sarah who remained at his side, without calling for anyone else from the family, at a New Jersey seashore resort, where he died. She spent a few months in Philadelphia after his death and was still in a very depressed state when she returned to Charleston in 1818. She had become attracted to the Quaker religion during her stay in Philadelphia, and after her permanent move North three years later, she was accepted into the Society of Friends at the age of thirty-one.

With Sarah in the North, Angelina in turn struggled against the restrictions of the narrow social world within which she moved; her efforts were more vigorous and overt than her older sister's had been. Despite a flurry of late-adolescent social engagements, Angelina continued to be disillusioned with Presbyterian church doctrine and troubled by the slave-owning practices she considered to be in conflict with Christian beliefs. When Sarah returned home on a visit in 1827, she found Angelina receptive to Quaker beliefs, and Angelina shortly followed her sister into the Society of

Friends. There were only a few, mostly older, Quakers in Charleston, and in 1829 Angelina traveled North to join her sister in Philadelphia.

In later years both sisters tended to project backward a deeper repugnance and rejection of slavery than they probably felt during their youth in Charleston. Lerner (1967) suggests that Sarah probably felt greater discontent on the grounds of her sex than on the issue of slavery. Her brother Thomas' departure for study at Yale when Sarah was twelve was not only the personal loss of a close sibling, but also an occasion that forced her to face the reality that, no matter how she longed for learning, she could not expect the family support that went naturally to her brother. Sarah recalled her own defiance of South Carolina law in teaching her maid at night, when she was supposed to be combing and brushing her hair. With the light out and the keyhole screened, the two girls lay flat on their stomachs before the fire, and Sarah taught the slave girl how to read and spell (Lerner 1967:23). But this was far from a unique occurrence in families of the antebellum South, as Anne Scott's analysis (1970:46–79) of Southern women's memoirs reveals. Yet few Southern women left their homes to make a lonely way for themselves in a Northern city, as Sarah and Angelina did.

The boldness that drove the sisters North should not be exaggerated. They did not establish a separate household, either alone or together, but lived with a variety of Quaker families in Philadelphia, enclosed in a world hardly more open to free intellectual inquiry than was the Charleston world they had left behind them. Nor did they have acute financial difficulties, since they had funds from home to take care of the necessities of life. The sisters were associated with the more orthodox side of the Society of Friends, and this circumstance contributed to their limited intellectual exposure. When Angelina visited Catherine Beecher's Hartford Female Academy, one of the best schools for young women in the country at the time, and expressed an interest in attending the school, her Quaker mentors in Philadelphia refused permission, on the ground that there were too many Presbyterians there, though Angelina was a woman of twenty-five at this time. Instead, the sisters tried their hand at a variety of activities in Philadelphia, teaching and caring for children in a small dame school, studying on their own to fill the deficiencies in their education. But they seem to have had a very limited range of interests or exposure to political events in the larger society; nor were they exposed to the lectures Fanny Wright was conducting in her tour of the Eastern cities during these years. Lerner (1967:95) suggests that, had they read Wright's work or heard her speeches, they might have been spared many years of intellectual struggle, for many of the points they painfully worked out on their own a few years later had been developed and advocated by Fanny Wright several years previously. The same point could be made concerning other writers on women who published prior to 1835—Martineau, Wollstonecraft, Macaulay—plus a variety of English periodicals during this early part of the nineteenth century.

The Grimké sisters did learn of the antislavery societies in Philadelphia and attended their meetings. As news of the Lane Seminary debates reached the East and sparked new debates, Sarah and Angelina heard of them and were distressed by the violent public reactions to speeches by abolitionists in New England. The act that started Angelina on the way to a public reputation was a letter she wrote to Garrison, which he published in *The Liberator*. Her orthodox Quaker friends were furious at the strong public stand Angelina had taken; her refusal to withdraw the letter was the symbolic act of Angelina's emancipation from the past.

This one firm step seemed to free both sisters for a rapidly escalating awareness of many restrictions upon their lives. Their physical and intellectual energies were soon fully expanded, as though they and their ideas had been suddenly released after a long period of germination. In their own special religious framework the sisters took no special credit for this awakening, for their explanations were in terms of "revelations" and "callings." Whatever the origin, Angelina was galvanized into an extensive two weeks of writing which yielded her *Appeal to the Christian Women of the South*. This work stands as one of her unique contributions to the abolition movement—not only the earliest but the only appeal by a Southern abolitionist woman to Southern women. It is written in a clear, bold style, with a minimum of the rhetoric fashionable in that period. Following the lead of the Northern abolitionists, Angelina argued that, since slavery was a sin, the Christian was absolved from the responsibility to obey the laws of the Southern states, for adherence to moral principles takes precedence over obedience to man-made law. She called upon the women of the South to learn all they could about the institution of slavery, to discuss the problem widely in their family and social circles, and to act consistently by denouncing slavery and releasing any slaves in their personal possession.

Word of the sisters' abolitionist sympathy and Angelina's writing soon reached the headquarters of the American Anti-Slavery Society in New York, and Elizur Wright invited them to come to the city as speakers in women's sewing circles and private homes. Agreeing to this plan, the sisters started their most vigorous two years in 1836 as the only women abolition agents in the movement. The training courses they attended, led by Theodore Weld, provided them with an experience important in several ways. They were at last in a social group of like-minded souls, particularly delighted to find Quakers attuned to their viewpoints; and undoubtedly they were easily captivated, as thousands of others had been, by Theodore Weld's instruction and preaching.

At the time the Grimké sisters set off on their speaking tour of New England in 1837, many sectors of the New England churches had already been long-standing supporters of colonization societies, and at first the sisters received a warm welcome. Indeed, what better appeal could there be than the living witness of two women from a prominent Southern family who had personally observed the horrors of slavery and who now denounced the institution as sinful? They were tangible demonstrations that the tactical campaign launched by the abolition societies was a good one. If Southern women could have a change of heart and mind on the issue, then surely Northerners could be easily won to the same persuasion. But the Grimké sisters went beyond denouncing slavery as sinful; they spoke against race prejudice as an indirect support of slavery, insisting that such prejudice had to be fought in the North as well as the South. Angelina argued that the female slaves

> are our countrywomen; they are our sisters; and to us as women, they have a right to look for sympathy with their sorrows and effort and prayer for their rescue.

To denounce slavery as sinful was one thing; to call on Northern Protestants to rid themselves of race prejudice was a rather strong idea to many New Englanders. Before the year was out, the Congregationalist ministers were refusing to read notices of abolitionist meetings from the pulpit.

During their Boston stay the sisters were clearly influenced and encouraged by Garrison to strengthen the positions they had espoused at the beginning of their tour. They quietly emphasized the point in their lectures that if women were to become effective in the abolition movement, they had to free themselves from the social restraints that had kept them numb and silent and learn to speak and act as fully responsible moral beings. Many people, clergymen in particular, were very skeptical of, if not openly hostile to, this view of women in the abolition movement. Garrison seems to have taken the discord as an opportunity to denounce the clergy and to identify himself as a strong supporter of woman's rights. It is difficult to be sure of the distribution of views within the abolition movement concerning the stress on woman's rights by antislavery agents, for G. H. Barnes (1957), one of the chief historians of this movement, is so clearly critical of Garrison that one must look cautiously beyond his textual account to the evidence itself, and that is ambiguous. The correspondence between Weld and Angelina Grimké makes it is clear that Weld was eager to open the leadership of the movement to women, since they could reach other women more effectively than men could. Angelina seemed to become increasingly convinced that there was a need to mobilize the reservoir of antislavery sentiment and potential for action among women in more general terms. Since the sisters were speaking many times a week as they toured New England, they were in the throes of an intensive process of politicization themselves, and much of the assurance with which they now wrote and defended their ideas was probably rooted in this experience. But Weld advised caution without departing from his principled support for women. Other officers of the society used a much sharper tone in their letters to the women. Whittier asked how they could forget "the great and dreadful wrongs of the slave in a selfish crusade against some paltry grievance . . . some trifling oppression, political or social, of their own" (Barnes 1957: 157).

Despite the warnings from abolition society officials, Sarah continued her work on a series of letters on the equality of the sexes and on her response to the angry pastoral

letter that denounced "the mistaken conduct of those who
encourage females to bear an obtrusive and ostentatious part
in measures of reform" (Barnes 1957:156).

There is no question but that the "woman issue" had
divisive impact on the abolition movement in 1837 and 1838.
Some people felt that the blending of the woman's issue with
the slavery issue contributed to the strength of both reforms,
but for many others it represented a potential split in the
abolition movement. What is not clear is the extent to which
the more inflammatory, radical tactics and views taken by
the Garrison abolitionists in Boston on all aspects of the
slavery agitation was at issue in the Boston-versus-New York
conflict or affected the issue of women which the Grimké
sisters brought to a head. Garrison has been described as an
opportunist, who supported woman's rights in public as one
more issue he could use to agitate and assert leadership. Certainly for someone who claimed to be so ardent a supporter
of women, he was remarkably lukewarm in supporting Angelina's acceptance of an invitation to speak before the
Massachusetts legislative committee. Weld, on the other
hand, was enthusiastic in both anticipation and in reaction
to the successful impact Angelina made upon that committee.

There was probably a blend of several factors in the complex situation: a moderate-versus-radical tactical difference
among men competing for leadership in the movement; a
reasonable concern for protecting the primary goal of the
movement by not compounding it unduly with another
equally emotional social issue; and a basic division on the
whole question of women in society. But what seems totally
unjustified is the implication in Barnes' account that Weld
either consciously or unconsciously solved the problem by
removing "Angelina from the controversy very effectually
by asking her to marry him" (Barnes 1957:158). Weld was no
johnny-come-lately to the woman's issue any more than to
the abolition issue. And from correspondence which passed
between himself and Angelina after he made his offer of
marriage, it is impossible to draw any conclusion other than
that his love for her was sincere and that it was a disruptive
revelation to himself about himself.

The correspondence affords a rare opportunity to lift even
a slight corner of the veil which Puritan theology imposed
upon sexuality and its expression, and I have rarely seen so
clear a depiction of the struggle sexual passion could repre-

sent for intensely religious, Calvinist-reared men and women
as the exchanges which flew between Angelina in Massachusetts and Theodore in New York during the weeks following
their declaration of love for each other. Angelina wrote from
Brookline in February 1838:

> Ought God to be *all in all* to us *on earth*? I tho't so,
> and am frightened to find He is not, that is, I feel some-
> thing else is necessary to my happiness. I laid awake
> thinking why it was that my heart longed and panted and
> reached after you as it does. Why my Savior and my God
> is not enough to *satisfy* me. Am I sinning, am I ungrate-
> ful, *am I an* IDOLATOR? I trust I am not, and yet—but I
> cannot tell how I feel. I am a mystery to myself. [Barnes
> and Dumond 1934:II, 553–554]

The sexual agitation and the complete novelty of such feelings are transparent in the imagery with which Theodore
wrote back from New York:

> The truth is Angelina . . . I have so long wrestled with
> myself like a blind giant stifling by violence all the in-
> tensities of my nature that when at last they found *vent*,
> and your voice of love proclaimed a *deliverance* so
> unlooked for, . . . it was as the life touch to one *dead*;
> all the pent up tides of my being so long shut out from
> light and air, broke forth at once and spurned controul.
> . . . I thought I had mastery of my spirit and power to
> quell its wildest insurrection . . . but your letter has
> taught me that I am a novice in one department of self
> restraint. In truth, till then I never had either observation,
> experience, or the least knowledge of myself in this re-
> spect. [Barnes and Dumond 1934:II, 555–556]

Four days later Angelina wrote in a similar vein, expressing
her intense emotional state and simultaneous anxiety in finding her most passionate feelings flowing toward Weld rather
than toward God, unwittingly suggesting the deep sublima-
tion of sexual passion that was channeled into religious
observance and feeling:

> I want to know why those of our own sex *cannot* fill the
> void in human hearts. This is a mystery I have yet to
> learn and I want to know why I find myself involuntarily
> applying to you the language which hitherto I had applied

to my blessed Master, for instance "I am my beloved's
and my beloved is mine," etc. . . . I shall look anxiously
for a letter *tomorrow*, for you promised to make some
suggestions on my IDOLATRY . . . and yet I feel *no* condemnation, but rather that the Lord smiles on these very
emotions. O! what a mystery to *myself* am I. [Barnes
and Dumond 1934:II,569]

Toward the end of this long letter, Angelina showed a comparable concern of an interesting sort. In the above section,
she is worried that love for a man may reduce her love of
God; next she worries lest their love detract from their commitment to abolition:

I trust the slave will lose nothing by our gain in each
other. Farewell—I am Thine—Deep calleth unto deep in
the ceaseless respondings of my heart to thine. [Barnes
and Dumond 1934:II,570]

Toward the end of the following month, March 1838,
Angelina again returned to the question of the effect of her
new love on the commitments that have absorbed her:

I tho't yesterday, perhaps our marriage was to be my dis-
mission from *public* service. O! how I should rejoice at it,
if the Master should say *"It is enough."* It is an encreasing
trial to me and most gladly would I retire from public
view and sink down into *sweet obscurity.* Perhaps the
slave needed my service in this way just when I was called
out, but the crisis is rapidly passing away and he will
need them *no longer.* Is it a temptation that I want to
pray it may be so? [Barnes and Dumond 1934:II,611]

Weld responded to this point very firmly. He would have
nothing to do with the suggestion that with love found, she
could relax her efforts and commitment to the slave and the
woman issues:

What Angelina! Shall my love prove a weakener of your
womanhood, diluting its strength, eclipsing its brightness
and causing it to droop with failing wings in its heaven-
ward soaring? Nay . . . it must not, shall not be. . . .
I feel an assured confidence that we shall gird to mightier
accomplishment each others souls, elevating to higher
attempt and quickening to stronger resolves and daring.
[Barnes and Dumond 1934:II,631]

There are no letters from Angelina to tell whether she was pleased, displeased, or ambivalent about Weld's firm insistence that she continue her involvement in reform. A month later he wrote a remarkable letter, in which he discussed the social significance of their marriage, warning her that people think her utterly spoiled for domestic life, so that thousands will be watching their "experiment." Poor Angelina! Like generations of women to follow, she is expected to meet impossible standards: she must continue her contribution to reform in the larger world, maintain a home and a happy marriage, and in due time, bear and rear children. In Angelina's case, a Southern background that provided her with few domestic skills and little interest in acquiring them up to this juncture in her life, a realistic expectation of a meager income, and no contraceptive devices whereby to control the number or spacing of children—none of these are auspicious indices that she could become the paragon of perfection and boundless energy Weld held out to her. It is a credit to Theodore that he applied the same stern standard to himself, for he viewed married life as a test of his ability to practice what he had long held in theory. The letter is sufficiently interesting to quote at somewhat greater length:

We have uncommon notoriety, you *especially*. At this moment probably no female in the country is so extensively known or so much the subject of remark everywhere as *you*. . . . We are very prominently identified with the great moral movements of the age. I mean the *reformations*, Moral reform, Temperance, Abolition, Rights and sphere of women, the reform in physical habits, food regimen and exercise and education, the battle with factitious life and aristocracy and thraldom of fashion, the great question of diversity of sects, anti Bible, etc. . . . Your being so generally known as a public lecturer to promiscuous assemblies, and especially as having addressed the legislature, all eyes are upon you and almost all mouths filled with cavil. Nine tenths of the community verily believe that you are utterly spoiled for domestic life. . . . My intercourse you know has been almost exclusively with my own sex, and I deem it no self conceit . . . to say that men I understand thoroughly and I know that the devil of dominion over woman will be one of the last that will be cast out of them; Beloved, on account of

your *doctrine* and *practice* touching the sphere of woman.
I will only add that you are the FIRST woman everywhere
known to be on this ground, to whom in the Providence
of God the *practical test* of married life will be applied
(if we are spared). Thousands and thousands will watch
for your halting and with a Satanic eagerness forestall if
possible the result of the *experiment* (!) by ill omen[ed]
croakings and prophecies of failure and downfall. I feel
also most solemnly that a peculiar responsibility rests on
ME too, on this very account. All who know me intimately know that I have always held and maintained the
same views of the sphere of woman. Married life will be
the touchstone to test me and to show how I reduce to
practice what I have long and perhaps pertinaciously
contended for in *theory*. [Barnes and Dumond, 1934:II,
636–638]

Angelina wrote only a brief reply to Theodore's long
warning. She suggested that "thou art blind to the danger of
marrying a woman who feels and acts out the principle of
equal rights," but she concurred with Weld in praying that
their marriage might demonstrate the merit of the principles
to the world:

May the Lord Jesus help me for thy sake, and for *woman's*
sake to prove that well regulated minds can with *equal
ease* occupy high and low stations and find *true happiness*
in both. Yes thou art trying a *dangerous experiment*, one
which I do believe *no other man* would try because I tho't
no other understands my principles or myself. [Barnes
and Dumond 1934:II,649]

Theodore and Angelina were married in May 1838 in
Philadelphia; they settled in a house in Fort Lee, New Jersey,
overlooking the Hudson above New York. Except for the
winter of 1853, Sarah continued as a member of the Weld
household throughout their lives. The sisters withdrew from
their public careers, feeling that they had to prove by their
attention to the home that they were fully competent in that
area. The first year was a busy one nonetheless, for both
sisters helped gather and organize the massive materials
Weld used for his book, *Slavery as It Is*.

Knowing from their early correspondence how keenly
self-conscious Theodore and Angelina were about their visi-

bility as an "experimental" new kind of partnership marriage, one can expect a good deal of reticence about (if not inability to recognize) problems or crises that were particular to the married state. There is little in their later correspondence to provide firm, direct evidence on whether either partner would revise their youthful declarations of principles concerning sex equality in light of their living the "experiment." Affection and loyalty seem to have continued strong; but there are suggestive hints of sex-linked difficulties. Angelina had a history of gynecological trouble, which Weld referred to as the "accidents" which weakened her, although there is no evidence of any "accidents" in the sense he implied. Lerner suggests that this phrasing may have been an evasion, for "accidents" could be viewed as providential, while gynecological disorder would have to be admitted as a sex-linked source of trouble that might complicate their ideology. A first child was born in 1839, the second in 1841, and the third and last in 1844. There were numerous periods of illness over the years which seem to have involved disorder of the uterus. Sarah was on the scene to help with maternal and household responsibilities.

But it was a hard and a poor life for the Weld family. Theodore was often absent from home entirely during the early years of the marriage, working in Washington, D. C., during the petition campaign to Congress in the abolition cause. He played an important, though backstage, role in this effort, preparing evidence, lobbying among the Congressmen, providing John Quincy Adams with material for his speeches on the Hill. These were undoubtedly gratifying years to the abolitionist, and one would expect that the successful end of the petition campaign, which meant that the slavery issue could come directly before the Congress without the guise of petition submission, would only increase the role that Weld could play on the Washington scene.

Yet in midwinter of 1843, and again in January 1844, he absolutely refused the entreaties of Adams, Tappan, and Giddings to return to Washington to help the cause. Barnes (1957) interprets this refusal as consistent with Weld's long-standing tendency to humility and a distaste for organizational prominence. This is not a convincing argument, however, for Weld's work in Washington would not have changed from what it had been earlier. He was needed for his encyclopedic knowledge of slavery, his mastery of the state laws, his writing and tactical skills, and his persuasiveness as a lobbyist in the quiet rounds of Congressmen's boarding houses.

I think a better explanation of his withdrawal to Fort Lee can be found by looking more closely to the dates involved from the perspective of events on the domestic scene. Weld left Washington in midwinter of 1843 and refused to return, despite urgent appeals from the capital. At home Angelina had been pregnant and ill, and her situation culminated in a miscarriage in February 1843. By summer she was pregnant again. When the call came from Washington to return in January 1844, Angelina was seven months pregnant. It seems highly plausible that it was concern for his wife that kept Weld at home through this period, and equally plausible that he would not refer even in private correspondence to the real reasons for abandoning the Washington work. To have done so would have been to admit to the same limitation of their principles of sex equality that the identification of gynecological disorder would have imposed.

This refusal to admit the influence of a private concern on a man's public decisions is hardly unique to the Welds or peculiar to the mid-nineteenth century. Even in the 1970s men generally give as their reasons for choosing a career or a new job such considerations as careerism, their own predilections, and the like; they take pride in the adaptability of their wives and children. Sociological theory itself has posited a lack of interdependence between family and occupational processes, with the former playing a passive, adaptive role.

For whatever reasons, Theodore Weld remained more closely tied to home from 1844 on. Financial difficulties pressed on the family, and eventually the Welds and Sarah Grimké began a new and taxing career, running a residential boarding school, first at their Fort Lee home and later at a new cooperative community, Raritan Bay Union. It is an interesting reflection of the close ties that bound the abolitionists together to note the identity of the youngsters who were first sent to the Welds' Belleville School at Fort Lee: Henry and Elizabeth Stanton sent two of their boys; Gerrit Smith from Peterboro, New York, and James Birney, who had run for the presidency on the Liberty Party ticket, each sent a son; a Grimké nephew came up from Charleston. In October 1851 life for the Grimké sisters was a long way from the public roles they had played in the years from 1836 to 1838; there were three young Weld children and twenty pupils, for whom the sisters did all the cooking, washing, cleaning, and mending, on top of teaching history and French (Lerner 1967:315). Yet one senses little pleasure and pride in this combination of teaching and domesticity. Instead, a note of exhaustion and anxiety sounds between the lines of their correspondence.

In reading about the mature middle years of the family, one wonders what held Sarah to the household. In an 1841 letter to a friend she used the language of her own religious creed to explain her confinement within the Weld household. She explained that she could not return to Massachusetts, as she had been invited to do, "because God has not called me to do so." Her comments then continue:

His loving kindness has provided me a sweet harbor of rest, after years of tossing and buffeting; he has given me two children with whom I enjoy sweet communion and who delight to do me good. [Barnes and Dumond 1934:II, 708]

Yet it seems doubtful that a *menage à trois* is ever a simple affair socially or psychologically. Undoubtedly there were strong and abiding ties to Angelina, and by extension, to her children. Sarah was a woman of forty-eight when her sister married, and the spirit of adventure that had marked their march through New England was more that of Angelina than of the more serious-minded Sarah. To leave Angelina for an independent life elsewhere might have seemed an empty and frightening prospect after the long years during which their lives had been closely connected. One suspects, too, that Theodore Weld was an important figure in Sarah's life in more than one respect. Relations between the sisters were not always smooth. In 1852 they took a critical turn, and Angelina admitted to being "weary of a conflict which has lasted 15 years." She expressed shame at her own ingratitude toward Sarah, but at the same time she felt it "unnatural that a wife and mother should ever thus be willing to share the affections of her dearest ones with any human being" (Lerner 1967:324).

Sarah went to Washington for the winter, but it must have been a sad and lonely time for her, cut off from the only people who meant anything to her. She wrote during this period that the children were a link that bound her to life. Several times she referred to her love "of Theodore's chil-

dren," only rarely calling them "Nina's children." In the
statement quoted above Angelina spoke not only of a mother
sharing her dearest ones, but of a wife as well. How much of
Angelina's conflict was rooted in a more than sisterly regard
by Sarah for Theodore is not at all clear. Lerner comments
that, after Sarah's return, the "strange trio continued in
Victorian harmony, tantalizing the biographer and historian
with a host of unanswered questions" (Lerner 1967:327).

Though pacifists of long standing, the threesome supported the Civil War as the only way to end the hated institution of slavery; it must have pained them to find that the
oldest son, Charles, took a position as conscientious objector
and refused to serve in the army or to pay for a substitute,
on the claim that the war was an "unjust cause." The sisters
lived on into the 1870s, occasionally participating in woman's-
rights conventions and other reforms that moved them to
action outside their teaching and domestic duties. Loyal to a
good cause to the very end of her life, Sarah Grimké at the
age of seventy-nine trudged up and down the countryside in
Massachusetts in order to sell one hundred and fifty copies
of John Stuart Mill's *The Subjection of Women*.

⚘ Angelina Grimké: Appeal to the ⚘ Christian Women of the South

I have thus, I think, clearly proved to you seven propositions, viz.: First, that slavery is contrary to the declaration
of our independence. Second, that it is contrary to the first
charter of human rights given to Adam, and renewed to Noah.
Third, that the fact of slavery having been the subject of
prophecy, furnishes *no* excuse whatever to slavedealers.
Fourth, that no such system existed under the patriarchal dispensation. Fifth, that *slavery never* existed under the Jewish
dispensation; but so far otherwise, that every servant was

From Angelina Emily Grimké, "Appeal to the Christian
Women of the South," *The Anti-Slavery Examiner*, Vol. 1, No. 2,
September 1836. Pp. 16–26.

placed under the *protection of law,* and care taken not only to prevent all *involuntary* servitude, but all *voluntary perpetual* bondage. Sixth, that slavery in America reduces a *man* to a *thing,* a "chattel personal," *robs him* of *all* his rights as a *human being,* fetters both his mind and body, and protects the *master* in the most unnatural and unreasonable power, whilst it *throws him out* of the protection of law. Seventh, that slavery is contrary to the example and precepts of our holy and merciful Redeemer, and of his apostles.

But perhaps you will be ready to query, why appeal to *women* on this subject? *We* do not make the laws which perpetuate slavery. *No* legislative power is vested in *us; we* can do nothing to overthrow the system, even if we wished to do so. To this I reply, I know you do not make the laws, but I also know that *you are the wives and mothers, the sisters and daughters of those who do;* and if you really suppose *you* can do nothing to overthrow slavery, you are greatly mistaken. You can do much in every way: four things I will name. 1st. You can read on this subject. 2d. You can pray over this subject. 3d. You can speak on this subject. 4th. You can *act* on this subject. I have not placed reading before praying because I regard it more important, but because, in order to pray aright, we must understand what we are praying for; it is only then we can "pray with the understanding and the spirit also."

1. Read then on the subject of slavery. Search the Scriptures daily, whether the things I have told you are true. Other books and papers might be a great help to you in this investigation, but they are not necessary, and it is hardly probable that your Committees of Vigilance will allow you to have any other. The *Bible* then is the book I want you to read in the spirit of inquiry, and the spirit of prayer. Even the enemies of Abolitionists, acknowledged that their doctrines are drawn from it. In the great mob in Boston, last autumn, when the books and papers of the Anti-Slavery Society, were thrown out of the windows of their office, one individual laid hold of the Bible and was about tossing it out to the ground, when another reminded him that it was the Bible he had in his hand. "O! 'tis all one," he replied, and out went the sacred volume, along with the rest. We thank him for the acknowledgment. Yes, "it is all one," for our books and papers are mostly commentaries on the Bible, and the Declaration. Read the *Bible* then, it contains the words of

Jesus, and they are spirit and life. Judge for yourselves whether *he sanctioned* such a system of oppression and crime.

2. Pray over this subject. When you have entered into your closets, and shut to the doors, then pray to your father, who seeth in secret, that he would open your eyes to see whether slavery is *sinful*, and if it is, that he would enable you to bear a faithful, open and unshrinking testimony against it, and to do whatsoever your hands find to do, leaving the consequences entirely to him, who still says to us whenever we try to reason away duty from the fear of consequences, *"What is that to thee, follow thou me."* Pray also for that poor slave, that he may be kept patient and submissive under his hard lot, until God is pleased to open the door of freedom to him without violence or bloodshed. Pray too for the master that his heart may be softened, and he made willing to acknowledge, as Joseph's brethren did, "Verily we are guilty concerning our brother," before he will be compelled to add in consequence of Divine judgment, "therefore is all this evil come upon us." Pray also for all your brethren and sisters who are laboring in the righteous cause of Emancipation in the Northern States, England and the world. There is great encouragement for prayer in these words of our Lord. "Whatsoever ye shall ask the Father *in my name*, he *will give* it to you"—Pray then without ceasing, in the closet and the social circle.

3. Speak on this subject. It is through the tongue, the pen, and the press, that truth is principally propagated. Speak then to your relatives, your friends, your acquaintances on the subject of slavery; be not afraid if you are conscientiously convinced it is *sinful*, to say so openly, but calmly, and to let your sentiments be known. If you are served by the slaves of others, try to ameliorate their condition as much as possible; never aggravate their faults, and thus add fuel to the fire of anger already kindled, in a master and mistress's bosom; remember their extreme ignorance, and consider them as your Heavenly Father does the *less* culpable on this account, even when they do wrong things. Discountenance *all* cruelty to them, all starvation, all corporal chastisement; these may brutalize and *break* their spirits, but will never bend them to willing, cheerful obedience. If possible, see that they are comfortably and *seasonably* fed, whether in the house or the field; it is unreasonable and cruel to expect slaves to wait for their breakfast until eleven o'clock, when they rise at five or

six. Do all you can, to induce their owners to clothe them well, and to allow them many little indulgences which would contribute to their comfort. Above all, try to persuade your husband, father, brothers and sons, that *slavery is a crime against God and man,* and that it is a great sin to keep *human beings* in such abject ignorance; to deny them the privilege of learning to read and write. The Catholics are universally condemned, for denying the Bible to the common people, but, *slaveholders must not* blame them, for *they* are doing the *very same thing,* and for the very same reason, neither of these systems can bear the light which bursts from the pages of that Holy Book. And lastly, endeavour to inculcate submission on the part of the slaves, but whilst doing this be faithful in pleading the cause of the oppressed.

> "Will *you* behold unheeding,
>   Life's holiest feelings crushed,
> Where *woman's* heart is bleeding,
>   Shall *woman's* voice be hushed?"

4. Act on this subject. Some of you *own* slaves yourselves. *If* you believe slavery is *sinful,* set them at liberty, "undo the heavy burdens and let the oppressed go free." If they wish to remain with you, pay them wages, if not let them leave you. Should they remain, teach them, and have them taught the common branches of an English education; they have minds and those minds, *ought to be improved.* So precious a talent as intellect, never was given to be wrapt in a napkin and buried in the earth. It is the *duty* of all, as far as they can, to improve their own mental faculties, because we are commanded to love God with *all our minds,* as well as with all our hearts, and we commit a great sin, if we *forbid or prevent* that cultivation of the mind in others, which would enable them to perform this duty. Teach your servants then to read &c, and encourage them to believe it is their *duty* to learn, if it were only that they might read the Bible.

But some of you will say, we can neither free our slaves nor teach them to read, for the laws of our state forbid it. Be not surprised when I say such wicked laws *ought to be no barrier* in the way of your duty, and I appeal to the Bible to prove this position. What was the conduct of Shiphrah and Puah, when the king of Egypt issued his cruel mandate, with regard to the Hebrew children? "*They* feared *God,* and did *not* as the King of Egypt commanded them, but saved the

men children alive." Did these *women* do right in disobeying
that monarch? "*Therefore* (says the sacred text,) *God dealt
well* with them, and made them houses" Ex. i. What was the
conduct of Shadrach, Meshach, and Abednego, when Ne-
buchadnezzar set up a golden image in the plain of Dura, and
commanded all people, nations, and languages, to fall down
and worship it? "Be it known, unto thee, (said these faithful
Jews) O king, that *we will not* serve thy gods, nor worship
the image which thou hast set up." Did these men *do right in
disobeying the law* of their sovereign? Let their miraculous deliverance from the burning fiery furnace, answer;
Dan.iii. . . .

But some of you may say, if we do free our slaves, they
will be taken up and sold, therefore there will be no use in
doing it. Peter and John might just as well have said, we will
not preach the gospel, for if we do, we shall be taken up
and put in prison, therefore there will be no use in our
preaching. *Consequences*, my friends, belong no more to *you*,
than they did to these apostles. Duty is ours and events are
God's. If you think slavery is sinful, all *you* have to do is to
set your slaves at liberty, do all you can to protect them, and
in humble faith and fervent prayer, commend them to your
common Father. He can take care of them; but if for wise
purposes he sees fit to allow them to be sold, this will afford
you an opportunity of testifying openly, wherever you go,
against the crime of *manstealing*. Such an act will be *clear
robbery*, and if exposed, might, under the Divine direction,
do the cause of Emancipation more good, than any thing that
could happen, for, "He makes even the wrath of man to
praise him, and the remainder of wrath he will restrain."

I know that this doctrine of obeying *God*, rather than
man, will be considered as dangerous, and heretical by many,
but I am not afraid openly to avow it, because it is the
doctrine of the Bible; but I would not be understood to advocate resistance to any law however oppressive, if, in obeying
it, I was not obliged to commit *sin*. If for instance, there
was a law, which imposed imprisonment or a fine upon me
if I manumitted a slave, I would on no account resist that
law, I would set the slave free, and then go to prison or pay
the fine. If a law commands me to *sin I will break it*; if it
calls me to *suffer*, I will let it take its course *unresistingly*.
The doctrine of blind obedience and unqualified submission
to *any human* power, whether civil or ecclesiastical, is the

doctrine of despotism, and ought to have no place among Republicans and Christians.

But you will perhaps say, such a course of conduct would inevitably expose us to great suffering. Yes! my christian friends, I believe it would, but this will *not* excuse you or any one else for the neglect of *duty*. If Prophets and Apostles, Martyrs, and Reformers had not been willing to suffer for the truth's sake, where would the world have been now? If they had said, we cannot speak the truth, we cannot do what we believe is right, because the *laws of our country or public opinion are against us*, where would our holy religion have been now? . . .

But you may say we are *women*, how can our hearts endure persecution? And why not? Have not women stood up in all the dignity and strength of moral courage to be the leaders of the people, and to bear a faithful testimony for the truth whenever the providence of God has called them to do so? Are there no *women* in that noble army of martyrs who are now singing the song of Moses and the Lamb? Who led out the women of Israel from the house of bondage, striking the timbrel, and singing the song of deliverance on the banks of that sea whose waters stood up like walls of crystal to open a passage for their escape? It was a *woman*: Miriam, the prophetess, the sister of Moses and Aaron. Who went up with Barak to Kadesh to fight against Jabin, King of Canaan, into whose hand Israel had been sold because of their iniquities? It was a *woman!* Deborah the wife of Lapidoth, the judge, as well as the prophetess of that backsliding people; Judges iv, 9. Into whose hands was Sisera, the captain of Jabin's host delivered? Into the hand of a *woman*. Jael the wife of Heber! Judges vi, 21. Who dared to *speak the truth* concerning those judgments which were coming upon Judea, when Josiah, alarmed at finding that his people "had not kept the word of the Lord to do after all that was written in the book of the Law," sent to enquire of the Lord concerning these things? It was a *woman*. Huldah the prophetess, the wife of Shallum; 2, Chron. xxxiv, 22. Who was chosen to deliver the whole Jewish nation from that murderous decree of Persia's King, which wicked Haman had obtained by calumny and fraud? It was a *woman*; Esther the Queen; yes, weak and trembling *woman* was the instrument appointed by God, to reverse the bloody mandate of the eastern monarch, and save the *whole visible church* from destruction. What human voice

first proclaimed to Mary that she should be the mother of
our Lord? It was a *woman!* Elizabeth, the wife of Zacharias;
Luke i, 42, 43. Who united with the good old Simeon in giving
thanks publicly in the temple, when the child, Jesus, was
presented there by his parents, "and spake of him to all them
that looked for redemption in Jerusalem?" It was a *woman!*
Anna the prophetess. Who first proclaimed Christ as the true
Messiah in the streets of Samaria, once the capital of the ten
tribes? It was a *woman!* Who ministered to the Son of God
whilst on earth, a despised and persecuted Reformer, in the
humble garb of a carpenter? They were *women!* Who followed the rejected King of Israel, as his fainting footsteps
trod the road to Calvary? "A great company of people and of
women;" and it is remarkable that to *them alone*, he turned
and addressed the pathetic language, "Daughters of Jerusalem,
weep not for me, but weep for yourselves and your children."
Ah! who sent unto the Roman Governor when he was set
down on the judgment seat, saying unto him, "Have thou
nothing to do with that just man, for I have suffered many
things this day in a dream because of him?" It was a *woman!*
the wife of Pilate. Although "*he knew* that for envy the Jews
had delivered Christ," yet *he* consented to surrender the Son
of God into the hands of a brutal soldiery, after having himself scourged his naked body. Had the *wife* of Pilate sat upon
that judgment seat, what would have been the result of the
trial of this "just person?". . .

And what, I would ask in conclusion, have *women* done
for the great and glorious cause of Emancipation? Who wrote
that pamphlet which moved the heart of Wilberforce to pray
over the wrongs, and his tongue to plead the cause of the
oppressed African? It was a *woman*, Elizabeth Heyrick. Who
labored assiduously to keep the sufferings of the slave continually before the British public? They were *women*. And
how did they do it? By their needles, paint brushes and pens,
by speaking the truth, and petitioning Parliament for the
abolition of slavery. And what was the effect of their labors?
Read it in the Emancipation bill of Great Britain. Read it, in
the present state of her West India Colonies. Read it, in the
impulse which has been given to the cause of freedom, in the
United States of America. Have English women then done so
much for the negro, and shall American women do nothing?
Oh no! Already are there sixty female Anti-Slavery Societies
in operation. These are doing just what the English women

did, telling the story of the colored man's wrongs, praying for his deliverance, and presenting his kneeling image constantly before the public eye on bags and needle-books, card-racks, pen-wipers, pin-cushions, &c. Even the children of the north are inscribing on their handy work, "May the points of our needles prick the slaveholder's conscience." Some of the reports of these Societies exhibit not only considerable talent, but a deep sense of religious duty, and a determination to persevere through evil as well as good report, until every scourge, and every shackle, is buried under the feet of the manumitted slave.

The Ladies' Anti-Slavery Society of Boston was called last fall, to a severe trial of their faith and constancy. They were mobbed by "the gentlemen of property and standing," in that city at their anniversary meeting, and their lives were jeoparded by an infuriated crowd; but their conduct on that occasion did credit to our sex, and affords a full assurance that they will *never* abandon the cause of the slave. The pamphlet, Right and Wrong in Boston, issued by them in which a particular account is given of that "mob of broad cloth in broad day," does equal credit to the head and the heart of her who wrote it. I wish my Southern sisters could read it; they would then understand that the women of the North have engaged in this work from a sense of *religious duty*, and that nothing will ever induce them to take their hands from it until it is fully accomplished. They feel no hostility to you, no bitterness or wrath; they rather sympathize in your trials and difficulties; but they well know that the first thing to be done to help you, is to pour in the light of truth on your minds, to urge you to reflect on, and pray over the subject. This is all *they* can do for you, *you* must work out your own deliverance with fear and trembling, and with the direction and blessing of God, *you can do it*. Northern women may labor to produce a correct public opinion at the North, but if Southern women sit down in listless indifference and criminal idleness, public opinion cannot be rectified and purified at the South. It is manifest to every reflecting mind, that slavery must be abolished; the era in which we live, and the light which is overspreading the whole world on this subject, clearly show that the time cannot be distant when it will be done. Now there are only two ways in which it can be effected, by moral power or physical force, and it is for *you* to choose which of these you prefer. Slavery always has, and always will produce in-

surrections wherever it exists, because it is a violation of the
natural order of things, and no human power can much longer
perpetuate it. . . .

· · ·

The *women of the South can overthrow* this horrible system of oppression and cruelty, licentiousness and wrong. Such
appeals to your legislatures would be irresistible, for there is
something in the heart of man which *will bend under moral
suasion*. There is a swift witness for truth in his bosom, which
will respond to truth when it is uttered with calmness and
dignity. If you could obtain but six signatures to such a petition in only one state, I would say, send up that petition, and
be not in the least discouraged by the scoffs and jeers of the
heartless, or the resolution of the house to lay it on the table.
It will be a great thing if the subject can be introduced into
your legislatures in any way, even by *women*, and *they* will
be the most likely to introduce it there in the best possible
manner, as a matter of *morals* and *religion*, not of expediency
or politics. You may petition, too, the different ecclesiastical
bodies of the slave states. Slavery must be attacked with the
whole power of truth and the sword of the spirit. You must
take it up on *Christian* ground, and fight against it with Christian weapons, whilst your feet are shod with the preparation
of the gospel of peace. And *you are now* loudly called upon
by the cries of the widow and the orphan, to arise and gird
yourselves for this great moral conflict, with the whole armour
of righteousness upon the right hand and on the left.

───────────────────────────────

[Something of the angry tone to clerical reaction to the
speeches by the Grimké sisters is captured in the following
excerpt. It is helpful background to the first of the letters
Sarah Grimké wrote on the equality of the sexes and the
conditions of women.]

From a Pastoral Letter, "The General Association of Massachusetts (Orthodox) to the Churches Under Their Care." 1837.

III. We invite your attention to the dangers which at present seem to threaten the female character with widespread and permanent injury.

The appropriate duties and influence of woman are clearly stated in the New Testament. Those duties and that influence are unobtrusive and private, but the source of mighty power. When the mild, dependent, softening influence of woman upon the sternness of man's opinions is fully exercised, society feels the effects of it in a thousand forms. The power of woman is her dependence, flowing from the consciousness of that weakness which God has given her for her protection, and which keeps her in those departments of life that form the character of individuals, and of the nation. There are social influences which females use in promoting piety and the great objects of Christian benevolence which we can not too highly commend.

We appreciate the unostentatious prayers and efforts of woman in advancing the cause of religion at home and abroad; in Sabbath-schools; in leading religious inquirers to the pastors for instruction; and in all such associated effort as becomes the modesty of her sex; and earnestly hope that she may abound more and more in these labors of piety and love. But when she assumes the place and tone of man as a public reformer, our care and protection of her seem unnecessary; we put ourselves in self-defence against her; she yields the power which God has given her for her protection, and her character becomes unnatural. If the vine, whose strength and beauty is to lean upon the trellis-work, and half conceal its clusters, thinks to assume the independence and the overshadowing nature of the elm, it will not only cease to bear fruit, but fall in shame and dishonor into the dust. We can not, therefore, but regret the mistaken conduct of those who encourage females to bear an obtrusive and ostentatious part in measures of reform, and countenance any of that sex who so far forget themselves as to itinerate in the character of public lecturers and teachers. We especially deplore the intimate acquaintance and promiscuous conversation of females with regard to things which ought not to be named; by which that modesty and delicacy which is the charm of domestic life, and which constitutes the true influence of woman in society, is consumed, and the way opened, as we apprehend, for degeneracy and ruin.

We say these things not to discourage proper influences against sin, but to secure such reformation as we believe is Scriptural, and will be permanent.

Sarah Grimké: Letters on the Equality
⋈   of the Sexes and the Condition   ⋉
of Women

Haverhill, 7th Mo. 1837.

Dear Friend,—

When I last addressed thee, I had not seen the Pastoral Letter of the General Association. It has since fallen into my hands, and I must . . . make some remarks on this extraordinary document. I am persuaded that when the minds of men and women become emancipated from the thraldom of superstition and "traditions of men," the sentiments contained in the Pastoral Letter will be recurred to with as much astonishment as the opinions of Cotton Mather and other distinguished men of his day, on the subject of witchcraft; nor will it be deemed less wonderful, that a body of divines should gravely assemble and endeavor to prove that woman has no right to "open her mouth for the dumb," than it now is that judges should have sat on the trials of witches, and solemnly condemned nineteen persons and one dog to death for witchcraft.

From Sarah M. Grimké, *Letters on the Equality of the Sexes and the Condition of Women.* Boston, 1838. Pp. 14–121.

But to the letter. It says, "We invite your attention to the dangers which at present seem to threaten the FEMALE CHARACTER with wide-spread and permanent injury." I rejoice that they have called the attention of my sex to this subject, because I believe if woman investigates it, she will soon discover that danger is impending, though from a totally different source from that which the Association apprehends, —danger from those who, having long held the reins of *usurped* authority, are unwilling to permit us to fill that sphere which God created us to move in, and who have entered into league to crush the immortal mind of woman. I rejoice, because I am persuaded that the rights of woman, like the rights of slaves, need only be examined to be understood and asserted, even by some of those, who are now endeavoring to smother the irrepressible desire for mental and spiritual freedom which glows in the breast of many, who hardly dare to speak their sentiments.

"The appropriate duties and influence of women are clearly stated in the New Testament. Those duties are unobtrusive and private, but the sources of *mighty power*. When the mild, *dependent*, softening influence of woman upon the sternness of man's opinions is fully exercised, society feels the effects of it in a thousand ways." No one can desire more earnestly than I do, that woman may move exactly in the sphere which her Creator has assigned her; and I believe her having been displaced from that sphere has introduced confusion into the world. It is, therefore, of vast importance to herself and to all the rational creation, that she should ascertain what are her duties and her privileges as a responsible and immortal being. The New Testament has been referred to, and I am willing to abide by its decisions, but must enter my protest against the false translation of some passages by the MEN who did that work, and against the perverted interpretation by the MEN who undertook to write commentaries thereon. I am inclined to think, when we are admitted to the honor of studying Greek and Hebrew, we shall produce some various readings of the Bible a little different from those we now have.

The Lord Jesus defines the duties of his followers in his Sermon on the Mount. He lays down grand principles by which they should be governed, without any reference to sex or condition.—"Ye are the light of the world. A city that is set on a hill cannot be hid. Neither do men light a candle and put it under a bushel, but on a candlestick, and it giveth light unto all that are in the house. Let your light so shine before men, that they may see your good works, and glorify your Father which is in Heaven." I follow him through all his precepts, and find him giving the same directions to women as to men, never even referring to the distinction now so strenuously insisted upon between masculine and feminine virtues: this is one of the anti-christian "traditions of men" which are taught instead of the "commandments of God." Men and women were CREATED EQUAL; they are both moral and accountable beings, and whatever is *right* for man to do, is *right* for woman.

But the influence of woman, says the Association, is to be private and unobtrusive; her light is not to shine before man like that of her brethren; but she is passively to let the lords of the creation, as they call themselves, put the bushel over it, lest peradventure it might appear that the world has been benefitted by the rays of *her* candle. So that her quenched light, according to their judgment, will be of more use than if it were set on the candlestick. "Her influence is the source of mighty power." This has ever been the flattering language of man since he laid aside the whip as a means to keep woman in subjection. He spares her body; but the war he has waged against her mind, her heart, and her soul, has been no less destructive to her as a moral being. How monstrous, how anti-christian, is the doctrine that woman is to be dependent on man! Where, in all the sacred Scriptures, is this taught? Alas! she has too well learned the lesson, which MAN has labored to teach her. She has surrendered her dearest RIGHTS, and been satisfied with the privileges which man has assumed to grant her; she has been amused with the show of power, whilst man has absorbed all the reality into himself. He has adorned the creature whom God gave him as a companion, with baubles and gewgaws, turned her attention to personal attractions, offered incense to her vanity, and made her the instrument of his selfish gratification, a plaything to please his eye and amuse his hours of leisure. "Rule by obedience and by submission sway," or in other words, study to be a hypocrite, pretend to submit, but gain your point, has been the code of household morality which woman has been taught. The poet has sung, in sickly strains, the loveliness of woman's dependence upon man, and now we find it reechoed by those who profess to teach the religion of the Bible. God says, "Cease ye from man whose breath is in his nostrils, for wherein is he to be accounted of?" Man says, depend upon me. God says, "HE will teach us of his ways." Man says, believe it not, I am to be your teacher. This doctrine of dependence upon man is utterly at variance with the doctrine of the Bible. In that book I find nothing like the softness of woman, nor the sternness of man: both are equally commanded to bring forth the fruits of the Spirit, love, meekness, gentleness, &c.

But we are told, "the power of woman is in her dependence, flowing from a consciousness of that weakness which God has given her for her protection." If physical weakness is alluded to, I cheerfully concede the superiority; if brute force is what my brethren are claiming, I am willing to let them have all the honor they desire; but if they mean to intimate, that mental or moral weakness belongs to woman, more than to man, I utterly disclaim the charge. Our powers of mind have been crushed, as far as man could do it, our sense of morality has been impaired by his interpretation of our duties; but no where does God say that he made any distinction between us, as moral and intelligent beings.

"We appreciate," say the Association, "the *unostentatious* prayers and efforts of woman in advancing the cause of religion at home and abroad, in leading religious inquirers TO THE PASTOR for instruction." Several points here demand attention. If public prayers and public efforts are necessarily ostentatious, then "Anna the prophetess, (or preacher,) who departed not from the temple, but served God with fastings and prayers night and day," "and spake of Christ to all them that looked for redemption in Israel," was ostentatious in her efforts. Then, the apostle Paul encourages women to be ostentatious in their efforts to spread the gospel, when he gives them directions how they should appear, when engaged in praying, or preaching in the public assemblies. Then, the whole association of Congregational ministers are ostentatious, in the efforts they are making in preaching and praying to convert souls.

But woman may be permitted to lead religious inquirers to the PASTORS for instruction. Now this is assuming that all pastors are better qualified to give instruction than woman. This I utterly deny. I have suffered too keenly from the teaching of man, to lead any one to him for instruction. The Lord Jesus says,—"Come unto me and learn of me." He points his followers to no man; and when woman is made the favored instrument of rousing a sinner to his lost and helpless condition, she has no right to substitute any teacher for Christ; all she has to do is, to turn the contrite inquirer to the "Lamb of God which taketh away the sins of the world." More souls have probably been lost by going down to Egypt for help, and by trusting in man in the early stages of religious experience, than by any other error. Instead of the petition being offered to God,—"Lead me in thy truth, and TEACH ME, for thou art the God of my salvation,"—instead of relying on the precious promises—"What man is he that feareth the Lord? him shall HE TEACH in the way that he shall choose"—"I will instruct thee and TEACH thee in the way which thou shalt go—I will guide thee with mine eye"—the young convert is directed to go to man, as if he were in the place of God, and his instructions essential to an advancement in the path of righteousness. That woman can have but a poor conception of the privilege of being taught of God, what he alone can teach, who would turn the "religious inquirer aside" from the fountain of living waters, where he might slake his thirst for spiritual instruction, to those broken cisterns which can hold no water, and therefore cannot satisfy the panting spirit. The business of men and women, who are ORDAINED OF GOD to preach the unsearchable riches of Christ to a lost and perishing world, is to lead souls to Christ, and not to Pastors for instruction.

The General Association say, that "when woman assumes the place and tone of man as a public reformer, our care and protection of her seem unnecessary; we put ourselves in self-defence against her, and her character becomes unnatural." Here again the unscriptural notion is held up, that there is a distinction between the duties of men and women as moral beings; that what is virtue in man, is vice in woman; and women who dare to obey the command of Jehovah, "Cry aloud, spare not, lift up thy voice like a trumpet, and show my people their transgression," are threatened with having the protection of the brethren withdrawn. If this is all they do, we shall not even know the time when our chastisement is inflicted; our trust is in the Lord Jehovah, and in him is ever-lasting strength. The motto of woman, when she is engaged in the great work of public reformation should be,— "The Lord is my light and my salvation; whom shall I fear? The Lord is the strength of my life; of whom shall I be afraid?" She must feel, if she feels rightly, that she is fulfilling one of the important duties laid upon her as an accountable being, and that her character, instead of being "unnatural," is in exact accordance with the will of Him to whom, and to no other, she is responsible for the talents and the gifts confided to her. As to the pretty simile, introduced into the "Pastoral Letter," "If the vine whose strength and beauty is to lean upon the trellis work, and half conceal its clusters, thinks to assume the independence and the overshadowing nature of the elm," &c. I shall only remark, that it might well suit the poet's fancy, who sings of sparkling eyes and coral lips, and knights in armor clad; but it seems to me utterly inconsistent with the dignity of a Christian body, to endeavor to draw such an anti-scriptural distinction between men and women. Ah! how many of my sex feel in the dominion, thus unrighteously exercised over them, under the gentle appellation of *protection*, that what they have leaned upon has proved a broken reed at best, and oft a spear.

Thine in the bonds of womanhood,

Sarah M. Grimké

Letter VIII

Brookline, 1837

. . . I shall now proceed to make a few remarks on the condition of women in my own country.

During the early part of my life, my lot was cast among the butterflies of the *fashionable* world; and of this class of women, I am constrained to say, both from experience and observation, that their education is miserably deficient; that they are taught to regard marriage as the one thing needful, the only avenue to distinction; hence to attract the notice and win the attention of men, by their external charms, is the chief business of fashionable girls. They seldom think that men will be allured by intellectual acquirements, because they find, that where any mental superiority exists, a woman is generally shunned and regarded as stepping out of her "appropriate sphere," which, in their view, is to dress, to dance, to set out to the best possible advantage her person, to read the novels which inundate the press, and which do more to destroy her character as a rational creature, than any thing else. Fashionable women regard themselves, and are regarded by men, as pretty toys or as mere instruments of pleasure; and the vacuity of mind, the heartlessness, the frivolity which is the necessary result of this false and debasing estimate of women, can only be fully understood by those who have mingled in the folly and wickedness of fashionable life. . . .

There is another and much more numerous class in this country, who are withdrawn by education or circumstances from the circle of fashionable amusements, but who are brought up with the dangerous and absurd idea, that *marriage* is a kind of preferment; and that to be able to keep their husband's house, and render his situation comfortable, is the end of her being. Much that she does and says and thinks is done in reference to this situation; and to be married is too often held up to the view of girls as the sine qua non of human happiness and human existence. For this purpose more than for any other, I verily believe the majority of girls are trained. This is demonstrated by the imperfect education which is bestowed upon them, and the little pains taken to cultivate their minds, after they leave school, by the little time allowed them for reading, and by the idea being constantly inculcated, that although all household concerns should be attended to with scrupulous punctuality at particular seasons, the improvement of their intellectual capacities is only a secondary consideration, and may serve as an occupation to fill up the odds and ends of time. In most families, it is considered a matter of far more consequence to call a girl off from making a pie, or a pudding, than to interrupt her whilst engaged in her studies. This mode of training necessarily exalts, in their view, the animal above the intellectual and spiritual nature, and teaches women to regard themselves as a kind of machinery, necessary to keep the domestic engine in order, but of little value as the *intelligent* companions of men.

Let no one think, from these remarks, that I regard a knowledge of housewifery as beneath the acquisition of women. Far from it: I believe that a complete knowledge of household affairs is an indispensable requisite in a woman's education,—that by the mistress of a family, whether married or single, doing her duty thoroughly and *understandingly*, the happiness of the family is increased to an incalculable degree, as well as a vast amount of time and money saved. All I complain of is, that our education consists so almost exclusively in culinary and other manual operations. I do long to see the time, when it will no longer be necessary for women to expend so many precious hours in furnishing "a well spread table," but that their husbands will forego some of their accustomed indulgences in this way, and encourage their wives to devote some portion of their time to mental cultivation, even at the expense of having to dine sometimes on baked potatoes, or bread and butter. . . .

The influence of women over the minds and character of *children* of both sexes, is allowed to be far greater than that of men. This being the case by the very ordering of nature, women should be prepared by education for the performance of their sacred duties as mothers and as sisters. . . .

There is another way in which the general opinion, that women are inferior to men, is manifested, that bears with tremendous effect on the laboring class, and indeed on almost all who are obliged to earn a subsistence, whether it be by mental or physical exertion—I allude to the disproportionate value set on the time and labor of men and of women. A man who is engaged in teaching, can always, I believe, command a higher price for tuition than a woman—even when he teaches the same branches, and is not in any respect superior to the woman. This I know is the case in boarding and other schools with which I have been acquainted, and it is so in every occupation in which the sexes engage indiscriminately. As for example, in tailoring, a man has twice, or three times as much for making a waistcoat or pantaloons as a woman, although the work done by each may be equally good. In those employments which are peculiar to women, their time is estimated at only half the value of that of men. A woman who goes out to wash, works as hard in proportion as a wood sawyer, or a coal heaver, but she is not generally able to make more than half as much by a day's work. The low remuneration which women receive for their work, has claimed the attention of a few philanthropists, and I hope it will continue to do so until some remedy is applied for this enormous evil. . . . There is yet another and more disastrous consequence arising from this unscriptural notion—women being educated, from earliest childhood, to regard themselves as inferior creatures, have not that self-respect which conscious equality would engender, and hence when their virtue is assailed, they yield to temptation with facility, under the idea that it rather exalts than debases them, to be connected with a superior being.

There is another class of women in this country, to whom I cannot refer, without feelings of the deepest shame and sorrow. I allude to our female slaves. Our southern cities are whelmed beneath a tide of pollution; the virtue of female slaves is wholly at the mercy of irresponsible tyrants, and women are bought and sold in our slave markets, to gratify the brutal lust of those who bear the name of Christians. In our slave States, if amid all her degradation and ignorance, a woman desires to preserve her virtue unsullied, she is either bribed or whipped into compliance, or if she dares resist her seducer, her life by the laws of some of the slave States may be, and has actually been sacrificed to the fury of disappointed passion. Where such laws do not exist, the power which is necessarily vested in the master over his property, leaves the defenceless slave entirely at his mercy, and the sufferings of some females on this account, both physical and mental, are intense. Mr. Gholson, in the House of Delegates of Virginia, in 1832, said, "He really had been under the impression that he owned his slaves. He had lately purchased four women and ten children, in whom he thought he had obtained a great bargain; for he supposed they were his own property, *as were his brood mares.*" But even if any laws existed in the United States, as in Athens formerly, for the protection of female slaves, they would be null and void, because the evidence of a colored person is not admitted against a white, in any of our Courts of Justice in the slave States. "In Athens, if a female slave had cause to complain of any want of respect to the laws of modesty, she could seek the protection of the temple, and demand a change of owners; and such appeals were never discountenanced, or neglected by the magistrate." In Christian America, the slave has no refuge from unbridled cruelty and lust.

S. A. Forrall, speaking of the state of morals at the South, says, "Negresses when young and likely, are often employed by the planter, or his friends, to administer to their sensual desires. This frequently is a matter of speculation, for if the offspring, a mulatto, be a handsome female, 800 or 1000 dollars may be obtained for her in the New Orleans market. It is an occurrence of no uncommon nature to see a Christian father sell his own daughter and the brother his own sister." . . . I will add but one more from the numerous testimonies respecting the degradation of female slaves, and the licentiousness of the South. It is from the Circular of the Kentucky Union, for the moral and religious improvement of the colored race. "To the female character among our black population, we cannot allude but with feelings of the bitterest shame. A similar condition of moral pollution and utter disregard of a pure and virtuous reputation, is to be found *only without the pale of Christendom*. That such a state of society should exist in a Christian nation, claiming to be the most enlightened upon earth, without calling forth any *particular attention* to its existence, though ever before our eyes and *in our* families, is a moral phenomenon at once unaccountable and disgraceful." Nor does the colored woman suffer alone: the moral purity of the white woman is deeply contaminated. In the daily habit of seeing the virtue of her enslaved sister sacrificed without hesitancy or remorse, she looks upon the crimes of seduction and illicit intercourse without horror, and although not personally involved in the guilt, she loses that value for innocence in her own, as well as the other sex, which is one of the strongest safeguards to virtue. She lives in habitual intercourse with men, whom she knows to be polluted by licentiousness, and often is she compelled to witness in her own domestic circle, those disgusting and heart-sickening jealousies and strifes which disgraced and distracted the family of Abraham. In addition to all this, the female slaves suffer every species of degradation and cruelty, which the most wanton barbarity can inflict; they are indecently divested of their clothing, sometimes tied up and severely whipped, sometimes prostrated on the earth, while their naked bodies are torn by the scorpion lash.

> "The whip on WOMAN's shrinking flesh!
> Our soil yet reddening with the stains
> Caught from her scourging warm and fresh."

Can any American woman look at these scenes of shocking licentiousness and cruelty, and fold her hands in apathy, and say, "I have nothing to do with slavery"? *She cannot and be guiltless*.

I cannot close this letter, without saying a few words on the benefits to be derived by men, as well as women, from the opinions I advocate relative to the equality of the sexes. Many women are now supported, in idleness and extravagance, by the industry of their husbands, fathers, or brothers, who are compelled to toil out their existence, at the counting house, or in the printing office, or some other laborious occupation, while the wife and daughters and sisters take no part in the support of the family, and appear to think that their sole

business is to spend the hard bought earnings of their male
friends. I deeply regret such a state of things, because I believe
that if women felt their responsibility, for the support of
themselves, or their families it would add strength and dignity to their characters, and teach them more true sympathy
for their husbands, than is now generally manifested,—a sympathy which would be exhibited by actions as well as words.
Our brethren may reject my doctrine, because it runs counter
to common opinions, and because it wounds their pride; but I
believe they would be "partakers of the benefit" resulting
from the Equality of the Sexes, and would find that woman,
as their equal, was unspeakably more valuable than woman
as their inferior, both as a moral and an intellectual being.

Thine in the bonds of womanhood,

Sarah M. Grimké

Letter XV

To perform our duties, we must comprehend our rights
and responsibilities; and it is because we do not understand,
that we now fall so far short in the discharge of our obligations. Unaccustomed to think for ourselves, and to search
the sacred volume, to see how far we are living up to the
design of Jehovah in our creation, we have rested satisfied
with the sphere marked out for us by man, never detecting
the fallacy of that reasoning which forbids woman to exercise some of her noblest faculties, and stamps with the reproach of indelicacy those actions by which women were
formerly dignified and exalted in the church.

I should not mention this subject again, if it were not to
point out to my sisters what seems to me an irresistible conclusion from the literal interpretation of St. Paul, without
reference to the context, and the peculiar circumstances and
abuses which drew forth the expressions, "I suffer not a
woman to teach"—"Let your women keep silence in the
church," i.e. congregation. It is manifest, that if the apostle
meant what his words imply, when taken in the strictest
sense, then women have no right to *teach* Sabbath or day
schools, or to open their lips to sing in the assemblies of the
people; yet young and delicate women are engaged in all
these offices; they are expressly trained to exhibit themselves,
and raise their voices to a high pitch in the choirs of our

places of worship. I do not intend to sit in judgment on my sisters for doing these things; I only want them to see, that they are as really infringing a *supposed* divine command, by instructing their pupils in the Sabbath or day schools, and by singing in the congregation, as if they were engaged in preaching the unsearchable riches of Christ to a lost and perishing world. Why, then, are we permitted to break this injunction in some points, and so seduously warned not to overstep the bounds set for us by our *brethren* in another? Simply, as I believe, because in the one case we subserve *their* views and *their* interests, and act *in subordination to them*; whilst in the other, we come in contact with their interests, and claim to be on an equality with them in the highest and most important trust ever committed to man, namely, the ministry of the word. It is manifest, that if women were permitted to be ministers of the gospel, as they unquestionably were in the primitive ages of the Christian church, it would interfere materially with the present organized system of spiritual power and ecclesiastical authority, which is now vested solely in the hands of men. It would either show that all the paraphernalia of theological seminaries, &c. &c. to prepare men to become evangelists, is wholly unnecessary, or it would create a necessity for similar institutions in order to prepare women for the same office; and this would be an encroachment on that learning, which our kind brethren have so ungenerously monopolized. I do not ask any one to believe my statements, or adopt my conclusions, because they are mine; but I do earnestly entreat my sisters to lay aside their prejudices, and examine these subjects *for themselves*, regardless of the "traditions of men," because they are intimately connected with their duty and their usefulness in the present important crisis.

All who know any thing of the present system of benevolent and religious operations, know that women are performing an important part in them, in *subserviency to men*, who guide our labors, and are often the recipients of those benefits of education we toil to confer, and which we rejoice they can enjoy, although it is their mandate which deprives us of the same advantages. Now, whether our brethren have defrauded us intentionally, or unintentionally, the wrong we suffer is equally the same. For years, they have been spurring us up to the performance of our duties. The immense usefulness and the vast influence of woman have been eulogized and called into exercise, and many a blessing has been lavished upon us, and many a prayer put up for us, because we have labored by day and by night to clothe and feed and educate young men, whilst our own bodies sometimes suffer for want of comfortable garments, and our minds are left in almost utter destitution of that improvement which we are toiling to bestow upon the brethren. . . .

If the sewing societies, the avails of whose industry are now expended in supporting and educating young men for the ministry, were to withdraw their contributions to these objects, and give them where they are *more needed*, to the advancement of their *own sex* in useful learning, the next generation might furnish sufficient proof, that in intelligence and ability to master the whole circle of sciences, woman is not inferior to man; and instead of a sensible woman being regarded as she now is, as a *lusses naturæ*, they would be quite as common as sensible men. I confess, considering the high claim men in this country make to great politeness and deference to women, it does seem a little extraordinary that we should be urged to work for the brethren. I should suppose it would be more in character with "the generous promptings of chivalry, and the poetry of romantic gallantry," for which Catherine E. Beecher gives them credit, for them to form societies to educate their sisters, seeing our inferior capacities require more cultivation to bring them into use, and qualify us to be helps meet for them. However, though I think this would be but a just return for all our past kindnesses in this way, I should be willing to balance our accounts, and begin a new course. Henceforth, let the benefit be reciprocated, or else let each sex provide for the education of their own poor, whose talents ought to be rescued from the oblivion of ignorance. Sure I am, the young men who are now benefitted by the handy work of their sisters, will not be less honorable if they occupy half their time in earning enough to pay for their own education, instead of depending on the industry of women, who not unfrequently deprive themselves of the means of purchasing valuable books which might enlarge their stock of useful knowledge, and perhaps prove a blessing to the family by furnishing them with instructive reading. If the minds of women were enlightened and improved, the domestic circle would be more frequently refreshed by intelligent conversation, a means of edification now deplorably neglected, for want of that cultivation which these intellectual advantages would confer.

Angelina Grimké: Letters to Catherine Beecher

Letter XI

. . . [T]he women of this country are not to be governed
by principles of duty, but by the effect their petitions produce
on the members of Congress, and by the opinions of these
men. If they deem them "obtrusive, indecorous, and unwise,"
they must not be sent. If *thou* canst consent to exchange the
precepts of the Bible for the opinions of *such a body of men*
as now sit on the destinies of this nation, I cannot. What is
this but *obeying man* rather than God, and seeking the *praise
of man* rather than of God? . . .

Another objection to woman's petitions is, that they may
"tend to bring females, as petitioners and partisans, into
every political measure that may tend to injure and oppress
their sex." As to their ever becoming partisans, i.e. sacrificing
principles to power or interest, I reprobate this under all circumstances, and in *both* sexes. But I trust my sisters may
always be permitted to *petition* for a redress of grievances.
Why not? The right of petition is the only political right that
women have: why not let them exercise it whenever they are
aggrieved? Our fathers waged a bloody conflict with England,
because *they* were taxed without being represented. This is
just what unmarried women of property now are. *They* were
not willing to be governed by laws which *they* had no voice
in making; but this is the way in which women are governed
in this Republic. If, then, *we* are taxed without being represented, and governed by laws *we* have no voice in framing,
then, surely, we ought to be permitted at least to remonstrate
against "every political measure that may tend to injure and
oppress our sex in various parts of the nation, and under the
various public measures that may hereafter be enforced."
Why not? Art thou afraid to trust the women of this country
with discretionary power as to petitioning? Is there not sound
principle and common sense enough among them, to regulate

From Angelina Emily Grimké, *Letters to Catherine Beecher.*
Boston, Isaac Knapp, 1836. Pp. 103–121.

the exercise of this right? I believe they will always use it wisely. I am not afraid to trust my sisters—not I.

Thou sayest, "In this country, petitions to Congress, in reference to official duties of legislators, seem, IN ALL CASES, to fall entirely without the sphere of female duty. Men are the proper persons to make appeals to the rulers whom they appoint," &c. Here I entirely dissent from thee. The fact that women are denied the right of voting for members of Congress, is but a poor reason why they should also be deprived of the right of petition. If their numbers are counted to swell the number of Representatives in our State and National Legislatures, the *very least* that can be done is to give them the right of petition in all cases whatsoever; and without any abridgement. If not, they are mere slaves, known only through their masters. . . .

Thy Friend,　　A. E. Grimké

Letter XII

The investigation of the rights of the slave has led me to a better understanding of my own. I have found the Anti-Slavery cause to be the high school of morals in our land—the school in which *human rights* are more fully investigated, and better understood and taught, than in any other. Here a great fundamental principle is uplifted and illuminated, and from this central light, rays innumerable stream all around. Human beings have *rights*, because they are *moral beings*: the rights of *all* men grow out of their moral nature; and as all men have the same moral nature, they have essentially the same rights. These rights may be wrested from the slave, but they cannot be alienated: his title to himself is as perfect *now*, as is that of Lyman Beecher: it is stamped on his moral being, and is, like it, imperishable. Now if rights are founded in the nature of our moral being, then the *mere circumstance of sex* does not give to man higher rights and responsibilities, than to woman. To suppose that it does, would be to deny the self-evident truth, that the "physical constitution is the mere instrument of the moral nature." To suppose that it does, would be to break up utterly the relations, of the two natures, and to reverse their functions, exalting the animal nature into a monarch, and humbling the moral into a slave; making the former a proprietor, and the latter its property. When human beings are regarded as *moral* beings, *sex*, instead of being en-

throned upon the summit, administering upon rights and responsibilities, sinks into insignificance and nothingness. . . .

This regulation of duty by the mere circumstance of sex,
rather than by the fundamental principle of moral being, has
led to all that multifarious train of evils flowing out of the
anti-christian doctrine of masculine and feminine virtues. By
this doctrine, man has been converted into the warrior, and
clothed with sternness, and those other kindred qualities,
which in common estimation belong to his character as a
man; whilst woman has been taught to lean upon an arm of
flesh, to sit as a doll arrayed in "gold, and pearls, and costly
array," to be admired for her personal charms, and caressed
and humored like a spoiled child, or converted into a mere
drudge to suit the convenience of her lord and master. Thus
have all the diversified relations of life been filled with "confusion and every evil work." This principle has given to man
a charter for the exercise of tyranny and selfishness, pride and
arrogance, lust and brutal violence. It has robbed woman of
essential rights, the right to think and speak and act on all
great moral questions, just as men think and speak and act;
the right to share their responsibilities, perils and toils; the
right to fulfil the great end of her being, as a moral, intellectual and immortal creature, and of glorifying God in her body
and her spirit which are His. Hitherto, instead of being a help
meet to man, in the highest, noblest sense of the term, as a
companion, a co-worker, an equal; she has been a mere appendage of his being, an instrument of his convenience and
pleasure, the pretty toy with which he wiled away his leisure
moments, or the pet animal whom he humored into playfulness and submission. Woman, instead of being regarded as
the equal of man, has uniformly been looked down upon as
his inferior, a mere gift to fill up the measure of his happiness. In "the poetry of romantic gallantry," it is true, she has
been called "the last *best* gift of God to man." . . . Where is
the scripture warrant for this "rhetorical flourish, this splendid absurdity?" Let us examine the account of her creation.
"And the rib which the Lord God had taken from man, made
he a woman, and brought her unto the man." Not as a gift—
for Adam immediately recognized her *as a part of himself*—
("this is now bone of my bone, and flesh of my flesh")—a
companion and equal, not one hair's breadth beneath him in
the majesty and glory of her moral being; not placed under
his authority as a *subject*, but by his side, on the same platform of human rights, under the government of God only.

This idea of woman's being "the last best gift of God to man," however pretty it may sound to the ears of those who love to discourse upon "the poetry of romantic gallantry, and the generous promptings of chivalry," has nevertheless been the means of sinking her from an *end* into a mere *means*—of turning her into an *appendage* to man, instead of recognizing her as *a part of man*—of destroying her individuality, and rights, and responsibilities, and merging her moral being in that of man. Instead of *Jehovah* being *her* king, *her* lawgiver, and *her* judge, she has been taken out of the exalted scale of existence in which He placed her, and subjected to the despotic control of man. . . .

. . . I recognize no rights but *human* rights—I know nothing of men's rights and women's rights; for in Christ Jesus, there is neither male nor female. It is my solemn conviction, that, until this principle of equality is recognised and embodied in practice, the church can do nothing effectual for the permanent reformation of the world. Woman was the first transgressor, and the first victim of power. In all heathen nations, she has been the slave of man, and Christian nations have never acknowledged her rights. Nay more, no Christian denomination or Society has ever acknowledged them on the broad basis of humanity. I know that in some denominations, she is permitted to preach the gospel; not from a conviction of her rights, nor upon the ground of her equality as a *human being*, but of her equality in spiritual gifts—for we find that woman, even in these Societies, is allowed no voice in framing the Discipline by which she is to be governed. Now, I believe it is woman's right to have a voice in all the laws and regulations by which she is to be *governed*, whether in Church or State; and that the present arrangements of society, on these points, are *a violation of human rights, a rank usurpation of power*, a violent seizure and confiscation of what is sacredly and inalienably hers—thus inflicting upon woman outrageous wrongs, working mischief incalculable in the social circle, and in its influence on the world producing only evil, and that continually. *If* Ecclesiastical and Civil governments are ordained of God, *then* I contend that woman has just as much right to sit in solemn counsel in Conventions, Conferences, Associations and General Assemblies, as man—just as much right to sit upon the throne of England, or in the Presidential chair of the United States.

The Blackwell Clan

The name of Blackwell is important in the history of American women on a number of issues: moral reform, abolition, higher education and professional opportunities, political rights. There were nine Blackwell children who survived childhood and three women who married men in the family; together they comprise a fascinating set of individuals and a remarkably cohesive family group. In the sibling set itself were the first two women to practice medicine in the United States to have earned American medical degrees—Elizabeth and Emily Blackwell. Their older sister Anna was probably the first woman foreign correspondent. A younger sister Ellen was a talented artist and writer. Their younger brother Samuel married Antoinette Brown, one of the first American women to attend college and the first woman to be ordained and to hold her own ministry. Henry Blackwell, prominent in abolition and suffrage history in his own right, married Lucy Stone, a classmate and friend of Antoinette Brown at Oberlin College and among the first women to speak in public on women's rights. Their daughter Alice Stone Blackwell became well-known as a speaker, suffrage campaigner, and editor of the Boston *Woman's Journal*. Women in this family were active advocates of one or another cause for over a hundred years, from Lucy Stone's spirited first public speeches in defense of woman's rights in the mid-1840s to her daughter Alice's equally spirited participation in the last stages of the suffrage movement in the 1910s, and as a supporter of Sacco and Vanzetti and defender of the Soviet Union in the decades before her death in 1950. (See Figure 4 for a graphic sketch of the lifelines of the nine Blackwell siblings and their wives, and Figure 5 for the Blackwell genealogy.)

Thus the Blackwell family was prominent in efforts toward two key developments affecting women in the nineteenth century: to secure political and legal rights for women and to expand the educational rights of women to college and professional training. In the background of these endeavors was a longer history of family involvement in the reform

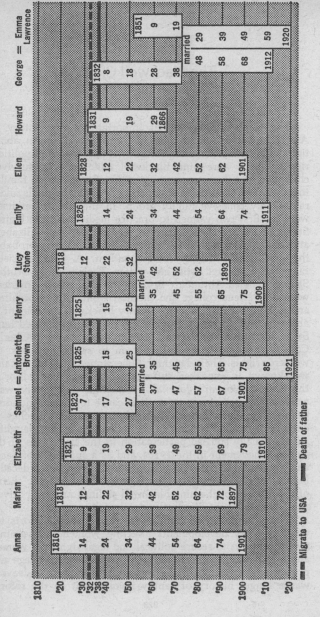

Figure 4. Life Line of the Blackwell Sibling Set and In-Laws

causes of the early part of the nineteenth century. The father, Samuel Blackwell, was an English religious dissenter and an antislavery man; he tried to refine sugar from beets to avoid British economic dependence on cane sugar from the slave plantations of the West Indies. Within months of the family's arrival in the United States in 1832 the Blackwell family was participating in New York temperance and antislavery societies.

The two best-known members of the family have been Elizabeth Blackwell, widely known as the first American woman physician, and Lucy Stone, the early woman's-rights advocate. The image of the Blackwell family that has come down to us has been colored by Elizabeth's autobiography, published in 1914, and the biography of Lucy Stone, written by her daughter Alice in 1930. Both were highly romanticized accounts, filtered through the very special Blackwell perception. A more recent book, *Those Extraordinary Blackwells,* is based heavily on the voluminous correspondence among the Blackwell brothers and sisters (Hays 1967).

There are two characteristics of the Blackwell clan that make it interesting to study from a sociographic perspective. For one, it is difficult to focus on a particular member of the family, since to know one member invariably involves becoming acquainted with the whole extensive family circle. Even as middle-aged adults, the Blackwell siblings remained in constant touch with each other through visits and a voluminous correspondence. Well into their later years they continued an early pattern of circulating letters between any given pair among the rest of the sibling set; decisions that might typically be made by an individual or a married couple were the subjects of discussion in the wider circle of siblings. It has been an intriguing exercise in social and psychological investigation to try to penetrate this cohesive family structure and to understand the roles the individuals played in each other's lives.

The second fact is that none of the five women in the Blackwell sibling set ever married, nor did the one child of the family most closely molded in the Blackwell image— Henry and Lucy's daughter Alice. Students of women's lives have sometimes claimed that spinsterhood and childlessness are the price such women paid for the unusual career paths they pursued. But this seems an inadequate explanation for the total absence of marriages among all the women in a

Figure 5. The Blackwell Genealogy

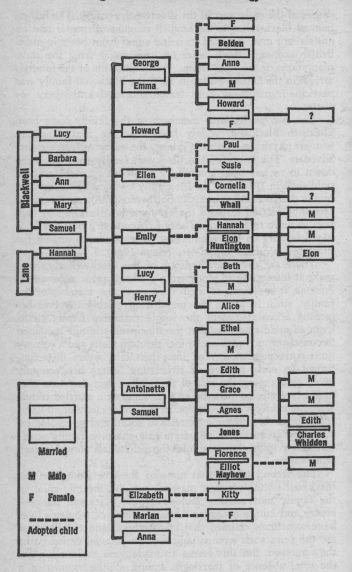

large sibling set. It was especially significant in the 1830s and 1840s in Cincinnati, a western city, where the sex ratio was tipped so far in favor of men that social pressure must have been very great on all the city's women to marry.

It may be thought that the fact of singleness was itself the source of the Blackwell sisters' retention of close family ties. But the three brothers who did marry clearly demonstrated a closeness to each other and their sisters that seems as intense as the feelings of the unmarried sisters for each other and their brothers' families.

The view that spinsterhood is simply a price paid for unusual career choices assumes that the course of female development is such that normal socialization in childhood and adolescence raises in the girl conventional expectations that she will marry; independent of this normal development, she acquires the training and the commitment to a career, which then lowers the probability that any man will choose her. In other words, the direction of effect is assumed to be from career choice to subsequent spinsterhood. But the Blackwell sisters chose their careers after an adolescence and early adulthood with at least some social opportunities to marry, which they turned down. The decisions against marriage, then, seem to have occurred prior to the development of their unusual occupational choices. Some evidence of the relationship between these two life decisions can be seen in Elizabeth's autobiography.

As she tells it, she was twenty-four years old and just returned from a teaching assignment in Kentucky when the suggestion was first made that she study medicine. The immediate stimulus occurred on a visit to a woman friend dying from a painful gynecological disorder. This friend pointed out that her own worst sufferings would have been spared if she had had a woman doctor to administer the medical treatment, and she suggested that Elizabeth consider the profession of medicine for herself. Elizabeth's initial reaction is surprising in a future physician:

I hated everything connected with the body and could not bear the sight of a medical book. This was so true, that I had been always foolishly ashamed of any form of illness. . . . As a schoolgirl I had tried to harden the body by sleeping on the floor at night, and even passing a couple of days without food, with the foolish notion

> of thus subduing one's physical nature . . . . The very thought of dwelling on the physical structure of the body and its various ailments filled me with disgust. [E. Blackwell 1914:22]

It is perhaps significant that Emily, who was to follow her sister Elizabeth into a medical career, showed the same early repugnance toward the body and its ills. In 1851, when she was called home from a teaching assignment to care for her ill mother, she confided in her diary that, though she tried to be patient and gentle, she found her mother and herself "far apart" and she could not "lay aside her strong natural repugnance toward those toward whom she was not drawn" (Hays 1967:97). This reaction on Emily's part was apparently so severe that another sister, Marian, had to return home to nurse her mother.

Elizabeth's account of her final decision to seek a medical degree moves from the description of her early repugnance toward the body to her adolescent susceptibility to the "other sex." It is difficult to determine the extent of retrospective fantasy involved here. She claims that her choice of medicine became linked in her own mind with the need to devote herself to "some absorbing occupation." This phrasing implies that she sought a career as a means to "control" her own normal yearning for marriage; yet during the preceding year, while teaching in Kentucky, she had effectively alienated the young people in the community by laughing at their "sentimental doings," and she admitted in a letter to her mother that she liked to make her contemporaries "a little afraid" of her (Hays 1967:60). She also confessed in her memoirs that

> whenever I became sufficiently intimate with any individual to be able to realise what a life association might mean, I shrank from the prospect disappointed or repelled. [E. Blackwell 1914:22]

This particular passage was written when she was an older woman, but she also quotes from her journal, written during the years when she was struggling to reach a decision concerning a medical career:

> I felt more determined than ever to become a physician, and thus place a strong barrier between me and all ordinary marriage. I must have something to engross my

thoughts, some object in life which will fill this vacuum and prevent this sad wearing away of the heart. [E. Blackwell 1914:23]

Here she clearly suggests that, for reasons she cannot articulate to herself, she is repelled by the thought of the intimate association of marriage and is moving toward a choice of medicine as a barrier between herself and the normal life of a married woman. So too she uses a revealing phrase in discussing the possibility of medical study in France: "I hesitate as if I were about to take the veil" (E. Blackwell 1914:25), with the implication, once again, not only that becoming a physician would close the door to marriage, but that medical study might be undertaken *in order to* close that door.

Elizabeth, far from confining her latent emotional opposition to marriage to herself, extended it to her siblings. While Emily was teaching in New York, she became interested in a young man. Elizabeth wrote the family that she had spoken to Emily,

urging her by all means to go home at once, promising her eight and forty students to drive out any presumptuous coat and pants that may perchance have found their way to her heart. [Hays 1967:54]

When she learned of her younger brother Henry's romantic involvement with a Miss Guilford, she protested to him that his woman friend was "too fashionable" and that her mother was frivolous and somewhat coarse. She argued that Henry must share her "dread of the weary horrors of an unhappy marriage" (Hays 1967:54). Elizabeth played the same role when her older sister Marian had a suitor. In this case the young man had plans to go to India as a missionary and had urged Marian to marry him and join him in his missionary endeavors. Elizabeth wrote her sister in protest against the idea of going so far away: "it seems to me so terrible, that I would charge you never to entertain it" (Hays 1967:53). Yet a year earlier she had suggested to Marian that some time in the future they might live together and even "lead out a missionary colony . . . to far away India." Thus, it appears to have been marriage and not distance that Elizabeth objected to.

The oldest of the Blackwell women, Anna, was the most adventurous of the sisters, a woman of great superficial gaiety with a life-long series of "enthusiasms"—Fourierism, free love, spiritualism, vegetarianism. Anna, too, had had marriage possibilities that she rejected. She spent the summer and fall of 1845 at Brook Farm, which stimulated her enthusiasm for "free association." She wrote long afterward about these months:

> those days were the happiest of my life. . . . Everyone was so genial, so happy. . . . A good deal of love-making went on, and nothing delighted the rest so much as when it ended, as happened several times, in marriage. [Hays 1967:56–57]

But it was this same sister who was personally wistful about her own sexual inadequacy, writing once that she was herself "not of a passionate nature" and that "all of the women in our family were deficient in that way" (Hays 1967:57). With much the same wistful air her sister Marian once posed the question in a letter, when she was herself only thirty-two, "how is it that all girls but those of our own family seem to be so full of spirits and fun?" (Hays 1967:81).

It would appear from these various bits of evidence that marriage was not looked upon by the Blackwell sisters as the height of fulfillment for themselves. Elizabeth took perhaps the strongest position of them all. Though she never became active in the woman's-rights movement as her famous sisters-in-law did, she certainly gave evidence in many ways of anti-male sentiment. In an amusing example of her feelings in this regard, she once reacted very intensely to her brother Samuel's attempt to make her financial affairs "intelligible" to her. She replied angrily, with a revealing slip of the pen:

> I do declare that the arrogance of the male sect [sic] is something astounding—though I've had fifty years experience of it, it constantly strikes me with fresh surprise. [Hays 1967:199]

It is also clear that the Blackwell women tried to foist their own views toward marriage on the next generation of Blackwells. There was much criticism by the sisters of Antoinette Brown's rearing of her five daughters, and they feared for the outcome when the girls reached adolescence. Elizabeth once wrote from England to suggest that Florence, the oldest of the nieces, be sent to England, where Elizabeth would help "cure her" of her excessive interest in men. After a year's trial, the niece was sent back to the United States, with a comment from Elizabeth:

> if any of Sam's children could come over to me *before* the instinct of sex has got an upper hand in them, I could do very much more in the way of radical benefit. [Hays 1967:194]

Although the Blackwell clan worked hard to prevent it, three of these nieces eventually did marry. It would appear that their mother, Antoinette Brown, had rather different attitudes toward sexuality and marriage than the Blackwell sisters did. Indeed, Nettie Brown is the only woman in the Blackwell clan who seemed to have a sexually gratifying relationship. She wrote to her husband while on a speaking tour that, much as she loved and missed the children, it was Sam she yearned for most of all. While she was at the Blackwells' summer home on Martha's Vineyard for some weeks before her husband could join her, Nettie was so lonesome for him that her niece Alice commented, "such a pair of lovers I never saw."

A number of factors help to explain the Blackwell sisters' negative attitude toward marriage and sexuality. The earliest clues can be found in the atmosphere and composition of the household during their childhood in England, before the family migrated to the United States. Included in this household were their father's four unmarried sisters. These aunts may have been important in the lives of the nieces on more than one count. Not only were they unmarried, but they apparently did a rather poor job of the traditional women's jobs they tried to fill. The Blackwell children attended day schools run by two of their aunts and apparently suffered at their incompetent hands; another aunt did the family "sewing" and was so poor a seamstress that the Blackwell girls were embarrassed to wear the dresses she made for them. In addition, the household included their paternal grandfather and grandmother. The grandfather was an authoritative, peppery old gentleman, and the grandmother took pride in the fact that her daughters did not marry, since in her view marriage was dreadful. The influence of the aunts and grandmother might have been countered had the girls' mother been warmly encouraging of their development. But Hannah Blackwell was hardly a maternal figure in this regard. She was a very strict and religious woman; under her supervision the girls' religious training included frightful stories of the devil waiting to snatch bad children; Anna later reported that these tales had so frightened her that she woke screaming in the night. The mother was also committed to the view that vanity was to be prevented at all costs in the rearing of children. When her daughters were complimented about their appearance, she could say, "yes, mama's babies are always pretty; but unfortunately they are like pig's babies, that grow uglier every day" (Hays 1967:8).

The women who grew up in that household were molded in its image. Hannah's correspondence with her children over the years remained fixed on concern for their immortal souls and her fears that they were not living pure lives to prepare for the afterlife. In one revealing letter Elizabeth wrote to assure her mother that she was retaining her strong faith despite her exposure to medical training, and she commented:

> Do you think I care about medicine? Nay, verily, It's just to kill the devil, whom I hate so heartily—that's the fact, mother. [Hays 1967:75]

In Elizabeth's lexicon the devil may have been equated with the hated body and human sexuality. I suspect that, at deeper levels of Elizabeth's personality, she grew up with a psychological incapacity to relate to men in any intimate way. Though she began her memoirs with a tribute to her happy large family, another sister held a different view. Anna claimed that she utterly detested "everything connected with my constrained, held in, undeveloped girlhood" (Hays 1967:6). Much the same description holds for Elizabeth's childhood, however much she glossed it over with sentiment.

Thus several factors in the early Blackwell household predisposed the young sisters to their eventual career-filled spinsterhood: a grandmother denouncing marriage; a mother withholding any praise and encouragement for her daughters' sexual and reproductive nature, while herself experiencing thirteen pregnancies in sixteen years; unmarried aunts to warn by their example against the unhappy plight of single women without training; a father who—though a far less somber personality, able to rhyme and play with the children—migrated each time economic setbacks caused his business to suffer. When the father died in 1838, shortly after the family settled in Cincinnati, the young Blackwells were deprived not only of economic support, but also of his leavening influence to soften the impact of their mother's somber religiosity.

Freud, asked what qualities were most conducive to a satis-factory life, once answered, *"Lieben und arbeiten."* The Black-well sisters showed great capacity for work, but not for love. Women of considerable accomplishment, they were yet im-poverished in their more deeply personal lives. Judging from the evidence of their early family life, the Blackwell sisters did not acquire more than superficial expectations for mar-riage, beneath which was an emotional vacuum that propelled them toward spheres of activity to which they could devote their lives. Far from unusual career choices causing their spinsterhood, I believe their psychological antipathy to mar-rage caused them to seek out careers.

This process does not detract from the very real achieve-ments of the Blackwell women. Many women equally anti-pathetic to marriage did in fact marry; still others remained single but never attempted to reach the goals the Blackwell sisters set for themselves. It took enormous courage and a passionate commitment to a high moral cause to motivate Elizabeth and Emily to fight for the right to a medical educa-tion. Yet it is also true that once their goals were attained, both women began to doubt whether medicine was really the cause they wished to devote their lives to. Elizabeth worked as a practicing physician for a very short period of time, moving quickly into hospital administration, then into public health and sanitation reform. Emily remained a practicing physician and teacher for most of her life, but it is not clear whether she derived much inner satisfaction from this work. After some time as a physician she confided in her diary:

> An agony of doubt has burnt in my heart for months. Oh my God, is the end of all my aspirations . . . to be that this long earnest struggle has been a mistake—that this life of a physician is so utterly not my life? [Hays 1967: 143]

Even two years later Elizabeth noted that her sister had "taken an extreme dislike" to medicine and hoped to collect a "small competency" to enable her to travel and devote herself to art, though Emily never achieved this goal. The younger sister Ellen was sufficiently interested in art in her youth to travel alone to study with John Ruskin in London; but she soon showed the same sharp drop in enthusiasm and the sud-den conviction that art was not what she wished to do after all.

Hays postulates that for such women as Elizabeth and Emily Blackwell the major attraction to medicine was the battle more than the career in the profession. On the surface this theory comes close to Elizabeth's self-assessment when she wrote that winning her medical degree "gradually assumed the aspect of a great moral struggle, and the moral fight possessed immense attraction to me" (E. Blackwell 1914:23). If the moral struggle was in any sense the counterpart to her mother's lifelong struggle to prepare for "heaven," both women may have been involved in a psychological avoidance of deep personal commitments in the here and now. The focus on heaven can be a lifetime pursuit, and there is no way to test whether the goal was worth the effort, as the choice of a medical degree was tested in actual professional practice.

The concept that a personal incapacity for intimate relations played a role in propelling the Blackwell sisters to their unusual career choices may also touch on a reason for their lesser gratification from medical practice than from medical studies. The women were merely "tolerated" as students in medical school, so that their relationships to male fellow students and their professors were extremely impersonal and formal. As practicing physicians, they faced very different demands, for they spent their days with women patients who brought them their most intimate physical and emotional problems. The doctor-patient relationship may have called for a personal response neither woman could give.

This same incapacity may have been the root of the dislike of teaching which four of the Blackwell sisters shared. Their lack of personal warmth may have held off their young students and reduced an important source of gratification in the teaching experience. In a letter Elizabeth wrote home from her first teaching assignment in Kentucky she touched on her strong need for solitude:

> the whole family have treated me with kindness to the extent of their knowledge, one portion of which is never to leave me alone, and I, who so love a hermit life for a good part of the day, find myself living in public, and almost losing my identity. [E. Blackwell 1914:14]

Spending a "good part of the day" alone is hardly a good omen for gratification either in teaching or doctoring; it may adversely affect relations with both students and patients.

Many years later one of the Blackwell nieces, Anne Belden, commented that "the Blackwells were and are an awfully reserved lot, who rarely make friends with whom they feel entirely at home" (Hays 1967:260). So too Ellen had commented in a diary entry when she was only twenty-two: "it seemed to me I need never expect much real, lasting friendship out of our own family" (Hays 1967:80). The youngest brother, George, also put his finger on this quality of the Blackwells. Though writing to Elizabeth about two other sisters, his comment applies as much to Elizabeth as to Anna and Marian:

> it is not that they *cannot* enjoy what others do, but that they will not, and the persistent holding aloof makes them feel as though they *could* not take part. [Hays 1967:263]

If the thesis that the Blackwell women were incapable of intimate relations is correct, what are we to make of the fact that they seemed to have such close relations within the family? A superficial reading of their lives and relations to each other invokes an image of a large, close extended family. But behind that lovely image may often lurk a dependency on blood ties which compensates for an incapacity to relate intimately with others. Kinsmen have an obligatory claim on each other; equivalent claims must be "earned" in nonkin relations. Ellen bemoaned the fact that real friendships would only be found within the family; it may be that she could not gain social acceptance from anyone but her family.

The diaries of the Blackwell sisters are full of their loneliness and need for the family, which led to the constant passage of one Blackwell or another across the continent and the ocean for prolonged visits with each other. One of the mechanisms the clan adopted to facilitate these contacts was the purchase of land on Martha's Vineyard, where numerous Blackwell cottages were built and the clan gathered each summer for prolonged visits, itself an interesting institutional device that blurs the boundaries of nuclear families and encourages the younger people to relate to each other more like siblings than as cousins. In their old age there was a drawing together into closer proximity, but always with the particular Blackwell style. Thus, when Elizabeth settled in Bristol, England, her two older sisters eventually settled nearby. The three sisters did not live together, however: Elizabeth had her own household, while Anna and Marian purchased a semidetached house where they could "live together yet apart." Family cohesion may thus mask psychological dependency.

Still another characteristic of the Blackwells is consistent with the thesis of a restricted capacity for intimacy: the high incidence of informal adoption of children by the unmarried sisters. The first of these adoptions was initiated by Elizabeth, and we can compare her public account with a more private one. The comparison affords an insight into Elizabeth's personality and the quality of her relationship to young Kitty. In her official autobiography Elizabeth explained:

> The utter loneliness of life became intolerable, and in October of 1854 I took a little orphan girl from the great emigrant depot of Randall's Island to live with me. This congenial child I finally adopted. . . . I desperately needed the change of thought she compelled me to give her. It was a dark time, and she did me good—her genial, loyal, Irish temperament suited me. [E. Blackwell 1914: 160]

At the time she took Kitty into her home, she wrote her sister Emily along rather less romantic and more practical lines:

> I must tell you of a little item that I've introduced into my own domestic economy in the shape of a small girl . . . whom I mean to train up into a valuable domestic, if she proves on sufficient trial to have the qualities I give her credit for. . . . I gave a receipt for her, and the poor little thing trotted after me like a dog. . . . she is very bright, has able little fingers that are learning to dust, and wash up, and sew. . . . Of course she is more trouble than use at present, and quite bewildered me at first, but still I like on the whole to have her. [Hays 1967:104–105]

Kitty was about seven years old at this time and shared Elizabeth's life and household for over fifty years. Elizabeth never legally adopted her, as she claimed in the autobiography, nor did Kitty ever call her "mother" or even "Elizabeth" but always simply "Doctor." She took the name of Blackwell for her own only several years after Elizabeth's death.

As can be readily seen in the Blackwell genealogy in Figure 5, there were a number of other informal adoptions in the family, none of them legal. Emily adopted a girl and Ellen adopted three children, two girls and a boy. Lucy and Henry adopted a girl to help in their household and in the hope of providing companionship for their only child, Alice. George and Emma also added an orphaned girl to their own three children. While these adopted children no doubt enjoyed far better lives in the Blackwell households than they would have led in orphan asylums, they nonetheless met rather practical needs of the Blackwell women for domestic help. Beyond such help, they provided the sisters with a living presence—"living together yet apart"—with safe limits to any emotional claims on them.

In later years, when these children were all grown, the Blackwell sisters became great devotees of dogs; Ellen, Elizabeth, Marian, and Anna, all had dogs on which they lavished excessive attention. Their niece Alice later wrote that she would

> no more adopt a dog, after the frightful examples I have seen in the case of three of my aunts, of an hereditary tendency toward an excess in dogs, than I should dare to drink if I knew there was dipsomania in the family. [Hays 1967:261]

True to her Blackwell heritage, Alice as a young girl wrote of her plans to live together with Kitty when they were "old" and to adopt two orphan babies. Like her aunts, Alice Blackwell lived a long life devoted to numerous social causes, but she never married.

Thus, though the Blackwell women showed a cultivated intelligence and considerable drive and commitment to the work they chose for themselves, these qualities were built on a shaky emotional base. The men in the family were far less dynamic and purposive than their sisters. Henry and Samuel were "middle" children, boys still in their teens when their father died in 1838. They had grown up in a household of women: four aunts, a grandmother, a mother, three older sisters, and two sisters somewhat younger than themselves. Their hopes for college training and professional careers were temporarily dashed when their father died, though the teaching efforts of their sisters sent Henry at least off to college. But he seemed as lacking in steady commitment to study and employment as his father before him. He ran a hardware store, tried with his brother Samuel to make a go of beet-sugar refinement as their father had, worked as a salesman, and finally became reasonably comfortable in real-estate investment and home construction. The only real financial success among the men in the family was the youngest son, George, who eventually amassed a considerable fortune and helped to guide the real-estate investments of the whole Blackwell clan. Significantly, George was the only sibling who did not share the Blackwell passion for moral reform.

The two middle Blackwell brothers, Samuel and Henry, married women as unusual in their way as their own sisters. I suspect, however, that Lucy Stone fit the Blackwell mold far better than did Antoinette Brown, and it is interesting to examine the family backgrounds of these two women. Lucy Stone's background resembled the Blackwells' in its sternness and repressive atmosphere; she too was brought up in a household that emphasized piety and purity. Lucy told her daughter that "there was only one will in our home and that was my father's" (L. S. Blackwell 1930:9). In a revealing letter to her brother Bowman in later years, discussing the upbringing of his child, she wrote:

> I want that you . . . should praise Willy if he ever does anything to deserve it. . . . Judging from my own experience, and from observation I know that one word of approval will do more to make a child good than all the scoldings and whippings in the world put together. [Hays 1961:15]

Her father was very much opposed to her desire to obtain a college education but at the same time had a very low opinion of her ability to attract a husband. He is reputed to have said openly: "Lucy's face is like a blacksmith's apron; it keeps off sparks" (Hays 1961:20–21).

The dedication with which Lucy devoted her energies to combat male supremacy and to speak out strongly for woman's rights may well have had its roots in her private rebellion from her father. It is curious to find her, thirty years after her marriage, showing the same distrust when she changed her will to leave the bulk of her considerable property to her daughter rather than to her husband. Henry was to receive their Dorchester home and two thousand dollars in stocks, but even this bequest was to be valid only after he returned to the estate six thousand dollars' worth of stocks and bonds he was holding (Hays 1961:32). Some degree of caution seems always to have been present in Lucy's relations with men, including her devoted husband.

Lucy's personality also harbored a degree of emotional insecurity which marriage and maternity seemed to aggravate. She had been plagued with severe headaches from her student days at Oberlin; with marriage and the birth of Alice, the headaches returned, along with periodic depressions—which caused her to withdraw into total silence—and spells during which she lost her voice. Her husband Henry always liked to claim that a "cheerful serenity" characterized his life with Lucy, though there are enough indications that the reality was quite otherwise. He describes, for example, occasions when he had to leave the house on business with a fear that some very serious consequences might develop from Lucy's depressed state. Yet on one such occasion, when Henry returned home, Lucy was bright and cheerful, and he learned that Angelina Grimké had paid a visit during the day. In his view, it was the "diversion of thought and feeling" and "revival of old associations" that dispelled the clouds from his wife's mind (Hays 1961:160). Lucy's withdrawal into depressed silence, however, may be seen as her latent withdrawal from such family roles as she was not psychologically comfortable with—wifehood and motherhood. For a few hours, with Angelina, she was able to return to the old spirited Lucy, woman's-rights advocate.

In the nineteenth century correspondence between husband and wife was seldom frank concerning intimate aspects of the marriage. One suspects, however, that Lucy is referring to a sexual withdrawal from her husband in the following letter, written to him while he was on one of his many business trips:

> I *am* trying to be a good wife and mother . . . but I have tried before, and my miserable failures hitherto make me silent now. But if I have conquered myself, or gained anything in all these weary weeks, you will find it in my actions—I hope to be more to you and better—when you come to me. [Hays 1961:161]

I have long felt that Lucy Stone might have lived a far less painful psychological existence if she had kept to her earlier resolve never to marry, as the Blackwell sisters did. For all the loneliness that haunted the lives of her unmarried sisters-in-law, they did not undergo the psychological terrors that held Lucy so long in their grip. I suspect that a psychological aversion to sex, linked with an emotional incapacity to sustain intimate relations, were characteristics Lucy shared with the Blackwell women and, further, that it was these personal qualities that fed into the conservative stands they all took on many public issues of their day. Under Lucy's and then her daughter Alice's editorship of the *Woman's Journal*, the periodical gave support to Anthony Comstock's campaign to suppress "vile" literature, advocated the use by colleges of expurgated editions of Greek and Latin literature to save susceptible students from "corruption," became an outlet for Elizabeth Blackwell's campaign for moral reform of sexual manners, and approved the militant, whiskey-spilling, hymn-singing stage of the temperance movement.

Antoinette Brown was a very different kind of woman. Unlike Lucy, Nettie had the good fortune to grow up in a liberal family in Henrietta, New York. Her father was a prosperous farmer and local justice of the peace, a convert to Charles Finney's evangelical preaching in Rochester, and a supporter of all the liberal causes of the day. In her old age Nettie remembered that her father subscribed to every reform paper he knew of, including the moral-reform journal edited by women in New York, antislavery papers in which Harriet Stowe published *Uncle Tom's Cabin*, and liberal political newspapers. The conversion by Finney helped pave the way for family support of Nettie's dream of a college education and of her choice of Oberlin, for Charles Finney was then a professor of theology at the college. Of her mother, she makes an assessment unusual for this generation of pioneer women:

> She was a natural business woman of much executive ability, able to carry through any undertaking. If she had lived in modern times she would certainly have been a power. [Gilson 1909:15]

Nettie's memories of these rural childhood years in New York were far from dull and monotonous: cheese and candle making; fruit drying; wheat farming; an experiment in cultivating silk worms; yarn dying and pickling; and the forest surrounding the farm—all were exciting elements in her fond memories. In addition, with a baby at home, her mother let her attend school with her older brothers and sisters when she was not yet three years of age. She remembers "sitting on my teacher's lap and reciting lessons" (Gilson 1909:38).

Nettie gives an interesting account of her adolescent years at school. Her county was one of the first in the state to have its own high school, and it was the custom for children from surrounding farms to live together in the town close to the Academy, returning home just for Sundays. This practice clearly provided training in independence on the part of the young people. She describes this local pattern:

> children from three different families all of our own school district kept house, each family for itself in a building nearest to the Academy. At first there was a man and his wife living in the house. We saw little of them; they were never expected to supervise us in any way and they soon disappeared. In one of these child families were two, sometimes three, sisters and a brother; in another two sisters and a brother and a young niece; in ours an older sister and myself. Most of the cooking for all of us was done at home and we did little more than warm up the food, which came to us on Monday mornings or was brought to us on Thursdays. We were all trusted to take care of ourselves and each other, and we did so with fair satisfaction to everybody. Other young people in the neighborhood kept house and went to school in the same way. It was not thought anything peculiar or not adapted to the times. [Gilson 1909:42]

After a few years of teaching in surrounding communities, Nettie attended Oberlin College. Unlike Lucy Stone, her effort had her family's support and encouragement. One example from her account of these college years is particularly interesting in reflecting the independence and resolve of both Lucy and Nettie. During Nettie's first year at Oberlin she and her friends began an informal debating and speaking society, since the college, though teaching writing to the women students, offered no aspect of elocution. At the same time Lucy was teaching in a Negro school in Oberlin, with many ex-slaves and their children among her students. The debating society met on the outskirts of the town in the home of one of Lucy's women pupils, to which the Oberlin women walked quietly by ones and twos to keep their proceedings unnoticed by the college and the local people. Also indicative of an early commitment to the cause of women, Nettie's senior class essay, later published in the *Oberlin Quarterly Review*, was an exegisis of the biblical injunction "let women keep silence in the churches." In her essay Nettie argued that the Greek word *"alein"* meant inconsequential talk or babbling, not serious talk; only this interpretation, Nettie reasoned, is consistent with the further fact that ancient prophetesses were called of the Lord to become teachers of Israel.

After graduation Nettie returned to Oberlin for three years of graduate study in the theological department. Yet when she was finally ordained and had her own little parish in South Butler, New York, she underwent a profound change of thinking on theological issues, during her very first year as a minister. It probably did not help matters that in that fall and winter of 1853 her reading included Darwin and Spencer's new ideas about human evolution. By spring she reported:

> the whole groundwork of my faith had dropped away from me. I found myself absolutely believing nothing, not even in my own continuous personal existence. [Gilson 1909:180]

This loss of faith was serious enough to cause Nettie to resign from her parish, and she went on to work for Horace Greeley in New York as a reporter and writer.

That issues of marriage and public roles as reformers were often discussed with her friend Lucy during their years at Oberlin is caught in this recollection:

> It had seemed to both Lucy Stone and myself in our student days that marriage would be a hindrance to our public work. I at least had accepted celibacy as my destiny and I think she had also at an early age. If I had remained orthodox I should probably have considered marriage out of the question, a hindrance to the best usefulness. But when the early faith seemed wholly lost and the new and stronger belief not yet obtained, there seemed no good reason for not accepting the love and help of a good man. [Gilson 1909:180–181]

Samuel Blackwell had visited with Nettie at South Butler while she was undergoing her most serious doubts, and it was to him she turned a few years later. A letter she wrote to him just before their marriage gives interesting early expression to their uniquely cooperative marriage:

you asked me one day if it seemed like giving up much for your sake. Only leave me free, as free as you are and everyone ought to be, and it is giving up nothing. It will not be so very hard to have a dear quiet own home with one's husband to love and be loved by. . . . You may sigh for a more domestic wife. And yet to have me merely go into New York to preach Sundays or gone on a lecturing tour of a few days or weeks won't be so very bad, will it? [Gilson 1909:187]

The marriages of Lucy and Nettie to the two Blackwell brothers took place within months of each other, as did the birth of their first children. I can find no record of Nettie's own response to pregnancy, but a revealing letter to her from Lucy warns of its psychological hazards:

I sympathize with you and respect the moods, silent or otherwise, which these months will give. I am glad that you are so well. Don't blame yourself, Nettie, if you find that all the original sin seems to try and manifest itself in you for even Margaret Fuller with all her strength and philosophy says she was "never so unreasonable and desponding." Blame the circumstances, though maybe the Furies will not haunt you, as they often do the very best. I hope that everything will go pleasantly and that another new year will find your heart made glad and warm and large by a mother's love. For myself I almost despair. Will you give me one of your seven? I expect some new phases of life this summer and shall try to get the honey from each moment. [Gilson 1909:222]

This letter, though not dated, clearly refers to Nettie's first pregnancy; hence Lucy's reference to "one of your seven" must refer to previous talk about how many children they hoped to have. Lucy's "despair" is not specified, but it was indeed the case that she had no other child than Alice after she lost one stillborn son, while Nettie went on to have six other pregnancies and five daughters who survived childhood.

Antoinette Brown Blackwell is the least well-known but in my view the most interesting of these early pioneers in the woman's movement in the nineteenth century. She had a far more finely honed intellect than most of the early leaders, as sharp in purely intellectual reasoning as Elizabeth

Stanton's was in political and ideological thinking. It is to bring back into more general circulation some of Nettie's work that a selection is included in this volume from a collection of her papers on sex and evolution, in which she argued Darwin's and Spencer's use of the veneer of "science" to claim that women were inferior physically and mentally to men, thus grounding themselves and their generation anew upon "the moss grown foundations of ancient dogma." In "Trial by Science" she derides the lack of any psychology of womanhood and argues that the mental abilities of the sexes cannot be compared, since the mental life of women of the past has left almost no record of itself, while contemporary differences provide no proof of innate differences "unless we first determine that the work was done under equivalent conditions equally favorable to each" (A. B. Blackwell 1875:238–239).

In a telling passage, amply expanded upon in the selection to follow, Antoinette sums up her criticism of Darwin's evolutionary theories and illustrates her cogent reasoning:

> Mr. Darwin . . . has failed to hold definitely before his mind the principle that the difference of sex, whatever it may consist in, must itself be subject to natural selection and to evolution. Nothing but the exacting task before him of settling the Origin of all Species and the Descent of Man, through all the ages, could have prevented his recognition of ever-widening organic differences evolved in two distinct lines. With great wealth of detail, he has illustrated his theory of how the male has probably acquired additional masculine characters; but he seems never to have thought of looking to see whether or not the females had developed equivalent feminine characters. [A. B. Blackwell 1875:16]

Long before scientific research in genetics permitted adequate substantiation, Antoinette Brown argued that

> all characters, being equally transmitted to descendants of both sexes, may remain undeveloped in either, or may be developed subject to sexual modifications; and yet, as a whole, the males and females of the same species, from mollusk up to man, may continue their related evolution, as true equivalents. . . . If this . . . can be shown to have sufficient basis in nature, then Mr. Spencer and Mr.

Darwin are both wrong in the conclusion, that, in the processes of Evolution, man has become the superior of woman. [A. B. Blackwell 1875:21–22]

It is curious to note that it was Antoinette Brown Blackwell, trained in theology, who was writing in a completely naturalistic framework by the 1870s, while Elizabeth Blackwell, trained in medicine, was waging a moral crusade for a sexual physiology rooted in Christian morality. In 1894 Elizabeth published an interesting, and at the time controversial, book entitled *The Human Element in Sex*. In it she argued for the exact equivalence between the male sperm-producing system and the female ovum-producing system. It followed that "menstruation in the female and natural sperm emission in the male are analogous and beneficial functions" (E. Blackwell 1894:22). Hence, nocturnal emission, a source of worry to many mothers of adolescent boys in those days, was a "natural relief and independent outlet of that steady action of the generative organs in the male which secures . . . the constant aptitude for reproduction distinctive of the human race" (E. Blackwell 1894:24). In Elizabeth's view these natural functions are perfectly healthy and degenerate into states of disease only through "ignorance of physiological law" and "impure thoughts." Hence, while masturbation is immoral, nocturnal emission is natural and an "aid to adult self-government."

Another passage anticipates Freud's later emphasis on vaginal orgasm in the female. Elizabeth comments that, since the genitalia are external in the male but internal in the female, this difference suggests to the young boy "the meaning of action of the lower animals," while the girl "may grow up to full womanhood in complete unconsciousness of their signification" (E. Blackwell 1894:20):

This failure to recognise the equivalent value of internal with external structure has led to such a crude fallacy as a comparison of the penis with such a vestige as the clitoris, whilst failing to recognise that vast amount of erectile tissue, mostly internal, in the female, which is the direct seat of sexual spasm. [E. Blackwell 1894:20–21]

But Elizabeth is much in advance of her day in pointing out that sexual pleasure in a healthy woman can increase with time and experience, "whilst the total deprivation of it produces irritability" (E. Blackwell 1894:51).

Elizabeth Blackwell's major contribution to feminism does not stem from her work on moral reform in the sexual area. Rather, the work she and her sister Emily performed in establishing the first infirmary for women and children in New York, run by women physicians, and their own medical school in connection with that infirmary established their place in feminist history. The first woman to earn a medical degree in the United States, she had the gratification of knowing that by the time she died in 1910, there were over seven thousand women physicians in the United States. It therefore seems most appropriate to include a selection from Elizabeth and Emily Blackwell's *Medicine as a Profession for Women*. These arguments have a disturbingly contemporary ring, perhaps for the reason that women still represent so small a proportion of American physicians.

Elizabeth and Emily Blackwell: Medicine as a Profession for Women

The idea of the education of women in medicine is not now an entirely new one; for some years it has been discussed by the public, institutions have been founded professing to accomplish it, and many women are already engaged in some form of medical occupation. Yet the true position of women in medicine, the real need which lies at the bottom of this movement, and the means necessary to secure its practical usefulness and success, are little known. We believe it is now time to bring this subject forward and place it in its true light, as a matter not affecting a few individuals only, but of serious importance to the community at large; and demanding such support as will allow of the establish-

From Elizabeth Blackwell and Emily Blackwell, *Medicine as a Profession for Women*. New York, New York Infirmary for Women, 1860.

ment of an institution for the thorough education of women in medicine.

When the idea of the practice of medicine by women is suggested, the grounds on which we usually find sympathy expressed for it are two. The first is, that there are certain departments of medicine in which the aid of *women* physicians would be especially valuable to women. The second argument is, that women are much in need of a wider field of occupation, and if they could successfully practice any branches of medicine it would be another opening added to the few they already possess. In some shape or other, these two points are almost universally regarded (where the matter has been considered at all) as the great reasons to be urged in its behalf.

Now, we believe that both these reasons are valid, and that experience will fully confirm them; but we believe also that there is a much deeper view of the question than this; and that the thorough education of a class of women in medicine will exert an important influence upon the life and interests of women in general, an influence of a much more extended nature than is expressed in the above views. . . .

. . . The interests and occupations of women, as they actually are at present, may be referred to four distinct forms of efforts:—Domestic life; the education of youth; social intercourse, and benevolent effort of various kinds. All these avocations, by unanimous consent, are especially under the superintendence of women, and every woman, as she takes her place in society, assumes the responsibility of participation in some of them.

While these pursuits have always formed the central interest of the majority of women, their character, and the requirements which they make for their proper performance, have widened, with the advance of modern society, in a remarkable degree. Social intercourse—a very limited thing in a half civilized country, becomes in our centres of civilization a great power, establishing customs more binding than laws, imposing habits and stamping opinions, a tribunal from whose judgment there is hardly an appeal. All who are familiar with European life, and the life of our great cities, know what an organized and powerful force it ever tends to become.

In like manner, benevolent efforts have little influence in new countries, but in Europe, especially in England, the extent of such work, and the amount of it which is done by women would be incredible, did we not see here, in our midst, the commencement of a similar state of things.

Domestic life is not less affected by the growth of the age; the position and duties of the mother of a family call for very different qualifications, in the wide and complicated relations of the present, from what was needed a century ago.

Now it is evident that the performance of all these forms of work, extended and organized as they are, is in its practical nature a business requiring distinct knowledge and previous preparation, as much as actual trades and professions. This fact would be more commonly recognized were it not that there is so much moral and spiritual life interwoven into woman's work by the relations upon which it is founded, and out of which it grows, as to make it more difficult to separate this business aspect of her work from her personal life, than is the case with the business life of men; consequently its practical character is too often considered entirely subordinate, or lost sight of. Every woman, however, who brings thought and conscience to the performance of everyday duties, soon realizes it in her own experience. The wider the view she takes of life, the higher her ideal of her domestic and social relations, the more keenly she will feel the need of knowledge with regard to this matter of fact basis upon which they rest. The first and most important point in which she will feel the want of this previous training will be in her ignorance of physiological and sanitary science, in their application to practical life; of the laws of health and physical and mental development; of the connection between moral and physical conditions, and the influences which our social and domestic life exert upon us. These and similar questions will meet her at every step, from the commencement of her maternal life, when the care of young children and of her own health bring to her a thousand subjects of perplexity, to the close of her career, when her children, assuming their positions as men and women, look to her as their natural counsellor.

It may be said, at first sight, that in these things it is not so much knowledge as common sense and earnestness that is wanted; that as health is the natural condition, it will be secured by simply using our judgment in not positively disregarding what our natural instincts teach us in regard to our lives. This would be true if civilization were a simple state directed by instinct; but every advance in social progress removes us more and more from the guidance of instinct, obliging us to depend upon reason for the assurance that our habits are really agreeable to the laws of health, and compelling us to guard against the sacrifice of our physical or moral nature while pursuing the ends of civilization. . . .

In education, as in domestic life, the same necessity for hygienic knowledge exists. Statistics show that nine-tenths of our teachers are women, and it is obviously a matter of great importance that they should be familiar with the nature and needs of the great body of youth which is intrusted to their care. It is not possible that our systems of education should be really suited to childhood, training its faculties without cramping or unduly stimulating the nature, unless those by whom this work is done understand the principles of health and growth upon which school training should be based. Our school education ignores, in a thousand ways, the rules of healthy development; and the results, obtained with much labor and expense, are gained very generally at the cost of physical and mental health.

If, then, it be true that health has its science as well as disease; that there are conditions essential for securing it, and that every-day life should be based upon its laws; if, moreover, women, by their social position, are important agents in this practical work, the question naturally arises, how is this knowledge to be widely diffused among them? At present there exists no method of supplying this need. Physiology and all branches of science bearing upon the physical life of man are pursued almost exclusively by physicians, and from these branches of learning they deduce more or less clear ideas with regard to the conditions of health in every-day life. But it is only the most enlightened physicians who do this work for themselves; a very large proportion of the profession, who are well acquainted with the bearing of this learning upon disease, would find it a difficult matter to show its relation to the prevention of disease, and the securing of health, by its application to daily life. If this be the case with regard to physicians, it must evidently be impossible to give to the majority of women the wide scientific training that would enable them from their own knowledge to deduce practical rules of guidance. This must be done by those whose avocations require wide scientific knowledge—by physicians. Yet the medical profession is at present too far removed from the life of women; they regard these subjects from such a different stand-point that they can not supply the want. The application of scientific knowledge to women's necessities in actual life can only be done by women who possess at once the scientific learning of the physician, and as women a thorough acquaintance with women's requirements—that is, by women physicians.

That this connecting link between the science of the medical profession and the every-day life of women is needed, is proved by the fact that during the years that scientific knowledge has been accumulating in the hands of physicians, while it has revolutionized the science of medicine, it has had so little direct effect upon domestic life. Twenty years ago, as now, their opinion was strongly expressed with regard to the defects in the adaptation of modern life and education to the physical well being of society, and particularly of its injurious results to women. Yet, as far as these latter are concerned, no change has been effected. In all such points women are far more influenced by the opinions of society at large, and of their elder women friends, than by their physician, and this arises from the fact that physicians are too far removed from women's life; they can criticize but not guide it. On the other hand, it is curious to observe that, as within the last few years the attention of a considerable number of women has been turned to medicine, the first use they have made of it has been to establish a class of lectures on physiology and hygiene for women. They are scattered all over the country; the lectures are generally as crude and unsatisfactory as the medical education out of which they have sprung; but the impulse is worthy of note, as showing the instinctive perception of women, as soon as they acquire even a slight acquaintance with these subjects, how directly they bear upon the interests of women, and the inclination which exists to attempt, at least, to apply them to their needs. As teachers, then, to diffuse among women the physiological and sanitary knowledge which they need, we find the first work for women physicians.

The next point of interest to be noticed is the connection of women with public charities and benevolent institutions.

In all civilized nations women have always taken an active share in these charities; indeed, if we include those employed in the subordinate duties of nurses, matrons, etc., the number of women actually engaged would much outnumber that of men. How large a part of the character of these institutions, and of the influence exerted by them upon society, is dependent upon this great body of women employed in them and connected with them, may readily be imagined. Yet it is certain, and admitted by all who have any acquaintance with the matter, that this influence at present is far from being a good one. It is well known how much the efficiency of women as managers or supporters of public institutions is impaired by the lack of knowledge and practical tact to second their zeal; and business men who have dealings with them in these relations are very apt to regard them as troublesome and uncertain allies, rather than as efficient co-workers. . . .

. . . In England, where all public institutions, hospitals—civil and military—workhouses, houses for reformation, prisons, penitentiaries, etc., form a great system, dealing with the poorer classes to an immense extent, and having a social importance too serious to be overlooked, the question has assumed sufficient weight to be discussed earnestly by government and the public at large.

In Catholic countries this is accomplished to a certain extent—that is, as far as the domestic and nursing departments are concerned—by the religious orders, the sisters of charity and others. . . .

It is very common among both Catholics and Protestants to consider these sisterhoods as the result entirely of religious enthusiasm, and to assert that large bodies of women can only be induced to accept these occupations, and carry them out in this efficient manner from this motive. When efforts have been made in England and Germany to establish any thing of the kind among Protestants, it is always to the religious element that the appeal has been made. . . . In England, the results have been very imperfect, and have entirely failed to secure any thing approaching in practical efficiency to the Catholic sisterhoods.

Now these failures are very easily comprehended by any one who has seen much of these sisters in actual work, for such persons will soon perceive that the practical success of these orders does not depend upon religious enthusiasm, but upon an excellent business organization. Religious feeling there is among them, and it is an important aid in filling their ranks and keeping up their interest; but the real secret of their success is in the excellent opening afforded by them for all classes of women to a useful and respected social life. The inferior sisters are plain, decent women, nothing more, to whom the opportunity of earning a support, the companionship, protection and interest afforded by being members of a respected order, and the prospect of a certain provision for age, are the more powerful ties to the work, from the fact that they are generally without means, or very near connexions, and would find it difficult to obtain a better or so good a living. The superior sisters are usually women of character and education, who, from want of family ties, misfortune, or need of occupation, find themselves lonely or unhappy in ordinary life; and to them the church, with its usual sagacity in availing itself of all talents, opens the attractive prospect of active occupation, personal standing and authority, social respect, and the companionship of intelligent co-workers, both men and women—the feeling of belonging to the world, in fact, instead of a crippled and isolated life. For though it is common to speak of the sisters as renouncing the world, the fact is, that the members of these sisterhoods have a far more active participation in the interests of life than most of them had before. No one can fully realize the effect this has upon them, unless they have at once seen them at their work, and are aware how welcome to great numbers of women would be an active, useful life, free from pecuniary cares, offering sympathy and companionship in work and social standing to all its members, with scope for all talents, from the poorest drudge to the intelligent and educated woman—an offer so welcome as to be quite sufficient to overcome the want of attraction in the work itself at first sight.

As we have said, every effort so far to introduce a corresponding class of women into English institutions has proved a failure, for there is no such organization in external life in Protestant churches as there is in the Catholic. . . .

The only way to meet the difficulty, to give a centre to women who are interested in such efforts, and to connect intelligent women with these institutions, is to introduce women into them as physicians. If all public charities were open to *well* educated women physicians, they would exert upon them the same valuable influence that is secured by the presence and services of the superiors of these orders; they would bring in a more respectable class of nurses and train them, which no men can do; they would supervise the domestic arrangements, and give the higher tone of womanly influence so greatly needed. . . .

We come now to the position of women in medicine itself. The fact that more than half of ordinary medical practice lies among women and children, would seem to be, at first sight, proof enough that there must be here a great deal that women could do for themselves, and that it is not a natural arrangement that in what so especially concerns themselves, they should have recourse entirely to men. Accordingly we find that, from the very earliest ages, a large class of women has always existed occupying certain departments of medical practice. Until within half a century, a recognized position was accorded to them, and midwives were as distinct a class, as doctors. Even now, in most European countries, there are government schools for their instruction, where they are most carefully trained in their own speciality. This training is always given in connexion with a hospital, of which the pupils perform the actual practice, and physicians of standing are employed as their instructors. . . . The whole idea of their education, however, planned and molded entirely by men, was not to enable these women to do all they could in medicine, but to make them a sort of supplement to the profession, taking off a great deal of laborious poor practice, and supplying a certain convenience in some branches where it was advantageous to have the assistance of skilful women's hands. With the advance of medical science, however, and its application to all these departments of medicine, this division of the directing head, and the subordinate hand, became impossible. Physicians dismissed, as far as possible, these half-educated assistants, excluded them from many opportunities of instruction under their authority, and in the government schools, which popular custom still upholds, they have materially curtailed their education. Nor is it possible or desirable to sanction the practice of any such intermediate class. The alternative is unavoidable of banishing women from medicine altogether, or giving them the education and standing of the physician. The broad field of general medical science underlies all specialities, and an acquaintance with it is indispensable for the successful pursuit of every department. If the popular instinct that called women so widely to this sort of work represent a real need, it can only be met now by a class of women whose education shall correspond to the wider requirements of our present medical science.

Moreover, experience very soon shows that it is not these special branches of practice that will chiefly call for the attention of women in medicine. The same reason which especially qualifies women to be the teachers of women, in sanitary and physiological knowledge, viz., that they can better apply it to the needs of women's life, holds good in regard to their action as physicians. . . . At present, when women need medical aid or advice, they have at once to go out of their own world, as it were; the whole atmosphere of professional life is so entirely foreign to that in which they live that there is a gap between them and the physician whom they consult, which can only be filled up by making the profession no longer an exclusively masculine one. Medicine is so broad a field, so closely interwoven with general interests, dealing as it does with all ages, sexes, and classes, and yet of so personal a character in its individual applications, that it must be regarded as one of those great departments of work in which the coöperation of men and women is needed to fulfill all its requirements. It is not only by what women will do themselves in medicine, but also by the influence which they will exert on the profession, that they will lead it to supply the needs of women as it can not otherwise. . . .

It is often objected to this idea of professional and scientific pursuits for women that it is too much out of keeping with their general life, that it would not harmonize with their necessary avocations in domestic and social life; that the advantages to be gained from the services of women physicians would not compensate for the injurious effect it would have upon the women themselves who pursued the profession, or the tendency it might have to induce others to undervalue the importance of duties already belonging to them.

This objection, the prominent one which we usually meet, appears to us based on an entire misapprehension of what is the great want of women at the present day. All who know the world must acknowledge how far the influence of women in the home, and in society, is from what it should be. How often homes, which should be the source of moral and physical health and truth, are centers of selfishness or frivolity! How often we find women, well meaning, of good intelligence and moral power, nevertheless utterly unable to influence their homes aright. The children, after the first few years of life, pass beyond the influence of the mother. The sons have an entire life of which she knows nothing, or has only uneasy misgivings that they are not growing up with the moral truthfulness that she desires. She has not the width of view—that broad knowledge of life, which would enable her to comprehend the growth and needs of a nature and position so different from hers; and if she retain their personal affection, she can not acquire that trustful confidence which would enable her to be the guardian friend of their early manhood. Her daughters also lack that guidance which would come from broader views of life, for she can not give them a higher perception of life than she possesses herself. How is it, also, with the personal and moral goodness attributed to woman, that the tone of social intercourse, in which she takes so active a part, is so low? That, instead of being a counterpoise to the narrowing or self-seeking spirit of business life, it only adds an element of frivolity and dissipation. . . .

. . . The more connections that are established between the life of women and the broad interests and active progress of the age, the more fully will they realize this wider view of their work. The profession of medicine which, in its practical details, and in the character of its scientific basis, has such intimate relations with these every-day duties of women, is peculiarly adapted as such a means of connection. For what is done or learned by one class of women becomes, by virtue of their common womanhood, the property of all women. It tells upon their thought and action, and modifies their relations to other spheres of life, in a way that the accomplishment of the same work by men would not do. Those women who pursued this life of scientific study and practical activity, so different from woman's domestic and social life and yet so closely connected with it, could not fail to regard these avocations from a fresh stand-point, and to see in a new light the noble possibilities which the position of woman opens to her; and though they may be few in number, they will be enough to form a new element, another channel by which women in general may draw in and apply to their own needs the active life of the age.

⤝ Antoinette Brown Blackwell: ⤜
Sex and Evolution

It is the central theory of the present volume that the sexes in each species of beings compared upon the same plane, from the lowest to the highest, are always true equivalents—equals but not identicals in development and in relative amounts of all normal force. This is an hypothesis which must be decided upon the simple basis of fact.

If the special class of feminine instincts and tendencies is a fair offset in every grade of life to corresponding masculine traits, this is a subject for direct scientific investigation. It is a question of pure quantity; of comparing unlike but strictly measurable terms. In time it can be experimentally decided, and settled by rigidly mathematical tests. We do not weigh lead and sunbeams in the same balance; yet the *savants* can estimate their equivalent forces on some other basis than avoirdupois. So if the average female animal is the natural equivalent of the average male of its own type in the whole aggregate of their differentiated qualities, science, by turning concentrated attention to this problem, and applying the adequate tests, can yet demonstrate this fact beyond controversy.

Or if the male is everywhere the established superior, then science in time can undoubtedly affirm that truth upon a basis of such careful and exact calculation that every opponent must learn to acquiesce.

But the question is still very far from reaching the point of accurate solution. It is decided on both sides by inferences drawn from yet untested data. . . .

. . . [E]ach writer can best treat of any subject from his own standpoint, and hence, in the present paper, the equivalence of the sexes is considered in the light of certain theories of development.

Mr. Spencer and Mr. Darwin, the accredited exponents of Evolution, are both constructive reasoners. Each, with a special line of investigation, is intent upon the unfolding of related facts and conclusions; and every fresh topic is

From Antoinette Brown Blackwell, *The Sexes Throughout Nature*. New York, G. P. Putnam's Sons, 1875. Pp. 11–137.

destined to be examined as to its bearing upon the central points of *the system*.

Any positive thinker is compelled to see everything in the light of his own convictions. The more active and dominant one's opinions, the more liable they must be to modify his rendering of related facts—roping them inadvertently into the undue service of his theories. Add to this the immense concentrated work which both these famous investigators have undertaken for years past, and one may readily understand that on certain points to which they have not given special attention, these great men may be equally liable with lesser ones to form mistaken judgments. When, therefore, Mr. Spencer argues that women are inferior to men because their development must be earlier arrested by reproductive functions, and Mr. Darwin claims that males have evolved muscle and brains much superior to females, and entailed their pre-eminent qualities chiefly on their male descendants, these conclusions need not be accepted without question, even by their own school of evolutionists. . . .

. . .

Mr. Darwin, . . . eminently a student of organic structures, and of the causes which have produced them, with their past and present characters, has failed to hold definitely before his mind the principle that the difference of sex, whatever it may consist in, must itself be subject to *natural selection* and to evolution. Nothing but the exacting task before him of settling the Origin of all Species and the Descent of Man, through all the ages, could have prevented his recognition of ever-widening organic differences evolved in two distinct lines. With great wealth of detail, he has illustrated his theory of how the male has probably acquired additional masculine characters; but he seems never to have thought of looking to see whether or not the females had developed equivalent feminine characters.

The older physiologists not only studied nature chiefly, being generally men—but they interpreted facts by the accepted theory that the male is the representative type of the species—the female a modification preordained in the interest of reproduction, and in that interest only or chiefly. To them, physiology was an adjunct of the special creation theory. They believed that Sovereign Power and Wisdom had created one vessel to honor, and the other to dishonor. Evolutionists depart widely from this time-honored basis. But how are we to understand the want of balance in their interpretation of natural methods? It is difficult to perceive what self-adjusting forces, in the organic world, have developed men everywhere the superiors of women, males characteristically the superiors of females.

Other things equal, children of the same parents must begin embryo life on the same plane. As many successive stages of growth have arisen between primordial forms and women, as between these and men. Mr. Spencer reasons, that the cost of reproduction being greater for the female than the male, female development is earlier arrested in proportion. Hence woman can never equal man, physically or mentally.

Mr. Darwin's theory of Sexual Selection supposes that a male superiority has been evolved in the male line, and entailed chiefly to the male descendants. The females, sometimes, inherit characters originally acquired by the males; but this form of evolution is carried forward principally from father to son, from variety to variety, and from species to species, beginning with the lowest unisexual beings and continuing upwards to man. With a few inconsiderable exceptions, the more active progressive male bears off the palm, among all higher animals in size, and among all animals high and low, in development of muscles, in ornamentation, in general brightness and beauty, in strength of feeling, and in vigor of intellect. Weighed, measured, or calculated, the masculine force always predominates.

Possibly the cause to which Mr. Spencer assigns the *earlier arrest of feminine development* may be alleged as the sufficient reason for Mr. Darwin's *male evolution*. At any rate, Mr. Spencer scientifically *subtracts from the female,* and Mr. Darwin as scientifically *adds to the male.* The inequality between them is steadily increasing along the whole length of all the internodes; and it seems to grow both upwards and downwards, as plants do, from all the nodes. Unless it meet with a check in some unknown law, the causes which originally superinduced the inequality between the sexes must continue to increase it to a degree which it is startling to contemplate!

These philosophers both believe that inheritance is limited in a large degree to the same sex, and both believe in mathematical progression. Where, then, is male superiority to end? Are all the races, because of it, threatened with decadence and death somewhere in the remote future? Or must the time arrive when inferior males will be systematically chosen, and the superior ones thus eliminated from existence? But would this be Evolution? Moreover, if we must fall back upon certain natural checks which will be able in the future to prevent too great an inequality between the sexes, it cannot be preposterous to suppose that in the past and in the present similar natural checks always have been, and still are, in active operation. These, from the beginning, may have been able, progressively, to maintain a due balance, an approximate equilibrium and equivalence of forces, between the males and females of each species, as it has been successively evolved. To point out the nature of these functional checks, to show that they have produced many various structural modifications in different species, corresponding in each with varying habits and development, but all tending to maintain a virtual equivalence of the sexes, is the aim of the present paper.

The facts of Evolution may have been misinterpreted, by giving undue prominence to such as have been evolved in the male line; and by overlooking equally essential modifications which have arisen in the diverging female line. It is claimed that average males and females, in every species, always have been approximately equals, both physically and mentally. It is claimed that the extra size, the greater beauty of color, and wealth of appendages, and the greater physical strength and activity in males, have been in each species mathematically offset in the females by corresponding advantages—such as more highly differentiated structural development; greater rapidity of organic processes; larger relative endurance, dependent upon a more facile adjustment of functions among themselves, thus insuring a more prompt recuperation after every severe tax on the energies. It is claimed that the stronger passional force in the male finds its equivalent in the deeper parental and conjugal affection of the female; and that, in man, the more aggressive and constructive intellect of the male, is balanced by a higher intellectual insight, combined with a greater facility in coping with details and reducing them to harmonious adjustment, in the female. It is also claimed that in morals—development still modified by the correlative influences of sex—unlike practical virtues and vices and varied moral perceptions, must still be regarded as scientific equivalents.

All characters, being equally transmitted to descendants of both sexes, may remain undeveloped in either, or may be developed subject to sexual modifications; and yet, as a whole, the males and females of the same species, from mollusk up to man, may continue their related evolution, as true equivalents in all modes of force, physical and psychical. If this hypothesis can be shown to have a sufficient basis in nature, then Mr. Spencer and Mr. Darwin are both wrong in the conclusion that, in the processes of Evolution, man has become the superior of woman.

I do not underrate the charge of presumption which must attach to any woman who will attempt to controvert the great masters of science and of scientific inference. But there is no alternative! Only a woman can approach the subject from a feminine standpoint; and there are none but beginners among us in this class of investigations. However great the disadvantages under which we are placed, these will never be lessened by waiting. . . .

. . .

. . . [A]dult males and females of every species are differentiated *just in proportion to their general development*. They are evolved not in parallel but in adapted diverging lines. Apparently there exists a definite ratio between the evolution of a species and its sexual divergence. Every detail of each structure becomes somewhat diversely modified, and every function, with its related organs, more definitely unlike its analogue in the opposite sex. In the highest group, the mammals, the sexes differ more widely than with birds or fishes, and these than any class of invertebrates. At the head of the ascending series, men and women are more broadly unlike physiologically and psychologically than any lower class. . . .

If we consider *external characters only*, the larger relative size, brighter plumage, and more showy ornaments of male birds distinguish them from their females more obviously than any kindred differences among the mammalia. But when we turn to *the facts of structure and their related modifications in function*, no physiologist can doubt for a moment that wider differences of sex have been evolved in correlation with the general development. These "differentiations" increase in number, and are more elaborately wrought out in detail, extending to slight but well-defined modifications in the whole general system, in addition to becoming more distinctive in primary and secondary sexual characters. . . .

. . . No male of any species, high or low, is known to afford *direct nutriment* to the young—to first assimilate the food, and then transfer it to the offspring. The nearest approach to this is among pigeons. With these birds, both parents eject half digested food from the crop to feed their young. But there is no female of any species, plant, or animal, which does not in some form elaborate food and effect a direct transfer of it to the seed, the egg, the growing embryo, or the living young. This distinction is universal: *The male never affords direct nurture to offspring; the female always affords direct nurture to offspring.* . . .

The terrestrial carnivora are nearly always monogamous. The male forages for the family—that is, while the female supplies the *direct nurture* of offspring, the male provides largely for their *indirect nurture*. Among vegetable-eaters, this division of labor is impracticable; then natural selection fixes upon some other division of commensurate duties or acquirements which will be of greatest benefit to the particular species, such as greater beauty of coloring, superior size and strength of muscle, and increased activity of brain. In brief, the evolution of secondary sexual characters developed in the male line, which Mr. Darwin has recognized and followed out extensively, assigning their origin chiefly to sexual selection, we may attribute chiefly to the broader Natural Selection, which, *securing both the survival and the advancement of the fittest, gradually selects secondary or indirect characters which enable average males, equally with average females, to contribute to the general advancement of offspring.* . . .

By the survival of the fittest, the nearest approximations to equivalents in the sexes would leave the greatest number of offspring, and those best adapted to survive. The higher the development of the species and the more differentiated in structure and functions, the greater need would there be of a complex opposite polarity of activities in the uniting elements. Therefore natural selection, acting during immense periods of time, would be able to maintain, through the survival of the fittest, an approximate equality between the sexes at all stages of their development. It would be a differentiated and mutually adjusted equivalence—ultimating in an unlike modification of each which must extend to every function and to every adapted organ, to every thought and action of either sex. . . .

Finally, complex organisms are differentiated to perpetuate—not each one, another entire organism like itself—but dividing the work: one perpetuates the class of elements which may be called the incident forces of the new organism, and the other the opposed or complimentary forces. Thus, with unlike functions acted upon by unlike conditions, the sexes become more and more widely, though definitely, differentiated; each tending always to the perpetuation of all acquired characters, by transmitting those elements which are the incident forces to the opposite sex.

The status of each new resulting unit must be determined by the ability or the inability of the co-operative elements each to balance the other in their entirety. If their mutual adaptations enable them to do this, the child will combine in modified form all the qualities of both parents at their best. This is Evolution in its highest definite significance. . . .

Somewhere within the division Vertebrate runs a dividing line separating the more highly organized animals on the one side, and all the more lowly organized classes, including vegetable life, on the other. On the upper side of this line the males are habitually larger than the females; on the lower side the law is reversed—the females are habitually larger than the males. A fact so broad and well defined as this must be significant in its bearing upon the equilibrium of the sexes. Moreover, in the division where the males predominate in size, the females are invariably the more heterogeneous in structure and in functions. In the lower division, the characteristic structure of the females is still sometimes the more heterogeneous, but in a comparatively less degree; and there are counteracting conditions to be pointed out hereafter which obviously must influence their comparative size. With some small quadrupeds, birds, and reptiles, the size of the two sexes is about the same; but it is in the neighborhood of these classes that our dividing line threads its winding way.

Mr. Darwin is himself the authority for the following statements. Among quadrupeds, when there is any marked difference in the size of the sexes, the males are always the larger. This whole division, therefore, lies either upon or above the line. Birds also are generally, not always, on the upper side. Reptiles are grouped more immediately about the line, above or below. The females of all snakes are slightly the larger. The rule is reversed with lizards. Some male turtles are the larger, and among frogs, toads, etc., neither sex greatly excels.

Below the line are all fishes; for no male of any species is known to exceed the female in size. Here also are all invertebrates of every class, a very few insects excepted. The rule holds equally in the sea with its hosts of curious swarming tribes, and, on land, with every variety of crawling, jumping, or flying creatures without jointed backbones. . . .

This law would continue up to the point at which *heterogeneity of structure and functions* is able to balance *direct nutrition* in importance as means to the advancement of the species. At some fixed point, varying within certain limits, according to the conditions and habits of the species, there would arise an equilibrium between these two antagonisms— the direct and the indirect sustenance of offspring. So long as the conditions of life are simple, nature directly favors the female; and it is she who attains the larger growth. But with added complexity of functions and a higher division of labor, the indirect sustenance of the species, represented by the raw material of food, and by the greater strength and activity of muscle and brain to meet the higher conditions of existence, becomes of equal or even of paramount importance. Here, selecting characters according to varying conditions of the species, it becomes useful that the male should attain to the larger growth and the greater activity.

But this antagonism or opposition of the functions of sex, though real and continuous, is in reality a balance of activities—an equilibrium which requires that at all stages of development there shall be a virtual equivalence of sex in every species. This is claimed to be the true meaning of all the curious and varied modifications on either side. *Nature is forced to provide for a balanced expenditure between the sexes of all the greater divisions of force—to maintain not only a differentiated moving equilibrium in each, but also a still wider equilibrium between the two. . . .*

. . . There is, then, a wide sense in which it may be said that the feminine and the masculine, with their opposed tensions and polarities of forces, are combined in every organism; but among all higher beings begins from the first *the division of functions* analogous to that which we see in the flower with its separation of stamens and pistils. The en-

tire organism and all modes of activity being, then, necessarily
modified diversely in correspondence with one or other of the
two phases of the differentiated function, this resulting modification, and this only, whether greater or less in degree
—as in high or low organisms—may be properly called *the
difference* arising from sex. We do not consider that the
balanced actions and reactions which work together in the
inorganic world are distinctions of sex; that of the two elements in a compound one is masculine and the other feminine.
Nor can we so regard them, for these elements and these
forces are continually changing sides, entering into indefinite
rearrangements in conjunction with other forces. Thus what
might be distinguished as masculine in one case, would become feminine in the next.

* * *

Mr. Spencer designates a "stable equilibrium" as that in
which "any excess of one of the forces at work, itself generates, by the deviation it produces, certain counter forces that
eventually outbalance it, and initiate an opposite deviation."
This is an admirable statement of my idea of the balanced
relations of the opposite sexes. In every type of beings the
sexes are necessarily in "stable equilibrium." Thus, in the
flower of a plant, as the pistil is in the central, best nourished,
and most protected position, the stamens are usually many
more in number, even when the pistil is compound or several
in a group. An ovale has gathered about the germ an expensive supply of nutriment; but, on the other hand, the pollen
grains are a multitude, most of which are wasted of necessity.
We may regard this simply as an extra provision for insuring
the fructification of the seed; but there is also some ground
for supposing that it is a mode of expending equal amounts
of the unlike forces, in maintenance of the necessary equilibrium; for when the two sexes are borne upon separate
plants, the amount of pollen is enormously increased, while
on the companion tree the flower is more or less shorn of all
superfluous parts, and is sometimes reduced, as in the cones,
to a simple naked scale.

Comparisons can be also made among the higher types
where sex and individuality are both complete and associated.
And yet here the equation must be much less direct and
simple. As both sexes become more complex in structure and
functions, and also more characteristically unlike in propor-

tion, one class of activities must be often balanced by some very different class. Thus greater complexity of structure may be offset by greater bulk and strength, or by any excess of activity in one or in several directions. From the conservation of force, the convertibility of like modes of force, a perpetual readjustment is essential. The many possible combinations, varying with unlike conditions, often render the equation extremely difficult of statement. Of course it can be only approximate as applied to individuals; but in a species, or in a large number of averages, it may be literally accurate. . . .

MAN.

Males.	Females.
− Structure,	+ Structure,
+ Size,	− Size,
+ Strength,	− Strength,
+ Amount of Activity,	− Amount of Activity,
− Rate of Activity,	+ Rate of Activity,
+ Amount of Circulation,	− Amount of Circulation,
− Rate of Circulation,	+ Rate of Circulation,
− Endurance,	+ Endurance,
− Products,	+ Products,
− Direct Nurture,	+ Direct Nurture,
+ Indirect Nurture,	− Indirect Nurture,
+ Sexual Love,	− Sexual Love,
± Parental Love,	+ Parental Love,
+ Reasoning Powers,	− Reasoning Powers,
− Direct Insight of Facts,	+ Direct Insight of Facts,
− Direct Insight of Relations,	+ Direct Insight of Relations,
+ Thought,	± Thought,
± Feeling,	± Feeling,
± Moral Powers,	± Moral Powers.

Result in every Species.

The Females   =   The Males.

Comprehensive Result.

Sex   =   Sex.

Or,

Organic Equilibrium in Physiological and Psychological Equivalence of the Sexes.

These approximate equations are largely collated from Mr. Darwin's extended comparisons of secondary sexual characters. Fixing attention, as he does, upon masculine characters only, there seems to be no equilibrium of sex; but, holding the feminine characters up beside the others in a balanced view, the equilibrium is restored. The two leading philosophers of Evolution, each after his own method of investigation, being intent upon explaining the wider equilibrium between organic nature and its external conditions, it becomes fairly credible that they may have failed to give satisfactory attention to the lesser equilibria of sex, of each individual organism, and of every organic cell. If these are not each moving points of simpler adjustments within wider and wider systems of more complex adjustments, then I fail utterly to comprehend the first principle of organization. . . .

. . . [I]f all those instincts tending to the propagation of the race, on which Mr. Darwin has laid such stress in "Sexual Selection," are most active in the male line, there are corresponding traits in nearly all females, equally important and of equal significance in mental evolution. All insect mothers act with the utmost wisdom and good faith, and with a beautiful instinctive love towards a posterity which they are directly never to caress or nurture, as mothers do who are higher up in the scale of being. These tiny creatures work with the skill of carpenters and masons, and often with a prudence and forethought which is even more than human; for they never suffer personal ease or advantage to prevent their making proper provision for their young. Some of them merely deposit their eggs where there will be abundant nourishment for the larva; others search for the proper food—perhaps the young of other creatures—and seal them up together in nests, or by similar marvellous devices promote the survival of their race. . . .

. . . [A]ll the accessories, physical and psychical, which accompany female instincts in the invertebrates (parental love) must be considered as fairly equal to correlative male instincts (sexual love). The one impels to the initiation, the other to the preservation, of offspring; the one leads to vivid, concentrated impulses; the other to calmer, self-forgetting, steady affection: both united, to the higher and higher development of the race. We need only compare one such picture of instinctive parental love, as that drawn by Professor Agassiz, of the common horse-hair worm, sewing herself like a living threaded needle again and again through the mass of eggs she was trying to protect, when they were successively broken up and taken from her, with Mr. Darwin's repeated citations of courtship, as a strong phase of Evolution. We shall comprehend that the more placid love of offspring is an equivalent equally needed in combination in all higher development, male and female; and everywhere accompanied with at least as much intelligence in its manifestations. The great majority of the "homes without hands," among the highest evidences that we have of animal intelligence, as expended in their construction, are in whole or in part the work of females. The undeveloped female constructs the cell of the bee, and probably of all kindred species; and birds work together in nest-building, the little mother generally taking upon herself the larger share of duty. It requires a great amount of male surplus activity, to be expended physically in motion and psychically in emotion, as well as a good deal of extra ornamentation and brilliancy of coloring, to balance the extra direct and indirect nurture, the love, and the ingenuity which the mother birds, and even the insects, bestow upon their young.

• • •

Now as to the balance of qualities in men and women. The special adaptations and economies of Nature are in active operation from the first. The future woman is not destined to attain to the size of the man; Nature therefore adds atom to atom in the new organism with dainty care, rejecting the unfit more rigidly than with the boy. But the work is done with equal energy; for within a smaller compass there is to be wrought out a structure, part for part the analogue of his, not less perfect in every detail, but supplemented by yet other organs which are unique—the male developing only their merest rudiments. This smaller, more complex structure must therefore be the more delicately elaborated. . . .

But when nearly grown, the girl, who has never before equalled her brother in size, suddenly overtakes or even outstrips him in bulk. Why? Because, the work of organic development completed, the simpler task of adding like increments can be rapidly accomplished. Nature has already begun the process of storing up force, which is on demand, should it be needed in the growth of offspring. If it is not

needed, there shortly begins the periodical work of elimination. If it is needed, it is appropriated as provided. It appears
that the appropriation is not made—is not intended to be
made, at least—at the expense of the mother's own proper
supply of nutritive force, or of force devoted to any other
purpose in the economy of the feminine organism, with its
totality of functions. An elaborate, highly-developed reproductive system, with its own proper and complete nutritive
relations, has been evolved as one special function of the
feminine organism.

The nutrition which is continually and functionally stored
up for reproductive processes can doubtless in any exigency
—so close is the relation of every function to every other—
be diverted from its appropriate use. When the system is
over-taxed, underfed, impaired by sickness or by any other
course, this provision may be drawn upon for general purposes; yet the abnormal diversion will be accompanied by
the same kind of disturbance as follows the perversion of
any other nutriment. When the brain is excessively used, it
robs the body, which is weakened in proportion; or if muscle
is over-exercised, the brain suffers; or if there is an over-tax
of the reproductive functions, the whole organism is depleted.
Physiologists now admit that every great nervous centre
must be maintained in balanced activity, that it may draw its
proper nutritive supply. The digestive organs themselves
must work and rest alternately, so must every nerve and
member; for all act in correlation. The feminine functions
find their place in the system, co-ordinated with all the
others; equally normal, equally healthful, and even more
fundamental. Periodicity of function, maternity, lactation, all
being organically provided for, each in relation to the other,
neither should cause the least disturbance to health; neither
should subtract anything from the general functions of nutrition, and all should add, as all other balanced activity
does, to a larger vigor both of mind and body. The legitimate
use of any and of every faculty is strengthening, not exhausting. How can there exist a more fundamental antagonism
between individual wellbeing and the balanced exercise of
one function, than between it and any or every other function? They have all grown together in mutual adaptation. A
disturbance of one is the disturbance of all.

The girl attains physical maturity earlier than the boy.
May not this be because there is less to mature, because all

the processes, smaller in quantity, yet driven with equal force, have been accelerated in activity. Her circulation and respiration are more rapid. So are her mental processes. Why? Let science investigate the whole subject quantitatively. It may be found, process for process, in detail and in totality, that the average woman is equal to the average man. By all means let the sexes be studied mathematically.

At present, under the prevailing theory of the proper weakness and helplessness of the girl, we forget that food and oxygen are measures of force, and exercise largely the measure of appetite and digestion. The girl, starved by conventionality in body and mind, hinders the evolution of the race, or entails upon it a weak and unbalanced constitution. One writer says: "The monster who is in the way of woman's progress is not man, so much as the idle women who want somebody else to think for them, work for them, do for them, and even dress them." True; but the great underlying cause of all is a false theory that, because women are to be the mothers of the race, therefore they are not to be the thinkers or the pioneers in enterprise. This ancient dogma enfeebles one class of women and degrades the other. We believe in a fairly equal division of duties between men and women; but not that the wife of a laboring man, who accepts ten hours of daily toil as his share of family duty, is bound by her duty to spend twenty-four hours among the pots and the children, with no absolute rest and without fitting recreation. If woman's sole responsibility is of the domestic type, one class will be crushed by it, and the other throw it off as a badge of poverty. The poor man's motto, "Woman's work is never done," leads inevitably to its antithesis—ladies' work is never begun.

Let us suppose that natural selection has continually averaged the duty of the sexes to offspring, by modification and adjustment of each organism to its appropriate functions. At maturity, then, males and females would be true equivalents, each equally well fortified to meet its own responsibilities. Woman's share of duties must involve direct nutrition, man's indirect nutrition. She should be able to bear and nourish their young children, at a cost of energy equal to the amount expended by him as household provider. Beyond this, if human justice is to supplement Nature's provisions, all family duties must be shared equitably, in person or by proxy. Work, alternated with needful rest, is the salvation of man or woman. Far be it from me to encourage one human being as an idler! But *in the scientific distribution of work*, the males, not the females, must be held primarily responsible for the proper *cooking of food*, as for the *production* of it. Since we cannot thrive on the raw materials, like the lower animals, culinary processes must be *allied to indirect nutrition*.

In the progress of functions, the human mother must contribute much more towards the direct sustenance of offspring than any class of inferior beings. For many months before and for many months after its birth, her system must elaborate the entire food of her child. Its growth and activity are supplemental to her own, and are absolutely at her expense as is the growth of her own right arm. But Nature has provided for that by giving her a smaller frame of her own, and less disposition to great activity personally, with less need of it in the interest of perfect health. Nature is just enough; but men and women must comprehend and accept her suggestions. For the best fulfilment of maternal duties, the mother must have comfortable surroundings provided for her without a large personal tax on her own energies. Therefore it seems to me to be scientifically demonstrable that fathers are equitably bound to contribute indirect sustenance to offspring in the shape of good edible food for the mother. To this we might add ready-made clothing and fires lighted on cold winter mornings!

Undoubtedly, in the division of the many complex duties of life, it may be equitable and decidedly best in many households that the wives should be responsible for the family cooking and sewing; yet it should be understood that they both belong more properly to the category of masculine function, and pertain to the indirect nurture of the youthful scions of the household. Every nursing mother, in the midst of her little dependent brood, has far more right to whine, sulk, or scold, as temperament dictates, because beefsteak and coffee are not prepared for her and exactly to her taste, than any man ever had or ever can have during the present stage of human evolution. Other things equal—during the whole child-bearing age, at least—if family necessity compels to extra hours of toil or care, these must belong to the husband, never to the wife. The interests of their children *must not be sacrificed* by her over-exhaustion, even though she were willing and eager for the sacrifice of herself.

On the other hand, as highly complex beings, women

must be taught to exercise all their functions, that they may develop and strengthen all their faculties healthfully and symmetrically. *A regimen of sofas* must be as utterly demoralizing as would be a regimen of soft bread and milk, appropriate enough to the yearling baby. Mental torpor must be still more fatal, and aimless restlessness of body or mind, if possible, worse than either. In brief, then, let woman take part in any human enterprise which is at once attractive, feasible, *compatible with a fair division of family duties*, and thoroughly honorable in its character. Let her choose her own work and learn to do it in her own way, instructed only to maintain the natural balance of all her many admirably-appointed faculties; that she and her descendants after her may be alike subject to the laws of health. If anybody's *brain* requires to be sacrificed to those two Molochs, sewing-machine and cooking-stove, it is not hers! Nature's highest law is evolution, and no hereditary evolution is possible except through the prolonged maternal supervention.

The mother may transmit male characters to her son; but there is much evidence that a correlative feminine equivalent must first have found some place in her own nature. The pollen of a widely alien plant cannot fertilize a seed, nor can the wisest man bequeath intellect to children through the agency of a weak-minded or characterless mother. . . .

. . . Thus has Nature been forced to maintain the average equality of sex. Defrauded womanhood, as unwittingly to herself as to man, has been everywhere avenged for the system of arrogant repression under which she has always stifled hitherto; the human race, forever retarding its own advancement, because it could not recognize and promote a genuine, broad, and healthful equilibrium of the sexes. . . .

Fortunately, Nature is so tenacious of her ends, that a vast amount of inherent feminine vitality must persist, though never voluntarily exercised. Organic processes will tend to utilize the latent energies, and a doll or a drudge, with qualities which might have made a noble woman, may possibly become the mother of very noble children. But it must be sheer folly to believe that the offspring of such an one will not be defrauded of the increase which should revert to them from the exercise of parental talent.

There is a special directness in feminine perception which is in curious correspondence with the organic functions. The rapid intuitions with which women are credited, are simply direct perceptions. Their minds incline to the *direct reading* of all facts, from the simplest to the most complex and involved. They are quick to detect the dawning sentiments of a little child, or to divine the disguised opinions of the consummate man or woman of the world; to catch the details of a leaf at sight, or to gather at a glance the salient points of a landscape. Some man says, he never made his toilsome way up to any vantage-ground without finding a woman there in advance of him. The statement may be more than a compliment. A woman finds the natural lay of the land almost unconsciously; and not feeling it incumbent on her to be guide and philosopher to any successor, she takes little pains to mark the route by which she is making her ascent. John Stuart Mill, the life-long student of philosophy, must be credited with sincerity when he so earnestly reiterates that his wife was often his leader in abstract thinking, his superior in finding the truths after which they were both searching. He was emphatically a logician; she had quick perceptive powers. The one was a strong man, the other a strong woman.

* * *

There is a convenient hypothesis that the intellect of the female, among all the higher orders of being, has acquired a development intermediate between the young of the species and the males, as their bodies and brains are intermediate in size. It is a theory closely akin to the time-honored assumption that the male is the normal type of his species; the female the modification to a special end. Also, it is nearly allied to any scheme of Evolution which believes that progress is affected chiefly through the acquirement and transmission of masculine characters. . . .

It may be demonstrated that the nervous system, which is the primary organ of mind, has acquired greater *special development* in the woman than in the man. The differentiation between woman and child is much greater *in kind* than between man and child; the difference in *quantity* remains with the man. The female organism, selected during countless ages to elaborate much larger amounts of reproductive elements, in correspondence with this fact, has been progressively furnished with a graduated supply of blood-vessels, feeders of the special organs, and all these have their closely-attendant nerves. Thus, a progressively modified nervous system has kept pace in growth and development with the evolutions of the reproductive functions, till, in the mammalia, there is more than one nervous plexus well developed in adult females which is only rudimentary in the young and in the mature males. Now, if these nerve-ganglia and their added ramifications must be considered as partially automatic, they are yet allied to consciousness; exerting a profound influence over the whole sentient nature, and capable of elevating or depressing the entire mental activity. The brain is not, and cannot be, the sole or complete organ of thought and feeling.

Herbert Spencer's theory, that, as the male exhales relatively more carbonic acid than the female, this fact must be taken as the measure of oxygen consumed, and therefore of the amount of force evolved, takes no account of a differentiation of functions. The feminine system has other methods of eliminating waste matter along with the surplus nutritive elements, and perhaps even with the waste from the embryonic processes. Besides, at all ages of a woman's life, the skin and other tissues must be the more active in expelling refuse matter.

Conventionality has indeed curtailed feminine force by hindering healthful and varied activity; but Nature is continually devising compensations for that loss. When, from deficient action of mind or body, there is less appetite, less food consumed, and less strength evolved, there is also less expended. And whenever there is an excessive drain on any set of functions, psychical or physical, the feminine economy has made it easier to restore the balance than with men, for whom there is no equal organic provision. It seems to be an offset to his superior strength and activity, and it gives to the weaker and less active of the two the greater relative power of endurance, and the ability to bear a much wider departure from normal conditions comparatively unharmed. Therefore loss of sleep, loss of food, great fatigue, or great indolence of mind or body, are less exhausting to the female organism than to the male—a much-needed provision, especially in the ruder barbaric ages, when might was the most easily-recognized patent of right. It will be also an excellent additional safeguard to the feminine brain-workers of a more intellectual era.

* * *

Possibly, in adaptation to her smaller size, the woman may have a greater relative development of nerve-tissue than the man. The facts need careful investigation. Science has not determined in regard to it. I do not know that it has ever sought to do so, that it has ever raised the question as to woman's actual equality, or as to her relative equality in the total of nerve-tissue and of nerve-force. It has sought to compare the relative size and power of the average male and female brain; but the brain-system is no more shut up within the cranium than the great system of blood-vessels is shut up within the heart. Psychical action can no more be fairly measured or estimated in its modes of activity by the size and action of the brain alone, than the amount and rate of the circulation of the blood could be learned from the heart alone. Harvey discovered the wonderful facts of the blood circulation by tracing it in its whole complicated round through the system. The neurologists have discovered how the nerves act in conducting nerve force to and fro from the nerve-centres, not by watching the brain alone, but by comprehensive investigation of the whole co-operative nervous system. And yet I cannot learn that any scientist has proposed to estimate the psychical force of males and females on any other basis than that of the relative size of their brains and muscles. This mode of inference may suffice in comparing men with the lower animals, because the whole nervous system in its development keeps pace with the increasing size and complexity of the cranial mass; but the male nervous system is progressively differentiated from the female in the rising chain of species. In the human race the difference has become so important that when it is wholly ignored, and the comparison made by taking only two of the factors—size of brain and size of body—great injustice must be done to the female whose nervous system has become the more complex and is not aggregated to an equal extent within the cranium. . . .

It is currently known that the emotional and intellectual processes in woman are *more closely in relation* than in man. A more direct and frequent interchange seems to have been established between them. Thought and feeling work together more inseparably than in man. This is a fact learned by everyday experience, learned by comparing the masculine and feminine methods of working. Comparative anatomy of their modified nervous systems must suggest corresponding facts of structure.

Women's thoughts are impelled by their feelings. Hence the sharp-sightedness, the direct insight, the quick perceptions; hence also their warmer prejudices and more unbalanced judgments, and their infrequent use of the masculine methods of ratiocination. In this the child is like the woman. Its feelings directly impel its actions. The immediate sensation or perception seems also to be the impelling power of the savage and of all animal instincts. Call it automatic activity if you will; yet the incident force is real feeling, is perception, is intelligence, and is, as I believe, ordinarily accompanied by volition which has acquired more or less development towards such mastery of the situation that it may choose or reject on its own sovereign responsibility. . . .

But although thought and feeling are more nearly related in the child and woman than in the man, and though the latter, in his mature development, is thus differentiated from the child, I hold that the woman's mode of thinking and feeling is still more differentiated from that of childhood. The child is pre-eminently self-centred in all his psychical development. The law of grab is the primal law of infancy. "I want it," "I feel like it," is the impelling mainspring of its activity. It knows nothing of duty, and cares nothing for the interests or rights of others, till it is taught these things educationally.

Now the woman is not constitutionally self-centred in thought or feeling. Her sympathies have been functionally carried forward into an objective channel. Her instincts impel her to self-forgetfulness in thinking and acting for her children, and inherited habit has developed and extended the tendency to whatever person or subject demands her care and occupies her thoughts. Thus her nature must have been tending for many ages towards the objective in thought, the impersonal in feeling; towards the abstract in principle. Of course, human development is complex, subject to many cross complications, which neutralize each other. There are women of mature years who never, in mental development, get beyond childhood, with all its absorbing self-centredness or selfishness. We may charitably hope that their volitions, like their perceptive powers, are little more than rudimentary. There are men who have developed the transmitted feminine qualities, and by a more indirect route have become the most disinterested of their species. But, class for class, as the race now is, it is apparently easier for women to practice self-negation than for men, and more normal for them to develop an ob-

jective or perceptive intellect than a subjective or ratiocinative
intellect. There are certainly as many points of antithesis
between childhood and the highest female development, as
between childhood and the highest male development.

The mature woman is not incapable of appreciating the
most highly complex fact or the most abstract principle. She
learns easily to recognize all these, with their relative bearings; and can perceive existing relations as readily as she sees
the objects related. Her outlook is forward and backward,
with as wide a reach in either direction as man's. That she is
not his peer in all intellectual and moral capabilities, cannot
at least be very well proved until she is allowed an equally
untrammelled opportunity to test her own strength. It would
be possible to carry on a running comparison in detail; to
laud her untested powers, prophesying her future success in
executive ability, in abstract thinking, or in physical and
moral science; but I have no wish to do so. All doors are now
measurably open to her. Whatever her hand finds to do, let
her do it with her might, in demonstration of her capacity.

Morally certain it is that she will neither forego, nor
desire to forego, her domestic relations; nor will the average
woman seek to evade an equitable share of the burdens or
disabilities of her station, or shrink from sharing honorably
all the many duties which arise within the home-life. Evolution has given and is still giving to woman an increasing complexity of development which cannot find a legitimate field
for the exercise of all its powers within the household. There
is a broader, not a higher, life outside, which she is impelled
to enter, taking some share also in its responsibilities.

This need in no wise interfere with the everyday comforts,
the fostering mental influences, and the moral sanctities of
the home, nor with the highest good of the olive-plants which
will continue to bud and blossom in every household. The
restless, nervous woman of to-day may rather be expected to
attain a more contented and well-poised temperament with
the more symmetrical development. She will find opportunity to convert some of the smothered discontent, fostered
by superfluous sentiment with inaction, into the energy of
wider thought, purpose, and achievement.

If Evolution, as applied to sex, teaches any one lesson
plainer than another, it is the lesson that the monogamic
marriage is the basis of all progress. Nature, who everywhere
holds her balances with even justice, asks only that every

husband and wife shall co-operate to develop her most dilligently-selected characters. When she has endowed any woman with special talents, the balanced development of such a character requires the amplest exercise of these predominant gifts. Any prevailing tendency is itself evidence that the entire organism is adjusted to promote its superior activity. If it is a quality, just, honorable, desirable to be attained by the race, to hinder its highest development is to retard the normal rate of human progress; to interfere unwarrantably with a fundamental law of evolution. No theory of unfitness, no form of conventionality, can have the right to suppress any excellence which Nature has seen fit to evolve. Men and women, in search of the same ends, must co-operate in as many heterogeneous pursuits as the present development of the race enables them both to recognize and appreciate.

A Feminist Friendship:
Elizabeth Cady Stanton (1815–1902) and Susan B. Anthony (1820–1906)

The two women most closely associated with the emergence of the woman's-rights movement in the nineteenth century are Elizabeth Cady Stanton and Susan B. Anthony. From the spring of 1851, when they first met, until Elizabeth's death in 1902 they were the most intimate of friends and the closest collaborators in the battle for women's rights in the United States. Together they were Lyceum lecturers in the 1850s, founders of equal-rights and suffrage associations, organizers of annual conventions, hardy suffrage campaigners in the western states, and coeditors of the massive first three volumes of the *History of Woman Suffrage*; the contributions of these two pioneers are so intertwined that it is nearly impossible to speak of one without the other. They were in and out of each other's personal lives and households for more than fifty years. Their friendship and shared commitment to the cause of women's rights were the solid, central anchor in both their lives. As Elizabeth wrote to Susan in 1869, "no power in heaven, hell or earth can separate us, for our hearts are eternally wedded together" (Stanton and Blatch 1922:II, 125).

It is fitting, therefore, to introduce these two remarkable women in one essay and to focus on their friendship and the nature of their collaboration. The key to their effectiveness lies in the complementary nature of their skills. It can truly be said in this instance that the sum was greater than its parts, for either woman by herself would have had far less impact on the history of women's rights than they had in combination. Elizabeth had the intellect and ability to organize thought and evidence in a pungent, punchy prose. Susan was a master strategist, the "Napoleon" of the movement, as William Channing described her, superb at managing large-scale campaigns, quick and nimble in handling the give-and-take of convention meetings, and an effective public speaker. Elizabeth had only average stage presence and delivery as a speaker, and Susan's ability to conceptualize and develop her ideas was poor. Between them, Elizabeth's effective prose found its perfect outlet in Susan's public speaking. Elizabeth summed up their complementarity very well:

> In writing we did better work together than either could alone. While she is slow and analytical in composition, I am rapid and synthetic. I am the better writer, she the better critic. She supplied the facts and statistics, I the philosophy and rhetoric, and together we have made arguments that have stood unshaken by the storms of thirty long years. [HWS I,459]

Down through the years Susan turned to Elizabeth for help in drafting speeches, testimony, and letters for presentation to conventions on education, temperance, and women's rights. A good example of this pressure on Elizabeth is in a letter appealing for her help in preparing a speech for a convention of school teachers which Susan was invited to give in 1856:

> There is so much to say and I am so without constructive power to put in symmetrical order. So, for the love of me and for the saving of the reputation of womanhood, I beg you, with one baby on your knee and another at your feet, and four boys whistling, buzzing, hallooing "Ma, Ma," set yourself about the work. . . . Now will you load my gun, leaving me to pull the trigger and let fly the powder and ball? Don't delay one mail to tell me what you will do, for I must not and will not allow these school masters to say: "See, these women can't or won't do anything when we give them a chance." No, they sha'n't say that, even if I have to get a man to write it. But no man can write from my standpoint, nor no woman but you; for all, all would base their strongest argument on the unlikeness of the sexes. . . . And yet, in the schoolroom more than any other place, does the difference of sex, if there is any, need to be forgotten. . . . Do get all on fire and be as cross as you please. [Stanton and Blatch 1922:II,64–66]

The letter captures several of Susan's qualities: blunt speech, a badgering of her associates to give her the help she needs (always in a hurry), a fighting spirit, and an ability to point to a central theme she wishes stressed. Elizabeth's response to this particular call for help came just five days later. She says in part:

> Your servant is not dead but liveth. Imagine me, day in and day out, watching, bathing, dressing, nursing, and promenading the precious contents of a little crib in the corner of the room. I pace up and down these two chambers of mine, like a caged lioness longing to bring to a close nursing and housekeeping cares. . . . Is your speech to be exclusively on the point of educating the sexes together, or as to the best manner of educating women? I will do what I can to help you with your lecture. [Stanton and Blatch 1922:II,66–67]

The "baby" referred to is five-month-old Harriot, Elizabeth's sixth child, and the speech, entitled "Co-education," was written by Elizabeth and delivered by Susan less than two months later.

This particular collaborative effort differed from most of their team work only in that it involved no face-to-face working out of the ideas to be developed in the speech. In most of their joint efforts they worked together more closely; Susan often visited the Stanton home in Seneca Falls for this purpose. Elizabeth described these occasions:

> whenever I saw that stately Quaker girl coming across my lawn, I knew that some happy convocation of the sons of Adam were to be set by the ears, by one of our appeals or resolutions. The little portmanteau stuffed with facts was opened. . . . Then we would get out our pens and write articles for papers, or a petition to the Legislature, letters to the faithful . . . call on *The Una, The Liberator,* and *The Standard,* to remember our wrongs as well as those of the slave. We never met without issuing a pronunciamento on some question. [HWS I,458–459]

Thirty years later, when Elizabeth was no longer burdened with housekeeping and child-rearing responsibilities, she commented that in the 1850s, had it not been for Susan, who provided her with enough evidence of injustice to "turn any woman's thoughts from stockings and puddings," she might in time, "like too many women, have become wholly absorbed in a narrow family selfishness."

But a supportive friend who applied continual pressure to produce speeches and resolutions and articles for the press would hardly suffice to carry Elizabeth through the arduous years of child-rearing, from 1842 to the Civil War. During these years she not only bore seven children, but did a good deal of entertaining, produced reams of written material, served in temperance and abolition societies, lectured widely with the Lyceum circuit, and ran the household in Seneca Falls for long stretches of time without a man in the house. Elizabeth was clearly a woman of enormous physical energy coupled with a very strong will; these were needed to cope with such a regimen and to thrive on it. She was not a woman easily threatened by new experiences. Indeed, one of the best examples of her independence of mind and strength of body is the selection that follows, which describes her first experience of maternity. The reader will see how readily Elizabeth exercised her own judgment, even if it meant over-riding medical advice. She seems to have given birth to all seven children with no aid beyond that of a friend and a nurse, commenting in a letter to Lucretia Mott after the fifth child's birth:

> Dear me, how much cruel bondage of mind and suffering of body poor woman will escape when she takes the liberty of being her own physician of both body and soul!
> [Stanton and Blatch 1922:II,45]

Among Elizabeth's prescriptions for a healthy womanhood was one she clearly followed herself, but which it would take many decades for medicine and psychiatry to learn: she insightfully put her finger on an important cause of hysteria and illness among the women of her day, in a 1859 letter to a Boston friend:

> I think if women would indulge more freely in vituperation, they would enjoy ten times the health they do. It seems to me they are suffering from repression. [Stanton and Blatch 1922:II,73–74]

Elizabeth was not a woman to suffer from such repression herself. She showed none of the modern ambivalence about complaining when her responsibilities became onerous. One feels sure that in the intimacy of a friendly visit she let off steam in much the way she did in her letters during the 1850s, either by frankly admitting that she longed to be "free from housekeeping and children, so as to have some time to read and think and write" or by chafing at some affront to women and writing to Susan: "I am at a boiling point! If I do not find some day the use of my tongue on this question I shall die of an intellectual repression, a woman's rights convulsion" (Stanton and Blatch 1922:II,41).

There was probably not another woman in the nineteenth century who put her tongue and pen to better use than Elizabeth Stanton. She and Susan clearly viewed themselves as rebels in a good fight for justice and equality for women. They wrote each other in martial terms full of "triggers," "powder and balls," "Thunderbolts." Locust Hill, Elizabeth's home in Seneca Falls, was dubbed the "center of the rebellion" and from here Elizabeth "forged the thunderbolts" and Susan "fired them."

But even a close friend was no solution to the heavy family responsibilities Elizabeth carried throughout the 1850s. In the early years of her residence in Seneca Falls she was full of complaints about the unreliability of household servants, falling back on a dream of some "cooperative housekeeping in a future time that might promise a more harmonious domestic life" for women. But from 1851 on she had the help of a competent housekeeper, Amelia Willard, a capable woman who could readily substitute for Elizabeth herself. It was unquestionably this household arrangement which released Elizabeth for at least periodic participation in lecture tours and convention speeches during the years of heavy family responsibilities.

> It was while living in Seneca Falls, and at one of the most despairing periods of my young life, that one of the best gifts of the gods came to me in the form of a good, faithful housekeeper. She was indeed a treasure, a friend and comforter, a second mother to my children, and understood all life's duties and gladly bore its burdens. She could fill any department in domestic life, and for thirty years was the joy of our household. But for this noble, self sacrificing woman, much of my public work would have been quite impossible. If by word or deed I have made the journey of life easier for any struggling soul, I must in justice share the meed of praise accorded me with my little Quaker friend Amelia Willard. [Stanton and Blatch 1922:II,174]

It is curious that it may be the help of a housekeeper and a friend that facilitates a woman's life's work, while the closest analogy to Elizabeth's tribute one would find from the pen of a man is typically a tribute to his wife.

It is an interesting aspect of the friendship between Elizabeth and Susan that, while Susan was extremely critical of the energy her woman's-rights friends gave to homemaking and "baby-making," as she put it, there is no written evidence that Elizabeth exerted any pressure on Susan to marry and have a family of her own, though Susan was only in her thirties during the first decade of their friendship. Elizabeth seems, in fact, to have been remarkably accepting of Susan exactly as she was; only a teasing quality in a few letters expressed any criticism of her. Susan, by contrast, showed little understanding of, and no hesitation in expressing herself strongly about, the diversion of her friends' energies away from reform causes. In the same 1856 letter in which she calls for Elizabeth's aid in writing a speech on coeducation Susan comments:

> Those of you who have the talent to do honor to poor womanhood, have all given yourself over to baby-making; and left poor brainless me to do battle alone. It is a shame. Such a body as I might be spared to rock cradles. But it is a crime for you and Lucy Stone and Antoinette Brown to be doing it. [Stanton and Blatch 1922:II,65]

In response, Elizabeth urged her friend to let "Lucy and Antoinette rest awhile in peace and quietness," since "we cannot bring about a moral revolution in a day or year" (Stanton and Blatch 1922:II,67). This advice from Elizabeth had no effect on Susan, however. Two years later, in learning of the birth of Antoinette Brown's second child, she wrote the following revealing letter to Nettie (emphasis is by Susan):

April 22, 1858

Dear Nettie:

A note from Lucy last night tells me that you have another *daughter*. Well, so be it. I rejoice that you are past the trial hour.

Now Nettie, *not another baby* is my *peremptory command, two* will solve the problem whether a *woman can* be anything more than a *wife* and *mother* better than a half dozen or *ten even*.

I am provoked at Lucy, just to think that she will attempt to speak in a course with such intellects as Brady, Curtis, and Chapin, and then as her special preparation, take upon herself in addition to baby cares, quite too absorbing for careful close and continued intellectual effort—the entire work of her house. A woman who is and must of necessity continue for the present at least, the representative woman, has no right to disqualify herself for such a representative occasion. I do feel it is so foolish for her to put herself in the position of *maid of all work and baby tender.* . . .

Nettie, I don't really want to be a downright scolder, but I can't help looking after the married sheep of the flock a wee bit. [Gilson 1909:223–224]

Three weeks later Susan sent another note to Nettie, this time adding a postscript to report:

Mrs. Stanton sends love, and says "if you are going to have a large family go right on and finish up at once," as she has done. She has only devoted 18 years out of the very heart of existence here to the great work. But *I say stop now,* once and for all. Your life work will be arduous enough with two. [Gilson 1909:225]

Elizabeth Stanton softened this message with her own warm congratulations in an undated letter to Nettie that must have been written during this same spring:

How many times I have thought of you since reading your pleasant letter to Susan. I was so happy to hear that you had another daughter. In spite of all Susan's admonitions, I do hope you and Lucy will have all the children you desire. I would not have one less than seven, in spite of all the abuse that has been heaped upon me for such extravagance. [Gilson 1909:233]

Quite another aspect of the place their friendship held in their personal lives is suggested by their terms of address and reference to each other. They were not terms of "sisterhood" but of "marriage." Their hearts "are eternally wedded together," as Elizabeth put it. In 1870, when the press circulated rumors that their partnership was "dissolving," Elizabeth wrote her friend, half in jest:

Have you been getting a divorce out in Chicago without notifying me? I should like to know my present status. I shall not allow any such proceedings. I consider that our relations are to last for life; so make the best of it. [Stanton and Blatch 1922:II,127]

Two such passionate and committed women were bound to have differences of opinion, but once again, Elizabeth drew the analogy to marriage in explaining their conviction that differences should be confined to their private exchanges while they presented a united front in public:

So entirely one are we, that in all our associations, ever side by side on the same platform, not one feeling of jealousy or envy has ever shadowed our lives. We have indulged freely in criticism of each other when alone, and hotly contended whenever we have differed, but in our friendship of thirty years there has never been a break of one hour. To the world we always seem to agree and uniformly reflect each other. Like husband and wife, each has the feeling that we must have no differences in public. [HWS I,459]

During these years the two women were firm in their belief that the differences between men and women were rooted purely in social custom; it may be that the cultural model of differences between husband and wife made the complementary of marital roles a closer analogy to the nature of their own relationship than the presumed similarity of sisterhood. There is nevertheless some psychological validity in the symbolic use of the marriage bond to describe their friendship. Susan Anthony never married, and Elizabeth Stanton, though married for forty-six years, clearly received only shallow emotional support and no political support for her convictions from Henry Stanton. A warmth and effusiveness pervades Elizabeth's autobiography and her correspondence when she speaks of her children and of her close friends, but in hundreds of pages devoted to her personal life no comparable sentiment of warmth and mutuality appears in her rare references to her husband. It is not even clear whether Susan's frequent visits to the Stanton home coincided with Henry's stays at home. A politician, reformer, and journalist, he was clearly a traveling man. Seven children were born between 1842 and 1859, but there was a thinly disguised conflict between husband and wife on nonfamily matters. In 1855 Elizabeth wrote a few letters that permit a crack to show in the surface harmony. She had been developing plans that year to give a series of lectures on the Lyceum circuit and reports an exchange with her father concerning this plan in a letter to her cousin Elizabeth:

> We had a visit a little while ago from my venerable sire. . . . As we sat alone one night, he asked me: "Elizabeth, are you getting ready to lecture before lyceums?" "Yes sir," I answered. "I hope," he continued, "you will never do it during my lifetime, for if you do, be assured of one thing, your first lecture will be a very expensive one." "I intend," I replied, "that it shall be a very profitable one." [Stanton and Blatch 1922:II,61]

Her father did in fact disinherit her at this time, though he relented before his death and altered his will once again. Elizabeth does not give vent to her acute distress over this altercation with her father in writing to her cousin, but during the same month she wrote in quite a different vein to Susan. Referring to a "terrible scourging" on her last meeting with her father, she wrote:

> I cannot tell you how deep the iron entered my soul. I never felt more keenly the degradation of my sex. To think that all in me of which my father would have felt a proper pride had I been a man, is deeply mortifying to him because I am a woman. That thought has stung me to a fierce decision—to speak as soon as I can do myself credit. But the pressure on me just now is too great. Henry sides with my friends, who oppose me in all that is dearest to my heart. They are not willing that I should write even on the woman question. But I will both write and speak. I wish you to consider this letter strictly confidential. Sometimes, Susan, I struggle in deep waters. [Stanton and Blatch 1922:II,59–60]

This letter is a revealing one concerning both men in her life. Elizabeth had deeply ambivalent feelings toward her father. On the one hand she admired him for his mental abilities, was grateful for the understanding he gave her of the law, and was indebted to him for his continual financial support of her and her family over the years after her marriage. On the other hand she deeply resented the fact that none of her abilities or successes either as a schoolgirl or an adult could gain any praise at all from him. The same profile seems to hold for her marriage to Henry Stanton. Though they were both active in temperance and abolition agitation, they were completely at odds on her ideas and political activity on the woman's-rights issue. In the letter quoted above, the association of "father" and "husband" is immediate (Henry was ten years her senior), and Elizabeth feels herself a lone rebel in an unsympathetic social circle of family and neighbors, reaching out to the one sure friend who shares her commitments.

In this connection Henry Stanton's memoirs are interesting for what they leave unsaid. Though he wrote in the 1880s, when he was himself in his eighties, he seems unable to even mention the words "woman's rights." His wife is as absent from these pages as he is from her memoirs. The only reference in the entire book to Elizabeth's role in the woman's-rights movement is the following passage, with its oblique reference to her leadership role—"in another department."

> The celebrity in this country and Europe of two women in another department has thrown somewhat into the shade the distinguished service they rendered to the slave in the four stormy years preceding the war and in the four years while the sanguinary conflict was waged in the field. I refer to Elizabeth Cady Stanton and Susan B. Anthony. [H. Stanton 1887:68]

The submerged conflict in the Stanton household was not confined to the husband and wife, for the seven children were drawn in as well. It is interesting to compare their separate memoirs on this point. Of the seven, the first four and the last-born were boys; yet it was the fourth child, a fourth son, who was to be the closest of the sons to Elizabeth. In the kind of leap across time that is perhaps characteristic of women's memories of their children she wrote:

> I had a list of beautiful names for sons and daughters, from which to designate each newcomer; but, as yet, not one on my list had been used for my children. However, I put my foot down at number four, and named him Theodore, and, thus far, he has proved himself a veritable "gift of God," doing his uttermost, in every way possible, to fight the battle of freedom for woman. [Stanton and Blatch 1922:I,136]

It was Theodore who studied the women's movement in Europe, where he lived for many years; he wrote a book entitled *The Woman Question in Europe*. In her autobiography Elizabeth noted:

> To have a son interested in the question to which I have devoted my life, is a source of intense satisfaction. To say that I have realized in him all I could desire, is the highest praise a fond mother can give. [Stanton 1898:399–400]

Theodore's daughter was named Elizabeth Cady Stanton Jr. That Elizabeth took pride in her two daughters and lived in close contact with them, particularly Harriot, is clear throughout her memoirs. Both Harriot and her own daughter Nora were active in the suffrage movement, carrying Elizabeth's lead into the third generation.

In contrast, Henry Stanton makes no reference at all to the three children Elizabeth talked about so warmly, though he mentions the remaining four sons with pride. Speaking of his life as a lawyer, he added:

> I have shown my regard for the profession by inducting four of my sons into its intricacies. Daniel Cady Stanton was for one year a supervisor of registration, and for two years a member of the legislature of Louisiana, in the turbulent era of reconstruction. Henry Stanton, a graduate of the law school of Columbia College, is now the official attorney of the Northern Pacific Railway Company. Gerrit Smith Stanton and Robert Livingston Stanton are also graduates of the Columbia School. The former cultivates the soil and dispenses the law in Iowa. The latter practices his profession in the city of New York. [H. Stanton 1887:147]

These are the only references Henry makes to any of his children. One senses a divisive line-up within the Stanton household that widened as the children grew up: Henry Sr. with sons Daniel, Henry, Gerrit, and Robert on the one side; Elizabeth with Theodore, Margaret, and Harriot on the other. The division, at least on the surface indications left to us, was rooted in Elizabeth's involvement in the "woman question."

It is little wonder that Elizabeth's friendship with Susan took on such intensity. While Elizabeth was torn between the love of her children and a sense of duty to home and spouse on the one hand, and the rebellious desire to be up and out fighting the battles dearest to her convictions on the other, Susan was a vital link that held these two worlds together in Elizabeth's heart and mind. Always the one to speak for both of them, and able to acknowledge tender sentiments to a far greater extent than the more purposive Susan, Elizabeth sums up the importance of their friendship:

> So closely interwoven have been our lives, our purposes, and experiences that, separated, we have a feeling of incompleteness—united, such strength of self-assertion that no ordinary obstacles, difficulties, or dangers ever appear to us insurmountable. [Stanton and Blatch 1922:I,157]

The emotional quality of this assessment is one normally associated with the ideal, if not the reality, of a marital relationship; it is also a forerunner of the sisterly solidarity experienced in numerous feminist friendships in the 1970s.

It is much more difficult to gain a sense of Susan Anthony as a private person than it is of Elizabeth Stanton. Though she clearly reciprocated the deep friendship Elizabeth described, her personal style was quite different. The pressures on Susan were far more of a public than a private nature throughout her life, nor did she experience the deeply ambivalent relationship to a parent as Elizabeth did. Since she did not marry, Susan had no adult conflict of loyalties between family and a public career. Indeed, she showed great impatience with her women friends in the reform movements as they married and took on family responsibilities. That reticence in an autobiographic sense may be rooted in a past of greater serenity and lack of conflict is an insight for which we are indebted to Gordon Allport:

> autobiographical writing seems to be preoccupied with conflict . . . happy, peaceful periods of time are usually passed over in silence. A few lines may tell of many serene years whereas pages are devoted to a single humiliating episode or to an experience of suffering. Writers seem driven to elaborate on the conditions that have wrecked their hopes and deprived them of satisfactions. [Allport 1942:78]

This point may apply to correspondence as much as to autobiographies; and it is consistent that, from all one knows of

Susan Anthony's family background, it was far more serene and conflict-free than Elizabeth's.

Susan Anthony's parents were happily married, and her father was a strong and beloved figure throughout her life. He was a strong supporter of temperance and antislavery, even at the risk of financial penalty to himself. He took an active role in the rearing and education of his children, with consistent encouragement of their independence and initiative, and drew no distinction in such matters between sons and daughters. He supported the girls in any desire to acquire skills, believing that every girl should be trained to be self-supporting—a view the Anthony neighbors clearly did not share. Susan's first biographer and friend, Ida Harper, suggests that Daniel Anthony saw in Susan an

> ability of a high order and that same courage, persistence and aggressiveness which entered into his own character. He encouraged her desire to go into the reforms which were demanding attention, gave her financial backing when necessary, moral support upon all occasions and was ever her most interested friend and faithful ally. [Harper 1898:I,57–58]

While many parents of the early woman's-movement leaders shared commitments to temperance and abolition, few were full supporters of the woman's-rights movement. Susan's family was exceptional in this regard; her parents and sister attended the earliest convention on woman's rights in Rochester and were among those signing petitions in support of the convention resolutions.

Drive, executive ability, and a single-mindedness of purpose became enduring characteristics of Susan Anthony. She was impatient with whatever did not contribute directly to the battles she waged in her various campaigns for reform. She began as a teacher at the age of seventeen, and for many years she was a critical observer and then vigorous participant at teachers'-association conventions.

An early example of her courage and ability to press to the main point of an argument can be seen in her role at the 1853 state convention of schoolteachers. At this time women teachers could attend but could not speak at the convention meetings. Susan listened to a long discussion on why the profession of teaching was not as respected as those of law, medicine, and the ministry. When she could stand it no longer, she rose from her seat and called out, "Mr. President!" After much consternation about recognizing her, she was asked what she wished. When informed that she wished to speak to the question under discussion, a half-hour's debate and a close vote resulted in permission. Then she said:

> It seems to me, gentlemen, that none of you quite comprehend the cause of the disrespect of which you complain. Do you not see that so long as society says a woman is incompetent to be a lawyer, minister or doctor, but has ample ability to be a teacher, that every man of you who chooses this profession tacitly acknowledges that he has no more brains than a woman? And this, too, is the reason that teaching is a less lucrative profession, as here men must compete with the cheap labor of woman. Would you exalt your profession, exalt those who labor with you. Would you make it more lucrative, increase the salaries of the women engaged in the noble work of educating our future Presidents, Senators and Congressmen (HWS I, 514).

Susan's point on the wage scale of occupations in which many women are employed is as pertinent in the 1970s as it was in the 1850s. Equal pay for equal work continues to be seen as applying to equal pay for men and women in the same occupation, while the larger point of continuing relevance in our day is that some occupations have depressed wages because women are the chief employees. The former is a pattern of sex discrimination, the latter of institutionalized sexism.

Stanton and Anthony were of one mind on the issue of political rights for women, and this unanimity was at the core of their concerted organizational efforts during the long decades of the suffrage campaigns. Beyond this collaboration, however, they had complementary secondary interests. As a single woman and a Quaker, Susan was deeply concerned with opening the doors to women in the professions and with improving the pay scale of women workers. As a married woman and the more radical thinker of the two, Elizabeth was concerned with legislative reform of marriage, divorce, and property laws. There was much debate in the inner circle of woman's-rights leaders in the 1850s on the expediency of pressing an issue such as divorce at woman's-rights conventions, for it triggered far more violent responses from the public and was more divisive within their associa-

tions than even the political-rights issue. It was also the case
that the early leaders were not in agreement among themselves on the importance of marriage and divorce law reform
or the solutions to sex inequity in the family sphere.

To trace these women leaders' views on marriage and divorce issues over the years would constitute a fascinating
analysis that must remain for future scholars. I suspect,
though only as a hypothesis, that the long-range trend of
the woman's-rights movement toward a narrower focus on
the single issue of the vote was partially rooted in the aging
of the leaders. Not only did these early pioneers live to a very
old age, but they retained leadership positions in the movement well into their seventies. With increasing age, they may
have felt far less personal involvement in such issues as
marriage, child care, divorce, employment, and household
management than they did in questions of political rights.
Lucy Stone and Elizabeth Stanton were most concerned to
press the issue of a woman's right to her own body in the
1850s, when they were young enough to be personally concerned. Thirty years later, the issue was no longer of high
priority to them either personally or politically.

Some suggestion of the link between personal age and
family status on the one hand and views on sex and maternity
on the other can be seen in the following excerpts from
writings of Elizabeth Stanton at various moments during her
life. Elizabeth's age is recorded in parentheses along with the
year in which she made each statement.

> 1853 (38) [Letter to Susan Anthony]. Man in his lust has
> regulated long enough this whole question of sexual
> intercourse. Now let the mother of mankind, whose
> prerogative it is to set bounds to his indulgence rouse
> up and give this whole matter a thorough, fearless ex-
> amination. . . . I feel, as never before, that this whole
> question of woman's rights turns on the pivot of the
> marriage relation, and, mark my word, sooner or later,
> it will be the topic for discussion. I would not hurry it
> on, nor would I avoid it. [Stanton and Blatch 1922:11,
> 49]

> 1860 (45) [Letter to Susan Anthony]. Woman's degrada-
> tion is in man's idea of his sexual rights. Our religion,
> laws, customs are all founded on the belief that woman
> was made for man. Come what will, my whole soul

rejoices in the truth that I have uttered. One word of thanks from a suffering woman outweighs with me the howls of all Christendom. How this marriage question grows on me. It lies at the very foundation of all progress. I never read a thing on this subject until I had arrived at my present opinion. My own life, observation, thought, feeling, reason, brought me to the conclusion. So fear not that I shall falter. I shall not grow conservative with age. [Stanton and Blatch 1922:II,82–83]

1870 (55) [Letter to Susan Anthony]. Not only have I finished my lecture on marriage and divorce, but I have delivered it. . . . Women respond to this divorce speech as they never did to suffrage. In a word, I have had grand meetings. Oh, how the women flock to me with their sorrows. Such experiences as I listen to, plantation never equaled. [Stanton and Blatch 1922:II, 127]

1883 (68) [Excerpt from Diary]. I have been reading *Leaves of Grass*. Walt Whitman seems to understand everything in nature but woman. In "There is a Woman Waiting for Me," he speaks as if the female must be forced to the creative act, apparently ignorant of the great natural fact that a healthy woman has as much passion as a man, that she needs nothing stronger than the law of attraction to draw her to the male. [Stanton and Blatch 1922:II,210]

1890 (75) [Excerpt from Diary]. Our trouble is not our womanhood, but the artificial trammels of custom under false conditions. We are, as a sex, infinitely superior to men, and if we were free and developed, healthy in body and mind, as we should be under natural conditions, our motherhood would be our glory. That function gives women such wisdom and power as no male ever can possess. When women can support themselves, have their entry to all the trades and professions, with a house of their own over their heads and a bank account, they will own their bodies and be dictators in the social realm. [Stanton and Blatch 1922:II,270]

There is an interesting progression in Elizabeth's ideas over the forty years covered by these excerpts, reflecting, one feels sure, not only the continuing evolution of her thought but also the subtle impact of her changing age and family status. Let us go back over these excerpts and try to see a connection between her ideas and the developmental stage she had reached in her own personal life.

The first two excerpts focus on sex and the power of men to impose their sexual demands on women: these are years during which Elizabeth was herself sexually active, with two pregnancies still ahead of her at the time of the 1853 writing, and a last birth just a year before she wrote the second excerpt in 1860.

The growing concern she felt for divorce reform was particularly apparent in the 1860s, culminating in the speech she delivered on marriage and divorce laws at numerous Lyceum lectures in 1870: with her own children now ranging in age from eleven to twenty-eight, she herself may have emerged from her peak dependent years. Indeed, since she was fifty-five years old in 1870, she was probably postmenopausal. Marital stability and termination now absorb her.

By 1883 there is a sharp shift in emphasis, with an image of woman as possessing a healthy sexual passion to match that of men: despite her age—sixty-eight—she had read and traveled widely and given much thought to the question of sexuality; but she no longer had any personal need to act upon them. She was now fully independent of her husband, seldom traveling with him, and perhaps learning a more modern view of sexuality from her own married children, Theodore and Harriot.

By 1890 the view of maternity had again shifted, and a strong positive view of women emerges: now she is no longer focusing on what women are deprived of by men or subjected to by men—a topic which had absorbed her as a younger woman; rather, she is taking pride in what women have that men do not have. Perhaps her own independence and the circumstance of married children who acknowledge her prominence and share her interests now permit her to see the power and privilege that flow from maternity at a more mature age. It may also be significant that by this date she is living in New York City, in an apartment overlooking the Hudson River, which she shared with her daughter Margaret and her youngest son, Robert. But it is also a tribute to the openness of her intellect at seventy-five that she could envisage the significance to women of an independent household and independent income, some thirty-five years before

Virginia Woolf argued that "500 guineas" and a "room of one's own" were the symbols of what women needed to achieve real emancipation.

Elizabeth and Susan began their lives in the same social and political climate of central New York State, absorbing the perspectives on benevolent reform that marked the region during the 1820s and 1830s. A critical difference between them was rooted in their families: Susan's family applied the lofty reformist values to their own personal lives, whereas Elizabeth's did not. Hence, when the two women turned to the cause of their own sex, it was a rebellious step for Elizabeth but an acting-out of parental values for Susan. This difference between the two women had consequences that showed throughout their lives. The more rebellious Elizabeth was in part motivated by the discord rankling within her as a result of the ambivalence in her relations with her parents and husband. She was driven to a search for a better vision of a better life, one grounded in cooperation and marked by domestic harmony. Her intellect was opened outward to the future, while her political action was held in check by the necessities of organization and the pressure of her far more conservative supporters. Since her past did not nourish her as Susan's did, the impulse to open inquiry and acceptance of change continued strong. For Susan the world looked rather different. She had no inner rebellious feelings rooted in her early family experiences, since she enjoyed the support and praise of the people important in her private life. She was therefore the executor of the reform ideas developed by her friend. But her mission was to make the system work, while Elizabeth was drawn to social innovation and more fundamental change in the system. From all the evidence available, Elizabeth seems to have been correct when she wrote, at the age of seventy-nine, that "I get more radical as I grow older, while she [Susan] seems to get more conservative" (Stanton and Blatch 1922:II,254).

This account of the friendship between Elizabeth Stanton and Susan Anthony is a partial one at best, and the interested reader can find more detail and a better chronology of their individual lives in several biographies on Anthony (Harper 1898; K. Anthony 1954; Lutz 1959), and both biographies (Lutz 1940; Stanton and Blatch 1922) and memoirs by Elizabeth Stanton herself (E. C. Stanton 1898). The best introduction to the political and organizational efforts of these two friends is in the volumes of the *History of Woman Suffrage* themselves, from which several selections will be found in the section "Along the Suffrage Trail."

In addition to the selection by Stanton which describes her first experience with maternity, we have chosen the introduction to her last book, *The Woman's Bible.* This less well-known undertaking of Elizabeth's caused a considerable stir when it was published in 1895, almost on a par with the denunciation and ridicule the early pioneers experienced when they first passed resolutions on the political rights of women in 1848. It has some special relevance to the 1970s as women renew the battle Elizabeth began in 1895 by seeking a wider role for women in the churches and synagogues of the country.

⚭ Elizabeth Cady Stanton: Motherhood ⚭

. . . Though motherhood is the most important of all the professions—requiring more knowledge than any other department in human affairs—there was no attention given to preparation for this office. If we buy a plant of a horticulturist we ask him many questions as to its needs, whether it thrives best in sunshine or in shade, whether it needs much or little water, what degrees of heat or cold; but when we hold in our arms for the first time a being of infinite possibilities, in whose wisdom may rest the destiny of a nation, we take it for granted that the laws governing its life, health, and happiness are intuitively understood, that there is nothing new to be learned in regard to it. Here is a science to which philosophers have as yet given but little attention. An important fact has only been discovered and acted upon within the last ten years; that children come into the world tired, and not hungry, exhausted with the perilous journey. Instead of being kept on the rack while the nurse makes a prolonged

From Theodore Stanton and Harriot Stanton Blatch, editors, *Elizabeth Cady Stanton: As Revealed in Her Letters, Diary and Reminiscences.* New York, Harper & Brothers, 1922. Vol. I, pp. 109–124.

toilet and feeds it some nostrum supposed to have much-
needed medicinal influence, the child's face, eyes, and mouth
should be carefully washed, and the rest of its body thoroughly oiled, and then it should be slipped into a soft pillow
case, wrapped in a blanket, and laid to sleep. Ordinarily, in
the proper conditions, with its face uncovered in a cool, pure
atmosphere, it will sleep twelve hours. Then it should be
bathed, fed, and clothed in a high-neck, long-sleeved silk
shirt and a blanket. As babies lie still most of the time for
the first six weeks, they need no elaborate dressing. I think
the nurse was a full hour bathing and dressing my first-born,
who protested with a melancholy wail every blessed minute.

Ignorant myself of the initiative steps on the threshold of
time, I supposed this proceeding was approved by the best
authorities. However, I had been thinking, reading, observing,
and had as little faith in the popular theories in regard to
babies as on any other subject. I saw them, on all sides, ill
half the time, pale and peevish, dying early, having no joy in
life. I heard parents complaining of weary days and sleepless
nights, while each child in turn ran the gauntlet of red gum,
whooping cough, chicken pox, mumps, measles, and fits.
Everyone seemed to think these inflictions were a part of the
eternal plan—that Providence had a kind of Pandora's box,
from which he scattered these venerable diseases most liberally among those whom he especially loved. Having gone
through the ordeal of bearing a child, I was determined, if
possible, to keep him, so I read everything I could find on
babies. But the literature on this subject was as confusing
and unsatisfactory as the longer and shorter catechism and
the Thirty-nine Articles of our faith. I had recently visited our
dear friends, Theodore and Angelina Grimké-Weld, and they
warned me against books on this subject. They had been so
misled by one author, who assured them that the stomach of
a child could only hold one tablespoonful, that they nearly
starved their first-born to death. Though the child dwindled
day by day, and, at the end of a month looked like a little old
man, yet they still stood by the distinguished author. Fortunately, they both went off one day and left the child with
"Sister Sarah," who thought she would make an experiment
and see what a child's stomach could hold, as she had grave
doubts about the tablespoonful theory. To her surprise the
baby took a pint bottle full of milk, and had the sweetest
sleep thereon he had known in his earthly career. After that

he was permitted to take what he wanted, and "the author" was informed of his libel on the infantile stomach.

So here again I was entirely afloat, launched on the seas of doubt without chart or compass. The life and well-being of the race seemed to hang on the slender thread of such traditions as were handed down by ignorant mothers and nurses. One powerful ray of light illuminated the darkness; it was the work of Andrew Combe on *Infancy*. He had evidently watched some of the manifestations of man in the first stages of his development, and could tell at least as much of babies as naturalists could of beetles and bees. He did give young mothers some hints of what to do, and the whys and wherefores of certain lines of procedure. I read several chapters to the nurse. Although out of her ten children she had buried five, she still had too much confidence in her own wisdom and experience to pay much attention to any new idea that might be suggested to her. Among other things, Combe said that a child's bath should be regulated by the thermometer, in order to be always of the same temperature. She ridiculed the idea, and said her elbow was better than any thermometer, and, when I insisted on its use, she would invariably, with a smile of derision, put her elbow in first, to show how exactly it tallied with the thermometer.

When I insisted that the child should not be bandaged, she rebelled outright, and said she would not take the responsibility of caring for a child without a bandage. I said: "Pray, sit down, dear nurse, and let us reason together. Do not think I am setting up my judgment against yours, with all your experience. I am simply trying to act on the opinions of a distinguished physician, who says there should be no pressure on a child anywhere; that the limbs and body should be free; that it is cruel to bandage an infant from hip to armpit, as is usually done in America; or both body and legs, as is done in Europe; or strap them to boards, as is done by savages on both continents. Can you give me one good reason, nurse, why a child should be bandaged?" "Yes," she said emphatically, "I can give you a dozen." "I only asked for one," I replied. "Well," said she, after much hesitation, "the bones of a newborn infant are soft, like cartilage, and, unless you pin them up snugly there is danger of their falling apart." "It seems to me," I replied, "you have given the strongest reason why they should be carefully guarded against the slightest pressure. It is very remarkable that kittens and

puppies should be so well put together that they need no artificial bracing, and the human family be left wholly to the
mercy of a bandage. Suppose a child was born where you
could not get a bandage, what then? Now, I think this child
will remain intact without a bandage, and, if I am willing to
take the risk, why should you complain?" "Because," said
she, "if the child should die, it would injure my name as a
nurse. I therefore wash my hands of all these new-fangled
notions."

So she put a bandage on the child every morning, and I as
regularly took it off. It has been fully proved since to be as
useless an appendage as the vermiform. She had several cups
with various concoctions of herbs standing in the chimney
corner, ready for insomnia, colic, indigestion, etc., etc., all
of which were spirited away when she was at her dinner. . . .
I told her that if she would wash the baby's mouth with pure
cold water morning and night, and give it a teaspoonful to
drink occasionally during the day, there would be no danger
of red gum; that if she would keep the blinds open and let
in the air and sunshine, keep the temperature of the room at
sixty-five degrees, leave the child's head uncovered so that
it could breathe freely, stop rocking and trotting it, and
singing such melancholy hymns as "Hark, from the tombs a
doleful sound!" the baby and I would both be able to weather
the cape. I told her I should nurse the child once in two hours,
and that she must not feed it any of her nostrums in the
meantime; that a child's stomach, being made on the same
general plan as our own, needed intervals of rest as well as
ours. She said it would be racked with colic if the stomach
was empty any length of time, and that it would surely have
rickets if it were kept too still. I told her if the child had no
anodynes, nature would regulate its sleep. She said she could
not stay in a room with the thermometer at sixty-five degrees,
so I told her to sit in the next room and regulate the heat to
suit herself; that I would ring a bell when her services were
needed. . . .

Besides the obstinacy of the nurse, I had the ignorance of
physicians to contend with. When the child was four days old
we discovered that the collar bone was bent. The physician,
wishing to get a pressure on the shoulder, braced the bandage
round the wrist. "Leave that," he said, "ten days, and then it
will be all right." Soon after he left I noticed that the child's
hand was blue, showing that the circulation was impeded.

"That will never do," said I; "nurse, take it off." "No, indeed," she answered, "I shall never interfere with the doctor." So I took it off myself, and sent for another doctor, who was said to know more of surgery. He expressed great surprise that the first physician called should have put on so severe a bandage. "That," said he, "would do for a grown man, but ten days of it on a child would make him a cripple." However, he did nearly the same thing, only fastening it round the hand instead of the wrist. I soon saw that the ends of the fingers were all purple, and that to leave that on ten days would be as dangerous as the first. So I took it off.

"What a woman!" exclaimed the nurse. "What do you propose to do?" "Think out something better myself; so brace me up with some pillows and give the baby to me." She looked at me aghast. "Now," I said, talking partly to myself and partly to her, "what we want is a little pressure on that bone; that is what both of those men have aimed at. How can we get it without involving the arm, is the question?" "I am sure I don't know," said she, rubbing her hands and taking two or three brisk turns around the room. "Well, bring me three strips of linen, four double." I then folded one, wet in arnica and water, and laid it on the collar bone, put two other bands, like a pair of suspenders over the shoulder, crossing them both in front and behind, pinning the ends to the diaper, which gave the needed pressure without impeding the circulation anywhere. As I finished she gave me a look of budding confidence, and seemed satisfied that all was well. Several times, night and day, we wet the compress and readjusted the bands, until all appearance of inflammation had subsided.

At the end of ten days the two sons of Æsculapius appeared and made their examination, and said all was right, whereupon I told them how badly their bandages worked, and what I had done myself. They smiled at each other, and one said, "Well, after all, a mother's instinct is better than a man's reason." "Thank you, gentlemen, there was no instinct about it. I did some hard thinking before I saw how I could get pressure on the shoulder without impeding the circulation, as you did." Thus, in the supreme moment of a young mother's life, when I needed tender care and support, the whole responsibility of my child's supervision fell upon me; but though uncertain at every step of my own knowledge, I learned another lesson in self-reliance. I trusted neither men nor books absolutely after this, either in regard to the heavens above or the earth beneath, but continued to use my "mother's instinct," if "reason" is too dignified a term to apply to a woman's thoughts. My advice to every mother is, above all other arts and sciences, study first what relates to babyhood, as there is no department of human action in which there is such lamentable ignorance.

Elizabeth Cady Stanton: Introduction to *The Woman's Bible*

From the inauguration of the movement for woman's emancipation the Bible has been used to hold her in the "divinely ordained sphere," prescribed in the Old and New Testaments.

The canon and civil law; church and state; priests and legislators; all political parties and religious denominations have alike taught that woman was made after man, of man, and for man, an inferior being, subject to man. Creeds, codes, Scriptures and statutes, are all based on this idea. The fashions, forms, ceremonies and customs of society, church ordinances and discipline all grow out of this idea.

Of the old English common law, responsible for woman's civil and political status, Lord Brougham said, "it is a disgrace to the civilization and Christianity of the Nineteenth Century." Of the canon law, which is responsible for woman's status in the church, Charles Kingsley said, "this will never be a good world for women until the last remnant of the canon law is swept from the face of the earth."

The Bible teaches that woman brought sin and death into the world, that she precipitated the fall of the race, that she was arraigned before the judgment seat of Heaven, tried, condemned and sentenced. Marriage for her was to be a condition of bondage, maternity a period of suffering and anguish, and in silence and subjection, she was to play the role of a

From Elizabeth Cady Stanton, editor, *The Woman's Bible*. New York, European Publishing Company, 1895. Part 1, pp. 7–13.

dependent on man's bounty for all her material wants, and for all the information she might desire on the vital questions of the hour, she was commanded to ask her husband at home. Here is the Bible position of woman briefly summed up.

Those who have the divine insight to translate, transpose and transfigure this mournful object of pity into an exalted, dignified personage, worthy our worship as the mother of the race, are to be congratulated as having a share of the occult mystic power of the eastern Mahatmas.

The plain English to the ordinary mind admits of no such liberal interpretation. The unvarnished texts speak for themselves. The canon law, church ordinances and Scriptures, are homogeneous, and all reflect the same spirit and sentiments.

These familiar texts are quoted by clergymen in their pulpits, by statesmen in the halls of legislation, by lawyers in the courts, and are echoed by the press of all civilized nations, and accepted by woman herself as "The Word of God." So perverted is the religious element in her nature, that with faith and works she is the chief support of the church and clergy; the very powers that make her emancipation impossible. When, in the early part of the Nineteenth Century, women began to protest against their civil and political degradation, they were referred to the Bible for an answer. When they protested against their unequal position in the church, they were referred to the Bible for an answer.

This led to a general and critical study of the Scriptures. Some, having made a fetish of these books and believing them to be the veritable "Word of God," with liberal translations, interpretations, allegories and symbols, glossed over the most objectionable features of the various books and clung to them as divinely inspired. Others, seeing the family resemblance between the Mosaic code, the canon law, and the old English common law, came to the conclusion that all alike emanated from the same source; wholly human in their origin and inspired by the natural love of domination in the historians. Others, bewildered with their doubts and fears, came to no conclusion. While their clergymen told them on the one hand, that they owed all the blessings and freedom they enjoyed to the Bible, on the other, they said it clearly marked out their circumscribed sphere of action: that the demands for political and civil rights were irreligious, dangerous to the stability of the home, the state and the church. Clerical appeals were circulated from time to time conjuring members of their churches to take no part in the anti-slavery or woman suffrage movements, as they were infidel in their tendencies, undermining the very foundations of society. No wonder the majority of women stood still, and with bowed heads, accepted the situation.

Listening to the varied opinions of women, I have long thought it would be interesting and profitable to get them clearly stated in book form. To this end six years ago I proposed to a committee of women to issue a Woman's Bible, that we might have women's commentaries on women's position in the Old and New Testaments. It was agreed on by several leading women in England and America and the work was begun, but from various causes it has been delayed, until now the idea is received with renewed enthusiasm, and a large committee has been formed, and we hope to complete the work within a year.

Those who have undertaken the labor are desirous to have some Hebrew and Greek scholars, versed in Biblical criticism, to gild our pages with their learning. Several distinguished women have been urged to do so, but they are afraid that their high reputation and scholarly attainments might be compromised by taking part in an enterprise that for a time may prove very unpopular. Hence we may not be able to get help from that class.

Others fear that they might compromise their evangelical faith by affiliating with those of more liberal views, who do not regard the Bible as the "Word of God," but like any other book, to be judged by its merits. If the Bible teaches the equality of Woman, why does the church refuse to ordain women to preach the gospel, to fill the offices of deacons and elders, and to administer the Sacraments, or to admit them as delegates to the Synods, General Assemblies and Conferences of the different denominations? They have never yet invited a woman to join one of their Revising Committees, nor tried to mitigate the sentence pronounced on her by changing one count in the indictment served on her in Paradise.

The large number of letters received, highly appreciative of the undertaking, is very encouraging to those who have inaugurated the movement, and indicate a growing self-respect and self-assertion in the women of this generation. But we have the usual array of objectors to meet and answer. One correspondent conjures us to suspend the work, as it is "ridiculous" for "women to attempt the revision of the

Scriptures." I wonder if any man wrote to the late revising committee of Divines to stop their work on the ground that it was ridiculous for men to revise the Bible. Why is it more ridiculous for women to protest against her present status in the Old and New Testament, in the ordinances and discipline of the church, than in the statutes and constitution of the state? Why is it more ridiculous to arraign ecclesiastics for their false teaching and acts of injustice to women, than members of Congress and the House of Commons? Why is it more audacious to review Moses than Blackstone, the Jewish code of laws, than the English system of jurisprudence? Women have compelled their legislators in every state in this Union to so modify their statutes for women that the old common law is now almost a dead letter. Why not compel Bishops and Revising Committees to modify their creeds and dogmas? Forty years ago it seemed as ridiculous to timid, time-serving and retrograde folk for women to demand an expurgated edition of the laws, as it now does to demand an expurgated edition of the Liturgies and the Scriptures. Come, come, my conservative friend, wipe the dew off your spectacles, and see that the world is moving. Whatever your views may be as to the importance of the proposed work, your political and social degradation are but an outgrowth of your status in the Bible. When you express your aversion, based on a blind feeling of reverence in which reason has no control, to the revision of the Scriptures, you do but echo Cowper, who, when asked to read Paine's "Rights of Man," exclaimed, "No man shall convince me that I am improperly governed while I *feel* the contrary."

Others say it is not *politic* to rouse religious opposition. This much-lauded policy is but another word for *cowardice.* How can woman's position be changed from that of a subordinate to an equal, without opposition, without the broadest discussion of all the questions involved in her present degradation? For so far-reaching and momentous a reform as her complete independence, an entire revolution in all existing institutions is inevitable.

Let us remember that all reforms are interdependent, and that whatever is done to establish one principle on a solid basis, strengthens all. Reformers who are always compromising, have not yet grasped the idea that truth is the only safe ground to stand upon. The object of an individual life is not to carry one fragmentary measure in human progress, but to utter the highest truth clearly seen in all directions, and thus to round out and perfect a well balanced character. Was not the sum of influence exerted by John Stuart Mill on political, religious and social questions far greater than that of any statesman or reformer who has sedulously limited his sympathies and activities to carrying one specific measure? We have many women abundantly endowed with capabilities to understand and revise what men have thus far written. But they are all suffering from inherited ideas of their inferiority; they do not perceive it, yet such is the true explanation of their solicitude, lest they should seem to be too self-asserting.

Again there are some who write us that our work is a useless expenditure of force over a book that has lost its hold on the human mind. Most intelligent women, they say, regard it simply as the history of a rude people in a barbarous age, and have no more reverence for the Scriptures than any other work. So long as tens of thousands of Bibles are printed every year, and circulated over the whole habitable globe, and the masses in all English-speaking nations revere it as the word of God, it is vain to belittle its influence. The sentimental feelings we all have for those things we were educated to believe sacred, do not readily yield to pure reason. I distinctly remember the shudder that passed over me on seeing a mother take our family Bible to make a high seat for her child at table. It seemed such a desecration. I was tempted to protest against its use for such a purpose, and this, too, long after my reason had repudiated its divine authority.

To women still believing in the plenary inspiration of the Scriptures, we say give us by all means your exegesis in the light of the higher criticism learned men are now making, and illumine the Woman's Bible, with your inspiration.

Bible historians claim special inspiration for the Old and New Testaments containing most contradictory records of the same events, of miracles opposed to all known laws, of customs that degrade the female sex of all human and animal life, stated in most questionable language that could not be read in a promiscuous assembly, and call all this "The Word of God."

The only points in which I differ from all ecclesiastical teaching is that I do not believe that any man ever saw or talked with God, I do not believe that God inspired the Mosaic code, or told the historians what they say he did about woman, for all the religions on the face of the earth degrade her, and so long as woman accepts the position that they assign her, her emancipation is impossible. Whatever the Bible may be made to do in Hebrew or Greek, in plain English it does not exalt and dignify woman. My standpoint for criticism is the revised edition of 1888. I will so far honor the revising committee of nine men who have given us the best exegesis they can according to their ability, although Disraeli said the last one before he died, contained 150,000 blunders in the Hebrew, and 7,000 in the Greek.

But the verbal criticism in regard to woman's position amounts to little. The spirit is the same in all periods and languages, hostile to her as an equal.

There are some general principles in the holy books of all religions that teach love, charity, liberty, justice and equality for all the human family, there are many grand and beautiful passages, the golden rule has been echoed and re-echoed around the world. There are lofty examples of good and true men and women, all worthy our acceptance and example whose lustre cannot be dimmed by the false sentiments and vicious characters bound up in the same volume. The Bible cannot be accepted or rejected as a whole, its teachings are varied and its lessons differ widely from each other. In criticising the peccadilloes of Sarah, Rebecca and Rachel, we would not shadow the virtues of Deborah, Huldah and Vashti. In criticising the Mosaic code we would not question the wisdom of the golden rule and the fifth Commandment. Again the church claims special consecration for its cathedrals and priesthood, parts of these aristocratic churches are too holy for women to enter, boys were early introduced into the choirs for this reason, women singing in an obscure corner closely veiled. A few of the more democratic denominations accord women some privileges, but invidious discriminations of sex are found in all religious organizations, and the most bitter outspoken enemies of woman are found among clergymen and bishops of the Protestant religion.

The canon law, the Scriptures, the creeds and codes and church discipline of the leading religions bear the impress of fallible man, and not of our ideal great first cause, "the Spirit of all Good," that set the universe of matter and mind in motion, and by immutable law holds the land, the sea, the planets, revolving round the great centre of light and heat, each in its own elliptic, with millions of stars in harmony all singing together, the glory of creation forever and ever.

Along the Suffrage Trail

The single most impressive fact about the attempt by American women to obtain the right to vote is how long it took. From its earliest beginnings in the public speaking of Fanny Wright in the 1820s and the Grimké sisters in the 1830s, through the complex history of equal rights and suffrage associations led by such woman's-rights pioneers as Lucy Stone, Susan Anthony, and Elizabeth Stanton, it was indeed a "century of struggle" (Flexner 1959) before the suffrage amendment to the Constitution was ratified and women could first participate in a national election. Of the first generation pioneers, only Antoinette Brown Blackwell lived to cast her ballot in that first election in 1920.

Since the leaders of the woman's-rights movement were above all "activists," it is fitting to document their history by selecting accounts they themselves wrote of the campaigns, conventions, testimonies, and speeches that occupied them throughout the second half of the nineteenth century. But in orienting the reader to this long seventy-two-year history of the suffrage effort, it may be helpful to provide some "anchor" dates:

1848 to Civil War. Grass-roots organization following Seneca Falls Convention in 1848, with a proliferation of state and national woman's-rights conventions throughout the 1850s.

1861–1865. Temporary halt to woman's-rights conventions; the Woman's National Loyalty League was formed to assist in the war effort and to press for the full emancipation of the slave.

1866. The national Woman's Rights Convention was transformed into the American Equal Rights Association, to "bury the woman in the citizen."

1869. Split in the woman's-rights movement between the New York-based group which formed the National Suffrage Association, with Elizabeth Stanton as its first president, and the Boston-based group which formed the American Woman Suffrage Association, with Henry Ward Beecher holding its first presidency. The NWSA, under Anthony and Stanton, concentrated its efforts on the national Constitutional amendment level, while the AWSA, under the more conservative influence of Beecher, Stone, Blackwell, and Howe, focused on the popular vote in the states.

1890. The twenty-one-year split in the movement was ended with the formation of the American National Woman Suffrage Association.

1900. Susan Anthony stepped down as president of ANWSA and was replaced by Carrie Chapman Catt, who handled the last phase of the suffrage campaigns until the Constitutional amendment was fully ratified.

The selections to follow all come from the first two of the six volumes of the *History of Woman Suffrage.* The task of writing this history began in 1876 under the editorship of Elizabeth Stanton, Susan Anthony, and Matilda Joslyn Gage. Why these leaders chose to write a history before the suffrage had actually been attained is itself a complex story. They were not so innocent as to believe that the right to vote would soon be theirs. Nor had the women in any sense retired from their own active role within the movement and were thus motivated to write an equivalent of personal memoirs. Anthony, for example, only retired from the presidency of NAWSA in 1900, twenty or more years later. When they began their editing, Stanton and Anthony anticipated a task they could work at during the four months of the year when they were not on the lecture circuit, and they believed that it would yield a few hundred pages. The project, like the struggle for the vote itself, was to consume many times that amount of time and effort. The first three volumes were written over the course of the decade from 1876 to 1886, while the fourth volume went to press sixteen years later, in 1902, edited by Susan Anthony and Ida Husted Harper. The last two volumes were published in 1922 under the editorship of Ida Harper.

It is clear that Susan Anthony was as concerned for the impact of the *History* upon the contemporary movement of the 1880s as she was to provide a detailed reference work for future historians. She planned to give away, free of charge, hundreds of copies of the volumes to libraries and individuals in England and America, to serve as a good reference source for their contemporaries in ongoing suffrage campaigns. Stanton and Gage did not see eye to eye with Anthony on the plan to distribute so many volumes without cost, since they felt that the volumes had considerable sales potential. Susan Anthony shrewdly shifted the copyright from a joint one, shared with Stanton and Gage when the first two volumes were published in 1881 and 1882, to a copyright in her own name alone for the third volume in 1886; she retained this practice when she shared the editing with Ida Husted Harper to produce the fourth volume in 1902.

There was no money to cover the expenses connected with the production of the *History* when the women began their task. Ever the optimist where financial matters were concerned, Anthony undertook the work in the conviction that somehow or other the money would eventually be forthcoming. In 1882 her optimism was confirmed, for she received a legacy from Eliza Jackson Eddy of Boston to use "for the advancement of woman's cause." This legacy was used to carry out Anthony's project of extensive free distribution of the volumes; hundreds of copies were sent out to libraries and countless individuals Anthony thought could put them to good use in the woman's cause.

The bulk of the editing of the first three volumes took place during the years of a split within the suffrage movement. As a result, the account given is partial and onesided. The NWSA activities and leaders figure far more prominently in the *History* than do the women and men active in AWSA. By the time the fourth volume was produced, the two organizations had merged into the NAWSA, and the reader can learn about the suffrage activities of Lucy Stone, Mary Livermore, Julia Ward Howe, and their associates in New England.

The volumes themselves consist of a diverse range of materials either accumulated by the editors themselves during their quarter-century of active leadership in the movement, or specifically solicited for the volume in the late 1870s. Thousands of letters were sent out to former participants, requesting information, a check on accuracy of details, or personal reminiscences. There are meticulous accounts of the long series of petition campaigns, annual conventions, government testimonies; letters, speeches, and personal reminiscences; articles from newspapers and government records; and steel engravings by the score of individual women suffragists. Throughout all four volumes countless names acknowledge the contributions of men and women in all the state and national campaigns and conventions. Like the pages of a small-town newspaper, the books provided many thousands of women with a footnote in history, a printed reminder of their contribution to the suffrage cause between 1848 and 1902.

In making selections from the close to four thousand pages of the *History of Woman Suffrage,* our goal has been to permit the reader to participate in that movement through the eyes of its members as they recorded those events in the 1880s. Six selections have been made from the first two volumes:

Seneca Falls Convention. The first convention in the woman's movement was held at Seneca Falls in 1848. The *History*'s account of the convention includes the "call" to the convention, a description of the preparation for it and of the event itself, and the Declaration of Sentiments which Stanton drafted with her friends the week before the convention and read to the men and women gathered at the little Wesleyan chapel.

Reminiscences of Emily Collins. Such names as Stanton, Anthony, Stone, Gage, Blackwell, and Catt have become familiar through the years. Behind such prominent names were thousands of women and men, comprising the movement itself, who were little-known outside the pages of the *History.* Emily Collins was one of these lesser-known figures, and her reminiscences illustrate the way in which individual women, fired with a new consciousness of themselves as women, slowly began to assert themselves as political actors, first in the small circle of friends in their neighborhood, then growing to wider circles of surrounding towns, with a longer reach outward through petitions to the state legislature and affiliation with state and national suffrage associations. Emily Collins lived in a small town in western New York, but in 1848 she read about the Seneca Falls convention, studied the Declaration of Sentiments, and set to work in her own world as an agent of social change on the issue of woman's rights.

The Akron Convention of 1851. The Akron Convention was a noteworthy one in the history of the suffrage movement. The second to be held in the state of Ohio, it was presided over by Frances Dana Gage, an Ohio reformer, lecturer and writer who subsequently presided over a national covention held in Cleveland in 1853. It was this same Frances Gage who translated her concern for abolition into direct work with some five hundred freedmen on Parris Island, South Carolina, during the Civil War. It was from her observations at the Akron Convention that she wrote out, as best she could remember it, the famous "And Ain't I a Woman?" speech of Sojourner Truth.

The Newport Convention of 1869. This very brief news note from the pen of Elizabeth Stanton appeared in the short-lived publication *Revolution.* After a successful convention at Saratoga, New York, earlier in the summer, the Anthony-Stanton forces decided to invade a second upper-class summer resort at Newport, Rhode Island. Stanton clearly felt the Saratoga and Newport conventions were a new venture into unfamiliar turf, "to awaken thought among a new class of people," as she put it.

The Kansas Campaign of 1867. The 1867 action was critical in the history of the suffrage movement. In that year hopes had been raised in all segments of the woman's-rights movement that Kansas would be the first state to remove from its constitution the franchise restrictions on the grounds of sex and race. When word got out that a referendum would be put to the citizens of Kansas, the suffrage forces began an intensive campaign to arrange speakers, raise funds, and publish thousands of pamphlets to pour into Kansas. Lucy Stone and Henry Blackwell wrote optimistic letters back to the Eastern offices during their spring speaking tour, full of details that permit the reader to sense the hardiness required of the suffrage worker on tour in the Western states during these post-Civil War years.

In the spring of 1867 the suffrage leaders fully expected the Republicans and Abolitionists to give strong support to the suffrage cause in Kansas. For twenty years there had been close political and personal relationships between the abolitionist and the suffrage movement. With the Civil War behind them, the suffrage leaders felt that their time had now come. They were destined to be bitterly disappointed, for the pressure was strong within Republican ranks to assure national strength to the party by granting the vote to the Southern Negro. Republican men feared that support for the vote for women would jeopardize the chances of securing the vote for the Negro, and Southern Negro votes were needed to strengthen Republican representation in the Congress. Hence the Eastern Republicans withheld any support for the women's efforts in the Kansas campaign, beginning the long cry of "This is the Negro's hour" that was to ring through the years until the Fourteenth and Fifteenth Amendments were passed.

The failure of the suffrage referendum in Kansas was a bitter lesson in the hard facts of American party politics for the suffragists, stirring Elizabeth Stanton to an angry and memorable warning to future generations of women:

> woman must lead the way to her own enfranchisement, and work out her own salvation with a hopeful courage and determination. . . . She must not put her trust in man in this transition period, since, while regarded as his subject, his inferior, his slave, their interests must be antagonistic. [HWS II, 268]

Beneath the fine rhetoric a decision was forming in one wing of the suffrage movement: to cease relying on the Republicans alone but to seek political allies for the suffrage cause wherever they were to be found. By 1869 this issue was to split the suffrage movement for the next twenty years.

Questions and Answers Concerning Political Equality for Women. The "Introduction" to the *History of Woman Suffrage* is itself a remarkable distillation of the arguments the suffrage leaders encountered over three decades of writing and speaking against extreme opposition. In this brief essay the leaders review the major objections they have heard so repeatedly and the best of the arguments they developed in rebuttal.

Selections from the *History of Woman Suffrage*

Seneca Falls Convention

WOMAN'S RIGHTS CONVENTION.—A Convention to discuss the social, civil, and religious condition and rights of woman, will be held in the Wesleyan Chapel, at Seneca Falls, N.Y., on Wednesday and Thursday, the 19th and 20th of July, current; commencing at 10 o'clock A.M. During the first day the meeting will be exclusively for women, who are earnestly invited to attend. The public generally are invited to be present on the second day, when Lucretia Mott, of Philadelphia, and other ladies and gentlemen, will address the convention.

This call, without signature, was issued by Lucretia Mott, Martha C. Wright, Elizabeth Cady Stanton, and Mary Ann McClintock. At this time Mrs. Mott was visiting her sister Mrs. Wright, at Auburn, and attending the Yearly Meeting of Friends in Western New York. Mrs. Stanton, having recently removed from Boston to Seneca Falls, finding the most congenial associations in Quaker families, met Mrs. Mott incidentally for the first time since her residence there. They at once returned to the topic they had so often discussed, walking arm in arm in the streets of London, and Boston, "the propriety of holding a woman's convention." These four ladies, sitting round the tea-table of Richard Hunt, a prominent Friend near Waterloo, decided to put their long-talked-of resolution into action, and before the twilight deepened into night, the call was written, and sent to the *Seneca County Courier*. On Sunday morning they met in Mrs. McClintock's parlor to write their declaration, resolutions, and to consider subjects for speeches. As the convention was to assemble in three days, the time was short for such productions; but having no experience in the *modus*

From Elizabeth C. Stanton, Susan B. Anthony, and Matilda J. Gage, editors, *History of Woman Suffrage*. Rochester, New York, Charles Mann. Vol 1 (1881), pp. 67–74, 88–94, 111–117; Vol. 2 (1882), pp. 403–404, 229–268; Vol. 1, pp. 13–24.

operandi of getting up conventions, nor in that kind of literature, they were quite innocent of the herculean labors they proposed. On the first attempt to frame a resolution; to crowd a complete thought, clearly and concisely, into three lines; they felt as helpless and hopeless as if they had been suddenly asked to construct a steam engine. And the humiliating fact may as well now be recorded that before taking the initiative step, those ladies resigned themselves to a faithful perusal of various masculine productions. The reports of Peace, Temperance, and Anti-Slavery conventions were examined, but all alike seemed too tame and pacific for the inauguration of a rebellion such as the world had never before seen. They knew women had wrongs, but how to state them was the difficulty, and this was increased from the fact that they themselves were fortunately organized and conditioned; they were neither "sour old maids," "childless women," nor "divorced wives," as the newspapers declared them to be. While they had felt the insults incident to sex, in many ways, as every proud, thinking woman must, in the laws, religion, and literature of the world, and in the invidious and degrading sentiments and customs of all nations, yet they had not in their own experience endured the coarser forms of tyranny resulting from unjust laws, or association with immoral and unscrupulous men, but they had souls large enough to feel the wrongs of others, without being scarified in their own flesh.

After much delay, one of the circle took up the Declaration of 1776, and read it aloud with much spirit and emphasis, and it was at once decided to adopt the historic document, with some slight changes such as substituting "all men" for "King George." Knowing that women must have more to complain of than men under any circumstances possibly could, and seeing the Fathers had eighteen grievances, a protracted search was made through statute books, church usages, and the customs of society to find that exact number. Several well-disposed men assisted in collecting the grievances, until, with the announcement of the eighteenth, the women felt they had enough to go before the world with a good case. One youthful lord remarked, "Your grievances must be grievous indeed, when you are obliged to go to books in order to find them out."

The eventful day dawned at last, and crowds in carriages and on foot, wended their way to the Wesleyan church.

When those having charge of the Declaration, the resolutions, and several volumes of the Statutes of New York arrived on the scene, lo! the door was locked. However, an embryo Professor of Yale College was lifted through an open window to unbar the door; that done, the church was quickly filled. It had been decided to have no men present, but as they were already on the spot, and as the women who must take the responsibility of organizing the meeting, and leading the discussions, shrank from doing either, it was decided, in a hasty council round the altar, that this was an occasion when men might make themselves pre-eminently useful. It was agreed they should remain, and take the laboring oar through the Convention.

James Mott, tall and dignified, in Quaker costume, was called to the chair; Mary McClintock appointed Secretary, Frederick Douglass, Samuel Tillman, Ansel Bascom, E. W. Capron, and Thomas McClintock took part throughout in the discussions. Lucretia Mott, accustomed to public speaking in the Society of Friends, stated the objects of the Convention, and in taking a survey of the degraded condition of woman the world over, showed the importance of inaugurating some movement for her education and elevation. Elizabeth and Mary McClintock, and Mrs. Stanton, each read a well-written speech; Martha Wright read some satirical articles she had published in the daily papers answering the diatribes on woman's sphere. Ansel Bascom, who had been a member of the Constitutional Convention recently held in Albany, spoke at length on the property bill for married women, just passed the Legislature, and the discussion on woman's rights in that Convention. Samuel Tillman, a young student of law, read a series of the most exasperating statutes for women, from English and American jurists, all reflecting the *tender mercies* of men toward their wives, in taking care of their property and protecting them in their civil rights.

The Declaration having been freely discussed by many present, was re-read by Mrs. Stanton, and with some slight amendments adopted.

Declaration of Sentiments. When, in the course of human events, it becomes necessary for one portion of the family of man to assume among the people of the earth a position different from that which they have hitherto occupied, but one to which the laws of nature and of nature's God entitle them, a decent respect to the opinions of mankind requires that they should declare the causes that impel them to such a course.

We hold these truths to be self-evident: that all men and women are created equal; that they are endowed by their Creator with certain inalienable rights; that among these are life, liberty, and the pursuit of happiness; that to secure these rights governments are instituted, deriving their just powers from the consent of the governed. Whenever any form of government becomes destructive of these ends, it is the right of those who suffer from it to refuse allegiance to it, and to insist upon the institution of a new government, laying its foundation on such principles, and organizing its powers in such form, as to them shall seem most likely to effect their safety and happiness. Prudence, indeed, will dictate that governments long established should not be changed for light and transient causes; and accordingly all experience hath shown that mankind are more disposed to suffer, while evils are sufferable, than to right themselves by abolishing the forms to which they were accustomed. But when a long train of abuses and usurpations, pursuing invariably the same object evinces a design to reduce them under absolute despotism, it is their duty to throw off such government, and to provide new guards for their future security. Such has been the patient sufferance of the women under this government, and such is now the necessity which constrains them to demand the equal station to which they are entitled.

The history of mankind is a history of repeated injuries and usurpations on the part of man toward woman, having in direct object the establishment of an absolute tyranny over her. To prove this, let facts be submitted to a candid world.

He has never permitted her to exercise her inalienable right to the elective franchise.

He has compelled her to submit to laws, in the formation of which she had no voice.

He has withheld from her rights which are given to the most ignorant and degraded men—both natives and foreigners.

Having deprived her of this first right of a citizen, the elective franchise, thereby leaving her without representation in the halls of legislation, he has oppressed her on all sides.

He has made her, if married, in the eye of the law, civilly dead.

He has taken from her all right in property, even to the wages she earns.

He has made her, morally, an irresponsible being, as she can commit many crimes with impunity, provided they be done in the presence of her husband. In the covenant of marriage, she is compelled to promise obedience to her husband, he becoming, to all intents and purposes, her master—the law giving him power to deprive her of her liberty, and to administer chastisement.

He has so framed the laws of divorce, as to what shall be the proper causes, and in case of separation, to whom the guardianship of the children shall be given, as to be wholly regardless of the happiness of women—the law, in all cases, going upon a false supposition of the supremacy of man, and giving all power into his hands.

After depriving her of all rights as a married woman, if single, and the owner of property, he has taxed her to support a government which recognizes her only when her property can be made profitable to it.

He has monopolized nearly all the profitable employments, and from those she is permitted to follow, she receives but a scanty remuneration. He closes against her all the avenues to wealth and distinction which he considers most honorable to himself. As a teacher of theology, medicine, or law, she is not known.

He has denied her the facilities for obtaining a thorough education, all colleges being closed against her.

He allows her in Church, as well as State, but a subordinate position, claiming Apostolic authority for her exclusion from the ministry, and, with some exceptions, from any public participation in the affairs of the Church.

He has created a false public sentiment by giving to the world a different code of morals for men and women, by which moral delinquencies which exclude women from society, are not only tolerated, but deemed of little account in man.

He has usurped the prerogative of Jehovah himself, claiming it as his right to assign for her a sphere of action, when that belongs to her conscience and to her God.

He has endeavored, in every way that he could, to destroy her confidence in her own powers, to lessen her self-respect, and to make her willing to lead a dependent and abject life.

Now, in view of this entire disfranchisement of one-half the people of this country, their social and religious degradation—in view of the unjust laws above mentioned, and because women do feel themselves aggrieved, oppressed, and fraudulently deprived of their most sacred rights, we insist that they have immediate admission to all the rights and privileges which belong to them as citizens of the United States.

In entering upon the great work before us, we anticipate no small amount of misconception, misrepresentation, and ridicule; but we shall use every instrumentality within our power to effect our object. We shall employ agents, circulate tracts, petition the State and National legislatures, and endeavor to enlist the pulpit and the press in our behalf. We hope this Convention will be followed by a series of Conventions embracing every part of the country.

The following resolutions were discussed by Lucretia Mott, Thomas and Mary Ann McClintock, Amy Post, Catharine A. F. Stebbins, and others, and were adopted:

WHEREAS, The great precept of nature is conceded to be, that "man shall pursue his own true and substantial happiness." Blackstone in his Commentaries remarks, that this law of Nature being coeval with mankind, and dictated by God himself, is of course superior in obligation to any other. It is binding over all the globe, in all countries and at all times; no human laws are of any validity if contrary to this, and such of them as are valid, derive all their force, and all their validity, and all their authority, mediately and immediately, from this original; therefore,

Resolved, That such laws as conflict, in any way, with the true and substantial happiness of woman, are contrary to the great precept of nature and of no validity, for this is "superior in obligation to any other."

Resolved, That all laws which prevent woman from occupying such a station in society as her conscience shall dictate, or which place her in a position inferior to that of man, are contrary to the great precept of nature, and therefore of no force or authority.

Resolved, That woman is man's equal—was intended to be so by the Creator, and the highest good of the race demands that she should be recognized as such.

Resolved, That the women of this country ought to be enlightened in regard to the laws under which they live, that they may no longer publish their degradation by declaring themselves satisfied with their present position, nor their ignorance, by asserting that they have all the rights they want.

Resolved, That inasmuch as man, while claiming for himself intellectual superiority, does accord to woman moral superiority, it is pre-eminently his duty to encourage her to speak and teach, as she has an opportunity, in all religious assemblies.

Resolved, That the same amount of virtue, delicacy, and refinement of behavior that is required of woman in the social state, should also be required of man, and the same transgressions should be visited with equal severity on both man and woman.

Resolved, That the objection of indelicacy and impropriety, which is so often brought against woman when she addresses a public audience, comes with a very ill-grace from those who encourage, by their attendance, her appearance on the stage, in the concert, or in feats of the circus.

Resolved, That woman has too long rested satisfied in the circumscribed limits which corrupt customs and a perverted application of the Scriptures have marked out for her, and that it is time she should move in the enlarged sphere which her great Creator has assigned her.

Resolved, That it is the duty of the women of this country to secure to themselves their sacred right to the elective franchise.

Resolved, That the equality of human rights results necessarily from the fact of the identity of the race in capabilities and responsibilities.

Resolved, therefore, That, being invested by the Creator with the same capabilities, and the same consciousness of responsibility for their exercise, it is demonstrably the right and duty of woman, equally with man, to promote every righteous cause by every righteous means; and especially in regard to the great subjects of morals and religion, it is self-evidently her right to participate with her brother in teaching them, both in private and in public, by writing and by speaking, by any instrumentalities proper to be used, and in any assemblies proper to be held; and this being a self-evident truth growing out of the divinely implanted principles of human nature, any custom or authority adverse to it, whether modern or wearing the hoary sanction of antiquity, is to be regarded as a self-evident falsehood, and at war with mankind.

At the last session Lucretia Mott offered and spoke to the following resolution:

Resolved, That the speedy success of our cause depends upon the zealous and untiring efforts of both men and women, for the overthrow of the monopoly of the pulpit, and for the securing to woman an equal participation with men in the various trades, professions, and commerce.

The only resolution that was not unanimously adopted was the ninth, urging the women of the country to secure to themselves the elective franchise. Those who took part in the debate feared a demand for the right to vote would defeat others they deemed more rational, and make the whole movement ridiculous.

But Mrs. Stanton and Frederick Douglass seeing that the power to choose rulers and make laws, was the right by which all others could be secured, persistently advocated the resolution, and at last carried it by a small majority.

Thus it will be seen that the Declaration and resolutions in the very first Convention, demanded all the most radical friends of the movement have since claimed—such as equal rights in the universities, in the trades, and professions; the right to vote; to share in all political offices, honors, and emoluments; to complete equality in marriage, to personal freedom, property, wages, children; to make contracts; to sue, and be sued; and to testify in courts of justice. At this time the condition of married women under the Common Law, was nearly as degraded as that of the slave on the Southern plantation. The Convention continued through two entire days, and late into the evenings. The deepest interest was manifested to its close.

The proceedings were extensively published, unsparingly ridiculed by the press, and denounced by the pulpit, much to the surprise and chagrin of the leaders. Being deeply in earnest, and believing their demands pre-eminently wise and just, they were wholly unprepared to find themselves the target for the jibes and jeers of the nation. The Declaration was signed by one hundred men, and women, many of whom withdrew their names as soon as the storm of ridicule began to break. The comments of the press were carefully preserved, and it is curious to see that the same old arguments, and objections rife at the start, are reproduced by the press of to-day. But the brave protests sent out from this Convention touched a responsive chord in the hearts of women all over the country.

Reminiscences of Emily Collins

I was born and lived almost forty years in South Bristol, Ontario County—one of the most secluded spots in Western New York; but from the earliest dawn of reason I pined for that freedom of thought and action that was then denied to all womankind. I revolted in spirit against the customs of society and the laws of the State that crushed my aspirations and debarred me from the pursuit of almost every object worthy of an intelligent, rational mind. But not until that meeting at Seneca Falls in 1848, of the pioneers in the cause, gave this feeling of unrest form and voice, did I take action. Then I summoned a few women in our neighborhood together and formed an Equal Suffrage Society, and sent petitions to our Legislature; but our efforts were little known beyond our circle, as we were in communication with no person or newspaper. Yet there was enough of wrong in our narrow horizon to rouse some thought in the minds of all.

In those early days a husband's supremacy was often enforced in the rural districts by corporeal chastisement, and it was considered by most people as quite right and proper—as much so as the correction of refractory children in like manner. I remember in my own neighborhood a man who was a Methodist class-leader and exhorter, and one who was esteemed a worthy citizen, who, every few weeks, gave his wife a beating with his horsewhip. He said it was necessary, in order to keep her in subjection, and because she scolded so much. Now this wife, surrounded by six or seven little children, whom she must wash, dress, feed, and attend to day and night, was obliged to spin and weave cloth for all the garments of the family. She had to milk the cows, make butter and cheese, do all the cooking, washing, making, and mending for the family, and, with the pains of maternity forced upon her every eighteen months, was whipped by her pious husband, "because she scolded." And pray, why should he not have chastised her? The laws made it his privilege—and the Bible, as interpreted, made it his duty. It is true, women repined at their hard lot; but it was thought to be fixed by a divine decree, for "The man shall rule over thee," and "Wives, be subject to your husbands," and "Wives, submit yourselves unto your husbands as unto the Lord," caused them to consider their fate inevitable, and to feel that it would be contravening God's law to resist it. It is ever thus; where Theology enchains the soul, the Tyrant enslaves the body. But can any one, who has any knowledge of the laws that govern our being—of heredity and pre-natal influences —be astonished that our jails and prisons are filled with criminals, and our hospitals with sickly specimens of humanity? As long as the mothers of the race are subject to such unhappy conditions, it can never be materially improved. Men exhibit some common sense in breeding all animals except those of their own species.

All through the Anti-Slavery struggle, every word of denunciation of the wrongs of the Southern slave, was, I felt, equally applicable to the wrongs of my own sex. Every argument for the emancipation of the colored man, was equally one for that of woman; and I was surprised that all Abolitionists did not see the similarity in the condition of the two classes. I read, with intense interest, everything that indicated an awakening of public or private thought to the idea that woman did not occupy her rightful position in the organization of society; and, when I read the lectures of Ernestine L. Rose and the writings of Margaret Fuller, and found that other women entertained the same thoughts that had been seething in my own brain, and realized that I stood not alone, how my heart bounded with joy! The arguments of that distinguished jurist, Judge Hurlburt, encouraged me to hope that men would ultimately see the justice of our cause, and concede to women their natural rights.

I hailed with gladness any aspiration of women toward an enlargement of their sphere of action. . . .

But, it was the proceedings of the Convention, in 1848, at Seneca Falls, that first gave a direction to the efforts of the many women, who began to feel the degradation of their subject condition, and its baneful effects upon the human race. They then saw the necessity for associated action, in order to obtain the elective franchise, the only key that would unlock the doors of their prison. I wrote to Miss Sarah C. Owen, Secretary of the Women's Protective Union, at Rochester, as to the line of procedure that had been proposed there. In reply, under date of October 1, 1848, she says:

Your letter has just reached me, and with much pleasure I reply to the echo of inquiry, beyond the bounds of those personally associated with us in this enterprise. It is indeed encouraging to hear a voice from South Bristol in such perfect unison with our own.

Possibly, extracts from my next letter to Miss Owen, dated Oct. 23, 1848, will give you the best idea of the movement:

I should have acknowledged the receipt of yours of the 1st inst. earlier, but wished to report somewhat of progress whenever I should write. Our prospects here are brightening. Every lady of any worth or intelligence adopts unhesitatingly our view, and concurs in our measures. On the 19th inst. we met and organized a Woman's Equal Rights Union. Living in the country, where the population is sparse, we are consequently few; but hope to make up in zeal and energy for our lack of numbers. We breathe a freer, if not a purer atmosphere here among the mountains, than do the dwellers in cities,—have more independence,—are less subject to the despotism of fashion, and are less absorbed with dress and amusements. . . . A press entirely devoted to our cause seems indispensable. If there is none such, can you tell me of any paper that advocates our claims more warmly than the *North Star*? A lecturer in the field would be most desirable; but how to raise funds to sustain one is the question. I never really wished for Aladdin's lamp till now. Would to Heaven that women could be persuaded to use the funds they acquire by their sewing-circles and fairs, in trying to raise their own condition above that of "infants, idiots, and lunatics," with whom our statutes class them, instead of spending the money in decorating their churches, or sustaining a clergy, the most of whom are striving to rivet the chains still closer that bind, not only our own sex, but the oppressed of every class and color.

The elective franchise is now the one object for which we

must labor; that once attained, all the rest will be easily acquired. Moral Reform and Temperance Societies may be multiplied *ad infinitum*, but they have about the same effect upon the evils they seek to cure, as clipping the top of a hedge would have toward extirpating it. Please forward me a copy of the petition for suffrage. We will engage to do all we can, not only in our own town, but in the adjoining ones of Richmond, East Bloomfield, Canandaigua, and Naples. I have promises of aid from people of influence in obtaining signatures. In the meantime we wish to disseminate some able work upon the enfranchisement of women. We wish to present our Assemblyman elect, whoever he may be, with some work of this kind, and solicit his candid attention to the subject. People are more willing to be convinced by the calm perusal of an argument, than in a personal discussion. . . .

Our Society was composed of some fifteen or twenty ladies, and we met once in two weeks, in each other's parlors, alternately, for discussion and interchange of ideas. I was chosen President; Mrs. Sophia Allen, Vice-President; Mrs. Horace Pennell, Treasurer; and one of several young ladies who were members was Secretary. Horace Pennell, Esq., and his wife were two of our most earnest helpers. We drafted a petition to the Legislature to grant women the right of suffrage, and obtained the names of sixty-two of the most intelligent people, male and female, in our own and adjoining towns, and sent it to our Representative in Albany. It was received by the Legislature as something absurdly ridiculous, and laid upon the table. We introduced the question into the Debating Clubs, that were in those days such popular institutions in the rural districts, and in every way sought to agitate the subject. I found a great many men, especially those of the better class, disposed to accord equal rights to our sex. And, now, as the highest tribute that I can pay to the memory of a husband, I may say that during our companionship of thirty-five years, I was most cordially sustained by mine, in my advocacy of equal rights to women. Amongst my own sex, I found too many on whom ages of repression had wrought their natural effect, and whose ideas and aspirations were narrowed down to the confines of "woman's sphere," beyond whose limits it was not only impious, but infamous to tread. "Woman's sphere" *then*, was to discharge the duties of a housekeeper, ply the needle, and teach a primary or ladies' school. From press, and pulpit, and platform, she was taught that "to be unknown was her highest praise," that "dependence was her best protection," and "her weakness her sweetest charm." She needed only sufficient intelligence to comprehend her husband's superiority, and to obey him in all things. It is not surprising, then, that I as often heard the terms "strong-minded" and "masculine" as opprobious epithets used against progressive women, by their own sex as by the other; another example only of the stultifying effect of subjection, upon the mind, exactly paralleled by the Southern slaves, amongst many of whom the strongest term of contempt that could be used was *"Free Nigger."* Our Equal Rights Association continued to hold its meetings for somewhat over a year, and they were at last suspended on account of bad weather and the difficulty of coming together in the country districts. We, however, continued to send petitions to the Legislature for the removal of woman's disabilities.

From 1858 to 1869 my home was in Rochester, N. Y. There, by brief newspaper articles and in other ways, I sought to influence public sentiment in favor of this fundamental reform. In 1868 a Society was organized there for the reformation of abandoned women. At one of its meetings I endeavored to show how futile all their efforts would be, while women, by the laws of the land, were made a subject class; that only by enfranchising woman and permitting her a more free and lucrative range of employments, could they hope to suppress the "social evil." My remarks produced some agitation in the meeting and some newspaper criticisms. In Rochester, I found many pioneers in the cause of Woman Suffrage, and from year to year we petitioned our Legislature for it.

Since 1869 I have been a citizen of Louisiana. Here, till recently, political troubles engrossed the minds of men to the exclusion of every other consideration. They glowed with fiery indignation at being, themselves, deprived of the right of suffrage, or at having their votes annulled, and regarded it as an intolerable outrage; yet, at the same time, they denied it to all women, many of whom valued the elective franchise as highly, and felt as intensely, as did men, the injustice that withheld it from them. In 1879, when the Convention met to frame a new Constitution for the State, we strongly petitioned it for an enlargement of our civil rights and for the ballot. Mrs. Elizabeth L. Saxon was indefatigable in her efforts, and went before the Convention in person and plead our cause. But the majority of the members thought there were cogent reasons for not granting our petitions; but they made women eligible to all school offices—an indication that Louisiana will not be the last State in the Union to deny women their inalienable rights.

The Akron Convention

Sojourner Truth, Mrs. Stowe's "Lybian Sibyl," was present at this Convention. Some of our younger readers may not know that Sojourner Truth was once a slave in the State of New York, and carries to-day as many marks of the diabolism of slavery, as ever scarred the back of a victim in Mississippi. Though she can neither read nor write, she is a woman of rare intelligence and common-sense on all subjects. She is still living, at Battle Creek, Michigan, though now 110 years old. Although the exalted character and personal appearance of this noble woman have been often portrayed, and her brave deeds and words many times re-hearsed, yet we give the following graphic picture of Sojourner's appearance in one of the most stormy sessions of the Convention, from reminiscences by Frances D. Gage.

Sojourner Truth. The leaders of the movement trembled on seeing a tall, gaunt black woman in a gray dress and white turban, surmounted with an uncouth sun-bonnet, march deliberately into the church, walk with the air of a queen up the aisle, and take her seat upon the pulpit steps. A buzz of disapprobation was heard all over the house, and there fell on the listening ear, "An abolition affair!" "Woman's rights and niggers!" "I told you so!" "Go it, darkey!"

I chanced on that occasion to wear my first laurels in public life as president of the meeting. At my request order was restored, and the business of the Convention went on. Morning, afternoon, and evening exercises came and went. Through all these sessions old Sojourner, quiet and reticent as the "Lybian Statue," sat crouched against the wall on the corner of the pulpit stairs, her sun-bonnet shading her eyes, her elbows on her knees, her chin resting upon her broad, hard palms. At intermission she was busy selling the "Life of Sojourner Truth," a narrative of her own strange and adventurous life. Again and again, timorous and trembling ones came to me and said, with earnestness, "Don't let her speak, Mrs. Gage, it will ruin us. Every newspaper in the land will have our cause mixed up with abolition and niggers, and we shall be utterly denounced." My only answer was, "We shall see when the time comes."

The second day the work waxed warm. Methodist, Baptist, Episcopal, Presbyterian, and Universalist ministers came in to hear and discuss the resolutions presented. One claimed superior rights and privileges for man, on the ground of "superior intellect"; another, because of the "manhood of Christ; if God had desired the equality of woman, He would have given some token of His will through the birth, life, and death of the Saviour." Another gave us a theological view of the "sin of our first mother."

There were very few women in those days who dared to "speak in meeting"; and the august teachers of the people were seemingly getting the better of us, while the boys in the galleries, and the sneerers among the pews, were hugely enjoying the discomfiture, as they supposed, of the "strongminded." Some of the tender-skinned friends were on the point of losing dignity, and the atmosphere betokened a storm. When, slowly from her seat in the corner rose Sojourner Truth, who, till now, had scarcely lifted her head. "Don't let her speak!" gasped half a dozen in my ear. She moved slowly and solemnly to the front, laid her old bonnet at her feet, and turned her great speaking eyes to me. There was a hissing sound of disapprobation above and below. I rose and announced "Sojourner Truth," and begged the audience to keep silence for a few moments.

The tumult subsided at once, and every eye was fixed on this almost Amazon form, which stood nearly six feet high, head erect, and eyes piercing the upper air like one in a dream. At her first word there was a profound hush. She spoke in deep tones, which, though not loud, reached every ear in the house, and away through the throng at the doors and windows.

"Wall, chilern, whar dar is so much racket dar must be somethin' out o' kilter. I tink dat 'twixt de niggers of de Souf and de womin at de Norf, all talkin' 'bout rights, de white men will be in a fix pretty soon. But what's all dis here talkin' 'bout?

"Dat man ober dar say dat womin needs to be helped into carriages, and lifted ober ditches, and to hab de best place everywhar. Nobody eber helps me into carriages, or ober mud-puddles, or gibs me any best place!" And raising herself to her full height, and her voice to a pitch like rolling thunder, she asked, "And a'n't I a woman? Look at me! Look at my arm! (and she bared her right arm to the shoulder, showing her tremendous muscular power). I have ploughed, and planted, and gathered into barns, and no man could head me! And a'n't I a woman? I could work as much and eat as much as a man—when I could get it— and bear de lash as well! And a'n't I a woman? I have borne thirteen chilern, and seen 'em mos' all sold off to slavery, and when I cried out with my mother's grief, none but Jesus heard me! And a'n't I a woman?

"Den dey talks 'bout dis ting in de head; what dis dey call it?" ("Intellect," whispered some one near.) "Dat's it, honey. What's dat got to do wid womin's rights or nigger's rights? If my cup won't hold but a pint, and yours holds a quart, wouldn't ye be mean not to let me have my little half-measure full?" And she pointed her significant finger, and sent a keen glance at the minister who had made the argument. The cheering was long and loud.

"Den dat little man in black dar, he say women can't have as much rights as men, 'cause Christ wan't a woman! Whar did your Christ come from?" Rolling thunder couldn't have stilled that crowd, as did those deep, wonderful tones, as she stood there with outstretched arms and eyes of fire. Raising her voice still louder, she repeated, "Whar did your Christ come from? From God and a woman! Man had nothin' to do wid Him." Oh, what a rebuke that was to that little man.

Turning again to another objector, she took up the defense of Mother Eve. I can not follow her through it all. It was pointed, and witty, and solemn; eliciting at almost every sentence deafening applause; and she ended by asserting: "If de fust woman God ever made was strong enough to turn the world upside down all alone, dese women togedder (and she glanced her eye over the platform) ought to be able to turn it back, and get it right side up again! And now dey is asking to do it, de men better let 'em." Long-continued cheering greeted this. " 'Bleeged to ye for hearin' on me, and now ole Sojourner han't got nothin' more to say."

Amid roars of applause, she returned to her corner, leaving more than one of us with streaming eyes, and hearts beating with gratitude. She had taken us up in her strong arms and carried us safely over the slough of difficulty turning the whole tide in our favor. I have never in my life seen anything like the magical influence that subdued the mobbish spirit of the day, and turned the sneers and jeers of an excited crowd into notes of respect and admiration. Hundreds rushed up to shake hands with her, and congratulate the glorious old mother, and bid her God-speed on her mission of "testifyin' agin concerning the wickedness of this 'ere people."

The Newport Convention

Susan B. Anthony having decided that neither age, color, sex, or previous condition could shield any one from this agitation—that neither the frosts of winter nor the heats of summer could afford its champions any excuse for halting on the way, our forces were commanded to be in marching order on the 25th of August, to besiege the "butterflies of fashion" in Newport. Having gleefully chased butterflies in our young days on our way to school, we thought it might be as well to chase them in our old age on the way to heaven. So, obeying orders, we sailed across the Sound one bright moonlight night with a gay party of the "disfranchised," and found ourselves quartered on the enemy the next morning as the sun rose in all its resplendent glory. Although trunk after trunk—not of gossamers, laces, and flowers, but of Suffrage ammunition, speeches, resolutions, petitions, tracts, John Stuart Mill's last work, and folios of *The Revolution* had been slowly carried up the winding stairs of the Atlantic—the brave men and fair women, who had tripped the light fantastic toe until the midnight hours, slept heedlessly on, wholly unaware that twelve apartments were already filled with invaders of the strong-minded editors, reporters, and the Hutchinson family to the third and fourth generation.

Suffice it to say the Convention continued through two days with the usual amount of good and bad speaking and debating, strong and feeble resolutions, fair and unfair reporting—but, with all its faults, an improvement on the general run of conventions called by the stronger sex. We say this not in a spirit of boasting, but with a heart overflowing with pity for the "men of the period." The chief speakers were Paulina Wright Davis, Isabella Beecher Hooker, Theodore Tilton, Francis D. Moulton, Rev. Phebe Hanaford, Lillie Devereux Blake, Elizabeth R. Churchill, the Hon. Mr. Stillman, of Rhode Island; and the editor and proprietor of *The Revolution*. The occasion was enlivened with the stirring songs of the Hutchinsons, and a reading by Mrs. Sarah Fisher Ames, the distinguished artist who moulded the bust of Abraham Lincoln which now adorns the rooms of the Union League.

The audience throughout the sittings of the Convention was large, fashionable, and as enthusiastic as the state of the weather would permit. From the numbers of *The Revolution* and John Stuart Mill's new work sold at the door, it is evident that much interest was roused on the question. We can say truly that we never received a more quiet and respectful hearing; and, from many private conversations with ladies and gentlemen of influence, we feel assured that we have done much by our gatherings in Saratoga and Newport to awaken thought among a new class of people. The *ennui* and utter vacuity of a life of mere pleasure is fast urging fashionable women to something better, and, when they do awake to the magnitude and far-reaching consequences of woman's enfranchisement, they will be the most enthusiastic workers for its accomplishment.

The Kansas Campaign of 1867

As Kansas was the historic ground where Liberty fought her first victorious battles with Slavery, and consecrated that soil forever to the freedom of the black race, so was it the first State where the battle for woman's enfranchisement was waged and lost for a generation. There never was a more hopeful interest concentrated on the legislation of any single State, than when Kansas submitted the two propositions to her people to take the words "white" and "male" from her Constitution.

Those awake to the dignity and power of the ballot in the hands of all classes, to the inspiring thought of self-government, were stirred as never before, both in Great Britain and America, upon this question. Letters from John Stuart Mill and other friends, with warm words of encouragement, were read to thousands of audiences, and published in journals throughout the State. Eastern women who went there to speak started with the full belief that their hopes so long deferred were at last to be realized. Some even made arrangements for future homes on that green spot where at last the sons and daughters of earth were to stand equal before the law. With no greater faith did the crusaders of old seize their shields and start on their perilous journey to wrest from the infidel the Holy Sepulcher, than did these defenders of a sacred principle enter Kansas, and with hope sublime consecrate themselves to labor for woman's freedom; to roll off of her soul the mountains of sorrow and superstition that had held her in bondage to false creeds, and codes, and customs for centuries. There was a solemn earnestness in the speeches of all who labored in that campaign. Each heart was thrilled with the thought that the youngest civilization in the world was about to establish a government based on the divine idea —the equality of all mankind—proclaimed by Jesus of Nazareth, and echoed by the patriots who watched the dawn of the natal day of our Republic. Here at last the mothers of the race, the most important actors in the grand drama of human progress were for the first time to stand the peers of men.

These women firmly believed that Republicans and Abolitionists who had advocated their cause for years would aid them in all possible efforts to carry the Constitutional Amendment that was to enfranchise the women of the State. They looked confidently for encouragement, and inspiring editorials in certain Eastern journals. With Horace Greeley at the head of the New York Tribune, Theodore Tilton of the Independent, and Wendell Phillips of the Anti-Slavery Standard, they felt they had a strong force in the press of the East to rouse the men of Kansas to their duty. But, alas! they all preserved a stolid silence, and the Liberals of the State were in a measure paralyzed by their example. Though the amendment to take the word "male" from the Constitution was a Republican measure, signed by a Republican Governor, and advocated by leading men of that party throughout the campaign, yet the Republican party, as such, the Abolitionists and black men were all hostile to the proposition, because they said to agitate the woman's amendment would defeat negro suffrage.

Eastern politicians warned the Republicans of Kansas that "negro suffrage" was a party measure in national politics, and that they must not entangle themselves with the "woman question." On all sides came up the cry, this is "the negro's hour." Though the Republican State Central Committee adopted a resolution leaving all their party speakers free to express their individual sentiments, yet they selected men to canvass the State, who were known to be unscrupulous and disreputable, and violently opposed to woman suffrage. The Democratic party was opposed to both amendments and to the new law on temperance, which it was supposed the women would actively support.

The Germans in their Conventions passed a resolution against the new law that required the liquor dealers to get the signatures of one-half the women, as well as the men, to their petitions before the authorities could grant them license. In suffrage for women they saw rigid Sunday laws and the suppression of their beer gardens. The liquor dealers throughout the State were bitter and hostile to the woman's amendment. Though the temperance party had passed a favorable resolution in their State Convention, yet some of their members were averse to all affiliations with the dreaded question, as to them, what the people might drink seemed a subject of greater importance than a fundamental principle of human rights. Intelligent black men, believing the sophistical statements of politicians, that their rights were imperiled by the agitation of woman suffrage, joined the opposition. Thus the campaign in Kansas was as protracted as many sided.

From April until November, the women of Kansas, and those who came to help them, worked with indomitable energy and perseverance. Besides undergoing every physical hardship, traveling night and day in carriages, open wagons, over miles and miles of the unfrequented prairies, climbing divides, and through deep ravines, speaking in depots, unfinished barns, mills, churches, schoolhouses, and the open air, on the very borders of civilization, wherever two or three dozen voters could be assembled.

Henry B. Blackwell and Lucy Stone opened the campaign

in April. The following letters show how hopeful they were
of success, and how enthusiastically they labored to that end.
Even the New York *Tribune* prophesied victory.

AT GOV. ROBINSON'S HOUSE, FOUR MILES NORTH OF
LAWRENCE, KANSAS, *April*, 5, 1867.

Dear Mrs. Stanton:

We report good news! After half a day's earnest debate,
the Convention at Topeka, by an almost unanimous vote,
refused to separate "the two questions" male and white. A
delegation from Lawrence came up specially to get the woman
dropped. The good God upset a similar delegation from
Leavenworth bent on the same object, and prevented them
from reaching Topeka at all. Gov. Robinson, Gov. Root, Col.
Wood, Gen. Larimer, Col. Ritchie, and "the old guard" generally were on hand. Our coming out did good. Lucy spoke
with all her old force and fire. Mrs. Nichols was there—a
strong list of permanent officers was nominated—and a State
Impartial Suffrage Association was organized. The right men
were put upon the committees, and I do not believe that the
Negro Suffrage men can well bolt or back out now.

The effect is wonderful. Papers which had been ridiculing
woman suffrage and sneering at "Sam Wood's Convention"
are now on our side. We have made the present Gov. Crawford President of the Association, Lieut.-Gov. Green Vice-
President. Have appointed a leading man in every judicial district member of the Executive Committee, and have some of
the leading Congregational, Old School, and New School Presbyterian ministers committed for both questions; have already
secured a majority of the newspapers of the State, and if Lucy
and I succeed in "getting up steam" as we hope in Lawrence,
Wyandotte, Leavenworth, and Atchison, the woman and the
negro will rise or fall together, and shrewd politicians say that
with proper effort we shall carry both next fall. . . .

We are announced to speak every night but Sundays from
April 7 to May 5 inclusive. We shall have to travel from
twenty to forty miles per day. If our voices and health hold
out, Col. Wood says the State is safe. We had a rousing convention—three sessions—at Topeka, and a crowded meeting
the night following. We find a very strong feeling against
Col. S. N. Wood among politicians, but they all respect and
dread him. He has warmer friends and bitterer enemies than

almost any man in the State. But he is true as steel. My judgment of men is rarely deceived, and I pronounce S. N. Wood
a great man and a political genius. Gov. Robinson is a masterly tactician, cool, wary, cautious, decided, and brave as a
lion. These two men alone would suffice to save Kansas. But
when you add the other good and true men who are already
pledged, and the influences which have been combined, I
think you will see next fall an avalanche vote—"the caving
in of the mighty sandbank" your husband once predicted on
a similar occasion.

Now, Mrs. Stanton, you and Susan and Fred. Douglass
must come to this State early next September; you must come
prepared to make *sixty speeches* each. You must leave your
notes *behind you.* These people won't have written sermons.
And you don't want notes. You are a natural orator, and
these people will give you inspiration! Everything has con-
spired to help us in this State. Gov. Robinson and Sam.
Wood have quietly set a ball in motion which nobody in
Kansas is now strong enough to stop. Politicians' hair here is
fairly on end. But the fire is in the prairie behind them, and
they are getting out their matches in self-defense to fire their
foreground. This is a glorious country, Mrs. S., and a glorious
people. If we succeed here, it will be the State of the Future.

> With kind regards,   Henry B. Blackwell

P.S.—So you see we have the State Convention committed
to the right side, and I do believe we shall carry it. All the old
settlers are for it. It is only the later comers who say, "If I
were a black man I should not want the woman question
hitched to me." These men tell what their wives have done,
and then ask, shall such women be left without a vote?

> L. S.

> D. R. ANTHONY'S HOUSE, LEAVENWORTH,
> April 10, 1867

Dear Mrs. Stanton:

We came here just in the nick of time. The papers were
laughing at "Sam Wood's Convention," the call for which
was in the papers with the names of Beecher, Tilton, Ben
Wade, Gratz Brown, E. C. Stanton, Anna Dickinson, Lucy
Stone, etc., as persons expected or invited to be at the convention. The papers said: "This is one of Sam's shabbiest

tricks. Not one of these persons will be present, and he knows it," etc., etc. Our arrival set a buzz going, and when I announced you and Susan and Aunt Fanny for the fall, they began to say "they guessed the thing would carry." Gov. Robinson said he could not go to the Topeka Convention, for he had a lawsuit involving $1,000 that was to come off that very day, but we talked the matter over with him, showed him what a glorious hour it was for Kansas, etc., etc., and he soon concluded to get the suit put off and go to the convention. Ex-Gov. Root, of Wyandotte, joined with him and us, though he had not intended to go. We went to Topeka; and the day and evening before the convention, pulled every wire and set every honest trap. Gov. Robinson has a long head, and he arranged the "platform" so shrewdly, carefully using the term "impartial," which he said meant right, and we must make them use it, so that there would be no occasion for any other State Association. In this previous meeting, the most prominent men of the State were made officers of the permanent organization. When the platform was read, with the names of the officers, and the morning's discussion was over, everybody then felt that the ball was set right. But in the P.M. came a Methodist minister and a lawyer from Lawrence as delegates, "instructed" to use the word "impartial," "as it had been used for the last two years," to make but one issue, and to drop the woman. The lawyer said, "If I was a negro, I would not want the woman hitched on to my skirts," etc. He made a mean speech. Mrs. Nichols and I came down upon him, and the whole convention, except the Methodist, was against him. The vote was taken whether to drop the woman, and only the little lawyer from Lawrence, with a hole in his coat and only one shoe on, voted against the woman. After that it was all one way. The papers all came out right, I mean the Topeka papers. One editor called on us, said we need not mention that he had called, but he wanted to assure us that he had always been right on this question. That the mean articles in his paper had been written by a subordinate in his office in his absence, etc. That the paper was fully committed, etc., etc. That is a fair specimen of the way all the others have done, till we got to this place. Here the Republicans had decided to drop the woman, Anthony with the others, and I think they are only waiting to see the result of our meetings, to announce their decision. But the Democrats all over the State are preparing to take us up. They are a small minority, with nothing to lose, and utterly unscrupulous, while all who will work with Sam Wood will work with anybody. I fully expect we shall carry the State. But it will be necessary to have a good force here in the fall, and you will have to come. Our meetings are everywhere crowded to overflowing, and in every case the papers speak well of them. We have meetings for every night till the 4th of May. By that time we shall be well tired out. But we shall see the country, and I hope have done some good. There is no such love of principle here as I expected to find. Each man goes for himself, and "the devil take the hindmost." The women here are grand, and it will be a shame past all expression if they don't get the right to vote. One woman in Wyandotte said she carried petitions all through the town for female suffrage, and not one woman in ten refused to sign. Another in Lawrence said they sent up two large petitions from there. So they have been at the Legislature, like the heroes they really are, and it is not possible for the husbands of such women to back out, though they have sad lack of principle and a terrible desire for office.

                                                        Yours,   L. S.

· · ·

Junction City, Kansas, April 21, 1867

Dear Friends, E. C. Stanton and Susan B. Anthony:

You will be glad to know that Lucy and I are going over the length and breadth of this State speaking every day, and sometimes twice, journeying from twenty-five to forty miles daily, sometimes in a carriage and sometimes in an open wagon, with or without springs. We climb hills and dash down ravines, ford creeks, and ferry over rivers, rattle across limestone ledges, struggle through muddy bottoms, fight the high winds on the high rolling upland prairies, and address the most astonishing (and astonished) audiences in the most extraordinary places. To-night it may be a log school house, tomorrow a stone church; next day a store with planks for seats, and in one place, if it had not rained, we should have held forth in an unfinished court house, with only four stone walls but no roof whatever.

The people are a queer mixture of roughness and intelligence, recklessness, and conservatism. One swears at women who want to wear the breeches; another wonders whether we ever heard of a fellow named Paul; a third is not going to put women on an equality with niggers. One woman told Lucy that no decent woman would be running over the country talking nigger and woman. Her brother told Lucy that "he had had a woman who was under the sod, but that if she had ever said she wanted to vote he would have pounded her to death!"

The fact is, however, that we have on our side all the shrewdest politicians and all the best class of men and women in this State. Our meetings are doing much towards organizing and concentrating public sentiment in our favor, and the papers are beginning to show front in our favor. We fought and won a pitched battle at Topeka in the convention, and have possession of the machine. By the time we get through with the proposed series of meetings, it will be about the 20th of May, if Lucy's voice and strength hold out. The scenery of this State is lovely. In summer it must be very fine indeed, especially in this Western section the valleys are beautiful, and the bluffs quite bold and romantic.

I think we shall probably succeed in Kansas next fall if the State is thoroughly canvassed, not else. We are fortunate in having Col. Sam N. Wood as an organizer and worker. We owe everything to Wood, and he is really a thoroughly noble, good fellow, and a hero. He is a short, rather thick set, somewhat awkward, and "slouchy" man, extremely careless in his dress, blunt and abrupt in his manner, with a queer inexpressive face, little blue eyes which can look dull or flash fire or twinkle with the wickedest fun. He is so witty, sarcastic, and cutting, that he is a terrible foe, and will put the laugh even on his best friends. The son of a Quaker mother, he held the baby while his wife acted as one of the officers, and his mother another, in a Woman's Rights Convention seventeen years ago. Wood has helped off more runaway slaves than any man in Kansas. He has always been *true* both to the negro and the woman. But the negroes dislike and distrust him because he has never allowed the word white to be struck out, unless the word male should be struck out also. He takes exactly Mrs. Stanton's ground, that the colored men and women shall enter the kingdom *together*, if at all. . . . I am glad to say that our friend D. R. Anthony is out for both propositions in the *Leavenworth Bulletin*. But his sympathies are so especially with the negro question that we must have

Susan out here to strengthen his hands. We must have Mrs. Stanton, Susan, Mrs. Gage, and Anna Dickinson, this fall. Also Ben Wade and Carl Schurz, if possible. We must also try to get 10,000 each of Mrs. Stanton's address, of Lucy Stone's address, and of Mrs. Mills article on the Enfranchisement of Women, printed for us by the Hovey Fund.

Kansas is to be *the battle ground* for 1867. *It must not be allowed to fail.*

The politicians here, except Wood and Robinson, are generally "on the fence." But they dare not oppose us openly. And the Democratic leaders are quite disposed to take us up. If the Republicans come out against us the Democrats will take us up. Do not let anything prevent your being here September 1 *for the campaign*, which will end in November. There will be a big fight and a great excitement. After the fight is over Mrs. Stanton will never have *use* for *notes* or *written* speeches any more.

Yours truly,   Henry B. Blackwell.

Fort Scott, May 1, 1867

Dear Susan:

. . . There is no time to write here. We ride all day, and lecture every night, and sometimes at noon too. So there is time for nothing else. I am sorry there is no one to help you, Susan, in New York. I always thought that when this hour of our bitter need come—this darkest hour before the dawn— Mr. Higginson would bring his beautiful soul and his fine, clear intellect to draw all women to his side; but if it is possible for him to be satisfied at *such* an hour with writing the best literary essays, it is because the power to help us has gone from him. The old lark moves her nest only when the farmer prepares to cut his grass himself. This will be the way with us; as to the *Standard*, I don't count upon it at all. Even if you get it, the circulation is so limited that it amounts almost to nothing. I have not seen a copy in all Kansas. But the *Tribune* and *Independent* alone could, if they would, urge *universal* suffrage, as they do negro suffrage, carry this whole nation upon the only just plane of equal human rights. What a power to hold, and not use! I could not sleep the other night, just for thinking of it; and if I had got up and written the thought that burned my very soul, I do believe that Greeley and Tilton would have echoed the cry of the old crusaders, "God wills it;" and rushing to our half-sustained standard, would plant it high and firm on immutable principles. *They* MUST take it up. I shall see them the very first thing when I go home. At your meeting next Monday evening, I think you should insist that all of the Hovey fund used for the *Standard* and Anti-Slavery purposes, since slavery is abolished, must be returned with interest to the three causes which by the express terms of the will were to receive *all* of the fund when slavery was abolished. You will have a good meeting, I am sure, and I hope you will not fail to rebuke the cowardly use of the terms "universal," and "impartial," and "equal," applied to hide a dark skin, and an unpopular client. All this talk about the infamous thirteen who voted against "negro suffrage" in New Jersey, is unutterably contemptible from the lips or pen of those whose words, acts, and votes are not against ignorant and degraded negroes, but against every man's mother, wife, and daughter. We have crowded meetings everywhere. I speak as well as ever, thank God! The audiences move to tears or laughter, just as in the old time. Harry makes capital speeches, and gets a louder cheer always than I do, though I believe I move a deeper feeling. The papers all over the State are discussing pro and con. The whole thing is working just right. . . .

Very truly, Lucy Stone

In a letter dated Atchison, May 9, 1867, Lucy Stone says:

. . . I can not send you a telegraphic dispatch as you wish, for just now there is a plot to get the Republican party to drop the word "male," and also to agree to canvass *only* for the word "white." There is a call, signed by the Chairman of the State Central Republican Committee, to meet at Topeka on the 15th, to pledge the party to the canvass on that single issue. As soon as we saw the call and the change of tone of some of the papers, we sent letters to all those whom we had found true to principle, urging them to be at Topeka and vote for both words. This effort of ours the Central Committee know nothing of, and we hope they will be defeated, as they will be sure to be surprised. So, till this action of the Republicans is settled, we can affirm nothing. Everywhere we go we have the largest and most enthusiastic meetings, and any one of our audiences would give a majority for woman suffrage. But the negroes are all against us. There has just now left us an ignorant black preacher named Twine, who is very confident that women ought not to vote. These men *ought not to be allowed to vote before we do*, because they will be just so much more dead weight to lift. . . .

Lucy Stone

P. S.—The papers here are coming down on us, and every prominent reformer, and charging us with being Free Lovers. I have to-day written a letter to the editor, saying that it has not the shadow of a foundation.

Rev. Olympia Brown arrived in the State in July, where her untiring labors for four months were never equaled by man or woman. Mrs. Stanton, Miss Anthony, and the Hutchinson family followed her early in September. What these speakers could not do with reason and appeal, the Hutchinsons, by stirring the hearts of the people with their sweet ballads, readily accomplished. Before leaving New York Miss Anthony published 60,000 tracts, which were distributed in Kansas with a liberal hand under the frank of Senators Ross and Pomeroy. Thus the thinking and unthinking in every school district were abundantly supplied with woman suffrage literature, such as Mrs. Mill's splendid article in the *Westminster Review*, the best speeches of John Stuart Mill, Theodore Parker, Wendell Phillips, George William Curtis, Elizabeth Cady Stanton's argument before the Constitutional Convention, Parker Pillsbury's "Mortality of Nations," Thomas Wentworth Higginson's "Woman and her Wishes," Henry Ward Beecher's "Woman's Duty to Vote," and Mrs. C. I. H. Nichols' "Responsibility of Woman." There was scarcely a log cabin in the State that could not boast one or more of these documents, which the liberality of a few eastern friends enabled the "Equal Rights Association" to print and circulate.

The opposition were often challenged to debate this question in public, but uniformly refused, knowing full well, since their powder in this battle consisted of vulgar abuse and ridicule, that they had no arguments to advance. But it chanced that on one occasion by mistake, a meeting was appointed for the opposing forces at the same time and place where Olympia Brown was advertised to speak. This gave her an opportunity of testing her readiness in debate with Judge Sears. Of this occasion a correspondent says:

Discussion at Oskaloosa.—To the Editor of the *Kansas State Journal:* For the first time during the canvass for Universal Suffrage, the opponents of the two wrongs, "Manhood Suffrage" and "Woman Suffrage," met in open debate at this place last evening. The largest church in the place was crowded to its utmost, every inch of space being occupied. Judge Gilchrist was called to the chair, and first introduced Judge Sears, who made the following points in favor of Manhood Suffrage:

1st. That in the early days of the Republic no discrimination was made against negroes on account of color.

He proved from the constitutions and charters of the original thirteen States, that all of them, with the exception of South Carolina, allowed the colored freeman the ballot, upon the same basis and conditions as the white man. That we were not conferring a right, but restoring one which the fathers in their wisdom had never deprived the colored man of. He showed how the word white had been forced into the State constitutions, and advocated that it should be stricken out, it being the last relic of the "slave power."

2d. That the negro needed the ballot for his protection and elevation.

3d. That he deserved the ballot. He fought with our fathers side by side in the war of the revolution. He did the same thing in the war of 1812, and in the war of the rebellion. He fought for us because he was loyal and loved the old flag. If any class of men had ever earned the enjoyment of franchise the negro had.

4th. The Republican party owed it to him.

5th. The enfranchisement of the negro was indispensable to reconstruction of the late rebellious States upon a basis that should secure to the loyal men of the South the control of the government in those States. Congress had declared it was necessary, and the most eminent men of the nation had failed to discover any other means by which the South could be restored to the Union, that should secure safety, prosperity, and happiness. There was not loyalty enough in the South among the whites to elect a loyal man to an inferior office.

Upon each one of these points the Judge elaborated at

length, and made really a fine speech, but his evident dis-
concertion showed that he knew what was to follow. It was
expected that when Miss Brown was introduced many would
leave, owing to the strange feeling against Female Suffrage
in and about Oscaloosa; but not one left, the crowd grew
more dense. A more eloquent speech never was uttered in
this town than Miss Brown delivered; for an hour and three-
quarters the audience was spell-bound as she advanced from
point to point. She had been longing for such an opportunity,
and had become weary of striking off into open air; and she
proved how thoroughly acquainted she was with her subject
as she took up each point advanced by her opponent, not
denying their truth, but showing by unanswerable logic that
if it were good under certain reasons for the negro to vote, it
was ten times better for the same reasons for the women to
vote.

The argument that the right to vote is not a natural right,
but acquired as corporate bodies acquire their rights, and that
the ballot meant "protection," was answered and explained
fully. She said the ballot meant protection; it meant much
more; it means education, progress, advancement, elevation
for the oppressed classes, drawing a glowing comparison
between the working classes of England and those of the
United States. She scorned the idea of an aristocracy based
upon two accidents of the body. She paid an eloquent tribute
to Kansas, the pioneer in all reforms, and said that it would
be the best advertisement that Kansas could have to give the
ballot to women, for thousands now waiting and uncertain,
would flock to our State, and a vast tide of emigration would
continually roll toward Kansas until her broad and fertile
prairies would be peopled. It is useless to attempt to report
her address, as she could hardly find a place to stop. When
she had done, her opponent had nothing to say, he had been
beaten on his own ground, and retired with his feathers
drooping. After Miss Brown had closed, some one in the
audience called for a vote on the female proposition. The vote
was put, and nearly every man and woman in the house rose
simultaneously, men that had fought the proposition from the
first arose, even Judge Sears himself looked as though he
would like to rise, but his principles, much tempted, forbade.
After the first vote, Judge Sears called for a vote on his, the
negro proposition, when about one-half the house arose.
Verily there was a great turning to the Lord that day, and

many would have been baptized, but there was no water. When Mrs. Stanton has passed through Oscaloosa, her fame having gone before her, we can count on a good majority for Female Suffrage. . . .

Oscaloosa, October 11, 1867

Salina, Kansas, Sept. 12, 1867

Dear Friend:

We are getting along splendidly. Just the frame of a Methodist church with sidings and roof, and rough cotton-wood boards for seats, was our meeting place last night here; and a perfect jam it was, with men crowded outside at all the windows. Two very brave young Kentuckian sprigs of the law had the courage to argue or present sophistry on the other side. The meeting continued until eleven o'clock. To-day we go to Ellsworth, the very last trading post on the frontier. A car load of wounded soldiers went East on the train this morning; but the fight was a few miles West of Ellsworth. No Indians venture to that point.

Our tracts gave out at Solomon, and the Topeka people failed to fill my telegraphic order to send package here. It is enough to exhaust the patience of any "Job" that men are so wanting in promptness. Our tracts do more than half the battle; reading matter is so very scarce that everybody clutches at a book of any kind. If only reformers would supply this demand with the right and the true—come in and occupy the field at the beginning—they might mould these new settlements. But instead they wait until everything is fixed, and the comforts and luxuries obtainable, and then come to find the ground preoccupied.

Send 2,000 of Curtis' speeches, 2,000 of Phillips', 2,000 of Beecher's, and 1,000 of each of the others, and then fill the boxes with the reports of our last convention; they are the best in the main because they have everybody's speeches together.

S. B. A.

Home of Ex-Gov. Robinson, Lawrence, Kansas, Sept. 15, 1867

I rejoice greatly in the $100 from the Drapers. That makes $250 paid toward the tracts. I am very sorry Mr. J. can not get off Curtis and Beecher. There is a perfect greed for our tracts. All that great trunk full were sold and given away at our first fourteen meetings, and we in return received $110, which a little more than paid our railroad fare—*eight cents per mile*—and hotel bills. Our collections thus far fully equal those at the East. I have been delightfully disappointed, for everybody said I couldn't raise money in Kansas meetings. I wish you were here to make the tour of this beautiful State, in which to live fifty years hence will be charming; but now, alas, the women especially see hard times; to come actually in contact with all their discomforts and privations spoils the poetry of pioneer life. The opposition, the "Anti-Female Suffragists," are making a bold push now; but all prophesy a short run for them. They held a meeting here the day after ours, and the friends say, did vastly more to make us converts than we ourselves did. The fact is nearly every man of the movers is like Kalloch, notoriously wanting in right action toward woman. Their opposition is low and scurrilous, as it used to be fifteen and twenty years ago at the East. Hurry on the tracts.

As ever,   S. B. A.

Seeing that the republican vote must be largely against the woman's amendment, the question arose what can be done to capture enough democratic votes to outweigh the recalcitrant republicans. At this auspicious moment George Francis Train appeared in the State as an advocate of woman suffrage. He appealed most effectively to the chivalry of the intelligent Irishmen, and the prejudices of the ignorant; conjuring them not to take the word "white" out of their constitution unless they did the word "male" also; not to lift the negroes above the heads of their own mothers, wives, sisters, and daughters. The result was a respectable democratic vote in favor of woman suffrage.

In a discussion with General Blunt at a meeting in Ottawa, Mr. Train said:

You say, General, that women in politics would lower the standard. Are politicians so pure, politics so exalted, the polls so immaculate, men so moral, that woman would pollute the ballot and contaminate the voters? Would revolvers, bowie-knives, whisky barrels, profane oaths, brutal rowdyism, be the feature of elections if women were present? Woman's presence purifies the atmosphere. Enter any Western hotel and what do you see, General? Sitting around the stove you will see dirty, unwashed-looking men, with hats on, and feet on the chairs; huge cuds of tobacco on the floor, spittle in pools all about; filth and dirt, condensed tobacco smoke, and a stench of whisky from the bar and the breath (applause, and "that's so,") on every side. This, General, is the manhood picture. Now turn to the womanhood picture; she, whom you think will debase and lower the morals of the elections. Just opposite this sitting room of the King, or on the next floor, is the sitting room of the Queen, covered chairs, clean curtains, nice carpets, books on the table, canary birds at the window, everything tidy, neat and beautiful, and according to your programme the occupants of this room will so demoralize the occupants of the other as to completely undermine all society.

Did man put woman in the parlor? Did woman put man in that bar room? Are the instincts of woman so low that unless man puts up a bar, she will immediately fall into man's obscene conversation and disreputable habits? No, General, women are better than men, purer, nobler, hence more exalted, and so far from falling to man's estate, give her power and she will elevate man to her level.

One other point, General, in reply to your argument. You say woman's sphere is at home with her children, and paint her as the sovereign of her own household. Let me paint the picture of the mother at the washtub, just recovering from the birth of her last child as the Empress. Six little children, half starved and shivering with cold, are watching and hoping that the Emperor will arrive with a loaf of bread, he having taken the wash money to the baker's. They wait and starve and cry, the poor emaciated Empress works and prays, when lo! the bugle sounds. It is the Emperor staggering into the yard. The little famished princesses' mouths all open are waiting for their expected food. Your friend, General, the Emperor, however, was absent minded, and while away at the polls voting for the license for his landlord, left the wash money on deposit with the bar-keeper (laughter) who wouldn't give it back again, and the little Queen birds must starve another day, till the wash-tub earns them a mouthful of something to eat. Give that woman a vote and she will keep the money she earns to clothe and feed her children, instead of its being spent in drunkenness and debauchery by her lord and master. . . .

You say, General, that you intend to vote for *negro suffrage* and against *woman suffrage.* In other words, not satisfied with having your mother, your wife, your sisters, your daughters, the equals *politically* of the negro—by giving him a vote and refusing it to woman, you wish to place your family politically still lower in the scale of citizenship and humanity. This particular twist, General, is working in the minds of the people, and the democrats, having got you where Tommy had the wedge, intend to hold you there. Again you say that Mrs. Cady Stanton was three days in advance of you in the border towns, calling you the Sir John Falstaff of the campaign. I am under the impression, General, that these strong minded woman's rights women *are more than three days in advance of you.* (Loud cheers.) Falstaff was a jolly old brick, chivalrous and full of gallantry, and were he stumping Kansas with his ragged regiment, he would do it as the champion of woman instead of against her. (Loud cheers.) Hence Mrs. Stanton owes an apology to Falstaff, not to General Blunt. (Laughter and cheers.)

One more point, General. You have made a terrific personal attack on Senator Wood, calling him everything that is vile. I do not know Mr. Wood. Miss Anthony has made all my arrangements; but perhaps you will allow me to ask you if Mr. Wood is a democrat? (Laughter and applause from the democrats.) Gen. Blunt—No, he is a republican, (laughter) and chairman of the woman suffrage committee. Mr. Train—Good. I understand you and your argument against Wood is so forcible, (and Mr. Train said this with the most biting sarcasm, every point taking with the audience.) I believe with you that Wood is a bad man, (laughter) a man of no principle whatever. (Laughter.) A man who has committed all the crimes in the calendar, (loud laughter) who, if he has done what you have said, ought to be taken out on the square and hung, and *well hung* too. (Laughter and cheers.) Having admitted that I am converted to the fact of Wood's villainy, (laughter) and you having admitted that he is not a democrat, but a republican, (laughter) I think it is time the honest democratic and republican voters should rise up in their might and wipe off all those corrupt republican leaders from the Kansas State committee. (Loud cheers.) Democrats do your duty on the fifth of November and vote for woman suffrage. (Applause.) The effect of turning the General's own words back upon his party was perfectly electric, and when the vote was put for woman's suffrage it was almost unanimous. Mr. Train saying amid shouts of laughter, that he supposed that a few henpecked men would say "No" here, because they didn't dare to say their souls were their own at home. . . .

Mr. Train continued: Twelve o'clock at night is a late hour to take up all your points, General; but the audience will have me talk. Miss Anthony gave you, General, a very sarcastic retort to your assertion that every woman ought to be married. (Laughter.) She told you that to marry, it was essential to find some decent man, and that could not be found among the Kansas politicians who had so gallantly forsaken the woman's cause. (Loud laughter.) She said, as society was organized there was not one man in a thousand worthy of marriage—marrying a man and marrying a whisky barrel were two distinct ideas. (Laughter and applause.) Miss Anthony tells me that your friend Kalloch said at Lawrence that *of all the infernal humbugs of this humbugging Woman's Rights question, the most absurd was that woman should assume to be entitled to the same wages for the same amount of labor performed, as man.* Do you mean to say that the school mistress, who so ably does her duty, should only receive three hundred dollars, while the school master, who performs the same duty, gets fifteen hundred? (Shame.) All the avenues of employment are blocked against women. Embroidering, tapestry, knitting-needle, sewing needle have all been displaced by machinery; and women speakers, women doctors, and women clerks, are ridiculed and insulted till every modest woman fairly cowers before her Emperor Husband, her King, her Lord, for fear of being called "strong minded." (Laughter and applause.) Why should not the landlady of that hotel over the way share the profits of their joint labors with the landlord? *She* works as hard—yet *he* keeps all the money, and she goes to him, instead of being an independent woman, for her share of the profits, as a *beggar* asking for ten dollars to buy a bonnet or a dress. (Applause from the ladies.) Nothing is more contemptible than this slavery to the husband on the question of money. (Loud applause.) . . .

Woman first, and negro last, is my programme; yet I am willing that intelligence should be the test, although some men have more brains in their hands than others in their heads. (Laughter.) Emmert's Resolution, introduced into your Legislature last year, disfranchising, after July 4, 1870, all of age who can not read the American Constitution, the State Constitution, and the Bible, in the language in which he was educated, (applause) expresses my views.

Again you alluded to the Foreign Emissary—who had no interest in Kansas. Do you mean me, General? General Blunt —No, sir. Thank you. The other four Foreign Emissaries are women, noble, self-sacrificing women, bold, never-tiring, un- blemished reputation; women who have left their pleasant Eastern homes for a grand idea, (loud applause.). . . .

No, General, these women are no foreign emissaries. They came expecting support. They thought the republicans hon- est. They forgot that the democrats alone were their friends. (Applause.) They forgot that it was the Republican party that publicly insulted them in Congress. That it was Charles Sumner who wished to insert the word "male" in the amend- ment of the Federal Constitution two years ago, when the old Constitution, by having neither male nor female, had left it an open question. No, Mrs. Cady Stanton, Miss Susan B. Anthony, Mrs. Lucy Stone, and Miss Olympia Brown are the "foreign emissaries" that will alone have the credit of emancipating women in Kansas. Your trimming politicians left them in the lurch. Not one of you was honest. (Applause.) Even those who assumed to be their friends by saying nothing on the woman, and everything on the negro, are worse than you and Kalloch. (Applause.) Mr. Kalloch and Leggett and Sears have helped the woman's cause by opposing it, (cheers,) while the milk-and-water republican committee and speakers and press have damaged woman by their sneaking, cowardly way of advocacy. (That's so.) . . .

But Kansas being republican by a large majority, there was no chance of victory. For although the women were sup- ported by some of the best men in the State, such as Gov. Crawford, Ex-Gov. Robinson, United States Senators Pome- roy and Ross, and a few of the ablest editors, the opposition was too strong to be conquered. With both parties, the press, the pulpit and faithless liberals as opponents, the hopes of the advocates of woman suffrage began to falter before the election.

The action of the Michigan Commission, in refusing to

submit a similar amendment to her people, and the adverse report of Mr. Greeley in the Constitutional Convention of New York, had also their depressing influence. Nevertheless, when election day came, the vote was nearly equal for both propositions. With all the enginery of the controlling party negro suffrage had a little over 10,000 votes, while woman suffrage without press or party, friends or politicians, had 9,000 and some over. And this vote for woman's enfranchisement represented the best elements in the State, men of character and conscience, who believed in social order and good government.

When Eastern Republicans learned that the action of their party in Kansas was doing more damage than the question of woman to the negro, since the pioneers, who knew how bravely the women had stood by their side amid all dangers, were saying, "if our women can not vote, the negro shall not;" they began to take in the situation, and a month before the election issued the following appeal, signed by some of the most influential men of the nation. It was published in the New York *Tribune* October 1st, and copied by most of the papers throughout the State of Kansas:

To the Voters of the United States:

In this hour of national reconstruction we appeal to good men of all parties, to Conventions for amending State Constitutions, to the Legislature of every State, and to the Congress of the United States, to apply the principles of the Declaration of Independence to women; "Governments derive their just powers from the consent of the governed." The only form of consent recognized under a Republic is suffrage. Mere tacit acquiescence is not consent; if it were, every despotism might claim that its power is justly held. Suffrage is the right of every adult citizen, irrespective of sex or color. Women are governed, therefore they are rightly entitled to vote.

The problem of American statesmanship is how to incorporate in our institutions a guarantee of the rights of every individual. The solution is easy. Base government on the consent of the governed, and each class will protect itself.

But the appeal was too late, the mischief done was irreparable. The action of the Republican party had created a hostile feeling between the women and the colored people. The men of Kansas in their speeches would say, "What would be to us the comparative advantage of the amendments? If negro suffrage passes, we will be flooded with ignorant, impoverished blacks from every State of the Union. If woman suffrage passes, we invite to our borders people of character and position, of wealth and education, the very element Kansas needs to-day. Who can hesitate to decide, when the question lies between educated women and ignorant negroes?" Such appeals as these were made by men of Kansas to hundreds of audiences. . . .

. . .

Blackheath Park, Kent, England, June 2, 1867

Dear Sir:

Being one who takes as deep and as continuous an interest in the political, moral, and social progress of the United States as if he were himself an American citizen, I hope I shall not be intrusive if I express to you as the executive organ of the Impartial Suffrage Association, the deep joy I felt on learning that both branches of the Legislature of Kansas had, by large majorities, proposed for the approval of your citizens an amendment to your constitution, abolishing the unjust political privileges of sex at one and the same stroke with the kindred privilege of color. We are accustomed to see Kansas foremost in the struggle for the equal claims of all human beings to freedom and citizenship. I shall never forget with what profound interest I and others who felt with me watched every incident of the preliminary civil war in which your noble State, then only a Territory, preceded the great nation of which it is a part, in shedding its blood to arrest the extension of slavery.

Kansas was the herald and protagonist of the memorable contest, which at the cost of so many heroic lives, has admitted the African race to the blessings of freedom and education, and she is now taking the same advanced position in the peaceful but equally important contest which, by relieving half the human race from artificial disabilities belonging to the ideas of a past age, will give a new impulse and improved character to the career of social and moral progress now opening for mankind. If your citizens, next November, give effect to the enlightened views of your Legislature, history will remember that one of the youngest States in the civilized world has been the first to adopt a measure of liberation destined to extend all over the earth, and to be looked back to (as is my fixed conviction) as one of the most fertile in beneficial consequences of all the improvements yet effected in human affairs. I am, sir, with the warmest wishes for the prosperity of Kansas,

Yours very truly,   J. Stuart Mill

To S. N. Wood, Topeka, Kansas, U. S. A.

• • •

Both propositions got about 10,000 votes, and both were defeated. After the canvass the excitement died away and the Suffrage Associations fell through, but the seed sown has silently taken root and sprung up everywhere. Or rather, the truths then spoken, and the arguments presented, sinking into the minds and hearts of the men and women who heard them, have been like leaven, slowly but surely operating until it seems to many that nearly the whole public sentiment of Kansas is therewith leavened. A most liberal sentiment prevails everywhere toward women. Many are engaged in lucrative occupations. In several counties ladies have been elected superintendents of public schools. In Coffey County, the election of Mary P. Wright, was contested on the ground that by the Constitution a woman was ineligible to the office. The case was decided by the Supreme Court in her favor. By our laws women vote on all school questions and avail themselves very extensively of the privilege. Our property laws are conceded to be the most just to women of any State in the Union. It is believed by many that were the question of woman suffrage again submitted to the people it would be carried by an overwhelming majority.

The following letter from Susan E. Wattles, the widow of the pioneer, Augustus Wattles, shows woman's interest in the great struggle to make Kansas the banner State of universal freedom and franchise.

Mound City, December 30, 1881

My Dear Miss Anthony:

Here, as in New York, the first in the woman suffrage cause were those who had been the most earnest workers for freedom. They had come to Kansas to prevent its being made a slave State. The most the women could do was to bear their privations patiently, such as living in a tent in a log cabin, without any floor all winter, or in a cabin ten feet square, and cooking out of doors by the side of a log, giving up their beds to the sick, and being ready, night or day, to feed the men who were running for their lives. Then there was the ever present fear that their husbands would be shot. The most obnoxious had a price set upon their heads. A few years ago a man said: "I could have got $1,000 once for shooting Wattles, and I wish now I had done it." When in Ohio, our house was often the temporary home of the hunted slave; but in Kansas it was the *white* man who ran from our door to the woods because he saw strangers coming.

After the question of a free State seemed settled, we who had thought and talked on woman's rights before we came to Kansas, concluded that now was the woman's hour. We determined to strive to obtain Constitutional rights, as they would be more secure than Legislative enactments. On the 13th of February, 1858, we organized the Moneka Woman's Rights Society. There were only twelve of us, but we went to work circulating petitions and writing to every one in the Territory whom we thought would aid us. Our number was afterwards increased to forty; fourteen of them were men. We sent petitions to Territorial Legislatures, Constitutional Conventions, State Legislatures, and Congress. Many of the leading men were advocates of women's rights. Governor Robinson, S. N. Wood, and Erastus Heath, with their wives, were constant and efficient workers. . . .

The last vigorous effort we made in circulating petitions was when Congress was about extending to the colored men the right to vote. Many signed then for the first time. One woman said, "I know my husband does not believe in women voting, but he hates the negroes, and would not want them placed over me." I saw in *The Liberator* that a bequest to the woman's rights cause had been made by a gentleman in Boston, and I asked Wendell Phillips if we could have some of it in Kansas. He directed me to Susan B. Anthony, and you gave us $100. This small sum we divided between two lecturers, and paying for tracts. . . .

When the question was submitted in 1867, and the men

were to decide whether women should be allowed to vote, we felt very anxious about the result. We strongly desired to make Kansas the banner State for Freedom. We did all we could to secure it, and some of the best speakers from the East came to our aid. Their speeches were excellent, and were listened to by large audiences, who seemed to believe what they heard; but when voting day came, they voted according to their prejudices, and our cause was defeated. My work has been very limited. I have only been able to talk and circulate tracts and papers. I took *The Una, The Lily, The Sybil, The Pittsburg Visitor, The Revolution, Woman's Journal, Ballot Box,* and *National Citizen;* got all the subscribers I could, and scattered them far and near. When I gave away *The Revolution,* my husband said, "Wife, that is a very talented paper; I should think you would preserve that." I replied: "They will continue to come until our cause is won, and I must make them do all the good they can." I am delighted with the "Suffrage History." I do not think you can find material to make the second volume as interesting. I knew of most of the incidents as they transpired, yet they are full of interest and significance to me now. My book is now lent where I think it will be highly appreciated.

• • •

After speaking in all the chief cities from Leavenworth to New York, Mrs. Stanton and Miss Susan B. Anthony turned their attention to the establishment in the city of New York of a woman suffrage paper, called *The Revolution.* The funds for this enterprise were provided by two Democrats, David Melliss, the financial editor of the *World,* and George Francis Train. The editors were Parker Pillsbury and Elizabeth Cady Stanton; the owner and publisher, Susan B. Anthony. This affiliation with Mr. Train and other Democrats, together with the aggressive tone of *The Revolution,* called down on Miss Anthony and Mrs. Stanton severe criticism from some of their friends, while they received sincere praise from others. In reviewing the situation, they have had no reason to regret their course, feeling that their determination to push their cause, and accept help from whatever quarter it was proffered, aroused lukewarm friends to action, who, though hostile at first to the help of Democrats, soon came to appreciate the difficulty of carrying on a movement with the press, pulpit, politicians, and philanthropists all in the opposition.

Abolitionists were severe in their denunciations against these ladies, because, while belonging to anti-slavery associations, they affiliated with the bitter enemies of the negro and all his defamers. To which they replied: "So long as opposition to slavery is the only test for a free pass to your platform and membership of your association, and you do not shut out all persons opposed to woman suffrage, why should we not accept all in favor of woman suffrage to our platform and association, even though they be rabid pro-slavery Democrats? Your test of unfaithfulness is the negro, ours is the woman; the broadest platform, to which no party has as yet risen, is humanity." Reformers can be as bigoted and sectarian and as ready to malign each other, as the Church in its darkest periods has been to persecute its dissenters.

So utterly had the women been deserted in the Kansas campaign by those they had the strongest reason to look to for help, that at times all effort seemed hopeless. The editors of the New York *Tribune* and the *Independent* can never know how wistfully, from day to day, their papers were searched for some inspiring editorials on the woman's amendment, but naught was there; there were no words of hope and encouragement, no eloquent letters from an Eastern man that could be read to the people; all were silent. Yet these two papers, extensively taken all over Kansas, had they been as true to woman as to the negro, could have revolutionized the State. But with arms folded, Greeley, Curtis, Tilton, Beecher, Higginson, Phillips, Garrison, Frederick Douglass, all calmly watched the struggle from afar, and when defeat came to both propositions, no consoling words were offered for woman's loss, but the women who spoke in the campaign were reproached for having "killed negro suffrage."

We wondered then at the general indifference to that first opportunity of realizing what all those gentlemen had advocated so long; and, in looking back over the many intervening years, we still wonder at the stolid incapacity of all men to understand that woman feels the invidious distinctions of sex exactly as the black man does those of color, or the white man the more transient distinctions of wealth, family, position, place, and power; that she feels as keenly as man the injustice of disfranchisement. Of the old abolitionists who stood true to woman's cause in this crisis, Robert Purvis, Parker Pillsbury, and Rev. Samuel J. May were the only Eastern men. Through all the hot debates during the period of reconstruction, again and again, Mr. Purvis arose and declared, that he would rather his son should never be enfranchised, unless his daughter could be also, that, as she bore the double curse of sex and color, on every principle of justice she should first be protected. These were the only men who felt and understood as women themselves do the degradation of disfranchisement.

Twenty years ago, as now, the Gibraltar of our difficulties was the impossibility of making the best men feel that woman is aggravated by the endless petty distinctions because of sex, precisely as the most cultivated man, black or white, suffers the distinctions of color, wealth, or position. Take a man of superior endowments, once powerful and respected, who through unfortunate circumstances is impoverished and neglected; he sees small men, unscrupulous, hard, grinding men taking places of trust and influence, making palace homes for themselves and children, while his family in shabby attire are ostracised in the circle where by ancestry and intelligence they belong, made to feel on all occasions the impassable gulf that lies between riches and poverty. That man feels for himself and doubly for his children the humiliation. And yet with the ever-turning wheel of fortune such distinctions are transient; yours to-day, mine to-morrow. . . .

When a colored man of education and wealth like Robert Purvis, of Philadelphia, surrounded with a family of cultivated sons and daughters, was denied all social communion with his neighbors, equal freedom and opportunity for himself and children, in public amusements, churches, schools, and means of travel because of race, he felt the degradation of color. The poor white man might have said; If I were Robert Purvis, with a good bank account, and could live in my own house, ride in my own carriage, and have my children well fed and clothed, I should not care if we were all as black as the ace of spades. But he had never tried the humiliation of color, and could not understand its peculiar aggravations, as he did those of poverty. It is impossible for one class to appreciate the wrongs of another. The coarser forms of slavery all can see and deplore, but the subjections of the spirit, few either comprehend or appreciate. In our day women carrying heavy burdens on their shoulders while men walk by their side smoking their pipes, or women harnessed to plows and carts with cows and dogs while men drive, are sights which need no eloquent appeals to move American men to pity and indignation. But the subtle humiliations of women possessed of wealth, education, and genius, men on the same plane can not see or feel, and yet can any misery be more real than invidious distinctions on the ground of sex in the laws and constitution, in the political, religious, and moral position of those who in nature stand the peers of each other? And not only do such women suffer these ever-recurring indignities in daily life, but the literature of the world proclaims their inferiority and divinely decreed subjection in all history, sacred and profane, in science, philosophy, poetry, and song.

And here is the secret of the infinite sadness of women of genius; of their dissatisfaction with life, in exact proportion to their development. A woman who occupies the same realm of thought with man, who can explore with him the depths of science, comprehend the steps of progress through the long past and prophesy those of the momentous future, must ever be surprised and aggravated with his assumptions of leadership and superiority, a superiority she never concedes, an authority she utterly repudiates. Words can not describe the indignation, the humiliation a proud woman feels for her sex in disfranchisement.

In a republic where all are declared equal an ostracised class of one half of the people, on the ground of a distinction founded in nature, is an anomalous position, as harassing to its victims as it is unjust, and as contradictory as it is unsafe to the fundamental principles of a free government. When we remember that out of this degraded political status, spring all the special wrongs that have blocked woman's success in the world of work, and degraded her labor everywhere to one half its value; closed to her the college doors and all opportunities for higher education, forbade her to practice in the professions, made her a cipher in the church, and her sex, her motherhood a curse in all religions; her subjection a text for bibles, a target for the priesthood; seeing all this, we wonder now as then at the indifference and injustice of our best men when the first opportunity offered in which the women of any State might have secured their enfranchisement.

It was not from ignorance of the unequal laws, and false public sentiment against woman, that our best men stood silent in this Kansas campaign; it was not from lack of chivalry that they thundered forth no protests, when they saw noble women, who had been foremost in every reform, hounded through the State by foul mouthed politicians; it was not from lack of money and power, of eloquence of pen and tongue, nor of an intellectual conviction that our cause was just, that they came not to the rescue, but because in their heart of hearts they did not grasp the imperative necessity of woman's demand for that protection which the ballot alone can give; they did not feel for *her* the degradation of disfranchisement.

The fact of their silence deeply grieved us, but the philosophy of their indifference we thoroughly comprehended for the first time and saw as never before, that only from woman's standpoint could the battle be successfully fought, and victory secured. "It is wonderful," says Swift, "with what patience some folks can endure the sufferings of others." Our liberal men counseled us to silence during the war, and we were silent on our own wrongs; they counseled us again to silence in Kansas and New York, lest we should defeat "negro suffrage," and threatened if we were not, we might fight the battle alone. We chose the latter, and were defeated. But standing alone we learned our power; we repudiated man's counsels forevermore; and solemnly vowed that there should never be another season of silence until woman had the same rights everywhere on this green earth, as man.

While we hold in loving reverence the names of such men as Charles Sumner, Horace Greeley, William Lloyd Garrison, Gerrit Smith, Wendell Phillips and Frederick Douglass, and would urge the rising generation of young men to emulate their virtues, we would warn the young women of the coming generation against man's advice as to their best interests, their highest development. We would point for them the moral of our experiences: that woman must lead the way to her own enfranchisement, and work out her own salvation with a hopeful courage and determination that knows no fear nor trembling. She must not put her trust in man in this transition period, since, while regarded as his subject, his inferior, his slave, their interests must be antagonistic.

But when at last woman stands on an even platform with man, his acknowledged equal everywhere, with the same freedom to express herself in the religion and government of the country, then, and not till then, can she safely take counsel with him in regard to her most sacred rights, privileges, and immunities; for not till then will he be able to legislate as wisely and generously for her as for himself.

Political Equality for Women

The prolonged slavery of woman is the darkest page in human history. A survey of the condition of the race through those barbarous periods, when physical force governed the world, when the motto, "might makes right," was the law, enables one to account for the origin of woman's subjection to man without referring the fact to the general inferiority of the sex, or Nature's law.

Writers on this question differ as to the cause of the universal degradation of woman in all periods and nations.

One of the greatest minds of the century has thrown a ray of light on this gloomy picture by tracing the origin of woman's slavery to the same principle of selfishness and love of power in man that has thus far dominated all weaker nations and classes. This brings hope of final emancipation, for as all nations and classes are gradually, one after another, asserting and maintaining their independence, the path is clear for woman to follow. The slavish instinct of an oppressed class has led her to toil patiently through the ages, giving all and asking little, cheerfully sharing with man all perils and privations by land and sea, that husband and sons might attain honor and success. Justice and freedom for herself is her latest and highest demand.

Another writer asserts that the tyranny of man over woman has its roots, after all, in his nobler feelings; his love, his chivalry, and his desire to protect woman in the barbarous periods of pillage, lust, and war. But wherever the roots may be traced, the results at this hour are equally disastrous to woman. Her best interests and happiness do not seem to have been consulted in the arrangements made for her protection. She has been bought and sold, caressed and crucified at the will and pleasure of her master. But if a chivalrous desire to protect woman has always been the mainspring of man's dominion over her, it should have prompted him to place in her hands the same weapons of defense he has found to be most effective against wrong and oppression.

It is often asserted that as woman has always been man's slave—subject—inferior—dependent, under all forms of government and religion, slavery must be her normal condition. This might have some weight had not the vast majority of men also been enslaved for centuries to kings and popes, and orders of nobility, who, in the progress of civilization, have reached complete equality. And did we not also see the great changes in woman's condition, the marvelous transformation in her character, from a toy in the Turkish harem, or a drudge in the German fields, to a leader of thought in the literary circles of France, England, and America!

In an age when the wrongs of society are adjusted in the courts and at the ballot-box, material force yields to reason and majorities.

Woman's steady march onward, and her growing desire for a broader outlook, prove that she has not reached her normal condition, and that society has not yet conceded all that is necessary for its attainment.

Moreover, woman's discontent increases in exact proportion to her development. Instead of a feeling of gratitude for rights accorded, the wisest are indignant at the assumption of any legal disability based on sex, and their feelings in this matter are a surer test of what her nature demands, than the feelings and prejudices of the sex claiming to be superior. American men may quiet their consciences with the delusion that no such injustice exists in this country as in Eastern nations, though with the general improvement in our institutions, woman's condition must inevitably have improved also, yet the same principle that degrades her in Turkey, *insults* her in this republic. Custom forbids a woman there to enter a mosque, or call the hour for prayers; here it forbids her a voice in Church Councils or State Legislatures. The same taint of her primitive state of slavery affects both latitudes.

The condition of married women, under the laws of all countries, has been essentially that of slaves, until modified, in some respects, within the last quarter of a century in the United States. The change from the old Common Law of England, in regard to the civil rights of women, from 1848 to the advance legislation in most of the Northern States in 1880, marks an era both in the status of woman as a citizen and in our American system of jurisprudence. When the State of New York gave married women certain rights of property, the individual existence of the wife was recognized, and the old idea that "husband and wife are one, and that one the husband," received its death-blow. From that hour the statutes of the several States have been steadily diverging from the old English codes. Most of the Western States copied the advance legislation of New York, and some are now even more liberal.

The broader demand for political rights has not commanded the thought its merits and dignity should have secured. While complaining of many wrongs and oppressions, women themselves did not see that the political disability of sex was the cause of all their special grievances, and that to secure equality anywhere, it must be recognized everywhere. Like all disfranchised classes, they began by asking to have certain wrongs redressed, and not by asserting their own right to make laws for themselves.

Overburdened with cares in the isolated home, women had not the time, education, opportunity, and pecuniary independence to put their thoughts clearly and concisely into propositions, nor the courage to compare their opinions with one another, nor to publish them, to any great extent, to the world.

It requires philosophy and heroism to rise above the opinion of the wise men of all nations and races, that to be *unknown,* is the highest testimonial woman can have to her virtue, delicacy and refinement.

A certain odium has ever rested on those who have risen above the conventional level and sought new spheres for thought and action, and especially on the few who demand complete equality in political rights. The leaders in this movement have been women of superior mental and physical organization, of good social standing and education, remarkable alike for their domestic virtues, knowledge of public affairs, and rare executive ability; good speakers and writers, inspiring and conducting the genuine reforms of the day; everywhere exerting themselves to promote the best interests of society; yet they have been uniformly ridiculed, misrepresented, and denounced in public and private by all classes of society.

Woman's political equality with man is the legitimate outgrowth of the fundamental principles of our Government, clearly set forth in the Declaration of Independence in 1776, in the United States Constitution adopted in 1784, in the prolonged debates on the origin of human rights in the anti-slavery conflict in 1840, and in the more recent discussions of the party in power since 1865, on the 13th, 14th, and 15th Amendments to the National Constitution; and the majority of our leading statesmen have taken the ground that suffrage is a natural right that may be regulated, but can not be abolished by State law.

Under the influence of these liberal principles of republicanism that pervades all classes of American minds, however vaguely, if suddenly called out, they might be stated, woman readily perceives the anomalous position she occupies in a republic, where the government and religion alike are based on individual conscience and judgment—where the natural rights of all citizens have been exhaustively discussed, and repeatedly declared equal.

From the inauguration of the government, representative women have expostulated against the inconsistencies between our principles and practices as a nation. Beginning with special grievances, woman's protests soon took a larger scope. Having petitioned State legislatures to change the statutes that robbed her of children, wages, and property, she demanded that the Constitutions—State and National—be so amended as to give her a voice in the laws, a choice in the rulers, and protection in the exercise of her rights as a citizen of the United States.

While the laws affecting woman's civil rights have been greatly improved during the past thirty years, the political demand has made but a questionable progress, though it must be counted as the chief influence in modifying the laws. The selfishness of man was readily enlisted in securing woman's civil rights, while the same element in his character antagonized her demand for political equality.

Fathers who had estates to bequeath to their daughters could see the advantage of securing to woman certain property rights that might limit the legal power of profligate husbands.

Husbands in extensive business operations could see the advantage of allowing the wife the right to hold separate property, settled on her in time of prosperity, that might not be seized for his debts. Hence in the several States able men championed these early measures. But political rights, involving in their last results equality everywhere, roused all the antagonism of a dominant power, against the self-assertion of a class hitherto subservient. Men saw that with political equality for woman, they could no longer keep her in social subordination, and "the majority of the male sex," says John Stuart Mill, "can not yet tolerate the idea of living with an equal." The fear of a social revolution thus complicated the discussion. The Church, too, took alarm, knowing that with the freedom and education acquired in becoming a component part of the Government, woman would not only outgrow the power of the priesthood, and religious superstitions, but would also invade the pulpit, interpret the Bible anew from her own stand-point, and claim an equal voice in all ecclesiastical councils. With fierce warnings and denunciations from the pulpit, and false interpretations of Scripture, women have been intimidated and misled, and their religious feelings have been played upon for their more complete subjugation. While the general principles of the Bible are in favor of the most enlarged freedom and equality of the race, isolated texts have been used to block the wheels of progress in all periods; thus bigots have defended capital punishment, intemperance, slavery, polygamy, and the subjection of woman. The creeds of all nations make obedience to man the corner-stone of her religious character. Fortunately, however, more liberal minds are now giving us higher and purer expositions of the Scriptures.

As the social and religious objections appeared against the demand for political rights, the discussion became many-sided, contradictory, and as varied as the idiosyncrasies of individual character. Some said, "Man is woman's natural protector, and she can safely trust him to make laws for her." She might with fairness reply, as he uniformly robbed her of all property rights to 1848, he can not safely be trusted with her personal rights in 1880, though the fact that he did make some restitution at last, might modify her distrust in the future. However, the calendars of our courts still show that fathers deal unjustly with daughters, husbands with wives, brothers with sisters, and sons with their own mothers. Though woman needs the protection of one man against his whole sex, in pioneer life, in threading her way through a lonely forest, on the highway, or in the streets of the metropolis on a dark night, she sometimes needs, too, the protection of all men against this one. But even if she could be sure, as she is not, of the ever-present, all-protecting power of one strong arm, that would be weak indeed compared with the subtle, all-pervading influence of just and equal laws for all women. Hence woman's need of the ballot, that she may hold in her own right hand the weapon of self-protection and self-defense.

Again it is said: "The women who make the demand are few in number, and their feelings and opinions are abnormal, and therefore of no weight in considering the aggregate judgment on the question." The number is larger than appears on the surface, for the fear of public ridicule, and the loss of private favors from those who shelter, feed, and clothe them, withhold many from declaring their opinions and demanding their rights. The ignorance and indifference of the majority of women, as to their status as citizens of a republic, is not remarkable, for history shows that the masses of all oppressed classes, in the most degraded conditions, have been stolid and apathetic until partial success had crowned the faith and enthusiasm of the few.

The insurrections on Southern plantations were always defeated by the doubt and duplicity of the slaves themselves. That little band of heroes who precipitated the American Revolution in 1776 were so ostracised that they walked the streets with bowed heads, from a sense of loneliness and apprehension. Woman's apathy to the wrongs of her sex, instead of being a plea for her remaining in her present condition, is the strongest argument against it. How completely demoralized by her subjection must she be, who does not feel her personal dignity assailed when all women are ranked in every State Constitution with idiots, lunatics, criminals, and minors; when in the name of Justice, man holds one scale for woman, another for himself; when by the spirit and letter of the laws she is made responsible for crimes committed against her, while the male criminal goes free; when from altars where she worships no woman may preach; when in the courts, where girls of tender age may be arraigned for the crime of infanticide, she may not plead for the most miserable of her sex; when colleges she is taxed to build and endow, deny her the right to share in their advantages; when she finds that which should be her glory—her possible motherhood—treated everywhere by man as a disability and a crime! A woman insensible to such indignities needs some transformation into nobler thought, some purer atmosphere to breathe, some higher stand-point from which to study human rights.

It is said, "the difference between the sexes indicates different spheres." It would be nearer the truth to say the difference indicates different duties in the same sphere, seeing that man and woman were evidently made for each other, and have shown equal capacity in the ordinary range of human duties. In governing nations, leading armies, piloting ships across the sea, rowing life-boats in terrific gales; in art, science, invention, literature, woman has proved herself the complement of man in the world of thought and action. This difference does not compel us to spread our tables with different food for man and woman, nor to provide in our common schools a different course of study for boys and girls. Sex pervades all nature, yet the male and female tree and vine and shrub rejoice in the same sunshine and shade. The earth and air are free to all the fruits and flowers, yet each absorbs what best ensures its growth. But whatever it is, it requires no special watchfulness on our part to see that it is maintained. This plea, when closely analyzed, is generally found to mean woman's inferiority.

The superiority of man, however, does not enter into the demand for suffrage, for in this country all men vote; and as the lower orders of men are not superior, either by nature or grace, to the higher orders of women, they must hold and exercise the right of self-government on some other ground than superiority to women.

Again it is said, "Woman when independent and self-asserting will lose her influence over man." In the happiest conditions in life, men and women will ever be mutually dependent on each other. The complete development of all woman's powers will not make her less capable of steadfast love and friendship, but give her new strength to meet the emergencies of life, to aid those who look to her for counsel and support. Men are uniformly more attentive to women of rank, family, and fortune, who least need their care, than to any other class. We do not see their protecting love generally extending to the helpless and unfortunate ones of earth. Wherever the skilled hands and cultured brain of woman have made the battle of life easier for man, he has readily pardoned her sound judgment and proper self-assertion. But the prejudices and preferences of man should be a secondary consideration, in presence of the individual happiness and freedom of woman. The formation of her character and its influence on the human race, is a larger question than man's personal liking. There is no fear, however, that when a superior order of women shall grace the earth, there will not be an order of men to match them, and influence over such minds will atone for the loss of it elsewhere.

An honest fear is sometimes expressed "that woman would degrade politics, and politics would degrade woman." As the influence of woman has been uniformly elevating in new civilizations, in missionary work in heathen nations, in schools, colleges, literature, and in general society, it is fair to suppose that politics would prove no exception. On the other hand, as the art of government is the most exalted of all sciences, and statesmanship requires the highest order of mind, the ennobling and refining influence of such pursuits must elevate rather than degrade woman. When politics degenerate into bitter persecutions and vulgar court-gossip, they are degrading to man, and his honor, virtue, dignity, and refinement are as valuable to woman as her virtues are to him.

Again, it is said, "Those who make laws must execute them; government needs force behind it,—a woman could not be sheriff or a policeman." She might not fill these offices in the way men do, but she might far more effectively guard the morals of society, and the sanitary conditions of our cities. It might with equal force be said that a woman of culture and artistic taste can not keep house, because she can not wash and iron with her own hands, and clean the range and furnace. At the head of the police, a woman could direct her forces and keep order without ever using a baton or a pistol in her own hands. "The elements of sovereignty," says Blackstone, "are three: wisdom, goodness, and power." Conceding to woman wisdom and goodness, as they are not strictly masculine virtues, and substituting moral power for physical force, we have the necessary elements of government for most of life's emergencies. Women manage families, mixed schools, charitable institutions, large boarding-houses and hotels, farms and steam-engines, drunken and disorderly men and women, and stop street fights, as well as men do. The queens in history compare favorably with the kings.

But, "in the settlement of national difficulties," it is said, "the last resort is war; shall we summon our wives and mothers to the battle-field?" Women have led armies in all ages, have held positions in the army and navy for years in disguise. Some fought, bled, and died on the battle-field in our late war. They performed severe labors in the hospitals and sanitary department. Wisdom would dictate a division of labor in war as well as in peace, assigning each their appropriate department.

Numerous classes of men who enjoy their political rights are exempt from military duty. All men over forty-five, all who suffer mental or physical disability, such as the loss of an eye or a forefinger; clergymen, physicians, Quakers, school-teachers, professors, and presidents of colleges, judges, legislators, congressmen, State prison officials, and all county, State and National officers; fathers, brothers, or sons having certain relatives dependent on them for support,—all of these summed up in every State in the Union make millions of voters thus exempted.

In view of this fact there is no force in the plea, that "if women vote they must fight." Moreover, war is not the normal state of the human family in its higher development, but merely a feature of barbarism lasting on through the transition of the race, from the savage to the scholar. When England and America settled the *Alabama* Claims by the Geneva Arbitration, they pointed the way for the future adjustment of all national difficulties.

Some fear, "If women assume all the duties political equality implies, that the time and attention necessary to the duties of home life will be absorbed in the affairs of State." The act of voting occupies but little time in itself, and the vast majority of women will attend to their family and social affairs to the neglect of the State, just as men do to their individual interests. The virtue of patriotism is subordinate in most souls to individual and family aggrandizement. As to offices, it is not to be supposed that the class of men now elected will resign to women their chances, and if they should to any extent, the necessary number of women to fill the offices would make no apparent change in our social circles. If, for example, the Senate of the United States should be entirely composed of women, but two in each State would be withdrawn from the pursuit of domestic happiness. For many reasons, under all circumstances, a comparatively smaller proportion of women than men would actively engage in politics.

As the power to extend or limit the suffrage rests now

wholly in the hands of man, he can commence the experiment with as small a number as he sees fit, by requiring any lawful qualification. Men were admitted on property and educational qualifications in most of the States, at one time, and still are in some—so hard has it been for man to understand the theory of self-government. Three-fourths of the women would be thus disqualified, and the remaining fourth would be too small a minority to precipitate a social revolution or defeat masculine measures in the halls of legislation, even if women were a unit on all questions and invariably voted together, which they would not. In this view, the path of duty is plain for the prompt action of those gentlemen who fear universal suffrage for women, but are willing to grant it on property and educational qualifications. While those who are governed by the law of expediency should give the measure of justice they deem safe, let those who trust the absolute right proclaim the higher principle in government, "equal rights to all."

Many seeming obstacles in the way of woman's enfranchisement will be surmounted by reforms in many directions. Co-operative labor and co-operative homes will remove many difficulties in the way of woman's success as artisan and housekeeper, when admitted to the governing power. The varied forms of progress, like parallel lines, move forward simultaneously in the same direction. Each reform, at its inception, seems out of joint with all its surroundings; but the discussion changes the conditions, and brings them in line with the new idea.

The isolated household is responsible for a large share of woman's ignorance and degradation. A mind always in contact with children and servants, whose aspirations and ambitions rise no higher than the roof that shelters it, is necessarily dwarfed in its proportions. The advantages to the few whose fortunes enable them to make the isolated household a more successful experiment, can not outweigh the difficulties of the many who are wholly sacrificed to its maintenance.

Quite as many false ideas prevail as to woman's true position in the home as to her status elsewhere. Womanhood is the great fact in her life; wifehood and motherhood are but incidental relations. Governments legislate for men; we do not have one code for bachelors, another for husbands and fathers; neither have the social relations of women any significance in their demands for civil and political rights. Custom and philosophy, in regard to woman's happiness, are alike based on the idea that her strongest social sentiment is love of children; that in this relation her soul finds complete satisfaction. But the love of offspring, common to all orders of women and all forms of animal life, tender and beautiful as it is, can not as a sentiment rank with conjugal love. The one calls out only the negative virtues that belong to apathetic classes, such as patience, endurance, self-sacrifice, exhausting the brain-forces, ever giving, asking nothing in return; the other, the outgrowth of the two supreme powers in nature, the positive and negative magnetism, the centrifugal and centripetal forces, the masculine and feminine elements, possessing the divine power of creation, in the universe of thought and action. Two pure souls fused into one by an impassioned love—friends, counselors—a mutual support and inspiration to each other amid life's struggles, must know the highest human happiness;—this is marriage; and this is the only corner-stone of an enduring home. Neither does ordinary motherhood, assumed without any high purpose or preparation, compare in sentiment with the lofty ambition and conscientious devotion of the artist whose pure children of the brain in poetry, painting, music, and science are ever beckoning her upward into an ideal world of beauty. They who give the world a true philosophy, a grand poem, a beautiful painting or statue, or can tell the story of every wandering star; a George Eliot, a Rosa Bonheur, an Elizabeth Barrett Browning, a Maria Mitchell—whose blood has flowed to the higher arches of the brain,—have lived to a holier purpose than they whose children are of the flesh alone, into whose minds they have breathed no clear perceptions of great principles, no moral aspiration, no spiritual life.

Her rights are as completely ignored in what is adjudged to be woman's sphere as out of it; the woman is uniformly sacrificed to the wife and mother. Neither law, gospel, public sentiment, nor domestic affection shield her from excessive and enforced maternity, depleting alike to mother and child;—all opportunity for mental improvement, health, happiness—yea, life itself, being ruthlessly sacrificed. The weazen, weary, withered, narrow-minded wife—mother of half a dozen children—her interests all centering at her fireside, forms a painful contrast in many a household to the liberal, genial, brilliant, cultured husband in the zenith of his power, who has never given one thought to the higher life, liberty, and happiness of the woman by his side; believing her self-abnegation to be Nature's law.

It is often asked, "if political equality would not rouse antagonism between the sexes?" If it could be proved that men and women had been harmonious in all ages and countries, and that women were happy and satisfied in their slavery, one might hesitate in proposing any change whatever. But the apathy, the helpless, hopeless resignation of a subjected class can not be called happiness. The more complete the despotism, the more smoothly all things move on the surface. "Order reigns in Warsaw." In right conditions, the interests of man and woman are essentially one; but in false conditions, they must ever be opposed. The principle of equality of rights underlies all human sentiments, and its assertion by any individual or class must rouse antagonism, unless conceded. This has been the battle of the ages, and will be until all forms of slavery are banished from the earth. Philosophers, historians, poets, novelists, alike paint woman the victim ever of man's power and selfishness. And now all writers on Eastern civilization tell us, the one insurmountable obstacle to the improvement of society in those countries, is the ignorance and superstition of the women. Stronger than the trammels of custom and law, is her religion, which teaches that her condition is Heaven-ordained. As the most ignorant minds cling with the greatest tenacity to the dogmas and traditions of their faith, a reform that involves an attack on that stronghold can only be carried by the education of another generation. Hence the self-assertion, the antagonism, the rebellion of woman, so much deplored in England and the United States, is the hope of our higher civilization. A woman growing up under American ideas of liberty in government and religion, having never blushed behind a Turkish mask, nor pressed her feet in Chinese shoes, can not brook any disabilities based on sex alone, without a deep feeling of antagonism with the power that creates it. The change needed to restore good feeling can not be reached by remanding woman to the spinning-wheel, and the contentment of her grandmother, but by conceding to her every right which the spirit of the age demands. Modern inventions have banished the spinning-wheel, and the same law of progress makes the woman of to-day a different woman from her grandmother.

With these brief replies to the oft-repeated objections made by the opposition, we hope to rouse new thoughts in minds prepared to receive them. That equal rights for woman have not long ago been secured, is due to causes beyond the control of the actors in this reform. "The success of a movement," says Lecky, "depends much less upon the force of its arguments, or upon the ability of its advocates, than the predisposition of society to receive it."

PART 3

Bread Comes First

PART 3

Bread Comes First

Introduction: Feminism and Class Politics

A marked change in political ideas, intellectual tone, and personal style sets in as we shift from the moral crusaders presented in Part 2 to the radicals and reformers who appear in Part 3. The woman's movement represented by Susan Anthony and Elizabeth Stanton drew deeply on its roots in small-town America and reacted far more strongly to what had been lost as the United States embarked on its romance with industrialization than to what the future might hold or to the price attached to industrialism for the millions of women less fortunate than themselves. Though they wrote and spoke as if they were equally concerned with women at all levels of society, the nineteenth-century woman's-rights spokeswomen rarely knew or deeply cared for the lot of women outside their own social class. Women's efforts in the temperance cause may in fact have been of more direct and immediate benefit to working-class women than their efforts in the woman's-rights movement during the last decades of the nineteenth century. Consequently their feminism was linked to status politics rather than to class politics. When the chips were down during the last stage of the suffrage movement, they did not draw back from the anti-immigrant ethos then abroad in the country but bent it to their own political ends, arguing that the best women of the country—middle class, educated, moral, Protestant—would, if given the vote, help counteract the political power of the growing numbers of new citizens among the immigrants.

The radical and reform feminists drew their ideas about women from a larger perspective on society. For one, they were intensely urban and cosmopolitan and saw the future within the framework of an urban, industrial society. Secondly, they were critical and questioning about the impact of social institutions upon human freedoms. They were also intensely secular, no longer involved in theology and the church. The passions that had been expended on religious issues by the moral-crusader feminists were expended on political issues and economic analysis and reform by the radical and reform feminists. While the moral crusaders shied away from a fundamental examination of the church or the family, the radicals simply assumed that religion was dead and that the family was either on the wane or in need of restructuring. Lastly—and this element was shared by radicals and reformers—their concern was as much for working-class women as for middle-class, educated women. Many had experienced working-class life in industrial cities at first hand and knew the price in human misery exacted by industrialization in England and America.

A very good example of a woman's response to the urban industrial scene can be seen in the life of Florence Kelley (Blumberg 1966; Kelley 1926; Kelley 1927). Born into a comfortable Philadelphia family and the daughter of a congressman, Kelley often accompanied her father on trips to the growing industrial cities. Congressman Kelley was, as she put it, "completely preoccupied with technical and financial development of the great American industries," while "the conservation of the human element was to remain a charge on the oncoming generation" (Kelley 1926). She described in detail her visits to the new steel mills and glass factories in Pennsylvania, noting "the utter unimportance of children compared with products in the minds of the people whom I was among." She found that the glass works depended even more on the labor of children than of men:

In front of the blower's oven stood the blower with his long blow-pipe and, at his feet sat the blower's boy, crouched so that his head was sometimes lower than the oven-opening with its molten glass. I did not then know that the trade name of these boys was "blower's dog," given them probably because they were compelled to respond instantly to the blower's whistle. The function of this boy was to take the blower's mold the instant the bottle or tumbler was removed from it, scrape it, and replace it perfectly smooth and clean for the next bottle or tumbler which the blower was already shaping in his pipe.

I have never found anyone who could tell me the limit of heat to which these pitiable victims could be exposed at the mouth of the blower's oven. How their little heads survived one night of exposure at close range, to that fearful glare, I cannot imagine as I think of the picture presented to me in 1871. Twenty years later, I was to encounter it again and again, when as Chief Inspector of Factories of the State of Illinois, I investigated the glasshouses and sought to obtain child labor laws to put an end to the practice. [Kelley 1927:57]

Florence Kelley was only twelve years old when she accompanied her father to inspect the new industrial processes that fascinated him; but she shared with many women of her generation of civic reformers the sense for detail and the concern for the "human element" that became a central motivating factor in her dedication to the protection of child labor and the establishment of standards for consumer goods.

A dedicated socialist for most of her life, Kelley was, however, not a political organizer and pamphleteer; her energies were devoted to hard battles for legislative reform. Revolution versus reform was not an issue for most of the women in the period from 1880 to 1910. Kelley was involved in radical socialist causes—she was, in fact, the first English translator of Friedrich Engels' *The Condition of the Working Class in England*—but her major energies went to the amelioration of the living conditions of women and children of her own day. There is no evidence that she was aware of the touch of male arrogance with which Engels took for granted her service as a translator. But having looked forward to meeting him on his visit to the United States in 1889, she was hurt that he had not taken the time to meet with her. Engels commented to a fellow radical:

[Florence Kelley] . . . seems to be hurt by a breach of etiquette and lack of gallantry towards ladies. But I do not allow the little women's rights ladies to demand gallantry from us; if they want men's rights they should also let themselves be treated as men. She will doubtless calm down. [Blumberg 1966:96]

Writing about the oppression of women in the family system, as Engels did, was many degrees removed from his personal life and the style with which he related to women in the radical movement—an attitude every bit as familiar to contemporary young radical women.

For women such as Florence Kelley, Jane Addams, Alice Hamilton, and Grace and Edith Abbott, concern for the plight of the working class was no empty mouthing of radical pieties; rather, it represented a central focus of their active involvement in reform movements. They did not romanticize the idea that proletarian marriages were "pure" compared to the oppressive impact of property factors upon bourgeois marriage, as Engels believed, for they saw at first hand the brutalizing impact on marriage of a grinding routine to earn a bare living, and they set out to do what they could to improve economic conditions in the urban setting, through unionization efforts, progressive-party formation, and legislative reform, in order to impose safety, wage, and product standards on the profit-seeking industrialists of their day.

It was difficult to choose representative people and the written evidence of their thought and action for this section. Many fascinating documents from the socialist and reform movements of the late-nineteenth and early-twentieth centuries that show the contributions of women have gone out of general circulation. Middle-class scholars have been far more interested in collecting and republishing the evidence of the middle-class woman's-rights movement than of the radical and reform women in American history.

We have chosen to divide the selections into two major categories. The first represents the *radical perspective*. Here an essential classic essay in socialistic history is Friedrich Engels' analysis of the origin of the family, private property, and the state. This essay provided the analytic underpinning for many of the radical critiques of the family and the connection between marriage and property on which later generations of radical thinkers have drawn. August Bebel's *Woman and Socialism* is far more of a "period" piece, emphasizing the particular demographic and economic trends he saw at the turn of the century that are no longer of very general interest. But as a self-educated worker and political organizer, Bebel had a vision of the position of women under socialism that remains relevant. No account of this period could be complete without some mention of Emma Goldman; her essay reprinted here seems to speak directly to our contemporary situation in its rare blend of radical analysis of the position of women and concern for the unique gratifications of maternity. Suzanne LaFollette's *Concerning Women* is the best example I have found of a radical libertarianism that shares in the anarchist suspicion of the bureaucratic state. It, too, speaks to our current situation.

The second part of this section presents the *reform per-*

spective. This term is not intended to indicate that the women involved were necessarily conservative or liberal rather than radical thinkers. It means only that their chief energies were devoted to amelioration, and their politics, while often socialist in ideology, did not center on agitation. Charlotte Gilman viewed herself as a socialist, but it was a non-Marxian, gentle form of socialism difficult to distinguish from the mild progressive politics of her period. Margaret Sanger was a radical socialist in her youth, but once she settled into her lifelong campaign for birth control, she lost all but the feminist passion for the right of women to control their own bodies. Jane Addams is the most representative of her generation of civic reformers. In basic social values she is closer to the moral crusaders of the nineteenth century than to other women in this section, but she shared with Goldman, Gilman, Kelley, and Sanger an intense involvement with urban issues and with the lives of working-class women and their families in the new urban America.

Marriage and Property:
Friedrich Engels (1820–1895)

Friedrich Engels and Karl Marx were lifelong friends, cofounders of scientific socialism, and active revolutionaries. Born into a prosperous commercial family in Barmen, Germany, Engels spent his youth in an extremely pious Protestant atmosphere. As a very young man he was attracted to the dissident currents of German intellectual and political life and contributed to periodicals in politics and philosophy. He left Germany in 1842 to work in a firm in Manchester, England, where his father had financial interests. Here, while Engels learned the inner workings of laissez-faire economics at first hand, he continued to contribute to English papers in support of the English Chartists and Owenites. In 1844, when he was twenty-two, he met Marx in Paris, and they began their association. The next few years were devoted to revolutionary work with underground radical groups on the Continent and to collaboration with Marx in a steady stream of political pamphlets, including the famous *Communist Manifesto*. After the failure of the revolution of 1848, Engels returned to England and the Manchester firm, where he earned enough to provide for himself and for Marx and his family during the years Marx was working on *Das Kapital*.

Engels retired from business in 1869 and devoted the remainder of his life to literary and revolutionary activity. Shortly after Marx's death in 1883 Engels worked over their joint notes on the origin and nature of the state and prepared the book that became an important link in the developing chain of socialist analyses of the connections among the major institutions of industrial society. It represents one of the first essays in which a critique of marriage and family structure was linked to the larger class system of society. First published in German in the 1880s, it did not receive American publication until 1902. It was therefore not accessible to most of the turn-of-century feminists who held a critical view of the family system.

Engels drew heavily on a source common to many late-nineteenth-century thinkers concerning the course of social evolution of human institutions. This was Lewis Morgan's *Ancient Society*, which first appeared in 1877. Engels and Marx joined their own conception of historical materialism to Morgan's evolutionary hypotheses in classical anthropology. It has been thought by some that when the early anthropological theories about human evolution were discredited, Engels' analysis was also discredited. But though Marx and Engels drew upon Morgan, their ideas on the nature of the state and the functions filled by monogamous marriage based on economic ties had been developed before they heard of Morgan and are not therefore dependent on the validity of Morgan's particular anthropological theories.

Thirty years before Engels wrote this essay, Marx and he had argued that the first division of labor was that between man and woman for the propogation of children. In the 1880s Engels added the concept that

> the first class opposition that appears in history coincides with the development of the antagonism between man and woman in monogamous marriage and the first class oppression coincides with that of the female sex by the male.

The family is therefore the "cellular form of civilized society," in which one can study "the oppositions and contradictions" of the larger economy and polity. Since marriage, like the structure of the state, is conditioned by the larger class system, Engels believed that marriage among the upper classes was always a marriage of "convenience" and often of a crass form of prostitution. The modern individual family was thus founded on the "open or concealed domestic slavery of the wife." Within the family the husband is the bourgeois, the wife the proletarian.

It was an easy step from Engels' analysis to planning a revolutionary society in which women would withdraw from private domestic service and return to socially meaningful participation in public production. But Engels, like Lenin, did not predict that the family would "wither away." On the contrary, both believed that by severing the link between marriage and property, and by absorbing women into public production, monogamous marriage based on individual attraction and love might come into being for the first time.

⚔ The Origin of the Family ⚔

. . . The original meaning of the word "family" (*familia*)
is not that compound of sentimentality and domestic strife
which forms the ideal of the present-day philistine; among
the Romans it did not at first even refer to the married pair
and their children, but only to the slaves. *Famulus* means domestic slave, and *familia* is the total number of slaves belonging to one man. As late as the time of Gaius, the *familia, id
est patrimonium* (family, that is, the patrimony, the inheritance) was bequeathed by will. The term was invented by
the Romans to denote a new social organism, whose head
ruled over wife and children and a number of slaves, and
was invested under Roman paternal power with rights of life
and death over them all.

This term, therefore, is no older than the iron-clad
family system of the Latin tribes, which came in after field
agriculture and after legalized servitude, as well as after
the separation of the Greeks and Latins. [Morgan, 474]

Marx adds:

The modern family contains in germ not only slavery
(*servitus*), but also serfdom, since from the beginning it is
related to agricultural services. It contains *in miniature* all
the contradictions which later extend throughout society
and its state.

Such a form of family shows the transition of the pairing
family to monogamy. In order to make certain of the wife's
fidelity and therefore of the paternity of the children, she is
delivered over unconditionally into the power of the husband. . . .
[The monogamous family developed] out of the pairing
family . . . in the transitional period between the upper

From Friedrich Engels, *The Origin of the Family, Private
Property, and the State*. New York, International Publishers,
1942. Pp. 51–74.

and middle stages of barbarism; its decisive victory is one of the signs that civilization is beginning. It is based on the supremacy of the man, the express purpose being to produce children of undisputed paternity; such paternity is demanded because these children are later to come into their father's property as his natural heirs. It is distinguished from pairing marriage by the much greater strength of the marriage tie, which can no longer be dissolved at either partner's wish. As a rule, it is now only the man who can dissolve it, and put away his wife. The right of conjugal infidelity also remains secured to him, at any rate by custom (the *Code Napoléon* explicitly accords it to the husband as long as he does not bring his concubine into the house), and as social life develops he exercises his right more and more; should the wife recall the old form of sexual life and attempt to revive it, she is punished more severely than ever.

We meet this new form of the family in all its severity among the Greeks. While the position of the goddesses in their mythology, as Marx points out, brings before us an earlier period when the position of women was freer and more respected, in the heroic age we find the woman already being humiliated by the domination of the man and by competition from girl slaves. Note how Telemachus in the *Odyssey* silences his mother. In Homer young women are booty and are handed over to the pleasure of the conquerors, the handsomest being picked by the commanders in order of rank; the entire *Iliad*, it will be remembered, turns on the quarrel of Achilles and Agamemnon over one of these slaves. If a hero is of any importance, Homer also mentions the captive girl with whom he shares his tent and his bed. These girls were also taken back to Greece and brought under the same roof as the wife, as Cassandra was brought by Agamemnon in Aeschylus; the sons begotten of them received a small share of the paternal inheritance and had the full status of freemen. . . . The legitimate wife was expected to put up with all this, but herself to remain strictly chaste and faithful. In the heroic age a Greek woman is, indeed, more respected than in the period of civilization, but to her husband she is after all nothing but the mother of his legitimate children and heirs, his chief housekeeper and the supervisor of his female slaves, whom he can and does take as concubines if he so fancies. It is the existence of slavery side by side with monogamy, the presence of young, beautiful slaves belonging unreservedly to the *man*, that stamps monogamy from the very beginning with its specific character of monogamy *for the woman only*, but not for the man. And that is the character it still has today. . . .

. . . [Monogamy] was not in any way the fruit of individual sex-love, with which it had nothing whatever to do; marriages remained as before marriages of convenience. It was the first form of the family to be based, not on natural, but on economic conditions—on the victory of private property over primitive, natural communal property. The Greeks themselves put the matter quite frankly: the sole exclusive aims of monogamous marriage were to make the man supreme in the family, and to propagate, as the future heirs to his wealth, children indisputably his own. Otherwise, marriage was a burden, a duty which had to be performed, whether one liked it or not, to gods, state, and one's ancestors. In Athens the law exacted from the man not only marriage but also the performance of a minimum of so-called conjugal duties.

Thus when monogamous marriage first makes its appearance in history, it is not as the reconciliation of man and woman, still less as the highest form of such a reconciliation. Quite the contrary. Monogamous marriage comes on the scene as the subjugation of the one sex by the other; it announces a struggle between the sexes unknown throughout the whole previous prehistoric period. In an old unpublished manuscript, written by Marx and myself in 1846, I find the words: "The first division of labor is that between man and woman for the propagation of children." And today I can add: The first class opposition that appears in history coincides with the development of the antagonism between man and woman in monogamous marriage, and the first class oppression coincides with that of the female sex by the male. Monogamous marriage was a great historical step forward; nevertheless, together with slavery and private wealth, it opens the period that has lasted until today in which every step forward is also relatively a step backward, in which prosperity and development for some is won through the misery and frustration of others. It is the cellular form of civilized society, in which the nature of the oppositions and contradictions fully active in that society can be already studied.

                              • • •

But if monogamy was the only one of all the known forms of the family through which modern sex-love could develop, that does not mean that within monogamy modern sexual love developed exclusively or even chiefly as the love of husband and wife for each other. That was precluded by the very nature of strictly monogamous marriage under the rule of the man. Among all historically active classes—that is, among all ruling classes—matrimony remained what it had been since the pairing marriage, a matter of convenience which was arranged by the parents. The first historical form of sexual love as passion, a passion recognized as natural to all human beings (at least if they belonged to the ruling classes), and as the highest form of the sexual impulse—and that is what constitutes its specific character—this first form of individual sexual love, the chivalrous love of the middle ages, was by no means conjugal. Quite the contrary. In its classic form among the Provençals, it heads straight for adultery, and the poets of love celebrated adultery. The flower of Provençal love poetry are the Albas (*aubades*, songs of dawn). They describe in glowing colors how the knight lies in bed beside his love—the wife of another man—while outside stands the watchman who calls to him as soon as the first gray of dawn (*alba*) appears, so that he can get away unobserved; the parting scene then forms the climax of the poem. The northern French and also the worthy Germans adopted this kind of poetry together with the corresponding fashion of chivalrous love; old Wolfram of Eschenbach has left us three wonderfully beautiful songs of dawn on this same improper subject, which I like better than his three long heroic poems.

Nowadays there are two ways of concluding a bourgeois marriage. In Catholic countries the parents, as before, procure a suitable wife for their young bourgeois son, and the consequence is, of course, the fullest development of the contradiction inherent in monogamy: the husband abandons himself to hetaerism and the wife to adultery. Probably the only reason why the Catholic Church abolished divorce was because it had convinced itself that there is no more a cure for adultery than there is for death. In Protestant countries, on the other hand, the rule is that the son of a bourgeois family is allowed to choose a wife from his own class with more or less freedom; hence there may be a certain element of love in the marriage, as, indeed, in accordance with Protestant hypocrisy, is always assumed, for decency's sake. Here the husband's hetaerism is a more sleepy kind of business, and adultery by the wife is less the rule. But since, in every kind of marriage, people remain what they were before, and since the bourgeois of Protestant countries are mostly philistines, all that this Protestant monogamy achieves, taking the average of the best cases, is a conjugal partnership of leaden boredom, known as "domestic bliss." The best mirror of these two methods of marrying is the novel—the French novel for the Catholic manner, the German for the Protestant. In both, the hero "gets" them: in the German, the young man gets the girl; in the French, the husband gets the horns. Which of them is worse off is sometimes questionable. This is why the French bourgeois is as much horrified by the dullness of the German novel as the German philistine is by the "immorality" of the French. However, now that "Berlin is a world capital," the German novel is beginning with a little less timidity to use as part of its regular stock-in-trade the hetaerism and adultery long familiar to that town.

In both cases, however, the marriage is conditioned by the class position of the parties and is to that extent always a marriage of convenience. In both cases this marriage of convenience turns often enough into crassest prostitution—sometimes of both partners, but far more commonly of the woman, who only differs from the ordinary courtesan in that she does not let out her body on piece-work as a wage-worker, but sells it once and for all into slavery. And of all marriages of convenience Fourier's words hold true: "As in grammar two negatives make an affirmative, so in matrimonial morality two prostitutions pass for a virtue." Sex-love in the relationship with a woman becomes, and can only become, the real rule among the oppressed classes, which means today among the proletariat—whether this relation is officially sanctioned or not. But here all the foundations of typical monogamy are cleared away. Here there is no property, for the preservation and inheritance of which monogamy and male supremacy were established; hence there is no incentive to make this male supremacy effective. What is more, there are no means of making it so. Bourgeois law, which protects this supremacy, exists only for the possessing class and their dealings with the proletarians. The law costs money and, on account of the worker's poverty, it has no validity for his relation to his

wife. Here quite other personal and social conditions decide.
And now that large-scale industry has taken the wife out of
the home onto the labor market and into the factory, and
made her often the bread-winner of the family, no basis for
any kind of male supremacy is left in the proletarian household—except, perhaps, for something of the brutality towards
women that has spread since the introduction of monogamy.
The proletarian family is therefore no longer monogamous in
the strict sense, even where there is passionate love and firmest loyalty on both sides, and maybe all the blessings of religious and civil authority. Here, therefore, the eternal at-
tendants of monogamy, hetaerism and adultery, play only an
almost vanishing part. The wife has in fact regained the right
to dissolve the marriage, and if two people cannot get on with
one another, they prefer to separate. In short, proletarian
marriage is monogamous in the etymological sense of the
word, but not at all in its historical sense.

Our jurists, of course, find that progress in legislation is
leaving women with no further ground of complaint. Modern
civilized systems of law increasingly acknowledge, first, that
for a marriage to be legal, it must be a contract freely entered
into by both partners, and, secondly, that also in the married
state both partners must stand on a common footing of equal
rights and duties. If both these demands are consistently
carried out, say the jurists, women have all they can ask.

This typically legalist method of argument is exactly the
same as that which the radical republican bourgeois uses to
put the proletarian in his place. The labor contract is to be
freely entered into by both partners. But it is considered to
have been freely entered into as soon as the law makes both
parties equal on *paper*. The power conferred on the one party
by the difference of class position, the pressure thereby
brought to bear on the other party—the real economic position of both—that is not the law's business. Again, for the
duration of the labor contract both parties are to have equal
rights, in so far as one or the other does not expressly surrender them. That economic relations compel the worker to
surrender even the last semblance of equal rights—here
again, that is no concern of the law.

In regard to marriage, the law, even the most advanced, is
fully satisfied as soon as the partners have formally recorded
that they are entering into the marriage of their own free
consent. What goes on in real life behind the juridical scenes,

how this free consent comes about—that is not the business
of the law and the jurist. And yet the most elementary comparative jurisprudence should show the jurist what this free
consent really amounts to. In the countries where an obligatory share of the paternal inheritance is secured to the children by law and they cannot therefore be disinherited—in
Germany, in the countries with French law and elsewhere—
the children are obliged to obtain their parents' consent to
their marriage. In the countries with English law, where parental consent to a marriage is not legally required, the parents on their side have full freedom in the testamentary
disposal of their property and can disinherit their children at
their pleasure. It is obvious that, in spite and precisely because
of this fact, freedom of marriage among the classes with
something to inherit is in reality not a whit greater in
England and America than it is in France and Germany.

As regards the legal equality of husband and wife in marriage, the position is no better. The legal inequality of the
two partners, bequeathed to us from earlier social conditions,
is not the cause but the effect of the economic oppression of
the woman. In the old communistic household, which comprised many couples and their children, the task entrusted to
the women of managing the household was as much a public
and socially necessary industry as the procuring of food by
the men. With the patriarchal family, and still more with the
single monogamous family, a change came. Household management lost its public character. It no longer concerned
society. It became a *private service*; the wife became the head
servant, excluded from all participation in social production.
Not until the coming of modern large-scale industry was the
road to social production opened to her again—and then only
to the proletarian wife. But it was opened in such a manner
that, if she carries out her duties in the private service of her
family, she remains excluded from public production and unable to earn; and if she wants to take part in public production and earn independently, she cannot carry out family
duties. And the wife's position in the factory is the position
of women in all branches of business, right up to medicine
and the law. The modern individual family is founded on the
open or concealed domestic slavery of the wife, and modern
society is a mass composed of these individual families as its
molecules.

In the great majority of cases today, at least in the possessing classes, the husband is obliged to earn a living and support his family, and that in itself gives him a position of supremacy, without any need for special legal titles and privileges. Within the family he is the bourgeois and the wife represents the proletariat. In the industrial world, the specific character of the economic oppression burdening the proletariat is visible in all its sharpness only when all special legal privileges of the capitalist class have been abolished and complete legal equality of both classes established. The democratic republic does not do away with the opposition of the two classes; on the contrary, it provides the clear field on which the fight can be fought out. And in the same way, the peculiar character of the supremacy of the husband over the wife in the modern family, the necessity of creating real social equality between them, and the way to do it, will only be seen in the clear light of day when both possess legally complete equality of rights. Then it will be plain that the first condition for the liberation of the wife is to bring the whole female sex back into public industry, and that this in turn demands the abolition of the monogamous family as the economic unit of society.

We thus have three principal forms of marriage which correspond broadly to the three principal stages of human development. For the period of savagery, group marriage; for barbarism, pairing marriage; for civilization, monogamy, supplemented by adultery and prostitution. Between pairing marriage and monogamy intervenes a period in the upper stage of barbarism when men have female slaves at their command and polygamy is practiced.

As our whole presentation has shown, the progress which manifests itself in these successive forms is connected with the peculiarity that women, but not men, are increasingly deprived of the sexual freedom of group marriage. In fact, for men group marriage actually still exists even to this day. What for the woman is a crime, entailing grave legal and social consequences, is considered honorable in a man or, at the worse, a slight moral blemish which he cheerfully bears. But the more the hetaerism of the past is changed in our time by capitalist commodity production and brought into conformity with it, the more, that is to say, it is transformed into undisguised prostitution, the more demoralizing are its effects. And it demoralizes men far more than women.

Among women, prostitution degrades only the unfortunate ones who become its victims, and even these by no means to the extent commonly believed. But it degrades the character of the whole male world. A long engagement, particularly, is in nine cases out of ten a regular preparatory school for conjugal infidelity.

We are now approaching a social revolution in which the economic foundations of monogamy as they have existed hitherto will disappear just as surely as those of its complement—prostitution. Monogamy arose from the concentration of considerable wealth in the hands of a single individual—a man—and from the need to bequeath this wealth to the children of that man and of no other. For this purpose, the monogamy of the woman was required, not that of the man, so this monogamy of the woman did not in any way interfere with open or concealed polygamy on the part of the man. But by transforming by far the greater portion, at any rate, of permanent, heritable wealth—the means of production—into social property, the coming social revolution will reduce to a minimum all this anxiety about bequeathing and inheriting. Having arisen from economic causes, will monogamy then disappear when these causes disappear?

One might answer, not without reason: far from disappearing, it will, on the contrary, be realized completely. For with the transformation of the means of production into social property there will disappear also wage-labor, the proletariat, and therefore the necessity for a certain—statistically calculable—number of women to surrender themselves for money. Prostitution disappears; monogamy, instead of collapsing, at last becomes a reality—also for men.

In any case, therefore, the position of men will be very much altered. But the position of women, of *all* women, also undergoes significant change. With the transfer of the means of production into common ownership, the single family ceases to be the economic unit of society. Private housekeeping is transformed into a social industry. The care and education of the children becomes a public affair; society looks after all children alike, whether they are legitimate or not. This removes all the anxiety about the "consequences," which today is the most essential social—moral as well as economic—factor that prevents a girl from giving herself completely to the man she loves. Will not that suffice to bring about the gradual growth of unconstrained sexual intercourse and with it a more tolerant public opinion in regard to a maiden's honor and a woman's shame? And, finally, have we not seen that in the modern world monogamy and prostitution are indeed contradictions, but inseparable contradictions, poles of the same state of society? Can prostitution disappear without dragging monogamy with it into the abyss?

Here a new element comes into play, an element which, at the time when monogamy was developing, existed at most in germ: individual sex-love.

Before the Middle Ages we cannot speak of individual sex-love. That personal beauty, close intimacy, similarity of tastes and so forth awakened in people of opposite sex the desire for sexual intercourse, that men and women were not totally indifferent regarding the partner with whom they entered into this most intimate relationship—that goes without saying. But it is still a very long way to our sexual love. Throughout the whole of antiquity, marriages were arranged by the parents, and the partners calmly accepted their choice. What little love there was between husband and wife in antiquity is not so much subjective inclination as objective duty, not the cause of the marriage, but its corollary. Love relationships in the modern sense only occur in antiquity outside official society. The shepherds of whose joys and sorrows in love Theocritus and Moschus sing, the Daphnis and Chloe of Longus are all slaves who have no part in the state, the free citizen's sphere of life. Except among slaves, we find love affairs only as products of the disintegration of the old world and carried on with women who also stand outside official society, with *hetairai*—that is, with foreigners or freed slaves: in Athens from the eve of its decline, in Rome under the Cæsars. If there were any real love affairs between free men and free women, these occurred only in the course of adultery. And to the classical love poet of antiquity, old Anacreon, sexual love in our sense mattered so little that it did not even matter to him which sex his beloved was.

Our sexual love differs essentially from the simple sexual desire, the Eros, of the ancients. In the first place, it assumes that the person loved returns the love; to this extent the woman is on an equal footing with the man, whereas in the Eros of antiquity she was often not even asked. Secondly, our sexual love has a degree of intensity and duration which makes both lovers feel that non-possession and separation are a great, if not the greatest, calamity; to possess one another, they risk high stakes, even life itself. In the ancient world this happened only, if at all, in adultery. And, finally, there arises a new moral standard in the judgment of a sexual relationship. We do not only ask, was it within or outside marriage? but also, did it spring from love and reciprocated love or not? Of course, this new standard has fared no better in feudal or bourgeois practice than all the other standards of morality—it is ignored. But neither does it fare any worse. It is recognized just as much as they are—in theory, on paper. And for the present it cannot ask anything more.

At the point where antiquity broke off its advance to sexual love, the Middle Ages took it up again: in adultery. We have already described the knightly love which gave rise to the songs of dawn. From the love which strives to break up marriage to the love which is to be its foundation there is still a long road, which chivalry never fully traversed. Even when we pass from the frivolous Latins to the virtuous Germans, we find in the *Nibelungenlied* that, although in her heart Kriemhild is as much in love with Siegfried as he is with her, yet when Gunther announces that he has promised her to a knight he does not name, she simply replies: "You have no need to ask me; as you bid me, so will I ever be; whom you, lord, give me as husband, him will I gladly take in troth." It never enters her head that her love can be even considered. Gunther asks for Brünhild in marriage, and Etzel for Kriemhild, though they have never seen them. . . . As a rule, the young prince's bride is selected by his parents, if they are still living, or, if not, by the prince himself, with the advice of the great feudal lords, who have a weighty word to say in all these cases. Nor can it be otherwise. For the knight or baron, as for the prince of the land himself, marriage is a political act, an opportunity to increase power by new alliances; the interest of the *house* must be decisive, not the wishes of an individual. What chance then is there for love to have the final word in the making of a marriage?

The same thing holds for the guild member in the medieval towns. The very privileges protecting him, the guild charters with all their clauses and rubrics, the intricate distinctions legally separating him from other guilds, from the members of his own guild or from his journeymen and apprentices, already made the circle narrow enough within which he could look for a suitable wife. And who in the circle was the most suitable was decided under this complicated system most certainly not by his individual preference but by the family interests.

In the vast majority of cases, therefore, marriage remained, up to the close of the middle ages, what it had been from the start—a matter which was not decided by the partners. In the beginning, people were already born married—married to an entire group of the opposite sex. In the later forms of group marriage similar relations probably existed, but with the group continually contracting. In the pairing marriage it was customary for the mothers to settle the marriages of their children; here, too, the decisive considerations are the new ties of kinship, which are to give the young pair a stronger position in the gens and tribe. And when, with the preponderance of private over communal property and the interest in its bequeathal, father-right and monogamy gained supremacy, the dependence of marriages on economic considerations became complete. The *form* of marriage by purchase disappears, the actual practice is steadily extended until not only the woman but also the man acquires a price—not according to his personal qualities, but according to his property. That the mutual affection of the people concerned should be the one paramount reason for marriage, outweighing everything else, was and always had been absolutely unheard of in the practice of the ruling classes; that sort of thing only happened in romance—or among the oppressed classes, who did not count.

Such was the state of things encountered by capitalist production when it began to prepare itself, after the epoch of geographical discoveries, to win world power by world trade and manufacture. One would suppose that this manner of marriage exactly suited it, and so it did. And yet—there are no limits to the irony of history—capitalist production itself was to make the decisive breach in it. By changing all things into commodities, it dissolved all inherited and traditional relationships, and, in place of time-honored custom and historic right, it set up purchase and sale, "free" contract. And the English jurist, H. S. Maine, thought he had made a tremendous discovery when he said that our whole progress in comparison with former epochs consisted in the fact that we had passed "from status to contract," from inherited to freely contracted conditions—which, in so far as it is correct, was already in *The Communist Manifesto*.

But a contract requires people who can dispose freely of

their persons, actions, and possessions, and meet each other on the footing of equal rights. To create these "free" and "equal" people was one of the main tasks of capitalist production. Even though at the start it was carried out only half-consciously, and under a religious disguise at that, from the time of the Lutheran and Calvinist Reformation the principle was established that man is only fully responsible for his actions when he acts with complete freedom of will, and that it is a moral duty to resist all coercion to an immoral act. But how did this fit in with the hitherto existing practice in the arrangement of marriages? Marriage, according to the bourgeois conception, was a contract, a legal transaction, and the most important one of all, because it disposed of two human beings, body and mind, for life. Formally, it is true, the contract at that time was entered into voluntarily: without the assent of the persons concerned, nothing could be done. But everyone knew only too well how this assent was obtained and who were the real contracting parties in the marriage. But if real freedom of decision was required for all other contracts, then why not for this? Had not the two young people to be coupled also the right to dispose freely of themselves, of their bodies and organs? Had not chivalry brought sex-love into fashion, and was not its proper bourgeois form, in contrast to chivalry's adulterous love, the love of husband and wife? And if it was the duty of married people to love each other, was it not equally the duty of lovers to marry each other and nobody else? Did not this right of the lovers stand higher than the right of parents, relations, and other traditional marriage-brokers and matchmakers? If the right of free, personal discrimination broke boldly into the Church and religion, how should it halt before the intolerable claim of the older generation to dispose of the body, soul, property, happiness, and unhappiness of the younger generation?

These questions inevitably arose at a time which was loosening all the old ties of society and undermining all traditional conceptions. The world had suddenly grown almost ten times bigger; instead of one quadrant of a hemisphere, the whole globe lay before the gaze of the West Europeans, who hastened to take the other seven quadrants into their possession. And with the old narrow barriers of their homeland fell also the thousand-year-old barriers of the prescribed medieval way of thought. To the outward and the inward eye of man opened an infinitely wider horizon. What did a young man care about the approval of respectability, or honorable guild privileges handed down for generations, when the wealth of India beckoned to him, the gold and the silver mines of Mexico and Potosí? For the bourgeoisie, it was the time of knight-errantry; they, too, had their romance and their raptures of love, but on a bourgeois footing and, in the last analysis, with bourgeois aims.

So it came about that the rising bourgeoisie, especially in Protestant countries, where existing conditions had been most severely shaken, increasingly recognized freedom of contract also in marriage, and carried it into effect in the manner described. Marriage remained class marriage, but within the class the partners were conceded a certain degree of freedom of choice. And on paper, in ethical theory and in poetic description, nothing was more immutably established than that every marriage is immoral which does not rest on mutual sexual love and really free agreement of husband and wife. In short, the love marriage was proclaimed as a human right, and indeed not only as a *droit de l'homme*, one of the rights of man, but also, for once in a way, as *droit de la femme*, one of the rights of woman.

This human right, however, differed in one respect from all other so-called human rights. While the latter, in practice, remained restricted to the ruling class (the bourgeoisie), and are directly or indirectly curtailed for the oppressed class (the proletariat), in the case of the former the irony of history plays another of its tricks. The ruling class remains dominated by the familiar economic influences and therefore only in exceptional cases does it provide instances of really freely contracted marriages, while among the oppressed class, as we have seen, these marriages are the rule.

Full freedom of marriage can therefore only be generally established when the abolition of capitalist production and of the property relations created by it has removed all the accompanying economic considerations which still exert such a powerful influence on the choice of a marriage partner. For then there is no other motive left except mutual inclination.

And as sexual love is by its nature exclusive—although at present this exclusiveness is fully realized only in the woman —the marriage based on sexual love is by its nature individual marriage. We have seen how right Bachofen was in regarding the advance from group marriage to individual marriage as primarily due to the women. Only the step from pairing marriage to monogamy can be put down to the credit of the men, and historically the essence of this was to make the position of the women worse and the infidelities of the men easier. If now the economic considerations also disappear which made women put up with the habitual infidelity of their husbands—concern for their own means of existence and still more for their children's future—then, according to all previous experience, the equality of woman thereby achieved will tend infinitely more to make men really monogamous than to make women polyandrous.

But what will quite certainly disappear from monogamy are all the features stamped upon it through its origin in property relations; these are, in the first place, supremacy of the man, and, secondly, indissolubility. The supremacy of the man in marriage is the simple consequence of his economic supremacy, and with the abolition of the latter will disappear of itself. The indissolubility of marriage is partly a consequence of the economic situation in which monogamy arose, partly tradition from the period when the connection between this economic situation and monogamy was not yet fully understood and was carried to extremes under a religious form. Today it is already broken through at a thousand points. If only the marriage based on love is moral, then also only the marriage in which love continues. But the intense emotion of individual sex-love varies very much in duration from one individual to another, especially among men, and if affection definitely comes to an end or is supplanted by a new passionate love, separation is a benefit for both partners as well as for society—only people will then be spared having to wade through the useless mire of a divorce case.

What we can now conjecture about the way in which sexual relations will be ordered after the impending overthrow of capitalist production is mainly of a negative character, limited for the most part to what will disappear. But what will there be new? That will be answered when a new generation has grown up: a generation of men who never in their lives have known what it is to buy a woman's surrender with money or any other social instrument of power; a generation of women who have never known what it is to give themselves to a man from any other considerations than real love, or to refuse to give themselves to their lover from fear of the economic consequences. When these people are in the world, they will care precious little what anybody today thinks they ought to do; they will make their own practice and their corresponding public opinion about the practice of each individual—and that will be the end of it.

Working-Class Socialist:
August Bebel (1840–1913)

While the momentum of the women's suffrage movement gathered for its final push to obtain the vote at the turn of the century, new voices were beginning to warn that the suffragists were doomed to disappointment when their goal was reached. August Bebel and Emma Goldman were prominent among these critical radical voices. A self-educated German worker, Bebel argued that the "bourgeois suffragists" deluded themselves in focusing on civil equality for men and women, and he predicted that, even with the vote in hand, countless women would still experience marriage as a form of sex slavery; that the vote would do nothing to abolish prostitution and nothing to abolish the economic dependence of wives. Bebel argued that even large increases in the number of bourgeois women entering higher education, the professions, and government would constitute only a minor improvement, for such a development would bring no help to the countless millions of working-class women in the Western countries who suffered from economic exploitation, damaged health, and marital misery.

Turn-of-the-century demographic trends were congenial to the political perspective Bebel brought to the problem. In the text of *Woman and Socialism* Bebel argued that contemporary trends in his day gave ample evidence that marriage was in a state of decline and dissolution, just as bourgeois society itself was. He noted several trends: the decline in the marriage and birth rates; the increase in the divorce rate; and the excess of females over males in most European adult populations. He concluded that such indices "proved" the institution of marriage and the structure of bourgeois society to be on the verge of collapse; they were signs of the coming revolution and the radical transformation of society. It was a foregone conclusion, in Bebel's view, that bourgeois society was "incompetent to abolish [such] evils and to liberate women."

A great deal has happened in the decades since Bebel

496

built his case for the need of a total socialist reconstruction of society and since he argued that such reconstruction would have to precede the emergence of any meaningful sex equality. Western bourgeois societies have shown great resilience and at least some capacity to effect significant internal reforms that have mitigated the harshness of life in the working classes. Many of the improvements Bebel thought could be attained in a capitalist society only by a small privileged class—comfort in the human dwelling, adequate nutrition and schooling, a safe workplace—are now enjoyed by all but a small proportion of the population in Western industrial societies.

Many of us have learned to our sorrow that there can be a considerable gap between political blueprints of a socialist society and the socialist reality following a revolution. Some of us, like numerous contemporary radical feminists, have not been familiar with these earlier attempts to state the case for socialism as a precondition for sex equality and have painstakingly groped for a new formulation in the 1970s.

The data Bebel used to build his case are no longer of interest to anyone but the specialist. But his statement of the case for socialism as it applied to the circumstances of women's lives and his vision of the "woman of the future" are of continuing interest, despite the bitter recognition of the fact that his vision of sixty years ago is yet to be realized anywhere on the globe.

ꝅ Woman and Socialism ꝅ

Introduction

We are living in an age of great social transformations that are steadily progressing. In all strata of society we perceive an unsettled state of mind and an increasing restlessness, denoting a marked tendency toward profound and radi-

From August Bebel, *Woman and Socialism*. Translated by Meta Stein. New York, Socialist Literature Company, 1910. Pp. 3–7; 466–472.

cal changes. Many questions have arisen and are being discussed with growing interest in ever widening circles. One of the most important of these questions and one that is constantly coming into greater prominence, is the *woman question*.

The woman question deals with the position that woman should hold in our social organism, and seeks to determine how she can best develop her powers and her abilities, in order to become a useful member of human society, endowed with equal rights and serving society according to her best capacity. From our point of view this question coincides with that other question: In what manner should society be organized to abolish oppression, exploitation, misery and need, and to bring about the physical and mental welfare of individuals and of society as a whole? To us then, the woman question is only one phase of the general social question that at present occupies all intelligent minds; its final solution can only be attained by removing social extremes and the evils which are a result of such extremes.

Nevertheless, the woman question demands our special consideration. What the position of woman has been in ancient society, what her position is to-day and what it will be in the coming social order, are questions that deeply concern at least one half of humanity. Indeed, in Europe they concern a majority of organized society, because women constitute a majority of the population. Moreover, the prevailing conceptions concerning the development of woman's social position during successive stages of history are so faulty, that enlightenment on this subject has become a necessity. Ignorance concerning the position of woman, chiefly accounts for the prejudice that the woman's movement has to contend with among all classes of people, by no means least among the women themselves. Many even venture to assert that there is no woman question at all, since woman's position has always been the same and will remain the same in the future, because nature has destined her to be a wife and a mother and to confine her activities to the home. Everything that is beyond the four narrow walls of her home and is not closely connected with her domestic duties, is not supposed to concern her.

In the woman question then we find two contending parties, just as in the labor question, which relates to the position of the workingman in human society. Those who wish to maintain everything as it is, are quick to relegate woman to her so-called "natural profession," believing that they have thereby settled the whole matter. They do not recognize that millions of women are not placed in a position enabling them to fulfill their natural function of wifehood and motherhood. . . . They furthermore do not recognize that to millions of other women their "natural profession" is a failure, because to them marriage has become a yoke and a condition of slavery, and they are obliged to drag on their lives in misery and despair. But these wiseacres are no more concerned by these facts than by the fact that in various trades and professions millions of women are exploited far beyond their strength, and must slave away their lives for a meagre subsistence. They remain deaf and blind to these disagreeable truths, as they remain deaf and blind to the misery of the proletariat, consoling themselves and others by the false assertion that it has always been thus and will always continue to be so. That woman is entitled, as well as man, to enjoy all the achievements of civilization, to lighten her burdens, to improve her condition, and to develop all her physical and mental qualities, they refuse to admit. When, furthermore, told that woman—to enjoy full physical and mental freedom—should also be economically independent, should no longer depend for subsistence upon the good will and favor of the other sex, the limit of their patience will be reached. Indignantly they will pour forth a bitter endictment of the "madness of the age" and its "crazy attempts at emancipation." These are the old ladies of both sexes who cannot overcome the narrow circle of their prejudices. They are the human owls that dwell wherever darkness prevails, and cry out in terror whenever a ray of light is cast into their agreeable gloom.

Others do not remain quite as blind to the eloquent facts. They confess that at no time woman's position has been so unsatisfactory in comparison to general social progress, as it is at present. They recognize that it is necessary to investigate how the condition of the self-supporting woman can be improved; but in the case of married women they believe the social problem to be solved. They favor the admission of unmarried women only into a limited number of trades and professions. Others again are more advanced and insist that competition between the sexes should not be limited to the inferior trades and professions, but should be extended to all higher branches of learning and the arts and sciences as well. They demand equal educational opportunities and that women should be admitted to all institutions of learning, including the universities. They also favor the appointment of women to government positions, pointing out the results already achieved by women in such positions, especially in the United States. A few are even coming forward to demand equal political rights for women. Woman, they argue, is a human being and a member of organized society as well as man, and the very fact that men have until now framed and administered the laws to suit their own purposes and to hold woman in subjugation, proves the necessity of woman's participation in public affairs.

It is noteworthy that all these various endeavors do not go beyond the scope of the present social order. The question is not propounded whether any of these proposed reforms will accomplish a decisive and essential improvement in the condition of women. According to the conceptions of bourgeois, or capitalistic society, the civic equality of men and women is deemed an ultimate solution of the woman question. People are either unconscious of the fact, or deceive themselves in regard to it, that the admission of women to trades and industries is already practically accomplished and is being strongly favored by the ruling classes in their own interest. But under prevailing conditions woman's invasion of industry has the detrimental effect of increasing competition on the labor market, and the result is a reduction in wages for both male and female workers. It is clear then, that this cannot be a satisfactory solution.

Men who favor these endeavors of women within the scope of present society, as well as the bourgeois women who are active in the movement, consider complete civic equality of women the ultimate goal. These men and women then differ radically from those who, in their narrow-mindedness, oppose the movement. They differ radically from those men who are actuated by petty motives of selfishness and fear of competition, and therefore try to prevent women from obtaining higher education and from gaining admission to the better paid professions. But there is no difference of class between them, such as exists between the worker and the capitalist.

If the bourgeois suffragists would achieve their aim and would bring about equal rights for men and women, they would still fail to abolish that sex slavery which marriage, in its present form, is to countless numbers of women; they would fail to abolish prostitution; they would fail to abolish the economic dependence of wives. To the great majority of women it also remains a matter of indifference whether a few thousand members of their sex, belonging to the more favored classes of society, obtain higher learning and enter some learned profession, or hold a public office. The general condition of the sex as a whole is not altered thereby.

The female sex as such has a double yoke to bear. Firstly, women suffer as a result of their social dependence upon men, and the inferior position allotted to them in society; formal equality before the law alleviates this condition, but does not remedy it. Secondly, women suffer as a result of their economic dependence, which is the lot of women in general, and especially of the proletarian women, as it is of the proletarian men.

We see, then, that all women, regardless of their social position, represent that sex which during the evolution of society has been oppressed and wronged by the other sex, and therefore it is to the common interest of all women to remove their disabilities by changing the laws and institutions of the present state and social order. But a great majority of women is furthermore deeply and personally concerned in a complete reorganization of the present state and social order which has for its purpose the abolition of wage-slavery, which at present weighs most heavily upon the women of the proletariat, as also the abolition of sex-slavery, which is closely connected with our industrial conditions and our system of private ownership.

The women who are active in the bourgeois suffrage movement, do not recognize the necessity of so complete a transformation. Influenced by their privileged social position, they consider the more radical aims of the proletarian woman's movement dangerous doctrines that must be opposed. The class antagonism that exists between the capitalist and working class and that is increasing with the growth of industrial problems, also clearly manifests itself then within the woman's movement. Still these sister-women, though antagonistic to each other on class lines, have a great many more points in common than the men engaged in the class struggle, and though they march in separate armies they may strike a united blow. This is true in regard to all endeavors pertaining to equal rights of woman under the present social order; that is, her right to enter any trade or profession adapted to her strength and ability, and her right to civic and political equality. These are, as we shall see, very important and very far-reaching aims. Besides striving for these aims, it is in the particular interest of proletarian women to work hand in hand with proletarian men for such measures and institutions that tend to protect the working woman from physical and mental degeneration, and to preserve her health and strength for a normal fulfillment of her maternal functions. Furthermore, it is the duty of the proletarian woman to join the men of her class in the struggle for a thorough-going transformation of society, to bring about an order that by its social institutions will enable both sexes to enjoy complete economic and intellectual independence.

Our goal then is, not only to achieve equality of men and women under the present social order, which constitutes the sole aim of the bourgeois woman's movement, but to go far beyond this, and to remove all barriers that make one human being dependent upon another, which includes the dependence of one sex upon the other. *This* solution of the woman question is identical with the solution of the social question. They who seek a complete solution of the woman question must, therefore, join hands with those who have inscribed upon their banner the solution of the social question in the interest of all mankind—the Socialists.

The Socialist Party is the only one that has made the full equality of women, their liberation from every form of dependence and oppression, an integral part of its program; not for reasons of propaganda, but from necessity. *For there can be no liberation of mankind without social independence and equality of the sexes.*

Woman in the Future

In the new society woman will be entirely independent, both socially and economically. She will not be subjected to even a trace of domination and exploitation, but will be free and man's equal, and mistress of her own lot. Her education will be the same as man's, with the exception of those deviations that are necessitated by the differences of sex and sexual functions. Living under normal conditions of life, she may fully develop and employ her physical and mental faculties. She chooses an occupation suited to her wishes, inclinations and abilities, and works under the same conditions as man. Engaged as a practical working woman in some field of industrial activity, she may, during a second part of the day, be educator, teacher or nurse, during a third she may practice a science or an art, and during a fourth she may perform some administrative function. She studies, works, enjoys pleasures and recreation with other women or with men, as she may choose or as occasions may present themselves.

In the choice of love she is as free and unhampered as man. She woos or is wooed, and enters into a union prompted by no other considerations but her own feelings. This union is a private agreement, without the interference of a functionary, just as marriage has been a private agreement until far into the middle ages. Here Socialism will create nothing new, it will merely reinstate, on a higher level of civilization and under a different social form, what generally prevailed before private property dominated society.

Man shall dispose of his own person, provided that the gratification of his impulses is not harmful or detrimental to others. The satisfaction of the sexual impulse is as much the private concern of each individual, as the satisfaction of any other natural impulse. No one is accountable to any one else, and no third person has a right to interfere. What I eat and drink, how I sleep and dress is my private affair, and my private affair also is my intercourse with a person of the opposite sex. Intelligence and culture, personal independence,—qualities that will become natural, owing to the education and conditions prevailing in the new society,—will prevent persons from committing actions that will prove detrimental to themselves. Men and women of future society will possess far more self-control and a better knowledge of their own natures, than men and women of to-day. The one fact alone, that the foolish prudery and secrecy connected with sexual matters will disappear, will make the relation of the sexes a far more natural and healthful one. If between a man and woman, who have entered into a union, incompatibility, disappointment or revulsion should appear, morality commands a dissolution of the union which has become unnatural, and therefore immoral. As all those circumstances will have vanished that have so far compelled a great many women either

to choose celibacy or prostitution, men can no longer dominate over women. On the other hand, the completely changed
social conditions will have removed the many hindrances and
harmful influences that affect married life to-day and frequently prevent its full development or make it quite impossible.

The impediments, contradictions and unnatural features
in the present position of woman are being recognized by
ever wider circles, and find expression in our modern literature on social questions, as well as in modern fiction; only
the form in which it is expressed sometimes fails to answer
the purpose. That present day marriage is not suited to its
purpose, is no longer denied by any thinking person. So it is
not surprising that even such persons favor a free choice of
love and a free dissolution of the marriage relation, who are
not inclined to draw the resulting conclusions that point to a
change of the entire social system. They believe that freedom
in sexual intercourse is justifiable among members of the
privileged classes only. . . .

. . . Compulsory marriage is the normal marriage to
bourgeois society. It is the only "moral" union of the sexes;
any other sexual union is "immoral." Bourgeois marriage is,
—this we have irrefutably proved,—the result of bourgeois
relations. Closely connected with private property and the
right of inheritance, it is contracted to obtain "legitimate"
children. Under the pressure of social conditions it is forced
also upon those who have nothing to bequeath. It becomes a
social law, the violation of which is punished by the state,
by imprisonment of the men or women who have committed
adultery and have become divorced.

But in Socialistic society there will be nothing to bequeath, unless house furnishings and personal belongings
should be regarded as hereditary portions; so the modern
form of marriage becomes untenable from this point of view
also. This also settles the question of inheritance, which
Socialism will not need to abolish. Where there is no private
property, there can be no right of inheritance. So woman
will be *free*, and the children she may have will not impair
her freedom, they will only increase her pleasure in life.
Nurses, teachers, women friends, the rising female generation, all these will stand by her when she is in need of
assistance. . . .

. . . For thousands of years human society has passed

thru all phases of development, only to return to its starting point: communistic property and complete liberty and fraternity; but no longer only for the members of the gens, but for all human beings. That is what the great progress consists of. What bourgeois society has striven for in vain, in what it failed and was bound to fail,—to establish liberty, equality and fraternity for all,—will be realized by Socialism. Bourgeois society could merely advance the theory, but here, as in many other things, practice was contrary to the theories. Socialism will unite theory and practice.

But as mankind returns to the starting point of its development, it will do so on an infinitely higher level of civilization. If primitive society had common ownership in the gens and the clan, it was but in a coarse form and an undeveloped stage. The course of development that man has since undergone, has reduced common property to small and insignificant remnants, has shattered the gens and has finally atomized society; but in its various phases it has also greatly heightened the productive forces of society and the extensiveness of its demands; it has transformed the gentes and the tribes into nations, and has thereby again created a condition that is in glaring contradiction to the requirements of society. It is the task of the future to remove this contradiction by re-establishing the common ownership of property and the means of production on the broadest basis.

Society takes back what it has at one time possessed and has itself created, but it enables all to live in accordance with the newly created conditions of life on the highest level of civilization. In other words, it grants to all what under more primitive conditions has been the privilege of single individuals or classes. Now woman, too, is restored to the active position maintained by her in primitive society; only she no longer is mistress, but man's equal.

"The end of the development of the state resembles the beginnings of human existence. Primitive equality is reinstated. The maternal material existence opens and closes the cycle of human affairs." Thus Backofen, in his book on The Matriarchate.

Red Emma on Women:
Emma Goldman (1869–1940)

Emma Goldman was perhaps the most passionate rebel among the women represented in this volume. An anarchist committed to the view that "revolution is but thought carried into action," she stands in the line of other flaming spirits, such as Fanny Wright, Margaret Fuller, and Margaret Sanger, though she outshines them all in her charismatic ardor. From the hanging of four Chicago anarchists in 1887, which galvanized her thought into a commitment to action, to her death fifty years later, she lived in a whirl of radical thought and action in both Europe and America.

Emma Goldman was born in Russia in 1869, the daughter of a despotic father with a violent temper, which he discharged most often in conflict with Emma. Her own summary of her development applies equally well to her whole life—"largely in revolt." When repression at home was compounded by repression of Jews following the assassination of Czar Alexander II, she fled with a sister to the United States, where they settled in Rochester, New York. Working ten-hour days in an overcoat factory for $2.50 a week, she soon became as disillusioned with America as she had been with Russia. When she was seventeen she married a fellow immigrant, Jacob Kershner, found marriage equally disillusioning, and fled to New York for an active life as a revolutionary. Political study with Johann Most, editor of the German-language radical newspaper *Freiheit*, gave her her "voice," and she began her political life as a speaker, organizer, and agitator.

Many people who went to hear her speak came out of curiosity to see the firebrand in action but left impressed with her sincerity and integrity. A good example was Roger Baldwin, the civil-libertarian, who went to hear her when he was fresh out of Harvard. He later reported:

It was the eye-opener of my life. Never before had I heard such social passion, such courageous exposure of basic evils, such electric power behind words, such a sweeping challenge to all values I had been taught to hold highest. From that day forth I was her admirer. [Ishill 1957:22–23]

Goldman's skeptical view of the suffragists was no different from her skeptical view of most of the groups she analyzed and addressed. Combative by nature, she lectured on atheism to churchmen and free love to moralists, just as she denounced the ballot to suffrage campaigners. In her speeches, as in her writings in the journal *Mother Earth*, which she founded and edited from 1906 to 1918, she was always the ardent antagonist and critic. As she put it, "the more opposition I encountered, the more I was in my element."

Her views toward suffrage for women are aptly summarized in one of her essays:

I am not opposed to woman suffrage on the conventional ground that she is not equal to it. I see neither physical, psychological, nor mental reasons why woman should not have the equal right to vote with man. But that can not possibly blind me to the absurd notion that woman will accomplish that wherein man has failed. If she would not make things worse, she certainly could not make them better. To assume, therefore, that she would succeed in purifying something which is not susceptible of purification is to credit her with supernatural powers. [Goldman 1970: 53–54]

Goldman was active in the campaign for birth control several years before Margaret Sanger began her concerted campaign. In 1916 Goldman was arrested for giving public instruction in the use of contraceptives, but she went right back to deliver the same lecture again once she was released from jail.

Her political life was one long series of enthusiastic hopes followed by acute disillusionment, from the encounter with the United States to her experience with Communism in the Soviet Union and Spain. When she was deported with other anarchists to Russia in 1919, it was only two years before she became disenchanted with the Soviet experiment on the grounds of the suppression of free speech and party elitism. Ever the anarchist libertarian, she believed that the "triumph of the state meant the defeat of the Revolution." There were few people to hear her message during the romance with centralism in the 1930s, for her ideas on decentralization and libertarianism were then in total eclipse.

She was also a feminist visionary who speaks to the mood and the goals of feminism in the 1970s far better than she did to the women of her own day. In the following selection she speaks out with a very special voice, acceptable neither to the woman's-rights feminists, who accepted the society and merely wished to see more room made for women, nor to those feminists who rejected the traditional commitments of women to love and maternity. Goldman sought a blend of her own, the best that women could contribute to the world as women, but joined with men in the struggle for the utmost political, economic, and social freedom in some sane society of the future.

The reader who wishes to know Emma Goldman better will find a good range of available materials, including Alix Shulman's excellent recent collection of her writings and speeches (Shulman 1972), Drinnon's biography (1961), and Goldman's own fascinating autobiography, *Living My Life* (1931).

ᐩ The Tragedy of Woman's Emancipation ᐤ

I begin with an admission: Regardless of all political and economic theories, treating of the fundamental differences between various groups within the human race, regardless of class and race distinctions, regardless of all artificial boundary lines between woman's rights and man's rights, I hold that there is a point where these differentiations may meet and grow into one perfect whole.

With this I do not mean to propose a peace treaty. The general social antagonism which has taken hold of our entire public life today, brought about through the force of opposing and contradictory interests, will crumble to pieces when the

From Alix Kates Shulman, ed., *Red Emma Speaks: Selected Writings and Speeches by Emma Goldman*. New York, Vintage, 1972. Pp. 133–142.

reorganization of our social life, based upon the principles of economic justice, shall have become a reality.

Peace or harmony between the sexes and individuals does not necessarily depend on a superficial equalization of human beings; nor does it call for the elimination of individual traits and peculiarities. The problem that confronts us today, and which the nearest future is to solve, is how to be one's self and yet in oneness with others, to feel deeply with all human beings and still retain one's own characteristic qualities. This seems to me to be the basis upon which the mass and the individual, the true democrat and the true individuality, man and woman, can meet without antagonism and opposition. The motto should not be: Forgive one another; rather, Understand one another. The oft-quoted sentence of Madame de Staël: "To understand everything means to forgive everything," has never particularly appealed to me; it has the odor of the confessional; to forgive one's fellow-being conveys the idea of pharisaical superiority. To understand one's fellow-being suffices. The admission partly represents the fundamental aspect of my views on the emancipation of woman and its effect upon the entire sex.

Emancipation should make it possible for woman to be human in the truest sense. Everything within her that craves assertion and activity should reach its fullest expression; all artificial barriers should be broken, and the road towards greater freedom cleared of every trace of centuries of submission and slavery.

This was the original aim of the movement for woman's emancipation. But the results so far achieved have isolated woman and have robbed her of the fountain springs of that happiness which is so essential to her. Merely external emancipation has made of the modern woman an artificial being, who reminds one of the products of French arboriculture with its arabesque trees and shrubs, pyramids, wheels, and wreaths; anything, except the forms which would be reached by the expression of her own inner qualities. Such artificially grown plants of the female sex are to be found in large numbers, especially in the so-called intellectual sphere of our life.

Liberty and equality for woman! What hopes and aspirations these words awakened when they were first uttered by some of the noblest and bravest souls of those days. The sun in all his light and glory was to rise upon a new world; in this world woman was to be free to direct her own destiny

—an aim certainly worthy of the great enthusiasm, courage, perseverance, and ceaseless effort of the tremendous host of pioneer men and women, who staked everything against a world of prejudice and ignorance.

My hopes also move towards that goal, but I hold that the emancipation of woman, as interpreted and practically applied today, has failed to reach that great end. Now, woman is confronted with the necessity of emancipating herself from emancipation, if she really desires to be free. This may sound paradoxical, but is, nevertheless, only too true.

What has she achieved through her emancipation? Equal suffrage in a few States. Has that purified our political life, as many well-meaning advocates predicted? Certainly not. Incidentally, it is really time that persons with plain, sound judgment should cease to talk about corruption in politics in a boarding-school tone. Corruption of politics has nothing to do with the morals, or the laxity of morals, of various political personalities. Its cause is altogether a material one. Politics is the reflex of the business and industrial world, the mottos of which are: "To take is more blessed than to give"; "buy cheap and sell dear"; "one soiled hand washes the other." There is no hope even that woman, with her right to vote, will ever purify politics.

Emancipation has brought woman economic equality with man; that is, she can choose her own profession and trade; but as her past and present physical training has not equipped her with the necessary strength to compete with man, she is often compelled to exhaust all her energy, use up her vitality, and strain every nerve in order to reach the market value. Very few ever succeed, for it is a fact that women teachers, doctors, lawyers, architects, and engineers are neither met with the same confidence as their male colleagues, nor receive equal remuneration. And those that do reach that enticing equality generally do so at the expense of their physical and psychical well-being. As to the great mass of working girls and women, how much independence is gained if the narrowness and lack of freedom of the home is exchanged for the narrowness and lack of freedom of the factory, sweat-shop, department store, or office? In addition is the burden which is laid on many women of looking after a "home, sweet home"—cold, dreary, disorderly, uninviting—after a day's hard work. Glorious independence! No wonder that hundreds of girls are so willing to accept the first offer of marriage, sick and tired of their "independence" behind the counter, at the sewing or typewriting machine. They are just as ready to marry as girls of the middle class, who long to throw off the yoke of parental supremacy. A so-called independence which leads only to earning the merest subsistence is not so enticing, not so ideal, that one could expect woman to sacrifice everything for it. Our highly praised independence is, after all, but a slow process of dulling and stifling woman's nature, her love instinct, and her mother instinct.

Nevertheless, the position of the working girl is far more natural and human than that of her seemingly more fortunate sister in the more cultured professional walks of life— teachers, physicians, lawyers, engineers, etc., who have to make a dignified, proper appearance, while the inner life is growing empty and dead.

The narrowness of the existing conception of woman's independence and emancipation; the dread of love for a man who is not her social equal; the fear that love will rob her of her freedom and independence; the horror that love or the joy of motherhood will only hinder her in the full exercise of her profession—all these together make of the emancipated modern woman a compulsory vestal, before whom life, with its great clarifying sorrows and its deep, entrancing joys, rolls on without touching or gripping her soul.

Emancipation, as understood by the majority of its adherents and exponents, is of too narrow a scope to permit the boundless love and ecstasy contained in the deep emotion of the true woman, sweetheart, mother, in freedom.

The tragedy of the self-supporting or economically free woman does not lie in too many, but in too few experiences. True, she surpasses her sister of past generations in knowledge of the world and human nature; it is just because of this that she feels deeply the lack of life's essence, which alone can enrich the human soul, and without which the majority of women have become mere professional automatons.

That such a state of affairs was bound to come was foreseen by those who realized that, in the domain of ethics, there still remained many decaying ruins of the time of the undisputed superiority of man; ruins that are still considered useful. And, what is more important, a goodly number of the emancipated are unable to get along without them. Every movement that aims at the destruction of existing institutions

and the replacement thereof with something more advanced,
more perfect, has followers who in theory stand for the most
radical ideas, but who, nevertheless, in their every-day practice, are like the average Philistine, feigning respectability
and clamoring for the good opinion of their opponents. There
are, for example, Socialists, and even Anarchists, who stand
for the idea that property is robbery, yet who will grow indignant if anyone owe them the value of a half-dozen pins.

The same Philistine can be found in the movement for
woman's emancipation. Yellow journalists and milk-and-
water littérateurs have painted pictures of the emancipated
woman that make the hair of the good citizen and his dull
companion stand up on end. Every member of the woman's
rights movement was pictured as a George Sand in her absolute disregard of morality. Nothing was sacred to her. She
had no respect for the ideal relation between man and woman.
In short, emancipation stood only for a reckless life of lust
and sin, regardless of society, religion, and morality. The exponents of woman's rights were highly indignant at such misrepresentation, and, lacking humor, they exerted all their
energy to prove that they were not at all as bad as they were
painted, but the very reverse. Of course, as long as woman
was the slave of man, she could not be good and pure, but
now that she was free and independent she would prove how
good she could be and that her influence would have a purifying effect on all institutions in society. True, the movement
for woman's rights has broken many old fetters, but it has
also forged new ones. The great movement of *true* emancipation has not met with a great race of women who could look
liberty in the face. Their narrow, puritanical vision banished
man, as a disturber and doubtful character, out of their emotional life. Man was not to be tolerated at any price, except
perhaps as the father of a child, since a child could not very
well come to life without a father. Fortunately, the most rigid
Puritans never will be strong enough to kill the innate craving
for motherhood. But woman's freedom is closely allied with
man's freedom, and many of my so-called emancipated sisters seem to overlook the fact that a child born in freedom
needs the love and devotion of each human being about him,
man as well as woman. Unfortunately, it is this narrow conception of human relations that has brought about a great
tragedy in the lives of the modern man and woman.

About fifteen years ago appeared a work from the pen of

the brilliant Norwegian Laura Marholm, called *Woman, a Character Study*. She was one of the first to call attention to the emptiness and narrowness of the existing conception of woman's emancipation, and its tragic effect upon the inner life of woman. In her work Laura Marholm speaks of the fate of several gifted women of international fame: the genius Eleonora Duse; the great mathematician and writer Sonya Kovalevskaia; the artist and poet-nature Marie Bashkirtzeff, who died so young. Through each description of the lives of these women of such extraordinary mentality runs a marked trail of unsatisfied craving for a full, rounded, complete, and beautiful life, and the unrest and loneliness resulting from the lack of it. Through these masterly psychological sketches one cannot help but see that the higher the mental development of woman, the less possible it is for her to meet a congenial mate who will see in her, not only sex, but also the human being, the friend, the comrade and strong individuality, who cannot and ought not lose a single trait of her character.

The average man with his self-sufficiency, his ridiculously superior airs of patronage towards the female sex, is an impossibility for woman as depicted in the *Character Study* by Laura Marholm. Equally impossible for her is the man who can see in her nothing more than her mentality and her genius, and who fails to awaken her woman nature.

A rich intellect and a fine soul are usually considered necessary attributes of a deep and beautiful personality. In the case of the modern woman, these attributes serve as a hindrance to the complete assertion of her being. For over a hundred years the old form of marriage, based on the Bible, "Till death doth part," has been denounced as an institution that stands for the sovereignty of the man over the woman, of her complete submission to his whims and commands, and absolute dependence on his name and support. Time and again it has been conclusively proved that the old matrimonial relation restricted woman to the function of man's servant and the bearer of his children. And yet we find many emancipated women who prefer marriage, with all its deficiencies, to the narrowness of an unmarried life; narrow and unendurable because of the chains of moral and social prejudice that cramp and bind her nature.

The explanation of such inconsistency on the part of many advanced women is to be found in the fact that they never truly understood the meaning of emancipation. They thought that all that was needed was independence from external tyrannies; the internal tyrants, far more harmful to life and growth—ethical and social conventions—were left to take care of themselves; and they have taken care of themselves. They seem to get along as beautifully in the heads and hearts of the most active exponents of woman's emancipation, as in the heads and hearts of our grand-mothers.

These internal tyrants, whether they be in the form of public opinion or what will mother say, or brother, father, aunt, or relative of any sort; what will Mrs. Grundy, Mr. Comstock, the employer, the Board of Education say? All these busybodies, moral detectives, jailers of the human spirit, what will they say? Until woman has learned to defy them all, to stand firmly on her own ground and to insist upon her own unrestricted freedom, to listen to the voice of her nature, whether it call for life's greatest treasure, love for a man, or her most glorious privilege, the right to give birth to a child, she cannot call herself emancipated. How many emancipated women are brave enough to acknowledge that the voice of love is calling, wildly beating against their breasts, demanding to be heard, to be satisfied.

The French writer Jean Reibrach, in one of his novels, *New Beauty*, attempts to picture the ideal, beautiful, eman-cipated woman. This ideal is embodied in a young girl, a physician. She talks very cleverly and wisely of how to feed infants; she is kind, and administers medicines free to poor mothers. She converses with a young man of her acquaint-ance about the sanitary conditions of the future, and how various bacilli and germs shall be exterminated by the use of stone walls and floors, and by the doing away with rugs and hangings. She is, of course, very plainly and practically dressed, mostly in black. The young man, who, at their first meeting, was overawed by the wisdom of his emancipated friend, gradually learns to understand her, and recognizes one fine day that he loves her. They are young, and she is kind and beautiful, and though always in rigid attire, her appearance is softened by a spotlessly clean white collar and cuffs. One would expect that he would tell her of his love, but he is not one to commit romantic absurdities. Poetry and the enthusiasm of love cover their blushing faces before the pure beauty of the lady. He silences the voice of his nature, and remains correct. She, too, is always exact, always rational, always well behaved. I fear if they had formed a union, the young man would have risked freezing to death. I must confess that I can see nothing beautiful in this new beauty, who is as cold as the stone walls and floors she dreams of. Rather would I have the love songs of romantic ages, rather Don Juan and Madame Venus, rather an elopement by ladder and rope on a moonlight night, followed by the father's curse, mother's moans, and the moral comments of neighbors, than correctness and propriety measured by yardsticks. If love does not know how to give and take without restrictions, it is not love, but a transaction that never fails to lay stress on a plus and a minus.

The greatest shortcoming of the emancipation of the present day lies in its artificial stiffness and its narrow respectabilities, which produce an emptiness in woman's soul that will not let her drink from the fountain of life. I once remarked that there seemed to be a deeper relationship between the old-fashioned mother and hostess, ever on the alert for the happiness of her little ones and the comfort of those she loves, and the truly new woman, than between the latter and her average emancipated sister. The disciples of emancipation pure and simple declared me a heathen, fit only for the stake. Their blind zeal did not let them see that my comparison between the old and the new was merely to prove that a goodly number of our grandmothers had more blood in their veins, far more humor and wit, and certainly a greater amount of naturalness, kind-heartedness, and simplicity, than the majority of our emancipated professional women who fill the colleges, halls of learning and various offices. This does not mean a wish to return to the past, nor does it condemn woman to her old sphere, the kitchen and the nursery.

Salvation lies in an energetic march onward towards a brighter and clearer future. We are in need of unhampered growth out of old traditions and habits. The movement for woman's emancipation has so far made but the first step in that direction. It is to be hoped that it will gather strength to make another. The right to vote, or equal civil rights, may be good demands, but true emancipation begins neither at the polls nor in courts. It begins in woman's soul. History tells us that every oppressed class gained true liberation from its masters through its own efforts. It is necessary that woman learn that lesson, that she realize that her freedom will reach as far as her power to achieve her freedom reaches. It is, therefore, far more important for her to begin with her inner regeneration, to cut loose from the weight of prejudices, traditions, and customs. The demand for equal rights in every vocation of life is just and fair; but, after all, the most vital right is the right to love and be loved. Indeed, if partial emancipation is to become a complete and true emancipation of woman, it will have to do away with the ridiculous notion that to be loved, to be sweetheart and mother, is synonymous with being a slave or subordinate. It will have to do away with the absurd notion of the dualism of the sexes, or that man and woman represent two antagonistic worlds.

Pettiness separates; breadth unites. Let us be broad and big. Let us not overlook vital things because of the bulk of trifles confronting us. A true conception of the relation of the sexes will not admit of conqueror and conquered; it knows of but one great thing: to give of one's self boundlessly, in order to find one's self richer, deeper, better. That alone can fill the emptiness, and transform the tragedy of woman's emancipation into joy, limitless joy.

The Right to One's Body:
Margaret Sanger (1879–1966)

Without the means to prevent, and to control the timing of, conception, economic and political rights have limited meaning for women. If women cannot plan their pregnancies, they can plan little else in their lives during the long period from age twelve to fifty, while they are "at procreative risk." So long as sexual pleasure could not be enjoyed without the anxiety of a possible pregnancy, women seeking wider and more demanding participation in professions or politics really had an either-or choice of marriage *or* a career, while those who attempted the combination did so with a sense of anxiety that can be anathema to creativity in work. Sexual abstinence has never been a banner that could attract very many women or men, even in the nineteenth century, much less in the twentieth.

As perhaps the greatest champion of woman's freedom to control her own life and body, Margaret Sanger has a central place in any overview of feminist history and thought. From the first issue of her magazine, *Woman Rebel*, in March 1914 to the financial and organizational support she gave to research in hormonal anovulants in the post-World War II period, her life was dedicated to a passionate single-minded commitment to bring the best birth-control methods to ever larger numbers of women around the world.

There is little need for a long personal introduction to Margaret Sanger in this book. She was not a modest person who avoided the limelight, but a self-proclaimed heroine who sought it. She had a romantic flair for dramatizing herself and keeping the public spotlight on her activities. This was of course by intent, for it was to challenge regulations and laws that suppressed the free circulation of contraceptive information that she dedicated her efforts in the first stage of the birth-control movement. Deeply alienated from the society around her, she was drawn to

radical political circles in New York and again in France
during the years just before World War I. The proposals of Rosa Luxemburg in Germany and Anatole France
in France that workers undertake a "birth strike" to stop
the flow of exploited manpower into industrial-military
work, revealed to her an opportunity to blend several of her
own goals: to alleviate the misery of workers' lives, to contribute to the emancipation of women, and to aggravate the
class struggle that would eventuate in revolutionary upheaval
and change. Emma Goldman had talked about women's
need for contraception in the previous decade, but it was
Margaret Sanger who took this issue as her own for a lifetime of effort. Further, Margaret Sanger has told her own
story of the fight for birth control in a style that communicates as much about herself as a person as about the movement itself (Sanger 1920; Sanger 1931).

Her writings have been supplemented in the past few
years by two excellent new books on her life and work
(Douglas 1970; Kennedy 1970). Both of the recent studies
have corrected many points of exaggeration in Sanger's own
telling of her story, but the courage and rebellious quality
of the woman are best caught in her own words. For this
reason two major passages have been selected from her
account of the early struggle. One describes the obstetric
case which led to her decision to quit nursing and seek an
active role as publicist and educator on birth-control matters;
the other is her own account of the opening of the first birth-control clinic in the Brownsville section of Brooklyn. Kennedy
(1970:16–19) may be correct in suggesting that Sanger's romantic tendencies led her to exaggerate the significance of the
particular case of Sadie Sacks and that her own psychological
need for attention from the world led her to commit many
factual distortions. On the other hand, a rebel is a rebel, not
a Machiavellian tactician engaging in a shrewd calculus of
what would best enhance her own prestige. Kennedy's
analysis of these points reveals more about Kennedy than
about Sanger.

Women in the middle class had a more varied knowledge
of contraceptive methods than Sanger was aware of in the
early years, and it is clear that she did not have to go to
Europe in 1914 to inform herself about medical knowledge
concerning contraception. Her claim that New York libraries
had no such information has been disproved in Kennedy's

check (1970,18–19) on such library holdings years before Sanger claimed to have checked them. Her goal, however, was to effect changes, not in the middle class, but in working-class life, where the hardships produced by excessive fertility on very low wages took their worst toll of life and health. The production of her sixteen-page pamphlet, *Family Limitation*, shows the contrast between Sanger's willingness to be martyred for her cause and the timidity of men even among the radical printers she knew through political circles in New York. Several printers told her the pamphlet could never be printed, since it was a "Sing Sing job." When she finally found one courageous enough to undertake the work, it had to be done in secret, and the hundred thousand copies had to be wrapped and transported to storage in several cities, waiting for word from her to release them. Her plan was to insure simultaneous, rapid distribution, so that the pamphlets would reach people even after her arrest. The pamphlet itself is an interesting document, giving advice on douching, the use of the condom, the French pessary, sponges, and vaginal suppositories. She included names and addresses where women could write for further information or actually purchase supplies, as well as the recipe for home production of vaginal suppositories, which she had learned in Europe.

Some of her information has since been superceded by more accurate knowledge of conception, of course. Even for that day, her douching recommendations were not considered reliable. But two characteristics of the pamphlet have special appeal. One was consistent with her politics—its direct approach to the interests of working-class women. She notes in the introduction, for example:

Don't be over sentimental in this important phase of hygiene. The inevitable fact is that unless you prevent the male sperm from entering the womb, you are going to become pregnant. Women of the working class, especially wage workers, should not have more than two children at most. The average working man can support no more and the average working woman can take care of no more in decent fashion. . . . The working woman can use direct action by refusing to supply the market with children to be exploited, by refusing to populate the earth with slaves. It is also the one most direct method for you working women to help yourself *today*. [Sanger 1917:3]

The second characteristic is a criticism of *coitus interruptus* as a contraceptive device on the ground that it deprives women of sexual satisfaction:

> No one can doubt that this is a perfectly safe method; and it is not considered so dangerous to the man as some authorities have formerly viewed it, but it requires a man of the strongest will power to be certain that he has withdrawn before any of the semen is deposited in the vagina. It is very difficult to determine exactly whether this has been done. The greatest objection to this is the evil effect upon the woman's nervous condition. If she has not completed her desire, she is under a highly nervous tension, her whole being is perhaps on the verge of satisfaction. She is then left in this dissatisfied state. This does her injury. A mutual and satisfied sexual act is of great benefit to the average woman, the magnetism of it is health giving. When it is not desired on the part of the woman and she has no response, *it should not take place*. This is an act of prostitution and is degrading to the woman's finer sensibility, all the marriage certificates on earth to the contrary notwithstanding. Withdrawal on the part of the man should be substituted by some other means that does not injure the woman. [Sanger 1917:6]

Sanger was clearly communicating more than technical information in her pamphlet. Throughout it is pervaded by a view of the right of women to sexual gratification and control over the workings of their own bodies.

In the book from which our second selection comes, Sanger addressed herself to the larger issues of women's potential contribution to society and the relevance of control over her reproductive life to that contribution. Here she poses the question of whether birth control is an issue to be left exclusively in the hands of women or whether it should be shared with men. The question looms again in the 1970s as the question is debated whether men should be partners to decisions on whether to abort an unwanted pregnancy. Like today, then too strong voices such as Sanger's sided with the view that women themselves must have full and exclusive control of whether or not to become mothers, for it is the woman who must carry the major burden of rearing the child. "No woman can call herself free who does not own and control her body" was Sanger's consistent view throughout this work.

Sanger's vision was not narrowly focused on the dissemination of birth-control devices. She believed that the whole modern movement toward new sex ideas was bound to be challenged by the conservative forces of society. In her view, sex morals for women had been one-sided, purely negative, inhibitory, and repressive, "fixed by agencies which have sought to keep women enslaved; which have been determined . . . to use woman solely as an asset to the church, the state and the man." [Sanger 1920:179]

Sanger's activities in the birth-control movement extended over five decades. In the 1920s she traveled to Japan, China, and England in connection with international birth-control conferences; in 1927 she went to Geneva for a World Population Conference; in the 1930s her energies were devoted to a concerted push to change federal legislation and to traveling to Russia and India for further international conferences. She lived to see a good part of her hopes realized as the courts decided physicians could prescribe contraceptives for a "patient's general well being" (thus making federal legislation no longer necessary); by 1937 even a Committee on Contraception of the American Medical Association took the view that physicians had a legal right to give contraceptives to their patients. In 1959 Gregory Pincus inscribed a report on oral contraceptives "to Margaret Sanger with affectionate greetings—this product of her pioneering resoluteness."

The most serious problems that confront the world in the 1970s will not be solved by military generals and international statesmen. The environmental crisis of air and water pollution and the serious threat of an exploding world population call for the skills of charismatic leaders and technical experts. One of the earliest of these leaders whom future historians will have to credit with solving the population crisis will be Margaret Sanger. But women do not have to wait for the next century to acknowledge their indebtedness to Margaret Sanger: millions of us live fuller and more rewarding lives because of her work, as have two generations of women in this century.

ﾡ My Fight For Birth Control ﾡ

Awakening and Revolt

Early in the year 1912 I came to a sudden realization that my work as a nurse and my activities in social service were entirely palliative and consequently futile and useless to relieve the misery I saw all about me. . . .

Were it possible for me to depict the revolting conditions existing in the homes of some of the women I attended in that one year, one would find it hard to believe. There was at that time, and doubtless is still today, a sub-stratum of men and women whose lives are absolutely untouched by social agencies.

The way they live is almost beyond belief. They hate and fear any prying into their homes or into their lives. They resent being talked to. The women slink in and out of their homes on their way to market like rats from their holes. The men beat their wives sometimes black and blue, but no one interferes. The children are cuffed, kicked and chased about, but woe to the child who dares to tell tales out of the home! Crime or drink is often the source of this secret aloofness, usually there is something to hide, a skeleton in the closet somewhere. The men are sullen, unskilled workers, picking up odd jobs now and then, unemployed usually, sauntering in and out of the house at all hours of the day and night.

The women keep apart from other women in the neighborhood. Often they are suspected of picking a pocket or "lifting" an article when occasion arises. Pregnancy is an almost chronic condition amongst them. I knew one woman who had given birth to eight children with no professional care whatever. The last one was born in the kitchen, witnessed by a son of ten years who, under his mother's direction, cleaned the bed, wrapped the placenta and soiled articles in paper, and threw them out of the window into the court below. . . .

In this atmosphere abortions and birth become the main

From Margaret Sanger, *My Fight For Birth Control*. New York, Farrar-Rinehart, 1931. Pp. 46–56, 152–160.

theme of conversation. On Saturday nights I have seen groups of fifty to one hundred women going into questionable offices well known in the community for cheap abortions. I asked several women what took place there, and they all gave the same reply: a quick examination, a probe inserted into the uterus and turned a few times to disturb the fertilized ovum, and then the woman was sent home. Usually the flow began the next day and often continued four or five weeks. Sometimes an ambulance carried the victim to the hospital for a curetage, and if she returned home at all she was looked upon as a lucky woman.

This state of things became a nightmare with me. There seemed no sense to it all, no reason for such waste of mother life, no right to exhaust women's vitality and to throw them on the scrap-heap before the age of thirty-five.

Everywhere I looked, misery and fear stalked—men fearful of losing their jobs, women fearful that even worse conditions might come upon them. The menace of another pregnancy hung like a sword over the head of every poor woman I came in contact with that year. The question which met me was always the same: What can I do to keep from it? or, What can I do to get out of this? Sometimes they talked among themselves bitterly.

"It's the rich that know the tricks," they'd say, "while we have all the kids." Then, if the women were Roman Catholics, they talked about "Yankee tricks," and asked me if I knew what the Protestants did to keep their families down. When I said that I didn't believe that the rich knew much more than they did I was laughed at and suspected of holding back information for money. They would nudge each other and say something about paying me before I left the case if I would reveal the "secret.". . .

Finally the thing began to shape itself, to become accumulative during the three weeks I spent in the home of a desperately sick woman living on Grand Street, a lower section of New York's East Side.

Mrs. Sacks was only twenty-eight years old; her husband, an unskilled worker, thirty-two. Three children, aged five, three and one, were none too strong nor sturdy, and it took all the earnings of the father and the ingenuity of the mother to keep them clean, provide them with air and proper food, and give them a chance to grow into decent manhood and womanhood.

Both parents were devoted to these children and to each other. The woman had become pregnant and had taken various drugs and purgatives, as advised by her neighbors. Then, in desperation, she had used some instrument lent to her by a friend. She was found prostrate on the floor amidst the crying children when her husband returned from work. Neighbors advised against the ambulance, and a friendly doctor was called. The husband would not hear of her going to a hospital, and as a little money had been saved in the bank a nurse was called and the battle for that precious life began.

It was in the middle of July. The three-room apartment was turned into a hospital for the dying patient. Never had I worked so fast, never so concentratedly as I did to keep alive that little mother. Neighbor women came and went during the day doing the odds and ends necessary for our comfort. The children were sent to friends and relatives and the doctor and I settled ourselves to outdo the force and power of an outraged nature.

Never had I known such conditions could exist. July's sultry days and nights were melted into a torpid inferno. Day after day, night after night, I slept only in brief snatches, ever too anxious about the condition of that feeble heart bravely carrying on, to stay long from the bedside of the patient. . . .

At the end of two weeks recovery was in sight, and at the end of three weeks I was preparing to leave the fragile patient to take up the ordinary duties of her life, including those of wifehood and motherhood. Everyone was congratulating her on her recovery. All the kindness of sympathetic and understanding neighbors poured in upon her in the shape of convalescent dishes, soups, custards, and drinks. Still she appeared to be despondent and worried. She seemed to sit apart in her thoughts as if she had no part in these congratulatory messages and endearing welcomes. I thought at first that she still retained some of her unconscious memories and dwelt upon them in her silences.

But as the hour for my departure came nearer, her anxiety increased, and finally with trembling voice she said: "Another baby will finish me, I suppose."

"It's too early to talk about that," I said, and resolved that I would turn the question over to the doctor for his advice. When he came I said: "Mrs. Sacks is worried about having another baby."

"She well might be," replied the doctor, and then he stood before her and said: "Any more such capers, young woman, and there will be no need to call me."

"Yes, yes—I know, Doctor," said the patient with trembling voice, "but," and she hesitated as if it took all of her courage to say it, "*what* can I do to prevent getting that way again?"

"Oh ho!" laughed the doctor good naturedly, "You want your cake while you eat it too, do you? Well, it can't be done." Then, familiarly slapping her on the back and picking up his hat and bag to depart, he said: "I'll tell you the only sure thing to do. Tell Jake to sleep on the roof!"

With those words he closed the door and went down the stairs, leaving us both petrified and stunned.

Tears sprang to my eyes, and a lump came in my throat as I looked at that face before me. It was stamped with sheer horror. I thought for a moment she might have gone insane, but she conquered her feelings, whatever they may have been, and turning to me in desperation said: "He can't understand, can he?—he's a man after all—but you do, don't you? You're a woman and you'll tell me the secret and I'll never tell it to a soul."

She clasped her hands as if in prayer, she leaned over and looked straight into my eyes and beseechingly implored me to tell her something—something *I really did not know*. It was like being on a rack and tortured for a crime one had not committed. To plead guilty would stop the agony; otherwise the rack kept turning.

I had to turn away from that imploring face. I could not answer her then. I quieted her as best I could. She saw that I was moved by the tears in my eyes. I promised that I would come back in a few days and tell her what she wanted to know. The few simple means of limiting the family like *coitus interruptus* or the condom were laughed at by the neighboring women when told these were the means used by men in the well-to-do families. That was not believed, and I knew such an answer would be swept aside as useless were I to tell her this at such a time.

A little later when she slept I left the house, and made up my mind that I'd keep away from those cases in the future. I felt helpless to do anything at all. I seemed chained hand and foot, and longed for an earthquake or a volcano to shake the world out of its lethargy into facing these monstrous atrocities.

The intelligent reasoning of the young mother—how to *prevent* getting that way again—how sensible, how just she had been—yes, I promised myself I'd go back and have a long talk with her and tell her more, and perhaps she would not laugh but would believe that those methods were all that were really known.

But time flew past, and weeks rolled into months. That wistful, appealing face haunted me day and night. I could not banish from my mind memories of that trembling voice begging so humbly for knowledge she had a right to have. I was about to retire one night three months later when the telephone rang and an agitated man's voice begged me to come at once to help his wife who was sick again. It was the husband of Mrs. Sacks, and I intuitively knew before I left the telephone that it was almost useless to go.

I dreaded to face that woman. I was tempted to send someone else in my place. I longed for an accident on the subway, or on the street—anything to prevent my going into that home. But on I went just the same. I arrived a few minutes after the doctor, the same one who had given her such noble advice. The woman was dying. She was unconscious. She died within ten minutes after my arrival. It was the same result, the same story told a thousand times before —death from abortion. She had become pregnant, had used drugs, had then consulted a five-dollar professional abortionist, and death followed.

The doctor shook his head as he rose from listening for the heart beat. I knew she had already passed on; without a groan, a sigh or recognition of our belated presence she had gone into the Great Beyond as thousands of mothers go every year. I looked at that drawn face now stilled in death. I placed her thin hands across her breast and recalled how hard they had pleaded with me on that last memorable occasion of parting. The gentle woman, the devoted mother, the loving wife had passed on leaving behind her a frantic husband, helpless in his loneliness, bewildered in his helplessness as he paced up and down the room, hands clenching his head, moaning "My God! My God! My God!"

The Revolution came—but not as it has been pictured nor as history relates that revolutions have come. It came in my own life. It began in my very being as I walked home that night after I had closed the eyes and covered with a sheet the body of that little helpless mother whose life had been sacrificed to ignorance.

After I left that desolate house I walked and walked and walked; for hours and hours I kept on, bag in hand, thinking, regretting, dreading to stop; fearful of my conscience, dreading to face my own accusing soul. At three in the morning I arrived home still clutching a heavy load the weight of which I was quite unconscious.

I entered the house quietly, as was my custom, and looked out of the window down upon the dimly lighted, sleeping city. As I stood at the window and looked out, the miseries and problems of that sleeping city arose before me in a clear vision like a panorama: crowded homes, too many children; babies dying in infancy; mothers overworked; baby nurseries; children neglected and hungry—mothers so nervously wrought they could not give the little things the comfort nor care they needed; mothers half sick most of their lives— "always ailing, never failing"; women made into drudges; children working in cellars; children aged six and seven pushed into the labor market to help earn a living; another baby on the way; still another; yet another; a baby born dead—great relief; an older child dies—sorrow, but nevertheless relief—insurance helps; a mother's death—children scattered into institutions; the father, desperate, drunken; he slinks away to become an outcast in a society which has trapped him. . . .

. . . For hours I stood, motionless and tense, expecting something to happen. I watched the lights go out, I saw the darkness gradually give way to the first shimmer of dawn, and then a colorful sky heralded the rise of the sun. I knew a new day had come for me and a new world as well.

It was like an illumination. I could now see clearly the various social strata of our life; all its mass problems seemed to be centered around uncontrolled breeding. There was only one thing to be done: call out, start the alarm, set the heather on fire! Awaken the womanhood of America to free the motherhood of the world! I released from my almost paralyzed hand the nursing bag which unconsciously I had clutched, threw it across the room, tore the uniform from my body, flung it into a corner, and renounced all palliative work forever.

I would never go back again to nurse women's ailing bodies while their miseries were as vast as the stars. I was now finished with superficial cures, with doctors and nurses and social workers who were brought face to face with this overwhelming truth of women's needs and yet turned to pass on the other side. They must be made to see these facts. I resolved that women should have knowledge of contraception. They have every right to know about their own bodies. I would strike out—I would scream from the housetops. I would tell the world what was going on in the lives of these poor women. I *would* be heard. No matter what it should cost. *I would be heard.*

A "Public Nuisance"

The selection of a place for the first birth control clinic was of the greatest importance. No one could actually tell how it would be received in any neighborhood. I thought of all the possible difficulties: The indifference of women's organizations, the ignorance of the workers themselves, the resentment of social agencies, the opposition of the medical profession. Then there was the law—the law of New York State.

Section 1142 was definite. It stated that *no one* could give information to prevent conception to *anyone* for any reason. There was, however, Section 1145, which distinctly stated that physicians (*only*) could give advice to prevent conception for the cure or prevention of disease. I inquired about the section, and was told by two attorneys and several physicians that this clause was an exception to 1142 referring only to venereal disease. But anyway, as I was not a physician, it could not protect me. Dared I risk it?

I began to think of the doctors I knew. Several who had previously promised now refused. I wrote, telephoned, asked friends to ask other friends to help me find a woman doctor to help me demonstrate the need of a birth control clinic in New York. None could be found. No one wanted to go to jail. No one cared to test out the law. Perhaps it would have to be done without a doctor. But it had to be done; that I knew.

Fania Mindell, an enthusiastic young worker in the cause, had come on from Chicago to help me. Together we tramped the streets on that dreary day in early October, through a driving rainstorm, to find the best location at the cheapest terms possible. We stopped to inquire about vacant stores of the officials in one of the milk stations. "Don't come over here." "Keep out of this section." "We don't want any trouble over here." These and other pleasantries were hurled at us as we darted in and out of the various places asking for advice, hoping for a welcome.

Finally at 46 Amboy Street, in the Brownsville section of Brooklyn, we found a friendly landlord with a good place vacant at fifty dollars a month rental; and Brownsville was settled on. It was one of the most thickly populated sections. It had a large population of working class Jews, always interested in health measures, always tolerant of new ideas, willing to listen and to accept advice whenever the health of mother or children was involved. I knew that here there would at least be no breaking of windows, no hurling of insults into our teeth; but I was scarcely prepared for the popular support, the sympathy and friendly help given us in that neighborhood from that day to this.

The Brownsville section of Brooklyn in 1916 was a hive of futile industry—dingy, squalid, peopled with hard-working men and women, the home of poverty which was steadily growing worse in the tide of increasing responsibilities. Early every morning, weary-eyed men poured from the low tenement houses that crouched together as if for warmth, bound for ten or twelve hours of work. At the same time, or earlier, their women rose to set in motion that ceaseless round of cooking, cleaning, and sewing that barely kept the young generation alive. A fatalistic, stolid, and tragic army of New Yorkers dwelt here, most of them devout Jews or Italians, all of them energetic and ambitious,—but trapped by nature's despotism. . . .

We determined to open a birth control clinic at 46 Amboy Street to disseminate information where it was poignantly required by human beings. Our inspiration was the mothers of the poor; our object, to help them.

With a small bundle of handbills and a large amount of

zeal, we fared forth each morning in a house-to-house canvass of the district in which the clinic was located. Every family in that great district received a "dodger" printed in English, Yiddish and Italian. . . .

It was on October 16, 1916, that the three of us—Fania Mindell, Ethel Byrne and myself—opened the doors of the first birth control clinic in America. I believed then and do today, that the opening of those doors to the mothers of Brownsville was an event of social significance in the lives of American womanhood.

News of our work spread like wildfire. Within a few days there was not a darkened tenement, hovel or flat but was brightened by the knowledge that motherhood could be voluntary; that children need not be born into the world unless they are wanted and have a place provided for them. For the first time, women talked openly of this terror of unwanted pregnancy which had haunted their lives since time immemorial. The newspapers, in glaring headlines, used the words "birth control," and carried the message that somewhere in Brooklyn there was a place where contraceptive information could be obtained by all overburdened mothers who wanted it.

Ethel Byrne, who is my sister and a trained nurse, assisted me in advising, explaining, and demonstrating to the women how to prevent conception. As all of our 488 records were confiscated by the detectives who later arrested us for violation of the New York State law, it is difficult to tell exactly how many more women came in those few days to seek advice; but we estimate that it was far more than five hundred. As in any new enterprise, false reports were maliciously spread about the clinic; weird stories without the slightest foundation of truth. We talked plain talk and gave plain facts to the women who came there. We kept a record of every applicant. All were mothers; most of them had large families.

It was whispered about that the police were to raid the place for abortions. We had no fear of that accusation. We were trying to spare mothers the necessity of that ordeal by giving them proper contraceptive information. It was well that so many of the women in the neighborhood knew the truth of our doings. Hundreds of them who had witnessed the facts came to the courtroom afterward, eager to testify in our behalf.

One day a woman by the name of Margaret Whitehurst came to us. She said that she was the mother of two children and that she had not money to support more. Her story was a pitiful one—all lies, of course, but the government acts that way. She asked for our literature and preventives, and received both. Then she triumphantly went to the District Attorney's office and secured a warrant for the arrest of my sister, Mrs. Ethel Byrne, our interpreter, Miss Fania Mindell, and myself.

The crusade was actually under way! It is no exaggeration to call this period in the birth control movement the most stirring period up to that time, perhaps the most stirring of all times, for it was the only period during which we had experienced jail terms, hunger strikes, and intervention by the Chief Executive of the state. It was the first time that there was any number of widespread, popular demonstrations in our behalf. . . .

The arrest and raid on the Brooklyn clinic was spectacular. There was no need of a large force of plain clothes men to drag off a trio of decent, serious women who were testing out a law on a fundamental principle. My federal arrest, on the contrary, had been assigned to intelligent men. One had to respect the dignity of their mission; but the New York city officials seem to use tactics suitable only for crooks, bandits and burglars. We were not surprised at being arrested, but the shock and horror of it was that a *woman*, with a squad of five plain clothes men, conducted the raid and made the arrest. A woman—the irony of it!

I refused to close down the clinic, hoping that a court decision would allow us to continue such necessary work. I was to be disappointed. Pressure was brought upon the landlord, and we were dispossessed by the law as a "public nuisance." In Holland the clinics were called "public utilities."

When the policewoman entered the clinic with her squad of plain clothes men and announced the arrest of Miss Mindell and myself (Mrs. Byrne was not present at the time and her arrest followed later), the room was crowded to suffocation with women waiting in the outer room. The police began bullying these mothers, asking them questions, writing down their names in order to subpoena them to testify against us at the trial. These women, always afraid of trouble which the very presence of a policeman signifies,

screamed and cried aloud. The children on their laps
screamed, too. It was like a panic for a few minutes until I
walked into the room where they were stampeding and
begged them to be quiet and not to get excited. I assured
them that nothing could happen to them, that I was under
arrest but they would be allowed to return home in a few
minutes. That quieted them. The men were blocking the
door to prevent anyone from leaving, but I finally persuaded
them to allow these women to return to their homes, un-
molested though terribly frightened by it all.

Crowds began to gather outside. A long line of women
with baby carriages and children had been waiting to get into
the clinic. Now the streets were filled, and police had to see
that traffic was not blocked. The patrol wagon came rattling
through the streets to our door, and at length Miss Mindell
and I took our seats within and were taken to the police
station.

As I sat in the rear of the car and looked out on that
seething mob of humans, I wondered, and asked myself
what had gone out of the race. Something had gone from
them which silenced them, made them impotent to defend
their rights. I thought of the suffragists in England, and
pictured the results of a similar arrest there. But as I sat in
this mood, the car started to go. I looked out at the mass
and heard a scream. It came from a woman wheeling a baby
carriage, who had just come around the corner preparing to
visit the clinic. She saw the patrol wagon, realized what had
happened, left the baby carriage on the walk, rushed through
the crowd to the wagon and cried to me: "Come back! Come
back and save me!" The woman looked wild. She ran after
the car for a dozen yards or so, when some friends caught
her weeping form in their arms and led her back to the
sidewalk. That was the last thing I saw as the Black Maria
dashed off to the station.

Birth Control—A Parents' Problem or Woman's?

The problem of birth control has arisen directly from the effort of the feminine spirit to free itself from bondage. Woman herself has wrought that bondage through her reproductive powers and while enslaving herself has enslaved the world. The physical suffering to be relieved is chiefly woman's. Hers, too, is the love life that dies first under the blight of too prolific breeding. Within her is wrapped up the future of the race—it is hers to make or mar. All of these considerations point unmistakably to one fact—it is woman's duty as well as her privilege to lay hold of the means of freedom. Whatever men may do, she cannot escape the responsibility. For ages she has been deprived of the opportunity to meet this obligation. She is now emerging from her helplessness. Even as no one can share the suffering of the overburdened mother, so no one can do this work for her. Others may help, but she and she alone can free herself.

The basic freedom of the world is woman's freedom. A free race cannot be born of slave mothers. A woman enchained cannot choose but give a measure of that bondage to her sons and daughters. No woman can call herself free who does not own and control her body. No woman can call herself free until she can choose consciously whether she will or will not be a mother.

It does not greatly alter the case that some women call themselves free because they earn their own livings, while others profess freedom because they defy the conventions of sex relationship. She who earns her own living gains a sort of freedom that is not to be undervalued, but in quality and in quantity it is of little account beside the untrammeled choice of mating or not mating, of being a mother or not being a mother. She gains food and clothing and shelter, at least, without submitting to the charity of her companion, but the earning of her own living does not give her the development of her inner sex urge, far deeper and more

From Margaret Sanger, *Woman and the New Race*. New York, Brentano, 1920. Pp. 93–100.

powerful in its outworkings than any of these externals. In order to have that development, she must still meet and solve the problem of motherhood.

With the so-called "free" woman, who chooses a mate in defiance of convention, freedom is largely a question of character and audacity. If she does attain to an unrestricted choice of a mate, she is still in a position to be enslaved through her reproductive powers. Indeed, the pressure of law and custom upon the woman not legally married is likely to make her more of a slave than the woman fortunate enough to marry the man of her choice.

Look at it from any standpoint you will, suggest any solution you will, conventional or unconventional, sanctioned by law or in defiance of law, woman is in the same position, fundamentally, until she is able to determine for herself whether she will be a mother and to fix the number of her offspring. This unavoidable situation is alone enough to make birth control, first of all, a woman's problem. On the very face of the matter, voluntary motherhood is chiefly the concern of the woman.

It is persistently urged, however, that since sex expression is the act of two, the responsibility of controlling the results should not be placed upon woman alone. Is it fair, it is asked, to give her, instead of the man, the task of protecting herself when she is, perhaps, less rugged in physique than her mate, and has, at all events, the normal, periodic inconveniences of her sex?

We must examine this phase of her problem in two lights —that of the ideal, and of the conditions working toward the ideal. In an ideal society, no doubt, birth control would become the concern of the man as well as the woman. The hard, inescapable fact which we encounter to-day is that man has not only refused any such responsibility, but has individually and collectively sought to prevent woman from obtaining knowledge by which she could assume this responsibility for herself. She is still in the position of a dependent to-day because her mate has refused to consider her as an individual apart from his needs. She is still bound because she has in the past left the solution of the problem to him. Having left it to him, she finds that instead of rights, she has only such privileges as she has gained by petitioning, coaxing and cozening. Having left it to him, she is exploited, driven and enslaved to his desires.

While it is true that he suffers many evils as the consequence of this situation, she suffers vastly more. While it is true that he should be awakened to the cause of these evils, we know that they come home to her with crushing force every day. It is she who has the long burden of carrying, bearing and rearing the unwanted children. . . . It is her heart that the sight of the deformed, the subnormal, the undernourished, the overworked child smites first and oftenest and hardest. It is *her* love life that dies first in the fear of undesired pregnancy. It is her opportunity for self expression that perishes first and most hopelessly because of it.

Conditions, rather than theories, facts, rather than dreams, govern the problem. They place it squarely upon the shoulders of woman. She has learned that whatever the moral responsibility of the man in this direction may be, he does not discharge it. She has learned that, lovable and considerate as the individual husband may be, she has nothing to expect from men in the mass, when they make laws and decree customs. She knows that regardless of what ought to be, the brutal, unavoidable fact is that she will never receive her freedom until she takes it for herself.

Having learned this much, she has yet something more to learn. Women are too much inclined to follow in the footsteps of men, to try to think as men think, to try to solve the general problems of life as men solve them. If after attaining their freedom, women accept conditions in the spheres of government, industry, art, morals and religion as they find them, they will be but taking a leaf out of man's book. The woman is not needed to do man's work. She is not needed to think man's thoughts. She need not fear that the masculine mind, almost universally dominant, will fail to take care of its own. Her mission is not to enhance the masculine spirit, but to express the feminine; hers is not to preserve a man-made world, but to create a human world by the infusion of the feminine element into all of its activities.

Woman must not accept; she must challenge. She must not be awed by that which has been built up around her; she must reverence that within her which struggles for expression. Her eyes must be less upon what is and more clearly upon what should be. She must listen only with a frankly questioning attitude to the dogmatized opinions of man-made society. When she chooses her new, free course of action, it must be in the light of her own opinion—of her own intuition. Only so can she give play to the feminine spirit. Only thus can she free her mate from the bondage which he wrought for himself when he wrought hers. Only thus can she restore to him that of which he robbed himself in restricting her. Only thus can she remake the world. . . .

Woman must have her freedom—the fundamental freedom of choosing whether or not she shall be a mother and how many children she will have. Regardless of what man's attitude may be, that problem is hers—and before it can be his, it is hers alone.

She goes through the vale of death alone, each time a babe is born. As it is the right neither of man nor the state to coerce her into this ordeal, so it is her right to decide whether she will endure it. That right to decide imposes upon her the duty of clearing the way to knowledge by which she may make and carry out the decision.

Birth control is woman's problem. The quicker she accepts it as hers and hers alone, the quicker will society respect motherhood. The quicker, too, will the world be made a fit place for her children to live.

Beware the State:
Suzanne LaFollette (b. 1893)

An introduction to the life and work of Suzanne LaFollette must differ from all other introductions in this volume. I had known and admired her 1926 book, *Concerning Women*, since I discovered it in 1970, but during this editing project my attempts to find some information about the life of its author were fruitless. Of the many libraries in the area only my own college had a copy of her book. Biographic dictionaries did not include her. A newspaper search yielded the information that she had been a political candidate in a Congressional district in lower Manhattan in the early part of the 1960s. Before long I was dialing a New York number and, to my delight, hearing her crisp voice responding to my questions. Since my work that summer had been an almost total submersion in the nineteenth century, it was a great and special pleasure to hear the living voice of one of my authors. At the age of seventy-eight, Suzanne LaFollette was alive and well in New York City.

Suzanne LaFollette agreed to write a brief account of her life; toward the end of July 1971 I received her delightful letter. I shall draw freely on this letter and on a subsequent telephone conversation in the following description.

Suzanne LaFollette was born in 1893 on a wheat and fruit ranch in the state of Washington; she spent most of her childhood in the wildly beautiful and sparsely settled Snake River canyon. With four brothers and two sisters she "grew up on horseback," riding handsome little animals known as Cayuse ponies, who roamed the unfenced ranges of her pioneer community. As she crisply characterized these turn-of-century years in the Northwest, they were a time when "the automobile had not yet come in and the family had not yet gone out." A central figure in her early life was her mother's father, who lived with the LaFollettes, a "forty-niner, an old Indian fighter and former stock man." Her sense of the importance to children of close contact with grandparents is caught in the following tribute to her maternal grandfather:

> No one . . . who has not known that inestimable privilege can possibly realize what good fortune it is to grow up in a home where there are grandparents. Our parents were busy, hard-working people with a large family. They had little time and not much patience. But there was always Grandpa, who had both in abundance, who was gay, lovable and understanding and whose love never failed us. I shall never cease to be grateful for the sense of security he gave us.

As LaFollette reached her teens, her grandfather died; her father rented out his wheat ranches and retired from active farming and built a new house in the college town of Pullman, where he "prepared to see his family through college." Suzanne LaFollette did not live in that new home for very long, however, for her father was elected to the lower House of Congress. Consequently, for eight years, including the years of World War I and the final push to secure the suffrage, the LaFollette family lived in Washington, D. C. These were critical years of early exposure to politics for Suzanne LaFollette, during which she finished her schooling at Trinity College on the outskirts of Washington and did a good deal of work in her father's office in the House of Representatives and in the office of the elder Senator Robert LaFollette, her father's first cousin. The two LaFollette families were not only kin but also close friends; they lived together in a huge old house on Sixteenth Street for four of the eight years Suzanne's father served in the House. She remembers the elder Senator LaFollette as patient and dedicated to the inclusion of the young members of the family in all discussions concerning politics, so that she acquired a keen feeling of participation in the political process.

The four adults in the household during these years were "good feminists," in Suzanne's judgment. Her letter includes one vivid recollection of her first participation in the women's movement:

> The women's movement was very busy in Washington when we went there. I met several of its leaders, although I was too young to know them well. I remember vividly

the first of my modest contributions to the cause, which taught me something of what women were up against in the struggle for their rights.

The women's movement arranged to have a big parade up Pennsylvania Avenue the day before President Wilson was inaugurated, and I was invited to be on a float which represented some aspect of repression—I forget which. Our float was somewhere around the middle of the parade, which was long, and before the avenue came in sight we realized that our movement was extremely slow; also that the noise from the avenue was deafening—and not cheering. When at last we entered it the view was appalling. There was no division between the parade and the crowd, and the crowd was a seething mob of men who surged around the struggling marchers, shouting obscenities. There were few police in sight, and those who were in sight were making no effort to control the crowd. It was an obscene spectacle, and it lasted from one end of the avenue to the other; that is, it lasted for hours.

The scandal of that parade reverberated throughout the country, and the inadequacy and inaction of the police came in for merciless condemnation. A couple of months later I participated in another parade, this time to the Capital Rotunda where we presented a petition to Congress. There were 300 women marchers, and the avenue was lined by 600 policemen.

Looking back from the perspective of 1971, Suzanne LaFollette is not sure that her experience in the suffrage parades had anything to do with the later writing of her book on women. Rather, she attributes the most important influence on this turn in her professional life to Albert Jay Nock, under whose supervision she began her career as a journalist and editor. From 1919 on, her life centered in New York, where she began her work in the magazine field with a job on the staff of the *Nation*. When Nock left that magazine to cofound a new weekly, *The Freeman*, LaFollette followed and worked closely with Nock for four years. As so often happens with such periodicals, *The Freeman* had a short life; when it discontinued publication in 1924, LaFollette began work on her book, *Concerning Women*, which appeared two years later. She commented in a phone conversation that the

timing of publication for both the books she has written left
much to be desired. By 1926 there was little public concern
for the "women issue," so that her book was "reviewed here
and there . . . the rest was silence."

Immediately after the publication of *Concerning Women*
LaFollette left for France, where she spent a year studying
art, history, and economics, with occasional brief visits to
Germany and England. Under the guidance of the American
painter and critic Walter Pach, she learned a good deal about
art in general and American art in particular, and she responded to Albert Nock's suggestion that she write a history
of American art. This second book, *Art in America*, was published in 1929, "just in time for the market crash which
ushered in the Great Depression," as she wryly puts it. (This
book on the history of American art became a little classic
in its field and was republished in 1968 by Harper.)

During the Depression years, when LaFollette was herself
in her late thirties and early forties, she continued work in
the magazine field, editing the reactivated *New Freeman*
for a few years; traveled to Europe on a Guggenheim Fellowship as preparation for a book on the economics of art (a book
she never wrote, though she remembers having a firm belief
that it would be her *magnum opus*); continued her keen interest in international politics; and occasionally wrote for
the *Nation*.

The major effort in her life during the 1930s was working
on the commission established, under John Dewey's chair-
manship, to investigate the charges against Leon Trotsky
during Stalin's purges of his former comrades in the Moscow
Trials. LaFollette had joined the Committee for Defense of
Leon Trotsky to secure asylum for him when his Norwegian
asylum was withdrawn and to work for the formation of an
investigative commission. As secretary of this commission,
she attended the interrogation of Trotsky in Mexico and
played a major role in the final writing of the commission's
report, *Not Guilty*. Looking back on those years, she comments that they entailed the "hardest work I have ever done.
. . . After thirteen months it was finished and so—almost—
was I."

In the years since World War II, Suzanne LaFollette did
freelance work for magazines, including four years on the
National Review, until she retired in 1959. Since then, she
writes,

I have planned much, and done little except watch with
growing concern the disintegration of the Western World
—above all our own country—and the steady growth of
totalitarian influence and power, the fight against which
absorbed my best energies for thirty irretrievable years.

Suzanne LaFollette has traveled a long way from her
Snake River canyon home in the 1890s to her New York
apartment in the 1970s, but there has been a consistent theme
in her political perspective on the world: a fundamental
libertarianism that is suspicious of dependence on government even in the interests of human welfare, whether in the
United States or in the Soviet Union. In *Concerning Women,*
she argued a strong case against protective legislation for
women, on the grounds that safe standards must be equally
provided for men lest the protective laws prevent women's
having an equal chance in industrial employment. In an incisive analysis of such legislation, she saw a tacit recognition
of economic injustice:

One would naturally expect that the conditions which
move people to seek protective legislation would move
them to question the nature of an economic system which
permits such rapacity that any class of employees requires
to be protected from it. [LaFollette 1926:178]

On issue after issue LaFollette comes down on the side of the
least degree of state interference in the lives of men and
women and a consistent belief that it is only through full
economic independence and personal autonomy that sex
equality will be achieved.

⚖ Concerning Women ⚖

The Beginnings of Emancipation

It will be foolish to assume that women are free, until
books about them shall have ceased to have more than an

From Suzanne LaFollette, *Concerning Women.* New York, Albert & Charles Boni, 1926. Pp. 1–15, 56–92, 93–149, 263–306.

antiquarian interest. All such books, including this one, imply by their existence that women may be regarded as a class in society; that they have in common certain characteristics, conditions or disabilities which, predominating over their individual variations, warrant grouping them on the basis of sex. No such assumption about men would be thinkable. . . . Such books may one day appear, but when they do it will mean that society has passed from its present state through a state of sex-equality and into a state of female domination. In that day, in place of the edifying spectacle of men proclaiming that woman is useful only as a bearer of children, society may behold the equally edifying spectacle of women proclaiming that man is useful only as a begetter of children; since it seems to be charateristic of the dominant sex to regard the other sex chiefly as a source of pleasure and as a means of reproduction. It seems also to be characteristic of the dominant sex . . . to regard itself as humanity, and the other sex as a class of somewhat lower beings created by Providence for its convenience and enjoyment; just as it is characteristic of a dominant class, such as an aristocracy, to regard the lower classes as being created solely for the purpose of supporting its power and doing its will. When once a social order is well established, no matter what injustice it involves, those who occupy a position of advantage are not long in coming to believe that it is the only possible and reasonable order, and imposing their belief, by force if necessary, on those whom circumstances have placed in their power. There is nothing more innately human than the tendency to transmute what has become customary into what has been divinely ordained. . . .

She [woman] was humble and subservient, as a matter of fact, for an incredibly long time; so long that there exists a general suspicion even at the present day that there is something in her nature which makes her want to be subject to man and to live as it were at second hand. This thought would be even more alarming than it is, perhaps, if it were not true that men themselves have stood for a good deal of subjection during the world's known history. Chattel slavery and serfdom were abolished from the civilized world only at about the time that the subjection of women began to be modified; and men still endure, not only with resignation but with positive cheerfulness, a high degree of industrial and political slavery. The man who is entirely dependent for his livelihood upon the will of an employer is an industrial slave, and the man who may be drafted into an army and made to fight and perhaps die for a cause in which he can have no possible interest is the slave of the State. . . . What the slavery of men, as of women, implies is the existence of an economic and social order that is inimical to their interests as human beings; and it implies nothing more than this.

Nor does the opposition to the emancipation of women which still finds expression in this country and in Europe, prove anything more than that superstitious addiction to custom of which I have already spoken. Those anxious critics who protest that women have got more freedom than is good for Society make the mistake of supposing that Society can exist only if its organization remains unchanged. The same conservatism has opposed all the revolutionary adaptations which have fitted the social order to the breakdown of old forms and their replacement by new ones. . . .

Certainly the present tendency of woman to assume a position of equality with man involves, and will continue even more to involve, profound psychic and material readjustments. But to assume that such readjustments will injure or destroy Society is to adopt toward Society an attitude of philosophical realism, to attribute to it a personality, to suppose that it is equally capable of destruction with the individual, and that it may in some mystical way derive benefit from the sacrifice of the individual's best interests. But what is Society save an aggregation of individuals, half male, half female? Where you have a handful of people forming a community, there you have Society; and if the individuals are enlightened and humane it may be called a civilized Society, if they are ignorant and brutal it will be uncivilized. To assume that its "interests" may be promoted by the enslavement of one-half its members, is unreasonable. One may be permitted the doubtful assumption that this enslavement promotes the welfare of the other half of Society, but it is obvious that it can not promote the welfare of the whole, unless we assume that slavery is beneficial to the slave (the classic assumption, indeed, where the slaves have been women). When we consider the political organization known as the State, we have a different matter. The State always represents the organized interest of a dominant class; therefore the subjection of other classes may be said to benefit the

State, and their emancipation may be opposed as a danger
to the State. . . .

The conscious movement towards freedom for women
may be said to have originated in the great emancipatory
movement which found expression in the American and
French revolutions. The revolutionists did not succeed in
establishing human freedom; they poured the new wine of
belief in equal rights for all men into the old bottle of privilege
for some; and it soured. But they did succeed in creating
political forms which admitted, in theory at least, the principle of equality. Their chief contribution to progress was
that they dramatically and powerfuly impressed the idea of
liberty upon the minds of men, and thus altered the whole
course of human thought. Mary Wollstonecraft's book, "A
Vindication of the Rights of Women," revolutionary though
it seemed in its day, was a perfectly natural and logical
application of this idea of liberty to the situation of her sex.
This remarkable book may be said to have marked the
beginning of the conscious movement towards the emancipation of women.

The unconscious movement was the outgrowth of the
revolution in industry, brought about by the introduction of
the machine. Women had always been industrial workers,
but their work, after the break-up of the gilds, was for the
most part carried on at home. When the factory supplanted
the family as the producing unit in society, the environment
of women was altered; and the change affected not only
those women who followed industry to the factories, but
also those who remained housewives, for where these had
before been required to perform, or at least to superintend, a
large amount of productive work, they now found their function, as the family became a consuming unit, reduced to the
superintendence of expenditures and the operation of the
household machinery—a labour which was increasingly lightened by the progress of invention. With domestic conditions
so changed, what was more natural than that the daughters
should go into the factory; or, if the family were well-to-do,
into the schools, which were forced reluctantly to open their
doors to women? And what was more natural than that
women, as their minds were developed through education,
should perceive the injustice and humiliation of their position,
and organize to defend their right to recognition as human
beings? . . .

Women in the factories and shops; women in the schools —from this it was only a moment to their invasion of the professions, and not a very long time until they would be invading every field that had been held the special province of men. This is the great unconscious and unorganized woman's movement which has aroused such fear and resentment among people who saw it without understanding it.

The organized movement may be regarded simply as an attempt to get this changing relation of women to their environment translated into the kind of law that the eighteenth century had taught the world to regard as just: law based on the theory of equal rights for all human beings. The opposition that the movement encountered offers ample testimony to the fact that "acceptance in principle" is more than a mere subterfuge of diplomats and politicians. The eighteenth and nineteenth centuries resolutely clung to the theory of equality, and as resolutely opposed its logical application. This is not surprising; most people, no doubt, when they espouse human rights, make their own mental reservations about the proper application of the word "human.". . . The shadow of this old superstition still clouded the minds of men: therefore it is hardly surprising that the egalitarians of the French Revolution excluded women from equal political and legal rights with men; and that the young American republic which had adopted the Declaration of Independence, continued to sanction the slavery of negroes and the subjection of women. . . .

If the conscious feminists bore the brunt of the resentment aroused by woman's changing relation to the world about her, it was because their opponents did them the honour of believing that they were responsible for the change. It was a strangely incurious attitude that permitted such an assumption to be held; for it really takes a very feeble exercise of intelligence to perceive that a handful of feminist agitators could hardly coax millions of women into industry —under conditions often extremely disadvantageous—into business, the schools and the professions. I believe the cause of this incuriousness lay in the very fear aroused by these changes and the social revaluations which they implied; fear for a relation between the sexes which, having been established for so long, seemed the only reasonable, or indeed possible, relation. Filled as they were with this fear of change, which is one of the strongest human emotions, the opponents of woman's emancipation were incapable of objectivity. Their intellectual curiosity was paralyzed.

Institutional Marriage and Its Economic Aspects

1. Marriage, by a strictly technical definition, is a natural habit; that is to say, it is a relationship proceeding out of the common instinct of male and female to mate, and to remain together until after the birth of one or more children. Organized society, on the other hand, always makes it a civil institution, and sometimes a religious institution. So long as man remained in the natural state, roaming about in search of his food as do the apes today, it may be supposed that marriage was based on personal preference and involved only the selective disposition of the individual man and woman and their common concern for the safety of their offspring. But as advancing civilization enabled mankind more easily to obtain and augment its food-supply, and consequently to secure greater safety and also to satisfy its gregarious instinct by living in numerous communities, the habit of marriage underwent a process of sanction and regulation by the group, and was thus transformed into a civil institution. While society remains ethnical, the family exercises supervision over the sexual relations of its members, but always subject to the approval or disapproval of the larger group—the tribe or clan. When the political State emerges, this function continues to be exercised by the family, but it is subject to sanction by the State and is gradually absorbed by it. Yet even where the State has usurped almost all the prerogatives of the family, custom continues to give powerful sanction to interference in marriage both by relatives and by the community. . . .

Thus there may be, and in most civilized societies there is, a fourfold interference in marriage: interference by the family, by the community, by the State, and by the Church. An old Russian song had it that marriages were contracted

> By the will of God,
> By decree of the Czar,
> By order of the Master,
> By decision of the community

—with not a word about the two persons immediately concerned. Nor is this strange, for marriage is not generally conceived of among either primitive or highly civilized peoples as a personal relationship. It is an economic arrangement, an alliance between families, a means for getting children. To allow so unruly a passion as love to figure in the selection of a mate, is an irregularity which may under certain circumstances be tolerated, but one which is nevertheless likely to be regarded with extreme disapproval. As individualism makes progress against group-tyranny, the preliminaries and the actual contracting of marriage become less the affair of God, the State, the family and the community, and more the affair of the two people chiefly interested; but once contracted, the marriage can hardly be said, even in the most civilized community, to be free of considerable regulation by these four influences. The time which Spencer foresaw, when "the union by affection will be held of primary moment and the union by law as of secondary moment," has by no means arrived. . . .

It is significant of the unspiritual estimate generally put upon marriage, that incompatibility is rarely allowed as a legal ground of divorce. Violation of the sexual monopoly that marriage implies; prenuptial unchastity on the part of the woman; impotence; cruelty; desertion; failure of support; insanity; all of these or some of them are the grounds generally recognized where divorce is allowed at all. This is to say that society demands a specific grievance of one party against the other, a grievance having physical or economic consequences, as a prerequisite to freedom from the marriage-bond. The fact that marriage may be a failure spiritually is seldom taken into account. Yet there is no difficulty about which less can be done. Infidelity may be forgiven and in time forgotten; the deserter may return; the delinquent may be persuaded to support his family; the insane person may recover; even impotence may be cured. But if two people are out of spiritual correspondence, if they are not at ease in one another's society, there is nothing to be done about it. . . . The gradual liberalization of the divorce-laws which our moralists regard as a symptom of modern disrespect for the sacredness of marriage, is in fact a symptom of a directly opposite tendency—the tendency to place marriage on a higher spiritual plane than it has hitherto occupied.

The State assumes the right either to allow artificial limitation of offspring or to make it a crime; and it exercises this assumption according to its need for citizens or the complexion of its religious establishment. It also fixes the relative status and rights of the two parties. In several American States, for instance, a married woman is incompetent to make contracts or to fix her legal residence. . . . On the other hand, the husband is everywhere required by law to support his wife. Such laws, of course, like most laws, are felt only when the individual comes into conflict with them. The State does not interfere in many cases where married couples subvert its regulations—for example, the law which entitles the husband to his wife's services in the home and permits him to control her right to work outside the home, does not become binding save in cases where the husband sees fit to invoke it. . . .

The sanctions of interference by the family, save in the contracting of marriage by minors, are at present those of custom, affection, and (in so far as it exists and may be made effective) economic power. When two persons have decided to marry, for instance, it remains quite generally customary for the man to go through the formality of asking the woman's nearest male relation for her hand. This is of course a survival from the period when a woman's male guardian had actual power to prevent her marrying without his consent. The influence of affection is too obvious to require illustration; it is the subtlest and most powerful sanction of family interference. Economic power is perhaps most commonly used to prevent or compel the contracting of marriage. It may make itself felt, where parents or other relatives are well-to-do, in threats of disinheritance if prospective heirs undertake to make marriages which are displeasing to them. . . . It is not uncommon for legators to stipulate that legatees shall or shall not marry before a certain age under penalty of losing their inheritance.

These influences do not always, of course, take the same direction. At present, for example, artificial limitation of offspring receives irregular but effective community-sanction in face of opposition by Church and State. Or again, public opinion almost universally condemns the idea that a father may, by his will, remove his children from the custody of their mother. . . . But, however much they may check one another, these influences are all constantly operating to restrict and regulate marriage away from its original intention as a purely personal relationship, and to keep it in the groove of economic and social institutionalism. The reasons for this are to be found in the vestigiary fear of sex, love of power, love of the habitual, religious superstition, and above all in the notion that the major interests of the group are essentially opposed to those of the individual and are more important than his. . . .

2. If one be an apologist for the present economic and social order, there is little fault to be found with this endless and manifold regulation of the most intimate concern of the individual, save that it is not as effective as it once was. Society, we are being constantly reminded, is founded in the family. No one, I think, will quarrel with this statement, particularly at this stage of the world's rule by the exploiting State. . . .

The reason why marriage is "an incomparable protection to society" lies in the fact that the continuance of the power of the exploiting State depends upon the relative helplessness of its exploited subjects; and nothing renders the subject more helpless against the dominance of the State than marriage. For monopoly, under the protection of the State, has rendered the support of a family extremely difficult, by closing free access of labour to natural resources and thus enabling the constant maintenance of a labour-surplus. Where there is little or no land not legally occupied, access to the soil is impossible save on terms that render it, if not downright prohibitive, at least unprofitable. The breadwinner who has neither land nor capital is thus forced to take his chance in a labour-market overcrowded by applicants for work who are in exactly his position: they are shut out from opportunity to work for themselves, and obliged to accept such employment as they can get at a wage determined not by their capacity to produce, but by the number of their competitors. Not only is the wage-earner thus obliged to content himself with a small share of what his labour produces; he is forced to pay out of that share further tribute to monopoly in most of the things he buys. . . .

Such disadvantages tend not only to keep wages near the subsistence-level, but to keep opinions orthodox—or if not orthodox, unexpressed. For the wage-earner gets his living on sufferance: while he continues to please his employer he may earn a living, however inadequate, for himself and family; but if he show signs of discontent with the established order, by which his employer benefits or thinks he benefits, he is likely to find himself supplanted by some other worker whose need makes him more willing to conform, in appearance at least. . . . [T]he average wage-earner with a family to support will be under much greater pressure to dissemble than will the worker who has no family; for where the single worker risks privation for himself alone, the married worker takes this risk for his family as well. Nor does economic pressure operate only towards the appearance of conformity; it operates towards actual conformity, for the person who has children to rear and educate will be strongly impelled towards conservatism by his situation. If he can get along at all under the present order, the mere *vis inertiae* will incline him to fear for the sake of his family the economic dislocation attendant upon any revolutionary change, and to choose rather to keep the ills he has. . . .

Thus the economic conditions brought about by the State operate to make marriage the State's strongest bulwark; and those who believe that the preservation of the State, or of a particular form of it, is a sacred duty—their number among its victims is legion—are quite logical in taking alarm at the increasing unwillingness of men and women to marry, or if they do marry, to have children. They are logical not only because marriage and children make for endurance of established abuses, but because . . . it is important for the State to have as many subjects as possible, to keep up a labour-surplus at home and to fight for the interests of its privileged class abroad; that is, so long as industry is able to meet the exactions of monopoly and still pay interest and wages. . . .

* * *

. . . Meretricious standards of respectability, among them the idea that a married woman must not work outside her home even when she is childless, tend to make marriage from the outset a burden on the man of the middle class. For it must be remembered that since the so-called feminine occupations have been taken out of the home, a man no longer gains an economic asset in taking unto himself a wife. Rather, he assumes a liability. This is especially true among the middle classes, where social standing has come to be gauged to some extent by the degree in which wives are economically unproductive. It is a commonplace in this country that women form the leisure class; and this leisure class of women, like leisured classes everywhere, has its leisure at the expense of other people, who in this case are the husbands. Moreover, it is among the middle classes that the standards of education are highest and the rearing of children therefore most expensive; and this burden is usually borne by the husband alone. Hence the emergence of the type of harassed *pater familias* at whom our comic artists poke much sympathetic fun, who meets his family now and then on Sundays, foots their bills, and is rewarded for his unremitting toil in their behalf by being regarded much in the light of a cash-register. . . .

. . . The rearing of children, if justice is to be done them, is one of the most exacting tasks that can be undertaken. The adjustment that is required to fit parents to the personalities of their children and children to those of their parents and of one another, is in itself a most delicate and difficult process, and one upon which the nature of the child's adjustment to the larger world greatly depends. Such a process naturally involves friction, and therefore, if it is to be successful, calls for no little tact and patience in the parents; and cramped quarters, sordid poverty, and exhausting labour are hardly conducive to the possession of either of these qualities. Children of the middle class, it is remarked often enough, hardly know their harassed, overworked fathers; but children of the labouring class are likely to know neither of their parents, or to know them only as fretful, quarrelsome people, brutalized by overwork. . . .

If responsibility for the upbringing of children is to continue to be vested in the family, then the rights of children will be secured only when parents are able to make a living for their families with so little difficulty that they may give their best thought and energy to the child's development and the problem of helping it to adjust itself to the complexities of the modern environment. Such a condition is not utopian, but quite possible of attainment, as I shall show later. But for the present, and for some time to come, marriage and parenthood will continue to make men and women virtual slaves of the economic order which they help to perpetuate. . . .

Both as a personal relationship and as an institution, marriage is at present undergoing a profound modification resulting from the changing industrial and social position of women. The elevation of woman from the position of a chattel to that of a free citizen must inevitably affect the institution in which her subordinate position has been most strongly emphasized—which has been, indeed, the chief instrument of her subordination. The woman who is demanding her rightful place in the world as man's equal, can no longer be expected to accept without question an institution under whose rules she is obliged to remain the victim of injustice. There is every reason therefore, assuming that the process of emancipation shall not be interrupted, to expect a continuous alteration in the laws and customs bearing on marriage, until some adjustment shall be reached which allows scope for the individuality of both parties, instead of one only. The psychological conflict involved in the adaptation of marriage to woman's changing position and the changing mentality that results from it, is not to be underrated. At present the process of adjustment is needlessly complicated and this attendant conflict immensely exaggerated, by an economic injustice which bears most heavily on married people. Individualism is developing in modern society to such an extent that marriage based on anything but affection seems degrading; but economic injustice is progressing simultaneously with such strides that marriage based on nothing but affection is likely to end in disaster; for affection and the harassment of poverty are hardly compatible. If this complication were removed, as it could be, we should probably find that the adjustment of marriage to shifting ideals and conditions would come about in a natural and advantageous manner, as adjustments usually do when vexing and hampering conditions are removed. The question will settle itself in any case. Just how, no one, of course, can tell; but however revolutionary the adaptation to new conditions may be, it will not *seem* revolutionary to the people of the future because "the minds of men will be fitted to it." This is an all-important fact, and one that is too little respected; for the desire to enforce our own moral and spiritual criteria upon posterity is quite as strong as the desire to enforce them upon contemporaries. It is a desire which finds a large measure of fulfilment—where is the society which does not struggle along under a dead weight of tradition and law inherited from its grandfathers? All political and religious systems have their root and their strength in the innate conservatism of the human mind, and its intense fear of autonomy. Because of this conservatism, people never

move towards revolution; they are pushed towards it by
intolerable injustices in the economic and social order under
which they live. There were, and are, such injustices in the
laws and customs of the Christian world governing marriage
and the relations of the sexes; hence the changes which have
already begun, and may conceivably proceed until they shall
prove as far-reaching as those by which marriage in the
past was transformed from an instinctive habit into an
institution subject to regulation by everyone except the two
people most intimately concerned.

Woman and Marriage

1. Perhaps the most pronounced conventional distinction
between the sexes is made in their relation to marriage. For
man, marriage is regarded as a state; for woman, as a vocation. For man, it is a means of ordering his life and perpetuating his name, for woman it is considered a proper and
fitting aim of existence. This conventional view is yielding
before the changing attitude of women toward themselves;
but it will be long before it ceases to colour the instinctive
attitude of the great majority of people toward women. It is
because of the usual assumption that marriage is woman's
special province, that I have discussed its general aspect
somewhat at length before considering its relation to women
in particular. This assumption, I may remark, has been
justified expressly or by implication by all those advocates of
freedom for women who have assured the world that
woman's "mission" of wifehood and motherhood would be
better fulfilled rather than worse through an extension of her
rights. If we imagine the signers of the Declaration of Independence, in place of proclaiming the natural right of all men
to life, liberty, and the pursuit of happiness, arguing with
King George that a little more freedom would make them
better husbands and fathers, we shall imagine a pretty exact
parallel for this kind of argument on behalf of the emancipation of women.

The belief that marriage and parenthood are the especial
concern of women is rooted in the idea that the individual
exists for the sake of the species. Biologically, this is of
course true; but it is equally true of male and female. . . .
Among civilized peoples . . . where individuation has pro-

gressed farthest, it is not usual to look upon the male as existing solely for the species; but it is usual for the female to be so regarded, because, having had less freedom than the male, she has not been able to assert to the same extent her right to live for herself. The one-sided view that the future of the race depends solely on women has curious results: a nation may send the best of its male youth to be destroyed in war without overmuch anxiety being manifested in any quarter over the effect of this wholesale slaughter upon future generations; but if the idea of enlisting women in military service be so much as broached, there is an immediate outcry about the danger to posterity that such a course would involve. Yet it requires only a moderate exercise of intelligence to perceive that if there must be periodic slaughter it would be better, both for the survivors and for posterity, if the sexes were to be slaughtered in equal numbers; and more especially is this true, for obvious reasons, where monogamy is the accepted form of marriage. . . .

The view of woman as a biological function might be strongly defended on the ground of racial strength if that function were respected and she were free in discharging it. But it is not respected and she is not free. The same restrictions that have kept her in the status of a function have denied her freedom and proper respect even in the exercise of that function. Motherhood, to be sure, receives a great deal of sentimental adulation, but only if it is committed in accordance with rules which have been prescribed by a predominantly masculine society. *Per se* it is accorded no respect whatever. When it results from a sexual relationship which has been duly sanctioned by organized society, it is holy, no matter how much it may transgress the rules of decency, health, or common sense. Otherwise it is a sin meriting social ostracism for the mother and obloquy for the child—an ostracism and an obloquy, significantly enough, in which the father does not share.

The motives behind the universal condemnation of extra-legal motherhood are various and complex; but I believe it is safe to say that the strongest is masculine jealousy. Motherhood out of wedlock constitutes a defiance of that theory of male proprietorship on which most societies are based; it implies on the part of woman a seizure of sexual freedom which, if it were countenanced, would threaten the long-established dominance of the male in sexual matters, a dominance which has been enforced by imposing all manner of unnatural social and legal disabilities upon women, such, for example, as the demand for virginity before marriage and chastity after it. The woman who bears an illegitimate child violates one of these two restrictions. On the other hand, the man who begets an illegitimate child violates no such restriction, for society demands of him neither virginity nor chastity; therefore he is not only not punished by social ostracism, but he is often protected by law from being found out.

. . .

Instead of joining in the universal condemnation of illegitimacy, it seems more reasonable to question the ethics of a society which permits it to exist. Certainly no social usage could be more degrading to women as mothers of the race than that which makes it a sin to bear a child; and nothing could be more grotesquely unjust than a code of morals, reinforced by laws, which relieves men from responsibility for irregular sexual acts, and for the same acts drives women to abortion, infanticide, prostitution and self-destruction. I know of no word that may be said in justification of such a code or of a society that tolerates it. As marriage ceases to be a vested interest with women, and as their growing freedom enables them to perceive the insult to their humanity that this kind of morality involves, they will refuse to stand for it. Those who prefer to regard woman as a function will devote their energy to securing conditions under which she may bear and bring up children with a greater degree of freedom and self-respect than conventional morality allows her. As for those who prefer to regard her as a human being, they will naturally demand the abolition of all discriminations based on sex; while all women must certainly repudiate the barbarous injustice of organized society to the illegitimate child.

2. The assumption that justice to motherhood and childhood will undermine the institution of marriage implies that marriage as an institution is based on injustice; which is to assume that it is fundamentally unsound. . . . But this notion implies something more: it implies that marriage is acceptable to women only or chiefly because it offers them a position of privilege—the privilege of exemption from the social and economic consequences of illegitimate motherhood.

There is some show of reason in this; for the disabilities which marriage puts on women are in most communities humiliating and onerous, more particularly since the unmarried woman has so generally succeeded in establishing her right to be treated as a free agent. The abolition of illegitimacy may conceivably undermine institutional marriage; yet hardly before women are economically free. For her need of society's protection against itself in the discharge of her maternal function has certainly had less to do with woman's long acquiescence in the disabilities which marriage involves than the fact that marriage offered the only career which society approved for her or gave her much opportunity to pursue. She was under enormous economic and social pressure to accept those disabilities, and she yielded, precisely as thousands of men who have been under analogous pressure to get their living under humiliating conditions, have yielded, rather than not get it at all.

. . . The married mother, particularly in modern times, is the object of a sickly pawing and adulation and enjoys a certain formal respect—not, however, as a mother, but as a mother of legitimate children. While she continues to live with her husband, she may exercise considerable supervision over the rearing of her offspring; indeed in some communities she is, by force of custom, supreme in this province. But in case of separation or the death of her husband, she may find herself without any legal claim to their guardianship or custody, for until recently children born in wedlock have been generally held to belong exclusively to the father. The principle of joint guardianship is coming to be recognized in modern jurisprudence, but there are communities where the old laws still hold. . . . In this respect the unmarried mother is better off than the mother of legitimate children, for in most countries, as the only legal parent of her child, she exercises the right of guardianship and control and possesses full claim to their services and earnings. The unmarried mother, in a word, bears her own children; the married mother bears the children of her husband. . . .

So much for the disabilities of the married mother. Her compensations are the immunity that marriage affords her from society's displeasure and consequent persecution; the inestimable advantage of her husband's co-operation in making a home for her children, and in rearing and educating them; and the fact that they have a legal claim upon him for support and inheritance. . . .

The claim for alimony which at present constitutes such a fecund source of injustice to men and corruption among women, implies the assumption that a woman is economically helpless, that she is a natural dependent whose support, having been undertaken by her husband, must be continued even after divorce, until she dies or finds another husband to support her. It does not take into account the woman's rightful claim to any property that she may have helped her husband to accumulate, for the question whether or not she shall receive alimony is within the discretion of the court. On the other hand, the awarding of alimony may give a woman a claim to income from property possessed by her husband before marriage and therefore not rightfully to be enjoyed by her; it may, furthermore, give her an equally unjustifiable lien on his future earnings. Thus it allows woman at once too little and too much. . . .

I have given only a partial list of the economic disabilities enforced upon a good many millions of married women. Their status in the various countries of the civilized world ranges all the way from complete subjection to their husbands to complete equality with them. The subjection of women, like all slavery, has been enforced by legally established economic disadvantages; and upon the married woman these disadvantages, or some of them, are still binding in most communities. The law deprived her of the right to her own property and her own labour, and in return gave her a claim upon her husband for bare subsistence, which is the claim of a serf. Since woman's partial emergence from her subjection, and the consequent modification of the discriminations against her, laws which were logical and effective when her status was that of a chattel have been allowed to survive other laws which made them necessary. The result is a grotesque hodge-podge of illogical and contradictory provisions which involve injustice to both sexes, and should be abolished by the simple expedient of making men and women equal in all respects before the law, and sweeping away all legal claims which they now exercise against one another by virtue of the marriage-bond.

This would mean, of course, that a woman might no longer legally claim support from her husband by virtue of her wifehood; nor should she in fairness be able to do so when all his claims to her property and services had been abolished. There is no reason why the disabilities which marriage imposes on women should be done away with and those which it imposes on men retained. To take such a course would be to turn the tables and place women in a position of privilege. The fact that women are still at considerable disadvantage in the industrial world might appear to justify such a position; but there is a better way of dealing with their economic handicaps than the way of penalizing husbands and demoralizing a large number of women by degrading marriage, for them, to the level of a means of livelihood, gained sometimes through virtual blackmail. Given complete equality of the sexes, so that prejudice may no longer avail itself of legal sanction for excluding women from the occupations in which they may elect to engage, the economic handicaps from which they may still suffer will be those resulting from the overcrowded condition of the general labour-market. The ultimate emancipation of woman, then, will depend not upon the abolition of the restrictions which have subjected her to man—that is but a step, though a necessary one—but upon *the abolition of all those restrictions of natural human rights that subject the mass of humanity to a privileged class* . . .

The wife would no longer be humiliated by the assumption that as a married woman she is the natural inferior of her husband, and entitled to society's protection against the extreme results of the disabilities that her status involves. If she became his housekeeper, she would do so by free choice, and not because her services were his legal property; and her resultant claim on his purse would be fixed by mutual arrangement rather than by laws allowing her the claims of a serf. The marriage, if it became an economic partnership, would be so by mutual consent and arrangement, and would thus no longer be a one-sided contract, legally defined, in which all the rights were on the side of the husband, but compensated in too many cases by unjust privileges on that of the wife. At the same time, the temptation to marry for economic security or ease would be lessened. This temptation besets both men and women, though not in the same degree, because men, through the economic advantage enjoyed by their sex, are oftener in a position of ease than women are. . . .

More general and binding, even, than the economic obligations that marriage entails are the personal claims that it creates. In so far as these claims are psychological—those of affection and habit, or attachment to children—their regulation and abrogation will always afford a problem which must be solved by the two persons concerned. There is at present a strong tendency to equalize the incidence of the laws whereby the State defines these relations and imposes them on married people. The old assumption of feminine inferiority in sexual rights is gradually yielding to a single standard for both sexes. So, also, the requirement that the wife shall in all matters subordinate her will and judgment to the will and judgment of her husband, tends to be modified by the new view of woman as a free agent rather than a mere adjunct to man. Qualifications for marriage and grounds for divorce tend to become the same for both sexes as the State is forced to relinquish its right to regard as offences in one sex actions which it does not recognize as offences in the other. . . .

I have not forgotten the children. One could hardly do so in an age when sentimentalism offers them as the final and unanswerable reason for continuing to tolerate the injustice involved in institutionalized marriage. . . . [W]hen one hears the argument that marriage should be indissoluble for the sake of children, one cannot help wondering whether the protagonist is really such a firm friend of childhood, or whether his concern for the welfare of children is merely so much protective coloration for a constitutional and superstitious fear of change.

Children are really as helpless as women have always been held to be; and in their case the reason is not merely supposition. Woman was supposed to be undeveloped man. The child *is* undeveloped man or woman; and because of its lack of development it needs protection. To place it in the absolute power of its parents as its natural protectors and assume that its interests will invariably be well guarded, would be as cruel as was the assumption that a woman rendered legally and economically helpless and delivered over to a husband or other male guardian, was sure of humane treatment. No human being, man, woman, or child, may safely be entrusted to the power of another; for no human being may safely be trusted with absolute power. It is fair, therefore, that in the case of those whose physical or mental immaturity renders them comparatively helpless, there should be a watchful third person who from the vantage-point of a disinterested neutrality may detect and stop any infringement of their rights by their guardians, be they parents or other people. Here, then, is a legitimate office for the community: to arbitrate, in the interest of justice, between children and their guardians.

But the community has a more direct and less disinterested concern in the welfare of children: every child is a potential power for good or ill; what its children become, that will the community become. It is knowledge of this that prompts the establishment of public schools and colleges, and all the manifold associational activities intended to promote the physical and spiritual welfare of children. . . . From all this activity it is only a step to the assumption by the community of entire responsibility for the upbringing and education of every child. This idea has some advocates; it is a perfectly logical corollary of the modern conception of the child's relation to the community. Yet it invites a wary and conditional acceptance. It is fair that the community should assume the burden of the child's support and education, particularly so long as the community sanctions an economic system which makes this burden too heavy for the great majority of parents, and a political system which may force male children to sacrifice their lives in war as soon as parents have completed the task of bringing them up. But the advisability of accomplishing this purpose through the substitution of institutionalized care for parental care is more than a little doubtful; for to institutionalize means in great degree to mechanize. To establish such a system and make it obligatory, would be to remove many children from the custody of parents entirely unfitted to bring them up; but it would likewise involve the removal of many children from the custody of parents eminently well fitted for such a responsibility. It would imply an assumption that the people who might be engaged to substitute for parents would be better qualified for their task than the parents themselves; and such an assumption would be dangerous so long as the work of educators continues to be as little respected and as poorly paid as it now is. Moreover, so long as society remains organized in the exploiting State, the opportunity to corrupt young minds and turn out rubber-stamp patriots would be much greater than that which is now afforded by the public school system, whose influence intelligent parents are sometimes able to neutralize.

Perhaps the best argument against such a system is that it would not work. If experience teaches anything, it is that what the community undertakes to do is usually done badly. This is due in part to the temptation to corruption that such enterprises involve, but even more, perhaps, to the lack of personal interest on the part of those engaged in them. Those people who advocate bringing up children in institutions do not take into account the value of parental interest in the child; nor do they respect the parental affection which would cause many parents to suffer keenly if they were forced to part with their children. The family is by no means always the best milieu for young people; but before we seek to substitute a dubious institutionalism, it would be wise to ascertain whether the change is imperative. . . . [P]arents are at present under heavy economic handicaps in discharging their parental duties, handicaps which not only render those duties a heavy burden, but lengthen inordinately the period for which they must be undertaken. Until those handicaps are removed, it will not be fair to say that the family is a failure; and until they are removed, we may be certain that any other institution charged with the care of the young will be a failure, for it will be filled with people who are there less because of their understanding of children and their peculiar fitness to rear them, than because such work offers an avenue of escape from starvation.

These same considerations apply to the argument that the rearing of children should be institutionalized in order to emancipate women from the immemorial burden of "woman's work." There is a simpler way of dealing with this problem, a way which eliminates an element that dooms to failure any scheme of human affairs in which it is involved, namely: the element of coercion. To contend that all mothers should be forced to devote themselves exclusively to the rearing of children, or that they should be forcibly relieved of this responsibility, is to ignore the right of the individual to free choice in personal matters. There is no relation more intimately personal than that of parents to the child they have brought into the world; and there is therefore no relationship in which the community should be slower to interfere. This is a principle universally recognized: the community at present interferes only when the interest of the child, or that of the community in the child, is obviously suffering. The emancipation of women by no means necessitates the abandonment of this principle. It necessitates nothing more than a guarantee to women of free choice either to undertake themselves the actual work of caring for their children, or to delegate that work to others. There is nothing revolutionary about this: well-to-do parents have always exercised this choice. In mediaeval Europe people of the upper classes regularly sent their children to be brought up by other people, and took the children of other people into their own houses. . . . In modern times people who can afford it often place their children in boarding schools at an early age, and keep them at home only during vacations—when they do not place them in camps. Under a system of free economic opportunity all people, instead of a few, would have this alternative to rearing their children at home, for they would all be able to afford it. Even under the present economic order it would be possible if the system of children's assistance were extended to include every child, whether the parents were living or not. But under a system of free opportunity there would be greater certainty that the child would not suffer through separation from its parents; for the paid educator would be in his position because it interested him. If it did not, he would take advantage of the opportunity, freely open to him, to do something that did.

* * *

The modifications which institutionalized marriage has been undergoing since the partial emergence of woman, its chief victim, have been in the direction of equality and freedom. The relative ease with which divorce may now be had marks a long step towards recognition of marriage as a personal rather than a social concern; and so does the tendency to abolish the legal disabilities resulting from the marriage-bond. Nothing augurs better for the elevation of marriage to a higher plane than the growing economic independence of women and the consequent improvement in the social position of the unmarried woman; for only when marriage is placed above all considerations of economic or social advantage will it be in a way to satisfy the highest demands of the human spirit.

But the emergence of women has had another significant effect, namely: an increase in frankness concerning extra-legal sexual relations, if not in their number. Of late there has been much public discussion of the wantonness of our modern youth; which, being interpreted, means the disposition of our girls to take the same liberty of indulgence in pre-nuptial sexual affairs that has always been countenanced in boys. This tendency is an entirely natural result of woman's increased freedom. The conditions of economic and social life have undergone revolutionary change in the past half-century; and codes of morals always yield before economic and social exigency, for this is imperious. . . .

If there is about this attitude an element of bravado, akin to that of the youth who thinks it clever and smart to carry a hip-pocket flask, it bears testimony, not to the dangers of freedom, but to the bankruptcy of conventional morality. The worst effect of tutelage is that it negates self-discipline, and therefore people suddenly released from it are almost bound to make fools of themselves. The women who are emerging from it, if they have not learned to substitute an enlightened self-interest for the morality of repression, are certainly in danger of carrying sexual freedom to dishevelling extremes, simply to demonstrate to themselves their emancipation from unjust conventions. There is no reason to expect that women, emerging from tutelage, will be wiser than men. One should expect the contrary. It is necessary to grow accustomed to freedom before one may walk in it sure-footedly. . . . This so-called wantonness, this silly bravado, simply shows that the new freedom is a step ahead of the self-discipline that will eventually take the place of surveillance and repression. . . .

What Is To Be Done

The whole point of the foregoing . . . is this: It is impossible for a sex or a class to have economic freedom until everybody has it, and until economic freedom is attained for everybody, there can be no real freedom for anybody. Without economic freedom, efforts after political and social freedom are nugatory and illusive, except for what educational value they may have for those concerned with them. . . .

The organized feminist movement in England and America has concerned itself pretty exclusively with securing political rights for women; that is to say, its conception of freedom has been based on the eighteenth century misconception of it as a matter of suffrage. Women have won the vote, and now they are proceeding to use their new political power to secure the removal of those legal discriminations which still remain in force against their sex. This is well enough; it is important that the State should be forced to renounce its pretension to discriminate against women in favour of men. But even if we assume that the establishment of legal equality between the sexes would result in complete social and economic equality, we are obliged to face the fact that under such a régime women would enjoy precisely that degree of freedom which men now enjoy—that is to say, very little. I have remarked that those who control men's and women's economic opportunity control men and women. The State represents the organized interest of those who control economic opportunity; and while the State continues to exist, it may be forced to renounce all legal discriminations against one sex in favour of the other without in any wise affecting its fundamental discrimination against the propertyless, dependent class—*which is made up of both men and women*—in favour of the owning and exploiting classes. Until this fundamental discrimination is challenged, the State may, without danger to itself, grant, in principle at least, the claims to political and legal equality of all classes under its power. . . . The emancipation of women within the political State will leave them subject, like the negro, to an exploitation enhanced by surviving prejudices against them. The most that can be expected of the removal of discriminations subjecting one class to another within the exploiting State, is that it will free the subject class from dual control—control by the favoured class and by the monopolist of economic opportunity.

Even this degree of emancipation is worth a good deal; and therefore one is bound to regret that it has no guarantee of permanence more secure than legal enactment. Rights that depend on the sufferance of the State are of uncertain tenure; for they are in constant danger of abrogation either through the failure of the State to maintain them, through a gradual modification of the laws on which they depend, or through a change in the form of the State. At the present moment the third of these dangers, which might have seemed remote ten years ago, may be held to be at least equally pressing with the other two. It is a misfortune of the woman's movement that it has succeeded in securing political rights for women at the very period when political rights are worth less than they have been at any time since the eighteenth century. Parliamentary government is breaking down in Europe, and the guarantees of individual rights which it supported are disappearing with it. Republicanism in this country has not yet broken down, but public confidence in it has never been so low, and it seems certainly on the way to disaster. No system of government can hope long to survive the cynical disregard of both law and principle which government in America regularly exhibits. Under these circumstances, no legal guarantee of rights is worth the paper it is written on, and the women who rely upon such guarantees to protect them against prejudice and discrimination are leaning on a broken reed. They will do well to bear this in mind as they proceed with their demands for equality, and to remember that however great may be their immediate returns from the removal of their legal disabilities, they can hardly hope for security against prejudice and discrimination until their natural rights, not as women but as human beings, are finally established.

The "Militant Madonna":
Charlotte Perkins Gilman (1860–1935)

It is often a shock to meet someone for the first time whose published work we have read before the personal encounter, for all too frequently the two images of the person seem at odds: someone who is forceful and assertive in face-to-face encounters may be the gentle poet in print, while a small, slight person with a soft voice may be behind a forthright and forceful prose style. Charlotte Perkins Gilman was of the latter type; she was described by one of her listeners on a speaking tour as the "militant madonna," a woman who gave the impression of a gentle quiet soul but whose writings have the force of a closely argued pamphlet of social and political criticism.

The book Charlotte Gilman is best known for is _Women and Economics_, which she wrote in a marathon stint of a few months and published in 1898. There are interesting parallels between this very successful book and the equally successful Friedan's _The Feminine Mystique_, published sixty-five years later, in 1963. Both women had been professional writers before the publication of their first major book. Both books struck a responsive chord in the reading public; both went into numerous editions and were translated into several foreign languages. Neither book was hysterical with shrill feminism or antimale sentiment, and both gave a pungent analysis of the situations in which women were living at the time each book was written.

So too, both books gave social recognition to changes in American society that had already taken place rather than prophesying great and significant change in the future. Millions of women were already employed when Gilman wrote calling for changes in the institutions of child rearing and home maintenance to ease the burdens of working women. She was, in fact, one of the first writers to perceive the societal need for institutional innovation in the functions that had been absorbed by the family system in the past. The return of large numbers of older women to the labor force had already taken place and become a daily fact in the lives of millions of American women by the time Friedan published *The Feminine Mystique*. She also foresaw the need for changes in institutional arrangements that would facilitate more continuity of work involvement by women during the earlier stages of child rearing.

Yet Friedan's book hit the American scene as a forceful new message to the nation. She pricked the bubble of social myth that saw the suburban ranch home and four healthy, well-adjusted children as a sufficient goal for all American girls to dream of attaining for themselves. To millions of her American readers, unfamiliar with their own history as women and ignorant of the nineteenth-century pioneers who struggled in the woman's cause, Friedan's analysis sounded new and startling. Friedan herself showed no awareness of this historical past. There are no references in *The Feminine Mystique* to acknowledge the fact that Gilman, two generations before Friedan, had argued the same case. The responsive chord was waiting to be plucked in the American reading public in 1963, and Friedan helped her readers to recognize the nature of the "problem without a name," just as Gilman's readers had been ripe for her analysis of the position of women in an advanced industrial society in 1898.

Charlotte Gilman's book built on the grand theories of social structure and process that social Darwinists had been propounding since the middle of the nineteenth century. Herbert Spencer in England and Lester Ward in America were but two among a legion of theorists who saw evidence of a unilateral development of the human species in the changes taking place in industrializing Western societies. Gilman dedicated her 1911 book, *The Man-Made World*, with "reverent love and gratitude" to Lester Ward. She seized upon Ward's version of social evolution in particular because Ward had a theory that the male-dominant society of the Christian era (based on what he called the androcentric theory of life) had replaced an earlier stage of development of the human species when women were dominant (what he called the gynaecocentric theory of life). In Ward's view, women were the true and original "race type," while men were a later "sex type" (Ward 1903). What was startling in the 1890s is much less so now that research on fetal development supports the key element in this idea—i.e., that all embryos begin as "female," male development being contingent on a subtle process of hormonal triggering mechanisms (Hamilton *et al.* 1962; Sherfey 1972; Money and Ehrhardt, 1972). It has become more "reasonable" to argue that Adam was made from Eve than vice versa! Gilman believed that a future industrial society and the successful reabsorption of women into productive life could and would spell the end of the androcentric phase of human history. Thus her major book, *Women and Economics*, and the later books which for the most part served primarily to amplify her basic earlier analysis, built on the dominant currents of her era, with its belief in social evolution, unilinear progress, and a progressive commitment to equality of opportunity.

As a result of this major work, Gilman became the leading intellectual in the women's movement in the United States during the first two decades of the twentieth century. She played only a minimal role in the actual political movement for woman's rights. She was a "transitional" type, who stood between the turn-of-century era—when educated women wrote, spoke, and engaged in civic reform—and the post-World War I period, when similarly educated and intellectual women became lost to public view as they retired into the cloistered world of academe as "professional scholars." Thus, in her day Charlotte Gilman was the "intellectual" above the battles waged by the suffragists and reformers, though she felt sympathy with the work and goals of Addams and Kelley and others. But she was not by any means secluded in an academic office. She wrote, lectured, traveled, and published a journal that tried to reach the wider public. Significantly, she did not consider herself a "feminist," preferring the self-designation of "sociologist," again like the women who would follow her in the period marking the early stage of the professional careers of such women as Margaret Mead and Simone de Beauvoir.

Charlotte Gilman shared the characteristics of the Enlightenment Feminists in that she was an intensely "private" person rather than a reforming activist. It is difficult to imagine her as an activist devoting her energies to a political movement that required give and take, an ability to compromise or to shelve pet theories out of concern for implementing a specific legislative goal. Her forte was as a public speaker, a critic, a writer, and a publicist, not as an active participant in a political movement.

In a number of respects Gilman showed a personal profile

rather similar to that of Lucy Stone. Both came from emotionally impoverished families, in which they were deprived of the early foundation of trust and love that women like Antoinette Brown or Lucretia Mott could take for granted. As a consequence, both were unable to make the transition to adult life with an easy or mature acceptance of themselves as women, and this difficulty manifested itself in an undercurrent of psychological rejection of adult sexuality and maternity. In Charlotte Gilman's case, her early marriage to Charles Stetson, a young artist, was contracted after considerable hesitation and was followed by a long period of psychological despondency, which increased with pregnancy and the birth of a daughter. Unlike Lucy Stone, her marriage and home life were not in the context of an extended and warping clan; she was already "emancipated" from such family ties. Instead, she had to confront her pregnancy and the time of caring for an infant essentially on her own. She found that the depression that plagued her lifted when she traveled alone to California for rest and convalescence, away from her husband and child; when she returned to the East, the depression returned. In Charlotte's era, the proper course of action in such circumstances was to seek psychiatric counsel. Her therapist advised prolonged rest and complete withdrawal from intellectual activity. Gilman later stated that this prescription "almost drove her to madness." It was beyond the ken of contemporary psychiatric theories that a problem might reside in restricted life choices and that Charlotte was chafing from, and their prescriptions exacerbated, this handicap. It does not seem to have been her intellectual efforts and interests, but an acceptance of marriage and maternity, uncongenial to her personality, that was at the root of Charlotte Gilman's "problem."

Gilman eventually separated from and divorced Charles Stetson, who later married a close friend of hers. Their relationship after the divorce seems to have remained quite amicable. She married a second time at the age of forty, a few years after the successful publication of *Women and Economics*. She had known her second husband, George Houghton Gilman, for many years, since he was her first cousin. Once again, her memoirs have little to say about the personal side of this marriage. Her husband is an apparently loved figure in the private background of her life, accepting of the life she had developed as a speaker, writer, and journalist.

For some seven years she tried her hand at publishing a journal, *The Forerunner*, but this was not a collaborative effort like the *Woman's Journal* in Boston or the brief two-year fling at journalism of Stanton and Anthony in the *Revolution*. Gilman wrote almost the entire contents of the magazine herself; and she abandoned it after a seven-year trial on the premise that it did not make "sociological sense" to continue an enterprise that had no natural appeal to a wide enough reading public.

Gilman's ideas, which she expressed so ably in the late 1890s, were not centered on a narrow conception of "women's rights"; they swept broadly across human history, social process, and institutional change. But by the 1920s Freudianism had come "in" intellectually, and Gilman was all but "out." She was out of tune with the spirit of the decade, as she no doubt would be with many segments of contemporary society in the 1970s. Her life's dedication was to social service and the subordination of the individual to society. This was the foundation of her attraction to socialist ideas and her rejection of Freudian theories about sexuality, not to mention the ego-centered explorations of young people in the 1920s and the 1970s. To Gilman, as to many of her predecessors in feminist history American style, sex was not a source of recreative pleasure but a purely procreative function.

Like the Blackwell women in personality, Gilman was not able to establish deeply intimate (and hence mutually dependent) personal relationships. Thus she could argue, as many women then and now could not, that children needed greater freedom in order to acquire responsibility, self-reliance, and self-discipline. Her book on child rearing, *Concerning Children*, which she published in 1900, carried this message—an important one in an era when women were pouring excessive amounts of psychic and physical energies into maternity, but also one congenial to Charlotte Gilman's own personality (Gilman 1935).

On the other hand, though she had an incisive grasp of the nature of cultural conditioning to which girls and boys were subjected, she still held the view that, as a result of women's biological function as childbearers, it was much more likely that women were the peaceful, cooperative, steady sex, while men constituted the aggressive, competitive, and restless sex. Her mind was attuned to tracing out the consequences for social roles of the biological givens which characterized the sexes through long stretches of history and close proximity to the physiological pressures of selection and survival. There are any number of ideas in Gilman's writings that were the beginnings of an intellectually innovative view of sex differences and their origins, yet they remained undeveloped and have not yet been seized upon as significant problems in an intellectual history of human conceptions of basic sex differences. Her intellectual dedication to "sociology" led Charlotte Gilman to stress the cultural plasticity of human nature, but she kept a sensible, close contact with the biological tradition of theory and research represented by the intellectual descendants of Darwin.

With the hindsight of fifty years of social-science research, one is humbled by the experience of reading Gilman's early ideas and their implications. She was spared the full burden of those fifty years of research which built on a far purer model of human plasticity, one which argued far more strongly than Gilman did at the turn of the century that men and women are the products of social experiences and early molding within the family. An intellectual opportunity was lost by the 1930s to formulate serious questions concerning the interactive effect of physiology and culture upon the formation of the human personality. The beginnings of a return of research interest in this theoretical approach is only just visible on the intellectual horizon of the present decade (Bardwick 1971; Money and Ehrhardt 1972). It may well be that, as feminist thinking and research stimulates new formulations of problems, we shall be able in a few years to return to the writings of Antoinette Brown and Charlotte Gilman with a sense that they have become even more "contemporary" than we judge them to be in 1973.

Gilman carried her own sense of being "in control of her destiny" into the last years of her life. When she discovered in 1932 that she had breast cancer, she bought enough chloroform to give her control over her life. After her husband's death in 1934 she went to live with her daughter Katherine in California, and there, in August 1935, she ended her life with the chloroform she had purchased three years earlier.

Two references may be of interest to the reader who wishes to learn more about the life and work of Charlotte Gilman. Her own 1935 autobiography—*The Living of Charlotte Perkins Gilman*—remains a fascinating introduction,

while the introduction by Carl Degler to the republication of
Women and Economics (Degler 1966) gives a brief overview
of her life and work which will serve excellently until a fuller
biography and interpretation are written.

∂ Women and Economics ∠

1

The economic status of the human race in any nation,
at any time, is governed mainly by the activities of the male:
the female obtains her share in the racial advance only
through him.

Studied individually, the facts are even more plainly
visible, more open and familiar. From the day laborer to the
millionaire, the wife's worn dress or flashing jewels, her
low roof or her lordly one, her weary feet or her rich equipage,
—these speak of the economic ability of the husband. The
comfort, the luxury, the necessities of life itself, which the
woman receives, are obtained by the husband, and given her
by him. And, when the woman, left alone with no man to
"support" her, tries to meet her own economic necessities,
the difficulties which confront her prove conclusively what
the general economic status of the woman is. . . . But we
are instantly confronted by the commonly received opinion
that, although it must be admitted that men make and distribute the wealth of the world, yet women earn their share
of it as wives. This assumes either that the husband is in the
position of employer and the wife as employee, or that
marriage is a "partnership," and the wife an equal factor
with the husband in producing wealth. . . .

Women consume economic goods. What economic product
do they give in exchange for what they consume? The claim
that marriage is a partnership, in which the two persons

From Charlotte Perkins Gilman, *Women and Economics*. Boston, Small, Maynard & Company, 1898. Pp. 9–21, 49–57, 63–69,
86–91, 113–121, 138–144, 181–198, 202–216, 242–244, 255–256,
270, 290.

married produce wealth which neither of them, separately, could produce, will not bear examination. A man happy and comfortable can produce more than one unhappy and uncomfortable, but this is as true of a father or son as of a husband. To take from a man any of the conditions which make him happy and strong is to cripple his industry, generally speaking. But those relatives who make him happy are not therefore his business partners, and entitled to share his income.

Grateful return for happiness conferred is not the method of exchange in a partnership. The comfort a man takes with his wife is not in the nature of a business partnership, nor are her frugality and industry. A housekeeper, in her place, might be as frugal, as industrious, but would not therefore be a partner. Man and wife are partners truly in their mutual obligation to their children,—their common love, duty, and service. But a manufacturer who marries, or a doctor, or a lawyer, does not take a partner in his business, when he takes a partner in parenthood, unless his wife is also a manufacturer, a doctor, or a lawyer. . . .

If the wife is not, then, truly a business partner, in what way does she earn from her husband the food, clothing, and shelter she receives at his hands? By house service, it will be instantly replied. This is the general misty idea upon the subject,—that women earn all they get, and more, by house service. Here we come to a very practical and definite economic ground. Although not producers of wealth, women serve in the final processes of preparation and distribution. Their labor in the household has a genuine economic value.

For a certain percentage of persons to serve other persons, in order that the ones so served may produce more, is a contribution not to be overlooked. The labor of women in the house, certainly, enables men to produce more wealth than they otherwise could; and in this way women are economic factors in society. But so are horses. The labor of horses enables men to produce more wealth than they otherwise could. The horse is an economic factor in society. But the horse is not economically independent, nor is the woman. . . .

The labor which the wife performs in the household is given as part of her functional duty, not as employment. The wife of the poor man, who works hard in a small house, doing all the work for the family, or the wife of the rich man, who wisely and gracefully manages a large house and administers its functions, each is entitled to fair pay for services rendered.

To take this ground and hold it honestly, wives, as earners through domestic service, are entitled to the wages of cooks, housemaids, nursemaids, seamstresses, or housekeepers, and to no more. This would of course reduce the spending money of the wives of the rich, and put it out of the power of the poor man to "support" a wife at all, unless, indeed, the poor man faced the situation fully, paid his wife her wages as house servant, and then she and he combined their funds in the support of their children. He would be keeping a servant: she would be helping keep the family. But nowhere on earth would there be "a rich woman" by these means. Even the highest class of private housekeeper, useful as her services are, does not accumulate a fortune. . . .

But the salient fact in this discussion is that, whatever the economic value of the domestic industry of women is, they do not get it. The women who do the most work get the least money, and the women who have the most money do the least work. Their labor is neither given nor taken as a factor in economic exchange. It is held to be their duty as women to do this work; and their economic status bears no relation to their domestic labors, unless an inverse one. Moreover, if they were thus fairly paid,—given what they earned, and no more,—all women working in this way would be reduced to the economic status of the house servant. Few women—or men either—care to face this condition. The ground that women earn their living by domestic labor is instantly forsaken, and we are told that they obtain their livelihood as mothers. This is a peculiar position. We speak of it commonly enough, and often with deep feeling, but without due analysis. . . .

If this is so, if motherhood is an exchangeable commodity given by women in payment for clothes and food, then we must of course find some relation between the quantity or quality of the motherhood and the quantity and quality of the pay. This being true, then the women who are not mothers have no economic status at all; and the economic status of those who are must be shown to be relative to their motherhood. This is obviously absurd. The childless wife has as much money as the mother of many,—more; for the children of the latter consume what would otherwise be hers; and the inefficient mother is no less provided for than the efficient one. Visibly, and upon the face of it, women are not maintained in economic prosperity proportioned to their motherhood. Motherhood bears no relation to their economic status. . . . The claim of motherhood as a factor in economic exchange is false to-day. But suppose it were true. Are we willing to hold this ground, even in theory? Are we willing to consider motherhood as a business, a form of commercial exchange? Are the cares and duties of the mother, her travail and her love, commodities to be exchanged for bread?

It is revolting so to consider them; and, if we dare face our own thoughts, and force them to their logical conclusion, we shall see that nothing could be more repugnant to human feeling, or more socially and individually injurious, than to make motherhood a trade. Driven off these alleged grounds of women's economic independence; shown that women, as a class, neither produce nor distribute wealth; that women, as individuals, labor mainly as house servants, are not paid as such, and would not be satisfied with such an economic status if they were so paid; that wives are not business partners or co-producers of wealth with their husbands, unless they actually practise the same profession; that they are not salaried as mothers, and that it would be unspeakably degrad-ing if they were,—what remains to those who deny that women are supported by men? This . . . —that the function of maternity unfits a woman for economic production, and, therefore, it is right that she should be supported by her husband. . . .

. . . Because of her maternal duties, the human female is said to be unable to get her own living. As the maternal duties of other females do not unfit them for getting their own living and also the livings of their young, it would seem that the human maternal duties require the segregation of the entire energies of the mother to the service of the child during her entire adult life, or so large a proportion of them that not enough remains to devote to the individual interests of the mother. . . .

Is this the condition of human motherhood? Does the human mother, by her motherhood, thereby lose control of brain and body, lose power and skill and desire for any other work? Do we see before us the human race, with all its females segregated entirely to the uses of motherhood, con-secrated, set apart, specially developed, spending every power of their nature on the service of their children?

We do not. We see the human mother worked far harder than a mare, laboring her life long in the service, not of her children only, but of men; husbands, brothers, fathers, whatever male relatives she has; for mother and sister also; for the church a little, if she is allowed; for society, if she is able; for charity and education and reform,—working in many ways that are not the ways of motherhood.

It is not motherhood that keeps the housewife on her feet from dawn till dark; it is house service, not child service. Women work longer and harder than most men, and not solely in maternal duties. . . . Many mothers, even now, are wage-earners for the family, as well as bearers and rearers of it. And the women who are not so occupied, the women who belong to rich men,—here perhaps is the exhaustive devotion to maternity which is supposed to justify an admitted economic dependence. But we do not find it even among these. Women of ease and wealth provide for their children better care than the poor woman can; but they do not spend more time upon it themselves, nor more care and effort. They have other occupation.

In spite of her supposed segregation to maternal duties, the human female, the world over, works at extra-maternal duties for hours enough to provide her with an independent living, and then is denied independence on the ground that motherhood prevents her working!

2

. . . [I]t is in our common social relations that the predominance of sex-distinction in women is made most manifest. The fact that, speaking broadly, women have, from the very beginning, been spoken of expressively enough as "the sex," demonstrates clearly that this is the main impression which they have made upon observers and recorders. Here one need attempt no farther proof than to turn the mind of the reader to an unbroken record of facts and feelings perfectly patent to every one, but not hitherto looked at as other than perfectly natural and right. So utterly has the status of woman been accepted as a sexual one that it has remained for the woman's movement of the nineteenth century to devote much contention to the claim that women are persons! That women are persons as well as females,—an unheard of proposition! . . .

From the time our children are born, we use every means known to accentuate sex-distinction in both boy and girl; and the reason that the boy is not so hopelessly marked by it as the girl is that he has the whole field of human expression open to him besides. In our steady insistence on proclaiming sex-distinction we have grown to consider most human attributes as masculine attributes, for the simple reason that they were allowed to men and forbidden to women. . . .

All the varied activities of economic production and distribution, all our arts and industries, crafts and trades, all our growth in science, discovery, government, religion,—these are along the line of self-preservation: these are, or should be, common to both sexes. To teach, to rule, to make, to decorate, to distribute,—these are not sex-functions: they are race-functions. Yet so inordinate is the sex-distinction of the human race that the whole field of human progress has been considered a masculine prerogative. What could more absolutely prove the excessive sex-distinction of the human race? That this difference should surge over all its natural boundaries and blazon itself across every act of life, so that every step of the human creature is marked "male" or "female,"—surely, this is enough to show our over-sexed condition. . . .

But while with the male the things he fondly imagined to be "masculine" were merely human, and very good for him, with the female the few things marked "feminine" were feminine, indeed; and her ceaseless reiterance of one short song, however sweet, has given it a conspicuous monotony. In garments whose main purpose is unmistakably to announce her sex; with a tendency to ornament which marks exuberance of sex-energy, with a body so modified to sex as to be grievously deprived of its natural activities; with a manner and behavior wholly attuned to sex-advantage, and frequently most disadvantageous to any human gain; with a field of action most rigidly confined to sex-relations; with her overcharged sensibility, her prominent modesty, her "eternal femininity,"—the female of genus homo is undeniably over-sexed. . . .

Our peculiar inversion of the usual habit of species, in

which the male carries ornament and the female is dark and plain, is not so much a proof of excess indeed, as a proof of the peculiar reversal of our position in the matter of sex-selection. With the other species the males compete in ornament, and the females select. With us the females compete in ornament, and the males select. If this theory of sex-ornament is disregarded, and we prefer rather to see in masculine decoration merely a form of exuberant sex-energy, expending itself in non-productive excess, then, indeed, the fact that with us the females manifest such a display of gorgeous adornment is another sign of excessive sex-distinction. In either case the forcing upon the girl-children of an elaborate ornamentation which interferes with their physical activity and unconscious freedom, and fosters a premature sex-consciousness, is as clear and menacing a proof of our condition as could be mentioned. That the girl-child should be so dressed as to require a difference in care and behavior, resting wholly on the fact that she is a girl,—a fact not otherwise present to her thought at that age,—is a precocious insistence upon sex-distinction, most unwholesome in its results. Boys and girls are expected, also, to behave differently to each other, and to people in general,—a behavior to be briefly described in two words. To the boy we say, "Do"; to the girl, "Don't." The little boy must "take care" of the little girl, even if she is larger than he is. "Why?" he asks. Because he is a boy. Because of sex. Surely, if she is the stronger, she ought to take care of him, especially as the protective instinct is purely feminine in a normal race. It is not long before the boy learns his lesson. He is a boy, going to be a man; and that means all. "I thank the Lord that I was not born a woman," runs the Hebrew prayer. She is a girl, "only a girl," "nothing but a girl," and going to be a woman,—only a woman. Boys are encouraged from the beginning to show the feelings supposed to be proper to their sex. When our infant son bangs about, roars, and smashes things, we say proudly that he is "a regular boy!" When our infant daughter coquettes with visitors, or wails in maternal agony because her brother has broken her doll, whose sawdust remains she nurses with piteous care, we say proudly that "she is a perfect little mother already!" What business has a little girl with the instincts of maternity? No more than the little boy should have with the instincts of paternity. They are sex-instincts, and should not appear till the period of adolescence. The most normal girl is the "tom-boy,"—whose numbers increase among us in these wiser days,—a healthy young creature, who is human through and through, not feminine till it is time to be. The most normal boy has calmness and gentleness as well as vigor and courage. He is a human creature as well as a male creature, and not aggressively masculine till it is time to be. Childhood is not the period for these marked manifestations of sex. That we exhibit them, that we admire and encourage them, shows our over-sexed condition.

. . .

4

With the growth of civilization, we have gradually crystallized into law the visible necessity for feeding the helpless female; and even old women are maintained by their male relatives with a comfortable assurance. But to this day —save, indeed, for the increasing army of women wage-earners, who are changing the face of the world by their steady advance toward economic independence—the personal profit of women bears but too close a relation to their power to win and hold the other sex. From the odalisque with the most bracelets to the débutante with the most bouquets, the relation still holds good,—woman's economic profit comes through the power of sex-attraction.

When we confront this fact boldly and plainly in the open market of vice, we are sick with horror. When we see the same economic relation made permanent, established by law, sanctioned and sanctified by religion, covered with flowers and incense and all accumulated sentiment, we think it innocent, lovely, and right. The transient trade we think evil. The bargain for life we think good. But the biological effect remains the same. In both cases the female gets her food from the male by virtue of her sex-relationship to him. In both cases, perhaps even more in marriage because of its perfect acceptance of the situation, the female of genus homo, still living under natural law, is inexorably modified to sex in an increasing degree. . . .

. . . The human female has been restricted in range from the earliest beginning. Even among savages, she has a much more restricted knowledge of the land she lives in. She moves with the camp, of course, and follows her primitive industries in its vicinity; but the war-path and the hunt are the man's. He has a far larger habitat. The life of the female savage is freedom itself, however, compared with the increasing constriction of custom closing in upon the woman, as civilization advanced, like the iron torture chamber of romance. Its culmination is expressed in the proverb: "A woman should leave her home but three times,—when she is christened, when she is married, and when she is buried." Or this: "The woman, the cat, and the chimney should never leave the house." The absolutely stationary female and the wide-ranging male are distinctly human institutions. . . .

To reduce so largely the mere area of environment is a great check to race-development; but it is not to be compared in its effects with the reduction in voluntary activity to which the human female has been subjected. Her restricted impression, her confinement to the four walls of the home, have done great execution, of course, in limiting her ideas, her information, her thought-processes, and power of judgment; and in giving a disproportionate prominence and intensity to the few things she knows about; but this is innocent in action compared with her restricted expression, the denial of freedom to act. A living organism is modified far less through the action of external circumstances upon it and its reaction thereto, than through the effect of its own exertions. Skin may be thickened gradually by exposure to the weather; but it is thickened far more quickly by being rubbed against something, as the handle of an oar or of a broom. To be surrounded by beautiful things has much influence upon the human creature: to make beautiful things has more. To live among beautiful surroundings and make ugly things is more directly lowering than to live among ugly surroundings and make beautiful things. What we do modifies us more than what is done to us. The freedom of expression has been more restricted in women than the freedom of impression, if that be possible. Something of the world she lived in she has seen from her barred windows. . . . But in the ever-growing human impulse to create, the power and will to make, to do, to express one's new spirit in new forms,—here she has been utterly debarred. She might work as she had worked from the beginning,—at the primitive labors of the household; but in the inevitable expansion of

even those industries to professional levels we have striven to
hold her back. To work with her own hands, for nothing,
in direct body-service to her own family,—this has been
permitted,—yes, compelled. But to be and do anything
further from this she has been forbidden. Her labor has
not only been limited in kind, but in degree. Whatever she
has been allowed to do must be done in private and alone,
the first-hand industries of savage times.

Our growth in industry has been not only in kind, but
in class. The baker is not in the same industrial grade with
the house-cook, though both make bread. To specialize any
form of labor is a step up: to organize it is another step.
Specialization and organization are the basis of human
progress, the organic methods of social life. They have been
forbidden to women almost absolutely. The greatest and most
beneficent change of this century is the progress of women
in these two lines of advance. The effect of this check in
industrial development, accompanied as it was by the constant inheritance of increased racial power, has been to
intensify the sensations and emotions of women, and to
develop great activity in the lines allowed. The nervous
energy that up to present memory has impelled women to
labor incessantly at something, be it the veriest folly of
fancy work, is one mark of this effect.

5

Another instance of so grossly unjust, so palpable, so
general an evil that it has occasionally aroused some protest
even from our dull consciousness is this: the enforced attitude
of the woman toward marriage. To the young girl, as has
been previously stated, marriage is the one road to fortune,
to life. She is born highly specialized as a female: she is
carefully educated and trained to realize in all ways her
sex-limitations and her sex-advantages. What she has to
gain even as a child is largely gained by feminine tricks and
charms. Her reading, both in history and fiction, treats of the
same position for women; and romance and poetry give it
absolute predominance. Pictorial art, music, the drama, society, everything, tells her that she is *she,* and that all depends
on whom she marries. Where young boys plan for what they

will achieve and attain, young girls plan for whom they will achieve and attain. . . .

With such a prospect as this before her; with an organization specially developed to this end; with an education adding every weight of precept and example, of wisdom and virtue, to the natural instincts; with a social environment the whole machinery of which is planned to give the girl a chance to see and to be seen, to provide her with "opportunities"; and with all the pressure of personal advantage and self-interest added to the sex-instinct,—what one would logically expect is a society full of desperate and eager husband-hunters, regarded with popular approval.

Not at all! Marriage is the woman's proper sphere, her divinely ordered place, her natural end. It is what she is born for, what she is trained for, what she is exhibited for. It is, moreover, her means of honorable livelihood and advancement. *But*—she must not even look as if she wanted it! She must not turn her hand over to get it. She must sit passive as the seasons go by, and her "chances" lessen with each year. Think of the strain on a highly sensitive nervous organism to have so much hang on one thing, to see the possibility of attaining it grow less and less yearly, and to be forbidden to take any step toward securing it! This she must bear with dignity and grace to the end. . . .

The cruel and absurd injustice of blaming the girl for not getting what she is allowed no effort to obtain seems unaccountable; but it becomes clear when viewed in connection with the sexuo-economic relation. Although marriage is a means of livelihood, it is not honest employment where one can offer one's labor without shame, but a relation where the support is given outright, and enforcement by law in return for the functional service of the woman, the "duties of wife and mother." Therefore no honorable woman can ask for it. . . .

. . . Since women are viewed wholly as creatures of sex even by one another, and since everything is done to add to their young powers of sex-attraction; since they are marriageable solely on this ground, unless, indeed, "a fortune" has been added to their charms,—failure to marry is held a clear proof of failure to attract, a lack of sex-value. And, since they have no other value, save in a low order of domestic service, they are quite naturally despised. What else is the creature good for, failing in the functions for which it was created? The scorn of male and female alike falls on this sexless thing: she is a human failure.

It is not strange, therefore, though just as pitiful,—this long chapter of patient, voiceless, dreary misery in the lives of women; and it is not strange, either, to see the marked and steady change in opinion that follows the development of other faculties in woman besides those of sex. Now that she is a person as well as a female, filling economic relation to society, she is welcomed and accepted as a human creature, and need not marry the wrong man for her bread and butter. So sharp is the reaction from this unlovely yoke that there is a limited field of life to-day wherein women choose not to marry, preferring what they call "their independence,"— a new-born, hard-won, dear-bought independence. That any living woman should prefer it to home and husband, to love and motherhood, throws a fierce light on what women must have suffered for lack of freedom before.

This tendency need not be feared, however. It is merely a reaction, and a most natural one. It will pass as naturally, as more and more women become independent, when marriage is not the price of liberty. The fear exhibited that women generally, once fully independent, will not marry, is proof of how well it has been known that only dependence forced them to marriage as it was. There will be needed neither bribe nor punishment to force women to true marriage with independence.

6

. . . Legitimate sex-competition brings out all that is best in man. To please her, to win her, he strives to do his best. But the economic dependence of the female upon the male, with its ensuing purchasability, does not so affect a man: it puts upon him the necessity for getting things, not for doing them. In the lowest grades of labor, where there is no getting without doing and where the laborer always does more than he gets, this works less palpable evil than in the higher grades, the professions and arts, where the most valuable work is always ahead of the market, and where to work for the market involves a lowering of standards. The young artist or poet or scientific student works for his work's sake, for art, for science, and so for the best good of society. But the artist or student married must get gain, must work for those who will pay; and those who will pay are not those who lift and bear forward the standard of progress. Community of interest is quite possible with those who are working most disinterestedly for the social good; but bring in the sex-relation, and all such solidarity disintegrates,—resolves itself into the tiny groups of individuals united on a basis of sex-union, and briskly acting in their own immediate interests at anybody's or everybody's expense.

The social perception of the evil resultant from the intrusion of sex-influence upon racial action has found voice in the heartless proverb, "There is no evil without a woman at the bottom of it." When a man's work goes wrong, his hopes fail, his ambitions sink, cynical friends inquire, "Who is she?" It is not for nothing that a man's best friends sigh when he marries, especially if he is a man of genius. This judgment of the world has obtained side by side with its equal faith in the ennobling influence of woman. The world is quite right. It does not have to be consistent. Both judgments are correct. Woman affecting society through the sex-relation or through her individual economic relation is an ennobling influence. Woman affecting society through our perverse combination of the two becomes a strange influence, indeed. . . .

. . . Half the human race is denied free productive expression, is forced to confine its productive human energies to the same channels as its reproductive sex-energies. Its creative skill is confined to the level of immediate personal bodily service, to the making of clothes and preparing of food for individuals. No social service is possible. While its power of production is checked, its power of consumption is inordinately increased by the showering upon it of the "unearned increment" of masculine gifts. For the woman there is, first, no free production allowed; and, second, no relation maintained between what she does produce and what she consumes. She is forbidden to make, but encouraged to take. Her industry is not the natural output of creative energy, not the work she does because she has the inner power and strength to do it; nor is her industry even the measure of her gain. She has, of course, the natural desire to consume;

and to that is set no bar save the capacity or the will of her husband.

Thus we have painfully and laboriously evolved and carefully maintain among us an enormous class of nonproductive consumers,—a class which is half the world, and mother of the other half. We have built into the constitution of the human race the habit and desire of taking, as divorced from its natural precursor and concomitant of making. . . . To consume food, to consume clothes, to consume houses and furniture and decorations and ornaments and amusements, to take and take and take forever,—from one man if they are virtuous, from many if they are vicious, but always to take and never to think of giving anything in return except their womanhood,—this is the enforced condition of the mothers of the race. What wonder that their sons go into business "for what there is in it"! What wonder that the world is full of the desire to get as much as possible and to give as little as possible! . . .

. . . [T]he consuming female, debarred from any free production, unable to estimate the labor involved in the making of what she so lightly destroys, and her consumption limited mainly to those things which minister to physical pleasure, creates a market for sensuous decoration and personal ornament, for all that is luxurious and enervating, and for a false and capricious variety in such supplies, which operates as a most deadly check to true industry and true art. As the priestess of the temple of consumption, as the limitless demander of things to use up, her economic influence is reactionary and injurious. Much, very much, of the current of useless production in which our economic energies run waste—man's strength poured out like water on the sand—depends on the creation and careful maintenance of this false market, this sink into which human labor vanishes with no return. Woman, in her false economic position, reacts injuriously upon industry, upon art, upon science, discovery, and progress. The sexo-economic relation in its effect on the constitution of the individual keeps alive in us the instincts of savage individualism which we should otherwise have well outgrown. It sexualizes our industrial relation and commercializes our sex-relation. And, in the external effect upon the market, the over-sexed woman, in her unintelligent and ceaseless demands, hinders and perverts the economic development of the world.

7

. . . [T]he period of women's economic dependence is drawing to a close, because its racial usefulness is wearing out. We have already reached a stage of human relation where we feel the strength of social duty pull against the sex-ties that have been for so long the only ties that we have recognized. The common consciousness of humanity, the sense of social need and social duty, is making itself felt in both men and women. The time has come when we are open to deeper and wider impulses than the sex-instinct; the social instincts are strong enough to come into full use at last. This is shown by the twin struggle that convulses the world to-day,—in sex and economics,—the "woman's movement" and the "labor movement.". . .

The woman's movement rests not alone on her larger personality, with its tingling sense of revolt against injustice, but on the wide, deep sympathy of women for one another. It is a concerted movement, based on the recognition of a common evil and seeking a common good. So with the labor movement. It is not alone that the individual laborer is a better educated, more highly developed man than the stolid peasant of earlier days, but also that with this keener personal consciousness has come the wider social consciousness, without which no class can better its conditions. The traits incident to our sexuo-economic relation have developed till they forbid the continuance of that relation. In the economic world, excessive masculinity, in its fierce competition and primitive individualism; and excessive femininity, in its inordinate consumption and hindering conservatism; have reached a stage where they work more evil than good. . . .

To-day . . . the social consciousness is at last so vital a force in both men and women that we feel clearly that our human life cannot be fully lived on sex-lines only. We are so far individualized, so far socialized, that men can work without the tearing spur of exaggerated sex-stimulus, work for some one besides mate and young; and women can love and serve without the slavery of economic dependence,—love better and serve more. Sex-stimulus begins and ends in individuals. The social spirit is a larger thing, a better thing, and brings with it a larger, nobler life than we could ever know on a sex-basis solely. . . .

The woman's movement, then, should be hailed by every right-thinking, far-seeing man and woman as the best birth of our century. The banner advanced proclaims "equality before the law," woman's share in political freedom; but the main line of progress is and has been toward economic equality and freedom. While life exists on earth, the economic conditions must underlie and dominate each existing form and its activities; and social life is no exception. A society whose economic unit is a sex-union can no more develop beyond a certain point industrially than a society like the patriarchal, whose political unit was a sex-union, could develop beyond a certain point politically.

* * *

9

Human motherhood is more pathological than any other, more morbid, defective, irregular, diseased. Human childhood is similarly pathological. We, as animals, are very inferior animals in this particular. When we take credit to ourselves for the sublime devotion with which we face "the perils of maternity," and boast of "going down to the gates of death" for our children, we should rather take shame to ourselves for bringing these perils upon both mother and child. The gates of death? They are the gates of life to the unborn; and there is no death there save what we, the mothers, by our unnatural lives, have brought upon our own children. Gates of death, indeed, to the thousands of babies late-born, prematurely born, misborn, and still-born for lack of right motherhood. In the primal physical functions of maternity the human female cannot show that her supposed specialization to these uses has improved her fulfilment of them, rather the opposite. The more freely the human mother mingles in the natural industries of a human creature, as in the case of the savage woman, the peasant woman, the working-woman everywhere who is not overworked, the more rightly she fulfils these functions.

The more absolutely woman is segregated to sex-functions only, cut off from all economic use and made wholly dependent on the sex-relation as means of livelihood, the more pathological does her motherhood become. The over-development of sex caused by her economic dependence on

the male reacts unfavorably upon her essential duties. She is
too female for perfect motherhood! Her excessive specialization in the secondary sexual characteristics is a detrimental
element in heredity. Small, weak, soft, ill-proportioned
women do not tend to produce large, strong, sturdy, well-
made men or women. . . . The female segregated to the uses
of sex alone naturally deteriorates in racial development,
and naturally transmits that deterioration to her offspring.
The human mother, in the processes of reproduction, shows
no gain in efficiency over the lower animals, but rather a loss,
and so far presents no evidence to prove that her specialization to sex is of any advantage to her young. . . .

Motherhood in its fulfilment of educational duty can be
measured only by its effects. If we take for a standard the
noble men and women whose fine physique and character we
so fondly attribute to "a devoted mother," what are we to
say of the motherhood which has filled the world with the
ignoble men and women, of depraved physique and character? If the good mother makes the good man, how about
the bad ones? When we see great men and women, we give
credit to their mothers. When we see inferior men and
women,—and that is a common circumstance,—no one presumes to question the motherhood which has produced them.
When it comes to congenital criminality, we are beginning
to murmur something about "heredity"; and, to meet gross
national ignorance, we do demand a better system of education. But no one presumes to suggest that the mothering of
mankind could be improved upon; and yet there is where the
responsibility really lies. If our human method of reproduction is defective, let the mother answer. She is the main factor in reproduction. If our human method of education is
defective, let the mother answer. She is the main factor in
education.

To this it is bitterly objected that such a claim omits the
father and his responsibility. When the mother of the world
is in her right place and doing her full duty, she will have no
ground of complaint against the father. In the first place, she
will make better men. In the second, she will hold herself
socially responsible for the choice of a right father for her
children. In the third place, as an economic free agent, she
will do half duty in providing for the child. Men who are not
equal to good fatherhood under such conditions will have no

chance to become fathers, and will die with general pity instead of living with general condemnation. In his position, doing all the world's work, all the father's, and half the mother's, man has made better shift to achieve the impossible than woman has in hers. She has been supposed to have no work or care on earth save as mother. She has really had the work of the mother and that of the world's house service besides. But she has surely had as much time and strength to give to motherhood as man to fatherhood; and not until she can show that the children of the world are as well mothered as they are well fed can she cast on him the blame for our general deficiency. . . .

. . . When we see how some families improve, while others deteriorate, and how uncertain and irregular is such improvement as appears, we know that we could make better progress if all children had the same rich endowment and wise care that some receive. And, when we see how much of our improvement is due to gains made in hygienic knowledge, in public provision for education and sanitary regulation, none of which has been accomplished by mothers, we are forced to see that whatever advance the race has made is not exclusively attributable to motherhood. The human mother does less for her young, both absolutely and proportionately, than any kind of mother on earth. She does not obtain food for them, nor covering, nor shelter, nor protection, nor defence. She does not educate them beyond the personal habits required in the family circle and in her limited range of social life. The necessary knowledge of the world, so indispensable to every human being, she cannot give, because she does not possess it. All this provision and education are given by other hands and brains than hers. Neither does the amount of physical care and labor bestowed on the child by its mother warrant her claims to superiority in motherhood: this is but a part of our idealism of the subject. . . .

An extra-terrestrial sociologist, studying human life and hearing for the first time of our so-called "maternal sacrifice" as a means of benefiting the species, might be touched and impressed by the idea. "How beautiful!" he would say. "How exquisitely pathetic and tender! One-half of humanity surrendering all other human interests and activities to concentrate its time, strength, and devotion upon the functions of maternity! To bear and rear the majestic race to which they can never fully belong! To live vicariously forever, through their sons, the daughters being only another vicarious link! What a supreme and magnificent martyrdom!". . .

If the position of woman is to be justified by the doctrine of maternal sacrifice, surely society, or the individual, or both, would make some preparation for it. No such preparation is made. . . .

The education of young women has no department of maternity. It is considered indelicate to give this consecrated functionary any previous knowledge of her sacred duties. This most important and wonderful of human functions is left from age to age in the hands of absolutely untaught women. It is tacitly supposed to be fulfilled by the mysterious working of what we call "the divine instinct of maternity." Maternal instinct is a very respectable and useful instinct common to most animals. It is "divine" and "holy" only as all the laws of nature are divine and holy; and it is such only when it works to the right fulfilment of its use. If the race-preservative processes are to be held more sacred than the self-preservative processes, we must admit all the functions and faculties of reproduction to the same degree of reverence,—the passion of the male for the female as well as the passion of the mother for her young. And if, still further, we are to honor the race-preservative processes most in their highest and latest development, which is the only comparison to be made on a natural basis, we should place the great, disinterested, social function of education far above the second-selfishness of individual maternal functions. Maternal instinct, merely as an instinct, is unworthy of our superstitious reverence. It should be measured only as a means to an end, and valued in proportion to its efficacy. . . .

Women enter a position which gives into their hands direct responsibility for the life or death of the whole human race with neither study nor experience, with no shadow of preparation or guarantee of capability. So far as they give it a thought, they fondly imagine that this mysterious "maternal instinct" will see them through. Instruction, if needed, they will pick up when the time comes: experience they will acquire as the children appear. . . . The record of untrained instinct as a maternal faculty in the human race is to be read on the rows and rows of little gravestones which crowd our cemeteries. The experience gained by practising on the child is frequently buried with it.

10

. . . How can a young girl know a good prospective father, we ask. That she is not so educated as to know proves her unfitness for her great task. That she does not think or care proves her dishonorable indifference to her great duty. She can in no way shirk the responsibility for criminal carelessness in choosing a father for her children, unless indeed there were no choice,—no good men left on earth. Moreover, we are not obliged to leave this crucial choice in the hands of young girls. Motherhood is the work of grown women, not of half-children; and, when we honestly care as much for motherhood as we pretend, we shall train the woman for her duty, not the girl for her guileless manoeuvres to secure a husband. We talk about the noble duties of the mother, but our maidens are educated for economically successful marriage.

· · ·

Economic independence for women necessarily involves a change in the home and family relation. But, if that change is for the advantage of individual and race, we need not fear it. It does not involve a change in the marriage relation except in withdrawing the element of economic dependence, nor in the relation of mother to child save to improve it. But it does involve the exercise of human faculty in women, in social service and exchange rather than in domestic service solely. This will of course require the introduction of some other form of living than that which now obtains. It will render impossible the present method of feeding the world by means of millions of private servants, and bringing up children by the same hand. . . .

Perhaps it is worth while to examine the nature of our feeling toward that social institution called "the family," and the probable effect upon it of the change in woman's economic status.

Marriage and "the family" are two institutions, not one, as is commonly supposed. We confuse the natural result of marriage in children, common to all forms of sex-union, with the family,—a purely social phenomenon. Marriage is a form of sex-union recognized and sanctioned by society. It is a relation between two or more persons, according to the custom of the country, and involves mutual obligations. Although made by us an economic relation, it is not essentially so, and will exist in much higher fulfilment after the economic phase is outgrown. . . .

The family is a decreasing survival of the earliest grouping known to man. Marriage is an increasing development of high social life, not fully evolved. So far from being identical with the family, it improves and strengthens in inverse ratio to the family. . . . There was no conception of marriage as a personal union for life of two well-matched individuals during the patriarchal era. Wives were valued merely for child-bearing. The family needed numbers of its own blood, especially males; and the man-child was the price of favor to women then. . . . Its bonds of union were of the loosest,—merely common paternity, with a miscellaneous maternity of inimical interests. Such a basis forever forbade any high individualization, and high individualization with its demands for a higher marriage forbids any numerical importance to the family. Marriage has risen and developed in social importance as the family has sunk and decreased. . . .

11

If there should be built and opened in any of our large cities to-day a commodious and well-served apartment house for professional women with families, it would be filled at once. The apartments would be without kitchens; but there would be a kitchen belonging to the house from which meals could be served to the families in their rooms or in a common dining-room, as preferred. It would be a home where the cleaning was done by efficient workers, not hired separately by the families, but engaged by the manager of the establishment; and a roof-garden, day nursery, and kindergarten, under well-trained professional nurses and teachers, would insure proper care of the children. The demand for such provision is increasing daily, and must soon be met, not by a boarding-house or a lodging-house, a hotel, a restaurant, or any makeshift patching together of these; but by a permanent provision for the needs of women and children, of family privacy with collective advantage. This must be offered on a business basis to prove a substantial business success; and it will so prove, for it is a growing social need. . . .

In suburban homes this purpose could be accomplished much better by a grouping of adjacent houses, each distinct and having its own yard, but all kitchenless, and connected by covered ways with the eating-house. No detailed prophecy can be made of the precise forms which would ultimately prove most useful and pleasant; but the growing social need is for the specializing of the industries practised in the home and for the proper mechanical provision for them. . . .

Meals could of course be served in the house as long as desired; but, when people become accustomed to pure, clean homes, where no steaming industry is carried on, they will gradually prefer to go to their food instead of having it brought to them. It is a perfectly natural process, and a healthful one, to go to one's food. And, after all, the changes between living in one room, and so having the cooking most absolutely convenient; going as far as the limits of a large house permit, to one's own dining-room; and going a little further to a dining-room not in one's own house, but near by,—these differ but in degree. Families could go to eat together, just as they can go to bathe together or to listen to music together; but, if it fell out that different individuals presumed to develop an appetite at different hours, they could meet it without interfering with other people's comfort or sacrificing their own. Any housewife knows the difficulty of always getting a family together at meals. Why try? Then arises sentiment, and asserts that family affection, family unity, the very existence of the family, depend on their being together at meals. A family unity which is only bound together with a table-cloth is of questionable value.

12

Our domestic privacy is held to be . . . threatened by the invasion of professional cleaners. We should see that a kitchenless home will require far less cleaning than is now needed, and that the daily ordering of one's own room could be easily accomplished by the individual, when desired.

Many would so desire, keeping their own rooms, their personal inner chambers, inviolate from other presence than that of their nearest and dearest. . . . Of all popular paradoxes, none is more nakedly absurd than to hear us prate of privacy in a place where we cheerfully admit to our tabletalk and to our door service—yes, and to the making of our beds and to the handling of our clothing—a complete stranger. . . .

This stranger all of us who can afford it summon to our homes, . . . —with this observing and repeating army lodged in the very bosom of the family, may we not smile a little bitterly at our fond ideal of "the privacy of the home"? The swift progress of professional sweepers, dusters, and scrubbers, through rooms where they were wanted, and when they were wanted, would be at least no more injurious to privacy than the present method. Indeed, the exclusion of the domestic servant, and the entrance of woman on a plane of interest at once more social and more personal, would bring into the world a new conception of the sacredness of privacy, a feeling for the rights of the individual as yet unknown.

13

In reconstructing in our minds the position of woman under conditions of economic independence, it is most difficult to think of her as a mother.

We are so unbrokenly accustomed to the old methods of motherhood, so convinced that all its processes are interrelative and indispensable, and that to alter one of them is to endanger the whole relation, that we cannot conceive of any desirable change.

When definite plans for such change are suggested,—ways in which babies might be better cared for than at present,—we either deny the advantages of the change proposed or insist that these advantages can be reached under our present system. Just as in cooking we seek to train the private cook and to exalt and purify the private taste, so in baby-culture we seek to train the individual mother, and to call for better conditions in the private home; in both cases ignoring the relation between our general system and its particular phenomena. Though it may be shown, with clearness, that in physical conditions the private house, as a place in which to raise children, may be improved upon, yet all the more stoutly do we protest that the mental life, the emotional life, of the home is the best possible environment for the young.

There was a time in human history when this was true. While progress derived its main impetus from the sex-passion, and the highest emotions were those that held us together in the family relation, such education and such surroundings as fostered and intensified these emotions were naturally the best. But in the stage into which we are now growing, when the family relation is only a part of life, and our highest duties lie between individuals in social relation, the child has new needs. . . .

. . . [W]e have reached a stage where individual and racial progress is best served by the higher specialization of individuals and by a far wider sense of love and duty. This change renders the psychic condition of home life increasingly disadvantageous. We constantly hear of the inferior manners of the children of to-day, of the restlessness of the young, of the flat treason of deserting parents. It is visibly not so easy to live at home as it used to be. Our children are not more perversely constituted than the children of earlier ages, but the conditions in which they are reared are not suited to develop the qualities now needed in human beings.

This increasing friction between members of families should not be viewed with condemnation from a moral point of view, but studied with scientific interest. If our families are so relatively uncomfortable under present conditions, are there not conditions wherein the same families could be far more comfortable? . . . It is in the training of children . . . that the private home has ceased to be sufficient, or the isolated, primitive, dependent woman capable. Not that the mother does not have an intense and overpowering sense of loyalty and of duty; but it is duty to individuals, just as it was in the year one. What she is unable to follow, in her enforced industrial restriction, is the higher specialization of labor, and the honorable devotion of human lives to the development of their work. . . .

She cannot teach what she does not know. She cannot in any sincerity uphold as a duty what she does not practise. The child learns more of the virtues needed in modern life—

of fairness, of justice, of comradeship, of collective interest and action—in a common school than can be taught in the most perfect family circle. We may preach to our children as we will of the great duty of loving and serving one's neighbor; but what the baby is born into, what the child grows up to see and feel, is the concentration of one entire life—his mother's—upon the personal aggrandizement of one family, and the human service of another entire life—his father's—so warped and strained by the necessity of "supporting his family" that treason to society is the common price of comfort in the home. . . .

And this is the atmosphere in which the wholly home-bred, mother-taught child grows up. Why should not food and clothes and the comforts of his own people stand first in his young mind? Does he not see his mother, the all-loved, all-perfect one, peacefully spending her days in the arrangement of these things which his father's ceaseless labor has procured? Why should he not grow up to care for his own, to the neglect and willing injury of all the rest, when his earliest, deepest impressions are formed under such exclusive devotion?

It is not the home as a place of family life and love that injures the child, but as the centre of a tangled heap of industries, low in their ungraded condition, and lower still because they are wholly personal. Work the object of which is merely to serve one's self is the lowest. Work the object of which is merely to serve one's family is the next lowest. Work the object of which is to serve more and more people, in widening range . . . is social service in the fullest sense, and the highest form of service that we can reach. . . .

We suffer also, our lives long, from an intense self-consciousness, from a sensitiveness beyond all need; we demand measureless personal attention and devotion, because we have been born and reared in a very hot-bed of these qualities. A baby who spent certain hours of every day among other babies, being cared for because he was a baby, and not because he was "my baby," would grow to have a very different opinion of himself from that which is forced upon each new soul that comes among us by the ceaseless adoration of his own immediate family. What he needs to learn at once and for all, to learn softly and easily, but inexorably, is that he is one of many. We all dimly recognize this in our praise of large families, and in our saying that "an only child is apt to be selfish." So is an only family. The earlier and more easily a child can learn that human life means many people, and their behavior to one another, the happier and stronger and more useful his life will be.

This could be taught him with no difficulty whatever, under certain conditions, just as he is taught his present sensitiveness and egotism by the present conditions. It is not only temperature and diet and rest and exercise which affect the baby. "He does love to be noticed," we say. "He is never so happy as when he has a dozen worshippers around him." But what is the young soul learning all the while? What does he gather, as he sees and hears and slowly absorbs impressions? With the inflexible inferences of a clear, young brain, unsupplied with any counter-evidence until later in life, he learns that women are meant to wait on people, to get dinner, and sweep and pick up things; that men are made to bring home things, and are to be begged of according to circumstances; that babies are the object of concentrated admiration; that their hair, hands, feet, are specially attractive; that they are the heated focus of attention, to be passed from hand to hand, swung and danced and amused most violently, and also be laid aside and have nothing done to them, with no regard to their preference in either case. . . .

. . . [W]hile we flatter ourselves that things remain the same, they are changing under our very eyes from year to year, from day to day. Education, hiding itself behind a wall of books, but consisting more and more fully in the grouping of children and in the training of faculties never mentioned in the curriculum,—education, which is our human motherhood, has crept nearer and nearer to its true place, its best work,—the care and training of the little child. Some women there are, and some men, whose highest service to humanity is the care of children. Such should not concentrate their powers upon their own children alone,—a most questionable advantage,—but should be so placed that their talent and skill, their knowledge and experience, would benefit the largest number of children. . . .

As we now arrange life, our children must take their chances while babies, and live or die, improve or deteriorate, according to the mother to whom they chance to be born. An inefficient mother does not prevent a child from having a good college education; but the education of babyhood, the most important of all, is wholly in her hands. It is futile to say that mothers should be taught how to fulfil their duties. You cannot teach every mother to be a good school educator or a good college educator. Why should you expect every mother to be a good nursery educator? . . .

The growth and change in home and family life goes steadily on under and over and through our prejudices and convictions; and the education of the child has changed and become a social function, while we still imagine the mother to be doing it all. . . .

We think no harm of motherhood because our darlings go out each day to spend long hours in school. The mother is not held neglectful, nor the child bereft. It is not called a "separation of mother and child." There would be no further harm or risk or loss in a babyhood passed among such changed surroundings and skilled service as should meet its needs more perfectly than it is possible for the mother to meet them alone at home.

Better surroundings and care for babies, better education, do not mean, as some mothers may imagine, that the tiny monthling is to be taught to read, or even that it is to be exposed to cabalistical arrangements of color and form and sound which shall mysteriously force the young intelligence to flower. It would mean, mainly, a far quieter and more peaceful life than is possible for the heavily loved and violently cared for baby in the busy household; and the impressions which it did meet would be planned and maintained with an intelligent appreciation of its mental powers. The mother would not be excluded, but supplemented, as she is now, by the teacher and the school. . . .

. . . The mother as a social servant instead of a home servant will not lack in true mother duty. She will love her child as well, perhaps better, when she is not in hourly contact with it, when she goes from its life to her own life, and back from her own life to its life, with ever new delight and power. She can keep the deep, thrilling joy of motherhood far fresher in her heart, far more vivid and open in voice and eyes and tender hands, when the hours of individual work give her mind another channel for her own part of the day. From her work, loved and honored though it is, she will return to the home life, the child life, with an eager, ceaseless pleasure, cleansed of all the fret and fraction and weariness that so mar it now.

Pioneer on the Urban Frontier:
Jane Addams (1860–1935)

The two most widely known and respected American women in the twentieth century have probably been Jane Addams and Eleanor Roosevelt. They represent exceptions to the general tendency to leave untold the contributions of women to American national life. Both women were public heroines to many of their contemporaries, who saw in them the personification of the best blend of moral commitment and public service that American women could aspire to. They are direct descendants of a long line of American women who channeled morality and the need to be useful into public causes, from the moral reforms of Lucretia Mott in the 1830s to the temperance reform of Emma Willard in the 1880s. With the opening of higher education to women in the post-Civil War period, the reform impulse became linked to social service on the urban scene; Eleanor Roosevelt would later carry it to the international level through her work for UNESCO.

Jane Addams was by no means the sole woman of her generation to be successful in a career of public service. Lillian Wald was surely as eminent in her work—the professionalization of nursing and the foundation of the federal Children's Bureau—as Jane Addams was in her choice: social work and the settlement-house movement symbolized by Hull House. Florence Kelley probably had a more incisive mind, and her organizational genius in the campaigns of the National Consumers' League was fully the equal of Jane Addams' administrative skills. Alice Hamilton single-handedly founded the field of industrial medicine. Grace and Edith Abbott contributed as much as Jane Addams to the understanding and amelioration of the lot of immigrants to American cities at the turn of the century. But none of these women had the charisma of Jane Addams, who became for millions of Americans a "universally accepted popular conscience" (Conway 1964:765).

Jane Addams and the public-spirited women of her generation represent the first generation of educated American women who turned their reforming zeal to the unmet needs of the urban population. In the 1880s, when the rural frontier closed and the long-range trend toward an industrial urban society was well under way, women had acute problems in applying their new fund of knowledge and training. Since they accepted the American view that knowledge which does not lead to an active life is meaningless, these pragmatists sought channels through which to be useful to the world around them. That world was no longer the small town or rural farm, but the large and growing cities.

Jane Addams was herself extremely critical of the education she received at Rockford Seminary in Illinois. When she was a young women, her prime mission in life seemed to be to please her father, to meet his masculine standards of rectitude. With his death when she was twenty-one, followed by a long illness and a trip to Europe with her stepmother, she underwent a physical and emotional crisis in defining what meaning to give her life, what use to make of her education. She objected that education had been a "snare of preparation" that led her to view life through a veil of "irrelevant abstractions." Part of the impulse behind the establishment of Hull House was to create a house in the slums where educated girls like herself could learn what their schools did not teach, a kind of postgraduate course in the real conditions of life (Addams 1910:84; Lasch 1967:24–25).

Hofstadter (1955:151–152) has suggested that such young people as Jane Addams had an ability to understand the viewpoints of the poor and the immigrants because their own middle-class families had been cut off from the centers of power in American society, and this loss of status enabled them to understand the point of view of people who never had power to lose. Once again, then, status deprivation is posited as a social source for the emergence of reform movements; Hofstadter sees this circumstance in the background of the emergence of progressivism in the 1890s, as it has been seen in the background of the emergence of the abolition, temperance, and woman's-rights movements in an earlier period. Status deprivation is often linked with generational conflict between parents and children; behind Jane Addams' romance with the potential of the industrial city was a rejection of the confines of the small-town extended family she knew so well. Lasch has suggested that her own resistance to the pressure to marry following college graduation and her rejection of the life of ease and comfort as a leisured woman of the middle class sensitized Jane Addams to the gap between the generations which became a principal theme in her writings. She saw her own American version of the parent-child conflict acted out in the lives of immigrant parents and their children, first-generation Americans, whom she observed and tried to help in Chicago (Lasch 1967:36–37).

Women of Jane Addams' generation were responsible for the blossoming in the 1890s of a wide variety of voluntary social services: they created the institutions of police matrons, settlement houses, juvenile courts (Smith 1970:22). These urban pioneers in civic reform poured their energies into campaigns to ameliorate the unhealthy and exploitative environments in which immigrant women and children worked in the 1890s with the same spirit with which the Grimké sisters invoked Christian morality and sought to ameliorate the working conditions of Southern slaves. But there was this difference: the early pioneers went on very quickly to denounce the institution of slavery all told, while the civic reformers of the period from 1880 to 1920 did not arrive at any denunciation of an economic system that produced so much human misery. The factory manager did not become the ogre that the slave owner had been. Only a minority of reforming women joined the radical movements of the turn of the century in denouncing capitalism as a "monster institution" the way slavery or masonry had been denounced in the earlier generations. As these reforming women saw it, the need was for legislation to "protect" women, to restrict the age at which children could work, to set standards of safety and cleanliness in industrial workplaces, and in the consumer goods they produced. But the activist women saw industry and technology themselves as necessary and beneficial, as the social and economic means to a future urban life of plenty and leisure for all. Hence the impulse behind the public service of two generations of American women was a reformist impulse that rested on a firm acceptance of a Spencerian brand of Darwinian evolution and progress of "the race."

Jane Addams had a very special blend of characteristics that spanned the two earlier types of feminists covered in this volume. Like the Enlightenment feminists, she was a solitary thinker and social observer trying to make sense of

her own experience and the society around her. Like the
Moral Crusader feminists, she was an insatiable activist,
plunging into the thick of Chicago political and industrial
life to wring from the elite the money and power to implement her reformist plans. Her own seasonal shifts between
Chicago and Bar Harbor, Maine, symbolize these two characteristics. During the winter she was the activist crusader,
working at Hull House in Chicago; the shrewd administrator
skillful in translating the creative ideas of her associates and
staff members into funded projects. During the summer she
was the Enlightenment thinker and writer, withdrawn from
the hectic urban life in a contemplative rural Maine setting.
In her writings she helped Americans surmount the confusion
of values that flowed from the closing of the Western frontier and the opening of the urban frontier. She personified in
action and analyzed in prose what Whitman captured in
poetry—the romance and potential of the American city and
its diverse peoples. As Conway (1964:768–769) summed up
this key to the adulation of Addams by the nation:

> She had a real and creative vision of urban life based on
> profound disillusionment with her own small town ori-
> gins, and she wrote about cities and their growth in an
> edifying and comforting way. Urban life was the new
> decree of an evolutionary providence and was not to be
> decried or feared, but defined and understood. The city
> was an exciting and creative event in man's evolution, not
> a tragic falling off from an idyllic rural past. . . . In an
> urban world, man created his own environment. Man was
> therefore no longer dimly striving to understand God's
> creation but could control and direct a world which he
> had created for himself.

Addams was deeply committed to the view that women
had a special contribution to make to the world; as spelled
out in the selection to follow, it was a view of municipal
government as "housekeeping on a large scale." Women's
concern with cleanliness, teaching of the young, management of detail, and caring for the sick could find an outlet on
the urban scene to replace the productive work that kept the
rural woman of the past as busy a contributor to the domestic economy as her husband in the fields. The older virtues of
thrift and industry seemed to lack meaning to middle-class

urban and educated women in the 1890s; their domestic chores were lightened as much by the cheap labor of Irish and Polish immigrant domestic help as by the shift from producing to purchasing the goods consumed in the home. The surplus energy and sense of utility now found its outlets in charity. There it would remain for several decades, until social service itself was professionalized and bureaucratized under New Deal legislation.

Jane Addams had the good fortune to have administrative skills to organize, and the writing skills to communicate to a society hungry for the message she brought. Being respectable and single, she gained as much admiration from men as from women. She ruffled no feathers, since her views carried no threat to the basic institutional structure of society. She would "improve" it, take out the kinks, Americanize the immigrants while respecting the folk values and skills they brought from their European peasant background.

But she did have one set of values that, when acted upon in the 1910s, led to a temporary cooling of national admiration of her. She was deeply committed to pacifism, which she linked to her views on the position of women in society. In Addams' view the control of violence was essential if women were to be freed from their inferior status, since their lesser physical strength could never permit them to be men's equal in a society that sanctioned violence. She believed, as a result, that the hopes for equal status of women depended on eradicating violence from the world. With the outbreak of World War I, she poured her energies and organizing talents into the peace movement, and unlike many of her associates in that movement, she persisted in her peace efforts even after the entry of the United States into the war. Much of the adulation she had enjoyed from the nation underwent a temporary eclipse as a consequence, until, during the last years of her life, the Depression and the coming to power of the New Deal brought Addams back once again to national prominence. She was feted on her seventy-fifth birthday as probably no other woman in American history has been, before or since. She was an American heroine in the uniquely American tradition of reform.

The literature on the life and work of Jane Addams is voluminous. For the interested reader, the best introduction is her own account, *Twenty Years at Hull House* (1910). A recent biography (Tims 1961) and two essays (Lasch 1967:3–37; and Conway 1964:761–780) will lay open a wider range of information and interpretation on the woman and her work.

⤳ Utilization of Women in ⤶ City Government

We are told many times that the industrial city is a new thing upon the face of the earth, and that everywhere its growth has been phenomenal, whether we look at Moscow, Berlin, Paris, New York, or Chicago. With or without the mediaeval foundation, modern cities are merely resultants of the vast crowds of people who have collected at certain points which have become manufacturing and distributing centres.

For all political purposes, however, the industrial origin of the city is entirely ignored, and political life is organized exclusively in relation to its earlier foundations.

As the city itself originated for the common protection of the people and was built about a suitable centre of defense which formed a citadel, such as the Acropolis at Athens or the Kremlin at Moscow, so we can trace the beginning of the municipal franchise to the time when the problems of municipal government were still largely those of protecting the city against rebellion from within and against invasion from without. A voice in city government, as it was extended from the nobles, who alone bore arms, was naturally given solely to those who were valuable to the military system. There was a certain logic in giving the franchise only to grown men when the existence and stability of the city depended upon their defence, and when the ultimate value of the elector could be reduced to his ability to perform military duty. It was fair that only those who were liable to a sudden call to arms should be selected to decide as to the relations which the city should bear to rival cities, and that the vote for war

From Jane Addams, *Newer Ideals of Peace.* Chatauqua, New York, The Chatauqua Press, 1907. Pp. 180–207.

should be cast by the same men who would bear the brunt of battle and the burden of protection. . . .

But rival cities have long since ceased to settle their claims by force of arms, and we shall have to admit, I think, that this early test of the elector is no longer fitted to the modern city, whatever may be true, in the last analysis, of the basis for the Federal Government.

It has been well said that the modern city is a stronghold of industrialism, quite as the feudal city was a stronghold of militarism, but the modern city fears no enemies, and rivals from without and its problems of government are solely internal. Affairs for the most part are going badly in these great new centres in which the quickly congregated population has not yet learned to arrange its affairs satisfactorily. Insanitary housing, poisonous sewage, contaminated water, infant mortality, the spread of contagion, adulterated food, impure milk, smoke-laden air, ill-ventilated factories, dangerous occupations, juvenile crime, unwholesome crowding, prostitution, and drunkenness are the enemies which the modern city must face and overcome would it survive. Logically, its electorate should be made up of those who can bear a valiant part in this arduous contest, of those who in the past have at least attempted to care for children, to clean houses, to prepare foods, to isolate the family from moral dangers, of those who have traditionally taken care of that side of life which, as soon as the population is congested, inevitably becomes the subject of municipal consideration and control.

To test the elector's fitness to deal with this situation by his ability to bear arms, is absurd. A city is in many respects a great business corporation, but in other respects it is enlarged housekeeping. If American cities have failed in the first, partly because office holders have carried with them the predatory instinct learned in competitive business, and cannot help "working a good thing" when they have an opportunity, may we not say that city housekeeping has failed partly because women, the traditional housekeepers, have not been consulted as to its multiform activities? The men of the city have been carelessly indifferent to much of this civic housekeeping, as they have always been indifferent to the details of the household. They have totally disregarded a candidate's capacity to keep the streets clean, preferring to

consider him in relation to the national tariff or to the necessity for increasing the national navy, in a pure spirit of
reversion to the traditional type of government which had to
do only with enemies and outsiders.

It is difficult to see what military prowess has to do with
the multiform duties, which, in a modern city, include the
care of parks and libraries, superintendence of markets,
sewers, and bridges, the inspection of provisions and boilers,
and the proper disposal of garbage. Military prowess has
nothing to do with the building department which the city
maintains to see to it that the basements be dry, that the
bedrooms be large enough to afford the required cubic feet of
air, that the plumbing be sanitary, that the gas-pipes do not
leak, that the tenement-house court be large enough to afford
light and ventilation, and that the stairways be fireproof. The
ability to carry arms has nothing to do with the health department maintained by the city, which provides that children be vaccinated, that contagious diseases be isolated and
placarded, that the spread of tuberculosis be curbed, and that
the water be free from typhoid infection. Certainly the military conception of society is remote from the functions of the
school boards, whose concern it is that children be educated,
that they be supplied with kindergartens and be given a
decent place in which to play. The very multifariousness and
complexity of a city government demands the help of minds
accustomed to detail and variety of work, to a sense of obligation for the health and welfare of young children, and to a
responsibility for the cleanliness and comfort of others.

Because all these things have traditionally been in the
hands of women, if they take no part in them now, they are
not only missing the education which the natural participation in civic life would bring to them, but they are losing
what they have always had. From the beginning of tribal life
women have been held responsible for the health of the
community, a function which is now represented by the
health department; from the days of the cave dwellers, so far
as the home was clean and wholesome, it was due to their
efforts, which are now represented by the bureau of tenement-house inspection; from the period of the primitive village, the only public sweeping performed was what they
undertook in their own dooryards, that which is now represented by the bureau of street cleaning. Most of the departments in a modern city can be traced to woman's traditional

activity, but in spite of this, so soon as these old affairs were turned over to the care of the city, they slipped from woman's hands, apparently because they then became matters for collective action and implied the use of the franchise. Because the franchise had in the first instance been given to the man who could fight, because in the beginning he alone could vote who could carry a weapon, the franchise was considered an improper thing for a woman to possess.

Is it quite public spirited for women to say, "We will take care of these affairs so long as they stay in our own houses, but if they go outside and concern so many people that they cannot be carried on without the mechanism of the vote, we will drop them. It is true that these activities which women have always had, are not at present being carried on very well by the men in most of the great American cities, but because we do not consider it 'ladylike' to vote shall we ignore their failure"?

Because women consider the government men's affair and something which concerns itself with elections and alarms, they have become so confused in regard to their traditional business in life, the rearing of children, that they hear with complacency a statement made by Nestor of sanitary reformers, that one-half of the tiny lives which make up the city's death rate each year might be saved by a more thorough application of sanitary science. Because it implies the use of the suffrage, they do not consider it women's business to save these lives. Are we going to lose ourselves in the old circle of convention and add to that sum of wrong-doing which is continually committed in the world because we do not look at things as they really are? Old-fashioned ways which no longer apply to changed conditions are a snare in which the feet of women have always become readily entangled. . . .

Why is it that women do not vote upon the matters which concern them so intimately? Why do they not follow these vital affairs and feel responsible for their proper administration, even though they have become municipalized? What would the result have been could women have regarded the suffrage, not as a right or a privilege, but as a mere piece of governmental machinery without which they could not perform their traditional functions under the changed conditions of city life? Could we view the whole situation as a matter of obligation and of normal development, it would be much simplified. We are at the beginning of a prolonged effort to incorporate a progressive developing life founded upon a response to the needs of all the people, into the requisite legal enactments and civic institutions. To be in any measure successful, this effort will require all the intelligent powers of observation, all the sympathy, all the common sense which may be gained from the whole adult population.

The statement is sometimes made that the franchise for women would be valuable only so far as the educated women exercised it. This statement totally disregards the fact that those matters in which woman's judgment is most needed are far too primitive and basic to be largely influenced by what we call education. The sanitary condition of all the factories and workshops, for instance, in which the industrial processes are at present carried on in great cities, intimately affect the health and lives of thousands of workingwomen.

It is questionable whether women to-day, in spite of the fact that there are myriads of them in factories and shops, are doing their full share of the world's work in the lines of production which have always been theirs. Even two centuries ago they did practically all the spinning, dyeing, weaving, and sewing. They carried on much of the brewing and baking and thousands of operations which have been pushed out of the domestic system into the factory system. But simply to keep on doing the work which their grandmothers did, was to find themselves surrounded by conditions over which they have no control. . . .

When the family constituted the industrial organism of the day, the daughters of the household were carefully taught in reference to the place they would take in that organism, but as the household arts have gone outside the home, almost nothing has been done to connect the young women with the present great industrial system. This neglect has been equally true in regard to the technical and cultural sides of that system.

The failure to fit the education of women to the actual industrial life which is carried on about them has had disastrous results in two directions. First, industry itself has lacked the modification which women might have brought to it had they committed the entire movement to that growing concern for a larger and more satisfying life for each member of the community, a concern which we have come to regard as legitimate. Second, the more prosperous women would have been able to understand and adjust their own difficulties of household management in relation to the producer of factory products, as they are now utterly unable to do. . . .

. . . At a conference held at Lake Placid by employers of household labor, it was contended that future historical review may show that the girls who are to-day in domestic service are the really progressive women of the age; that they are those who are fighting conditions which limit their freedom, and although they are doing it blindly, at least they are demanding avenues of self-expression outside their work; and that this struggle from conditions detrimental to their highest life is the ever-recurring story of the emancipation of first one class and then another. It was further contended that in this effort to become sufficiently educated to be able to understand the needs of an educated employer from an independent standpoint, they are really doing the community a great service, and did they but receive co-operation instead of opposition, domestic service would lose its social ostracism and attract a more intelligent class of women. And yet this effort, perfectly reasonable from the standpoint of historic development and domestic tradition, receives little help from the employing housekeepers, because they know nothing of industrial development.

The situation could be understood only by viewing it, first, in the relation to recent immigration and, second, in connection with the factory system at the present stage of development in America. A review of the history of domestic service in a fairly prosperous American family begins with the colonial period, when the daughters of the neighboring farmers came in to "help" during the busy season. This was followed by the Irish immigrant, when almost every kitchen had its Nora or Bridget, while the mistress of the household retained the sweeping and dusting and the Saturday baking. Then came the halcyon days of German "second girls" and cooks, followed by the Swedes. The successive waves of immigration supply the demand for domestic service, gradually obliterating the fact that as the women became more familiar with American customs, they as well as their men folk, entered into more skilled and lucrative positions.

In these last years immigration consists in ever-increasing numbers of South Italians and of Russian, Polish, and Rumanian Jews, none of whom have to any appreciable extent entered into domestic service. The Italian girls are married between the ages of fifteen and eighteen, and to live in any house in town other than that of her father seems to an Italian girl quite incomprehensible. The strength of the family tie, the need for "kosher" foods, the celebration of religious festivities, the readiness with which she takes up the sewing trades in which her father and brother are already largely engaged, makes domestic service a rare occupation for the daughters of the recent Jewish immigrants. Moreover, these two classes of immigrants have been quickly absorbed, as, indeed, all working people are, by the increasing demand for the labor of young girls and children in factory and workshops. The paucity of the material for domestic service is therefore revealed at last, and we are obliged to consider the material for domestic service which a democracy supplies, and also to realize that the administration of the household has suffered because it has become unnaturally isolated from the rest of the community.

The problems of food and shelter for the family, at any given moment, must be considered in relation to all the other mechanical and industrial life of that moment, quite as the intellectual life of the family finally depends for its vitality upon its relation to the intellectual resources of the rest of the community. When the administrator of the household deliberately refuses to avail herself of the wonderful inventions going on all about her, she soon comes to the point of priding herself upon the fact that her household is administered according to traditional lines and of believing that the moral life of the family is so enwrapped in these old customs as to be endangered by any radical change. Because of this attitude on the part of contemporary housekeepers, the household has firmly withstood the beneficent changes and healing innovations which applied science and economics would long ago have brought about could they have worked naturally and unimpeded. . . .

. . . If American women could but obtain a liberating knowledge of that history of industry and commerce which is so similar in every country of the globe, the fact that so much factory labor is performed by immigrants would help to bring them nearer to the immigrant woman. Equipped with "the informing mind" on the one hand and with experience on the other, we could then walk together through the marvelous streets of the human city, no longer conscious whether we are natives or aliens, because we have become absorbed in a fraternal relation arising from a common experience.

And this attitude of understanding and respect for the worker is necessary, not only to appreciate what he produces, but to preserve his power of production, again showing the necessity for making that substitute for war—human labor— more aggressive and democratic. We are told that the conquered races everywhere, in their helplessness, are giving up the genuine practise of their own arts. In India, for instance, where their arts have been the blossom of many years of labor, the conquered races are casting them aside as of no value in order that they may conform to the inferior art, or rather, lack of art, of their conquerors. . . . This lack of respect and understanding of the primitive arts found among colonies of immigrants in a modern cosmopolitan city, produces a like result in that the arts languish and disappear. We have made an effort at Hull-House to recover something of the early industries from an immigrant neighborhood, and in a little exhibit called a labor museum, we have placed in historic sequence and order methods of spinning and weaving from a dozen nationalities in Asia Minor and Europe. The result has been a striking exhibition of the unity and similarity of the earlier industrial processes. Within the narrow confines of one room, the Syrian, the Greek, the Italian, the Russian, the Norwegian, the Dutch, and the Irish find that the differences in their spinning have been merely putting the distaff upon a frame or placing the old hand-spindle in a horizontal position. A group of women representing vast differences in religion, in language, in tradition, and in nationality, exhibit practically no difference in the daily arts by which, for a thousand generations, they have clothed their families. When American women come to visit them, the quickest method, in fact almost the only one, of establishing a genuine companionship with them, is through this same industry, unless we except that still older occupation, the care of little children. Perhaps this experiment may claim to have made a genuine effort to find the basic experiences upon which a cosmopolitan community may unite at least on the industrial side. The recent date of the industrial revolution and our nearness to a primitive industry are shown by the fact that Italian mothers are more willing to have their daughters work in factories producing textile and food stuffs than in those which produce wood and metal. They interpret the entire situation so simply that it appears to them just what it is—a mere continuation of woman's traditional work under changed conditions. . . .

We certainly may hope for two results if women enter formally into municipal life. First, the opportunity to fulfill their old duties and obligations with the safeguard and the consideration which the ballot alone can secure for them under the changed conditions, and, second, the education which participation in actual affairs always brings. As we believe that woman has no right to allow what really belongs to her to drop away from her, so we contend that ability to perform an obligation comes very largely in proportion as that obligation is conscientiously assumed.

PART 4

Sex Is a Many-Sided Thing

Introduction:
Feminism and Intellectual Complexity

It has been claimed by many historians that when the suffrage movement ended and women had secured the right to vote in national elections, the ardent women who participated in the campaigns folded away their mementoes in their attic trunks—and feminism "died." O'Neill subtitled his 1969 book on the woman's movement "The Rise and Fall of Feminism in America," just as Simone de Beauvoir in the late 1940s considered feminism "all but over."

But was this really the case? As a family sociologist, concerned professionally with issues of human development and value transmission between parents and their children, my assumption is that personality, human motivation, and values change very slowly over long stretches of time. It is the exceptional rather than the usual pattern for very marked change to occur between proximate generations. If this is so, then one would not expect the daughters of suffragists in the 1920s and 1930s to suddenly reject the aspirations and values that guided their mothers, any more than I expect my own daughters to reject feminist ideas they have absorbed from me when they are adult women in the 1970s and 1980s.

We have had a recent reminder of the intergenerational stability of basic values in studies of radical youth in the 1960s. It had been assumed by many people that these dissenting young people were "Oedipal rebels" against their fathers, who held a set of political and personal beliefs radically different from their parents'. Research has shown the case to be quite otherwise; there is, in fact, a good deal of value continuity from parents to their contemporary activist children. The parents of radical youth are liberal though apathetic politically and their children have carried those same values into the streets and the movements for social justice and a peaceful world (Keniston 1967, 1968; Flacks 1967; Haan et al. 1968; Brewster-Smith 1968).

I see little reason to expect the children of activists to be radically different from their parents. Consequently I doubt

615

that the daughters of the suffragists, radical socialists, or civic reformers among the turn-of-the-century feminists underwent any fundamental change in personality or values compared to their mothers. Among the pioneer leaders and thinkers studied in this volume, there is probably a larger proportion of women rebelling against their parents, but a movement is not comprised merely of leaders; it consists of thousands of women more moderately involved in the cause. Even among the pioneers we have studied, one or both parents of many of them were ardent defenders of the rights of women. The chances are great that they shared many similar values with their mothers.

I would suggest, however, that there may well be a generational dialectic in the spheres of life in which those values are acted out. It may be that the public heroines of one generation are the private heroines of the next. The reason researchers such as O'Neill see discontinuity through time may be rooted in the fact that historians confine their major attention to the public roles of men and women. As a result, they may perceive and report public discontinuity in a movement over time rather than private continuity between the generations. There is no question but that public political behavior of women was quite different in the 1920s from what it had been for the preceding two decades. Feminist ideas are not, after all, the same as the suffrage movement, and the generation that followed the activist generation of suffragists may have been consolidating feminist ideas into the private stuff of their lives and seeking new outlets for the expression of the values that prompted their mothers' public behavior.

If we take a very loose overview of the whole history of feminism over the past hundred years, there seem to have been three peaks of activity, roughly separated by fifty years: a first peaking in the 1850s; a second in the period 1900–1920; and a third peak beginning in the late 1960s. An alternating generational phenomenon is suggested in this dialectic pattern, with the feminist impulse acted out publicly in one generation and more privately in the next. Thus the late 1870s and 1880s were decades of great expansion in women's higher education and in white-collar clerical and professional jobs for women. The daughters of the 1850s activists may have been deflected from direct political activity and public visibility into private education and employment.

Even the elder stateswomen of the movement, such as Susan Anthony and Elizabeth Stanton, devoted a good deal of their energies in the 1880s to the writing of the *History of Woman Suffrage*. Many of the daughters of suffragists seem to have done the same in the 1930s; they retreated into private consolidation of the gains made by their mothers. Some of them became academic scholars, specializing in their mothers' generation. During the 1930s, when feminism was supposedly dead, women earned the highest proportion of advanced degrees in the history of American higher education. So too, the proportion of women in the labor force continued to climb dramatically throughout the 1940s and 1950s, and they came to a disproportionate degree from the ranks of married women.

This last point bears significantly on the probability of political activity among women. Except for political office-holders, political activity in America is an extracurricular indulgence over and above responsibilities in work and family. Strong-minded descendants of the suffragists between 1920 and 1960 were pouring much of their energy into education and employment, and if they were married, they did double duty at work and at home; such a profile leaves little time and energy for political involvement.

Depression and war contribute complex additional factors to the picture. During periods of economic stress women lose ground in the economy as pressure builds for a "one job per family" view so that the limited amount of work can be spread around. During periods of great economic expansion, there may be pressure for a sharp polarization among women. Some women whose skills become highly marketable in the expanding economy will be drawn into the labor force, thus restricting their political activity. For other women the pressure will be quite different; economic expansion and rapid growth means that men overinvest time and energy in work, and their wives may be pressed to overinvest in consumption, home, and maternal responsibilities in order to compensate for their men's decreased involvement in home life.

War has a rather different impact upon the social fabric of society, with important and frequently tragic consequences for women as well as men. The drum-beating martial mood of wartime is often followed by a pot-stirring and baby-rocking domestic ethos in its aftermath. This alternation has been noted many times in the past and suggests a

pendulum swing from great energy in public and national
service during a time of emergency to an equally strong
retraction into private lives of cave and clan after war's end.
But war has several important consequences of particular
relevance to women: the normal cultural timing of marriage
and parenthood is disturbed; family members are separated
as people become geographically mobile through service in
the armed forces or civilian war industry; marriages break
up; and a postwar imbalance sets in in the sex ratio among
young people. Wartime casualties result in an increase in the
numbers of unmarried women, young widows, and bread-
winner-wives with physically incapacitated husbands. For
every war widow there may be several dozen wives who cope
with the physical and emotional damage inflicted by war on
their husbands and sons. Among the young unmarried at
war's end, a shortage of potential husbands may sharpen the
competition of women for men and indirectly stimulate a
trend toward a more seductive style in clothes and invidious
competition of women with each other, all pressing for more
traditional conceptions of sex roles.

It would be a delicate job of historical analysis to disen-
tangle the various national events of the period from 1920 to
1960 as they affected American women. A good starting place
for historical examination might be to sample the lives of the
children and grandchildren of feminist women of the past.
Such strong-minded women were never the majority, even in
decades of peak feminist activism, and their descendants
would also be a minority among women. But it has never
taken more than a minority to affect larger sectors of society
than they represent numerically, even before the days of
instant communications. I suspect that many early feminists'
daughters would be found among the educated women in the
academic world, government service, and the professions. It
is also the case that feminists' written works are noted at
all only to the extent that there is some receptivity in the
larger society. Awareness of the publication of such books
depends on whether the larger category of women is turned
inward toward conventional domesticity or *outward* to the
larger society. There were, in fact, a number of excellent
feminist books published in the 1920s, of which Suzanne
LaFollette's *Concerning Women* and Virginia Woolf's *A
Room of One's Own* are only two notable examples, but all
enjoyed only very small sales at the time of publication.

Friedan's *The Feminine Mystique* makes an interesting comparison with Myron Brenton's *The American Male* (1966). Friedan struck a responsive chord in 1963, while Brenton's analogous critique of the masculinity trap went largely ignored. In the early 1960s women were *open* to a critical examination of their lives, but men were *closed* to the counterpart analysis of theirs.

To define the dynamics of the generational dialectic suggested above would require much more sociographic analysis of feminists' lives than now exists. As a social scientist, I have wondered whether the phenomenon isolated by Hansen (1952) in studies of ethnic assimilation might provide a clue to the fluctuations in the history of the women's movement. He noted that ethnic historical societies emerged roughly sixty years, or two generations, after a peak in a particular group's immigration to the United States, just as Southern history and literature flourished two generations after the Civil War. If sons forget what grandsons wish to remember, perhaps daughters, too, forget what granddaughters wish to remember. The striving second generation may struggle for status while the third generation seeks to recapture the thirst for freedom or social justice or women's rights of the first generation. Many early abolitionists in the 1830s were the grandchildren of Revolutionary soldiers, and today many young feminists may be the granddaughters of the suffragists and radical reformers who made their mark early in the twentieth century. The quiet second generation, unnoted by historians, may consolidate gains and provide the foundation on which the third generation takes off again into public and historical notice. After a generation of testing feminists' ideas in work and in the family, the limitations of those ideas may be realized, and the third generation returns again to challenge and action. How many of the young feminists today, one wonders, have their grandmothers' suffrage mementoes in some attic trunks? After Nora slammed the door, perhaps her daughter stayed quietly at home and at work, while her granddaughter is noisily slamming doors again.

One last characteristic of the 1920–1960 period is of particular relevance to the selections to follow. These were not only years of vast expansion of higher education and the professions; it was also a period in which a particular set of values was held among scholars and intellectuals. It was a period of academic specialization of knowledge, during which the area of competence in which one acquired skills became increasingly narrow and pressure was strong against poaching on the turf of even closely related specialties. Any meaningful analysis of women almost by definition requires a broader perspective than that provided by any one special field. Academic scholarly values, then, almost precluded an analytic overview of sex roles. Secondly, the underlying assumption in scholarship was that of value neutrality, and there were vigorous attempts on the part of the social sciences and the humanities to be as "pure" as they thought the natural sciences to be. Lastly, the postwar period of economic affluence created a great market for "culture," and women writers and painters were absorbed in great numbers in the literary and artistic "ranch-home industries" of the twentieth century. (See Chafe 1972 for one of the few treatments of women in the 1920–1970 period.)

A relativist perspective on human values is also resistant to purposive social change and encourages a static equilibrium conception of social structure. Hence all problems had many sides and many solutions. A status quo mentality swept through the theoretical systems of one after another academic discipline. Intellectual complexity and narrow specialization were "in" in the world of research and scholarship.

It is in this context that one finds Beauvoir arguing in the early 1950s that feminine literature was no longer animated by demands for women's rights but by an effort "toward clarity and understanding." "Understanding," however, is not a foundation for action if the terms in which a problem is "understood" tend toward acceptance of the status quo or an assumption that women already live in the best of all possible worlds. Coupled with the myth of an open society of equal opportunity for all, this assumption encouraged women to attribute any failure in family or school or work roles to themselves rather than to the larger social structure.

Though social anthropology was itself a specialty, its historical thrust has been to see a culture "whole," and it has tended to explore how its various elements hang together to form that whole. Unlike psychology and sociology in the post-World War II period, social anthropology brought an intellectual framework to the analysis of sex roles that was fresh and full of surprises to a parochial America which gave little thought to cultures outside the framework of Western civilization. Hence Margaret Mead's work on sex and temperament was a contribution to intellectual understanding of men and women that carried an important challenge to the twin academic gods of functionalism and psychoanalysis. Her work, represented here by the conclusion to *Sex and Temperament,* paved the way for the feminist critique of both functionalism and psychoanalysis in Friedan's *The Feminine Mystique.* While Virginia Woolf's *A Room of One's Own* contains a touch of the old feminism in that it carries an implicit demand for future change in women's lives, Margaret Mead's early work in the 1940s, like Simone de Beauvoir's work in the 1950s, represents the best of the work done in the transitional period, when intellectual complexity was sought after and respected but which carried no message, no sense of urgency, for social change *now.* And it is important to note that two of the three important survivors of that transitional period, Woolf and Beauvoir, are scholars who worked *outside* the walls of the highly specialized world of academe. All three of the transitional writers—Woolf, Mead, and Beauvoir—have been important in the early stages of intellectual development of the contemporary generation of feminists, whose aspirations are in part to effect a change in the style and content of research, scholarship, and teaching *inside* the ivied walls.

Guineas and Locks:
Virginia Woolf (1882–1941)

A Room of One's Own represents the reworking of two papers on "Women and Fiction" which Virginia Woolf delivered at Newnham and Girton, Cambridge University's only colleges for women at that time. The book, first published by Hogarth Press in 1929, appeared during a period of great artistic productivity in Virginia Woolf's life. Within the preceding decade she had published *Monday or Tuesday* (1921), *Jacob's Room* (1922), *Mrs. Dalloway* (1925), *To the Lighthouse* (1927), and *Orlando* (1928). Within a year following *A Room of One's Own*, *The Waves* (1931) was also completed. In 1929 the novelist drew upon a lifetime of creative and critical observations of men and women and their relationship to each other to enlarge on her college lectures.

Virginia Woolf had only limited contact with political efforts in the feminist cause, such as a brief period of work in 1910 with the Adult Suffrage movement (Bell 1972:161). The focus, in her life as in her writing, was on the private sphere of women's roles and the relations between the sexes. *A Room of One's Own* was not, however, her only attempt to speak directly to the issues of feminism. In a later essay, "Professions for Women," she returned to the problem of creative achievement for women and put her finger incisively on two difficulties that plague the woman writer (V. Woolf 1942). One was that a young woman must conceal the fact that she "had a mind of her own, so that no man should be shocked or offended," and the second that there are many things a woman may not freely say about what she physically feels or she will arouse severe masculine disapproval (Pippett 1957:30–31).

On a broader scale, in *Three Guineas* (1938) she considered the social role of all middle-class women, or "daughters of educated men." *Three Guineas* comments in turn on education for women, their place in the professions, and their potential contributions to national culture, from which Woolf insisted they had been excluded throughout history. Written in the shadow of the Spanish Civil War and the growth of European fascism, *Three Guineas* was dismissed by many of Virginia's friends as a distraction from the larger, more important issues of the day, and it has never been as widely read as *A Room of One's Own* (Bell 1972:204–205). But the questions it asks about the role of women in a war economy have a sharply contemporary ring, and they are well worth the attention of readers today.

Virginia Woolf's life spanned the late Victorian and Edwardian period and centered on the world of literature and criticism. Despite the gulf of time and culture that separates us from her, the passion with which she wrote about men and women perhaps speaks to us in the 1970s better than it did to women in the 1920s. It may be that the beat to which we as women respond in the writing of other women is tuned to a level of human experience that changes very little through time or across cultures. Virginia Woolf places a subtle finger on the anger that lurks just below the surface of many writings by men about women, and the corresponding anger in women's response to male writers and to the behavior of men toward women. *A Room of One's Own* is filled with examples of the ridicule and contempt many men unwittingly show toward women, and of the humiliations women are subjected to in the course of daily life simply because they are women. The thousands of small ways in which women are made to feel unwelcome in the world of the intellect and the institutions in which human rationality is enshrined —libraries, universities, eating clubs—still speak poignantly to female sensibility today. Furthermore, the associative style of her writing is an important precursor to what is now called "consciousness-raising," providing her with leaps of empathic identification with the feeling tone of social situations and a shocked recognition of a general social pattern beneath what one took to be a uniquely personal experience. The particularly intimate quality of the essay which follows is noted by Virginia's nephew, Quentin Bell, in his recent biography of her:

. . . in *A Room of One's Own* one hears Virginia speaking. In her novels she is thinking. In her critical works one can sometimes hear her voice, but it is always a little formal, a little editorial. In *A Room of One's Own* she gets very close to her conversational style. [Bell 1972:144]

The points Woolf elaborates in her essay can be stated quite simply: there is more emotion than cool analysis in the published literature on women; there is distortion in the view of women when men do the observing and writing; and above all, a woman has two requirements for creativity in any endeavor—money and a room of her own, "guineas and locks." The money symbolizes economic independence, and the room the solitude and autonomy to turn off the world of family and community and to withdraw into the self to think and write. Both are simple, basic needs for any creative attempt by men or women. They are also conditions which most Western societies have denied to women far more often than to men. The whole thrust of the sociological literature on women points to their economic dependency—in job choices, hiring, salary, advancement, and so on. The literature on family life also documents the cultural assumption that women should be instantly available and of service to all other family members. Painstakingly documented and quantified in the social sciences, these points are powerful but flat in that literature. They are no match for the experience of watching Virginia Woolf develop them in her inimitable way in the Newnham-Girton lectures.

For this reason, none of the selections in this collection gave as much difficulty in the process of abridgment as did *A Room of One's Own*. Abridgment of any published book or essay is an assault, a cutting or pruning by one mind of the work of another. But a social scientist feels a special awe when confronted with the task of abridging a work as closely knit and subtly balanced as the writings of a creative artist like Woolf. One can only hope the violation has not been too great and urge readers to go on to the full work.

Virginia Woolf was the third of four children by the second marriage of Leslie Stephen and Julia Duckworth, and grew up in a highly intellectual home, where reading and writing were as natural as breathing or eating. The Stephen household was a complex one in which even a hardy child would have had difficulty growing up: a publicly prominent but personally difficult father; endless social and psychological demands from relatives who streamed in and out of their daily lives; marked contrasts in personality and values between the older Duckworth half-siblings and the younger Stephen children; indecent sexual explorations of both

Virginia and her sister Vanessa by an overbearing older half-brother George Duckworth (Bell 1972:42–43)—all combined to place severe strains on a sensitive child like Virginia. The implication of Bell's biography is that this household warped Virginia's psychosexual development and contributed to the episodes of madness that burdened her life and work. It was also a household in which personal tragedy was a frequent visitor: Virginia lost her mother at age thirteen, her older step-sister Stella Duckworth at fifteen, and her father when she was twenty-two.

Virginia also had considerable experience with the disadvantages suffered by women. While her brother Thoby went up to Cambridge as a matter of course, she remained at home with her sisters to study, read, think, paint—so long as these activities left ample room to conform to the heavy social demands placed upon women of their class. She was witness to her father's rapacious demands for sympathy and subordination from his daughters—Stella and Vanessa in particular—after the death of his wife. While her father projected a public image of calm and reasonableness, in his private life he bellowed against his widowed fate and screamed for sympathy from the women in the family (Bell 1972:63).

After the death of Leslie Stephen in 1904, the four Stephen siblings—Thoby, Vanessa, Adrian, and Virginia—moved to the then unfashionable Bloomsbury district of London. Their household in Gordon Square bore the early seeds of what would later become known in literature as the Bloomsbury Group. Here the pendulum swung from the male-dominated household headed by their forceful father to a socially and intellectually free atmosphere of peers, as Thoby gathered his former Cambridge friends about him for the famous "Thursday Evenings," and Vanessa and Virginia slowly moved into a complex set of relationships with these young intellectuals. It was in this circle of Thoby's friends that Virginia and Vanessa met the men they later married—Leonard Woolf and Clive Bell.

Virginia married Leonard Woolf in 1912 and shortly afterward completed work on her first novel, *The Voyage Out* (1915). In the years that followed there were periods of light and creativity, with their resulting novels and critical essays, broken by illness and the dark demons that tormented her. With perhaps more detail than one really wishes for, Quentin Bell has chronicled that life, and Leonard Woolf has written a remarkable autobiography in five volumes, in which long stretches are devoted to tracing the course of Virginia's work and illnesses, sensitively showing how "terrifyingly thin is the fabric of thought" that separates creative inspiration and madness. Having watched anxiously through two of the three major breakdowns Virginia Woolf experienced and through innumerable illnesses just short of breakdowns, Leonard Woolf was in a unique position to describe the torment in his wife's personal life and to sense the close similarity of her creative moods in writing and conversation and the content of her fantasies while ill. In her *Writer's Diary* (1954:165), Virginia illustrates her own awareness of this similarity:

Saturday, February 7th

Here in the few minutes that remain I must record, heaven be praised, the end of *The Waves*. I wrote the words O Death fifteen minutes ago, having reeled across the last ten pages with some moments of such intensity and intoxication that I seemed only to stumble after my own voice, or almost, after some sort of speaker (as when I was mad). I was almost afraid, remembering the voices that used to fly ahead.

Leonard Woolf describes similar flights of inspiration during the course of daily conversation, when he felt she suddenly "left the ground" and

gave some fantastic, entrancing, amusing, dreamlike, almost lyrical description of an event, a place, or a person. . . . The ordinary mental processes stopped, and in their place the waters of creativeness and imagination welled up and, almost undirected, carried her and her listeners into another world. [L. Woolf 1963:30–31]

Writing itself under such circumstances was a perpetual menace to Virginia's mental stability, and her husband watched anxiously through the predictable stages of tension and exhaustion that accompanied that writing. She had finished the last words of *Between the Acts* just a month before she committed suicide by drowning herself in the river Ouse.

⊱ A Room of One's Own ⊰

Chapter 2

. . . I must ask you to imagine a room, like many thousands, with a window looking across people's hats and vans and motor-cars to other windows, and on the table inside the room a blank sheet of paper on which was written in large letters WOMEN AND FICTION, but no more. . . . Why did men drink wine and women water? Why was one sex so prosperous and the other so poor? What effect has poverty on fiction? What conditions are necessary for the creation of works of art?—a thousand questions at once suggested themselves. But one needed answers, not questions; and an answer was only to be had by consulting the learned and the unprejudiced, who have removed themselves above the strife of tongue and the confusion of body and issued the result of their reasoning and research in books which are to be found in the British Museum. If truth is not to be found on the shelves of the British Museum, where, I asked myself, picking up a notebook and a pencil, is truth? . . .

. . . Have you any notion how many books are written about women in the course of one year? Have you any notion how many are written by men? Are you aware that you are, perhaps, the most discussed animal in the universe? Here had I come with a notebook and a pencil proposing to spend a morning reading, supposing that at the end of the morning I should have transferred the truth to my notebook. But I should need to be a herd of elephants, I thought, and a wilderness of spiders, desperately referring to the animals that are reputed longest lived and most multitudinously eyed, to cope with all this. I should need claws of steel and beak of brass even to penetrate the husk. How shall I ever find the grains of truth embedded in all this mass of paper? I asked myself, and in despair began running my eye up and down the long list of titles. Even the names of the books gave me food for thought. Sex and its nature might well attract doc-

From Virginia Woolf, *A Room of One's Own.* London, Hogarth Press, 1931. Pp. 38–59; 62–86; 143–172.

tors and biologists; but what was surprising and difficult of explanation was the fact that sex—woman, that is to say—also attracts agreeable essayists, light-fingered novelists, young men who have taken the M.A. degree; men who have taken no degree; men who have no apparent qualification save that they are not women. Some of these books were, on the face of it, frivolous and facetious; but many, on the other hand, were serious and prophetic, moral and hortatory. Merely to read the titles suggested innumerable schoolmasters, innumerable clergymen mounting their platforms and pulpits and holding forth with a loquacity which far exceeded the hour usually allotted to such discourse on this one subject. It was a most strange phenomenon; and apparently —here I consulted the letter M—one confined to the male sex. Women do not write books about men—a fact that I could not help welcoming with relief, for if I had first to read all that men have written about women, then all that women have written about men, the aloe that flowers once in a hundred years would flower twice before I could set pen to paper. So, making a perfectly arbitrary choice of a dozen volumes or so, I sent my slips of paper to lie in the wire tray, and waited in my stall, among the other seekers for the essential oil of truth.

What could be the reason, then, of this curious disparity, I wondered, drawing cart-wheels on the slips of paper provided by the British taxpayer for other purposes. Why are women, judging from this catalogue, so much more interesting to men than men are to women? A very curious fact it seemed, and my mind wandered to picture the lives of men who spend their time in writing books about women; whether they were old or young, married or unmarried, red-nosed or hump-backed—anyhow, it was flattering, vaguely, to feel oneself the object of such attention, provided that it was not entirely bestowed by the crippled and the infirm—so I pondered until all such frivolous thoughts were ended by an avalanche of books sliding down on to the desk in front of me. . . . Why does Samuel Butler say, "Wise men never say what they think of women?" Wise men never say anything else apparently. But, I continued, leaning back in my chair and looking at the vast dome in which I was a single but by now somewhat harassed thought, what is so unfortunate is that wise men never think the same thing about women. Here is Pope:

Most women have no character at all.

And here is La Bruyère:

> Les femmes sont extrêmes; elles sont meilleures ou pires que les hommes—

a direct contradiction by keen observers who were contemporary. Are they capable of education or incapable? Napoleon thought them incapable. Dr. Johnson thought the opposite. Have they souls or have they not souls? Some savages say they have none. Others, on the contrary, maintain that women are half divine and worship them on that account. Some sages hold that they are shallower in the brain; others that they are deeper in the consciousness. Goethe honoured them; Mussolini despises them. Wherever one looked men thought about women and thought differently. . . .

. . . [W]hile I pondered I had unconsciously, in my listlessness, in my desperation, been drawing a picture where I should . . . have been writing a conclusion. I had been drawing a face, a figure. It was the face and the figure of Professor von X. engaged in writing his monumental work entitled *The Mental, Moral, and Physical Inferiority of the Female Sex*. He was not in my picture a man attractive to women. He was heavily built; he had a great jowl; to balance that he had very small eyes; he was very red in the face. His expression suggested that he was labouring under some emotion that made him jab his pen on the paper as if he were killing some noxious insect as he wrote, but even when he had killed it that did not satisfy him; he must go on killing it; and even so, some cause for anger and irritation remained. Could it be his wife, I asked, looking at my picture? Was she in love with a cavalry officer? Was the cavalry officer slim and elegant and dressed in astrachan? Had he been laughed at, to adopt the Freudian theory, in his cradle by a pretty girl? For even in his cradle the professor, I thought, could not have been an attractive child. Whatever the reason, the professor was made to look very angry and very ugly in my sketch, as he wrote his great book upon the mental, moral and physical inferiority of women. Drawing pictures was an idle way of finishing an unprofitable morning's work. Yet it is in our idleness, in our dreams, that the submerged truth sometimes comes to the top. A very elementary exercise in psychology,

not to be dignified by the name of psycho-analysis, showed
me, on looking at my notebook, that the sketch of the angry
professor had been made in anger. Anger had snatched my
pencil while I dreamt. But what was anger doing there?
Interest, confusion, amusement, boredom—all these emotions
I could trace and name as they succeeded each other throughout the morning. Had anger, the black snake, been lurking
among them? Yes, said the sketch, anger had. It referred me
unmistakably to the one book, to the one phrase, which had
roused the demon; it was the professor's statement about the
mental, moral and physical inferiority of women. My heart
had leapt. My cheeks had burnt. I had flushed with anger.
There was nothing specially remarkable, however foolish, in
that. One does not like to be told that one is naturally the
inferior of a little man. . . . One has certain foolish vanities.
It is only human nature, I reflected, and began drawing cart-
wheels and circles over the angry professor's face till he
looked like a burning bush or a flaming comet—anyhow, an
apparition without human semblance or significance. The
professor was nothing now but a faggot burning on the top
of Hampstead Heath. Soon my own anger was explained
and done with; but curiosity remained. How explain the
anger of the professors? Why were they angry? For when it
came to analysing the impression left by these books there
was always an element of heat. This heat took many forms;
it showed itself in satire, in sentiment, in curiosity, in
reprobation. But there was another element which was often
present and could not immediately be identified. Anger, I
called it. But it was anger that had gone underground and
mixed itself with all kinds of other emotions. To judge from
its odd effects, it was anger disguised and complex, not anger
simple and open.

Whatever the reason, all these books, I thought, surveying the pile on the desk, are worthless for my purposes. They
were worthless scientifically, that is to say, though humanly
they were full of instruction, interest, boredom, and very
queer facts about the habits of the Fiji Islanders. They had
been written in the red light of emotion and not in the white
light of truth. Therefore they must be returned to the central
desk and restored each to his own cell in the enormous honey-
comb. All that I had retrieved from the morning's work had
been the one fact of anger. The professors—I lumped them
together thus—were angry. But why, I asked myself, having

returned the books, why, I repeated, standing under the colonnade among the pigeons and the prehistoric canoes, why are they angry? And, asking myself this question, I strolled off to find a place for luncheon. What is the real nature of what I call for the moment their anger? I asked. Here was a puzzle that would last all the time that it takes to be served with food in a small restaurant somewhere near the British Museum. Some previous luncher had left the lunch edition of the evening paper on a chair, and, waiting to be served, I began idly reading the headlines. A ribbon of very large letters ran across the page. Somebody had made a big score in South Africa. Lesser ribbons announced that Sir Austen Chamberlain was at Geneva. A meat axe with human hair on it had been found in a cellar. Mr. Justice —— commented in the Divorce Courts upon the Shamelessness of Women. Sprinkled about the paper were other pieces of news. A film actress had been lowered from a peak in California and hung suspended in mid-air. The weather was going to be foggy. The most transient visitor to this planet, I thought, who picked up this paper could not fail to be aware, even from this scattered testimony, that England is under the rule of a patriarchy. Nobody in their senses could fail to detect the dominance of the professor. His was the power and the money and the influence. He was the proprietor of the paper and its editor and sub-editor. He was the Foreign Secretary and the Judge. He was the cricketeer; he owned the racehorses and the yachts. He was the director of the company that pays two hundred per cent to its shareholders. He left millions to charities and colleges that were ruled by himself. He suspended the film actress in mid-air. He will decide if the hair on the meat axe is human; he it is who will acquit or convict the murderer, and hang him, or let him go free. With the exception of the fog he seemed to control everything. Yet he was angry. I knew that he was angry by this token. When I read what he wrote about women I thought, not of what he was saying, but of himself. When an arguer argues dispassionately he thinks only of the argument; and the reader cannot help thinking of the argument too. If he had written dispassionately about women, had used indisputable proofs to establish his argument and had shown no trace of wishing that the result should be one thing rather than another, one would not have been angry either. One would have accepted the fact, as one accepts the fact that a

pea is green or a canary yellow. So be it, I should have said.
But I had been angry because he was angry. Yet it seemed
absurd, I thought, turning over the evening paper, that a
man with all this power should be angry. Or is anger, I
wondered, somehow, the familiar, the attendant sprite on
power? Rich people, for example, are often angry because
they suspect that the poor want to seize their wealth. The
professors, or patriarchs, as it might be more accurate to call
them, might be angry for that reason partly, but partly for
one that lies a little less obviously on the surface. Possibly
they were not "angry" at all; often, indeed, they were admiring, devoted, exemplary in the relations of private life. Possibly when the professor insisted a little too emphatically
upon the inferiority of women, he was concerned not with
their inferiority, but with his own superiority. That was what
he was protecting rather hot-headedly and with too much
emphasis, because it was a jewel to him of the rarest price.
Life for both sexes—and I looked at them, shouldering their
way along the pavement—is arduous, difficult, a perpetual
struggle. It calls for gigantic courage and strength. More
than anything, perhaps, creatures of illusion as we are, it
calls for confidence in oneself. Without self-confidence we
are as babes in the cradle. And how can we generate this
imponderable quality, which is yet so invaluable, most
quickly? By thinking that other people are inferior to oneself.
By feeling that one has some innate superiority—it may be
wealth, or rank, a straight nose, or the portrait of a grandfather by Romney—for there is no end to the pathetic devices of the human imagination—over other people. Hence
the enormous importance to a patriarch who has to conquer,
who has to rule, of feeling that great numbers of people, half
the human race indeed, are by nature inferior to himself. It
must indeed be one of the chief sources of his power. But
let me turn the light of this observation on to real life, I
thought. Does it help to explain some of those psychological
puzzles that one notes in the margin of daily life? Does it explain my astonishment the other day when Z, most humane,
most modest of men, taking up some book by Rebecca West
and reading a passage in it, exclaimed, "The arrant feminist!
She says that men are snobs!" The exclamation, to me so surprising—for why was Miss West an arrant feminist for making a possibly true if uncomplimentary statement about the
other sex?—was not merely the cry of wounded vanity; it

was a protest against some infringement of his power to believe in himself. Women have served all these centuries as looking-glasses possessing the magic and delicious power of reflecting the figure of man at twice its natural size. Without that power probably the earth would still be swamp and jungle. The glories of all our wars would be unknown. We should still be scratching the outlines of deer on the remains of mutton bones and bartering flints for sheep skins or whatever simple ornament took our unsophisticated taste. Supermen and Fingers of Destiny would never have existed. The Czar and the Kaiser would never have worn crowns or lost them. Whatever may be their use in civilised societies, mirrors are essential to all violent and heroic action. That is why Napoleon and Mussolini both insist so emphatically upon the inferiority of women, for if they were not inferior, they would cease to enlarge. That serves to explain in part the necessity that women so often are to men. And it serves to explain how restless they are under her criticism; how impossible it is for her to say to them this book is bad, this picture is feeble, or whatever it may be, without giving far more pain and rousing far more anger than a man would do who gave the same criticism. For if she begins to tell the truth, the figure in the looking-glass shrinks; his fitness for life is diminished. How is he to go on giving judgement, civilising natives, making laws, writing books, dressing up and speechifying at banquets, unless he can see himself at breakfast and at dinner at least twice the size he really is? . . .

But these contributions to the dangerous and fascinating subject of the psychology of the other sex—it is one, I hope, that you will investigate when you have five hundred a year of your own—were interrupted by the necessity of paying the bill. It came to five shillings and ninepence. I gave the waiter a ten-shilling note and he went to bring me change. There was another ten-shilling note in my purse; I noticed it, because it is a fact that still takes my breath away—the power of my purse to breed ten-shilling notes automatically. I open it and there they are. Society gives me chicken and coffee, bed and lodging, in return for a certain number of pieces of paper which were left me by an aunt, for no other reason than that I share her name.

My aunt, Mary Beton, I must tell you, died by a fall from her horse when she was riding out to take the air in Bombay. The news of my legacy reached me one night about the same time that the act was passed that gave votes to women. A solicitor's letter fell into the post-box and when I opened it I found that she had left me five hundred pounds a year for ever. Of the two—the vote and the money—the money, I own, seemed infinitely the more important. Before that I had made my living by cadging odd jobs from newspapers, by reporting a donkey show here or a wedding there; I had earned a few pounds by addressing envelopes, reading to old ladies, making artificial flowers, teaching the alphabet to small children in a kindergarten. Such were the chief occupations that were open to women before 1918. I need not, I am afraid, describe in any detail the hardness of the work, for you know perhaps women who have done it; nor the difficulty of living on the money when it was earned, for you may have tried. But what still remains with me as a worse infliction than either was the poison of fear and bitterness which those days bred in me. To begin with, always to be doing work that one did not wish to do, and to do it like a slave, flattering and fawning, not always necessarily perhaps, but it seemed necessary and the stakes were too great to run risks; and then the thought of that one gift which it was death to hide—a small one but dear to the possessor—perishing and with it my self, my soul,—all this became like a rust eating away the bloom of the spring, destroying the tree at its heart. However, as I say, my aunt died; and whenever I change a ten-shilling note a little of that rust and corrosion is rubbed off; fear and bitterness go. Indeed, I thought, slipping the silver into my purse, it is remarkable, remembering the bitterness of those days, what a change of temper a fixed income will bring about. No force in the world can take from me my five hundred pounds. Food, house and clothing are mine for ever. Therefore not merely do effort and labour cease, but also hatred and bitterness. I need not hate any man; he cannot hurt me. I need not flatter any man; he has nothing to give me. So imperceptibly I found myself adopting a new attitude towards the other half of the human race. It was absurd to blame any class or any sex, as a whole. Great bodies of people are never responsible for what they do. They are driven by instincts which are not within their control. They too, the patriarchs, the professors, had endless difficulties, terrible drawbacks to contend with. Their education had been in some ways as faulty as my own. It had bred in them defects as great. True, they had money and power, but only at the cost of harbouring in their breasts an eagle, a vulture, for ever tearing the liver out and plucking at the lungs—the instinct for possession, the rage for acquisition which drives them to desire other people's fields and goods perpetually; to make frontiers and flags; battleships and poison gas; to offer up their own lives and their children's lives. Walk through the Admiralty Arch (I had reached that monument), or any other avenue given up to trophies and cannon, and reflect upon the kind of glory celebrated there. Or watch in the spring sunshine the stockbroker and the great barrister going indoors to make money and more money and more money when it is a fact that five hundred pounds a year will keep one alive in the sunshine. These are unpleasant instincts to harbour, I reflected. They are bred of the conditions of life; of the lack of civilisation, I thought, looking at the statue of the Duke of Cambridge, and in particular at the feathers in his cocked hat, with a fixity that they have scarcely ever received before. And, as I realised these drawbacks, by degrees fear and bitterness modified themselves into pity and toleration; and then in a year or two, pity and toleration went, and the greatest release of all came, which is freedom to think of things in themselves. That building, for example, do I like it or not? Is that picture beautiful or not? Is that in my opinion a good book or a bad? Indeed my aunt's legacy unveiled the sky to me, and substituted for the large and imposing figure of a gentleman, which Milton recommended for my perpetual adoration, a view of the open sky.

So thinking, so speculating I found my way back to my house by the river.

Chapter 3

It was disappointing not to have brought back in the evening some important statement, some authentic fact. Women are poorer than men because—this or that. Perhaps now it would be better to give up seeking for the truth, and receiving on one's head an avalanche of opinion hot as lava, discoloured as dish-water. It would be better to draw the curtains; to shut out distractions; to light the lamp; to narrow the enquiry and to ask the historian, who records not opinions but facts, to describe under what conditions women lived, not throughout the ages, but in England, say in the time of Elizabeth.

For it is a perennial puzzle why no woman wrote a word of that extraordinary literature when every other man, it seemed, was capable of song or sonnet. What were the conditions in which women lived, I asked myself; for fiction, imaginative work that is, is not dropped like a pebble upon the ground, as science may be; fiction is like a spider's web, attached ever so lightly perhaps, but still attached to life at all four corners. Often the attachment is scarcely perceptible; Shakespeare's plays, for instance, seem to hang there complete by themselves. But when the web is pulled askew, hooked up at the edge, torn in the middle, one remembers that these webs are not spun in mid-air by incorporeal creatures, but are the work of suffering human beings, and are attached to grossly material things, like health and money and the houses we live in.

I went, therefore, to the shelf where the histories stand and took down one of the latest, Professor Trevelyan's *History of England*. Once more I looked up Women, found "position of" and turned to the pages indicated. "Wife-beating," I read, "was a recognised right of man, and was practised without shame by high as well as low. . . . Similarly," the historian goes on, "the daughter who refused to marry the gentleman of her parents' choice was liable to be locked up, beaten and flung about the room, without any shock being inflicted on public opinion. Marriage was not an affair of personal affection, but of family avarice, particularly in the 'chivalrous' upper classes. . . . Betrothal often took place while one or both of the parties was in the cradle, and marriage when they were scarcely out of the nurses' charge." That was about 1470, soon after Chaucer's time. The next reference to the position of women is some two hundred years later, in the time of the Stuarts. "It was still the exception for women of the upper and middle class to choose their own husbands, and when the husband had been assigned, he was lord and master, so far at least as law and custom could make him. Yet even so," Professor Trevelyan concludes, "neither Shakespeare's women nor those of authentic seventeenth-century memoirs, like the Verneys and the Hutchinsons, seem wanting in personality and character." Certainly, if we consider it, Cleopatra must have had a way with her; Lady Macbeth, one would suppose, had a will of her own;

Rosalind, one might conclude, was an attractive girl. Professor Trevelyan is speaking no more than the truth when he remarks that Shakespeare's women do not seem wanting in personality and character. Not being a historian, one might go even further and say that women have burnt like beacons in all the works of all the poets from the beginning of time— Clytemnestra, Antigone, Cleopatra, Lady Macbeth, Phèdre, Cressida, Rosalind, Desdemona, the Duchess of Malfi, among the dramatists; then among the prose writers: Millamant, Clarissa, Becky Sharp, Anna Karenine, Emma Bovary, Madame de Guermantes—the names flock to mind, nor do they recall women "lacking in personality and character." Indeed, if woman had no existence save in the fiction written by men, one would imagine her a person of the utmost importance; very various; heroic and mean; splendid and sordid; infinitely beautiful and hideous in the extreme; as great as a man, some think even greater. But this is woman in fiction. In fact, as Professor Trevelyan points out, she was locked up, beaten and flung about the room.

A very queer, composite being thus emerges. Imaginatively she is of the highest importance; practically she is completely insignificant. She pervades poetry from cover to cover; she is all but absent from history. She dominates the lives of kings and conquerors in fiction; in fact she was the slave of any boy whose parents forced a ring upon her finger. Some of the most inspired words, some of the most profound thoughts in literature fall from her lips; in real life she could hardly read, could scarcely spell, and was the property of her husband.

It was certainly an odd monster that one made up by reading the historians first and the poets afterwards—a worm winged like an eagle; the spirit of life and beauty in a kitchen chopping up suet. But these monsters, however amusing to the imagination, have no existence in fact. What one must do to bring her to life was to think poetically and prosaically at one and the same moment, thus keeping in touch with fact—that she is Mrs. Martin, aged thirty-six, dressed in blue, wearing a black hat and brown shoes; but not losing sight of fiction either—that she is a vessel in which all sorts of spirits and forces are coursing and flashing perpetually. The moment, however, that one tries this method with the Elizabethan woman, one branch of illumination fails; one is held up by the scarcity of facts. One knows nothing detailed,

nothing perfectly true and substantial about her. History
scarcely mentions her. And I turned to Professor Trevelyan
again to see what history meant to him. I found by looking
at his chapter headings that it meant—

"The Manor Court and the Methods of Open-field Agri-
culture . . . The Cistercians and Sheep-farming . . . The
Crusades . . . The University . . . The House of Commons
. . . The Hundred Years' War . . . The Wars of the Roses
. . . The Renaissance Scholars . . . The Dissolution of the
Monasteries . . . Agrarian and Religious Strife . . . The
Origin of English Sea-power . . . The Armada . . ." and so
on. Occasionally an individual woman is mentioned, an Elizabeth, or a Mary; a queen or a great lady. But by no possible
means could middle-class women with nothing but brains
and character at their command have taken part in any one
of the great movements which, brought together, constitute
the historian's view of the past. Nor shall we find her in any
collection of anecdotes. . . . She never writes her own life
and scarcely keeps a diary; there are only a handful of her
letters in existence. She left no plays or poems by which we
can judge her. What one wants, I thought . . . is a mass of
information; at what age did she marry; how many children
had she as a rule; what was her house like; had she a room
to herself; did she do the cooking; would she be likely to
have a servant? All these facts lie somewhere, presumably,
in parish registers and account books; the life of the average
Elizabethan woman must be scattered about somewhere,
could one collect it and make a book of it. It would be ambitious beyond my daring, I thought, looking about the
shelves for books that were not there, to suggest to the students of those famous colleges that they should rewrite history, though I own that it often seems a little queer as it is,
unreal, lop-sided; but why should they not add a supplement
to history? calling it, of course, by some inconspicuous name
so that women might figure there without impropriety? . . .
Here am I asking why women did not write poetry in the
Elizabethan age, and I am not sure how they were educated;
whether they were taught to write; whether they had sitting-
rooms to themselves; how many women had children before
they were twenty-one; what, in short, they did from eight in
the morning till eight at night. They had no money evidently;
according to Professor Trevelyan they were married whether
they liked it or not before they were out of the nursery, at

fifteen or sixteen very likely. It would have been extremely odd, even upon this showing, had one of them suddenly written the plays of Shakespeare, I concluded, and I thought of that old gentleman, who is dead now, but was a bishop, I think, who declared that it was impossible for any woman, past, present, or to come, to have the genius of Shakespeare. He wrote to the papers about it. He also told a lady who applied to him for information that cats do not as a matter of fact go to heaven, though they have, he added, souls of a sort. How much thinking those old gentlemen used to save one! How the borders of ignorance shrank back at their approach! Cats do not go to heaven. Women cannot write the plays of Shakespeare.

Be that as it may, I could not help thinking, as I looked at the works of Shakespeare on the shelf, that the bishop was right at least in this; it would have been impossible, completely and entirely, for any woman to have written the plays of Shakespeare in the age of Shakespeare. Let me imagine, since facts are so hard to come by, what would have happened had Shakespeare had a wonderfully gifted sister, called Judith, let us say. Shakespeare himself went, very probably,—his mother was an heiress—to the grammar school, where he may have learnt Latin—Ovid, Virgil and Horace—and the elements of grammar and logic. He was, it is well known, a wild boy who poached rabbits, perhaps shot a deer, and had, rather sooner than he should have done, to marry a woman in the neighbourhood, who bore him a child rather quicker than was right. That escapade sent him to seek his fortune in London. He had, it seemed, a taste for the theatre; he began by holding horses at the stage door. Very soon he got work in the theatre, became a successful actor, and lived at the hub of the universe, meeting everybody, knowing everybody, practising his art on the boards, exercising his wits in the streets, and even getting access to the palace of the queen. Meanwhile his extraordinarily gifted sister, let us suppose, remained at home. She was as adventurous, as imaginative, as agog to see the world as he was. But she was not sent to school. She had no chance of learning grammar and logic, let alone of reading Horace and Virgil. She picked up a book now and then, one of her brother's perhaps, and read a few pages. But then her parents came in and told her to mend the stockings or mind the stew and not moon about with books and papers.

They would have spoken sharply but kindly, for they were substantial people who knew the conditions of life for a woman and loved their daughter—indeed, more likely than not she was the apple of her father's eye. Perhaps she scribbled some pages up in an apple loft on the sly, but was careful to hide them or set fire to them. Soon, however, before she was out of her teens, she was to be betrothed to the son of a neighbouring wool-stapler. She cried out that marriage was hateful to her, and for that she was severely beaten by her father. Then he ceased to scold her. He begged her instead not to hurt him, not to shame him in this matter of her marriage. He would give her a chain of beads or a fine petticoat, he said; and there were tears in his eyes. How could she disobey him? How could she break his heart? The force of her own gift alone drove her to it. She made up a small parcel of her belongings, let herself down by a rope one summer's night and took the road to London. She was not seventeen. The birds that sang in the hedge were not more musical than she was. She had the quickest fancy, a gift like her brother's, for the tune of words. Like him, she had a taste for the theatre. She stood at the stage door; she wanted to act, she said. Men laughed in her face. The manager—a fat, loose-lipped man—guffawed. He bellowed something about poodles dancing and women acting—no woman, he said, could possibly be an actress. He hinted—you can imagine what. She could get no training in her craft. Could she even seek her dinner in a tavern or roam the streets at midnight? Yet her genius was for fiction and lusted to feed abundantly upon the lives of men and women and the study of their ways. At last—for she was very young, oddly like Shakespeare the poet in her face, with the same grey eyes and rounded brows—at last Nick Greene the actor-manager took pity on her; she found herself with child by that gentleman and so—who shall measure the heat and violence of the poet's heart when caught and tangled in a woman's body?—killed herself one winter's night and lies buried at some cross-roads where the omnibuses now stop outside the Elephant and Castle.

That, more or less, is how the story would run, I think, if a woman in Shakespeare's day had had Shakespeare's genius. But for my part, I agree with the deceased bishop, if such he was—it is unthinkable that any woman in Shakespeare's day should have had Shakespeare's genius. For

genius like Shakespeare's is not born among labouring, uneducated, servile people. It was not born in England among
the Saxons and the Britons. It is not born to-day among the
working classes. How, then, could it have been born among
women whose work began, according to Professor Trevelyan,
almost before they were out of the nursery, who were forced
to it by their parents and held to it by all the power of law
and custom? Yet genius of a sort must have existed among
women as it must have existed among the working classes.
Now and again an Emily Brontë or a Robert Burns blazes
out and proves its presence. But certainly it never got itself
on to paper. When, however, one reads of a witch being
ducked, of a woman possessed by devils, of a wise woman
selling herbs, or even of a very remarkable man who had a
mother, then I think we are on the track of a lost novelist,
a suppressed poet, of some mute and inglorious Jane Austen,
some Emily Brontë who dashed her brains out on the moor
or mopped and mowed about the highways crazed with the
torture that her gift had put her to. Indeed, I would venture
to guess that Anon, who wrote so many poems without
signing them, was often a woman. It was a woman Edward
Fitzgerald, I think, suggested who made the ballads and the
folk-songs, crooning them to her children, beguiling her
spinning with them, or the length of the winter's night.

This may be true or it may be false—who can say?—
but what is true in it, so it seemed to me, reviewing the
story of Shakespeare's sister as I had made it, is that any
woman born with a great gift in the sixteenth century would
certainly have gone crazed, shot herself, or ended her days
in some lonely cottage outside the village, half witch, half
wizard, feared and mocked at. For it needs little skill in
psychology to be sure that a highly gifted girl who had tried
to use her gift for poetry would have been so thwarted and
hindered by other people, so tortured and pulled asunder by
her own contrary instincts, that she must have lost her health
and sanity to a certainty. No girl could have walked to
London and stood at a stage door and forced her way into the
presence of actor-managers without doing herself a violence
and suffering an anguish which may have been irrational—
for chastity may be a fetish invented by certain societies for
unknown reasons—but were none the less inevitable. Chastity
had then, it has even now, a religious importance in a
woman's life, and has so wrapped itself round with nerves

and instincts that to cut it free and bring it to the light of
day demands courage of the rarest. To have lived a free life
in London in the sixteenth century would have meant for a
woman who was poet and playwright a nervous stress and
dilemma which might well have killed her. Had she survived,
whatever she had written would have been twisted and
deformed, issuing from a strained and morbid imagination.
And undoubtedly, I thought, looking at the shelf where there
are no plays by women, her work would have gone unsigned.
That refuge she would have sought certainly. It was the relic
of the sense of chastity that dictated anonymity to women
even so late as the nineteenth century. Currer Bell, George
Eliot, George Sand, all the victims of inner strife as their
writings prove, sought ineffectively to veil themselves by
using the name of a man. Thus they did homage to the
convention, which if not implanted by the other sex was
liberally encouraged by them (the chief glory of a woman is
not to be talked of, said Pericles, himself a much-talked-of
man) that publicity in women is detestable. Anonymity runs
in their blood. The desire to be veiled still possesses them.
They are not even now as concerned about the health of
their fame as men are, and, speaking generally, will pass a
tombstone or a signpost without feeling an irresistible desire
to cut their names on it, as Alf, Bert or Chas. must do in
obedience to their instinct, which murmurs if it sees a fine
woman go by, or even a dog, Ce chien est à moi. And, of
course, it may not be a dog, I thought, remembering Parliament Square, the Sieges Allee and other avenues; it may be
a piece of land or a man with curly black hair. It is one of
the great advantages of being a woman that one can pass
even a very fine negress without wishing to make an
Englishwoman of her.

That woman, then, who was born with a gift of poetry
in the sixteenth century, was an unhappy woman, a woman
at strife against herself. All the conditions of her life, all
her own instincts, were hostile to the state of mind which
is needed to set free whatever is in the brain. But what is the
state of mind that is most propitious to the act of creation,
I asked? Can one come by any notion of the state that
furthers and makes possible that strange activity? Here I
opened the volume containing the Tragedies of Shakespeare.
What was Shakespeare's state of mind, for instance, when he
wrote *Lear* and *Antony and Cleopatra*? It was certainly the

state of mind most favourable to poetry that there has ever existed. But Shakespeare himself said nothing about it. We only know casually and by chance that he "never blotted a line." Nothing indeed was ever said by the artist himself about his state of mind until the eighteenth century perhaps. Rousseau perhaps began it. At any rate, by the nineteenth century self-consciousness had developed so far that it was the habit for men of letters to describe their minds in confessions and autobiographies. Their lives also were written, and their letters were printed after their deaths. Thus, though we do not know what Shakespeare went through when he wrote *Lear*, we do know what Carlyle went through when he wrote the *French Revolution;* what Flaubert went through when he wrote *Madame Bovary;* what Keats was going through when he tried to write poetry against the coming of death and the indifference of the world.

And one gathers from this enormous modern literature of confession and self-analysis that to write a work of genius is almost always a feat of prodigious difficulty. Everything is against the likelihood that it will come from the writer's mind whole and entire. Generally material circumstances are against it. Dogs will bark; people will interrupt; money must be made; health will break down. Further, accentuating all these difficulties and making them harder to bear is the world's notorious indifference. It does not ask people to write poems and novels and histories; it does not need them. It does not care whether Flaubert finds the right word or whether Carlyle scrupulously verifies this or that fact. Naturally, it will not pay for what it does not want. And so the writer, Keats, Flaubert, Carlyle, suffers, especially in the creative years of youth, every form of distraction and discouragement. A curse, a cry of agony, rises from those books of analysis and confession. "Mighty poets in their misery dead"—that is the burden of their song. If anything comes through in spite of all this, it is a miracle, and probably no book is born entire and uncrippled as it was conceived.

But for women, I thought, looking at the empty shelves, these difficulties were infinitely more formidable. In the first place, to have a room of her own, let alone a quiet room or a sound-proof room, was out of the question, unless her parents were exceptionally rich or very noble, even up to the beginning of the nineteenth century. Since her pin money, which depended on the goodwill of her father, was only

enough to keep her clothed, she was debarred from such
alleviations as came even to Keats or Tennyson or Carlyle, all
poor men, from a walking tour, a little journey to France,
from the separate lodging which, even if it were miserable
enough, sheltered them from the claims and tyrannies of their
families. Such material difficulties were formidable; but much
worse were the immaterial. The indifference of the world
which Keats and Flaubert and other men of genius have found
so hard to bear was in her case not indifference but hostility.
The world did not say to her as it said to them, Write if
you choose; it makes no difference to me. The world said
with a guffaw, Write? What's the good of your writing?
Here the psychologists of Newnham and Girton might come
to our help, I thought, looking again at the blank spaces
on the shelves. For surely it is time that the effect of discouragement upon the mind of the artist should be measured,
as I have seen a dairy company measure the effect of ordinary
milk and Grade A milk upon the body of the rat. They set
two rats in cages side by side, and of the two one was furtive,
timid and small, and the other was glossy, bold and big.
Now what food do we feed women as artists upon? . . .
To answer that question I had only to open the evening
paper and to read that Lord Birkenhead is of opinion—but
really I am not going to trouble to copy out Lord Birkenhead's opinion upon the writing of women. . . . I will quote,
however, Mr. Oscar Browning, because Mr. Oscar Browning
was a great figure in Cambridge at one time, and used to
examine the students at Girton and Newnham. Mr. Oscar
Browning was wont to declare "that the impression left on
his mind, after looking over any set of examination papers,
was that, irrespective of the marks he might give, the best
woman was intellectually the inferior of the worst man."
After saying that Mr. Browning went back to his rooms—and
it is this sequel that endears him and makes him a human
figure of some bulk and majesty—he went back to his rooms
and found a stable-boy lying on the sofa—"a mere skeleton,
his cheeks were cavernous and sallow, his teeth were black,
and he did not appear to have the full use of his limbs. . . .
'That's Arthur' [said Mr. Browning]. 'He's a dear boy really
and most high-minded.' " The two pictures always seem to
me to complete each other. And happily in this age of
biography the two pictures often do complete each other,

so that we are able to interpret the opinions of great men not only by what they say, but by what they do.

But though this is possible now, such opinions coming from the lips of important people must have been formidable enough even fifty years ago. Let us suppose that a father from the highest motives did not wish his daughter to leave home and become writer, painter or scholar. "See what Mr. Oscar Browning says," he would say; and there was not only Mr. Oscar Browning; there was the *Saturday Review*; there was Mr. Greg—the "essentials of a woman's being," said Mr. Greg emphatically, "are that *they are supported by, and they minister to, men*"—there was an enormous body of masculine opinion to the effect that nothing could be expected of women intellectually. Even if her father did not read out loud these opinions, any girl could read them for herself; and the reading, even in the nineteenth century, must have lowered her vitality, and told profoundly upon her work. There would always have been that assertion —you cannot do this, you are incapable of doing that—to protest against, to overcome. Probably for a novelist this germ is no longer of much effect; for there have been women novelists of merit. But for painters it must still have some sting in it; and for musicians, I imagine, is even now active and poisonous in the extreme. The woman composer stands where the actress stood in the time of Shakespeare. Nick Greene, I thought, remembering the story I had made about Shakespeare's sister, said that a woman acting put him in mind of a dog dancing. Johnson repeated the phrase two hundred years later of women preaching. And here, I said, opening a book about music, we have the very words used again in this year of grace, 1928, of women who try to write music. "Of Mlle. Germaine Tailleferre one can only repeat Dr. Johnson's dictum concerning a woman preacher, transposed into terms of music. 'Sir, a woman's composing is like a dog's walking on his hind legs. It is not done well, but you are surprised to find it done at all.' " So accurately does history repeat itself.

Thus, I concluded, shutting Mr. Oscar Browning's life and pushing away the rest, it is fairly evident that even in the nineteenth century a woman was not encouraged to be an artist. On the contrary, she was snubbed, slapped, lectured and exhorted. Her mind must have been strained and her vitality lowered by the need of opposing this, of disproving

that. For here again we come within range of that very
interesting and obscure masculine complex which has had so
much influence upon the woman's movement; that deep-
seated desire, not so much that *she* shall be inferior as that
he shall be superior, which plants him wherever one looks,
not only in front of the arts, but barring the way to politics
too, even when the risk to himself seems infinitesimal and
the suppliant humble and devoted. . . . The history of men's
opposition to women's emancipation is more interesting
perhaps than the story of that emancipation itself. An amusing book might be made of it if some young student at
Girton or Newnham would collect examples and deduce a
theory,—but she would need thick gloves on her hands, and
bars to protect her of solid gold.

But what is amusing now . . . had to be taken in desperate earnest once. Opinions that one now pastes in a book
labelled cock-a-doodle-dum and keeps for reading to select
audiences on summer nights once drew tears, I can assure
you. Among your grandmothers and great-grandmothers
there were many that wept their eyes out. Florence Night-
ingale shrieked aloud in her agony. Moreover, it is all very
well for you, who have got yourself to college and enjoy
sitting-rooms . . . of your own to say that genius should
disregard such opinions; that genius should be above caring
what is said of it. Unfortunately, it is precisely the men or
women of genius who mind most what is said of them.
Remember Keats. Remember the words he had cut on his
tombstone. Think of Tennyson; think—but I need hardly
multiply instances of the undeniable, if very unfortunate, fact
that it is the nature of the artist to mind excessively what is
said about him. Literature is strewn with the wreckage of
men who have minded beyond reason the opinions of others.

And this susceptibility of theirs is doubly unfortunate, I
thought, returning again to my original enquiry into what
state of mind is most propitious for creative work, because
the mind of an artist, in order to achieve the prodigious effort
of freeing whole and entire the work that is in him, must be
incandescent, like Shakespeare's mind, I conjectured, looking
at the book which lay open at *Antony and Cleopatra*. There
must be no obstacle in it, no foreign matter unconsumed.

For though we say that we know nothing about Shakespeare's state of mind, even as we say that, we are saying
something about Shakespeare's state of mind. The reason

perhaps why we know so little of Shakespeare—compared with Donne or Ben Jonson or Milton—is that his grudges and spites and antipathies are hidden from us. We are not held up by some "revelation" which reminds us of the writer. All desire to protest, to preach, to proclaim an injury, to pay off a score, to make the world the witness of some hardship or grievance was fired out of him and consumed. Therefore his poetry flows from him free and unimpeded. If ever a human being got his work expressed completely, it was Shakespeare. If ever a mind was incandescent, unimpeded, I thought, turning again to the bookcase, it was Shakespeare's mind.

Chapter 6

Next day the light of the October morning was falling in dusty shafts through the uncurtained windows, and the hum of traffic rose from the street. London then was winding itself up again; the factory was astir; the machines were beginning. It was tempting, after all this reading, to look out of the window and see what London was doing on the morning of the 26th of October 1928. And what was London doing? Nobody, it seemed, was reading *Antony and Cleopatra*. London was wholly indifferent, it appeared, to Shakespeare's plays. Nobody cared a straw—and I do not blame them—for the future of fiction, the death of poetry or the development by the average woman of a prose style completely expressive of her mind. If opinions upon any of these matters had been chalked on the pavement, nobody would have stooped to read them. The nonchalance of the hurrying feet would have rubbed them out in half an hour. . . .

At this moment, as so often happens in London, there was a complete lull and suspension of traffic. Nothing came down the street; nobody passed. A single leaf detached itself from the plane tree at the end of the street, and in that pause and suspension fell. Somehow it was like a signal falling, a signal pointing to a force in things which one had overlooked. It seemed to point to a river, which flowed past, invisibly, round the corner, down the street, and took people and eddied them along, as the stream at Oxbridge had taken the undergraduate in his boat and the dead leaves. Now it was bringing from one side of the street to the other diagonally a girl in patent leather boots, and then a young man in a maroon overcoat; it was also bringing a taxi-cab; and it brought all three together at a point directly beneath my window; where the taxi stopped; and the girl and the young man stopped; and they got into the taxi; and then the cab glided off as if it were swept on by the current elsewhere.

The sight was ordinary enough; what was strange was the rhythmical order with which my imagination had invested it; and the fact that the ordinary sight of two people getting into a cab had the power to communicate something of their own seeming satisfaction. The sight of two people coming down the street and meeting at the corner seems to ease the mind of some strain, I thought, watching the taxi turn and make off. Perhaps to think, as I had been thinking these two days, of one sex as distinct from the other is an effort. It interferes with the unity of the mind. Now that effort had ceased and that unity had been restored by seeing two people come together and get into a taxi-cab. The mind is certainly a very mysterious organ, I reflected, drawing my head in from the window, about which nothing whatever is known, though we depend upon it so completely. Why do I feel that there are severances and oppositions in the mind, as there are strains from obvious causes on the body? What does one mean by "the unity of the mind"? I pondered, for clearly the mind has so great a power of concentrating at any point at any moment that it seems to have no single state of being. It can separate itself from the people in the street, for example, and think of itself as apart from them, at an upper window looking down on them. Or it can think with other people spontaneously, as, for instance, in a crowd waiting to hear some piece of news read out. It can think back through its fathers or through its mothers, as I have said that a woman writing thinks back through her mothers. Again if one is a woman one is often surprised by a sudden splitting off of consciousness, say in walking down Whitehall, when from being the natural inheritor of that civilisation, she becomes, on the contrary, outside of it, alien and critical. Clearly the mind is always altering its focus, and bringing the world into different perspectives. But some of these states of mind seem, even if adopted spontaneously, to be less comfortable than others. In order to keep oneself continuing in them one is unconsciously holding something back, and gradually the repression becomes an effort. But there may be some state of mind in which one could continue without effort because nothing is required to be held back. And this perhaps, I thought, coming in from the window, is one of them. For certainly when I saw the couple get into the taxi-cab the mind felt as if, after being divided, it had come together again in a natural fusion. The obvious reason would be that it is natural for the sexes to co-operate. One has a profound, if irrational, instinct in favour of the theory that the union of man and woman makes for the greatest satisfaction, the most complete happiness. But the sight of the two people getting into the taxi and the satisfaction it gave me made me also ask whether there are two sexes in the mind corresponding to the two sexes in the body, and whether they also require to be united in order to get complete satisfaction and happiness? And I went on amateurishly to sketch a plan of the soul so that in each of us two powers preside, one male, one female; and in the man's brain the man predominates over the woman, and in the woman's brain the woman predominates over the man. The normal and comfortable state of being is that when the two live in harmony together, spiritually co-operating. If one is a man, still the woman part of the brain must have effect; and a woman also must have intercourse with the man in her. Coleridge perhaps meant this when he said that a great mind is androgynous. It is when this fusion takes place that the mind is fully fertilised and uses all its faculties. Perhaps a mind that is purely masculine cannot create, any more than a mind that is purely feminine, I thought. But it would be well to test what one meant by man-womanly, and conversely by woman-manly, by pausing and looking at a book or two.

Coleridge certainly did not mean, when he said that a great mind is androgynous, that it is a mind that has any special sympathy with women; a mind that takes up their cause or devotes itself to their interpretation. Perhaps the androgynous mind is less apt to make these distinctions than the single-sexed mind. He meant, perhaps, that the androgynous mind is resonant and porous; that it transmits emotion without impediment; that it is naturally creative, incandescent and undivided. In fact one goes back to Shakespeare's mind as the type of the androgynous, of the man-womanly mind, though it would be impossible to say what Shakespeare thought of women. And if it be true that it is one of the tokens of the fully developed mind that it does not think specially or separately of sex, how much harder it is to attain that condition now than ever before. Here I came to the books by living writers, and there paused and wondered if this fact were not at the root of something that had long puzzled me. No age can ever have been as stridently sex-conscious as our own; those innumerable books by men about women in the British Museum are a proof of it. The Suffrage campaign was no doubt to blame. It must have roused in men an extraordinary desire for self-assertion; it must have made them lay an emphasis upon their own sex and its characteristics which they would not have troubled to think about had they not been challenged. And when one is challenged, even by a few women in black bonnets, one retaliates, if one has never been challenged before, rather excessively. . . .

What, then, it amounts to, if this theory of the two sides of the mind holds good, is that virility has now become self-conscious—men, that is to say, are now writing only with the male side of their brains. It is a mistake for a woman to read them, for she will inevitably look for something that she will not find. It is the power of suggestion that one most misses, I thought, taking Mr. B the critic in my hand and reading, very carefully and very dutifully, his remarks upon the art of poetry. Very able they were, acute and full of learning; but the trouble was that his feelings no longer communicated; his mind seemed separated into different chambers; not a sound carried from one to the other. Thus, when one takes a sentence of Mr. B into the mind it falls plump to the ground—dead; but when one takes a sentence of Coleridge into the mind, it explodes and gives birth to all kinds of other ideas, and that is the only sort of writing of which one can say that it has the secret of perpetual life.

But whatever the reason may be, it is a fact that one must deplore. For it means—here I had come to rows of books by Mr. Galsworthy and Mr. Kipling—that some of the finest works of our greatest living writers fall upon deaf ears. Do what she will a woman cannot find in them that fountain of perpetual life which the critics assure her is there. It is not only that they celebrate male virtues, enforce male values and describe the world of men; it is that the emotion with which these books are permeated is to a woman incomprehensible. . . . So with Mr. Kipling's officers who turn their backs; and his Sowers who sow the Seed; and his Men who are alone with their Work; and the Flag—one blushes at all these capital letters as if one had been caught eavesdropping at some purely masculine orgy. The fact is that neither Mr. Galsworthy nor Mr. Kipling has a spark of the woman in him. Thus all their qualities seem to a woman, if one may generalise, crude and immature. They lack suggestive power. And when a book lacks suggestive power, however hard it hits the surface of the mind it cannot penetrate within. . . .

However, the blame for all this, if one is anxious to lay blame, rests no more upon one sex than upon the other. All seducers and reformers are responsible. . . . All who have brought about a state of sex-consciousness are to blame, and it is they who drive me, when I want to stretch my faculties on a book, to seek it in that happy age . . . when the writer used both sides of his mind equally. One must turn back to Shakespeare then, for Shakespeare was androgynous; and so were Keats and Sterne and Cowper and Lamb and Coleridge. Shelley perhaps was sexless. Milton and Ben Jonson had a dash too much of the male in them. So had Wordsworth and Tolstoi. In our time Proust was wholly androgynous, if not perhaps a little too much of a woman. But that failing is too rare for one to complain of it, since without some mixture of the kind the intellect seems to predominate and the other faculties of the mind harden and become barren. However, I consoled myself with the reflection that this is perhaps a passing phase; much of what I have said in obedience to my promise to give you the course of my thoughts will seem out of date; much of what flames in my eyes will seem dubious to you who have not yet come of age.

Even so, the very first sentence that I would write here, I said, crossing over to the writing-table and taking up the page headed Women and Fiction, is that it is fatal for anyone who writes to think of their sex. It is fatal to be a man or woman pure and simple; one must be woman-manly or man-womanly. It is fatal for a woman to lay the least stress on any grievance; to plead even with justice any cause; in any way to speak consciously as a woman. And fatal is no figure of speech; for anything written with that conscious bias is doomed to death. It ceases to be fertilised. Brilliant and effective, powerful and masterly, as it may appear for a day or two, it must wither at nightfall; it cannot grow in the minds of others. Some collaboration has to take place in the mind between the woman and the man before the art of creation can be accomplished. Some marriage of opposites has to be consummated. The whole of the mind must lie wide open if we are to get the sense that the writer is communicating his experience with perfect fullness. There must be freedom and there must be peace.

. . .

I told you in the course of this paper that Shakespeare had a sister; but do not look for her in Sir Sidney Lee's life of the poet. She died young—alas, she never wrote a word. She lies buried where the omnibuses now stop, opposite the Elephant and Castle. Now my belief is that this poet who never wrote a word and was buried at the cross-roads still lives. She lives in you and in me, and in many other women who are not here to-night, for they are washing up the dishes and putting the children to bed. But she lives; for great poets do not die; they are continuing presences; they need only the opportunity to walk among us in the flesh. This opportunity, as I think, it is now coming within your power to give her. For my belief is that if we live another century or so—I am talking of the common life which is the real life and not of the little separate lives which we live as individuals—and have five hundred a year each of us and rooms of our own; if we have the habit of freedom and the courage to write exactly what we think; if we escape a little from the common sitting-room and see human beings not always in their relation to each other but in relation to reality; and the sky, too, and the trees or whatever it may be in themselves; if we look past Milton's bogey, for no human being should shut out the view; if we face the fact, for it is a fact, that there is no arm to cling to, but that we go alone and that our relation is to the world of reality and not only to the world of men and women, then the opportunity will come and the dead poet who was Shakespeare's sister will put on the body which she has so often laid down. Drawing her life from the lives of the unknown who were her forerunners, as her brother did before her, she will be born. As for her coming without that preparation, without that effort on our part, without that determination that when she is born again she shall find it possible to live and write her poetry, that we cannot expect, for that would be impossible. But I maintain that she would come if we worked for her, and that so to work, even in poverty and obscurity, is worth while.

Cultural Stretch:
Margaret Mead (b. 1901)

Very few academic disciplines include women among their most prominent scholars. Anthropology clearly heads the small list of fields that do: Margaret Mead and Ruth Benedict have been known and respected, not only in anthropology, but far beyond the confines of their discipline. Few academic fields have so large a proportion of women as anthropology; in 1969–1970, for example, 38 percent of the graduate students in anthropology were women, compared to 18 percent in political science and a mere 5 percent in physics.

There is apparently something about the discipline that women find intellectually exciting and attractive, and something that encourages women more often than do other fields. Notably, the department of anthropology at Columbia University under Franz Boas welcomed Elise Parsons, Ruth Benedict, and Margaret Mead as students in the specialty of ethnology, and all three continued an association with the department for a long time after they earned their degrees. This acceptance of women seems to be part of a larger characteristic of anthropology, for the discipline has a long history of admitting strangers to its ranks. Dedication to the psychic unity of mankind may tend to the acceptance of diverse kinds of people. Mead suggests that this welcome is extended

> to those who came from distant disciplines, to members of minority groups in general . . . to the "over-mature," the idiosyncratic, and the capriciously gifted or experienced, to refugees from political or religious oppression. [Mead and Bunzel 1960:5]

She is careful to point out, however, that this liberality was not uniform either in the past or in the present. In earlier decades there were departments that considered anthropology a field for wealthy amateurs, "where penniless graduate students were advised to marry money or get out of anthropology."

In ethnology a passion for exacting detail is blended with a larger concern for the whole of a culture: the human body, language, archeological remains, and the living culture are all treated together. Whether this broader synthesis has a special fascination to women as women is hard to say. In the first volume of her autobiography, Mead makes an observation that is relevant to this point, though she was clearly not thinking of sex differences in this context. She observed:

> . . . most people prefer to carry out the kinds of experiments that allow the scientist to feel that he is in full control of the situation rather than surrendering himself to the situation, as one must in studying human beings as they actually live. [Mead 1972:293]

The scientific tradition in Western societies does not produce human observers willing to "surrender" to a situation or another culture, as Margaret Mead and her associates in anthropology were able to do. Understanding through mastery and control versus understanding through empathic projection and the absorption of the views of others—individual, class, or culture—may be a comparison that frequently differentiates the sexes even among those trained at a high level in the humane and scientific disciplines of the 1970s.

Margaret Mead has been prominent on the American anthropological scene for forty years. In 1973 she is a charismatic public figure to many Americans outside her own specialty in social anthropology. The special blend of intellectual brilliance and down-to-earth humanness, which her professional writings, public pronouncements, congressional testimony, and magazine columns have shown over the years, is more readily understood now that she has provided us with a personal account of her own early life and the family within which she grew to adulthood. Her roots are deep in the American Midwest, where her mother grew up in Illinois and her father's family in Ohio. Her parents met as graduate students at the University of Chicago, where her father studied economics and her mother sociology; she commented at one point in her memoirs, "I have been fortunate in being able to look up to my parents' minds well past my own middle years" (Mead 1972:44).

The first-born of five children, Margaret links her own

particular intellectual bent to her father—"I had my father's kind of mind" (Mead 1972:54). For most of his life, her father was a professor in the Wharton School of Finance and Commerce, and the family shifted from urban residence in Philadelphia during the academic year to rural living during the summer. As a graduate student, he had been concerned with theoretical economics and later worked on the quantity theory of money. But, Mead comments:

> . . . working on the quantity theory of money led him to look at gold itself, instead of treating it as a mere abstraction with special concrete properties. So he became interested in gold mining and even wrote a little book on the whole sequence of processes connected with it, *The Story of Gold*. [Mead 1972:33]

This movement from the abstract and theoretical to the concrete is the quality that marks the daughter's writing, as well. For example, in discussing the way in which American anthropology contrasts with other disciplines more susceptible to extreme specialization, Mead notes:

> The other human sciences from economics to biology, working within the parochial framework of our Euro-American tradition, have taken for granted many aspects of man's life. Consumption has been discussed without the details of fur and lace, carrots and caviar, family income without history, sex habits without language, color recognition as if it depended on biology, heredity as if it were a matter of gene pools alone and not also of the rules of mating. [Mead and Bunzel 1960:9]

More important than her father, however, were the two women in her early life: her mother and her paternal grandmother. Her grandmother lived with her parents from their marriage until her death in 1927, and was "the most decisive influence in my life" (Mead 1972:45). A woman of great intelligence and a firm will, with ideas about child-rearing and teaching far in advance of her day, Mead's grandmother had been a schoolteacher before her own marriage, was widowed at an early age, and reared her one son while fending for herself financially by returning to the classroom. From this grandmother, Margaret learned to respect others, to be a careful "observer of the world around me and to note what

I saw" (Mead 1972:47). As they went about daily household tasks, her grandmother told her many stories of family members from the past, and Mead comments:

> . . . there were a number of stern, impressive women and an occasional impressive man, but a lot of weak ones, too—that is the family picture. [Mead 1972:52–53]

Her mother was less tolerant of the world about her, a woman deeply dedicated to social and political causes, and, at least in the abstract, intolerant of certain types of women:

> . . . there were types of people . . . for whom she had no use—anti-suffragettes (women who probably kept poodles) or "the kind of woman who comes down at ten in the morning wearing a boudoir cap and who takes headache powders." [Mead 1972:25]

Where her daughter was concerned, however, the mother had an ungrudging generosity: "in my life I realized every one of her unrealized ambitions, and she was unambivalently delighted" (Mead 1972:29). The combined effect of these three key figures in Margaret Mead's early life is best described in her own words:

> I think it was my grandmother who gave me my ease in being a woman. She was unquestionably feminine—small and dainty and pretty and wholly without masculine protest or feminist aggrievement. She had gone to college when this was a very unusual thing for a girl to do, she had a firm grasp of anything she paid attention to, she had married and had a child, and she had a career of her own. All this was true of my mother, as well. But my mother was filled with passionate resentment about the condition of women, as perhaps my grandmother might have been had my grandfather lived and had she borne five children and had little opportunity to use her special gifts and training. As it was, the two women I knew best were mothers and had professional training. So I had no reason to doubt that brains were suitable for a woman. And as I had my father's kind of mind—which was also his mother's—I learned that the mind is not sex-typed. [Mead 1972:53–54]

Margaret Mead's professional career spans the period from 1929, when she earned her doctorate at Columbia, to perhaps today's newspaper, and almost certainly last month's magazine. Her intellectual and physical energy has been enormous during more than four decades of professional work. She was one of the first women anthropologists to attempt field work in the Pacific. Unlike some anthropologists who have never taken more than one field trip to gather data for a doctoral dissertation, Margaret Mead has been on numerous expeditions over a long span of time, from her first trips in 1925 to Samoa and 1928 to the Admiralty Islands to her eighth return to New Guinea in 1973. She studied a wide range of cultures in the Pacific, did pioneer work on culture and personality, was an early advocate and practitioner of the visual media in anthropological field work, directed a major project on contemporary cultures at Columbia University, and has served as curator of ethnology at the American Museum of Natural History for over forty years. Together with Gregory Bateson (to whom she was married), she produced some of the finest photographic records on childhood and Balinese character. The insights recorded by her pen, voice, and camera contributed much to the discovery and communication of cultural variation.

In the selection which follows Mead is critical of those who tend to portray woman as infinitely malleable, a creature "upon which mankind has draped every varying period-costume in keeping with which she wilted or waxed imperious, flirted or fled." Instead Mead has been insistent in pointing out that studies of women per se obscure the basic point—"the recognition that the cultural plot behind human relations is the way in which the roles of the two sexes are conceived and that the growing boy is shaped to a local and special emphasis as inexorably as is the growing girl."

Mead's studies of the Arapesh, Mundugumor, and Tchambuli were important in giving content to this basic view of the inexorable cultural pressure for both males and females to conform to the very specific gender rules of their society. Equally important, she found and reported the very considerable variation across societies in the content of gender roles. This was an important lesson to Western social scientists, who so often deluded themselves that innate characteristics predetermined the specific sex roles assigned to men and women in our own civilization.

There is much in the work of Margaret Mead that can contribute new qualities to the thinking of contemporary feminists. We find her warning as early as 1935 that "to insist that there are no sex-differences in a society that has always believed in them and depended upon them may be as subtle a form of standardizing personality as to insist that there are many sex-differences."

By 1972 she had a larger and more complex view of the skills that must be brought to bear in attempts to understand the human condition, including the differences between the sexes, a view allowing for the contribution of brain chemistry and physiology, as well as cultural patterns. Her vision for future work in her field is caught in the following passage:

> . . . if anthropologists today made full use of the magnificent new technology and went to the field prepared to build into their research the new conceptions about evolution, about man's instinctual equipment, and about the functioning of the brain, as well as all we have learned about the embodiment of patterning and the development of the individual personality, they could come back with materials that would immensely expand what we could do. [Mead 1972:295]

As a young woman, Margaret Mead called for a holistic approach to the study of a culture; now as a mature woman, she calls for a holistic approach to the intellectual disciplines themselves, cutting across the gaps that have separated the biological from the social sciences for so long.

⚐ Sex and Temperament ⚑

This study is not concerned with whether there are or are not actual and universal differences between the sexes, either quantitative or qualitative. It is not concerned with whether women are more variable than men, which was claimed before the doctrine of evolution exalted variability, or less variable, which was claimed afterwards. It is not a

From Margaret Mead, *Sex and Temperament in Three Primitive Societies*. New York, William Morrow & Company, 1935. Pp. xvi–xxii; 310–322.

treatise on the rights of women, nor an inquiry into the basis of femininism. It is, very simply, an account of how three primitive societies have grouped their social attitudes towards temperament about the very obvious facts of sex-difference. I studied this problem in simple societies because here we have the drama of civilization writ small, a social microcosm alike in kind, but different in size and magnitude, from the complex social structures of peoples who, like our own, depend upon a written tradition and upon the integration of a great number of conflicting historical traditions. Among the gentle mountain-dwelling Arapesh, the fierce cannibalistic Mundugumor, and the graceful head-hunters of Tchambuli, I studied this question. Each of these tribes had, as has every human society, the point of sex-difference to use as one theme in the plot of social life, and each of these three peoples has developed that theme differently. In comparing the way in which they have dramatized sex-difference, it is possible to gain a greater insight into what elements are social constructs, originally irrelevant to the biological facts of sex-gender.

Our own society makes great use of this plot. It assigns different roles to the two sexes, surrounds them from birth with an expectation of different behaviour, plays out the whole drama of courtship, marriage, and parenthood in terms of types of behaviour believed to be innate and therefore appropriate for one sex or for the other. We know dimly that these roles have changed even within our history. Studies like Mrs. Putnam's *The Lady* depict woman as an infinitely malleable lay figure upon which mankind has draped ever varying period-costumes, in keeping with which she wilted or waxed imperious, flirted or fled. But all discussions have emphasized not the relative social personalities assigned to the two sexes, but rather the superficial behaviour-patterns assigned to women, often not even to all women, but only to women of the upper class. A sophisticated recognition that upper-class women were puppets of a changing tradition blurred rather than clarified the issue. It left untouched the roles assigned to men, who were conceived as proceeding along a special masculine road, shaping women to their fads and whims in womanliness. All discussion of the position of women, of the character and temperament of women, the enslavement or the emancipation of women, obscures the basic issue—the recognition that the

cultural plot behind human relations is the way in which
the roles of the two sexes are conceived, and that the growing boy is shaped to a local and special emphasis as inexorably as is the growing girl. . . .

. . . We know that human cultures do not all fall into
one side or the other of a single scale and that it is possible
for one society to ignore completely an issue which two
other societies have solved in contrasting ways. Because a
people honour the old may mean that they hold children
in slight esteem, but a people may also, like the Ba Thonga
of South Africa, honour neither old people nor children;
or, like the Plains Indians, dignify the little child and the
grandfather; or, again, like the Manus and parts of modern
America, regard children as the most important group in
society. In expecting simple reversals—that if an aspect
of social life is not specifically sacred, it must be specifically secular; that if men are strong, women must be weak—
we ignore the fact that cultures exercise far greater licence
than this in selecting the possible aspects of human life which
they will minimize, overemphasize, or ignore. And while
every culture has in some way institutionalized the rôles of
men and women, it has not necessarily been in terms of contrast between the prescribed personalities of the two sexes,
nor in terms of dominance or submission. With the paucity
of material for elaboration, no culture has failed to seize upon
the conspicuous facts of age and sex in some way, whether
it be the convention of one Philippine tribe that no man can
keep a secret, the Manus assumption that only men enjoy
playing with babies, the Toda prescription of almost all
domestic work as too sacred for women, or the Arapesh insistence that women's heads are stronger than men's. In the
division of labour, in dress, in manners, in social and religious functioning—sometimes in only a few of these respects, sometimes in all—men and women are socially
differentiated, and each sex, as a sex, forced to conform to
the role assigned to it. In some societies, these socially defined roles are mainly expressed in dress or occupation, wtih
no insistence upon innate temperamental differences.
Women wear long hair and men wear short hair, or men
wear curls and women shave their heads; women wear skirts
and men wears trousers, or women wear trousers, and men
wear skirts. Women weave and men do not, or men weave
and women do not. Such simple tie-ups as these between

dress and occupation and sex are easily taught to every child and make no assumptions to which a given child cannot easily conform.

It is otherwise in societies that sharply differentiate the behaviour of men and of women in terms which assume a genuine difference in temperament. Among the Dakota Indians of the Plains, the importance of an ability to stand any degree of danger or hardship was frantically insisted upon as a masculine characteristic. From the time that a boy was five or six, all the conscious educational effort of the household was bent towards shaping him into an indubitable male. Every tear, every timidity, every clinging to a protective hand or desire to continue to play with younger children or with girls, was obsessively interpreted as proof that he was not going to develop into a real man. In such a society it is not surprising to find the *berdache*, the man who had voluntarily given up the struggle to conform to the masculine role and who wore female attire and followed the occupations of a woman. The institution of the *berdache* in turn served as a warning to every father; the fear that the son might become a *berdache* informed the parental efforts with an extra desperation, and the very pressure which helped to drive a boy to that choice was redoubled. The invert who lacks any discernible physical basis for his inversion has long puzzled students of sex, who when they can find no observable glandular abnormality turn to theories of early conditioning or identification with a parent of opposite sex. In the course of this investigation, we shall have occasion to examine the "masculine" woman and the "feminine" man as they occur in these different tribes, to inquire whether it is always a woman of dominating nature who is conceived as masculine, or a man who is gentle, submissive, or fond of children or embroidery who is conceived as feminine.

. . . [W]e shall be concerned with the patterning of sex-behaviour from the standpoint of temperament, with the cultural assumptions that certain temperamental attitudes are "naturally" masculine and others "naturally" feminine. In this matter, primitive people seem to be, on the surface, more sophisticated than we are. Just as they know that the gods, the food habits, and the marriage customs of the next tribe differ from those of their own people, and do not insist that one form is true or natural while the other is false or unnatural, so they often know that the temperamental pro-

clivities which they regard as natural for men or for women
differ from the natural temperaments of the men and women
among their neighbours. Nevertheless, within a narrower
range and with less of a claim for the biological or divine
validity of their social forms than we often advance, each
tribe has certain definite attitudes towards temperament, a
theory of what human beings, either men or women or both,
are naturally like, a norm in terms of which to judge and
condemn those individuals who deviate from it.

Two of these tribes have no idea that men and women
are different in temperament. They allow them different
economic and religious roles, different skills, different vul-
nerabilities to evil magic and supernatural influences. The
Arapesh believe that painting in colour is appropriate only to
men, and the Mundugumor consider fishing an essentially
feminine task. But any idea that temperamental traits of the
order of dominance, bravery, aggressiveness, objectivity, mal-
leability, are inalienably associated with one sex (as opposed
to the other) is entirely lacking. This may seem strange to a
civilization which in its sociology, its medicine, its slang, its
poetry, and its obscenity accepts the socially defined differences between the sexes as having an innate basis in temperament and explains any deviation from the socially
determined role as abnormality of native endowment or early
maturation. It came as a surprise to me because I too had
been accustomed to use in my thinking such concepts as
"mixed type," to think of some men as having "feminine"
temperaments, of some women as having "masculine" minds.
I set as my problem a study of the conditioning of the social
personalities of the two sexes, in the hope that such an
investigation would throw some light upon sex-differences.
I shared the general belief of our society that there was a
natural sex-temperament which could at the most only be
distorted or diverted from normal expression. I was innocent
of any suspicion that the temperaments which we regard as
native to one sex might instead be mere variations of human
temperament, to which the members of either or both sexes
may, with more or less success in the case of different individuals, be educated to approximate.

. . .

The knowledge that the personalities of the two sexes are
socially produced is congenial to every programme that looks

forward towards a planned order of society. It is a two-edged sword that can be used to hew a more flexible, more varied society than the human race has ever built, or merely to cut a narrow path down which one sex or both sexes will be forced to march, regimented, looking neither to the right nor to the left. . . .

There are at least three courses open to a society that has realized the extent to which male and female personality are socially produced. Two of these courses have been tried before, over and over again, at different times in the long, irregular, repetitious history of the race. The first is to standardize the personality of men and women as clearly contrasting, complementary, and antithetical, and to make every institution in the society congruent with this standardization. If the society declared that woman's sole function was motherhood and the teaching and care of young children, it could so arrange matters that every woman who was not physiologically debarred should become a mother and be supported in the exercise of this function. It could abolish the discrepancy between the doctrine that women's place is the home and the number of homes that were offered to them. It could abolish the discrepancy between training women for marriage and then forcing them to become the spinster supports of their parents.

Such a system would be wasteful of the gifts of many women who could exercise other functions far better than their ability to bear children in an already overpopulated world. It would be wasteful of the gifts of many men who could exercise their special personality gifts far better in the home than in the market-place. It would be wasteful, but it would be clear. It could attempt to guarantee to each individual the role for which society insisted upon training him or her, and such a system would penalize only those individuals who, in spite of all the training, did not display the approved personalities. There are millions of persons who would gladly return to such a standardized method of treating the relationship between the sexes, and we must bear in mind the possibility that the greater opportunities open in the twentieth century to women may be quite withdrawn, and that we may return to a strict regimentation of women.

The waste, if this occurs, will be not only of many women, but also of as many men, because regimentation of one sex carries with it, to greater or less degree, the regimentation

of the other also. Every parental behest that defines a way
of sitting, a response to a rebuke or a threat, a game, or an
attempt to draw or sing or dance or paint, as feminine, is
moulding the personality of each little girl's brother as well
as moulding the personality of the sister. There can be no
society which insists that women follow one special person-
ality-pattern, defined as feminine, which does not do violence
also to the individuality of many men.

Alternatively, society can take the course that has become
especially associated with the plans of most radical groups:
admit that men and women are capable of being moulded to a
single pattern as easily as to a diverse one, and cease to make
any distinction in the approved personality of both sexes.
Girls can be trained exactly as boys are trained, taught the
same code, the same forms of expression, the same occupations. This course might seem to be the logic which follows
from the conviction that the potentialities which different
societies label as either masculine or feminine are really potentialities of some members of each sex, and not sex-linked
at all. If this is accepted, is it not reasonable to abandon the
kind of artificial standardizations of sex-differences that have
been so long characteristic of European society, and admit
that they are social fictions for which we have no longer any
use? In the world today, contraceptives make it possible for
women not to bear children against their will. The most
conspicuous actual difference between the sexes, the difference
in strength, is progressively less significant. Just as the difference in height between males is no longer a realistic issue,
now that lawsuits have been substituted for hand-to-hand
encounters, so the difference in strength between men and
women is no longer worth elaboration in cultural institutions.

In evaluating such a programme as this, however, it is
necessary to keep in mind the nature of the gains that society
has achieved in its most complex forms. A sacrifice of distinctions in sex-personality may mean a sacrifice in complexity. The Arapesh recognize a minimum of distinction in personality between old and young, between men and women,
and they lack categories of rank or status. We have seen
that such a society at the best condemns to personal frustration, and at the worst to maladjustment, all of those men
and women who do not conform to its simple emphases. The
violent person among the Arapesh cannot find, either in the
literature, or in the art, or in the ceremonial, or in the history

of his people, any expression of the internal drives that are shattering his peace of mind. Nor is the loser only the individual whose own type of personality is nowhere recognized in his society. The imaginative, highly intelligent person who is essentially in tune with the values of his society may also suffer by the lack of range and depth characteristic of too great simplicity. The active mind and intensity of one Arapesh boy whom I knew well was unsatisfied by the laissez-faire solutions, the lack of drama in his culture. Searching for some material upon which to exercise his imagination, his longing for a life in which stronger emotions would be possible, he could find nothing with which to feed his imagination but tales of the passionate outbursts of the maladjusted, outbursts characterized by a violent hostility to others that he himself lacked.

Nor is it the individual alone who suffers. Society is equally the loser, and we have seen such an attenuation in the dramatic representations of the Mundugumor. By phrasing the exclusion of women as a protective measure congenial to both sexes, the Arapesh kept their *tamberan* cult, with the necessary audiences of women. But the Mundugumor developed a kind of personality for both men and women to which exclusion from any part of life was interpreted as a deadly insult. And as more and more Mundugumor women have demanded and been given the right of initiation, it is not surprising that the Mundugumor ceremonial life has dwindled, the actors have lost their audience, and one vivid artistic element in the life of the Mundugumor community is vanishing. The sacrifice of sex-differences has meant a loss in complexity to the society.

So in our own society. To insist that there are no sex-differences in a society that has always believed in them and depended upon them may be as subtle a form of standardizing personality as to insist that there are many sex-differences. This is particularly so in a changing tradition, when a group in control is attempting to develop a new social personality, as is the case today in many European countries. Take, for instance, the current assumption that women are more opposed to war than men, that any outspoken approval of war is more horrible, more revolting, in women than in men. Behind this assumption women can work for peace without encountering social criticism in communities that would immediately criticize their brothers or husbands if they took a similarly active part in peace propaganda. This belief that women are naturally more interested in peace is undoubtedly artificial, part of the whole mythology that considers women to be gentler than men. But in contrast let us consider the possibility of a powerful minority that wished to turn a whole society whole-heartedly towards war. One way of doing this would be to insist that women's motives, women's interests, were identical with men's, that women should take as bloodthirsty a delight in preparing for war as ever men do. The insistence upon the opposite point of view, that the woman as a mother prevails over the woman as a citizen at least puts a slight drag upon agitation for war, prevents a blanket enthusiasm for war from being thrust upon the entire younger generation. The same kind of result follows if the clergy are professionally committed to a belief in peace. The relative bellicosity of different individual clerics may be either offended or gratified by the prescribed pacific role, but a certain protest, a certain dissenting note, will be sounded in society. The dangerous standardization of attitudes that disallows every type of deviation is greatly reinforced if neither age nor sex nor religious belief is regarded as automatically predisposing certain individuals to hold minority attitudes. The removal of all legal and economic barriers against women's participating in the world on an equal footing with men may be in itself a standardizing move towards the wholesale stamping-out of the diversity of attitudes that is such a dearly bought product of civilization.

Such a standardized society, in which men, women, children, priests, and soldiers were all trained to an undifferentiated and coherent set of values, must of necessity create the kind of deviant that we found among the Arapesh and the Mundugumor, the individual who, regardless of sex or occupation, rebels because he is temperamentally unable to accept the one-sided emphasis of his culture. The individuals who were specifically unadjusted in terms of their psycho-sexual role would, it is true, vanish, but with them would vanish the knowledge that there is more than one set of possible values.

To the extent that abolishing the differences in the approved personalities of men and women means abolishing any expression of the type of personality once called exclusively feminine, or once called exclusively masculine, such a course involves a social loss. Just as a festive occasion is the gayer and more charming if the two sexes are dressed differently, so it is in less material matters. If the clothing is in itself a symbol, and a woman's shawl corresponds to a recognized softness in her character, the whole plot of personal relations is made more elaborate, and in many ways more rewarding. The poet of such a society will praise virtues, albeit feminine virtues, which might never have any part in a social Utopia that allowed no differences between the personalities of men and women.

To the extent that a society insists upon different kinds of personality so that one age-group or class or sex-group may follow purposes disallowed or neglected in another, each individual participant in that society is the richer. The arbitrary assignment of set clothing, set manners, set social responses, to individuals born in a certain class, of a certain sex, or of a certain colour, to those born on a certain day of the week, to those born with a certain complexion, does violence to the individual endowment of individuals, but permits the building of a rich culture. The most extreme development of a society that has attained great complexity at the expense of the individual is historical India, based, as it was, upon the uncompromising association of a thousand attributes of behaviour, attitude, and occupation with an accident of birth. To each individual there was given the security, although it might be the security of despair, of a set role, and the reward of being born into a highly complex society.

Furthermore, when we consider the position of the deviant individual in historical cultures, those who are born into a complex society in the wrong sex or class for their personalities to have full sway are in a better position than those who are born into a simple society which does not use in any way their special temperamental gifts. The violent woman in a society that permits violence to men only, the strongly emotional member of an aristocracy in a culture that permits downright emotional expression only in the peasantry, the ritualistically inclined individual who is bred a Protestant in a country which has also Catholic institutions—each one of these can find expressed in some other group in the society the emotions that he or she is forbidden to manifest. He is given a certain kind of support by the mere existence of these values, values so congenial to him and so inaccessible because of an accident of birth. For those who are content with a vicarious spectator-role, or with materials upon which to feast the creative imagination, this may be almost enough.

They may be content to experience from the sidewalks during a parade, from the audience of a theatre or from the nave of a church, those emotions the direct expression of which is denied to them. The crude compensations offered by the moving pictures to those whose lives are emotionally starved are offered in subtler forms by the art and literature of a complex society to the individual who is out of place in his sex or his class or his occupational group.

Sex-adjustments, however, are not a matter of spectator-ship, but a situation in which the most passive individual must play some part if he or she is to participate fully in life. And while we may recognize the virtues of complexity, the interesting and charming plots that cultures can evolve upon the basis of accidents of birth, we may well ask: Is not the price too high? Could not the beauty that lies in contrast and complexity be obtained in some other way? If the social insistence upon different personalities for the two sexes results in so much confusion, so many unhappy deviants, so much disorientation, can we imagine a society that abandons these distinctions without abandoning the values that are at present dependent upon them?

Let us suppose that, instead of the classification laid down on the "natural" bases of sex and race, a society had classi-fied personality on the basis of eye-colour. It had decreed that all blue-eyed people were gentle, submissive, and re-sponsive to the needs of others, and all brown-eyed people were arrogant, dominating, self-centred, and purposive. In this case two complementary social themes would be woven together—the culture, in its art, its religion, its formal per-sonal relations, would have two threads instead of one. There would be blue-eyed men, and blue-eyed women, which would mean that there were gentle, "maternal" women, and gentle, "maternal" men. A blue-eyed man might marry a woman who had been bred to the same personality as himself, or a brown-eyed woman who had been bred to the contrasting personality. One of the strong tendencies that makes for homosexuality, the tendency to love the similar rather than the antithetical persons, would be eliminated. Hostility be-tween the two sexes as groups would be minimized, since the individual interests of members of each sex could be woven together in different ways, and marriages of simi-larity and friendships of contrast need carry no necessary handicap of possible psycho-sexual maladjustment. The individual would still suffer a mutilation of his temperamental preferences, for it would be the unrelated fact of eye-colour that would determine the attitudes which he was educated to show. Every blue-eyed person would be forced into submissiveness and declared maladjusted if he or she showed any traits that it had been decided were only appropriate to the brown-eyed. The greatest social loss, however, in the classification of personality on the basis of sex would not be present in this society which based its classification on eye-colour. Human relations, and especially those which involve sex, would not be artificially distorted.

But such a course, the substitution of eye-colour for sex as a basis upon which to educate children into groups showing contrasting personalities, while it would be a definite advance upon a classification by sex, remains a parody of all the attempts that society has made through history to define an individual's role in terms of sex, or colour, or date of birth, or shape of head.

However, the only solution of the problem does not lie between an acceptance of standardization of sex-differences with the resulting cost in individual happiness and adjustment, and the abolition of these differences with the consequent loss in social values. A civilization might take its cues not from such categories as age or sex, race or hereditary position in a family line, but instead of specializing personality along such simple lines recognize, train, and make a place for many and divergent temperamental endowments. It might build upon the different potentialities that it now attempts to extirpate artificially in some children and create artificially in others.

Historically the lessening of rigidity in the classification of the sexes has come about at different times, either by the creation of a new artificial category, or by the recognition of real individual differences. Sometimes the idea of social position has transcended sex-categories. In a society that recognizes gradations in wealth or rank, women of rank or women of wealth have been permitted an arrogance which was denied to both sexes among the lowly or the poor. Such a shift as this has been, it is true, a step towards the emancipation of women, but it has never been a step towards the greater freedom of the individual. A few women have shared the upper-class personality, but to balance this a great many men as well as women have been condemned to a personality

characterized by subservience and fear. Such shifts as these
mean only the substitution of one arbitrary standard for
another. A society is equally unrealistic whether it insists
that only men can be brave, or that only individuals of rank
can be brave.

To break down one line of division, that between the
sexes, and substitute another, that between classes, is no
real advance. It merely shifts the irrelevancy to a different
point. And meanwhile, individuals born in the upper classes
are shaped inexorably to one type of personality, to an arrogance that is again uncongenial to at least some of them,
while the arrogant among the poor fret and fume beneath
their training for submissiveness. At one end of the scale is
the mild, unaggressive young son of wealthy parents who is
forced to lead, at the other the aggressive, enterprising child
of the slums who is condemned to a place in the ranks. If
our aim is greater expression for each individual temperament, rather than any partisan interest in one sex or its fate,
we must see these historical developments which have aided
in freeing some women as nevertheless a kind of development that also involved major social losses.

The second way in which categories of sex-differences
have become less rigid is through a recognition of genuine
individual gifts as they occurred in either sex. Here a real distinction has been substituted for an artificial one, and the
gains are tremendous for society and for the individual.
Where writing is accepted as a profession that may be pursued by either sex with perfect suitability, individuals who
have the ability to write need not be debarred from it by
their sex, nor need they, if they do write, doubt their essential masculinity or femininity. An occupation that has no
basis in sex-determined gifts can now recruit its ranks from
twice as many potential artists. And it is here that we can
find a ground-plan for building a society that would substitute real differences for arbitrary ones. We must recognize
that beneath the superficial classifications of sex and race the
same potentialities exist, recurring generation after generation, only to perish because society has no place for them.
Just as society now permits the practice of an art to members
of either sex, so it might also permit the development of
many contrasting temperamental gifts in each sex. It might
abandon its various attempts to make boys fight and to make
girls remain passive, or to make all children fight, and in-

stead shape our educational institutions to develop to the full the boy who shows a capacity for maternal behaviour, the girl who shows an opposite capacity that is stimulated by fighting against obstacles. No skill, no special aptitude, no vividness of imagination or precision of thinking would go unrecognized because the child who possessed it was of one sex rather than the other. No child would be relentlessly shaped to one pattern of behaviour, but instead there should be many patterns, in a world that had learned to allow to each individual the pattern which was most congenial to his gifts.

Such a civilization would not sacrifice the gains of thousands of years during which society has built up standards of diversity. The social gains would be conserved, and each child would be encouraged on the basis of his actual temperament. Where we now have patterns of behaviour for women and patterns of behaviour for men, we would then have patterns of behaviour that expressed the interests of individuals with many kinds of endowment. There would be ethical codes and social symbolisms, an art and a way of life, congenial to each endowment.

Historically our own culture has relied for the creation of rich and contrasting values upon many artificial distinctions, the most striking of which is sex. It will not be by the mere abolition of these distinctions that society will develop patterns in which individual gifts are given place instead of being forced into an ill-fitting mould. If we are to achieve a richer culture, rich in contrasting values, we must recognize the whole gamut of human potentialities, and so weave a less arbitrary social fabric, one in which each diverse human gift will find a fitting place.

A Not-So-Rebellious "Other":
Simone de Beauvoir (b. 1908)

Widely viewed as Europe's "leading feminist," Simone de Beauvoir was among some 300 Frenchwomen who signed a ringing manifesto in the spring of 1971 which publicly announced that they had at one time or another undergone an abortion. The manifesto was in defiance of a French law which provides for a punishment of from six to twenty-four months in jail and a considerable fine. This challenge to legal authority did not lead to any imprisonment of either Beauvoir or her associates in the feminist movement in France (Mouvement de Libération des Femmes). American commentators seized upon her involvement in this public act as further evidence of her role as the ardent feminist who began the current feminist renascence with the publication of *Le Deuxieme Sexe* in 1949 (issued as *The Second Sex* in the United States in 1952).

But *The Second Sex* was far from a call for feminist action. In her introduction to the book, Beauvoir wrote that the subject of women had become "irritating" and held the view that "enough ink had been spilled in the quarreling over feminism, now practically over." She argued that feminine literature was no longer animated by a "wish to demand our rights" but by an "effort toward clarity and understanding." Though the roots of her book went deep into her own personal life, the book was not a political analysis; rather, it was fully in keeping with the transitional era between the old and the new feminism, that period between the 1920s and the 1960s, when the romance in scholarship was with intellectual complexity and a value neutrality of a completely apolitical nature. Its tone is caught by a quotation from Kierkegaard which graced the introduction: "what a misfortune it is to be a woman! And yet the greatest misfortune when one is a woman is not to realize that it is one."

What was new and startling about *The Second Sex* to its first generation of readers was not its feminism, but the audacity of a scholar who violated the comfortable confines of specialization that had grown up in the academic disciplines. Like Beauvoir's recent book on aging, *The Coming of Age* (1972), *The Second Sex* roams among biology, history, literature, anthropology, and sociology, soaking up what such fields could illuminate about the position of women and the meaning of sex differences. In an age of specialization, such an attempt was a bold intellectual exercise, and it called for the eclectic mentality and a capacity for synthesis that French higher education seems to produce more frequently than English or American schooling. Such human characteristics as age and sex play havoc with the specialization that had the academic disciplines in its grip during the 1940s and 1950s, with the result that researchers often simply confined their attention to one particular age group and dropped women from their research altogether. Thus a typical sample of subjects in psychology or sociology for more than a decade consisted of young college-age males. It was therefore an exhilarating experience to encounter a book like *The Second Sex* during the 1950s; but in academic circles the very strength that flowed from its broad synthesizing framework was criticized as a weakness: since no one, the view went, could be a specialist in so many areas, the work was therefore suspect.

It was not suspect, however, in the personal lives of countless women who read the book. A reading of *The Second Sex* made one feel very angry with society and the power of men to determine so much of what women could do with their lives. Nevertheless, the book did not stimulate any political activity on the part of women readers, since it was itself apolitical and the pressure of social life in the 1950s was toward private life and individual progress in work rather than toward political dissent and action. My own copy of *The Second Sex* simply went back onto a dusty shelf and remained there until the mid-1960s. It is difficult to imagine young women in 1970 responding in this way to a first reading of Kate Millett's *Sexual Politics*. The sheer contrast in titles is a symbolic index to the very changed circumstances of the times and the very different political perspective of the two writers.

Partly because of the subject matter, partly because of an already established national reputation as a writer, and partly because of Beauvoir's connection with Sartre, the initial French publication of the first volume of *The Second Sex* triggered some 22,000 sales in a single week. French readers found Beauvoir's personal memoirs much more fascinating, however: more than half a million copies of *Memoirs of a Dutiful Daughter* (1959) have been sold in France alone. The emergence of the woman's movement in the 1960s led to many new printings of *The Second Sex*, which has been translated into nineteen different languages. Simone de Beauvoir now considers this book the one she is most proud of, but one cannot help wondering what the book would be like had she waited to write it for another decade.

The personal life out of which *The Second Sex* grew has been described in great detail by Beauvoir herself, and the reader not yet familiar with *The Memoirs of a Dutiful Daughter* (1959) or *The Prime of Life* (1962) has a rare reading treat in store.

A complex volume such as *The Second Sex* does not lend itself to any easy abridgment. I have therefore chosen to include only portions of the introduction and the conclusion to the book, in which Beauvoir establishes the perspective from which she approaches her study of women. This selection will also help to dispel the view that *The Second Sex* represents the "beginnings" of the feminist renascence. No feminist of the 1970s would claim in an introduction to her work that "we are no longer like our partisan elders; by and large we have won the game." *The Second Sex* is the product of the transitional period between the old and the new feminism; hence it makes an appropriate last entry in this *historical* collection of feminist writings.

⋊ The Second Sex ⋉

. . . What is a woman?

To state the question is, to me, to suggest, at once, a preliminary answer. The fact that I ask it is in itself signifi-

---

From Simone de Beauvoir, *The Second Sex*. Translated by H. M. Parshley. New York, Alfred A. Knopf, 1953. Pp. xv–xxix, 716–732.

cant. A man would never get the notion of writing a book on the peculiar situation of the human male. But if I wish to define myself, I must first of all say: "I am a woman"; on this truth must be based all further discussion. A man never begins by presenting himself as an individual of a certain sex; it goes without saying that he is a man. The terms *masculine* and *feminine* are used symmetrically only as a matter of form, as on legal papers. In actuality the relation of the two sexes is not quite like that of two electrical poles, for man represents both the positive and the neutral, as is indicated by the common use of *man* to designate human beings in general; whereas woman represents only the negative, defined by limiting criteria, without reciprocity. In the midst of an abstract discussion it is vexing to hear a man say: "You think thus and so because you are a woman"; but I know that my only defense is to reply: "I think thus and so because it is true," thereby removing my subjective self from the argument. It would be out of the question to reply: "And you think the contrary because you are a man," for it is understood that the fact of being a man is no peculiarity. A man is in the right in being a man; it is the woman who is in the wrong. It amounts to this: just as for the ancients there was an absolute vertical with reference to which the oblique was defined, so there is an absolute human type, the masculine. Woman has ovaries, a uterus; these peculiarities imprison her in her subjectivity, circumscribe her within the limits of her own nature. It is often said that she thinks with her glands. Man superbly ignores the fact that his anatomy also includes glands, such as the testicles, and that they secrete hormones. He thinks of his body as a direct and normal connection with the world, which he believes he apprehends objectively, whereas he regards the body of woman as a hindrance, a prison, weighed down by everything peculiar to it. "The female is a female by virtue of a certain *lack* of qualities," said Aristotle; "we should regard the female nature as afflicted with a natural defectiveness." And St. Thomas for his part pronounced woman to be an "imperfect man," an "incidental" being. This is symbolized in Genesis where Eve is depicted as made from what Bossuet called "a supernumerary bone" of Adam.

Thus humanity is male and man defines woman not in herself but as relative to him; she is not regarded as an autonomous being. Michelet writes: "Woman, the relative

being. . . ." And Benda is most positive in his *Rapport
d'Uriel*: "The body of man makes sense in itself quite apart
from that of woman, whereas the latter seems wanting in
significance by itself. . . . Man can think of himself without
woman. She cannot think of herself without man." And she
is simply what man decrees; thus she is called "the sex," by
which is meant that she appears essentially to the male as a
sexual being. For him she is sex—absolute sex, no less. She
is defined and differentiated with reference to man and not
he with reference to her; she is the incidental, the inessential
as opposed to the essential. He is the Subject, he is the
Absolute—she is the Other.

The category of the *Other* is as primordial as consciousness itself. In the most primitive societies, in the most ancient
mythologies, one finds the expression of a duality—that of
the Self and the Other. This duality was not originally attached to the division of the sexes; it was not dependent upon
any empirical facts. It is revealed in such works as that of
Granet on Chinese thought and those of Dumézil on the East
Indies and Rome. The feminine element was at first no more
involved in such pairs as Varuna-Mitra, Uranus-Zeus, Sun-
Moon, and Day-Night than it was in the contrasts between
Good and Evil, lucky and unlucky auspices, right and left,
God and Lucifer. Otherness is a fundamental category of
human thought.

Thus it is that no group ever sets itself up as the One
without at once setting up the Other over against itself. If
three travelers chance to occupy the same compartments, that
is enough to make vaguely hostile "others" out of all the rest
of the passengers on the train. In small-town eyes all persons
not belonging to the village are "strangers" and suspect; to
the native of a country all who inhabit other countries are
"foreigners"; Jews are "different" for the anti-Semite, Negroes are "inferior" for American racists, aborigines are "natives" for colonists, proletarians are the "lower class" for the
privileged.

Lévi-Strauss, at the end of a profound work on the various forms of primitive societies, reaches the following conclusion: "Passage from the state of Nature to the state of
Culture is marked by man's ability to view biological relations as a series of contrasts; duality, alternation, opposition,
and symmetry, whether under definite or vague forms, con-

stitute not so much phenomena to be explained as fundamental and immediately given data of social reality." These phenomena would be incomprehensible if in fact human society were simply a *Mitsein* or fellowship based on solidarity and friendliness. Things become clear, on the contrary, if, following Hegel, we find in consciousness itself a fundamental hostility toward every other consciousness; the subject can be posed only in being opposed—he sets himself up as the essential, as opposed to the other, the inessential, the object.

But the other consciousness, the other ego, sets up a reciprocal claim. The native traveling abroad is shocked to find himself in turn regarded as a "stranger" by the natives of neighboring countries. As a matter of fact, wars, festivals, trading, treaties, and contests among tribes, nations, and classes tend to deprive the concept *Other* of its absolute sense and to make manifest its relativity; willy-nilly, individuals and groups are forced to realize the reciprocity of their relations. How is it, then, that this reciprocity has not been recognized between the sexes, that one of the contrasting terms is set up as the sole essential, denying any relativity in regard to its correlative and defining the latter as pure otherness? Why is it that women do not dispute male sovereignty? No subject will readily volunteer to become the object, the inessential; it is not the Other who, in defining himself as the Other, establishes the One. The Other is posed as such by the One in defining himself as the One. But if the Other is not to regain the status of being the One, he must be submissive enough to accept this alien point of view. Whence comes this submission in the case of woman?

There are, to be sure, other cases in which a certain category has been able to dominate another completely for a time. Very often this privilege depends upon inequality of numbers—the majority imposes its rule upon the minority or persecutes it. But women are not a minority, like the American Negroes or the Jews; there are as many women as men on earth. Again, the two groups concerned have often been originally independent; they may have been formerly unaware of each other's existence, or perhaps they recognized each other's autonomy. But a historical event has resulted in the subjugation of the weaker by the stronger. The scattering of the Jews, the introduction of slavery into America, the conquests of imperialism are examples in point. In these cases

the oppressed retained at least the memory of former days;
they possessed in common a past, a tradition, sometimes a
religion or a culture.

The parallel drawn by Bebel between women and the
proletariat is valid in that neither ever formed a minority or
a separate collective unit of mankind. And instead of a single
historical event it is in both cases a historical development
that explains their status as a class and accounts for the membership of *particular individuals* in that class. But proletarians
have not always existed, whereas there have always been
women. They are women in virtue of their anatomy and
physiology. Throughout history they have always been subordinated to men, and hence their dependency is not the result
of a historical event or a social change—it was not something
that *occurred*. The reason why otherness in this case seems to
be an absolute is in part that it lacks the contingent or incidental nature of historical facts. A condition brought about at
a certain time can be abolished at some other time, as the
Negroes of Haiti and others have proved; but it might seem
that a natural condition is beyond the possibility of change.
In truth, however, the nature of things is no more immutably
given, once for all, than is historical reality. If woman seems
to be the inessential which never becomes the essential, it is
because she herself fails to bring about this change. Proletarians say "We"; Negroes also. Regarding themselves as
subjects, they transform the bourgeois, the whites, into
"others." But women do not say "We," except at some
congress of feminists or similar formal demonstration; men
say "women," and women use the same word in referring to
themselves. They do not authentically assume a subjective
attitude. The proletarians have accomplished the revolution
in Russia, the Negroes in Haiti, the Indo-Chinese are battling
for it in Indo-China; but the women's effort has never been
anything more than a symbolic agitation. They have gained
only what men have been willing to grant; they have taken
nothing, they have only received.

The reason for this is that women lack concrete means
for organizing themselves into a unit which can stand face
to face with the correlative unit. They have no past, no
history, no religion of their own; and they have no such
solidarity of work and interest as that of the proletariat. They
are not even promiscuously herded together in the way that
creates community feeling among the American Negroes, the

ghetto Jews, the workers of Saint-Denis, or the factory hands of Renault. They live dispersed among the males, attached through residence, housework, economic condition, and social standing to certain men—fathers or husbands—more firmly than they are to other women. If they belong to the bourgeoisie, they feel solidarity with men of that class, not with proletarian women; if they are white, their allegiance is to white men, not to Negro women. The proletariat can propose to massacre the ruling class, and a sufficiently fanatical Jew or Negro might dream of getting sole possession of the atomic bomb and making humanity wholly Jewish or black; but woman cannot even dream of exterminating the males. The bond that unites her to her oppressors is not comparable to any other. The division of the sexes is a biological fact, not an event in human history. Male and female stand opposed within a primordial *Mitsein*, and woman has not broken it. The couple is a fundamental unity with its two halves riveted together, and the cleavage of society along the line of sex is impossible. Here is to be found the basic trait of woman: she is the Other in a totality of which the two components are necessary to one another.

One could suppose that this reciprocity might have facilitated the liberation of woman. When Hercules sat at the feet of Omphale and helped with her spinning, his desire for her held him captive; but why did she fail to gain a lasting power? To revenge herself on Jason, Medea killed their children; and this grim legend would seem to suggest that she might have obtained a formidable influence over him through his love for his offspring. In *Lysistrata* Aristophanes gaily depicts a band of women who joined forces to gain social ends through the sexual needs of their men; but this is only a play. In the legend of the Sabine women, the latter soon abandoned their plan of remaining sterile to punish their ravishers. In truth woman has not been socially emancipated through man's need—sexual desire and the desire for offspring—which makes the male dependent for satisfaction upon the female.

Master and slave, also, are united by a reciprocal need, in this case economic, which does not liberate the slave. In the relation of master to slave the master does not make a point of the need that he has for the other; he has in his grasp the power of satisfying this need through his own action; whereas the slave, in his dependent condition, his

hope and fear, is quite conscious of the need he has for his
master. Even if the need is at botton equally urgent for both,
it always works in favor of the oppressor and against the
oppressed. That is why the liberation of the working class,
for example, has been slow.

Now, woman has always been man's dependent, if not his
slave; the two sexes have never shared the world in equality.
And even today woman is heavily handicapped, though her
situation is beginning to change. Almost nowhere is her legal
status the same as man's, and frequently it is much to her
disadvantage. Even when her rights are legally recognized in
the abstract, long-standing custom prevents their full expression in the mores. In the economic sphere men and
women can almost be said to make up two castes; other
things being equal, the former hold the better jobs, get higher
wages, and have more opportunity for success than their new
competitors. In industry and politics men have a great many
more positions and they monopolize the most important
posts. In addition to all this, they enjoy a traditional prestige
that the education of children tends in every way to support,
for the present enshrines the past—and in the past all history
has been made by men. At the present time, when women
are beginning to take part in the affairs of the world, it is still
a world that belongs to men—they have no doubt of it at all
and women have scarcely any. To decline to be the Other, to
refuse to be a party to the deal—this would be for women to
renounce all the advantages conferred upon them by their
alliance with the superior caste. Man-the-sovereign will provide woman-the-liege with material protection and will
undertake the moral justification of her existence; thus she
can evade at once both economic risk and the metaphysical
risk of a liberty in which ends and aims must be contrived
without assistance. Indeed, along with the ethical urge of
each individual to affirm his subjective existence, there is also
the temptation to forgo liberty and become a thing. This is an
inauspicious road, for he who takes it—passive, lost, ruined
—becomes henceforth the creature of another's will, frustrated in his transcendence and deprived of every value. But
it is in an easy road; on it one avoids the strain involved in
undertaking an authentic existence. When man makes of
woman the *Other*, he may, then, expect her to manifest deep-
seated tendencies toward complicity. Thus, woman may fail
to lay claim to the status of subject because she lacks definite

resources, because she feels the necessary bond that ties her to man regardless of reciprocity, and because she is often very well pleased with her role as the *Other*.

But it will be asked at once: how did all this begin? It is easy to see that the duality of the sexes, like any duality, gives rise to conflict. And doubtless the winner will assume the status of absolute. But why should man have won from the start? It seems possible that women could have won the victory; or that the outcome of the conflict might never have been decided. How is it that this world has always belonged to the men and that things have begun to change only recently? Is this change a good thing? Will it bring about an equal sharing of the world between men and women?

These questions are not new, and they have often been answered. But the very fact that woman *is the Other* tends to cast suspicion upon all the justifications that men have ever been able to provide for it. These have all too evidently been dictated by men's interest. A little-known feminist of the seventeenth century, Poulain de la Barre, put it this way: "All that has been written about women by men should be suspect, for the men are at once judge and party to the lawsuit." Everywhere, at all times, the males have displayed their satisfaction in feeling that they are the lords of creation. "Blessed be God . . . that He did not make me a woman," say the Jews in their morning prayers, while their wives pray on a note of resignation: "Blessed be the Lord, who created me according to His will." The first among the blessings for which Plato thanked the gods was that he had been created free, not enslaved; the second, a man, not a woman. But the males could not enjoy this privilege fully unless they believed it to be founded on the absolute and the eternal; they sought to make the fact of their supremacy into a right. "Being men, those who have made and compiled the laws have favored their own sex, and jurists have elevated these laws into principles," to quote Poulain de la Barre once more.

Legislators, priests, philosophers, writers, and scientists have striven to show that the subordinate position of woman is willed in heaven and advantageous on earth. The religions invented by men reflect this wish for domination. In the legends of Eve and Pandora men have taken up arms against women. They have made use of philosophy and theology, as the quotations from Aristotle and St. Thomas have shown. Since ancient times satirists and moralists have delighted in

showing up the weaknesses of women. We are familiar with
the savage indictments hurled against women throughout
French literature. Montherlant, for example, follows the tradition of Jean de Meung, though with less gusto. This hostility may at times be well founded, often it is gratuitous; but
in truth it more or less successfully conceals a desire for
self-justification. As Montaigne says, "It is easier to accuse
one sex than to excuse the other." Sometimes what is going
on is clear enough. For instance, the Roman law limiting the
rights of woman cited "the imbecility, the instability of the
sex" just when the weakening of family ties seemed to
threaten the interests of male heirs. And in the effort to
keep the married woman under guardianship, appeal was
made in the sixteenth century to the authority of St. Augus-
tine, who declared that "woman is a creature neither decisive
nor constant," at a time when the single woman was thought
capable of managing her property. Montaigne understood
clearly how arbitrary and unjust was woman's appointed lot:
"Women are not in the wrong when they decline to accept
the rules laid down for them, since the men make these rules
without consulting them. No wonder intrigue and strife
abound." But he did not go so far as to champion their
cause.

It was only later, in the eighteenth century, that genu-
inely democratic men began to view the matter objectively.
Diderot, among others, strove to show that woman is, like
man, a human being. Later John Stuart Mill came fervently
to her defense. But these philosophers displayed unusual impartiality. In the nineteenth century the feminist quarrel
became again a quarrel of partisans. One of the consequences
of the industrial revolution was the entrance of women into
productive labor, and it was just here that the claims of the
feminists emerged from the realm of theory and acquired an
economic basis, while their opponents became the more
aggressive. Although landed property lost power to some
extent, the bourgeoisie clung to the old morality that found
the guarantee of private property in the solidity of the family.
Woman was ordered back into the home the more harshly as
her emancipation became a real menace. Even within the
working class the men endeavored to restrain woman's liberation, because they began to see the women as dangerous
competitors—the more so because they were accustomed to
work for lower wages.

In proving woman's inferiority, the antifeminists then began to draw not only upon religion, philosophy, and theology, as before, but also upon science—biology, experimental psychology, etc. At most they were willing to grant "equality in difference" to the *other* sex. That profitable formula is most significant; it is precisely like the "equal but separate" formula of the Jim Crow laws aimed at the North American Negroes. As is well known, this so-called equalitarian segregation has resulted only in the most extreme discrimination. The similarity just noted is in no way due to chance, for whether it is a race, a caste, a class, or a sex that is reduced to a position of inferiority, the methods of justification are the same. "The eternal feminine" corresponds to "the black soul" and to "the Jewish character." True, the Jewish problem is on the whole very different from the other two—to the anti-Semite the Jew is not so much an inferior as he is an enemy for whom there is to be granted no place on earth, for whom annihilation is the fate desired. But there are deep similarities between the situation of woman and that of the Negro. Both are being emancipated today from a like paternalism, and the former master class wishes to "keep them in their place"—that is, the place chosen for them. In both cases the former masters lavish more or less sincere eulogies, either on the virtues of "the good Negro" with his dormant, childish, merry soul—the submissive Negro—or on the merits of the woman who is "truly feminine"—that is, frivolous, infantile, irresponsible —the submissive woman. In both cases the dominant class bases its argument on a state of affairs that it has itself created. As George Bernard Shaw puts it, in substance, "The American white relegates the black to the rank of shoeshine boy; and he concludes from this that the black is good for nothing but shining shoes." This vicious circle is met with in all analogous circumstances; when an individual (or a group of individuals) is kept in a situation of inferiority, the fact is that he *is* inferior. But the significance of the verb *to be* must be rightly understood here; it is in bad faith to give it a static value when it really has the dynamic Hegelian sense of "to have become." Yes, women on the whole *are* today inferior to men; that is, their situation affords them fewer possibilities. The question is: should that state of affairs continue?

Many men hope that it will continue; not all have given

up the battle. The conservative bourgeoisie still see in the emancipation of women a menace to their morality and their interests. Some men dread feminine competition. Recently a male student wrote in the *Hebdo-Latin*: "Every woman student who goes into medicine or law robs us of a job." He never questioned his rights in this world. And economic interests are not the only ones concerned. One of the benefits that oppression confers upon the oppressors is that the most humble among them is made to *feel* superior; thus, a "poor white" in the South can console himself with the thought that he is not a "dirty nigger"—and the more prosperous whites cleverly exploit this pride.

Similarly, the most mediocre of males feels himself a demigod as compared with women. It was much easier for M. de Montherlant to think himself a hero when he faced women (and women chosen for his purpose) than when he was obliged to act the man among men—something many women have done better than he, for that matter. And in September 1948, in one of his articles in the *Figaro littéraire*, Claude Mauriac—whose great originality is admired by all—could write regarding woman: "*We* listen on a tone [*sic!*] of polite indifference . . . to the most brilliant among them, well knowing that her wit reflects more or less luminously ideas that come from *us*." Evidently the speaker referred to is not reflecting the ideas of Mauriac himself, for no one knows of his having any. It may be that she reflects ideas originating with men, but then, even among men there are those who have been known to appropriate ideas not their own; and one can well ask whether Claude Mauriac might not find more interesting a conversation reflecting Descartes, Marx, or Gide rather than himself. What is really remarkable is that by using the questionable *we* he identifies himself with St. Paul, Hegel, Lenin, and Nietzsche, and from the lofty eminence of their grandeur looks down disdainfully upon the bevy of women who make bold to converse with him on a footing of equality. In truth, I know of more than one woman who would refuse to suffer with patience Mauriac's "tone of polite indifference."

I have lingered on this example because the masculine attitude is here displayed with disarming ingenuousness. But men profit in many more subtle ways from the otherness, the alterity of woman. Here is miraculous balm for those afflicted with an inferiority complex, and indeed no one is more arrogant toward women, more aggressive or scornful, than the man who is anxious about his virility. Those who are not fear-ridden in the presence of their fellow men are much more disposed to recognize a fellow creature in woman; but even to these the myth of Woman, the Other, is precious for many reasons. They cannot be blamed for not cheerfully relinquishing all the benefits they derive from the myth, for they realize what they would lose in relinquishing woman as they fancy her to be, while they fail to realize what they have to gain from the woman of tomorrow. Refusal to pose oneself as the Subject, unique and absolute, requires great self-denial. Furthermore, the vast majority of men make no such claim explicitly. They do not *postulate* woman as inferior, for today they are too thoroughly imbued with the ideal of democracy not to recognize all human beings as equals.

In the bosom of the family, woman seems in the eyes of childhood and youth to be clothed in the same social dignity as the adult males. Later on, the young man, desiring and loving, experiences the resistance, the independence of the woman desired and loved; in marriage, he respects woman as wife and mother, and in the concrete events of conjugal life she stands there before him as a free being. He can therefore feel that social subordination as between the sexes no longer exists and that on the whole, in spite of differences, woman is an equal. As, however, he observes some points of inferiority—the most important being unfitness for the professions—he attributes these to natural causes. When he is in a co-operative and benevolent relation with woman, his theme is the principle of abstract equality, and he does not base his attitude upon such inequality as may exist. But when he is in conflict with her, the situation is reversed: his theme will be the existing inequality, and he will even take it as justification for denying abstract equality.

So it is that many men will affirm as if in good faith that women *are* the equals of man and that they have nothing to clamor for, while *at the same time* they will say that women can never be the equals of man and that their demands are in vain. It is, in point of fact, a difficult matter for man to realize the extreme importance of social discriminations which seem outwardly insignificant but which produce in woman moral and intellectual effects so profound that they appear to spring from her original nature. The most sympathetic of men never fully comprehend woman's concrete situation. And there is no reason to put much trust in the men when they rush to the defense of privileges whose full extent they can hardly measure. We shall not, then, permit ourselves to be intimidated by the number and violence of the attacks launched against women, nor to be entrapped by the self-seeking eulogies bestowed on the "true woman," nor to profit by the enthusiasm for woman's destiny manifested by men who would not for the world have any part of it.

We should consider the arguments of the feminists with no less suspicion, however, for very often their controversial aim deprives them of all real value. If the "woman question" seems trivial, it is because masculine arrogance has made of it a "quarrel"; and when quarreling one no longer reasons well. People have tirelessly sought to prove that woman is superior, inferior, or equal to man. Some say that, having been created after Adam, she is evidently a secondary being; others say on the contrary that Adam was only a rough draft and that God succeeded in producing the human being in perfection when He created Eve. Woman's brain is smaller; yes, but it is relatively larger. Christ was made a man; yes, but perhaps for his greater humility. Each argument at once suggests its opposite, and both are often fallacious. If we are to gain understanding, we must get out of these ruts; we must discard the vague notions of superiority, inferiority, equality which have hitherto corrupted every discussion of the subject and start afresh.

Very well, but just how shall we pose the question? And, to begin with, who are we to propound it at all? Man is at once judge and party to the case; but so is woman. What we need is an angel—neither man nor woman—but where shall we find one? Still, the angel would be poorly qualified to speak, for an angel is ignorant of all the basic facts involved in the problem. With a hermaphrodite we should be no better off, for here the situation is most peculiar; the hermaphrodite is not really the combination of a whole man and a whole woman, but consists of parts of each and thus is neither. It looks to me as if there are, after all, certain women who are best qualified to elucidate the situation of woman. Let us not be misled by the sophism that because Epimenides was a Cretan he was necessarily a liar; it is not a mysterious essence that compels men and women to act in good or in bad faith, it is their situation that inclines them more or less toward the search for truth. Many of today's women, fortunate in the restoration of all the privileges pertaining to the estate of the human being, can afford the luxury of impartiality—we even recognize its necessity. We are no longer like our partisan elders; by and large we have won the game. In recent debates on the status of women the United Nations has persistently maintained that the equality of the sexes is now becoming a reality, and already some of us have never had to sense in our femininity an inconvenience or an obstacle. Many problems appear to us to be more pressing than those which concern us in particular, and this detachment even allows us to hope that our attitude will be objective. Still, we know the feminine world more intimately than do the men because we have our roots in it, we grasp more immediately than do men what it means to a human being to be feminine, and we are more concerned with such knowledge. I have said that there are more pressing problems, but this does not prevent us from seeing some importance in asking how the fact of being women will affect our lives. What opportunities precisely have been given us and what withheld? What fate awaits our younger sisters, and what directions should they take? It is significant that books by women on women are in general animated in our day less by a wish to demand our rights than by an effort toward clarity and understanding. As we emerge from an era of excessive controversy, this book is offered as one attempt among others to confirm that statement.

But it is doubtless impossible to approach any human problem with a mind free from bias. The way in which questions are put, the points of view assumed, presuppose a relativity of interest; all characteristics imply values, and every objective description, so called, implies an ethical background. Rather than attempt to conceal principles more or less definitely implied, it is better to state them openly at the beginning. This will make it unnecessary to specify on every page in just what sense one uses such words as *superior, inferior, better, worse, progress, reaction*, and the like. If we survey some of the works on woman, we note that one of the points of view most frequently adopted is that of the public good, the general interest; and one always means by this the benefit of society as one wishes it to be maintained or established. For our part, we hold that the only public good is that which assures the private good of the citizens; we shall pass judgment on institutions according to their effectiveness in giving concrete opportunities to individuals. But we do not confuse the idea of private interest with that of happiness, although that is another common point of view. Are not women of the harem more happy than women voters? Is not the housekeeper happier than the working-woman? It is not too clear just what the word *happy* really means and still less what true values it may mask. There is no possibility of measuring the happiness of others, and it is always easy to describe as happy the situation in which one wishes to place them.

In particular those who are condemned to stagnation are often pronounced happy on the pretext that happiness consists in being at rest. This notion we reject, for our perspective is that of existentialist ethics. Every subject plays his part as such specifically through exploits or projects that serve as a mode of transcendence; he achieves liberty only through a continual reaching out toward other liberties. There is no justification for present existence other than its expansion into an indefinitely open future. Every time transcendence falls back into immanence, stagnation, there is a degradation of existence into the *"en-soi"*—the brutish life of subjection to given conditions—and of liberty into constraint and contingence. This downfall represents a moral fault if the subject consents to it; if it is inflicted upon him, it spells frustration and oppression. In both cases it is an absolute evil. Every individual concerned to justify his existence feels that his existence involves an undefined need to transcend himself, to engage in freely chosen projects.

Now, what peculiarly signalizes the situation of woman is that she—a free and autonomous being like all human creatures—nevertheless finds herself living in a world where men compel her to assume the status of the Other. They propose to stabilize her as object and to doom her to immanence since her transcendence is to be overshadowed and forever transcended by another ego (*conscience*) which is essential and sovereign. The drama of woman lies in this conflict between the fundamental aspirations of every subject (ego)—who always regards the self as the essential—and the compulsions of a situation in which she is the inessential. How can a human being in woman's situation attain fulfillment? What roads are open to her? Which are blocked?

How can independence be recovered in a state of dependency? What circumstances limit woman's liberty and how can they be overcome? These are the fundamental questions on which I would fain throw some light. This means that I am interested in the fortunes of the individual as defined not in terms of happiness but in terms of liberty.

• • •

"No, woman is not our brother; through indolence and depravity we have made of her a being apart, unknown, having no weapon other than her sex, which not only means constant strife but is moreover an unfair weapon of the eternal little slave's mistrust—adoring or hating, but never our frank companion, a being set apart as if in *esprit de corps* and freemasonry."

Many men would still subscribe to these words of Laforgue; many think that there will always be "strife and dispute," as Montaigne put it, and that fraternity will never be possible. The fact is that today neither men nor women are satisfied with each other. But the question is to know whether there is an original curse that condemns them to rend each other or whether the conflicts in which they are opposed merely mark a transitional moment in human history.

We have seen that in spite of legends no physiological destiny imposes an eternal hostility upon Male and Female as such; even the famous praying mantis devours her male only for want of other food and for the good of the species: it is to this, the species, that all individuals are subordinated, from the top to the bottom of the scale of animal life. Moreover, humanity is something more than a mere species: it is a historical development; it is to be defined by the manner in which it deals with its natural, fixed characteristics, its *facticité*. Indeed, even with the most extreme bad faith in the world, it is impossible to demonstrate the existence of a rivalry between the human male and female of a truly physiological nature. Further, their hostility may be allocated rather to that intermediate terrain between biology and psychology: psychoanalysis. Woman, we are told, envies man his penis and wishes to castrate him; but the childish desire for the penis is important in the life of the adult woman only if she feels her femininity as a mutilation; and then it is as a symbol of all the privileges of manhood that she wishes to

appropriate the male organ. We may readily agree that her
dream of castration has this symbolic significance: she
wishes, it is thought, to deprive the male of his transcendence.

But her desire, as we have seen, is much more ambiguous:
she wishes, in a contradictory fashion, *to have* this transcendence, which is to suppose that she at once respects it
and denies it, that she intends at once to throw herself into
it and keep it within herself. This is to say that the drama
does not unfold on a sexual level; further, sexuality has never
seemed to us to define a destiny, to furnish in itself the key
to human behavior, but to express the totality of a situation
that it only helps to define. The battle of the sexes is not
immediately implied in the anatomy of man and woman. The
truth is that when one evokes it, one takes for granted that in
the timeless realm of Ideas a battle is being waged between
those vague essences the Eternal Feminine and the Eternal
Masculine; and one neglects the fact that this titanic combat
assumes on earth two totally different forms, corresponding
with two different moments of history.

The woman who is shut up in immanence endeavors to
hold man in that prison also; thus the prison will be confused
with the world, and woman will no longer suffer from being
confined there: mother, wife, sweetheart are the jailers.
Society, being codified by man, decrees that woman is inferior: she can do away with this inferiority only by destroying the male's superiority. She sets about mutilating, dominating man, she contradicts him, she denies his truth and his
values. But in doing this she is only defending herself; it was
neither a changeless essence nor a mistaken choice that
doomed her to immanence, to inferiority. They were imposed
upon her. All oppression creates a state of war. And this is
no exception. The existent who is regarded as inessential
cannot fail to demand the re-establishment of her sovereignty.

Today the combat takes a different shape; instead of
wishing to put man in a prison, woman endeavors to escape
from one; she no longer seeks to drag him into the realms of
immanence but to emerge, herself, into the light of transcendence. Now the attitude of the males creates a new conflict: it is with a bad grace that the man lets her go. He is
very well pleased to remain the sovereign subject, the absolute superior, the essential being; he refuses to accept his

companion as an equal in any concrete way. She replies to his lack of confidence in her by assuming an aggressive attitude. It is no longer a question of a war between individuals each shut up in his or her sphere: a caste claiming its rights goes over the top and it is resisted by the privileged caste. Here two transcendences are face to face; instead of displaying mutual recognition, each free being wishes to dominate the other.

This difference of attitude is manifest on the sexual plane as on the spiritual plane. The "feminine" woman in making herself prey tries to reduce man, also, to her carnal passivity; she occupies herself in catching him in her trap, in enchaining him by means of the desire she arouses in him in submissively making herself a thing. The emancipated woman, on the contrary, wants to be active, a taker, and refuses the passivity man means to impose on her. Thus Elise and her emulators deny the values of the activities of virile type; they put the flesh above the spirit, contingence above liberty, their routine wisdom above creative audacity. But the "modern" woman accepts masculine values: she prides herself on thinking, taking action, working, creating, on the same terms as men; instead of seeking to disparage them, she declares herself their equal.

In so far as she expresses herself in definite action, this claim is legitimate, and male insolence must then bear the blame. But in men's defense it must be said that women are wont to confuse the issue. A Mabel Dodge Luhan intended to subjugate D. H. Lawrence by her feminine charms so as to dominate him spiritually thereafter; many women, in order to show by their successes their equivalence to men, try to secure male support by sexual means; they play on both sides, demanding old-fashioned respect and modern esteem, banking on their old magic and their new rights. It is understandable that a man becomes irritated and puts himself on the defensive; but he is also double-dealing when he requires woman to play the game fairly while he denies them the indispensable trump cards through distrust and hostility. Indeed, the struggle cannot be clearly drawn between them, since woman is opaque in her very being; she stands before man not as a subject but as an object paradoxically endued with subjectivity; she takes herself simultaneously as *self* and as *other*, a contradiction that entails baffling consequences. When she makes weapons at once of her weakness

and of her strength, it is not a matter of designing calculation: she seeks salvation spontaneously in the way that has
been imposed on her, that of passivity, at the same time
when she is actively demanding her sovereignty; and no
doubt this procedure is unfair tactics, but it is dictated to
her by the ambiguous situation assigned her. Man, however,
becomes indignant when he treats her as a free and independent being and then realizes that she is still a trap for
him; if he gratifies and satisfies her in her posture as prey,
he finds her claims to autonomy irritating; whatever he does,
he feels tricked and she feels wronged.

The quarrel will go on as long as men and women fail to
recognize each other as peers; that is to say, as long as femininity is perpetuated as such. Which sex is the more eager to
maintain it? Woman, who is being emancipated from it,
wishes none the less to retain its privileges; and man, in that
case, wants her to assume its limitations. "It is easier to
accuse one sex than to excuse the other," says Montaigne. It
is vain to apportion praise and blame. The truth is that if the
vicious circle is so hard to break, it is because the two sexes
are each the victim at once of the other and of itself. Between two adversaries confronting each other in their pure
liberty, an agreement could be easily reached: the more so as
the war profits neither. But the complexity of the whole affair
derives from the fact that each camp is giving aid and comfort
to the enemy; woman is pursuing a dream of submission,
man a dream of identification. Want of authenticity does not
pay: each blames the other for the unhappiness he or she has
incurred in yielding to the temptations of the easy way; what
man and woman loathe in each other is the shattering frustration of each one's own bad faith and baseness.

We have seen why men enslaved women in the first
place; the devaluation of femininity has been a necessary
step in human evolution, but it might have led to collaboration between the two sexes; oppression is to be explained
by the tendency of the existent to flee from himself by means
of identification with the other, whom he oppresses to that
end. In each individual man that tendency exists today; and
the vast majority yield to it. The husband wants to find himself in his wife, the lover in his mistress, in the form of a
stone image; he is seeking in her the myth of his virility, of
his sovereignty, of his immediate reality. "My husband never
goes to the movies," says his wife, and the dubious masculine

opinion is graved in the marble of eternity. But he is himself
the slave of his double: what an effort to build up an image
in which he is always in danger! In spite of everything his
success in this depends upon the capricious freedom of
women: he must constantly try to keep this propitious to
him. Man is concerned with the effort to appear male, important, superior; he pretends so as to get pretense in return;
he, too, is aggressive, uneasy; he feels hostility for women
because he is afraid of them, he is afraid of them because he
is afraid of the personage, the image, with which he identifies himself. What time and strength he squanders in liqui-
dating, sublimating, transferring complexes, in talking about
women, in seducing them, in fearing them! He would be
liberated himself in their liberation. But this is precisely what
he dreads. And so he obstinately persists in the mystifications
intended to keep woman in her chains.

That she is being tricked, many men have realized. "What
a misfortune to be a woman! And yet the misfortune, when
one is a woman, is at bottom not to comprehend that it is
one," says Kierkegaard. For a long time there have been
efforts to disguise this misfortune. For example, guardianship
has been done away with: women have been given "protectors," and if they are invested with the rights of the old-
time guardians, it is in woman's own interest. To forbid her
working, to keep her at home, is to defend her against herself and to assure her happiness. We have seen what poetic
veils are thrown over her monotonous burdens of housekeeping and maternity: in exchange for her liberty she has
received the false treasures of her "femininity." Balzac illustrates this maneuver very well in counseling man to treat
her as a slave while persuading her that she is a queen. Less
cynical, many men try to convince themselves that she is
really privileged. There are American sociologists who seri-
ously teach today the theory of "low-class gain." In France,
also, it has often been proclaimed—although in a less scientific manner—that the workers are very fortunate in not
being obliged to "keep up appearances" and still more so the
bums who can dress in rags and sleep on the sidewalks,
pleasures forbidden to the Count de Beaumont and the
Wendels. Like the carefree wretches gaily scratching at their
vermin, like the merry Negroes laughing under the lash and
those joyous Tunisian Arabs burying their starved children
with a smile, woman enjoys that incomparable privilege:

irresponsibility. Free from troublesome burdens and cares, she obviously has "the better part." But it is disturbing that with an obstinate perversity—connected no doubt with original sin—down through the centuries and in all countries, the people who have the better part are always crying to their benefactors: "It is too much! I will be satisfied with yours!" But the munificent capitalists, the generous colonists, the superb males, stick to their guns: "Keep the better part, hold on to it!"

It must be admitted that the males find in woman more complicity than the oppressor usually finds in the oppressed. And in bad faith they take authorization from this to declare that she has *desired* the destiny they have imposed on her. We have seen that all the main features of her training combine to bar her from the roads of revolt and adventure. Society in general—beginning with her respected parents—lies to her by praising the lofty values of love, devotion, the gift of herself, and then concealing from her the fact that neither lover nor husband nor yet her children will be inclined to accept the burdensome charge of all that. She cheerfully believes these lies because they invite her to follow the easy slope: in this others commit their worst crime against her; throughout her life from childhood on, they damage and corrupt her by designating as her true vocation this submission, which is the temptation of every existent in the anxiety of liberty. If a child is taught idleness by being amused all day long and never being led to study, or shown its usefulness, it will hardly be said, when he grows up, that he chose to be incapable and ignorant; yet this is how woman is brought up, without ever being impressed with the necessity of taking charge of her own existence. So she readily lets herself come to count on the protection, love, assistance, and supervision of others, she lets herself be fascinated with the hope of self-realization without *doing* anything. She does wrong in yielding to the temptation; but man is in no position to blame her, since he has led her into the temptation. When conflict arises between them, each will hold the other responsible for the situation; she will reproach him with having made her what she is: "No one taught me to reason or to earn my own living"; he will reproach her with having accepted the consequences: "You don't know anything, you are an incompetent," and so on. Each sex thinks it can justify itself by taking the offensive; but the wrongs done by one do not make the other innocent.

The innumerable conflicts that set men and women against one another come from the fact that neither is prepared to assume all the consequences of this situation which the one has offered and the other accepted. The doubtful concept of "equality in inequality," which the one uses to mask his despotism and the other to mask her cowardice, does not stand the test of experience: in their exchanges, woman appeals to the theoretical equality she has been guaranteed, and man the concrete inequality that exists. The result is that in every association an endless debate goes on concerning the ambiguous meaning of the words *give* and *take*: she complains of giving her all, he protests that she takes his all. Woman has to learn that exchanges—it is a fundamental law of political economy—are based on the value the merchandise offered has for the buyer, and not for the seller: she has been deceived in being persuaded that her worth is priceless. The truth is that for man she is an amusement, a pleasure, company, an inessential boon; he is for her the meaning, the justification of her existence. The exchange, therefore, is not of two items of equal value.

This inequality will be especially brought out in the fact that the time they spend together—which fallaciously seems to be the same time—does not have the same value for both partners. During the evening the lover spends with his mistress he could be doing something of advantage to his career, seeing friends, cultivating business relationships, seeking recreation; for a man normally integrated in society, time is a positive value: money, reputation, pleasure. For the idle, bored woman, on the contrary, it is a burden she wishes to get rid of; when she succeeds in killing time, it is a benefit to her: the man's presence is pure profit. In a liaison what most clearly interests the man, in many cases, is the sexual benefit he gets from it: if need be, he can be content to spend no more time with his mistress than is required for the sexual act; but—with exceptions—what she, on her part, wants is to kill all the excess time she has on her hands; and—like the storekeeper who will not sell potatoes unless the customer will take turnips also—she will not yield her body unless her lover will take hours of conversation and "going out" into the bargain. A balance is reached if, on the whole, the cost does not seem too high to the man, and this depends, of course, on the strength of his desire and the importance he gives to what is to be sacrificed. But if the woman demands—offers—too much time, she becomes wholly intrusive, like the river overflowing its banks, and the man will prefer to have nothing rather than too much. Then she reduces her demands; but very often the balance is reached at the cost of a double tension: she feels that the man has "had" her at a bargain, and he thinks her price is too high. This analysis of course, is put in somewhat humorous terms; but—except for those affairs of jealous and exclusive passion in which the man wants total possession of the woman—this conflict constantly appears in cases of affection, desire, and even love. He always has "other things to do" with his time; whereas she has time to burn; and he considers much of the time she gives him not as a gift but as a burden.

As a rule he consents to assume the burden because he knows very well that he is on the privileged side, he has a bad conscience; and if he is of reasonable good will he tries to compensate for the inequality by being generous. He prides himself on his compassion, however, and at the first clash he treats the woman as ungrateful and thinks, with some irritation: "I'm too good to her." She feels she is behaving like a beggar when she is convinced of the high value of her gifts, and that humiliates her.

Here we find the explanation of the cruelty that woman often shows she is capable of practicing; she has a good conscience because she is on the unprivileged side; she feels she is under no obligation to deal gently with the favored caste, and her only thought is to defend herself. She will even be very happy if she has occasion to show her resentment to a lover who has not been able to satisfy all her demands: since he does not give her enough, she takes savage delight in taking back everything from him. At this point the wounded lover suddenly discovers the value *in toto* of a liaison each moment of which he held more or less in contempt: he is ready to promise her everything, even though he will feel exploited again when he has to make good. He accuses his mistress of blackmailing him: she calls him stingy; both feel wronged.

Once again it is useless to apportion blame and excuses: justice can never be done in the midst of injustice. A colonial administrator has no possibility of acting rightly toward the natives, nor a general toward his soldiers; the only solution is to be neither colonist nor military chief; but a man could not prevent himself from being a man. So there he is, culpable in spite of himself and laboring under the effects of a fault he did not himself commit; and here she is, victim and shrew in spite of herself. Sometimes he rebels and becomes cruel, but then he makes himself an accomplice of the injustice, and the fault becomes really his. Sometimes he lets himself be annihilated, devoured, by his demanding victim; but in that case he feels duped. Often he stops at a compromise that at once belittles him and leaves him ill at ease. A well-disposed man will be more tortured by the situation than the woman herself: in a sense it is always better to be on the side of the vanquished; but if she is well-disposed also, incapable of self-sufficiency, reluctant to crush the man with the weight of her destiny, she struggles in hopeless confusion.

In daily life we meet with an abundance of these cases which are incapable of satisfactory solution because they are determined by unsatisfactory conditions. A man who is compelled to go on materially and morally supporting a woman he no longer loves feels he is victimized; but if he abandons without resources the woman who has pledged her whole life to him, she will be quite as unjustly victimized. The evil originates not in the perversity of individuals—and bad faith first appears when each blames the other—it originates rather in a situation against which all individual action is powerless. Women are "clinging," they are a dead weight, and they suffer for it; the point is that their situation is like that of a parasite sucking out the living strength of another organism. Let them be provided with living strength of their own, let them have the means to attack the world and wrest from it their own subsistence, and their dependence will be abolished—that of man also. There is no doubt that both men and women will profit greatly from the new situation.

A world where men and women would be equal is easy to visualize, for that precisely is what the Soviet Revolution *promised*: women raised and trained exactly like men were to work under the same conditions and for the same wages. Erotic liberty was to be recognized by custom, but the sexual act was not to be considered a "service" to be paid for; woman was to be *obliged* to provide herself with other ways of earning a living; marriage was to be based on a free agreement that the spouses could break at will; maternity was to be voluntary, which meant that contraception and abortion were to be authorized and that, on the other hand, all mothers and their children were to have exactly the same rights, in or out of marriage; pregnancy leaves were to be paid for by the State, which would assume charge of the children, signifying not that they would be *taken away* from their parents, but that they would not be *abandoned* to them.

But is it enough to change laws, institutions, customs, public opinion, and the whole social context, for men and women to become truly equal? "Women will always be women," say the skeptics. Other seers prophesy that in casting off their femininity they will not succeed in changing themselves into men and they will become monsters. This would be to admit that the woman of today is a creation of nature; it must be repeated once more that in human society nothing is natural and that woman, like much else, is a product elaborated by civilization. The intervention of others in her destiny is fundamental: if this action took a different direction, it would produce a quite different result. Woman is determined not by her hormones or by mysterious instincts, but by the manner in which her body and her relation to the world are modified through the action of others than herself. The abyss that separates the adolescent boy and girl has been deliberately opened out between them since earliest childhood; later on, woman could not be other than what she *was made*, and that past was bound to shadow her for life. If we appreciate its influence, we see clearly that her destiny is not predetermined for all eternity.

We must not believe, certainly, that a change in woman's economic condition alone is enough to transform her, though this factor has been and remains the basic factor in her evolution; but until it has brought about the moral, social, cultural, and other consequences that it promises and requires, the new woman cannot appear. At this moment they have been realized nowhere, in Russia no more than in France or the United States; and this explains why the woman of today is torn between the past and the future. She appears most often as a "true woman" disguised as a man, and she feels herself as ill at ease in her flesh as in her masculine garb. She must shed her old skin and cut her own new clothes. This she could do only through a social evolution.

No single educator could fashion a *female human being* today who would be the exact homologue of the *male human being*; if she is raised like a boy, the young girl feels she is an oddity and thereby she is given a new kind of sex specification. Stendhal understood this when he said: "The forest must be planted all at once." But if we imagine, on the contrary, a society in which the equality of the sexes would be concretely realized, this equality would find new expression in each individual.

If the little girl were brought up from the first with the same demands and rewards, the same severity and the same freedom, as her brothers, taking part in the same studies, the same games, promised the same future, surrounded with women and men who seemed to her undoubted equals, the meanings of the castration complex and of the Œdipus complex would be profoundly modified. Assuming on the same basis as the father the material and moral responsibility of the couple, the mother would enjoy the same lasting prestige; the child would perceive around her an androgynous world and not a masculine world. Were she emotionally more attracted to her father—which is not even sure—her love for him would be tinged with a will to emulation and not a feeling of powerlessness; she would not be oriented toward passivity. Authorized to test her powers in work and sports, competing actively with the boys, she would not find the absence of the penis—compensated by the promise of a child —enough to give rise to an inferiority complex; correlatively, the boy would not have a superiority complex if it were not instilled into him and if he looked up to women with as much respect as to men. The little girl would not seek sterile compensation in narcissism and dreaming, she would not take her fate for granted; she would be interested in what she was *doing*, she would throw herself without reserve into undertakings.

I have already pointed out how much easier the transformation of puberty would be if she looked beyond it, like the boys, toward a free adult future: menstruation horrifies her only because it is an abrupt descent into femininity. She would also take her young eroticism in much more tranquil fashion if she did not feel a frightened disgust for her destiny as a whole; coherent sexual information would do much to help her over this crisis. And thanks to coeducational schooling, the august mystery of Man would have no occasion to enter her mind: it would be eliminated by everyday familiarity and open rivalry.

Objections raised against this system always imply respect for sexual taboos; but the effort to inhibit all sex curiosity and pleasure in the child is quite useless; one succeeds only in creating repressions, obsessions, neuroses. The excessive sentimentality, homosexual fervors, and platonic crushes of adolescent girls, with all their train of silliness and frivolity, are much more injurious than a little childish sex play and a few definite sex experiences. It would be beneficial above all for the young girl not to be influenced against taking charge herself of her own existence, for then she would not seek a demigod in the male—merely a comrade, a friend, a partner. Eroticism and love would take on the nature of free transcendence and not that of resignation; she could experience them as a relation between equals. There is no intention, of course, to remove by a stroke of the pen all the difficulties that the child has to overcome in changing into an adult; the most intelligent, the most tolerant education could not relieve the child of experiencing things for herself; what could be asked is that obstacles should not be piled gratuitously in her path. Progress is already shown by the fact that "vicious" little girls are no longer cauterized with a red-hot iron. Psychoanalysis has given parents some instruction, but the conditions under which, at the present time, the sexual training and initiation of woman are accomplished are so deplorable that none of the objections advanced against the idea of a radical change could be considered valid. It is not a question of abolishing in woman the contingencies and miseries of the human condition, but of giving her the means for transcending them.

Woman is the victim of no mysterious fatality; the peculiarities that identify her as specifically a woman get their importance from the significance placed upon them. They can be surmounted, in the future, when they are regarded in new perspectives. Thus, as we have seen, through her erotic experience woman feels—and often detests—the domination of the male; but this is no reason to conclude that her ovaries condemn her to live forever on her knees. Virile aggressiveness seems like a lordly privilege only within a system that in its entirety conspires to affirm masculine sovereignty; and woman *feels* herself profoundly passive in the sexual act only because she already *thinks* of herself as such. Many modern women who lay claim to their dignity as human beings still envisage their erotic life from the standpoint of a tradition of slavery: since it seems to them humiliating to lie beneath the man, to be penetrated by him, they grow tense in frigidity. But if the reality were different, the meaning expressed symbolically in amorous gestures and postures would be different, too: a woman who pays and dominates her lover can, for example, take pride in her superb idleness and consider that she is enslaving the male who is actively exerting himself. And here and now there are many sexually well-balanced couples whose notions of victory and defeat are giving place to the idea of an exchange.

As a matter of fact, man, like woman, is flesh, therefore passive, the plaything of his hormones and of the species, the restless prey of his desires. And she, like him, in the midst of the carnal fever, is a consenting, a voluntary gift, an activity; they live out in their several fashions the strange ambiguity of existence made body. In those combats where they think they confront one another, it is really against the self that each one struggles, projecting into the partner that part of the self which is repudiated; instead of living out the ambiguities of their situation, each tries to make the other bear the abjection and tries to reserve the honor for the self. If, however, both should assume the ambiguity with a clear-sighted modesty, correlative of an authentic pride, they would see each other as equals and would live out their erotic drama in amity. The fact that we are human beings is infinitely more important than all the peculiarities that distinguish human beings from one another; it is never the given that confers superiorities: "virtue," as the ancients called it, is defined at the level of "that which depends on us." In both sexes is played out the same drama of the flesh and the spirit, of finitude and transcendence; both are gnawed away by time and laid in wait for by death, they have the same essential need for one another; and they can gain from their liberty the same glory. If they were to taste it, they would no longer be tempted to dispute fallacious privileges, and fraternity between them could then come into existence.

I shall be told that all this is utopian fancy, because woman cannot be "made over" unless society has first made her really the equal of man. Conservatives have never failed in such circumstances to refer to that vicious circle; history, however, does not revolve. If a caste is kept in a state of inferiority, no doubt it remains inferior; but liberty can break the circle. Let the Negroes vote and they become worthy of having the vote: let woman be given responsibilities and she is able to assume them. The fact is that oppressors cannot be expected to make a move of gratuitous generosity; but at one time the revolt of the oppressed, at another time even the very evolution of the privileged caste itself, creates new situations; thus men have been led, in their own interest, to give partial emancipation to women: it remains only for women to continue their ascent, and the successes they are obtaining are an encouragement for them to do so. It seems almost certain that sooner or later they will arrive at complete economic and social equality, which will bring about an inner metamorphosis.

However this may be, there will be some to object that if such a world is possible it is not desirable. When woman is "the same" as her male, life will lose its salt and spice. This argument, also, has lost its novelty: those interested in perpetuating present conditions are always in tears about the marvelous past that is about to disappear, without having so much as a smile for the young future. It is quite true that doing away with the slave trade meant death to the great plantations, magnificent with azaleas and camellias, it meant ruin to the whole refined Southern civilization. The attics of time have received its rare old laces along with the clear pure voices of the Sistine *castrati*, and there is a certain "feminine charm" that is also on the way to the same dusty repository. I agree that he would be a barbarian indeed who failed to appreciate exquisite flowers, rare lace, the crystal-clear voice of the eunuch, and feminine charm.

When the "charming woman" shows herself in all her splendor, she is a much more exalting object than the "idiotic paintings, overdoors, scenery, showman's garish signs, popular chromos," that excited Rimbaud; adorned with the most modern artifices, beautified according to the newest techniques, she comes down from the remoteness of the ages, from Thebes, from Crete, from Chichén-Itzá; and she is also the totem set up deep in the African jungle; she is a helicopter and she is a bird; and there is this, the greatest wonder of all: under her tinted hair the forest murmur becomes a thought, and words issue from her breasts. Men stretch forth avid hands toward the marvel, but when they grasp it it is gone; the wife, the mistress, speak like everybody else through their mouths: their words are worth just what they are worth; their breasts also. Does such a fugitive miracle—and one so rare—justify us in perpetuating a situation that is baneful for both sexes? One can appreciate the beauty of flowers, the charm of women, and appreciate them at their true value; if these treasures cost blood or misery, they must be sacrificed.

But in truth this sacrifice seems to men a peculiarly heavy one; few of them really wish in their hearts for woman to succeed in making it; those among them who hold woman in contempt see in the sacrifice nothing for them to gain, those who cherish her see too much that they would lose. And it is true that the evolution now in progress threatens more than feminine charm alone: in beginning to exist for herself, woman will relinquish the function as double and mediator to which she owes her privileged place in the masculine universe; to man, caught between the silence of nature and the demanding presence of other free beings, a creature who is at once his like and a passive thing seems a great treasure. The guise in which he conceives his companion may be mythical, but the experiences for which she is the source or the pretext are none the less real: there are hardly any more precious, more intimate, more ardent. There is no denying that feminine dependence, inferiority, woe, give women their special character; assuredly woman's autonomy, if it spares men many troubles, will also deny them many conveniences; assuredly there are certain forms of the sexual adventure which will be lost in the world of tomorrow. But this does not mean that love, happiness, poetry, dream, will be banished from it.

Let us not forget that our lack of imagination always depopulates the future; for us it is only an abstraction; each one of us secretly deplores the absence there of the one who was himself. But the humanity of tomorrow will be living in its flesh and in its conscious liberty; that time will be its present and it will in turn prefer it. New relations of flesh and sentiment of which we have no conception will arise between the sexes; already, indeed, there have appeared between men and women friendships, rivalries, complicities, comradeships—chaste or sensual—which past centuries could not have conceived. To mention one point, nothing could seem to me more debatable than the opinion that dooms the new world to uniformity and hence to boredom. I fail to see that this present world is free from boredom or that liberty ever creates uniformity.

To begin with, there will always be certain differences between man and woman; her eroticism, and therefore her sexual world, have a special form of their own and therefore cannot fail to engender a sensuality, a sensitivity, of a special nature. This means that her relations to her own body, to that of the male, to the child, will never be identical with those the male bears to his own body, to that of the female, and to the child; those who make much of "equality in difference" could not with good grace refuse to grant me the possible existence of differences in equality. Then again, it is institutions that create uniformity. Young and pretty, the slaves of the harem are always the same in the sultan's embrace; Christianity gave eroticism its savor of sin and legend when it endowed the human female with a soul; if society restores her sovereign individuality to woman, it will not thereby destroy the power of love's embrace to move the heart.

It is nonsense to assert that revelry, vice, ecstasy, passion, would become impossible if man and woman were equal in concrete matters; the contradictions that put the flesh in opposition to the spirit, the instant to time, the swoon of immanence to the challenge of transcendence, the absolute of pleasure to the nothingness of forgetting, will never be resolved; in sexuality will always be materialized the tension, the anguish, the joy, the frustration, and the triumph of existence. To emancipate woman is to refuse to confine her to the relations she bears to man, not to deny them to her; let her have her independent existence and she will continue none the less to exist for him *also*: mutually recognizing each other as subject, each will yet remain for the other an *other*. The reciprocity of their relations will not do away with the miracles—desire, possession, love, dream, adventure —worked by the division of human beings into two separate categories; and the words that move us—giving, conquering, uniting—will not lose their meaning. On the contrary, when we abolish the slavery of half of humanity, together with the whole system of hypocrisy that it implies, then the "division" of humanity will reveal its genuine significance and the human couple will find its true form. "The direct, natural, necessary relation of human creatures is the *relation of man to woman,*" Marx has said. "The nature of this relation determines to what point man himself is to be considered as a *generic being,* as mankind; the relation of man to woman is the most natural relation of human being to human being. By it is shown, therefore, to what point the *natural* behavior of man has become *human* or to what point the *human* being has become his *natural* being, to what point his *human nature* has become his *nature.*"

The case could not be better stated. It is for man to establish the reign of liberty in the midst of the world of the given. To gain the supreme victory, it is necessary, for one thing, that by and through their natural differentiation men and women unequivocally affirm their brotherhood.

References

Note: An asterisk before an entry indicates that the item is among the selections abridged for this volume. The edition cited is the one from which abridgments were made.

*Adams, Charles Francis. 1854. *The Works of John Adams: With Life of the Author.* 10 volumes. Boston, Little Brown.

*Addams, Jane. 1907. *Newer Ideals of Peace.* New York, Macmillan.

————. 1910. *Twenty Years at Hull House.* New York, Macmillan.

Ahlstrom, Sidney. 1972. *A Religious History of the American People.* New Haven, Conn., Yale University Press.

Allport, Gordon W. 1942. *The Use of Personal Documents in Psychological Science.* Bulletin 49. New York, Social Science Research Council.

Ancilla, Sister Joseph. 1968. *The Political Theory of Mercy Otis Warren: A Study in American Constitutionalism.* Ph.D. Dissertation. St. Johns University.

Anonymous. 1895. Book review of *The Grasshoppers. The Athenaeum,* Journal of Literature, Science, the Fine Arts, Music and the Drama, No. 3522 (April 27, 1895).

Anthony, Katherine. 1954. *Susan B. Anthony: Her Personal History and Her Era.* Garden City, New York, Doubleday.

Anthony, Susan B. 1902. See *History of Woman Suffrage.*

Bardwick, Judith M. 1971. *Psychology of Women: A Study of Bio-Cultural Conflicts.* New York, Harper and Row.

Barnes, Gilbert Hobbs. 1957. *The Antislavery Impulse 1830–1844.* Gloucester, Mass., Peter Smith.

Barnes, Gilbert Hobbs, and Dwight L. Dumond. 1934. *Letters of Theodore Dwight Weld, Angelina Grimké Weld and Sarah Grimké 1822–1844.* Vol. 2. New York, Appleton-Century.

*Beauvoir, Simone de. 1957. *The Second Sex.* New York, Alfred A. Knopf.

————. 1959. *Memoirs of a Dutiful Daughter.* New York, World.

————. 1962. *The Prime of Life*. New York, World.

————. 1972. *The Coming of Age*. New York, G. P. Putnam's Sons.

*Bebel, August. 1910. *Woman and Socialism*. New York, Socialist Literature Company.

Bell, Quentin. 1972. *Virginia Woolf: A Biography*. New York, Harcourt Brace Jovanovich.

Benson, Lee. 1961. *The Concept of Jacksonian Democracy*. Princeton, N.J., Princeton University Press.

Benson, Mary. 1935. *Women in Eighteenth-Century America: A Study of Opinion and Social Usage*. New York, Columbia University Press.

Blackwell, Alice Stone. 1930. *Lucy Stone: Pioneer of Woman's Rights*. Boston, Little Brown.

*Blackwell, Antoinette Brown. 1875. *The Sexes throughout Nature*. New York, G. P. Putnam's Sons.

Blackwell, Elizabeth. 1894. *The Human Element in Sex, being a Medical Inquiry into the Relation of Sexual Physiology to Christian Morality*. London, J. & A. Churchill.

————. 1914. *Pioneer Work for Women*. New York, E. P. Dutton.

*Blackwell, Elizabeth, and Emily Blackwell. 1860. *Medicine as a Profession for Women*. New York, New York Infirmary for Women.

Blumberg, Dorothy Rose. 1966. *Florence Kelley: The Making of a Social Pioneer*. New York, Augustus M. Kelley.

Brenton, Myron. 1966. *The American Male*. New York, Coward-McCann.

Brewster-Smith, M., J. Block, and N. Haan, 1968. "Activism and Apathy in Contemporary Adolescents." In J. F. Adams, ed. *Understanding Adolescence*. Boston, Allyn and Bacon.

Brinton, Crane. 1959. *History of Western Morals*. New York, Harcourt Brace.

*Butterfield, L. H., ed. 1963. *The Adams Papers*, Series II: *Adams Family Correspondence*. Cambridge, Mass., Harvard University Press.

Calhoun, Arthur. 1918. *A Social History of the American Family*. 3 volumes. Cleveland, Arthur H. Clark.

Callahan, Sidney Cornelia. 1965. *The Illusion of Eve: Modern Woman's Quest for Identity*. New York, Sheed and Ward.

Catt, Carrie Chapman, and Nettie Rogers Shuler. 1926.

Woman Suffrage and Politics. New York, Charles Scribner's Sons.

Chafe, William. 1972. *The American Woman: Her Changing Social, Economic and Political Roles, 1920–1970.* New York, Oxford University Press.

Chapman, Maria Weston, ed. 1877. *Harriet Martineau's Autobiography.* Volume I. Boston, James R. Osgood.

Conway, Jill. 1964. "Jane Addams: An American Heroine." *Daedalus,* 93(2):761–800.

Coss, John Jacob, ed. 1924. *Autobiography of John Stuart Mill.* New York, Columbia University Press.

Cross, Whitney R, 1950. *The Burned-over District.* Ithaca, N. Y., Cornell University Press.

Daly, Mary. 1968. *The Church and the Second Sex.* New York, Harper & Row.

Degler, Carl N., ed. 1966. *Women and Economics* by Charlotte Perkins Gilman. New York, Harper & Row.

Dexter, Elisabeth A. 1931. *Colonial Women of Affairs: Women in Business and Professions in America before 1776.* Boston, Houghton, Mifflin.

———. 1950. *Career Women of America: 1776–1840.* Francestown, N. H.: M. Jones.

Donald, David. 1956. *Lincoln Reconsidered: Essays on the Civil War Era.* New York, Vintage Books.

Douglas, Emily Taft. 1970. *Margaret Sanger: Pioneer of the Future.* New York, Holt, Rinehart and Winston.

Drinnon, Joseph. 1961. *Rebel in Paradise.* Chicago, University of Chicago Press.

Elliot, Hugh S. R. 1910. *The Letters of John Stuart Mill.* London, Longmans, Green & Co.

*Engels, Friedrich. 1942. *The Origin of the Family, Private Property and the State.* New York, International Publishers.

Field, Vena Bernadette. 1931. *Constantia: A Study of the Life and Works of Judith Sargent Murray 1751–1820.* University of Maine Studies, Second Series, no. 17. Orono, Maine, University of Maine Press.

Flacks, Richard. 1967. "The Liberated Generation: an Exploration of the Roots of Student Protest." *Journal of Social Issues,* 23(3):52–75.

Fredrickson, George M. 1965. *The Inner Civil War: Northern Intellectuals and the Crisis of the Union.* New York, Harper & Row.

Flexner, Eleanor. 1959. *Century of Struggle: The Woman's Rights Movement in the United States*. Cambridge, Mass., Harvard University Press.

Friedan, Betty. 1963. *The Feminine Mystique*. New York, W. W. Norton.

Fuller, Arthur Buckminster. 1855. *Woman in the Nineteenth Century and Kindred Papers by Margaret Fuller Ossoli*. Boston, John P. Jewett.

*Fuller, Margaret. 1848. "The Great Lawsuit. Man versus Men. Woman versus Women." *The Dial*, 4(1):1–47.

*Gilman, Charlotte Perkins. 1898. *Women and Economics*. Boston, Small, Maynard.

——. 1900. *Concerning Children*. Boston, Small, Maynard.

——. 1911. *The Man-Made World or our Androcentric Culture*. New York, Charlton.

——. 1935. *The Living of Charlotte Perkins Gilman*. New York, D. Appleton-Century.

Gilson, Sarah. 1909. *Antoinette Brown Blackwell: Biographical Sketch*. Unpublished manuscript. Cambridge, Mass., Schlesinger Library, Radcliffe College.

Godwin, William. 1930. *Memoirs of Mary Wollstonecraft*. New York, Richard R. Smith.

Goldman, Emma. 1931. *Living My Life*. New York, A. A. Knopf.

——. 1970. *The Traffic in Women and Other Essays on Feminism*. New York, Times Change Press.

Grimes, Alan P. 1967. *The Puritan Ethic and Woman Suffrage*. New York, Oxford University Press.

*Grimké, Angelina Emily. 1836. "An Appeal to the Christian Women of the South." *The Anti-Slavery Examiner*, 1(2):16–26.

*——. 1836. *Letters to Catherine Beecher*. Boston, Isaac Knapp.

*Grimké, Sarah. 1838. *Letters on the Equality of the Sexes and the Condition of Women*. Boston, Isaac Knapp.

Grylls, R. Glynn. 1938. *Mary Shelley*. London, Oxford University Press.

Gusfield, Joseph R. 1963. *Symbolic Crusade: Status Politics and the American Temperance Movement*. Urbana, University of Illinois Press.

HWS. See *History of Woman Suffrage*.

Haan, Norma, M. Brewster-Smith, J. Block. 1968. "Moral

Reasoning in Young Adults: political-social behavior, family background and personality correlates." *Journal of Personality and Social Psychology*, 10(3):183–201.

Hamilton, W. J., J. O. Boyd, and H. W. Mossman. 1962. *Human Embryology*. Baltimore, Williams and Wilkins.

Hansen, Marcus Lee. 1952. "The Third Generation in America." *Commentary*, 14(5):492–500.

Hare, Lloyd C. M. 1937. *The Greatest American Woman: Lucretia Mott*. New York, The American Historical Society.

Harper, Ida H. 1898. *The Life and Work of Susan B. Anthony*. 3 volumes. Indianapolis, The Hollenbeck Press.

———. 1922. See *History of Woman Suffrage*.

Hayek, Friedrich A. 1951. *John Stuart Mill and Harriet Taylor: Their Friendship and Subsequent Marriage*. Chicago, University of Chicago Press.

Hays, Elinor R. 1961. *Morning Star: A Biography of Lucy Stone*. New York, Harcourt Brace.

———. 1967. *Those Extraordinary Blackwells*. New York, Harcourt Brace and World.

Higham, John, ed. 1962. *The Reconstruction of American History*. New York, Harper Torchbooks.

History of Woman Suffrage (HWS in text). Vols. I, II, and III: edited by Elizabeth Cady Stanton, Susan B. Anthony, and Matilda J. Gage. Rochester, N. Y., Charles Mann, 1881, 1882, 1886. Vol. IV: edited by Susan B. Anthony and Ida Husted Harper. Indianapolis, The Hollenbeck Press, 1902. Vols. V and VI: edited by Ida Husted Harper. New York, J. J. Little and Ives, 1922.

Hofstadter, Richard. 1955. *The Age of Reform*. New York, Alfred A. Knopf.

———. 1954. *American Political Tradition*. New York, Vintage Books.

Hooper, Mary Evans. 1970. *Earned Degrees Conferred: 1969–70, Institutional Data*. Washington, D. C., Department of Health, Education and Welfare, Office of Education, National Center for Educational Statistics.

Ishill, Joseph. 1957. *Emma Goldman: A Challenging Rebel*. Berkeley Heights, N. J., Oriole.

Kelley, Florence. 1926. "My Philadelphia." *The Survey Graphic Number*, October 1, 1926. Pp. 7–11, 50–57.

———. 1927. "When Co-Education was Young." *The Survey*

Graphic Number, February 1, 1927. Pp. 557–561, 602.

———. 1927. "My Novitiate." *The Survey Graphic Number,* April 1, 1927. Pp. 31–35.

———. 1927. "I Go to Work." *The Survey Graphic Number,* June 1, 1927. Pp. 271–275, 301.

Keniston, Kenneth. 1967. "The Sources of Student Dissent." *Journal of Social Issues,* 23(3):108–137.

———. 1968. *Young Radicals: Notes on Committed Youth.* New York, Harcourt Brace.

Kennedy, David M. 1970. *Birth Control in America: The Career of Margaret Sanger.* New Haven, Conn., Yale University Press.

Kraditor, Aileen S. 1965. *The Ideas of the Woman Suffrage Movement, 1890–1920.* New York, Columbia University Press.

*LaFollette, Suzanne. 1926. *Concerning Women.* New York, Albert & Charles Boni.

Lasch, Christopher. 1967. *The New Radicalism in America: 1889–1963.* New York, Vintage Books.

Lauer, Rosemary. 1963. "Women and the Church." *The Commonweal,* 79(13):365–368.

Lerner, Gerda. 1966. "Changes in the Status of Women: 1800–1840." Paper presented to the American Historical Association, Boston, Massachusetts.

———. 1967. *The Grimké Sisters from South Carolina.* Boston, Houghton Mifflin.

Lerner, Max. 1961. *Essential Works of John Stuart Mill.* New York, Bantam Books.

Lipset, Seymour Martin. 1963. *The First New Nation.* New York, Basic Books.

Lipset, Seymour Martin, ed. 1962. *Harriet Martineau: Society in America.* New York, Doubleday.

Lundberg, Ferdinand, and Marynia F. Farnham. 1947. *Modern Woman: The Lost Sex.* New York, Harper & Bros.

Lutz, Alma. 1940. *Created Equal. A Biography of Elizabeth Cady Stanton.* New York, John Day.

———. 1959. *Susan B. Anthony,* Boston, Beacon Press.

McLoughlin, William G. 1959. *Modern Revivalism.* New York, Ronald Press.

*Martineau, Harriet. 1837. *Society in America.* Volume III. London, Saunders & Otley.

———. 1838. *How to Observe Manners and Morals.* London, Charles Knight.

*Mead, Margaret. 1935. *Sex and Temperament in Three Primitive Societies*. New York, William Morrow.

————. 1972. *Blackberry Winter: My Earlier Years*. New York, William Morrow.

Mead, Margaret, and Ruth L. Bunzel. 1960. *The Golden Age of American Anthropology*. New York, George Braziller.

Millett, Kate. 1970. *Sexual Politics*. Garden City, N. Y., Doubleday.

Mineka, Francis E. 1944. *The Dissidence of Dissent*. Chapel Hill, University of North Carolina Press.

Mineka, Francis E., ed. 1963. *The Earlier Letters of John Stuart Mill 1812–1848*, Volumes 12 and 13 of *Collected Works of John Stuart Mill*. Toronto, University of Toronto Press.

Money, John, and Anke A. Ehrhardt. 1972. *Man & Woman. Boy & Girl*. Baltimore, The Johns Hopkins University Press.

*Murray, Judith Sargent. 1790. "On the Equality of the Sexes." *The Massachusetts Magazine*, March-April issue.

O'Neill, William L. 1969. *Everyone Was Brave: the Rise and Fall of Feminism in America*. New York, Quadrangle.

Perkins, A. J., and Theresa Wolfson. 1939. *Frances Wright, Free Enquirer: A Study of a Temperament*. New York, Harper & Bros.

Pippett, Aileen. 1957. *The Moth and the Star: a Biography of Virginia Woolf*. New York, Viking.

Pope-Hennessy, Una. 1929. *Three Englishwomen in America*. London, Ernest Benn.

Riegel, Robert E. 1963. *American Feminists*. Lawrence, University of Kansas Press.

Rinehart, Keith. 1953. "John Mill's Autobiography: Its Art and Appeal." *University of Kansas City Review*, 19:265–273.

Rivlin, Joseph B. 1947. *Harriet Martineau. A Bibliography of Her Separately Printed Books*. New York, The New York Public Library.

Robson, J. M., ed. 1965. *Collected Works of John Stuart Mill*, Vol. 3. Toronto, University of Toronto Press.

Rosenberg, Carroll Smith. 1971. "Beauty, the Beast and the Militant Woman: A Case Study in Sex Roles and Social Stress in Jacksonian America." *American Quarterly*, 23(4):562–584.

————. 1972. "Volition, Aggression and Conflict: Some Reflections on Hysteria and Women in 19th Century America." *Social Research*, 39.

*Rossi, Alice S., ed. 1970. *Essays on Sex Equality by John Stuart Mill and Harriet Taylor Mill*. Chicago, University of Chicago Press.

Rothstein, William G. 1972. *American Physicians in the Nineteenth Century: From Sects to Science*. Baltimore, The Johns Hopkins University Press.

Sanger, Margaret. 1917. *Family Limitation*. (Pamphlet.) New York.

*————. 1920. *Woman and the New Race*. New York, Brentano.

*————. 1931. *My Fight for Birth Control*. New York, Farrar-Rinehart.

Scott, Anne Firor. 1970. *The Southern Lady: From Pedestal to Politics, 1830–1930*. Chicago, University of Chicago Press.

Shelley, Mary Wollstonecraft. 1963. *Frankenstein*. London, J. M. Dent & Sons.

Sherfey, Mary Jane. 1972. *The Nature and Evolution of Female Sexuality*. New York, Random House.

*Shulman, Alix Kates. 1972. *Red Emma Speaks: Selected Writings and Speeches by Emma Goldman*. New York, Vintage Books.

Smith, Page. 1970. *Daughters of the Promised Land*. Boston, Little Brown.

Stanton, Elizabeth Cady. See *History of Woman Suffrage*.

*Stanton, Elizabeth Cady, ed. 1895. *The Woman's Bible*. New York, European.

————. 1898. *Eighty Years and More: Reminiscences of Elizabeth Cady Stanton*. London, T. Fisher Unwin.

Stanton, Henry B. 1887. *Random Recollections*. New York, Harper & Bros.

*Stanton, Theodore, and Harriot Stanton Blatch, eds. 1922. *Elizabeth Cady Stanton as Revealed in Her Letters, Diary and Reminiscences*. 2 volumes. New York, Harper & Bros.

Stephen, Sir Leslie, and Sir Sidney Lee, ed. 1921–22. "Catherine Macaulay." In *The Dictionary of National Biography*. Volume 12. London, Oxford University Press. Pp. 407–409.

Stillinger, Jack, ed. 1961. *The Early Draft of John Stuart Mill's Autobiography*. Urbana, Illinois, University of Illinois Press.

Taylor, George Rogers. 1951. *The Transportation Revolution: 1815–1860*. New York, Rinehart.

Tims, Margaret. 1961. *Jane Addams of Hull-House*. London, Allen and Unwin.

Tocqueville, Alexis de. 1959. *Democracy in America*. New York, Vintage Books.

Trollope, Frances. 1832. *Domestic Manners of the Americans*. London, Whittaker, Treacher.

Van den Berghe, Pierre. 1967. *Race and Racism: a Comparative Perspective*. New York, Wiley.

Wade, Mason. 1940. *Margaret Fuller: Whetstone of Genius*. New York, Viking.

———. 1941. *The Writings of Margaret Fuller*. New York, Viking.

Ward, Lester F. 1903. *Pure Sociology*. New York, Macmillan.

Wardle, Ralph M. 1951. *Mary Wollstonecraft, a Critical Biography*. Lawrence, University of Kansas Press.

———. 1966. *Godwin and Mary: Letters of William Godwin and Mary Wollstonecraft*. Lawrence, University of Kansas Press.

Warren, Mercy Otis. 1805. *History of the Rise, Progress and Termination of the American Revolution*. 3 volumes. Boston, Manning & Loring.

Waterman, William R. 1924. *Frances Wright*. New York, Columbia University Press.

Webb, R. K. 1960. *Harriet Martineau: A Radical Victorian*. New York, Columbia University Press.

Welter, Barbara. 1966. "The Cult of True Womanhood: 1820–1860." *American Quarterly*, 18(2:1):151–174.

Wheatley, Vera. 1957. *The Life and Work of Harriet Martineau*. London, Secker & Warburg.

*Wollstonecraft, Mary. 1967. *A Vindication of the Rights of Woman*. New York, W. W. Norton.

Woolf, Leonard, ed. 1954. *A Writer's Diary: Being Extracts From the Diary of Virginia Woolf*. New York, Harcourt Brace.

Woolf, Leonard. 1960. *Sowing*. New York, Harcourt Brace.

———. 1961. *Growing*. New York, Harcourt Brace.

———. 1963. *Beginning Again*. New York, Harcourt Brace.

———. 1967. *Downhill All the Way*. New York, Harcourt Brace.

———. 1969. *The Journey Not the Arrival Matters*. New York, Harcourt Brace.

*Woolf, Virginia. 1931. *A Room of One's Own*. London, Hogarth Press.

——. 1938. *Three Guineas*. New York, Harcourt Brace.

——. 1942. *The Death of the Moth and Other Essays*. New York, Harcourt Brace.

*Wright, Frances. 1821. *Views of Society and Manners in America, In a Series of Letters From That Country to a Friend in England, During the Years 1818, 1819, 1820*. London, Longman.

——. 1829. *Course of Popular Lectures*. New York, Free Enquirer.